DECOUPLING

Michelson's analysis of almost 150,000 divorce trials reveals routine and egregious violations of China's own laws upholding the freedom of divorce, gender equality, and the protection of women's physical security. Using "big data" computational techniques to scrutinize cases covering 2009–2016 from all 252 basic-level courts in two Chinese provinces, Henan and Zhejiang, Michelson reveals that women have borne the brunt of a dramatic intensification since the mid-2000s of a decades-long practice of denying divorce requests. This book takes the reader upstream to the institutional sources of China's clampdown on divorce and downstream to its devastating and highly gendered human toll, showing how judges in an overburdened court system clear their oppressive dockets at the expense of women's lawful rights and interests. This book is a must-read for anyone interested in Chinese courts, judicial decision-making, family law, gender violence, and the limits and possibilities of the globalization of law.

ETHAN MICHELSON is Professor of Sociology and Law at Indiana University Bloomington, where he has been teaching courses on law and society, law and authoritarianism, and contemporary Chinese society since 2003. He has won several awards for his published research on China's legal system.

CAMBRIDGE STUDIES IN LAW AND SOCIETY

Founded in 1997, Cambridge Studies in Law and Society is a hub for leading scholarship in socio-legal studies. Located at the intersection of law, the humanities, and the social sciences, it publishes empirically innovative and theoretically sophisticated work on law's manifestations in everyday life: from discourses to practices, and from institutions to cultures. The series editors have longstanding expertise in the inter-disciplinary study of law, and welcome contributions that place legal phenomena in national, comparative, or international perspective. Series authors come from a range of disciplines, including anthropology, history, law, literature, political science, and sociology.

Series Editors

Mark Fathi Massoud, *University of California, Santa Cruz*

Jens Meierhenrich, *London School of Economics and Political Science*

'Rachel E. Stern, *University of California, Berkeley*

A list of books in the series can be found at the back of this book.

CAMBRIDGE
STUDIES IN
LAW AND SOCIETY

DECOUPLING
Gender Injustice in China's Divorce Courts

Ethan Michelson

Indiana University Bloomington

CAMBRIDGE
UNIVERSITY PRESS

University Printing House, Cambridge CB2 8BS, United Kingdom

One Liberty Plaza, 20th Floor, New York, NY 10006, USA

477 Williamstown Road, Port Melbourne, VIC 3207, Australia

314–321, 3rd Floor, Plot 3, Splendor Forum, Jasola District Centre,
New Delhi – 110025, India

103 Penang Road, #05–06/07, Visioncrest Commercial, Singapore 238467

Cambridge University Press is part of the University of Cambridge.

It furthers the University's mission by disseminating knowledge in the pursuit of
education, learning, and research at the highest international levels of excellence.

www.cambridge.org
Information on this title: www.cambridge.org/9781108487856
DOI: 10.1017/9781108768177

First published 2022

A catalogue record for this publication is available from the British Library.

Library of Congress Cataloging-in-Publication Data
Names: Michelson, Ethan, author.
Title: Decoupling : gender injustice in China's divorce courts / Ethan Michelson, Indiana Unversity
Bloomington.
Description: Cambridge, United Kingdom ; New York, NY : Cambridge University Press, 2021. | Series:
Cambridge studies in law and society | Includes index.
Identifiers: LCCN 2021050097 (print) | LCCN 2021050098 (ebook) |
ISBN 9781108487856 (hardback) | ISBN 9781108738156 (paperback) |
ISBN 9781108768177 (ebook)
Subjects: LCSH: Divorce–China. | Divorce–Law and legislation–China. |
Women–China–Social conditions. | BISAC: LAW / General
Classification: LCC HQ940 .M53 2022 (print) | LCC HQ940 (ebook) |
DDC 306.89/30951–dc23/eng/20211112
LC record available at https://lccn.loc.gov/2021050097
LC ebook record available at https://lccn.loc.gov/2021050098

ISBN 978-1-108-48785-6 Hardback

To the teachers in my life, including those unaware they were teaching me

CONTENTS

FIGURES

TABLES

PREFACE AND ACKNOWLEDGMENTS

I first started learning about Chinese divorce litigation in the winter of 1995 as a graduate student. My predissertation fieldwork (with the support of the Social Science Research Council) examined the work of the Beijing law firm responsible for the well-known "Dear Lawyer Bao" legal advice column published weekly by the *Beijing Evening News*. In a sample I collected of almost 2,000 of its over 11,000 documented legal consultations between 1992 and 1995, over one-fifth concerned divorce. More than one-quarter of the over 750 legal cases it handled in court on behalf of clients in the same time period were divorces.

As I studied the struggle to divorce in China, I became palpably aware of a tension between the grim reality of divorce litigation in practice and its rosy representation to the public. On the one hand, the divorce-seekers who approached this law firm, three-quarters of whom were women, commonly faced abusive spouses and unhelpful courts. On the other hand, Lawyer Bao educated the public about China's growing arsenal of laws giving special consideration to the rights and interests of women and children. In other words, the lawyers who regularly counseled and represented women whose divorce efforts were stymied by courts simultaneously reassured readers that courts would protect them. Decades of public legal education in China have exposed countless millions of people to a unifying message exhorting and emboldening them to "use the law as a weapon." Aggrieved citizens who followed this advice, however, were often let down (Gallagher 2006, 2011, 2017; Michelson 2008, 2019b; Michelson and Read 2011). In the specific context of domestic violence, Chinese government agencies and media sources alike have inundated the public with the unambiguous message that an abuse victim need only go to court to present her case and obtain a divorce. For decades, battered women in China have been misled by this hollow promise that courts will protect their lawful rights and interests.

While carrying out dissertation field research on the Chinese legal profession in 2001, I invited Sally Merry to Beijing under the auspices of a Ford Foundation grant designed to strengthen the field of law and society in China. She gave two public lectures and held a seminar at the Chinese Academy of Social Sciences and Renmin University of China. In exchange, I offered my services arranging and interpreting interviews in support of her research. At the time, she was studying the local implementation of international legal norms protecting women from violence. Some of what she learned during her stay informed her book, *Human Rights and Gender Violence* (Merry 2006).

Professor Merry arrived in Beijing less than two weeks after the final amendment of China's Marriage Law was approved by the National People's Congress in late April 2001. After years of scholarly and activist efforts in pursuit of better legal mechanisms to combat violence against women, the term "domestic violence" finally entered Chinese law. Notwithstanding a general mood of cautious optimism about this legislative milestone, many scholars lamented the absence of both a clear definition of domestic violence and the criminalization of marital rape.

In the course of assisting Professor Merry's research in Beijing, I met some of China's leading family law scholars, including Xue Ninglan, whose work I cite in this book. I also met some of the institutional and individual actors in this book. For example, we visited the Domestic Violence Research, Intervention, and Prevention Project at the China Law Society, where Chen Min, a pioneer and leader in efforts to combat violence against women in China, was working at the time. We also visited Peking University's Center for Women's Law Studies and Legal Services, which had spearheaded China's first (and unsuccessful) "battered woman syndrome" criminal defense in a murder trial less than a year beforehand.

I regret that I never told Professor Merry about my project before her death in September 2020. As a former editor of the Cambridge Series in Law and Society, of which this book is a part, and as someone who helped attune me to the issues at the heart of this book, she was at the top of my list of people to whom I was going to send a copy with a personal note of gratitude.

Twenty years after her visit and the final amendment of China's Marriage Law in 2001, now is a good time to assess courts' legal obligation to grant relief to women seeking divorce on the grounds of domestic violence. Legally speaking, a convincing claim of domestic violence should be enough to obtain a divorce in court. Practically speaking, however, a claim of either domestic violence or irreconcilable differences is rarely sufficient for a divorce. Judges almost never affirm litigants' domestic violence allegations.

Now is also a good time to assess the current state of China's no-fault "breakdown of mutual affection" divorce standard, over 40 years after it was introduced in the 1980 version of the Marriage Law. The near-impossibility of divorce characterized China's imperial times (Baker 1979:45; Honig and Hershatter 1988:206) and most of the 1949–1976 Mao era (Huang 2005; Tsui 2001). Like no-fault divorce elsewhere in the world, the right to divorce on the grounds of irreconcilable differences in contemporary China obviates the legal requirement to prove wrongdoing. In practice, however, judges generally affirm the breakdown of mutual affection only when both sides are willing to divorce or after a plaintiff files for divorce the second time.

Xin He's research was my first exposure to this phenomenon. As far as I know, he was the first to introduce to English-language audiences Chinese courts' common practice of denying divorce requests the first time and granting them the second time. In the first of a long series of articles he published on Chinese divorce litigation, culminating in a book, *Divorce in China* (He 2021), published after I finished mine, Professor He (2009) showed that only about 70% of divorce requests adjudicated by courts were granted in the mid-2000s. As I show in this book, rates at which courts granted the divorce petitions they adjudicated dropped to about 40% in a matter of only one decade.

Prior to launching this research project, by far my greatest source of knowledge about Chinese divorce litigation and the raw deals women get in the process was my first Ph.D. student, Ke Li, currently on the faculty at the City University of New York's John Jay College of Criminal Justice. Her pathbreaking dissertation (Li 2015a) informed much of my initial research agenda as I set out to write this book. I am enormously grateful to Professor Li for reversing roles, teaching me about Chinese divorce litigation, and serving as a critically helpful sounding board as I worked through the data. Her own book, *Marriage Unbound*, on Chinese divorce litigation was forthcoming at the time I finished mine (Li 2022). My book is thus part of a wave of book publications on Chinese divorce.

The world has changed since I started writing. When I settled on this book's title, I used the word "decoupling" to describe the decoupling of spouses in the divorce process and the decoupling of judicial practices from ideals enshrined in the law. However, since mid-2019, in the wake of the US–China trade war, "decoupling" has taken on a new and very different meaning in public discourse: economic decoupling between the two countries. Furthermore, in 2020, the urgency and global relevance of domestic violence and divorce as an escape hatch for victims – issues at the heart of this book – spiked. Academic and media reports chronicle both an apparent surge in the prevalence of domestic violence and an apparent narrowing of avenues to divorce during the COVID-19 pandemic, not only in China but around the world. An already perilous situation has escalated. As I was writing this book over those two tumultuous years, I was mindful that two years is also how long it might take a woman in China to divorce her abusive husband.

I have many debts of gratitude. This project emerged from a fateful meeting organized and generously hosted by Benjamin Liebman at Columbia University on October 5, 2015. Without Peter Lorentzen's matchmaking services, Ben Liebman, Rachel Stern, and Alice Wang – and the court decisions from Henan Province they painstakingly amassed – would not have been paired with Margaret Roberts and her team at the San Diego Supercomputer Center. I am indebted to all of them for the invitation to join the initial effort, for generously sharing their collection of court decisions published by the Henan Provincial High Court, and for their support as I dove into the data over the next five years.

Kathryn Hendley helped jump-start this project by inviting me to present preliminary findings at the University of Wisconsin-Madison Law School in March 2017. I also benefitted from feedback I received when presenting pieces of this book at the Renmin University of China Law School (January 2018), the Association for Asian Studies Annual Conference (March 2018), the Sichuan University School of Law (May 2018), the Chinese Academy of Social Sciences' Institute of Sociology (May 2018), and the University of Hong Kong School of Law (April 2019). I am grateful to the many friends, including Gardner Bovingdon, Sara Friedman, Padraic Kenney, Jayanth Krishnan, Adam Liff, Christiana Ochoa, and John Yasuda, who indulged me in conversation about this project and served as helpful sounding boards over coffee, beer, and meals (before the pandemic).

I thank Laurel Bossen, my undergraduate mentor at McGill University, who first taught me about the Chinese family when I took her anthropology of Chinese society class in 1990. I thank Bill Parish for mentoring my pursuit of the sociology of China through graduate school. I thank Tom Gieryn for believing in me when, after congratulating me on my tenure and promotion over a decade ago, he said,

"I think your best work is ahead of you." I thank the editors of the Cambridge Studies in Law and Society series, Mark Massoud, Jens Meierhenrich, and Rachel Stern, for supporting this project. I am particularly grateful to Professor Stern for her endorsement and support. I thank Margaret Boittin and Margaret Woo for their outstanding comments and suggestions that made this book better than it otherwise would have been. I thank John Berger, who shepherded this project through the review and approval process at Cambridge University Press before retiring in 2019. I thank Matt Gallaway for catching the baton and putting it into print.

Hai Hu and Zuoyu Tian provided key technical assistance with the collection and preparation of data. Shimona Michelson cheerfully verified the accuracy of my maps and spent a few hours on a mindless data entry task. Keera Allendorf, Tim Bartley, Michael Palmer, and Brian Powell generously read drafts and provided valuable feedback. Additional thanks go to James Baker, Zhaodi Chen, Cynthia Col, Chao Deng, Jinting Deng, Vitor Dias, Sarah Donilon, Priyanka Durai, Susan Finder, Hualing Fu, Jackie Grant, Yiming Hu, Wen-ling Liu, Scott Long, Nicola Maclean, Annabel Maunder, Patricia McManus, Kiran Mishra, Trenton Mize, Benjamin Read, Fabio Rojas, Beth Shack, Gemma Smith, Ruojun Sun, Catherine Taylor, Suisui Wang, Yuening Wei, Deborah Widiss, Jianing Ying, Lianhan Zhang, Lanyi Zhu, and Weimin Zuo. Of course all errors in this book are entirely my own.

I thank the Indiana University Maurer School of Law for generous summer research fellowships to support my work on this book, the Indiana University East Asian Studies Center for a much-needed subvention grant, and the Indiana University Office of the Vice President for Research for a grant in aid.

When I accidentally wrote enough text for two books, Gretchen Knapp masterfully edited and cut it down to size as much as humanly possible. I thank her for reducing this book's burden on readers.

Portions of this book appeared previously in the *American Journal of Sociology* and *The Journal of Comparative Law*. The anonymous reviewers and editors provided extraordinarily helpful suggestions.

I want to thank my parents, Ellen and Bill, for raising me to be conscious of social inequality and injustice. Above all, I owe a massive debt of gratitude to my children, Rachel and Shimona, for their infinite forbearance as I slogged away on this book through weekends and holidays. They never once complained even though I disappeared into my office for a couple of years and cancelled summer travels and family reunions. With an understanding of the gravity of the issues in this book, they were never less than fully supportive of my determination to finish it. The writing process was even longer in dog years for poor Jewel, who did not get walked as often as she would have liked but who loves me anyway.

Supplementary online material, including the original Chinese names of all legal sources I cite in this book, is available at https://decoupling-book.org/. In Chinese names, surnames come first. In this book's body of text, the surnames of Chinese litigants, scholars, judges, political leaders, and so on precede their first names. Only in in-text citations do Chinese first names (or initials) precede surnames.

A final note to the reader: In this book I rely to a considerable degree on internet resources. For reference purposes, I use Perma.cc permalinks for case examples and court work reports. I reference many other online materials, however, using their original URLs (a few particularly long ones were shortened at https://tinyurl.com/). I urge readers who encounter dead URLs to search for them on https://archive.org/. They should all be there.

CHAPTER ONE

SISYPHUS GOES TO DIVORCE COURT

Not long after immersing myself in this project, I began to visualize Sisyphus going to divorce court. His fate is an apt metaphor for the protracted and sometimes futile uphill struggle of China's mostly female divorce plaintiffs, whose petitions will almost certainly fail at first – even in cases involving domestic violence, regardless of the severity of the allegations or the strength of the evidence.[1] Many plaintiffs give up on litigation, either resigning themselves to staying married to their abusers or pursuing divorce through civil government channels outside the court system. Of those who do return to court, most will eventually succeed, albeit sometimes only after multiple attempts and long delays.

My key tasks in this book are to trace the origins and chronicle the consequences of this highly institutionalized practice of denying first-time petitions (He 2009), which I call the "divorce twofer" because a court typically grants a divorce only after trying the same case twice. Obtaining a divorce after two (or more) attempts is no bargain for litigants, but, as we shall see later, denying divorce petitions has helped judges in a variety of ways. Courts and judges have enjoyed divorce litigation's "two for the price of one" quality, for which female plaintiffs have paid dearly. The divorce twofer's benefits to courts and judges have come at the expense of gender justice.

As I studied tens of thousands of courts' written divorce decisions, I was struck both by the high prevalence of domestic violence

---

[1] Throughout this book I use the term "domestic violence" instead of "intimate partner violence" because the scope of analysis is almost exclusively limited to married couples.

allegations and by judges' tendency to ignore them. I was surprised by the ubiquity of judges' brazen and inscrutable disregard for plaintiffs' well-documented claims of domestic violence. I was mystified by how commonly judges denied divorce petitions on the grounds that mutual affection had not broken down and reconciliation remained possible despite admissible evidence of horrific spousal abuse. A remarkable feature of Chinese court rulings to deny divorce petitions is the overwhelming extent to which they are based on judges' arbitrary assessments of the strength of the marital foundation and speculative prognostications about litigants' reconciliation prospects. For this reason, the divorce twofer extends unabated to cases involving domestic violence.

I was equally amazed to find that judges' tendency to deny first-attempt divorce petitions had increased dramatically beginning in the mid-2000s. In some ways, the contemporary struggle is a throwback to the Mao era when divorce was notoriously difficult (Tsui 2001:105–06). To my dismay, I discovered that, among all divorce-seekers, women have been hugely disadvantaged not only in their prospects of obtaining a divorce on the first try but also in gaining child custody. Women have borne the brunt of this judicial clampdown on divorce. Their formidable difficulties thus harken even further back to China's imperial days (Baker 1979:45; Honig and Hershatter 1988:206).

These parallels to earlier periods, however, are strictly confined to courts. The Sisyphean character of divorce *litigation* stands in stark contrast to a relatively quick and simple *administrative* pathway to uncontested divorce in the Civil Affairs Administration, which accounts for the vast majority of China's divorces. Indeed, the liberalization in 2003 of this extrajudicial pathway helped triple China's crude divorce rate within 15 years. A prerequisite of divorcing outside of court, however, is mutual consent – and agreement on all terms. Most divorce cases brought to court, therefore, are contested. A considerable share of them have been filed by women making allegations of domestic violence.

Why have courts become averse, and increasingly so, to granting first-attempt divorce petitions? Why have judges remained so unmoved by domestic violence allegations? Why have women's divorce litigation outcomes been so much worse than men's? These are the questions I set out to answer in this book.

In my quest for answers, the first place I looked was China's family laws. Widely dubbed "breakdownism," the ultimate legal standard for divorce is the "breakdown of mutual affection." Strictly according to the law, judges can grant divorce petitions only if their mediation efforts fail to reconcile the couple and they determine that "mutual affection has indeed broken down." Breakdownism is analogous to no-fault divorce elsewhere in the world insofar as judges can apply it to grant a unilateral divorce petition on the grounds of irreconcilable differences. If mediation fails, a judge need only take a plaintiff's claim of the breakdown of mutual affection at face value to grant a divorce. Chinese judges almost never apply the law this way, however. More often than not, they take a defendant's unwillingness to divorce as proof that mutual affection has not broken down.

The law provides additional divorce standards. A judge is supposed to grant a plaintiff's divorce petition if the defendant fails to show up and mediation cannot be carried out, or if the litigants satisfy a physical separation test. Most importantly, statutory wrongdoing – including domestic violence – automatically establishes the breakdown of mutual affection. Any one of a series of fault-based legal tests known collectively as "faultism" automatically satisfies the breakdownism standard and therefore provides sufficient grounds for an adjudicated divorce. Again, however, judges rarely apply the law this way.

On paper, Chinese family law adheres to global legal norms concerning women's rights in general and protections against domestic violence in particular. Since the 1980s, the law has fully empowered judges to grant a divorce on the fault-based grounds of domestic violence. Although the term "domestic violence" debuted in Chinese law in 2001, earlier legal provisions extended protections – particularly to women and children – against "maltreatment" and "abuse," and provided the right to divorce on this basis. Ambiguities in the law, however, have also provided a way out for judges disinclined to grant a divorce. Most judges tend to privilege breakdownism over faultism. Rather than affirming the breakdown of mutual affection on the basis of statutory wrongdoing, judges tend to do the opposite: they sideline plaintiffs' fault-based claims and rule to preserve abusive marriages by determining that the litigants' marital discord can be fixed and that mutual affection has therefore not completely broken down.

Denying divorce petitions solves a lot of problems for judges, who face pressures from many sources, perhaps the least of which is the law. Chinese judges are rewarded and punished according to how well they support the court system's dual imperative to maximize judicial efficiency and minimize social unrest. Like Lipsky's (2010) "street-level

3

bureaucrats," Chinese judges take advantage of their considerable discretion to bend and reinterpret formal rules. As street-level bureaucrats, they have developed unofficial "routines and simplifications" not only to complete their relentless work tasks but also to maximize their scores on measures their superiors use to evaluate their work performance (Lipsky 2010). In so doing they have produced informal de facto rules that deviate from official de jure rules.

The divorce twofer emerged as one of judges' creative coping strategies. By helping overworked judges to close cases quickly and thus to clear their oppressive dockets, the divorce twofer is a docket-shrinking machine. Most of the divorce petitions that judges swiftly deny on the first attempt do not come back to court as second-attempt petitions. Moreover, the cases that do come back are less fraught and contentious – and are thus easier to dispose of and less likely to lead to "extreme incidents" of violence and unrest. Finally, marital preservation supports China's political ideology of family harmony as a means of maintaining social stability.

Street-level bureaucrats also save time and effort by making snap judgments guided by prevailing stereotypes and biases (Lipsky 2010). Chinese judges sort litigants into cultural categories of credibility and deservingness in part according to patriarchal cultural beliefs. Because they deem women's claims to be less credible than those of men, judges attach less weight to women's allegations of domestic violence than to their alleged abusers' denials. They use batterers' apparent contrition as evidence of reconciliation potential and thus as grounds for denying victims' divorce petitions. They support the rural patriarchal order by granting child custody – particularly of sons – to fathers. Judges also fear for their own personal safety lest they upset a defendant with a history of violence. To some degree, judicial decision-making occurs in the shadow of threats of violent retribution.

In recent years, the annual number of contested divorce petitions adjudicated by Chinese courts has exceeded half a million (Ministry of Civil Affairs of China, various years), at least one-quarter of which involve claims of violence and other forms of abuse (Chen and Duan 2012; Li 2015b). Such cases, usually filed by women, usually result in a court ruling to preserve the marriage (Ministry of Civil Affairs of China, various years; Xu 2007). My empirical analyses of the written court decisions of almost 150,000 divorce adjudications spanning eight years in two Chinese provinces, Henan and Zhejiang, show that courts' long-standing practice of denying divorce requests on the first attempt

(He 2009) has intensified since the mid-2000s, and that China's judicial clampdown on divorce has disproportionately impacted women. They also show that when they do grant divorces, courts favor fathers over mothers with respect to child custody, in part because women who flee domestic violence often leave their children behind. Men who beat their wives are thus rewarded with child custody.

The tragic 18-year saga of He Jie, a woman from Dingxi County in Gansu Province, offers a preview of almost every theme of this book about the struggle of Chinese divorce litigation.

CURTAIN-RAISER

He Jie's husband, Zhang Dong, began to beat her soon after they registered their marriage in 1986. His violent temper did not wane following the birth of their son. When their son was six months old, Zhang Dong's beating left He Jie collapsed on the floor with a ruptured eardrum and urinary and bowel incontinence. When she got up after Zhang Dong demanded that she return to work, he beat her again. He Jie's screams alerted the neighbors, who reported the situation to her parents, who in turn rushed her to the hospital. In 1987, as a consequence of this episode, He Jie filed her first divorce petition with the Dingxi County People's Court.[2] While awaiting her trial, she left her son behind and stayed with a relative in the provincial capital of Lanzhou, where she looked for work. Zhang Dong traveled to Lanzhou to express his remorse. He pledged never to repeat his offenses, and if he did, to agree to divorce and provide economic compensation. He also begged He Jie's parents to persuade her to give him another chance, which they did. In consideration of Zhang Dong's contrition, the court denied He Jie's divorce petition on the grounds that mutual affection had not completely broken down.

The very next day after the court's adjudicated denial, Zhang Dong brutally attacked He Jie. Later, in 1988, he dumped a basin of foot-washing water over her head and, wielding a cleaver, chased her out of their home. Not knowing where else to go, she returned to her parents' home. That same year, He Jie filed her second divorce petition. She also sought the assistance of the local branch of the All-Women's

---

[2] In 2003, Dingxi County was renamed Anding District after it was absorbed by the newly established prefecture-level city of Dingxi.

Federation and the local People's Congress, both of which attempted to persuade her that countless couples experience the same thing, that physical fights are no big deal. Afterward, He Jie declared to Zhang Dong that she would move to Lanzhou and look for work while awaiting the court's ruling. After the court denied her second petition, Zhang Dong traveled to Lanzhou to retrieve her.

In 1993, the court denied He Jie's third divorce petition after yet another convincing display of remorse by Zhang Dong. In 1996, Zhang Dong chased He Jie again with a cleaver. This time, as she was trying to escape through the front door, he caught her by grabbing her hair. When he held the knife against her neck and moved it back and forth on her skin, she nearly lost three fingers when she tried to push the blade away. Her fingers remained attached by a small amount of sinew. Although she was bleeding profusely, he prevented her from going to the hospital. Only by pretending to use the bathroom was she able to escape to the hospital, where her fingers were reattached.

The fourth time she filed for divorce, He Jie was more determined than ever to succeed. She reasoned that if she used medical records as evidence of Zhang Dong's abuse, the court would be unable to use "mutual affection has not broken down" to deny her petition. Zhang Dong wrote a "pledge letter" admitting his mistakes, promising never to repeat them, and begging for one more chance. Under enormous pressure – from Zhang Dong's work unit, which wrote a formal statement and affixed its official red seal to vouch for his commitment to become a better person; from He Jie's older brother, who was moved by Zhang Dong's gestures; and from her precarious employment situation at her own work unit, which had started laying off employees – He Jie relented and withdrew her divorce petition.

A few years later she did indeed get laid off. After Zhang Dong was also let go by his work unit shortly afterward, he regularly got drunk and beat her. In 2002, Zhang Dong was arrested for hiring a prostitute. After He Jie bailed him out of jail, he beat her. After a few more years of abuse, He Jie resumed plans to file her fifth divorce petition. One day, in May 2005, when she returned home to discover Zhang Dong drinking with a friend, she ran to her mother's home, where she spent the night in order to avoid another beating. Several hours after He Jie returned home the following morning, Zhang Dong notified her mother that she had killed herself by drinking rat poison. He rushed her to the emergency room where she was pronounced dead. He Jie's family, suspecting that Zhang Dong murdered her, requested a forensic investigation. Because Zhang Dong and his son refused to grant permission to examine He Jie's stomach contents, the forensic pathologist's tests were inconclusive. He Jie's body was cremated.[3]

Owing to failures in the Chinese civil courts, divorce cases do lead to suicides and spawn criminal domestic violence cases, including homicides. In the grand scheme of divorce litigation, however, He Jie's tragedy is an extreme case in terms of both the number of times she filed for divorce and her ultimate fate. Other themes emerging from her case, however, are hardly aberrations from the utterly common experiences of abuse victims who file for divorce in court:

- In their divorce petitions, plaintiffs often present claims of domestic violence in gory, harrowing detail, and support them with legally admissible documentation.
- These plaintiffs commonly report their fruitless prior help-seeking efforts with the police, local government agencies, and the All-China Women's Federation.
- Plaintiffs often face pressure from all sides to withdraw their petitions.
- In order to justify their adjudicated denials of abuse victims' petitions for divorce, judges downplay and normalize domestic violence and underscore batterers' contrition. In so doing, judges reinforce the gaslighting efforts of husbands, parents, parents-in-law, other family members, police, and village leaders.
- Written court decisions are rife with judges' contorted efforts to establish mutual affection despite plaintiffs' claims and prima facie evidence of domestic violence. Judges commonly cite defendants' desire to stay together and remorse as proof that mutual affection has not broken down. Whereas pledge letters are supposed to be used as evidence of domestic violence, for purposes of establishing the *breakdown* of mutual affection, judges tend instead to use them as evidence of defendants' repentance, for purposes of establishing the *existence* of mutual affection.
- When plaintiffs return to court after an unsuccessful first attempt, they often report the intensification of domestic violence in the

---

[3] This account is a summary of details reported by Shi (2005). In another media report on the same case, the name He Jie (何洁) is reported as He Cailian (何彩莲; Chai and Zhu 2005).

interim and their efforts to escape it by staying with family or participating in labor migration.

- In child custody determinations, judges privilege physical possession over domestic violence allegations. The judges in He Jie's case never had to determine child custody because they never granted any of her divorce petitions. Had they done so, they likely would have granted child custody to the defendant because He Jie, like so many abuse victims, left her son in the physical possession of her husband when she fled to safety.

I encountered other cases similar to He Jie's. In 2014, Henan Province's Zhongmu County People's Court denied the petition of a woman on her fourth attempt. According to the court decision, she and her husband moved in together in 2007. Like many rural couples, they had a traditional wedding ceremony but did not officially register their marriage. Because the husband came from a poor family without the means to support the dominant rural practice of patrilocality, they moved in with her parents. Only in 2009, a year after giving birth to a son, did they retroactively register their marriage. In 2011, their twins – one boy and one girl – were born. According to the plaintiff, the defendant regularly punched and kicked her when things were not to his liking. On one occasion, during a fight, he allegedly cut her parents with a knife when they tried to calm him down. When the plaintiff filed her first petition in 2011, village leaders intervened to persuade her to reconcile. In consideration of their son and given that she was pregnant, she agreed to give him another chance. Later in the same year, after no change whatsoever, the plaintiff filed a second petition, which the court denied. She withdrew her third petition in 2012, when her in-laws persuaded her to reconcile. Her fourth trial, like many divorce trials in China, was held with her husband in absentia. To support her claims, the plaintiff submitted as evidence a police report documenting an unspecified emergency incident. In its decision, the court wrote:

> [O]wing to conflicts over family trifles, the plaintiff filed three previous divorce petitions that were resolved through mediated reconciliation. Moreover, their three children are young and need to be raised and cared for by both sides. In consideration of the physical and mental health of the children, the marriage still has reconciliation potential if both sides can forgive, compromise, and properly deal with marital conflict. The plaintiff's claim that mutual affection has

8

indeed broken down lacks sufficient evidence, and the court denies support of it. (Decision #1138764, March 8, 2014)[4]

Unless the defendant is AWOL, the first step of the Chinese divorce litigation process is judicial mediation for the purpose of marital reconciliation. In this case, village leaders and family members also intervened in the mediation process. They acted in concert with the court to gaslight the plaintiff by characterizing her claims of marital violence as "trifles." Their efforts to persuade her to give her abusive husband another chance for the sake of the children and family unity succeeded when the plaintiff withdrew her first and third petitions. The court denied by adjudication her second and fourth petitions. This case illustrates not only the importance of mediation and petition withdrawals but also the unimportance of domestic violence allegations. The police report documented a visit in response to a call for help from the plaintiff, but even when they do explicitly describe the contents of police reports in their court decisions, judges tend to ignore, downplay, or negate their relevance.

Most divorce cases in Henan and Zhejiang involve couples from rural locales. A couple from Henan's Huojia County held their marriage ceremony in 2011 and registered their marriage a year later. In her third divorce petition, filed in 2015, the plaintiff claimed she and the defendant had been separated since 2012 owing to his regular habit of late-night drinking, their incompatible personalities, and their lack of communication. In 2013, during their separation, when the defendant visited her at her workplace (a KTV club), the discussion became heated and he allegedly beat her, causing her eardrum to bleed. She filed for divorce the following month but ultimately withdrew her petition. In 2014, she withdrew her second divorce petition. In 2015, the plaintiff supported her third petition for divorce by submitting the diagnostic result of an ear endoscopy performed at the Huojia County

---

[4] Case ID (2013)牟民初字第3050号. All translations in this book are mine. Using its case ID in a search query on both the "China Judgements Online" website of China's Supreme People's Court (https://wenshu.court.gov.cn) and an alternative online repository, OpenLaw (https://openlaw.cn/), this particular decision was still accessible at the time I wrote this book, and is archived at https://perma.cc/24RL-FUMW. The Henan and Zhejiang provincial high court websites from which all the court decisions I analyze in this book were originally bulk downloaded ("scraped") took their collections offline in 2018 and 2019, respectively. Chapter 4 contains more methodological details about my sources of court decisions. I include Perma.cc links because there is no way of knowing how long court decisions will remain available on any Chinese website.

Red Cross Hospital showing an external injury to her left ear and bleeding from – but no obvious perforation of – her left eardrum. The court refused to affirm the evidence because "the medical documentation proves only that an injury occurred but not that the defendant caused it." With the defendant in absentia, the court denied the plaintiff's divorce petition on the grounds that her claims of physical separation and violence lacked sufficient proof (Decision #1386750, April 2, 2015).[5]

As a pretext for excluding admissible evidence of domestic violence, courts commonly hold that it fails to link the defendant to the plaintiff's injury. The previous two examples also illustrate the prevalence of in absentia divorce trials. A defendant's failure to participate in trial proceedings in no way diminishes a court's legal authority to grant a plaintiff's divorce petition. Nonetheless, courts can be reluctant to grant a divorce when the defendant is absent.

In her fourth divorce trial at the Xinchang County People's Court in Zhejiang Province, a plaintiff lamented her three unsuccessful prior attempts. She supported her claim of marital strife with a copy of a pledge letter, which she said proved that her husband beat her. In his defense, the defendant stated, "It's true that the plaintiff's previous three attempts to divorce were unsuccessful, but it's not true that I beat her. I believe mutual affection has not broken down and do not consent to divorce." He challenged the plaintiff's use of his pledge letter by saying, "I think I wrote it just to reconcile with the plaintiff." To justify its decision to deny the plaintiff's fourth petition, the court wrote:

> In this case the plaintiff and defendant have some conflict in their life together. The plaintiff filed three previous petitions in this court, but never provided evidence that marital affection has indeed broken down. … Plaintiff and defendant are lacking communication and contact, but the court believes they have reconciliation potential if they can treasure marital affection, attend to family interests, communicate more, interact more, and forgive and compromise. (Decision #4861687, November 11, 2016)[6]

Defendants in most cases deny allegations of violence made against them. Even when they admit, on the record, to beating their wives,

---

[5] Case ID (2015)获民初字第252号, archived at https://perma.cc/Z9EV-EVS8.
[6] Case ID (2016)浙0624民初3381号, archived at https://perma.cc/M3L5-DRF9.

they usually withhold their consent to divorce, which is all judges need to hold that plaintiffs' evidence is insufficient to prove the breakdown of mutual affection.

HOW MARITAL DECOUPLING INFORMS THEORIES OF INSTITUTIONAL DECOUPLING

Why have Chinese judges been so unwilling to apply the breakdownism standard to grant unilateral no-fault divorces? Why have they increasingly applied the breakdownism standard to deny rather than to grant divorce petitions? And why have they done so even when they were both empowered and obligated by law to apply faultism standards to grant divorce petitions on the basis of spousal wrongdoing? For decades, Chinese law has called on judges to grant divorces in cases involving spousal abuse. And yet, a Beijing court's 2013 ruling to grant a divorce to Kim Lee has been heralded as "landmark" not because the plaintiff was American, but rather because the court granted her divorce on the grounds of domestic violence (Fincher 2014:156; J. Jiang 2019:241–42). Only exceedingly rarely have judges granted first-attempt divorce petitions on fault-based grounds.

Previous research offers clues regarding Chinese courts' routine and egregious violations of global legal norms about the freedom of divorce, gender equality, and the protection of the physical security of women. The existing literature points in at least four possible directions of inquiry. First, we could consider the supply of China's domestic laws that address divorce rights and domestic violence (Htun and Weldon 2018; Hudson, Bowen, and Nielsen 2011; Wang and Schofer 2018). We would quickly strike off this explanation upon discovering China's arsenal of laws and policies rooted in a deep ideological commitment to gender equality common to communist states (Cheng and Wang 2018; Htun and Weldon 2018:297–301; Huang 2005; Tang and Parish 2000:237). Just as the "freedom of marriage" came to symbolize the liberation of women from the oppression of arranged marriages, bigamy, and other "feudal" practices, the "freedom of divorce" too became an enshrined legal principle, particularly for purposes of providing relief to women (Jiang 2009a; Palmer 1995:122; Tsui 2001:105).

Second, we could consider China's international legal commitments (Englehart and Miller 2014; Htun and Weldon 2018; Hudson, Bowen, and Nielsen 2011; Wang and Schofer 2018). This avenue is another dead end, given that China has strongly endorsed relevant global legal norms by signing all seven (and ratifying six) core UN international human rights treaties, including the Convention on the Elimination of All Forms of Discrimination against Women (CEDAW) (Runge 2015; Zhao and Zhang 2017). Numerous official reports and white papers detail China's pledges and concrete steps to support international goals concerning the status of women in general and the protection of women against violence in particular, and its ostensible progress fulfilling these commitments (e.g., Information Office of the State Council 2015; Rong 2016; Zhao 2016).

But, of course, the law is not self-enforcing. China's on-the-ground judicial practices that subvert its domestic laws and international legal commitments point to a third literature on "loose coupling" and "decoupling," a gap between policies and practices, form and substance, intentions and results, appearance and reality (Hafner-Burton and Tsutsui 2005; Hafner-Burton, Tsutsui, and Meyer 2008; Meyer et al. 1997). It has become a sociological truism that largely ritualistic and ceremonial conformity in organizational appearance belies enormous local variation in on-the-ground organizational behavior (DiMaggio and Powell 1983; Meyer and Rowan 1977). For over two decades, scholars in the "world society" tradition have demonstrated the global ubiquity of decoupling, sometimes called "ceremony without substance" (Cole 2013; Frank, Hardinge, and Wosick-Correa 2009; Meyer and Rowan 1977; Meyer et al. 1997; Schofer et al. 2012), and which can also be thought of as "empty promises" (Hafner-Burton and Tsutsui 2005) and "rights without remedies." World society scholars, also referred to collectively as the "Stanford school of sociological institutionalism" (Haley and Haley 2016; True and Mintrom 2001), focus on the "strong commonalities in international discourses on a wide range of topics, from human rights to environmentalism" (Schofer et al. 2012:59).

The word "decoupling" in this book's title is a double entendre. On the one hand, it refers to the "decoupling of married spouses" (Mortelmans 2020:2).[7] On the other hand, it refers to the decoupling of – or a gap between – official promises of the law and the degree to which courts fulfill them in practice. Most of the world society literature is devoted to measuring and explaining the global diffusion of stuff

---

[7] Family scholars more commonly use the word "uncoupling," which also includes breakups of unmarried couples as well as marital pauses and separations that do not lead to divorce (Vaughan 1986).

on the "official promises" side of the decoupling gap: exogenous norms of secular individualism, scientific rationality, universalism, equality, human rights, and the like (Boli and Lechner 2001; Boli and Thomas 1997; Boyle and Meyer 1998; Meyer et al. 1997; Wotipka and Ramirez 2008). More recent efforts in this tradition have sought to measure and explain the stuff on the "promise fulfillment" side of the decoupling gap. World society scholars have thus moved beyond their initial focus on the emergence and proliferation of standardized scripts governing organizational appearance and behavior to a new focus on the extent of their local implementation (Cole 2005; Hafner-Burton and Tsutsui 2005; Pope and Meyer 2016; Swiss 2009). In other words, world society research has shifted from describing superficial norm adoption to assessing its real-life impact (Schofer et al. 2012).

This third literature is reminiscent of the "gap and impact studies" of the 1960s and 1970s in the field of law and society (Gould and Barclay 2012:330). Gap studies can be traced even further back to the 1920s and 1930s, when legal realists sought to demonstrate that judicial decision-making can never be isolated from its social, cultural, and political contexts (Gould and Barclay 2012:324–25). A quip widely attributed to legal realist Jerome Frank – that a judge's ruling has less to do with the law than what he ate for breakfast – has been dubbed the "digestive theory of law" (Black 1989:5). By highlighting the gap between the law on the books and the law in action, gap studies helped define the early years of the law and society movement (Gould and Barclay 2012:324).

Critics of gap studies focused on a naïve and optimistic view of gaps as bugs that could be fixed. Law and society scholars subsequently came to treat gaps not only as bugs but also as features (Gould and Barclay 2012). A gap sometimes reflects the limits of good intentions, a will without a way: insufficient capacity to realize a well-intentioned local effort to adhere to world society norms such as human rights and gender equality (Cole 2015). A gap sometimes also reflects bad intentions and hypocrisy: the adoption of laws that symbolically advance gender equality for the purpose of obscuring the perpetuation of practices that undermine gender equality (Fallon, Aunio, and Kim 2018). Gaps deliberately engineered by state actors as institutional features have been called "radical decoupling" (Hafner-Burton and Tsutsui 2005) and "state-led decoupling" (Fallon, Aunio, and Kim 2018).

In some studies, domestic and international laws appear to reduce gender violence and improve gender justice (Htun and Weldon 2018;

13

Hudson, Bowen, and Nielsen 2011). Even when adopted by states with no intention of enforcing them, international treaties and conventions can, according to some scholars, shrink the gap between promises and practices (Cole 2013; Cole and Ramirez 2013). Such an outcome is the "paradox of empty promises" (Hafner-Burton and Tsutsui 2005), and happens because "the entire system 'drifts' toward legitimated models" (Schofer and Hironaka 2005:27). World society scholars similarly argue that the ratification of international treaties promoting women's rights and the enactment of gender-equal national divorce laws have promoted the freedom of divorce and in so doing helped drive rising divorce rates around the world (Wang and Schofer 2018). China poses a challenge to these optimistic accounts of the impact of global legal norms. We will see later that China's divorce explosion obscures durable local institutional forces militating against domestic laws promoting gender equality and the freedom of divorce. China's rising divorce rates are limited to mutual-consent divorces in the Civil Affairs Administration. Meanwhile, China's judicial clampdown on divorce reflects a widening gap between rights and protections formally provided to divorce-seekers and their practical application by courts.

Although courts contribute only a small share of all of China's more than four million divorces processed annually in recent years (Ministry of Civil Affairs of China, various years), they are the only place where people can take contested, unilateral, ex parte divorce requests that often stem from domestic violence. Courts contribute only a small and shrinking share of divorces in part because they have become increasingly averse to granting adjudicated divorces. Between 2000 and 2018, the annual number of divorce requests courts *granted* through adjudication shrank by 16%, while the annual number of divorce requests *denied* by court adjudication more than tripled, rising by 206% (Ministry of Civil Affairs of China, various years).

Despite being far outnumbered by uncontested, voluntary, mutual consent "divorces by agreement" (协议离婚) processed by marriage registration offices in the Civil Affairs Administration, divorce cases in courts exert an outsized influence that extends into and colors the nature of divorce outside court. Divorce litigation casts a long shadow over couples' negotiations (Mnookin and Kornhauser 1979). Divorce-seekers' spouses take advantage of and benefit from the divorce twofer. Courts' tendency to deny first-attempt petitions gives spouses of divorce-initiators enormous bargaining leverage over the terms of divorce agreements processed outside court. The freedom of divorce is anything but free. Even if divorce is relatively easy to obtain outside court, divorce-seekers, the majority of whom are women, often sacrifice marital property and child custody in exchange for their husbands' consent to divorce (Li 2022). Divorce in China thus illuminates and obfuscates the limits and possibilities of world society's influence on the freedom of divorce.

In contrast to world society scholars' focus on *exogenous* models, templates, scripts, and blueprints (Frank, Camp, and Boutcher 2010; Frank, Hironaka, and Schofer 2000; Frank and Moss 2017), a fourth literature brings into high relief the less obvious *endogenous* forces that animate organizational behavior (Bartley 2018; Bartley and Egels-Zandén 2016; Dezalay and Garth 2010; Haley and Haley 2016; Hallett 2010; Lazarus-Black 2007; Merry 2006; Pache and Santos 2013; Raynard, Lounsbury, and Greenwood 2013; Wimmer 2001).[8] According to legal endogeneity theory, organizations interpret, give meaning to, and thus shape the application of the very laws intended to govern their behavior. Law, particularly when it contains ambiguities, is often endogenous to organizational practices (Edelman 2016). After the passage of federal equal employment opportunity laws in the United States, private corporations responded by establishing organizational policies, structures, and practices that redefined legal compliance in terms of symbolic commitment to diversity. Laws intended to combat employment discrimination have thus served to obscure and enable employment discrimination (Edelman 2016). Likewise, when hospital personnel and patients' family members struggle to assert neonatal intensive care decision-making authority on the basis of competing legal norms and rules, organizational insiders usually prevail, owing to their greater power to define patient care routines and practices (Heimer 1999).

Chinese courts, too, offer an opportunity to assess the relative importance of competing norms and practices – some consistent with and some antithetical to world society models. Judges, as organizational insiders, have redefined, reinterpreted, and applied laws in ways that advance their own professional interests, courts' organizational interests, and the political interests of the party-state, and in so doing have undermined the lawful rights and interests of divorce-seekers. Whereas

---

[8] The word "endogenous" is used synonymously with "local," "domestic," and "indigenous" in much of the institutional literature devoted to untangling "exogenous" and "endogenous" processes and influences (e.g., Cole 2005; Meyer 2010; Wotipka and Ramirez 2008).

faultism is consistent with global norms about protecting female victims of marital violence and supports *granting* divorces, breakdownism, a competing no-fault legal standard, is consistent with local norms about protecting the institution of marriage, social stability, and the interests of judges, and supports *denying* divorces. To borrow the conceptual language of Edelman (2016) and Heimer (1999), we will see that China's domestic fault-based standards, consistent with world society norms, are "symbolic laws" containing "symbolic rights" that, in a twist of tragic irony, have largely failed to penetrate its own civil courts, whereas the routine application of a countervailing no-fault standard to deny the petitions of plaintiffs seeking to dissolve abusive marriages has largely stuck.

From a methodological standpoint, this fourth literature eschews efforts to draw macroscopic generalizations from superficial country-level indicators and points instead to in-depth, nuanced, contextually specific scrutiny of local processes animating organizational behavior as a more fruitful means of explaining the puzzle of decoupling (in both senses of the word) in China's civil courts. Studies such as those in the world society literature that aim to explain variation between dozens of countries in the implementation of laws and policies intended to advance human rights and gender equality must rely on a limited set of crude measures. Owing to this inherent limitation of macro-comparative cross-national research designs, studies that adopt them would have us search in the wrong places for explanations for Chinese courts' systematic failure to protect women seeking to divorce their abusive husbands. In our search for answers, we would consider China's bureaucratic capacity to enforce its domestic laws and international commitments (Cole 2015; Englehart and Miller 2014; Htun and Weldon 2018; True and Mintrom 2001). We would consider the availability and character of monitoring mechanisms (Cole 2005). We would consider foreign aid (Dawson and Swiss 2020; Wei and Swiss 2020). We would consider the strength and autonomy of domestic feminist movements (Htun and Weldon 2018). In the end, we would discover that none of these explanations helps us discern the most salient local obstacles Chinese divorce-seekers face in court.

In the Chinese context of divorce litigation, world society norms coexist with and are neutralized by orthogonal institutional logics. Chinese family law embodies world society norms of equal rights to marriage and divorce (Wang and Schofer 2018). At the same time, the divorce twofer – Chinese judges' tendency to deny first-attempt divorce petitions and to grant subsequent petitions – stems from three institutional pressures unrelated to world society: a political ideology that emphasizes family preservation; heavy court dockets; and performance evaluation systems that motivate judges to maximize measures of social stability and judicial efficiency and to support other political priorities. I also argue that their unequal treatment of female and male plaintiffs stems from a fourth institutional logic incongruous with world society: patriarchy. I thus build on scholarship, some of it in the world society tradition, calling for scrutiny of local values and practices inimical to the reception of global norms, including religious doctrine and misogyny (Boyle, McMorris, and Gómez 2002; Htun and Weldon 2018; Inglehart and Norris 2003; Inglehart, Ponarin, and Inglehart 2017; Pierotti 2013; Wang and Schofer 2018; Welzel 2013).

Vague and contradictory guidance from the law requires judges to exercise discretion. Legal ambiguity provides space for judges to apply the law in creative ways that serve their own interests. It also invites bias. Consider French divorce judges. As street-level bureaucrats overwhelmed by heavy caseloads and under pressure to meet quantitative productivity targets, they exercise discretion by disposing swiftly of cases they deem unworthy and by approving divorce agreements they know to be unfair to one of the parties (Biland and Steinmetz 2017:313–14). Remarkably similar dynamics are at play in China. Chinese law is ambiguous on what constitutes the breakdown of mutual affection; domestic violence; evidence sufficient to prove a legal claim; the unknown whereabouts of a defendant; an "important, complicated, and difficult" dispute requiring the application of the ordinary civil procedure by a three-member collegial panel; and the best interests of the child in custody disputes. When judges exploit legal ambiguity to cut corners and close cases quickly, they often do so at the cost of due process. Owing to pervasive patriarchal cultural beliefs, women seeking to divorce their abusive husbands have paid a disproportionate share of this cost.

I am not the first to grapple with decoupling in Chinese courts. Sida Liu (2006), for example, has shown that courts derive more legitimacy from their durable adherence to local practices such as mediation than from their symbolic adherence to global norms. The story that emerges from the evidence I present in this book is about (endogenous) local institutional norms and practices that serve to marginalize and even neutralize China's domestic laws consistent with (exogenous) global legal norms protecting the freedom of divorce and the equal rights of women. Although it is a China-specific and divorce-specific story, it points to generalizable conditions of decoupling that may be found in other institutional contexts elsewhere in the world. If we are sufficiently attuned to local institutional pressures and practices, we will likely find similarly durable and even intensifying institutional decoupling in other contexts characterized by the same basic conditions present in the Chinese context of divorce litigation: close symbolic alignment to exogenous world society norms, and local agents – such as street-level bureaucrats (Lipsky 2010) – motivated to uphold countervailing endogenous institutional norms.

For women seeking relief from abusive husbands, courts are not the solution but rather part of the problem. I argue that the key to understanding the marginal relevance of marital violence in Chinese divorce adjudication despite its importance in official state rhetoric and black-letter law lies in countervailing legal standards, institutional norms, and practices that overwhelm China's ceremonial commitments to protect vulnerable women. By privileging a no-fault legal standard of the "breakdown of mutual affection" over competing fault-based legal standards of spousal wrongdoing, including domestic violence, courts themselves are an obstacle to women's freedom of divorce. Courts subvert the very legal principles of divorce rights and gender equality they symbolically embrace. In China, no-fault divorce laws consistent with legitimized global models are perversely used at best to delay and at worst to suppress divorce in general and female-initiated divorce in particular, even when plaintiffs make claims of domestic violence and support them with evidence. Even if most divorce-seekers eventually find a way to achieve their goal, justice delayed is justice denied. We will see that the delay and denial of justice are highly gendered.

In the remainder of this chapter, I set the stage for the remainder of this book. First, I delineate the empirical scope of this book by situating divorce litigation within the larger backdrop of divorce procedures. I then describe the cast of characters – both human and institutional – who star in this drama. Finally, I map out the organization of the book.

THE LANDSCAPE OF DIVORCE IN CHINA: PROCEDURES AND TRENDS

Litigation is the act of making, defending, and disposing of claims in court, and is handled by a judge or panel of judges. The litigation process begins when a plaintiff files a legal complaint, which I also refer to as a petition. When litigation is processed by adjudication, the decision is binding regardless of whether any or all parties agree with it. Only a minority of civil lawsuits in China are disposed of by trial, however. Most are disposed of by judicial mediation and plaintiffs' dropping their lawsuits (Chapter 2). Judicial mediation is a Maoist legacy and remains a mainstay practice in China's courts (Huang 2006). When they mediate disputes, judges apply less formal, more ad hoc, and somewhat free-flowing procedures intended to facilitate negotiation and compromise. Mediated decisions are agreements reached, in principle, voluntarily by all litigants. Likewise, a plaintiff's "voluntary" request to withdraw her petition, another common outcome of judicial mediation, takes effect after the court approves it.

This book's empirical focus is adjudicated outcomes in basic-level courts. I use the words "trials" and "adjudications" synonymously. I analyze mediation and petition withdrawals to a far lesser extent because written court decisions are poorly suited for their study (Chapter 4). Figure 1.1 maps out the key steps of the divorce process. It puts the general role of courts and the specific role of court adjudication in perspective.

Because the Civil Affairs Administration, shown on the left side of Figure 1.1, can only process uncontested mutual-agreement divorces, courts are the only place in China to which people can take contested or unilateral divorces. Generally speaking, divorce is readily accessible outside the court system if both sides consent and can agree on all terms. In China, a more than threefold surge in the annual volume of divorces since the year 2003 is attributable entirely to an explosion in the routine, administrative processing of uncontested, mutual-consent divorces outside the court system in local Civil Affairs Bureaus (Ministry of Civil Affairs of China, various years). Prior to the implementation of the 2003 Marriage Registration Regulations, divorces in the Civil Affairs Administration required an introduction letter from a work unit or villagers' committee and a one-month approval period. In the first year after the 2003 Regulations took effect, the absolute number of Civil Affairs divorces rose by over 50%, and since then annual percentage growth has averaged over 10%. Between 1990 and 2018, Civil Affairs divorces as a proportion of all divorces more than doubled from 37% to 85%. Fewer than one in six divorces are processed by courts, and absolute numbers of divorces granted by courts (through both mediation and adjudication) have remained flat since 2003. Civil Affairs divorces have driven China's rapidly rising divorce rates.

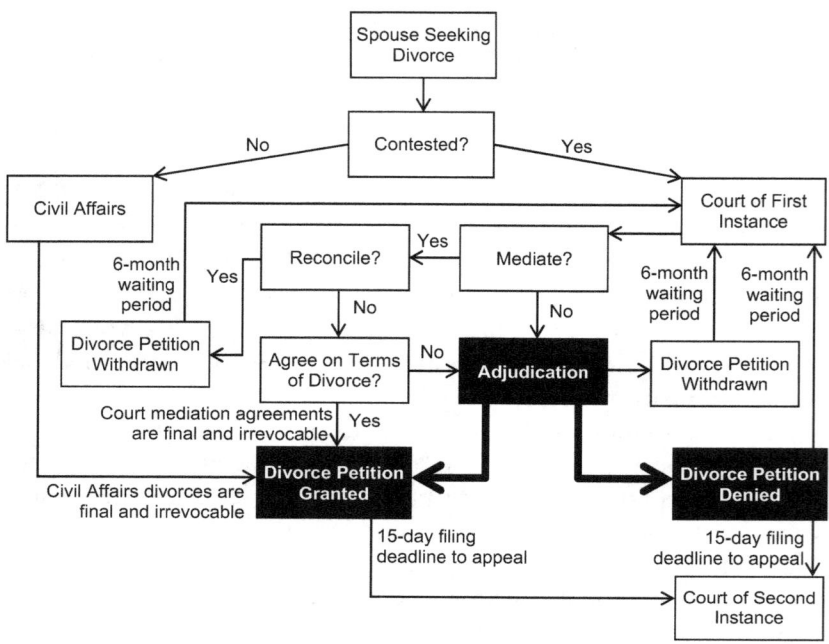

Figure 1.1 The divorce process
Note: Black boxes and thick lines denote the empirical focus of this book.

Court cases, shown on the right side of Figure 1.1, account for only a small fraction of all divorce outcomes in China. They nonetheless involved about 1.4 million couples in China in each year between 2015 and 2018 (Ministry of Civil Affairs of China, various years), many of whom were vulnerable abuse victims. Moreover, as mentioned earlier, courts' influence is vastly disproportionate to the share of divorce cases they process. Knowing that their odds of success in court would be slim on the first attempt, divorce-seekers, often in desperation, "voluntarily" accept unfavorable divorce agreement terms as a condition of a quick and certain Civil Affairs divorce.

A Civil Affairs divorce is considerably cheaper than divorce litigation. Some provinces and municipalities had already waived the ¥9 (about US$1.50) marriage and divorce registration fee before the Civil Affairs Administration abolished it nationwide in 2017 (Xinhua 2017).[9] A court divorce case, by contrast, can cost thousands of yuan

---

[9] The exchange rate was in the ¥6.2–6.8 range per US$1 over the period of time encompassing the court decisions analyzed in this book.

even when it does not result in a divorce. According to the 2007 Measures on Paying Litigation Fees, courts should charge between ¥50 and ¥300 for divorce cases that do not involve property division (Article 31, Item 1). Among the cases I analyze in this book, most litigants were charged the ¥300 regardless of whether their cases involved property claims. The following judicial practices reflect provisions in the 2007 Measures. Courts discount litigation fees by 50% when they apply the simplified civil procedure. When property claims are involved, courts may charge additional inspection, appraisal, and preservation fees according to the value of the property in dispute and which can total thousands of yuan. When a defendant's whereabouts are unknown, courts also charge a public notice fee. Absent an agreement between litigants, judges have discretion to order one party to pay court fees or both parties to share court fees. When they denied divorce petitions, courts almost always ordered plaintiffs to assume sole responsibility for court fees. When they granted divorces, courts were somewhat more likely to order defendants to pay all or half of court fees.

On top of court fees are legal service fees charged by lawyers and legal workers (who are discussed in more detail later in the chapter). Legal advocates were involved in at least half of the cases in my samples of first-attempt divorce adjudications. Legal workers in rural areas often charge a flat fee of several thousand yuan (Li 2015a:103, 107). Lawyers in urban areas often bill for their services according to the economic value of contested property on top of a base fee of several thousand yuan (Min 2017:180). Means-tested legal aid is available but uncommon in the divorce cases in my samples. Legal aid is provided by government legal aid centers, nonprofit and nongovernmental legal aid clinics, and private law firms fulfilling mandatory pro bono quotas.

Uncontested divorce cases rarely enter the court system. If a spouse is unable to appear in person at the local Civil Affairs Bureau's marriage registration office, the divorce-seeker would be forced to file for divorce in court even if her spouse agrees in writing both to the divorce and to all terms of the divorce. This is one of the few scenarios in which courts handle uncontested divorce petitions. Whereas both sides must be physically present for a Civil Affairs divorce, courts routinely proceed with divorce trials in the absence of defendants, and under special circumstances will even permit the representation of absentee plaintiffs in court proceedings.

Basic-level courts, as courts of first instance, are the first stop in the divorce litigation process. Similar to France's mandatory conciliation hearings, which are "the first procedural step for all disputed divorces" (Biland and Steinmetz 2017:314), judicial mediation with the aim of marital reconciliation is required by every version of China's Marriage Law (1950, 1980, and 2001) as well as the 2020 Civil Code that replaced it on January 1, 2021. Several judicial interpretations issued by the Supreme People's Court (SPC) echo this requirement.[10] A court can grant a divorce only if its mediation efforts have failed to achieve marital reconciliation (Huang 2005, 2006). A divorce granted by adjudication therefore implies the court's failure to salvage the marriage. This first step of the divorce process appears in Figure 1.1 as a choice, however, primarily because defendant absenteeism, a common occurrence, precludes the possibility of mediation. If mediation is successful, the plaintiff withdraws her petition, and the couple is considered to have reconciled. If mediation fails to bring forth this outcome, the court may redirect its mediation efforts toward helping the couple agree on the terms of divorce as amicably as possible. Mediation agreements approved by courts are final and cannot be appealed.

Courts generally do not publish approved mediation agreements because they are considered private settlements. When judges grant divorces, they sometimes indicate in their written decisions that mediation has failed to achieve marital reconciliation. Mediation also animates the adjudication process (Meng 2012:86). In the course of trial proceedings, a judge may informally cajole a litigant into backing down from an original demand or otherwise help the litigants work out a compromise. In their written decisions granting divorces, judges sometimes refer to and formalize such informal negotiations as a way of saying that their adjudicatory rulings on divorce terms reflect the voluntary will of the litigants. When they do so, however, the information they provide pertaining to judicial mediation is sparse and cryptic (Chapter 10). Ethnographic research designs are obviously better suited for the study of micro-processes in general and judicial

---

[10] Articles 92 and 145 of the 1992 Opinions of the SPC on Several Issues Concerning the Application of the Civil Procedure Law and the 2015 Interpretations of the SPC on the Application of the Civil Procedure Law, respectively, stipulate that "People's courts should carry out mediation in divorce litigation, but not indefinitely." The SPC's 2003 Judicial Interpretations on the Application of the Simplified Procedure in Civil Trials also stipulates the use of mediation before adjudication in domestic relations cases.

mediation in particular in Chinese divorce litigation (He 2017; He and Ng 2013a, 2013b; Li 2022; Ng and He 2014).

If mediation is not attempted (unlikely), fails to reconcile the couple (very likely), or is unable to produce an agreement on divorce terms (quite likely), the court will adjudicate the case unless the plaintiff withdraws her petition. Sometimes the court will adjudicate immediately after a half-hearted, pro forma reconciliation attempt. A plaintiff can withdraw her petition at any stage of the process, which is why a petition withdrawal is depicted in Figure 1.1 as a possible result of either mediation or adjudication.

Adjudication and its two primary outcomes – to grant or to deny the divorce petition – are denoted in black with thick lines in Figure 1.1 because they are the focus of my empirical scrutiny in this book. The vast majority of people whose divorce cases go to trial the first time will still be married at the end of the process. The "Divorce Petition Granted" box contains a secondary outcome to which I devote two empirical chapters: child custody. A litigant who is unhappy with her first-instance trial outcome may file an appeal with the municipal intermediate court, which is the court of second instance. Appeals are uncommon. When a plaintiff or defendant does file a second-instance petition, she usually seeks a more favorable ruling on child custody or property division after a first-instance verdict to dissolve her marriage. Sometimes a defendant unwilling to divorce will pursue a second-instance reversal of a first-instance court's decision to grant her spouse's divorce petition. For reasons discussed in Chapter 3, plaintiffs rarely appeal adjudicated denials. When plaintiffs do return to court following an adjudicated denial, they almost always do so to file a new first-instance petition after a six-month statutory waiting period. Plaintiffs who withdraw a first-instance divorce petition have the same right to refile after waiting six months. The right to file a new first-instance petition under these circumstances is unique to divorce cases (Chapter 3), gives rise to the feedback loops in Figure 1.1, and therefore enables the divorce twofer.

In Figure 1.1, the "Divorce Petition Granted" box is populated mostly by mediations, and the "Divorce Petition Denied" box is populated mostly by adjudications. Between 2015 and 2018, the slightly more than four million divorce cases that courts nationwide closed using mediation and adjudication were divided roughly evenly between these two modes of case disposal. However, courts tended to use mediation to *grant* divorces and to use adjudication to *deny* divorces.

In the same time period, courts granted 91% of all the divorce cases they closed by mediation but only 41% of all the divorce cases they closed by adjudication. As a consequence, court-mediated divorces outnumbered court-adjudicated divorces by a ratio of more than 2 to 1. Of all 17 million marital dissolutions in China processed over these four years both inside and outside courts, 11% were court-mediated, 5% were court-adjudicated, and 84% were processed in the Civil Affairs Administration. Courts' aversion to granting divorces by adjudication intensified dramatically beginning in the mid-2000s. Adjudicated approvals of divorce petitions as a proportion of all divorce adjudications dropped precipitously from 69% in 2000 to 38% in 2018. China's judicial clampdown on divorce simply reflects courts' growing unwillingness over time to grant first-attempt divorce petitions.[11]

DRAMATIS PERSONAE

The primary actors at the center of the divorce litigation stories I tell in this book include the litigants themselves, many of whom are victims of domestic violence. Courts are the stage set where judges decide litigants' legal fates. I also describe legal advocates even though they play only a cameo role in this book.

Litigants
Throughout this book I refer to divorce litigants as plaintiffs and defendants because they are referred to as such in all written court decisions. Plaintiffs initiate litigation by filing for divorce. As such, plaintiffs can also be thought of as petitioners or claimants. They make claims, which they are supposed to support with evidence. Defendants have an opportunity to respond to plaintiffs' claims, which are often accusations of wrongdoing. As such, defendants also can be thought of as respondents.

We know from the existing literature that wives have been more likely than husbands to file for divorce in China. According to Ke

---

[11] Divorces granted by court *approval* of mediation agreements as a proportion of all divorce cases courts *closed* by mediation remained stable at about 85% between 2000 and 2014 before climbing to 93% in 2018. Divorce petitions withdrawn by plaintiffs as a proportion of divorce petitions increased modestly from 19% in 2000 (and from 18% in each year between 2001 and 2006) to 25% in 2018. All figures in this paragraph are from the Ministry of Civil Affairs of China (various years).

Li (2015a:45), "in the countryside, it is primarily rural women, not men, who initiate divorce lawsuits, a pattern confirmed by scholars, judges, and court clerks." Female plaintiffs accounted for about 70% of all divorce plaintiffs throughout the 1980s (Robinson 1989), about two-thirds in the late 1980s (Palmer 1995:123), 73% in a sample of 1,000 divorces processed by Beijing courts in 1990 and 1991 (Liu and Li 1992), and 73% among over 2.8 million divorce cases across China in 2016 and 2017 (Judicial Big Data Research Institute 2018). Lest we think China is unique in this regard, women seem to be overrepresented among divorce-seekers elsewhere, too. In a study of divorces in Hong Kong between 1999 and 2011, about two-thirds were initiated by women (Law et al. 2019). In Scotland, 63% of divorce petitions were filed by women in a sheriff court (a self-divorce forum for simple cases) in 2002 (Breitenbach and Wasoff 2007:23). Studies consistently show that about 70% of divorces in the United States over the past 150 years were initiated by women (Brinig and Allen 2000; Pettit and Bloom 1984; Rosenfeld 2018). In some places, women's representation among divorce-seekers has grown over time. Japan, for example, appears to have moved in this direction only in recent decades (Alexy 2020). In England and Wales, 61% of divorce petitions were filed by women in the 1960s, an increase from below 50% in the 1940s and 55% in the 1950s (Smart 1984:33, 82).

Victims of Domestic Violence
In a sample of almost 2,000 divorce cases from a basic-level court in Chongqing in 2008–2010, 24% contained claims of domestic violence, and 85% of the victims in such claims were women (Chen and Duan 2012:29–30). In Ke Li's (2015b:168) sample of 60 divorce consultations in a law office in rural southwest China, 27% involved claims of domestic violence, all of which were made by women initiating the divorce process. And in her sample of 171 court divorce decisions, 35% involved claims of domestic violence, all of which were made by female plaintiffs (Li 2015b:171). Estimates of the incidence of domestic violence in the general population of married people (hovering around 30%) and of the composition of domestic violence victims (over 90% female) are generally consistent across studies (Htun and Weldon 2018:49; Parish et al. 2004:177; Runge 2015:32; Song, Zhang, and Zhang 2020; H. Zhang 2014:226; Zhao and Zhang 2017:193–94). Wives also beat their husbands, but far less often. Male victims of domestic violence are not a focus of this book.

Courts and Judges

This book studies basic-level courts in two Chinese provinces: Henan and Zhejiang. Basic-level courts are the lowest level of China's four-tier court system, which also includes municipal intermediate courts,[12] provincial high courts, and the SPC. As stipulated by the Organic Law of People's Courts, each county-level administrative unit – counties, county-level cities, urban districts, and their equivalents in minority nationality regions – has one regular basic-level court. According to one source, China had 2,856 such administrative units at the end of 2010 (xzqh.org 2011). According to another source, China had 2,888 regular basic-level courts in 2011 (Basic Level Legal Artisan 2016c). In addition to regular basic-level courts are courts of special jurisdiction, including railway transportation courts, maritime courts, forestry courts, and agricultural courts. Intellectual property courts, introduced in 2015 (Fu 2018:85), and internet courts, introduced in 2017 (Xinhua 2018), are China's newest courts of special jurisdiction. In 2010, China had 3,115 basic-level courts of all types, accounting for almost 90% of all courts in China (General Office of the SPC 2011). These numbers had hardly changed since 1991, when China had 3,015 basic-level courts (China Law Yearbook 1992:858). In the mid-2010s, Henan had 183 courts, of which 163 were basic-level courts, and Zhejiang had 105 courts, of which 93 were basic-level courts (Chapter 4). Numbers of basic-level courts had remained fairly stable since 1991, when Henan and Zhejiang had 164 and 87 basic-level courts, respectively (China Law Yearbook 1992:858).

Because they are courts of first resort, basic-level courts are generally synonymous with first-instance cases. With the exception of criminal cases eligible for sentences of life in prison or death, certain administrative cases, and other cases of great political importance, first-instance cases are generally handled by basic-level courts. Appellate cases are generally handled by intermediate courts. In every year between 2002 and 2016, basic-level courts were responsible for 90% of all cases, including appeals and retrials, and for 97–98% of all first-instance cases (SPC 2018). In 2010, basic-level courts' 148,000 judges accounted for about 80% of all judges in China (General Office of the SPC 2011). These numbers had not changed much over the preceding decade (Fu 2003:50). Although the population of judges dropped

---

[12] To be more precise, intermediate courts belong to prefectures and prefecture-level cities.

following the implementation of judicial personnel reforms completed in the second half of 2017 (Chapter 5), the number of courts in China remained stable because the number of counties and urban districts also remained stable.

Courts are divided into divisions, primarily civil, criminal, and administrative. In the mid-2010s, the vast majority of basic-level courts in Henan and Zhejiang had one criminal division and one administrative division. According to the official online profiles of basic-level courts in Henan and Zhejiang (described in Chapter 4), about half of Henan's basic-level courts and two-thirds of Zhejiang's basic-level courts had more than one civil division. The average number of civil divisions per basic-level court was 1.6 and 2.3 in each respective province. In Zhejiang, almost 40% of basic-level courts had at least three civil divisions. Because municipal intermediate and provincial high courts are so much larger and thus contain so many more civil divisions, they pushed up the overall average number of civil divisions among all courts to 6.2 and 4.3 in Henan and Zhejiang, respectively, in 2011 (Basic Level Legal Artisan 2016c). Some courts also had specialized divisions for domestic relations, juvenile matters (criminal, civil, and family cases involving minors), labor, traffic safety, bankruptcy, finance, real estate, and environmental resource cases.

In 2011, Henan and Zhejiang had 13,231 and 7,500 judges, respectively. Courts thus averaged 72 and 71 judges in the two respective provinces (Basic Level Legal Artisan 2016a). Crudely applying the rule of thumb that basic-level courts accounted for 80% of all judges (Basic Level Legal Artisan 2016b) yields an average of 58 and 57 judges per basic-level court in each respective province, which is practically identical to estimates I report in Chapter 6 using different sources. In each province, therefore, the average basic-level court served a population of about 600,000, and the average basic-level court judge served a population of about 9,000. Similarities between the two provinces end here. Although population-to-judge ratios were similar, the volume and character of court cases were vastly different across the two provinces. Zhejiang's courts developed an array of coping strategies, including the divorce twofer, in response to its far heavier caseloads (Chapters 5 and 6).

People's Tribunals (人民法庭 or 派出法庭) are sub-courts of basic-level courts that extend their reach into rural townships (乡), towns (镇), and urban subdistrict offices (街道办事处). They can be thought of as branches or outposts of the lowest level of the court system. The Organic Law of People's Courts stipulates that basic-level courts may create People's Tribunals according to local needs, population, and case characteristics (Article 26). Although they are not exclusively rural, their primary function is to enhance access to courts in remote rural areas, and they thus tend to be rural-facing (Liu 2006). In the mid-2000s, 90% of People's Tribunals were in rural areas (Du 2008). People's Tribunals have vastly increased the rural footprint of basic-level courts. Some urban districts contain People's Tribunals because they encompass rural outskirts containing towns and townships. Urban districts formerly designated as – or which annexed – rural counties or county-level cities often inherited People's Tribunals. For example, Henan's Nanyang County was redesignated as Wancheng District when the prefecture-level city of Nanyang was established in 1994. Its basic-level court, with jurisdiction over 927 square kilometers, has seven People's Tribunals for its heavily rural population (https://perma.cc/4SJT-X5JX). Likewise, Zhejiang's Fuyang County People's Court established four People's Tribunals in 1961. Fuyang County was redesignated as a county-level city in 1994 before it was absorbed by the provincial capital of Hangzhou as Fuyang District in 2015. Its basic-level court, with jurisdiction over 1,820 square kilometers, has maintained all of its original People's Tribunals for its overwhelmingly rural population (https://perma.cc/SXT7-ZUXH).

Rural counties and county-level cities, of course, are typically far more geographically expansive than urban districts. About 60–65% of Henan and Zhejiang's counties and county-level cities are larger than 1,000 square kilometers, and about 15–20% are larger than 2,000 square kilometers. Nanyang's Neixiang County People's Court, for example, has a jurisdiction of almost 2,500 square kilometers – much of it mountainous terrain – for its population of 630,000, 90% of which is rural. Its seven People's Tribunals covering 16 towns and townships have reduced the maximum distance between any village and any court outpost to a little over 60 kilometers (https://perma.cc/FF77-8UCM). By allowing villagers to file for divorce in towns and townships, People's Tribunals have obviated the need for villagers to travel long distances to basic-level courts. In Zhejiang, some coastal counties encompass hundreds of small islands. Mobile courts (巡回法庭) – widely referred to as "courts on horseback" (马背上的法庭), "van courts" (车载法庭), "mobile trial spots" (巡回审判点), and a means of "sending law to the countryside" (送法下乡) – have served China's rural areas since the time of the Chinese Communist Party's revolutionary base areas in the 1920s and 1930s (Gieryn 2018; Xu, Huang, and Lu 2011:144; Zhu 2016:8–10). In coastal fishing areas in provinces such as Zhejiang, they are also referred to as "fishing boat courts" (渔船法庭; https://perma.cc/H6CD-DLE9).

People's Tribunals merged and consolidated over time. Numbering 15,886 in 1987, they reached their apex of 18,000 in 1992, declined slightly to 17,411 in 1998, and had significantly shrunk in number to 11,220 in 2008, 10,023 in 2009, and to 9,880 in 2011 (Du 2008; General Office of the SPC 2011; Gu 2014:30n3; Yu and Gao 2015:21). In 2011, People's Tribunals in Henan and Zhejiang numbered 746 and 225, respectively (Basic Level Legal Artisan 2016c).[13] In 2020, People's Tribunals numbered 10,844 nationally, 699 in Henan, and 282 in Zhejiang.[14] Their numerical contraction over the past few decades, however, does not imply that their role has diminished. On the contrary, the SPC has continued to promote the role of People's Tribunals (Gu 2014; Wan and Lin 2020; Xinhua 2011; Yu and Gao 2015:22).

Given that divorce litigation is a predominantly rural phenomenon (Chapter 4) and that People's Tribunals are overwhelmingly rural, People's Tribunals handle about half of all divorce cases in the court system. According to official judicial statistics, domestic relations cases – marriage, family, and inheritance disputes, about 80% of which are divorce cases (Chapter 4) – were overrepresented in People's Tribunals. Between 2003 and 2016, People's Tribunals consistently handled 20–25% of basic-level courts' *total caseload*. At the same time, People's Tribunals have consistently handled the majority of basic-level courts' *domestic relations cases*. More specifically, the proportion of basic-level courts' domestic relations cases handled by People's Tribunals was close to 40% between 2003 and 2005, reached 50% in 2006, and plateaued at about 51–54% between 2007 and 2016 (SPC 2018). Despite their sizeable role in divorce litigation, People's Tribunals are generally unidentifiable in written court decisions. Only the basic-level courts to which they belong are disclosed. As we learn about judicial decision-making in this book, we should bear in mind that a large share of the divorce trials I analyze took place in these remote outpost court settings.

---

[13] The 2012 annual work report of Henan's provincial high court put its number of People's Tribunals at 729 (https://perma.cc/9B37-2FRQ).

[14] These numbers were reported by the National People's Tribunal Information Network (http://rmft.court.gov.cn/) as current as of November 8, 2020.

Judges include "frontline" judges (一线法官 or 办案法官) who handle cases and leaders who are responsible for court administration. In 2002, for example, an unnamed intermediate court had 192 employees in the state personnel system for civil servants (编制), of whom 103 had the title of judge, and of whom only 53 were frontline judges who did trial work. An additional 23 judges did case filing and enforcement work, meaning 74% of all judges were on the front lines (Xu and Jiang 2009:101). At the time, an estimated 75% of all nominal judges in China were frontline judges (Basic Level Legal Artisan 2016b). Officers of the court (干警) also include clerks (书记员) and bailiffs (法警).

Judges numbered about 200,000 prior to a quota reform launched in 2015. The new quota system drastically shrank the scope of who counts as a judge, reducing their numbers to about 125,000 by 2019. It also required court presidents, vice-presidents, and division heads, who had previously done little trial work, to join the ranks of frontline judges by doing at least some trial work. Even when cases are tried by court leaders, the written court decisions do not identify them as such. They are identified only as "associate judges" (审判员) and "assistant judges" (助理审判员). The foregoing points are elaborated in greater detail in Chapter 5.

The Chinese bench has feminized rapidly from a low base. Women accounted for 29% of all judges nationwide in 2013 (Zheng, Ai, and Liu 2017:169). In Henan and Zhejiang, female representation on the bench was 27% and 33% respectively, in the same year (Henan Provincial Bureau of Statistics 2014; Zheng, Ai, and Liu 2017:181). In Henan, female representation had increased to 30% in 2018 (Henan Provincial Bureau of Statistics 2019). Although written court decisions do not disclose judge sex, it can be inferred with imperfect accuracy from a judge's name. The extent to which judicial decision-making varies by judge sex is not a focus of this book.[15]

Finally, People's Lay Assessors (人民陪审员, hereafter "lay assessors") also participate in trials alongside judges as members of collegial panels. Although their status is nominally equal to that of judges, in practice they play a subordinate role (X. He 2016). Courts dramatically

---

[15] On the methodological challenges associated with testing judge gender effects, see Boyd, Epstein, and Martin (2010). These challenges are further compounded in the Chinese judicial context, where otherwise seemingly identical cases are variously tried by one judge, by three-judge panels, and by three-member mixed panels composed of judges and lay assessors.

increased their recruitment of lay assessors over the past decade as a means of coping with an acute imbalance between judges and cases (Chapter 5).

Legal Advocates

Although I have spent much of my career studying Chinese lawyers, they make only a cameo appearance in this book (in Chapter 9 on criminal domestic violence cases). Written court decisions contain the names of legal advocates and their firms, as well as varying amounts of personal information about them, including their sex, date of birth, ethnic group, and level of education.

Legal advocates are not limited to lawyers. Lawyers do not enjoy a monopoly over the Chinese market for legal services. They compete with a variety of alternative legal service providers (S. Liu 2011). In the realm of divorce, lawyers' primary source of competition is basic-level legal workers. Although China's 320,000 full-time lawyers (Ministry of Justice 2018) vastly outnumbered its 70,000 legal workers in 2017 (Jin and Zhou 2018), lawyers have been concentrated in larger cities (Liu, Liang, and Michelson 2014; Michelson 2012). Legal workers, by contrast, have been concentrated in townships, towns, and county seats of rural counties and county-level cities, serving rural areas where divorces are also concentrated and where lawyers are in short supply. When divorce litigants from the countryside have legal representation, it tends to come from legal workers "who attend to rural residents' struggles with divorce" (Li 2015b:158, 2016). With women accounting for only about 20% of lawyers through 2010, China's level of lawyer feminization has been relatively low in global comparative perspective (Michelson 2013:1083). Legal workers, too, are predominantly male (Li 2015a:152, 186). As mentioned earlier, legal aid lawyers play a very small role in the divorce litigation landscape.

Although, taken together, these various types of legal advocates commonly participate in the divorce litigation process, they are not a focus of this book. The impact of counsel is impossible to ascertain with cross-sectional information on concluded cases (Sandefur 2015). If, for example, we found that litigants represented by lawyers were more likely to win their cases, we would have no way of knowing whether lawyers strengthened their cases or simply selected strong cases and avoided weak cases. Furthermore, the voices of legal advocates are almost completely absent from the written court decisions. With only a tiny handful of exceptions, they did not make statements on the record to the court in divorce trial proceedings. Legal advocates may have a greater impact off the record by pressuring and persuading litigants: not to file for divorce, to withdraw their petitions, and to accept bad deals brokered by judges (Li 2015b, 2016, 2022). Such processes are obviously beyond the scope of my analyses of written court decisions.

MAIN ACTS: OVERVIEW OF THE BOOK

This book is roughly divided into two halves: (1) *causes* underlying the divorce twofer, the judicial clampdown on divorce, and judges' bias against women, and (2) gendered *consequences* of these problems, including women's dimmer prospects obtaining an adjudicated divorce, their worse child custody outcomes, and their greater risk of becoming a victim of criminal battery or murder following a divorce attempt. The book is also organized empirically according to two key decisions judges make in the divorce litigation process: (1) the *decision to grant or deny a plaintiff's divorce petition* and, when they do grant a divorce, (2) the *decision to grant child custody* to the mother, the father, or – in the case of siblinged children – both parents.

The next three chapters lay the groundwork for my empirical analyses of *marital decoupling*. Chapter 2 provides an overview of formal legal divorce rights, particularly as they pertain to gender equality and domestic violence.

Chapter 3 then identifies and explains countervailing institutional norms and pressures that have, at a minimum, blunted and, at most, neutralized the force of these formal legal rights, and that are therefore responsible for *institutional decoupling* inside China's divorce courts.

Chapter 4 contains details about my collection of 4.5 million written court decisions from two provinces and how I studied them. China's courts began posting their decisions online en masse for the most part in 2013 and 2014. At the time I finished writing this book, they had posted the text of over 90 million decisions and metadata of another 22 million decisions on the SPC's China Judgements Online website (https://perma.cc/9VH9-ZMH8). This book adds to growing sources of guidance on how to exploit this gold mine of information about judicial decision-making (Liebman et al. 2020).

Chapters 5 and 6 focus specifically on the causes and consequences of judges' heavy caseloads. My two-province comparative research design reveals that spectacular growth in civil litigation gave rise to the problem of "many cases, few judges." Judges adopted innovative coping strategies, including the divorce twofer, to deal with their crushing dockets. Divorce cases are casualties of clogged courts, and women are casualties of divorce cases. Whereas Chapter 6 shows how the divorce twofer *benefits* judges, subsequent chapters show how it *harms* women.

In Chapter 7, I begin my sustained empirical focus on gender injustice. After first quantitatively demonstrating the prevalence of domestic violence allegations in divorce petitions, I then qualitatively demonstrate their unimportance to judges.

Chapter 8 is a quantitative analysis of the decision to grant or deny a divorce petition. The content of judges' holdings was virtually identical regardless of whether plaintiffs made allegations of domestic violence. Men enjoyed various kinds of preferential treatment in divorce trial proceedings. Consequently, an adjudicated divorce on the first attempt was considerably less likely for a female plaintiff than for a male plaintiff. Female divorce-seekers' disadvantage, however, was limited to rural areas.

Chapter 9 explores two tragic consequences of decoupling in cases involving domestic violence. First, it has spawned a sizable population of female marital violence refugees who took flight from their abusive husbands. Second, it has spawned criminal cases. Judges' practice of denying divorce petitions as a means of protecting themselves and abuse victims has no basis whatsoever in law. Police intervention, including public security administrative punishment and enforcement of personal protection orders, is the primary legal mechanism for protecting abuse victims but has proven to be woefully ineffective in practice. With the more effective support of public authorities, including the police, judges would undoubtedly save lives by – precisely as stipulated by Chinese law – granting the divorce petitions of abuse victims. Courts revictimized abuse victims not only by denying their divorce petitions but also, as Chapters 10 and 11 show, by granting child custody to their abusers in the process of granting their divorce petitions.

Chapter 10 shifts the empirical focus to child custody determinations. Consistent with global legal norms, Chinese laws stipulate that child custody should be determined according to the best interests of the child. No Chinese law privileges fathers with respect to the custody rights of sons. In practice, however, courts tend to formalize the status quo. In so doing, they flout the best interests of the child doctrine as well as guidelines from the SPC directing them not to grant child custody to domestic batterers.

Chapter 11 reports the results of quantitative analyses of the decision to grant or deny child custody. Abused mothers were disadvantaged in child custody determinations, and women's child custody prospects were determined to a large extent by both the number and gender composition of children. Consistent with the logic of patriarchy, courts almost never granted child custody of only-sons to mothers. Mothers' best chances for child custody came from multiple children and from only-daughters. When there were multiple children, courts usually split them up between the parents. When multiple children included both genders, courts usually granted custody of sons to fathers and of daughters to mothers.

Chapter 12 concludes with lessons for research on the globalization of law. I discuss the substantive implications of scholars' methodological choices and constraints. Only by directly measuring judicial behavior and identifying the extrajudicial institutional forces that shape it – my key tasks in this book – can we properly assess the limits and possibilities of the local penetration of global legal norms.

CHAPTER TWO

THE RIGHT TO DECOUPLE

In this chapter, I provide a schematic overview of sources of law pertaining to the right to divorce, evidentiary standards, legal procedures, and how they are double-edged swords used to deny gender justice. Chinese law is replete with ambiguities and inconsistencies that enable almost limitless judicial discretion to deny legally deserving divorce petitions and to ignore domestic violence allegations (J. Zhang 2018).

As a primer on Chinese laws governing the divorce process, this chapter lays the groundwork for an assessment of how and how well China's courts implement those laws. Chinese judges arrive at their decisions not by applying case law, but rather by applying relevant legal provisions to the facts of a given case. As part of the civil law tradition, China's legal system operates not according to legal precedent at the center of Anglo-American common law systems but rather according to statutes enacted by China's legislature (the National People's Congress), rules and regulations promulgated by China's administrative agencies (ministries under the State Council), and judicial interpretations and opinions issued by the SPC, all of which carry the full force of law (Finder 1993; Hsia and Johnson 1986).[1] Judges' textual interpretations of the foregoing legal sources are hardly neutral, thanks to the judiciary's subordination to state interests and political priorities – a key defining feature of "rule by law" (Moustafa

---

[1] China's modern legal system was adapted from the civil law tradition of continental Europe in general and Germany in particular, via the influence of both Japan at the end of the Qing Dynasty and the Soviet Union in the 1950s (Xin 1999:319, 356, 473, 499–500).

2014) and "authoritarian legality" (Gallagher 2017; Solomon 2010) common to many illiberal political contexts. Judicial decision-making in China is colored generally by the strong civil service character of courts in civil law countries (Biland and Steinmetz 2017) and particularly by China's Leninist legacy of "socialist legality" (Baum 1986; Shih 1996).

Laws, rules, and judicial interpretations provide grounds on which judges can grant unilateral divorces and give women who cannot prove their domestic violence allegations the benefit of the doubt. At the same time, however, they provide judges with legal pretexts for denying divorce petitions even in cases involving domestic violence.

OVERVIEW OF RIGHTS

China is a poster child for laws protecting gender equality and the freedom of divorce. Following the establishment of the People's Republic of China in 1949, the first body of law enacted by the new government was the 1950 Marriage Law, which enshrined the principles of gender equality and the freedom of marriage based on love and consent, and which became a key weapon in early campaigns targeting arranged marriages, bride-buying, polygamy, concubinage, close cousin marriage, and other "feudal" marital practices (Diamant 2000b; Johnson 1983; Parish and Whyte 1978:158). The principle of the freedom of divorce has been an inextricable part of the principle of the freedom of marriage (Huang 2005; Li 2001:6), and facilitated a surge of divorces in the early 1950s, peaking at over one million in 1953 (Tsui 2001:110). Article 49 of China's Constitution and Article 103 of China's General Principles of Civil Law both explicitly prohibit any violation of or interference with the freedom of marriage.

In the time since the 1950 and 1980 versions of the Marriage Law, neither of which explicitly addressed domestic violence, legal provisions promoting gender equality in general and protecting victims of domestic violence in particular have emerged in a dizzying number of national laws in China, including the Constitution, the General Principles of Civil Law, the Civil Procedure Law, the Criminal Law, the Criminal Procedure Law, the National Security Law, the Law on the Protection of Women's Rights and Interests, the Law on the Protection of the Rights and Interests of Minors, the Law on the Protection of the Rights and Interests of the Elderly, and the Law Protecting Disabled Persons, not to mention national and local administrative regulations, measures, resolutions, notices, and circulars as well as SPC interpretations, opinions, instructions, and written replies to requests for guidance from lower courts – all of which generally have the force of law (Alford and Shen 2004:242; Chen and Duan 2012; Jiang 2016; Rong 2016; Runge 2015:34; H. Zhang 2012; Zhao and Zhang 2017:194–95). According to the 2008 Guidelines on Judging Marital Cases Involving Domestic Violence (hereafter, "the 2008 Guidelines"), published by the SPC's research arm, the China Institute of Applied Jurisprudence, "China has over 69 local laws and regulations to prevent, stop, and prohibit domestic violence" (Article 16). Its preamble reflects the strength of China's embrace of global norms of gender equality:

> Important instructions from Party and state leaders concerning "attaching importance to the protection of women's rights and bringing about gender mainstreaming" and "advancing gender equality and realizing common development," the emphasis of leaders of the Supreme People's Court on gender equality and judicial fairness, and policy documents from other relevant state agencies and social organizations on the implementation of principles of equality stipulated by the Constitution all provide policy support to these Guidelines.

The term "domestic violence" (家庭暴力) made its debut in Chinese law in the third and final version of the Marriage Law amended in 2001. It introduced several provisions related to domestic violence, including Article 46, a mechanism for claiming civil damages (Chen and Shi 2013; Chen, Shi, and He 2014; Chen, Shi, and Zhang 2016; Yang 2016). Article 46 is essentially preserved as Article 1091 in the 2020 Civil Code that took effect on January 1, 2021, superseding not only the Marriage Law but also the Inheritance Law, the Adoption Law, the General Principles of Civil Law, the Property Law, the Tort Law, the Guarantee Law, and the Contract Law. Although the 2001 Marriage Law and the 2020 Civil Code prohibit and punish domestic violence, they contain no clear definition of what constitutes domestic violence. This shortcoming was quickly remedied in the 2001 Interpretations of the SPC on Several Issues Regarding the Application of the Marriage Law (Li and Friedman 2016:156; H. Zhang 2014:225). Its definition of domestic violence includes "beating, tying-up, maiming and restricting personal freedom (for example by the use of force) such that mental or physical harm results" between spouses or between a spouse and a family member such as a child or parent-in-law (Article 1; Palmer 2007:683; also see

Cheng and Wang 2018:254–55). The 2005 amended version of the 1992 Law on Protecting the Rights and Interests of Women added a provision prohibiting – and requiring government agencies and grass-roots mass organizations to prevent and combat – domestic violence against women (Article 46).

The 2008 Guidelines further clarified the SPC's definition of domestic violence and brought it into alignment with international definitions of violence against women by including "actions between family members, but primarily between spouses, in which one side uses physical coercion, verbal degradation, economic control, or other means to carry out a violation of the other side's physical, sexual, psychological, or other rights of the person for the intended purpose of controlling the other side" (Article 2; H. Zhang 2014:226). Indeed, the 2008 Guidelines cite by name and quote directly from the United Nations 1993 Declaration on the Elimination of Violence against Women and the 2006 Secretary-General's In-Depth Study on All Forms of Violence against Women. One of its eight chapters is devoted to personal safety protection orders. The 2008 Guidelines even stipulate, "People's Courts may summon expert witnesses at the request of a litigant or on their own authority to explain the defining characteristics and unique patterns of domestic violence, including battered spouse syndrome. When necessary, experts may be questioned by judges and litigants on both sides. An expert opinion may be used as an important reference source in judicial rulings" (Article 44). We will see in Chapter 9 that Chinese courts, no different from courts in the United States and elsewhere (Fair 2018; Paradis 2017), do include expert witness testimony on battered woman syndrome in cases of women who killed their abusive husbands.

China had signaled its commitment to combatting domestic violence long before 2001. In February 1994, in preparation for 1995 World Conference on Women in Beijing, China's government submitted to the United Nations a report on the central document that emerged from the previous World Conference, namely the 1985 Nairobi Forward-Looking Strategies for the Advancement of Women. The Chinese report points out that "the elimination of all forms of violence against women is necessary to strengthen and advance China's social stability, and also to protect women's human rights." It also promises "gradually to improve the system of specialized, preventative, and administrative laws and regulations to eliminate violence against women as well as the system of enforcement and supervision" (Rong

2016:203–04). Following the Beijing conference, China along with over 180 other countries adopted the 1995 Beijing Declaration and the Platform for Action, in which violence against women is one of 12 "critical areas of concern" (Htun and Weldon 2018:63).

The 2008 Guidelines also urge courts to grant divorces when the legal standard for domestic violence is satisfied:

> The freedom of marriage includes both the freedom of marriage and the freedom of divorce. Marriage requires the mutual consent of both people, whereas divorce requires only that one person make a request that satisfies the conditions for divorce. The People's Court will not protect the freedom of marriage at the expense of neglecting the protection of the freedom of divorce. When one involved party initiates divorce litigation, the People's Court should grant the divorce through mediation or adjudication provided there are statutory grounds for divorce and mediation by a people's court failed to achieve marital reconciliation. Under circumstances in which the occurrence of domestic violence has been affirmed and one of the parties insists on divorcing, regardless of whether the petitioner is the offender or the victim, the People's Court should respect the party's desire, uphold the principle of the freedom of marriage, and grant the divorce as quickly as possible by mediation or adjudication in order to prevent the aggravation of violent injuries caused by a delay and lack of resolution. ... Even if a minority of such divorces resulted from people's rash decisions made impulsively, as adults they should accept responsibility for their actions. (Article 17)

As we will see, however, courts tend to do the opposite of what these guidelines prescribe. Judges sometimes fear that *granting* divorces may aggravate domestic violence and lead to "extreme incidents" such as murder and suicide (He 2017). Moreover, judges can and do disregard these guidelines because, as stated in the preamble, they are provided only for reference purposes to trial judges, lack the force of law, and thus cannot be the legal basis for court rulings (Deng 2017:109).

China's 2015 Anti-Domestic Violence Law, which took effect in March 2016, brings together and elaborates legal protections, including provisions on personal protection orders, previously scattered across a number of bodies of law, administrative regulations, and SPC interpretations. Indeed, it absorbed 12 out of all 38 articles of the 2008 Guidelines (Pan 2018). Although this law does not explicitly address divorce, it – like earlier laws, including Articles 100 and 154 of the 2012 Civil Procedure Law (which appeared as Articles 92 and

140 in the 2007 version) – gives women who want to separate from their abusive husbands the right to apply to courts for protection orders.[2]

Chinese law provides multiple grounds for divorce. Statutory wrongdoing, also known as "faultism," constitutes grounds for divorce. Physical separation can be grounds for divorce. A defendant's failure to respond to a public notice when his whereabouts are unknown is also grounds for divorce. Above all, the breakdown of mutual affection, also known as "breakdownism," is grounds; and consequently, judges assess the quality of the marital relationship and potential for reconciliation.

BREAKDOWNISM

In comparative historical perspective, China was a legal trailblazer in terms of liberal no-fault divorce standards. China's laws on the books have always allowed divorce when only one spouse wants it. China's 1950 Marriage Law stipulated: "If either husband or wife insists on divorce, the divorce will be granted when the district-level people's government and judicial organs fail to achieve marital reconciliation" (Article 17). The Chinese right to a unilateral ex parte divorce on grounds of "irreconcilable differences" has even deeper roots in the short-lived 1931–1937 Chinese Soviet Republic, which modeled its divorce laws on those of the Soviet Union, and predates the rise and spread of Western no-fault divorce by several decades (Chen 2005a:154, 156; Huang 2005:175).

Following a national campaign to enforce the Marriage Law in the early 1950s, however, the freedom of divorce became notoriously difficult to realize. Countervailing against the freedom of divorce were official concerns about its abuse and concomitant policies intended to discourage and limit its exercise. The call to "oppose" or "prevent frivolous divorce" (反对轻率离婚 or 防止轻率离婚; Chen 2005a; Ma and Luo 2014:39; Zhang 2009:28), which reverberates to this day, was justified by the work of Marx and Engels, and by Lenin's famous quip that "it is not at all difficult to understand that the recognition of the right of women to leave their husbands is not an invitation to all wives

---

[2] The use of these provisions for this purpose is explained both in the 2008 Guidelines and Liu (2013:79). Also see Runge (2015:37–38).

to do so!" (Liang 1982:19). The Chinese novel *Waiting* (Jin 2000) is frequently cited to illustrate a "legal system that substantively provides for the freedom of divorce but procedurally prohibits it" (Woo 2001; also see Alford and Shen 2004:250; Honig and Hershatter 1988:206; Huang 2005:187). This narrative of the Sisyphean challenge of divorce throughout the Mao era, although not entirely without challenge (Diamant 2000b, 2001), remains dominant (Honig and Hershatter 1988; Huang 2005; Johnson 1983; Stacey 1983; Wolf 1985). Despite a provision in the 1950 and 1980 versions of the Marriage Law (Article 17 and Article 24 respectively) requiring that divorce certificates be issued "without delay" (应即发给离婚证) when all legal conditions for divorce were satisfied, courts routinely denied divorce petitions or dragged out the process for years (Tsui 2001:108; Whyte and Parish 1984:150–51, 187).

Forces outside the Marriage Law undermined the realization of the freedom of divorce. Later in 1950, the Legal System Committee, under the now-defunct Government Administration Council of the Central People's Government, promulgated Answers to Several Issues Regarding the Implementation of the Marriage Law, which provided a condition under which courts could deny divorce petitions: "A divorce judgment should be rendered if there is a legitimate reason why marital relations cannot continue, otherwise a judgment denying the divorce may also be rendered" (Chen 2005a:154; Li 2001:7). Both the Legal System Committee's 1953 Answers to Questions about Divorce and the SPC's 1963 Opinions on Several Issues Regarding the Implementation and Enforcement of Civil Policies reaffirmed a court's ability to deny a divorce petition even if mediated reconciliation efforts failed, provided the court determined that the couple had not yet reached the point where life together was truly unsustainable (1953) or that marital relations (夫妻关系) and marital affection (夫妻感情) had not completely broken down beyond any hope of reconciliation (1963) (Chen 2005a:154–55; Li 2001:7). Judicial workers charged with deciding whether to grant divorce requests were reportedly vexed by the SPC's lack of clarity: "The rules looked like rules but at the same time were not rules; because they were ambiguous and cut both ways, were hard to get a handle on in judicial practice, and supported granting or denying the same divorce petition, judgments were inconsistent" (Chen 2005a:155). Legal ambiguity persists to the present day owing to multiple, competing standards for divorce against the backdrop of political and ideological pressures.

Animating China's history of family law legislation and practices over the past century are unresolved tensions between efforts to promote gender equality through the protection of divorce rights, and socialist morality and the legacy of Confucian family values. China's oxymoronic approach to divorce endeavors to "protect the freedom of divorce and prevent frivolous divorce" (Ma 2006:23; Ma and Luo 2014:39; W. Zhou 2018). The "freedom of marriage" is invoked in different ways. It often refers to the freedom of divorce. It is also a euphemism for marital preservation. Du Wanhua (杜万华), for example, a high-ranking member of the SPC's adjudication committee until the end of 2017, said in an interview: "In order to preserve family stability, should we get rid of the freedom of divorce and say marriages cannot end? Of course not. The freedom of marriage includes both the freedom to marry and the freedom to divorce. In order to maintain the stability of marriage and family we must also protect the freedom of marriage" (Wang and Luo 2016). In China, maintaining family stability through marital preservation is a political tool for maintaining social stability writ large (Chapter 3).

Although mutual consent has never been an absolute condition of divorce in any Chinese law, in practice it remains a virtual sine qua non of divorce, thanks to this legal test based on the current extent of – and future potential for – marital affection and love, known as "breakdownism." The 1980 Marriage Law removed the required step of extra-judicial mediation; those seeking to divorce could now go straight to court. At the same time, however, modeled after the standard I have already discussed in the earlier 1963 SPC Opinions, the "breakdown of mutual affection" (感情破裂) standard was added to the 1980 Marriage Law (Article 25). It remains in the 2001 version (Article 32) as well as the 2020 Civil Code (Article 1079) as follows: "If one party alone desires a divorce, the organization concerned may carry out mediation or the party may appeal directly to a People's Court to start divorce proceedings. In dealing with a divorce case, the People's Court shall carry out mediation; in cases of complete breakdown of mutual affection, and when mediation has failed, divorce should be granted."

By removing a burdensome extrajudicial mediation requirement and adding a variant of standardized global no-fault "irreconcilable differences" tests, the 1980 Marriage Law's breakdownism (破裂主义) appeared to lower barriers to divorce. Indeed, that was its original intent. As the deputy chair of the committee responsible for drafting the 1980 Marriage Law explained, forcibly preserving marriages "would only cause those involved to suffer, even for the contradictions to sharpen, and result possibly in homicides" (Huang 2005:186).

Paradoxically, however, breakdownism has also served to support the deep legislative spirit of "preventing frivolous divorce." The Marriage Law's promise of unilateral no-fault divorce was neutralized by its requirement that courts first determine whether a marriage is dead or viable. Chinese courts are distinguished by the wide discretion they wield to assess the extent and quality of marital affection. The legislative intent of the breakdownism standard was to allow "the courts both to loosen divorce requirements for those couples whose relationship offered no hope for reconciliation and to tighten them for spouses who sought divorce out of momentary anger" (Huang 2005:187). In practice, however, judges routinely rule that any marriage in which one party does not want to divorce has hope for reconciliation and therefore fails to meet the breakdownism standard – at least on the first filing (S. Guo 2018:113; Xu 2007:204; W. Zhou 2018).

Judges exercise enormous discretion and make arbitrary rulings when applying abstract, unmeasurable components of the breakdownism standard (Ma and Luo 2014:35). In 1989, to provide guidance to judges, the SPC promulgated Several Concrete Opinions on How to Determine in Divorce Trials Whether Marital Affection Has Indeed Broken Down, also informally dubbed the "Fourteen Articles" because it contains a list of 14 standards (Chen 2005a:155; Huang 2005:156; Li 2001:8). These opinions require that judges assess "the marriage's current condition and reconciliation potential" (有无和好的可能; Xu 2000).[3] Rather than offering clarity, the Fourteen Articles extended existing ambiguities by requiring judges to rule on divorce petitions according to unknowable, hypothetical future counterfactuals (Alford and Shen 2004:251; Chen 2005a:155).

> Holdings in adjudicated divorce decisions are extremely flexible, giving the law considerable room for the application of common sense. ... Whether or not there is reconciliation potential is the key reason for granting or denying a divorce. This is reflected in the following: First, when courts determine that there is reconciliation potential, they will deny the divorce petition. There can be no situation in which a court will affirm reconciliation potential and then grant a divorce. Second, if a couple in divorce litigation had previously reconciled through

---

[3] A "lack of reconciliation potential" appears in both the preamble and three of all 14 articles.

mediation and continued living together, the judge will often try to mediate again and then deny the divorce petition if mediation is unsuccessful. The reason for this is that judges can use previous reconciliation experience to form their judicial determination that the marital relationship can be reconciled. Whether there is reconciliation potential is entirely a matter of judicial discretion about – and a judicial determination of – the condition of a couple's mutual affection. For these reasons, both legal provisions and judicial discretion leave room for two or more divorce petitions from the same couple. (Jiang and Zhu 2014:82–83)

Scholars have widely decried the practical application of the breakdownism test as a "backward step" (倒退) and an unlawful assault on the freedom of divorce (Alford and Shen 2004:244–45, 252; Jiang 2009a:67; Ma 2006; Xu 2007; Yi and Tong 1998).

Mutual consent is often enough to establish the breakdown of mutual affection. Defendants sometimes (albeit rarely) agree on the divorce itself, even if they challenge its terms. According to Article 31 of the Marriage Law, a divorce should be granted if both sides want out. More often than not, judges take mutual consent as evidence of the breakdown of mutual affection and grant the divorce on these grounds (Jiang 2009b:19; Luo 2016:16). Judges, however, may also deny a divorce petition even when the defendant consents if they deem the case to be "frivolous" or "impulsive." They may also suspect the couple is conspiring to get a "fake divorce" and then to remarry after achieving their illicit goal of escaping debt, circumventing restrictions on the purchase of real estate, evading family planning policies, or receiving more housing demolition compensation (Cai and Qi 2019; Fu and Wang 2019; Jiang 2009b:19; Tan and Wang 2011). Most divorce fraud, however, occurs outside court in the Civil Affairs Administration (Min 2017:179).

FAULTISM

The breakdown of mutual affection can also be established on faultism grounds of statutory wrongdoing (过错主义; Ma and Luo 2014). Marital affection should be regarded as having broken down if any of the 14 standards itemized in the 1989 Fourteen Articles is met and the plaintiff insists on a divorce. The 14 breakdownism standards include sexual dysfunction, mental illness, "bride-buying" (买卖婚姻, also translated as "mercenary marriage"), and various forms of marriage fraud. Strictly speaking, not all of the 14 conditions on the list constitute wrongdoing. In addition to breakdownism and fault-ism, a third Chinese divorce standard is "purpose-ism" (目的主义). According to this standard, a divorce should be granted if one side wants it and marital conditions prohibit the realization of a primary purpose of marriage. According to one legal scholar, China's legal standards governing court judgments on divorce petitions have transitioned from a "simple breakdownism" (单一破裂主义) to a "complex breakdownism" (复合破裂主义) that also encompasses faultism and purpose-ism (Xue 2014:16).

Although a court will grant a divorce only when it holds that mutual affection has broken down, statutory wrongdoing and purpose-based standards can be the basis of such a holding. Any form of bad behavior listed in the Fourteen Articles should automatically satisfy the breakdownism test. If a court affirms the occurrence of statutory wrongdoing, marital affection, legally speaking, has broken down. Conspicuously absent from the 14 fault-based standards is domestic violence. As mentioned earlier, the term "domestic violence" first appeared in the 2001 Marriage Law. Only in the 2008 Guidelines is domestic violence framed as an issue of "coercive control" in accordance with global rights discourse and global legal norms. Prior to 2001, the words "mal-treatment" (虐待) and "abuse" (侮辱) were generally used to refer to violence against women and children. Every version of the Marriage Law refers to the maltreatment and desertion of family members, as do the Fourteen Articles and the Public Security Administrative Punishments Law.

In the Fourteen Articles, the modifier "truly" or "indeed" (确已) was added in front of "broken down": "mutual affection has indeed broken down" (感情确已破裂). This new language was incorporated into the 2001 Marriage Law and preserved in the 2020 Civil Code.[4] In their written court decisions, judges often use variants of a similar but even more restrictive modifier: "completely" (彻底 or 完全). Although the breakdownism test may appear to impose a higher bar than in the past

---

[4] In the legislative process of amending the 1980 Marriage Law, some legal scholars advocated in vain for replacing "mutual affection has indeed broken down" with "marital relations have indeed broken down" (婚姻关系确已破裂). Such efforts to lower barriers to no-fault divorce were unsuccessful (Ma 2006:23; Ma and Luo 2014:38). Much of the history of divorce-related lawmaking in China has been animated by debates between advocates of the prevailing "break-down of mutual affection doctrine" (感情破裂说) and advocates of a more liberal alternative "breakdown of marital relations doctrine" (婚姻关系破裂说) (Chen 2007:396; Luo 2016:14; Ma and Luo 2014; C. Xu 2012:42).

by virtue of the "truly" modifier, the various breakdownism standards in this body of law are nonetheless, in writing at least, far from insurmountable. In addition to reaffirming the earlier unilateral no-fault test of breakdownism (provided that the court first fails to achieve mediated reconciliation), it also incorporates and supplements some of the standards in the Fourteen Articles by itemizing three fault-based standards for unilateral divorce, namely, (1) bigamy or cohabitation with a third party, (2) domestic violence, or (3) chronic gambling, drug use, or other "odious and incorrigible habits" (恶习屡教). Article 32, Item 2 of the 2001 Marriage Law – and Article 1079, Item 2 of the 2020 Civil Code – stipulates that a court should grant a divorce request when any of these three itemized fault-based standards is satisfied and mediation fails. If a court affirms one of these forms of wrongdoing, it is supposed to view marital affection as having broken down.

Marital violence, regardless of which side is at fault, automatically establishes the breakdown of mutual affection and therefore should, according to this legal test, oblige courts to grant a unilateral divorce request (W. Chen 2013; Li, Liu, and Yang 2013:35; Ma 2006:24). Indeed, the 2001 Interpretations of the SPC on Several Issues Regarding the Application of the Marriage Law stipulates that judges' impulse to preserve marriages on the basis of breakdownism should be trumped by the requirement to grant divorces on the basis of faultism: "In divorce cases that 'should be granted' according to the conditions stipulated by Article 32, Item 2, a divorce request should not be denied when a litigant has committed wrongdoing" (Article 22; Cui 2015:184; Jiang 2009b:18). As we will see, however, China's fault-based legal standards are rarely used in practice to grant divorces even when claims of wrongdoing are supported by evidence and affirmed by judges.

A fundamental tension between protecting the rights of women and protecting the institution of marriage animates divorce litigation. Legal ambiguity enables judges to support the latter at the expense of the former. The scope and definition of domestic violence are limited and vague (H. Zhang 2012:51). For example, in the SPC's 2001 Interpretations cited earlier, the same article that defines domestic violence contains an additional sentence: "Domestic violence that is persistent and frequent [持续性、经常性] constitutes maltreatment" (Article 1; Palmer 2007:683). The absence of a clear definition of either "persistent" or "frequent" has given judges latitude to hold that spousal battery does not constitute domestic violence if it happened only once or rarely, and was thus neither persistent nor frequent (Chapter 7). As we will see later in this chapter, vague and competing standards of evidence create additional space for judicial discretion.

JURISDICTIONAL STANDING

Each county, county-level city, and urban district in China has one regular basic-level people's court. Plaintiffs, upon filing their petitions, are required to satisfy jurisdictional standing requirements. This means a court can consider a plaintiff's petition only if it has jurisdiction over the matter. A plaintiff must furnish a marriage certificate to prove she is lawfully married to the defendant.[5]

The Civil Procedure Law stipulates that court petitions should, under most circumstances, be filed in the defendant's place of residence (Article 21), which practically speaking usually means where the defendant's household is registered (place of *hukou*, 户口 or 户籍) and which, in the case of divorce, is usually also the plaintiff's place of residence. Plaintiffs filing first-attempt divorce petitions are, by and large, tethered to the basic-level courts in the counties, county-level cities, or urban districts of their officially registered residential addresses. Ke Li (2015a:98) reported that migrants from rural areas rarely file their divorces in urban courts: "due to jurisdictional restrictions, rural women who serve as migrant workers in cities and towns must return to their hometowns to file divorce petitions." The 2015 Interpretations of the SPC on the Application of the Civil Procedure Law provides the option for litigants who have been residing outside their place of *hukou* registration for over one year to file a divorce petition in their actual place of residence (Article 12). In practice, however, this right is rarely actualized (Chapter 4).

CIVIL PROCEDURES AND ASSIGNING JUDGES

Courts adjudicate divorce petitions according to one of two civil procedures: ordinary (普通程序, sometimes translated as the "normal procedure") or simplified (简易程序, sometimes translated as the

---

[5] Courts also handle the dissolution of nonmarital relationships. In some cases, courts regard couples who never registered their marriages as being in common law or de facto marriages (事实婚姻). In cases involving unmarried couples, courts can rule on property division and child custody.

"summary procedure"). When a plaintiff submits a divorce petition, the court's case filing division accepts it after establishing that standing requirements are met (i.e., the court has jurisdiction, the plaintiff and defendant are lawfully married to each other, etc.). Then, within five days of accepting the case, the court must deliver a copy of the plaintiff's petition and supporting evidence to the defendant. The defendant, after receiving them, has 15 days to submit a defense statement responding to the plaintiff's claims and evidence (according to Article 125 of the Civil Procedure Law). A defendant's failure to respond does not alter the trial process. Generally speaking, after the defendant's 15-day deadline passes, case filing division staff determine which civil procedure is used – ordinary or simplified – and assign judges accordingly. Case assignment and scheduling clerks (分案排期员) in the case filing division are generally responsible for carrying out these tasks under the supervision of judges (F. Ye 2015:126, 131).

The choice of civil procedure determines the number of judges who try the case. A single judge (独任法官) presides over cases tried using the simplified civil procedure, and a collegial panel of decision-makers (合议庭) is required when the ordinary civil procedure is applied. Decision-makers are judges and citizen lay assessors. The official primary function of lay assessors is to provide public oversight. As we will see in Chapter 5, in practice, they have also been used to alleviate judges' workload. Collegial panels must be composed of an odd number of members (almost always three). Lay assessor participation is limited to collegial panels in first-instance trials. So-called 1 + 2 panels consist of one judge and two lay assessors, whereas so-called 2 + 1 panels consist of two judges and one lay assessor. Collegial panels of five or seven decision-makers have been exceedingly rare (Ye 2004:29–30).

Cases tried using the simplified civil procedure must be closed within three months. If circumstances prohibit meeting this statutory deadline, the Civil Procedure Law allows for a change of procedure from simplified to ordinary (Article 163). Cases tried using the ordinary procedure must be closed within six months, with the option of a six-month extension in special circumstances with the approval of the court president (Article 149). According to the 2007 Measures on Paying Litigation Fees, court fees are discounted by 50% when the simplified civil procedure is utilized (Article 16). In the cases I analyze from Henan and Zhejiang, base court fees were typically ¥300

(US$45) with the application of the ordinary civil procedure and half this amount with the application of the simplified civil procedure.

The two civil procedures differ primarily in the use of solo judges versus collegial panels, the possibility of lay assessor participation, case closing deadlines, and court fees. In addition, the SPC permits simplified methods of communication and notification when the simplified civil procedure is applied. For example, litigants may provide oral statements, and judges may notify litigants of their trial dates and summon witness by telephone, email, fax, or social media messaging in the context of the simplified civil procedure (Chapter 5). In principle, the remainder – including trial procedures, evidentiary standards, requirements concerning written decisions, and so on – is generally the same.

PHYSICAL SEPARATION

Another statutory ground for the breakdown of mutual affection is physical separation for at least two years. According to the Fourteen Articles, courts are supposed to regard separation for at least three years or separation for at least one year following a court's adjudicated denial of a previous divorce request (Article 7) as tantamount to the breakdown of mutual affection. Article 32 of the 2001 Marriage Law relaxed this standard by shrinking the statutory physical separation period from three to two years for first-attempt petitions (Article 32, Item 4). The Fourteen Articles' one-year separation test following an adjudicated denial (Article 7) was incorporated into the 2020 Civil Code: "After the People's Court denies a divorce petition, the court should grant the divorce if one side files for divorce after both sides physically separate for another full year" (Article 1079). The plaintiff must also prove that the breakdown of mutual affection was the reason for the physical separation; separation due to labor migration, for example, fails to meet the statutory conditions. In practice, however, judges will often grant a divorce after inferring from a two-year separation that the breakdown of mutual affection was its consequence, if not its cause (C. Xu 2012:40).

DEFENDANT ABSENTEEISM

Article 32 of the 2001 Marriage Law – which became Article 1079 of the 2020 Civil Code – stipulates that a court should grant a divorce petition if it declares a defendant to be missing: "Where one party is declared to be missing and the other party starts divorce proceedings, divorce shall be granted." A missing person declaration from a court provides sufficient statutory grounds for a divorce and thus obviates the need for mutual consent or any other proof of the breakdown of mutual affection (Sun 2006:121). For a defendant to be declared missing according to Article 20 of the 1986 General Principles of the Civil Law (Sun 2006:122) and Article 185 of the 2012 Civil Procedure Law, he or she must be of unknown whereabouts (下落不明) for a full two years and fail to reappear after a court posts a public notice (公告) for three months. The 1987 Opinions of the SPC on Several Issues Concerning the Implementation of the General Principles of the Civil Law (Article 26) stipulates, "Unknown whereabouts refers to a situation in which a citizen has left his or her last place of residence without a word [没有音讯]" (Zhao 2018:187).

In practice, however, courts routinely grant divorces in absentia without first going to the trouble of formally declaring defendants missing. What matters is whether the conditions for a missing person declaration are satisfied. Even if a person seeking a divorce from a missing spouse does not request a missing person declaration, the court proceeds with a trial after serving the defendant via public notice (公告送达). The 1992 Opinions of the SPC on Several Issues Concerning the Application of the Civil Procedure Law stipulates that a formal missing person declaration is not required for a divorce trial to be conducted in absentia (缺席审理): "If the whereabouts of either husband or wife are unknown and the other side files a court petition, requests a divorce, and does not request that the defendant whose whereabouts are unknown be declared missing or dead, the court must accept the case and serve the defendant with court papers via public notice" (Article 151; Tan and Wang 2011:116–17; C. Xu 2012).[6] According to the 2012 Civil Procedure Law, a defendant is considered to have been served 60 days after a public notice is posted (Article 92).[7] According to the SPC's 1992 Opinions, a public notice can be placed on the court's bulletin board, posted in the location of the defendant's last known residence, or published in a newspaper (Article 88; Y. Wang 2012:120). The 2015 Interpretations of the SPC on the Application of

---

[6] This provision is duplicated verbatim as Article 217 of the 2015 Interpretations of the SPC on the Application of the Civil Procedure Law.

[7] This was Article 88 in the original 1991 Civil Procedure Law (Sun 2006:122).

the Civil Procedure Law extends approved locations for the placement of public notices to "the internet and other media" (Article 138). Searchable repositories of courts' public notices are now available online (e.g., https://rmfygg.court.gov.cn/).

The court need only serve a defendant with notice of his trial and make available a copy of the plaintiff's petition. Whether a defendant who has been served shows up for his day in court, submits a written response in lieu of appearing in person, or appoints a representative to speak on his behalf is not the court's responsibility and will not affect the court's adjudicatory role (Dong and Ji 2016:89). Article 62 of the Civil Procedure Law requires both sides of a divorce case, even when represented by legal counsel, to appear in court unless special circumstances prohibit them from doing so, in which case they are to submit their statements in writing. At the same time, however, according to Article 144 of the Civil Procedure Law, "When a defendant who has been served a court summons refuses to appear in court without due cause or leaves midway through the trial without the court's permission, the court may rule in absentia." Thus, even if a defendant whose whereabouts are known refuses to appear in court after successfully receiving a summons, the trial proceeds, and the court rules.

An "in absentia public notice divorce trial" (公告离婚, hereafter "public notice trial") constitutes the breakdown of mutual affection and can therefore serve as the statutory basis of a ruling to grant a divorce (Dong and Ji 2016:91–92). The Fourteen Articles stipulates that courts can grant divorces when defendants can be declared missing, which is to say, when "One side has been of unknown whereabouts for a full two years, the other side sues for divorce, and the court determines the whereabouts to be truly unknown after seeking them via public notice" (Article 12). A plaintiff can simultaneously satisfy the physical separation test and the unknown whereabouts test by claiming her spouse has been missing for two years. Because many defendants in public notice trials are alleged to have been missing for at least two years, public notice trials are often tantamount to physical separation. In practice, therefore, public notice divorce trials are often regarded as satisfying the breakdownism standard and, more often than not, lead to successful divorces.

Strictly speaking, however, the laws provide no clear definition of "unknown whereabouts," much less specify a minimum duration of time the defendant's whereabouts must be unknown before a court can issue a public notice (Xiong 2012:71). Public notice trials are yet another manifestation of judges' discretionary application of ambiguous rules.

Moreover, public notice trials must be conducted according to the ordinary civil procedure. According to the 1992 Opinions of the SPC on Several Issues Concerning the Application of the Civil Procedure Law, "In cases in which the defendant's whereabouts are unknown at the time the lawsuit is filed, the case may not be tried using the simplified procedure" (Article 169). Because they cannot be conducted by solo judges, public notice trials consume precious judicial resources. Zhejiang's courts have been far more overburdened than Henan's courts. Zhejiang's relatively acute shortage of judges may therefore help explain why public notice trials were less common in Zhejiang than in Henan (Chapter 8).

Divorce trials with AWOL defendants are concentrated in rural areas, where a large share of able-bodied adults participate in labor migration (Tao and Lu 2012; C. Xu 2012:42). Many defendants miss their trials not only because of service of process failures, but also because they opt out of them. Even when they receive a summons, defendants commonly fail to submit written statements or make oral defense statements in court (Zeng 2008:161).

STANDARDS OF EVIDENCE

Even if a plaintiff satisfies the statutory physical separation standard (two years in a first-attempt divorce petition and one year after a failed attempt), she may have trouble proving it to a judge's satisfaction. Convincing reluctant judges of the factual basis of a statutory claim that mutual affection has broken down is nearly futile without mutual consent. Judges overwhelmingly apply the breakdownism standard to justify their decisions to deny divorce petitions, typically using language such as: "Because the submitted evidence is insufficient to prove that mutual affection broke down, the claim lacks a factual basis, and the court therefore denies support of the plaintiff's petition" (Li, Liu, and Yang 2013:35).

> In judicial practice, common court holdings in adjudicated denials of divorce petitions are: "Although both sides frequently quarrel and there may exist some emotional distance, this falls far short of the breakdown of mutual affection. If both sides work to build mutual communication and mutual trust, and correctly deal with their conflicts, husband and

wife still have a chance to reconcile"; "Although conflicts have arisen for personality compatibility reasons, mutual affection has not completely broken down. If both sides treasure marital affection, give each other the benefit of the doubt, and learn to forgive and compromise, husband and wife still have a chance to reconcile completely." (Chen 2005a:155)

According to the 2008 Guidelines, judges are supposed to treat victims' claims of domestic violence as more credible than offenders' denials (Runge 2015:38) and to consider the interests of the more vulnerable side when ruling on evidence. In practice, however, the burden of proof tends to fall on the plaintiff according to the more general principle of "whoever makes the claim must prove it" (谁主张, 谁举证, paraphrasing Article 64 of the Civil Procedure Law; Hongxiang Li 2014:88). Judges rarely take plaintiffs at their word for claims of domestic violence, especially if the defendant denies the claim (Chen and Duan 2012:36; Hongxiang Li 2014:87), even though judges are fully empowered by the SPC to do so. The 2008 Guidelines call for treating victims' allegations as more credible than defendants' denials in "he said, she said" situations on the premise that "few people would risk the public shame of lying about being beaten and abused by one's spouse" (Article 41; also see Runge 2015:38). Another rationale for relaxing standards of proof in divorce cases involving domestic violence is that women are often reluctant to report abuse to the police, and may therefore lack documentation to support their claims (Hu et al. 2020; Wang, Fang, and Li 2013:35–36; Zeng and Zhou 2019). But judges often side with defendants who state, for example: "It's not true. She fell down on her own. Besides, it's not a bone fracture but a herniated disc. ... She's the one who grabbed the shovel and, when raising it to hit me, ended up hitting herself on the head. This was a fight over some trifling matter" (Li, Liu, and Yang 2013:34; also see Fincher 2014:152). As we will see, judges tend to treat men's denials of being perpetrators more seriously than women's claims of being victims of domestic violence.

Such widespread practices violate China's domestic legal standards and international commitments. According to relevant Chinese legal standards of evidence, judges should affirm a plaintiff's claim of domestic violence on the basis of even basic corroborating evidence if the defendant either does not deny the claim or fails to provide counterevidence (Chen and Duan 2012:35; Tan and Wang 2016:185). For example, judges should affirm as factual a claim of domestic violence if the plaintiff submits circumstantial evidence showing that both an injury occurred and a domestic dispute occurred the same day (Li, Liu, and Yang 2013:35). In either case, the burden of proof is supposed to fall on the defendant to support his denial of the plaintiff's claim (Li, Liu, and Yang 2013:35; Runge 2015:38; Tan and Wang 2016:185).[8]

To the dismay of scholars and activists, the draft version of the Anti-Domestic Violence Law circulated by the Legislative Affairs Office of the State Council in 2014 contained a provision on the reasonable distribution of the burden of proof that was subsequently deleted from the final version that took effect in 2016 (Deng 2017:108). Despite this legislative setback, the 2008 Guidelines already called on judges to shift the burden of proof to the defendant on the basis of existing legal sources (Deng 2017:109; J. Jiang 2019:232; Runge 2015:38). More specifically, Article 40 of the 2008 Guidelines calls on judges to follow the "preponderance of evidence" standard stipulated by Article 73 of the 2001 Several Provisions of the SPC Concerning Civil Procedure Evidence: when each side submits contradictory evidence that cannot disprove the other side's evidence, the court is supposed to determine which side's evidence is more convincing (Deng 2017:110). Article 64 of this judicial interpretation of the SPC calls on judges to use common sense and intuition to make this determination (S. Wang 2014:21). In US civil courts, establishing a preponderance of evidence "means to prove that something is more likely so than not so" and "that what is sought to be proved is more likely true than not true" (Simon and Mahan 1971:330n2). Judges in China are likewise supposed to rule in favor of one side when they are convinced that the probability is at least 51% that its claims are supported by the available evidence and therefore factual. In other words, the side with the more compelling evidence enjoys a probabilistic advantage and should prevail (Zeng and Zhou 2019). The preponderance of evidence standard was reaffirmed in Article 108 of the 2015 Interpretations of the SPC on the Application of the Civil Procedure Law.[9] Although it is supposed to

---

[8] The same legal reasoning applies to paternity claims. The court should support a plaintiff's claim that the defendant is the father of her child (or that the defendant is not the father) if she submits supporting evidence, the defendant refuses a paternity test, and the defendant fails to submit counterevidence (Yang 2011:41).

[9] When the SPC amended this judicial interpretation in 2019 (and it took effect in May 2020), the "preponderance of evidence" standard (referred to variously as 优势证据, 优势盖然性, and 高度盖然性) was replaced with a stricter "beyond reasonable doubt" standard (Article 86), which was already part of the 2012 Criminal Procedure Law (Article 53).

relax evidentiary standards and thereby reduce pressure on abuse victims to prove their claims (Y. Jiang 2019:20), we will see in Chapters 7 and 8 that judges almost never apply the preponderance of evidence standard in domestic violence cases.

Judges will not be persuaded by allegations of domestic violence if they lack an understanding of or choose to ignore its legal definition. For example, one court held that "the injury the defendant caused the plaintiff in an act of momentary agitation [一时冲动] is unlawful but not domestic violence" (Li, Liu, and Yang 2013:35). After affirming that the defendant had hit the plaintiff in the face, resulting in a contusion, another court ruled that "evidence submitted to the court by the plaintiff Xiao X proves only that the defendant Wang X beat the plaintiff one time with insignificant consequences, which counts as everyday marital squabbling [吵闹] and marital conflict with occasional physical fighting but without harm, and which cannot be affirmed as domestic violence" (J. Zhang 2018:109). In yet another case, after admitting into evidence police and hospital documentation of the plaintiff's injury, the court ruled that "in the course of living together, the defendant's everyday physical and verbal abuse [打骂], which occasionally causes minor bodily injury of no real consequence, cannot be affirmed as domestic violence" (J. Zhang 2018:109; also see Cheng and Wang 2018:262).

The case of a woman from Hunan Province illustrates courts' discretionary application of the SPC's requirement mentioned earlier in this chapter that domestic violence be "persistent and frequent" in order to constitute maltreatment. She lost significant eyesight owing to her husband's physical abuse. She also suffered a permanent disability after he broke two of her ribs. When he filed for divorce, she filed a separate private criminal prosecution in which she alleged maltreatment and claimed civil damages for associated medical expenses. In its ruling, the court held:

> It has already been verified as factual that the defendant battered the accuser ten times. However, the defendant's beatings of the accuser constitute occasional occurrences and do not possess the characteristics of frequent, persistent, and consistent [经常、连续、一贯性]. Furthermore, there were reasons for the occurrences of this type of behavior. The defendant's maltreatment of the accuser was not intentional, and therefore does not constitute the crime of maltreatment. (Li 2003:7)

The court also rejected her claim for civil damages. After she appealed, the court of second instance upheld the lower court's acquittal on the grounds that the "13 occurrences of maltreatment affirmed by the court happened for a reason" (Li 2003:8).[10]

In theory, evidence sufficient to support claims of domestic violence include medical documentation of injuries; photos documenting the injuries; audio or video recordings; text or online messages; physical wounds or scars on the victim for display in court; police reports; witness testimony; documentation from residents' committees or work units; and "remorse letters" (忏悔书, 悔过书), "pledge letters" (保证书), "promise letters" (承诺书), or "apology letters" (认错书), written by defendants as both confessions and cease and desist contracts (Chen and Duan 2012:35, 37; Li, Liu, and Yang 2013:35; Runge 2015:38; Su 2011). The 2015 Anti-Domestic Violence Law stipulates that judges can affirm the occurrence of domestic violence on the basis of a police record of a complaint, a police warning, or a police injury appraisal (Article 20). Although evidentiary standards for claiming civil damages from abuse are higher (Li, Liu, and Yang 2013), any one of these pieces of evidence should be sufficient to establish domestic violence and hence grounds for divorce. In practice, however, judges often exclude or ignore such evidence, particularly when the defendant denies the plaintiff's claim of abuse (Li, Liu, and Yang 2013:35). And, of course, courts cannot award civil damages for domestic violence if they fail to affirm its occurrence in the first place (Li, Liu, and Yang 2013:35).

Henan Province's Zhecheng County People's Court refused to affirm a 24-year-old plaintiff's claim of domestic violence despite an abundance of supporting evidence. On August 13, 2019, her husband viciously attacked her in their clothing store. Security video footage of the store interior documented her husband dragging her across the floor by her hair, slapping and punching her in the face, taking away her cell phone to prevent her from calling the police, and locking the door to prevent her from escaping. A second exterior security camera recorded her hitting the ground after she jumped out of the second-story window. Hospital and police records documented bone fractures in nine places. Most of the fractures, including those in both heels, tailbone, and several vertebrae, were caused by the fall, which

---

[10] Merry (2009:89–90) discusses the same case.

left her paralyzed below the waist. According to the police report, her left eye socket fracture was the result of her husband's fist. The local police who investigated the incident determined that she had jumped in a suicide attempt even though she insisted that she had jumped to escape with her life. Because the police could not reach a consensus on her husband's criminal culpability, they did not file criminal charges against him – a theme to which I return in Chapter 9. While undergoing inpatient hospital treatment, her father-in-law relayed a death threat: if her husband were sent to prison, he would murder her whole family upon his release.

On June 8, 2020, she filed for divorce. Exactly one week later, on June 15, the county procuracy filed a public prosecution against her husband for intentional injury. Perhaps the court had notified the procuracy of evidence of criminal wrongdoing it discovered in the plaintiff's civil petition. Although that is precisely what should happen according to the law, it rarely does (Chapter 9).

The divorce trial was held on July 14. The court should have granted her divorce petition on fault-based grounds. As in so many cases we will encounter throughout this book, however, her husband withheld his consent to divorce, the court swept aside her allegation of domestic violence, and it instead pursued marital reconciliation through mediation. The court cited two main reasons for refusing to entertain her domestic violence claim. First, the local police failed to attribute the injuries she sustained from the fall to her husband's violence. According to the police, she had jumped on her own volition after choosing to kill herself, not because her husband's violence had compelled her to flee for her life. As so often happens in Chinese divorce litigation (Chapter 7), the court accepted the police determination that her husband's punch caused her facial bone fracture but did not affirm domestic violence on this basis. Second, challenging her credibility and implicitly suggesting her petition was frivolous, the court questioned why – if indeed she was a victim of domestic violence – she had waited ten months to file for divorce. Her husband was arrested on July 21. On July 24, the court notified her that it would delay issuing a verdict on her divorce petition until after the conclusion of her husband's criminal trial. The civil division's decision on her divorce petition would hinge on whether the criminal division found that her husband had indeed committed domestic violence, and both verdicts would be issued together.

At around this time, facing an impasse, she shared her story, video footage, and hospital and police documentation with the media.

Within days her video footage had been viewed over one billion times and sparked public outrage at the court's unwillingness to grant her divorce request. If the public had known that courts ignored similarly compelling evidence of domestic violence in divorce litigation as a matter of course (Chapter 7), its outrage may have been greater and come sooner. On July 28, before the criminal trial had even begun, the court – under immense public pressure – suddenly reversed its position and issued a verdict granting the divorce, granting custody of their child to her, and ordering her husband to pay child support (Feng 2020; Guiyang Evening News 2020; S. Li 2020; Sohu.com 2020; Wee 2020; Xiaoxiang Morning News 2020; Xue 2020). I will return to the theme of the influence of public opinion on judicial decision-making in Chapter 9.

Judges' (mis)use of evidence turns laws and legal guidelines on their head in additional ways. Letters of apology and remorse for abuse should be used not as evidence of the *presence* of mutual affection but rather as evidence that domestic violence occurred and thus of the *absence* of mutual affection. According to the 2008 Guidelines:

> In the course of litigation, the abuser may provide to the victim in writing or orally an apology for his abuse or a promise never to commit abuse again. In the absence of any substantive, concrete acts of contrition, this should be regarded as a display of neither sincere repentance nor genuine abandonment of violent ways. On the contrary, it should be regarded as another means of maintaining control over the victim. For this reason, it should neither be treated as the abuser's remorse *nor used as evidence that mutual affection has not broken down.* (Article 42, emphasis added)

But as we will see from divorce cases in Henan and Zhejiang, judges sometimes improperly use defendants' apologies and promises to support their holding that mutual affection has not broken down and thus to justify their decisions to deny divorce petitions. Judges try to persuade plaintiffs to drop their lawsuits in exchange for their husbands' written expressions of remorse for – and promises to stop – beating them (Xu 2007:204).[11] Judges also frequently use defendants' unwillingness

---

[11] A husband's pledge to stop beating his wife is sometimes part of a "reconciliation agreement" (和好协议) written under the auspices of judicial mediation and culminating in the wife's withdrawal of her petition. See, for example, Decision #4154866, Jinhua Municipal Wucheng District People's Court, February 16, 2016, Case ID (2015)金婺汤民初字第00222号, archived at https://perma.cc/BV94-YMZ8.

to divorce as evidence of mutual affection and reconciliation potential. Judges even cite the free and voluntary nature of the marriage (自由恋爱), as opposed to an arranged or otherwise coerced marriage, and childbearing as evidence of mutual affection.

Judges exercise similar discretion when considering plaintiffs' claims of physical separation from defendants (Xu 2007:204). Some plaintiffs support claims of physical separation with documentation of a new residence (their own or the defendant's), while others hope the court will take them at their word (Luo 2016:22; C. Xu 2012). Meanwhile, plaintiffs' claims of defendants' unknown whereabouts are often supported by similarly shaky evidence, such as defendants' failure to be found when court personnel attempted to serve their court summons at the official addresses listed on their citizen identity cards, letters (of sometimes dubious provenance) from villagers' committees or residents' committees, or witness testimony from neighbors and relatives (Dong and Ji 2016:91; Sun 2006:122; Zhao 2018).

METHODS OF CLOSING CASES

Courts' respective use of adjudication and mediation to process the roughly 1.4 million divorce petitions they receive each year has ebbed and flowed dramatically over the past few decades. Figure 2.1 depicts time trends with respect to the court adjudication of divorce petitions, the empirical focus of this book. By displaying adjudications as a proportion of all concluded cases, it omits the residual categories of mediations and withdrawals.[12] Because the proportion of withdrawals has remained stable in recent years (accounting for a steady one-quarter of all the divorce petitions courts received), fluctuations in adjudication rates imply inverse fluctuations in mediation rates. In other words, declines in adjudication rates are commensurate with increases in mediation rates.

Two patterns are particularly noteworthy. First, court adjudication rates rose consistently from the late 1980s until the early 2000s before dropping equally consistently through the early 2010s, after which adjudication rates rose once again. The peaks and valleys in China's court system of alternating shifts between promoting adjudication and promoting mediation cannot be explained by changes in civil law

---

[12] Cases rejected by courts (驳回) and concluded by "other means" are additional residual categories that account for only about 1% of all divorce cases concluded by courts.

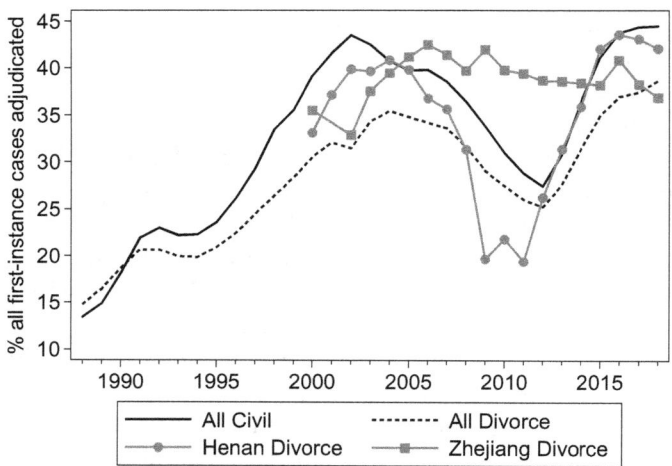

Figure 2.1 Adjudications as a proportion of all first-instance concluded cases
Sources: CLY, various years; Ministry of Civil Affairs of China, various years.

doctrine, in the composition of civil court dockets, or in the changing desires of litigants, much less in the influence of world society. Rather, they reflect the full extent to which courts fall in line with shifting policy directives from above. Like the rest of the state bureaucracy, courts in authoritarian political contexts are sensitive to the direction in which political winds blow and steer accordingly (Moustafa 2014:289).

Calls from top leadership beginning in 2003–2004 to "construct a harmonious society" ushered in the era of China's "turn against law" and "return to populist legality" by promoting populist courtroom mediation practices that blended elements of Maoism and Confucianism (Liebman 2011b, 2014; Minzner 2009, 2011). During this time, some courts even set targets of "zero adjudications" (零判决; X. Ye 2015; Zheng 2018:135), which is equivalent to 100% mediations and withdrawals. In Henan, some courts participated in zero adjudication competitions (Guo 2009; Yang 2010). As abruptly as it began, China's "mediation surge" ended in 2011–2012 after a new 2011 SPC opinion called for an end to the practice of intercepting and mediating cases before they had a chance to be filed and entered into court dockets (Li, Kocken, and van Rooij 2016: 14–15). This latest about-face was further supported by a series of

SPC opinions and guidelines on the proper use of mediation; an overhaul of performance evaluation systems that ended the practice of "overusing mediation and underusing adjudication" (重调轻判), including the widespread practice of forced mediation; the establishment of a "litigation system centered on adjudication" (以审判为中心) as part of the fourth five-year outline for judicial reform (2014–2018); and efforts to address a perceived crisis of low public confidence in courts made all the more urgent by calls beginning in 2013 from the top leadership "to let the masses experience fairness and justice in every judicial case" (让人民群众在每一个司法案件中都感受到公平正义; Xu, Huang, and Wang 2014:87–88, 93–94; Yan and Yuan 2015; Zhang 2016a:27).

In absolute numbers, divorce mediations increased steadily from 441,656 in 2004 to 612,304 in 2012, after which mediations declined steadily to 475,193 in 2018. Adjudication trends, of course, are in the reverse direction: between 2012 and 2018, following the end of the "mediation surge," the volume of court divorce adjudication rose by 70% from 314,468 to 534,589 cases. Judges' imperative to mediate has waned while their imperative to maximize efficiency and minimize unrest persists. Under growing pressure to clear their mounting divorce dockets efficiently while simultaneously promoting family and social stability, judges' commensurately growing tendency to deny divorce petitions – resulting in China's judicial clampdown on divorce (Chapter 6) – is not hard to understand.

Second, owing to the Marriage Law's emphasis on mediation, adjudication has been less common in divorce cases than in other civil cases. Nonetheless, when looking at China as a whole, divorce tracks with the larger category of civil cases of which it is a part. Figure 2.1 also includes adjudication trends for the two provinces I analyze in this book. While Henan mirrors the national pattern, Zhejiang's courts appear to have leap-frogged the "mediation surge" and used adjudication at fairly steady levels since 2005, at least in the context of divorce.

JUDICIAL WORK FLOW

Written court decisions afford a glimpse of how divorce cases move through the judicial pipeline. After a plaintiff files for divorce, the court must then approve and accept it. Lawsuits rejected by the court are not added to its docket, are not published, and are therefore beyond the scope of analysis. Courts typically accept divorce petitions on the same day plaintiffs file them. Upon accepting the case, the court issues a written notice to the plaintiff to this effect (受理通知书). The court may also issue a written notice requesting evidence in support of her claims (举证通知书). The court then provides service of process to the defendant by delivering: a copy of the plaintiff's petition, a notice requesting that he respond (应诉通知书) with a written defense statement within 15 days, and a notice requesting evidence in support of his counterclaims. Both plaintiff and defendant receive a court summons notifying them of their trial date (开庭传票 or 传唤). Court decisions indicate whether the defendant's whereabouts were unknown, whether it notified him via public notice, whether he responded within 60 days, and whether the trial was conducted in absentia. If both sides show up for their trial, the court will first attempt a mediated reconciliation. Reconciliation failures are often noted in written court decisions (调解未果, 调解无效, or 调解未成). Court decisions sometimes mention that mediated reconciliation was not attempted owing to the defendant's failure to appear for the trial. Court decisions usually indicate the trial date and whether the trial was open to the public (公开开庭) or closed (不公开开庭). The vast majority of trials were open to the public. When applying the simplified civil procedure, courts typically tried divorce cases about a month after accepting them in order to provide sufficient time for defendants to submit their responses and for both sides to submit supporting evidence. When applying the ordinary civil procedure, by contrast, courts typically tried divorce cases two or three months after accepting them. Recall that the ordinary civil procedure must be applied in public notice trials. Delays associated with the ordinary civil procedure are, above all, caused by the requirement that public notices be posted for 60 days when defendants' whereabouts are unknown. Courts usually issue their written adjudicated decisions within a month of the divorce trial. All told, the entire process from case filing to written decision typically lasts 30–60 days in simplified procedure cases and 100–150 days in ordinary procedure cases. Given that most first-attempt divorce petitions are denied, however, the entire divorce litigation process from initial filing to granted divorce often takes between one and two years (Chapter 9).

SUMMARY AND CONCLUSIONS

Even in the absence of mutual consent to dissolve a marriage, Chinese judges have a great deal of legal leeway to grant a unilateral divorce. They can choose to grant a divorce petition on the basis of break-downism, a no-fault legal standard permitting unilateral divorce owing to irreconcilable differences or physical separation. They can also use various faultism standards to grant a unilateral divorce petition on the grounds of domestic violence or other forms of bad spousal behavior. Finally, they should grant divorce petitions when defendants are AWOL. These various domestic legal tests are consistent with globally institutionalized legal models.

Yet, even when one of China's fault-based standards is satisfied, such as when a plaintiff supplies compelling evidence of marital violence, judges are far more likely to deny the petition using the breakdown-ism standard than to grant the divorce using an applicable faultism standard.

> The Marriage Law takes the "breakdown of mutual affection" as the basis for divorce. This standard, however, is subjective and mechanical. Although Article 32 of the Marriage Law lists [fault-based] conditions under which divorce "should" be granted, courts, influenced by the law's legislative spirit, tend to use the "breakdown of mutual affection" as grounds for divorce. (Hongxiang Li 2014:87)

The legislative spirit to which the author of this passage refers is the legal ambiguity baked into the Marriage Law, giving judges flexibility to heed ideological pressure to "oppose frivolous divorce" or to grant divorce petitions depending on their "ad hoc determinations that best suited the circumstances of specific cases and the policy emphases of the moment" (Huang 2005:187; also see W. Zhou 2018).

When judges deny divorce petitions on the basis of breakdownism, they often do so in a way that subverts China's own laws and global legal norms concerning the freedom of divorce. Owing to the wide discretion judges wield to determine the amount of love present and possible in the marriage, they typically treat a defendant's unwilling-ness to divorce as proof that mutual affection has not broken down. When a defendant withholds consent, a plaintiff's unilateral insistence on divorce is nearly futile regardless of whether her claim is based on the no-fault breakdownism test of incompatibility or the faultism test of domestic violence (Ma 2006:26; Xu 2007:204). Plaintiffs' claims of abuse and defendants' denials are often reduced to "she said, he said" scenarios in which judges deny the divorce petition unless the defendant consents to the divorce.

Judges' impulse to deny divorce petitions by denying that mutual affection broke down is further facilitated by their wide discretion to exclude or affirm evidence that litigation parties submit in support of their claims. As we will see in subsequent chapters of this book, domestic violence claims had no meaningful bearing on whether a court granted a divorce request and may have even been counterproductive (Chapters 7 and 8). Plaintiffs' best chances for getting divorced were either when their spouses consented or when their allegedly missing spouses were served by public notice. Mutual consent and public notice trials greatly boosted plaintiffs' chances of success. Even when – or especially when – plaintiffs made claims of marital violence and backed them with evidence, judges often downplayed as insufficient or altogether excluded the evidence in question and ruled against such claims. In their child custody determinations, judges likewise often excluded relevant evidence of horrific abuse on the grounds that it could not be authenticated or definitively linked to defendants (Chapter 10).

This chapter was devoted to the question of *how* judges undermine gender justice. The next chapter is devoted to the question of *why* judges do so.

CHAPTER THREE

THE DIVORCE TWOFER

Why Court Behavior Is Decoupled from the Right to Decouple

China's courts routinely deny divorce petitions filed for the first time and routinely grant divorce petitions filed for the second time (Chen 2005a; He 2009; He and Ng 2013a; Jiang and Zhu 2014; Luo 2016; Tan and Wang 2016).[1] Despite its ubiquity, this judicial phenomenon, which I call the "divorce twofer," has no basis in law. My task in this chapter is to explain its institutional roots.

Divorce is a microcosm of a general pattern in China's legal system of drifting simultaneously toward and away from global legal norms (Liu 2006; Minzner 2011), particularly with respect to gender equality (Chen 2007; He and Ng 2013a, 2013b; Li 2015b; Xu 2007). In the case of criminal justice, for example, laws on the books protecting the *globally* institutionalized due process rights of criminal suspects and their defense lawyers are overwhelmed by competing normative practices and cognitive scripts rooted in countervailing *local* institutional legacies (Liu and Halliday 2016; Michelson 2007). Laws conforming to *global* legal norms also coincide with spectacular *local* enforcement failures in the realms of labor (Bartley 2018; Gallagher 2017), food safety (Yasuda 2017), and environmental protection (van Rooij and Lo 2009; Stern 2013; A. L. Wang 2018), to name just a few examples.

In the context of Chinese divorce litigation, endogenous institutional logics similarly illuminate why courts obstruct the implementation of

---

[1] In Chinese, first-attempt denials are dubbed 第一次判不离 and 首次判不离, and the divorce twofer more generally is known variously as 二次离婚, 二次诉讼, 二次起诉, and 二次诉请.

domestic laws consistent with global legal norms. Given the general ubiquity of "logic pluralism" (Glynn and Raffaelli 2013; Thornton, Ocasio, and Lounsbury 2012:142), the institutional logic of laws protecting the freedom of divorce, gender equality, and victims of domestic violence is only one of many institutional pressures on Chinese judicial decision-makers. An acute imbalance between judges and cases is another source of institutional pressure giving rise to the divorce twofer. The decoupling of China's divorce courts from world society models is thus, to some measure, a function of bureaucratic capacity constraints and technical enforcement impediments (Cole 2015). To a greater extent it is also a function of closer alignment with alternative and competing local institutional logics.

THE DIVORCE TWOFER

In Chapter 1, we saw a feedback loop in the divorce litigation process (Figure 1.1). A feedback process by which litigation outputs return as new litigation inputs is unique to divorce cases. Divorce litigation represents an exception to the general rule – and a defining characteristic of China's court system – known as the "maximum of two decisions" or the "second-instance trial is always final" (两审终审制; Fu 2018:85; Xin 1999:522–24). According to this general rule stipulated by the Civil Procedure Law (Article 10) and the Criminal Procedure Law (Article 10), civil litigants and criminal defendants are given two chances in court. Civil first-instance cases are almost always filed in basic-level courts. Civil litigants who are unhappy with the first-instance outcome may appeal to an intermediate court. Although the SPC is China's court of last resort in a *technical* sense, the intermediate court is the court of last resort in a *practical* sense for most civil litigants. Divorces, however, are exempt from the general limit of one chance to request another trial. In the event a court denies a first-instance divorce petition, the process is reset following a statutory waiting period of six months. Article 124, Item 7, of the Civil Procedure Law has proven to be a gift to judges: "In divorce cases, where a judgment has been made to deny a divorce or where the parties reconciled through mediation … a new petition filed for the same case by the plaintiff within six months shall not be accepted without new developments or new grounds." Circumventing the six-month waiting period on the basis of "new developments" or "new grounds" is permitted but happens rarely in practice. Following an adjudicated denial, a subsequent divorce attempt counts as a new first-instance trial, and is almost always filed at and tried by the same court of first instance.

From a practical standpoint, therefore, in divorce litigation the court of last resort is usually the original court of first resort. Divorce provides the rare possibility of a litigation do-over, which, as we will see, has proven to be enormously valuable to judges (Chapter 6). Certain cases involving child adoptions are also eligible for do-overs, but they are unusual. For every other type of case, an undesirable outcome can, generally speaking, only be appealed and accepted as a second-instance trial. Of course, first-instance divorce judgments may also be appealed. However, the court of second instance can only assess the specific rulings made by the court of first instance. When a court of first instance denies a divorce petition without ruling on child custody, property division, or other pertinent matters, the best a court of second instance can do is to remand the case back to the original court for retrial, further delaying the process (He 2009). The worst a court of second instance can do is to uphold the original judgment, imperiling the plaintiff's effort to divorce (although not necessarily irretrievably).

A court of second instance cannot easily overturn a first-instance adjudicated denial of a divorce petition. In China, there is no official procedure by which judges can grant a divorce without also settling all terms of the divorce (He 2009:84; Li 2015a:148n12). Although all divorce-related matters are supposed to be bundled together when judges decide to grant a divorce request, they can be unbundled in post-divorce motions.[2] According to the 1992 Opinions of the SPC on Several Issues Concerning the Application of the Civil Procedure Law, "When a first-instance decision to deny a divorce petition is appealed and the second-instance people's court holds that the divorce should have been granted, litigants, in accordance with the principle of voluntarism, may mediate the terms of property division and child custody. If mediation fails, the case is remanded to the original court for retrial" (Article 189).[3] A mutual agreement on divorce terms during

---

[2] In the course of conducting research for this book, I discovered that judges nonetheless do routinely unbundle property division from the decision to grant a divorce when they are (or claim to be) unable to clarify ownership or the value of certain assets. In such cases, judges encourage litigants to file separate motions on property division. Shaoxia Wang (2013:174) makes the same observation.

[3] This provision reappears in Article 329 of the 2015 Explanations of the SPC on the Application of the Civil Procedure Law with an added provision allowing the court of second instance, with the approval of both plaintiff and defendant, to adjudicate property division and child custody (S. Guo 2018:113).

the second-instance trial is highly improbable for the same reason that the first-instance divorce petition was denied in the first place (e.g., the defendant's unwillingness to divorce or contentious claims concerning property division and/or child custody). From the plaintiff's standpoint, therefore, waiting six months for a second first-instance trial is far preferable to appealing the first-attempt judgment and extending the divorce process into a "three- to four-year marathon" (S. Guo 2018:113). Meanwhile, from the court's standpoint, giving litigants an extra six months to sort out their affairs greatly simplifies the litigation process. If, in the course of denying a first-attempt divorce petition, a judge assures the plaintiff he will grant the second-attempt petition on the condition that, during the statutory waiting period, both parties get their ducks in a row and return with an agreement on all terms of the divorce, the second first-instance trial should be relatively fast and straightforward, especially given that the basic facts of the case will not change, allowing the presiding judge to recycle a lot of text from the first court decision in the second one.

The second first-instance trial will thus benefit the judge's case volume and efficiency scores while simultaneously posing relatively little risk of an appeal, petition, or other sort of incident detrimental to a judge's performance evaluation (He 2009; J. Zhang 2018:109). The upshot is that "in judicial practice, when a husband or wife sues for divorce, the court will typically deny the petition on the first attempt, and only on the second or third attempt is there a possibility the court will grant it" (W. Zhang 2012:60).

To many judges, even if evidence is lacking, the very act of filing a second divorce petition is proof enough of the breakdown of mutual affection. A couple's failure to reconcile during the six-month statutory waiting period provides stronger legal grounds for the breakdown of mutual affection (Liu 2012; W. Zhou 2018:14). From a judge's perspective, a plaintiff sufficiently determined to file a second divorce petition is probably not acting frivolously, impulsively, or impetuously (Ye 2007:43). When ruling on second-attempt petitions, courts will often hold that "After the plaintiff's first divorce petition was denied, marital relations not only failed to improve but actually worsened. Neither side is fulfilling marital duties, both sides remain separated, and mutual affection has completely broken down" (Chen 2005a:155).

Long before the introduction of formal cooling-off periods in 2016, judges created informal cooling-off periods by denying divorce petitions. Typically, they declared that the marriage had merely experienced a bump in the road, was fundamentally healthy, and therefore did not satisfy any legal standard for divorce. They then advised the litigants to use the six-month statutory waiting period to work on their relationship skills. When they denied plaintiffs' divorce petitions, judges sometimes explicitly characterized the statutory six-month waiting period as a "cooling-off period" (冷静期; Liu 2012:84). In some cases, even those involving allegations of domestic violence supported by evidence, judges justified denying divorces by holding that a defendant's unwillingness to divorce called for a cooling-off period (e.g., Decision #2315222, Yueqing Municipal People's Court, Zhejiang Province, March 3, 2010).[4] In another typical example that foreshadows the influence of political ideology, the judge, in consideration of the plaintiff's claim that her husband beat her and committed domestic violence, held that the divorce should be denied "in order to give the litigants a chance to calm down and reconcile for the sake of maintaining marital and family stability" (Decision #1080860, Shangcheng County People's Court, Henan Province, December 15, 2013).[5]

Many plaintiffs therefore couch their second-attempt petitions accordingly, doing their utmost to convey their dashed hopes for marital improvement following the adjudicated denial of their first-attempt petitions. As we will see in Chapter 7, their claims along the lines of "following the court's denial of my divorce petition, the defendant not only failed to stop beating me, but his domestic violence intensified" are commonplace.

Observers have speculated about whether experimental cooling-off periods preceding trials will ultimately replace the six-month statutory waiting period. Rather than viewing cooling-off periods as raising the bar for divorce, thus making the divorce process even harder and more prolonged, some scholars have argued precisely the opposite. If the cooling-off period is a functional substitute for the statutory six-month waiting period following an adjudicated denial, they may come to replace the divorce twofer. By granting divorces on the first attempt after the conclusion of a cooling-off period, cooling-off periods may obviate the need for at least two trials and in so doing help conserve judicial resources (J. Guo 2018:28; He 2019; Hu 2019; Liu and Zheng

---

4 Case ID (2010)温乐柳民初字第17号, archived at https://perma.cc/KZ6G-EMYH.
5 Case ID (2013)商民初字第1129号, archived at https://perma.cc/QT9G-WYKF.

2018; J. Zhou 2018). In contrast to this expectation, however, the only two decisions published on China Judgements Online containing the term "notice of cooling-off period" (冷静期通知书), both from Hebei Province, were divorce denials following cooling-off periods.[6] As I was writing this book, the passage of the 2020 Civil Code appeared to bring to an end to cooling-off periods in divorce litigation: Article 1077 stipulates that 30-day cooling-off periods apply only to mutual-consent "divorces by agreement" processed by marriage registration offices in the Civil Affairs Administration (Du 2020).[7]

Women have borne the brunt of the divorce twofer. According to Hongxiang Li (2014:87), in practice "the breakdown of mutual affection test is based simply on the number of times a divorce has been requested ... which undermines women's right to the freedom of divorce." Family sociologist Xu Anqi underscores the costs borne by women from this routine practice:

> Judges wield excessive discretion with respect to whether litigants' mutual affection has broken down. Article 32 of the Marriage Law stipulates, "in cases of complete breakdown of mutual affection, and when mediation has failed, divorce should be granted." However, the *unwritten convention* in judicial practice – in first-attempt petitions when the defendant resolutely opposes the divorce – is to deny the divorce request on the grounds that mutual affection has not broken down. Under many circumstances this is perfectly appropriate, and may prevent frivolous divorce or the intensification of conflict. And yet, this *customary method* often results in the infringement of the physical rights of some women. For example, when in divorce litigation frequent offenders of domestic violence repeatedly admit wrongdoing and a desire to turn over a new leaf, judges typically try to persuade the female side to believe the defendant's remorse and his promise to mend his ways, and then deny the divorce petition on the grounds that mutual affection did not break down. In this process, some male litigants, after returning home, beat

---

6 Case ID (2017)冀0924民初601号, archived at https://perma.cc/83CC-SFF4, is an adjudicated denial following a two-month cooling-off period on the grounds that the litigants were experiencing a "marital crisis" that had not reached the point of breakdown. Case ID (2017)冀1127民初1650号, archived at https://perma.cc/9V96-PE9G, is an adjudicated denial following a three-month cooling-off period on the grounds that the defendant was unwilling to divorce and that neither side wanted custody of their son. I conducted this search on June 2, 2020.

7 The Ministry of Civil Affairs formalized this change in its 2020 Notice Concerning the Implementation of Marriage Registration Provisions in the Civil Code of the People's Republic of China, which took effect on January 1, 2021. In practice, however, courts continued to issue notices of cooling-off periods after the Civil Code took effect (Wang 2021; Yao 2021).

and abuse their wives with renewed intensity, resulting in the reoccurrence of serious physical and emotional violations. In fact, according to the amended [2001] Marriage Law, in the event of domestic violence or another form of wrongdoing, and if mediation fails, a divorce should be granted. The *prevailing practice* of denying a first-attempt divorce petition when one side withholds consent should be abolished. (Xu 2007:204, emphasis added)

The operative terms in the foregoing quotation are "unwritten convention," "customary method," and "prevailing practice." Elsewhere the divorce twofer has been called an "unspoken rule" (潜规则; J. Guo 2018:28; He 2019:91; Hu 2019; Liu 2012), "hidden rule" (隐规则; Deng 2017), an "open secret" (公开的秘密; Zhou and Qiu 2018), and a "rigid practice" (刚性做法; Liu 2012:84n1). It has been likened to a hammer wielded by judges who see every divorce petition as a nail (一刀切, meaning it is applied "across the board" or in a "one size fits all" manner; He 2019:92). Indeed, a judge in Jiangxi Province's Yongxiu County People's Court declared the divorce twofer to be a form of customary law lacking any basis in state law. According to this judge, the fault-based standards listed in Article 32 of the Marriage Law fail to encompass the most common reasons for divorce claimed by plaintiffs in their divorce petitions, namely incompatible personalities, financial disagreements, and poor relations with mothers-in-law. This judge argues that the divorce twofer emerged as a pragmatic, quasi-legal means to grant divorces in the absence of sufficient evidence of the breakdown of mutual affection. Judges inform plaintiffs frankly that they cannot grant the divorce on the first attempt. The private agreement is for the plaintiff to accept an adjudicated denial on the first attempt if the judge grants the divorce on the second attempt, even if the legal circumstances that prevented the judge from granting the divorce the first time persist. Doing so gives litigants an opportunity to cool off and reconcile during the six-month statutory waiting period, mollifies plaintiffs who are disappointed that they failed to achieve their goal on the first attempt, and allows judges to grant divorces to persistent plaintiffs. Thus, in this judge's account, the divorce twofer emerged as a form of "legal evasion" (法律规避) because it entails private agreements between judges and litigants (Huan 2014).

According to reports, in divorce disputes, if a court denies a divorce petition on the first attempt, the court will normally grant it the second time after the plaintiff files a new petition six months or so later. This is

71

known as the "two trial" rule of divorce litigation [离婚诉讼的"二次诉讼"规则]. This is a universal judicial phenomenon in basic-level courts across the country, and it is not based on any laws or judicial interpretations. (Zhang 2013)

Two judges from Henan's Jiaozuo Municipal Jiefang District People's Court explained their reluctance to grant first-attempt divorce petitions. In addition to citing plaintiffs' common failure to prove the breakdown of mutual affection, they also cited their fear of recalcitrant litigants.

> We discovered through our civil adjudication work that the majority of cases fall outside the scope of the conditions listed [in Article 32 of the Marriage Law]. For example, both sides constantly argue, they are physical separated for over one year but less than two years, one side withholds consent, they married shortly after meeting [闪婚, literally "flash marriage"], disagreements about property or relations with other family members led to the divorce petition, and so on. Moreover, in some cases in which the litigants and their family members ceaselessly argue, a fiercely disgruntled litigant, regardless of the outcome, will express an intent to appeal to a higher court or petition in the complaints system [上访]. The potential for upset litigants to end up in the petitioning system is a perennial threat lurking within cases such as these. Hard-pressed to know for certain whether mutual affection has indeed broken down, judges dare not adjudicate lightly. Thus, in order to avoid unnecessary trouble, judges tend to deny first-attempt divorce petitions. (Zhang and Fan 2011; also see Xu 2016)

As we will see later in this chapter, "upset" and "fiercely disgruntled litigants" may pose threats to judges' personal safety and performance evaluations. Judges do less to ascertain the extent and nature of marital conflict than they do to minimize litigant discontent (W. Zhou 2018:23).

When ruling on first-attempt divorce petitions, judges rarely support plaintiffs' unilateral claims that mutual affection broke down for reasons other than those stipulated by Article 32 of the Marriage Law. On the first attempt, plaintiffs' claims of marital discord will generally fall on deaf ears unless they are shared by defendants who consent to divorce or are supported by evidence either of statutory wrongdoing or a two-year physical separation (W. Zhou 2018). Even evidence of statutory wrongdoing, however, is rarely enough to stop judges from applying the divorce twofer. On the contrary, "judges' rulings in divorce cases involving domestic violence conspicuously show this sort of judicial inertia [司法惯性]." Judges tend to grant first-attempt divorce petitions involving domestic violence claims only when evidence of domestic violence is extraordinarily powerful or when mutual consent is achieved through mediation (Deng 2017:112; also see J. Jiang 2019:235).

In some parts of China, the divorce twofer has been formally codified. According to administrative regulations governing divorce cases in Guangdong Province (in a section on the "key conditions for denying divorces"), "Divorce petitions may be denied in first-attempt cases in which the defendant expresses an unwillingness to divorce, there is no fundamental conflict, marital affection has not completely broken down, and mediation fails to reconcile the couple." The regulations even stipulate that first-attempt divorce petitions should be denied in cases in which either side committed adultery, provided the defendant vehemently opposes the divorce (Zhang 2013). I found the same administrative regulations in other provinces.[8] Nonetheless, local administrative regulations lack the status of law.

First-attempt divorce verdicts do indeed tend to hinge on mutual consent. A judge in Anhui put it this way:

> When I first started working, I followed the practice of all courts by denying first-attempt petitions. During the initial trial, so long as none of the statutory conditions for divorce [in Article 32] was met, the instant I heard the words "I do not consent to divorce" I could start twiddling my thumbs. Seriously, from that point on I could stop listening and go straight to an adjudicated denial of the petition. This is the safest thing for judges to do. (Zhou and Qiu 2018)

Insofar as judges rarely grant divorces when defendants withhold their consent, defendants hold what amounts to a trump card overriding plaintiffs' domestic violence allegations. Peking University law professor Ma Yi'nan echoed this point:

> Judges are highly reluctant to grant a divorce when the petition is based on personality, temperament, and lifestyle incompatibilities or another reason that does not constitute a "fundamental conflict" [原则性分歧], or when the case involves housing, arrangements for a litigant with an illness or disability, or other complications that are difficult to resolve. So long as the other side resolutely opposes the divorce, judges for the most part will deny the petition, forcing the plaintiff to wait six months before filing a new petition. (Ma 2006:26)

---

[8] For two of many similar examples, see Henan High People's Court (2018) and Xiji County People's Court (2013). I thank Susan Finder for pointing out these rules to me.

Du Wanhua, a high-ranking official in the SPC, lamented the flipside, namely judges' tendency to grant divorces when defendants consent. His urging courts to do more to preserve marriages by denying divorce petitions foreshadows my discussion of political ideology later in this chapter.

> Marriage and family stability has not been emphasized enough in the context of social construction. Marriage and family are often regarded as private domains, and their importance is insufficiently recognized. ... When judges try a divorce case, the first thing they ask is whether [the defendant] consents. As soon as the defendant expresses a willingness to divorce, the trial immediately shifts to property division and child custody. Judges do not adequately investigate the question of repairing and restoring the litigants' marriage. (Wang and Luo 2016:3)

The case of a woman from Sichuan Province's Pingchang County (outside the city of Bazhong) illustrates a defendant's power to end a plaintiff's bid for divorce simply by withholding consent and expressing a desire to reconcile. Over the course of four years, she filed four divorce lawsuits, all of which were unsuccessful. When a newspaper reporter asked her why she was desperate to end her marriage, she stated tearfully, "It's too painful [太苦了]. At this point all I want is a divorce. I've given him so many opportunities." She pleaded with her husband, "I beg you to let me go, to let go of our life together." And she questioned him: "In recent years I've been roaming around for the sake of work, a vagabond without a home. You think this is easy for me? None of my three children is by my side, not a single family member is with me. Do you truly not know the real reason?" During the trial she even gave up all property division claims in the hopes of gaining custody of one of their children. Meanwhile, the defendant did his utmost to demonstrate affection for his wife. In court, immediately before the trial, he handed her a gift of new clothes, which she initially refused but later accepted on the insistence of a judge. (After the trial she left the gift behind.) When it was time to make his defense statement, the defendant turned to the plaintiff and said, "In the years since you left I've kept your clothes clean. I always carry photos from when we were together. Please come home with me!" When the court took a brief recess, the husband offered to buy water for his wife. None of his gestures went unnoticed by the court. Despite the plaintiff's determination to divorce, her husband's persistent unwillingness – to which his displays of care and affection lent further credence – was the basis of the court's string of rulings to deny her divorce petitions on the grounds that she had failed to prove the breakdown of mutual affection. The court's four adjudicated denials were supported by China's prevailing political ideology of marital preservation. As the head of the court division trying the case put it, "In every single divorce trial, we carry out mediation with the attitude of urging reconciliation and avoiding break-up [劝和不劝分]" (Yan 2016).

Beyond illustrating the importance of mutual consent, this case brings to the fore additional themes to which I will return in subsequent chapters. We cannot be certain the plaintiff in the foregoing case was a victim of domestic violence. We can be certain, however, that many women do escape domestic violence by "roaming around for the sake of work." The divorce twofer, by denying relief to women fleeing their abusive husbands, contributes to labor migration and the formation of a population of "marital violence refugees" (Chapter 9). Women who flee domestic violence often leave their children behind with their abusive husbands. Doing so puts them at a significant disadvantage in child custody disputes (Chapters 10 and 11). A defendant's power to upend his wife's divorce petition – even in cases involving domestic violence – gives him enormous bargaining leverage over the terms of divorce (Chapters 8, 9, 10, and 11).

Recall from Chapter 2 that the 2008 Guidelines urges judges not to take apologetic husbands at their word. In essence, it warns judges to treat "loving contrition" as a common aftereffect of an "acute battering incident," both of which are key stages of the archetypal "cycle of violence" (Walker 2017:97–98). Judges, however, generally fail to heed this warning. In their efforts to persuade abuse victims that their abusive husbands love them and are committed to improving themselves, Chinese judges, like judges elsewhere, help abusers gaslight their wives (Sweet 2019). When a woman leaves her abusive husband, parents on both sides will often work to reconcile the estranged couple (Wang, Qiao, and Yang 2013:32). The cultural stigma of divorce motivates some parents to do their utmost to prevent their children from divorcing; some parents "preferred a detestable son-in-law to a divorced daughter" (Honig and Hershatter 1988:224). According to a female police officer in Guizhou Province, when women report domestic violence to the police, "a lot of relatives and friends will show up and take part, trying all-out efforts or even cajole the wives to withdraw their domestic violence reports by brainwashing her with the cliché that 'every couple will fight and quarrel'" (J. Jiang 2019:234). Judges are thus part of a collective gaslighting effort (Chapter 9). Consider a divorce case filed by a woman beaten and injured by her husband. During her court trial, her father stood in for her abusive husband in court. The plaintiff and her father, as the defendant's representative, opposed each other in court. In his defense statement, the plaintiff's father described the defendant as a "good man and a good son-in-law," claimed their mutual affection had not completely broken down, characterized their current situation as the consequence of misunderstandings, and asked the court to deny his daughter's divorce petition. In typical fashion, the court denied the divorce petition on the grounds that "husband and wife still had reconciliation potential"; "their arguments over trivial matters had severely impacted marital affection" but "their foundation of affection was solid." The court further "recommended that both sides treasure their affection of many years, strengthen communication, and correctly resolve their conflicts" (Zhang 2013).

Despite the absence of any legal basis for the divorce twofer, it is a ubiquitous judicial practice that began to grow in the mid-2000s (Chapter 6). Unsupported by any sources of law, the divorce twofer only makes sense in terms of competing institutional pressures.

LIMITED JUDICIAL RESOURCES

Crushing workloads have incentivized Chinese judges to close cases as expeditiously as possible, and divorce petitions are easy targets owing in part to the highly discretionary and subjective breakdownism standard. For decades, a shortage of judges has been cited as a rationale for denying divorce petitions (Research Office of the Nanjing Municipal Intermediate Court 1987:16). According to a core tenet of the Stanford school of sociological institutionalism, the technical requirements of organizational work routines explain some measure of loose coupling between ceremonial conformity with globally legitimized norms and substantive organizational activities (Meyer and Rowan 1977). As the argument goes, legal systems around the world conform to the "universal ideal frame" embodied by global legal norms even when resource limitations and technical constraints limit their realization in practice (Boyle and Meyer 1998:217–18, 220). Evidence suggests that a state's bureaucratic capacity to fulfill its ceremonial commitments facilitates their implementation (Cole 2015). The case of Chinese courts appears to lend further support to this proposition.

A widening imbalance between the supply of and demand for judicial services is widely discussed as the problem of "many cases, few judges" (variously 案多人少, 官少案多, and 事多人少). Growth in the population of judges, which remained fairly stable at around 200,000 between 2000 and 2017 (Jiang 2015:26; Qu and Fan 2019:25; Zheng, Ai, and Liu 2017:169), has been far outstripped by growth in the volume of litigation. In 2009, when he delivered his annual work report to the National People's Congress, SPC President Wang Shengjun (王胜俊) stated that between 1978 and 2008, the annual number of closed cases at every level of the court system increased by a factor of 19.5, while the number of court personnel increased by a factor of only 1.68 (https://perma.cc/YL3Z-UH64). Elsewhere legal scholars reported that, between the late 1970s and the early 2010s, court dockets expanded by a factor of 20, while judge positions grew by only a factor of between two and three (Jiang 2015:26; Zheng 2018:130). Chapters 5 and 6 more fully assess the consequences of this growing imbalance between judges and cases. For now, I will briefly preview the argument that judges have embraced the divorce twofer as a coping strategy for their heavy caseloads.

It may seem counterintuitive that the divorce twofer, by multiplying court petitions, could help relieve the crushing pressure of China's court dockets. Indeed, granting first-time divorce petitions may seem like a more intuitive way for judges to clear their heavy dockets. After all, if a judge wants to put a divorce case behind him once and for all, swiftly granting the plaintiff's petition might seem more sensible than denying it. In contrast to such an expectation, however, the divorce twofer may enhance bureaucratic efficiency. Judges economize their time and effort by denying petitions, particularly ones that involve property division, child custody, and allegations of domestic violence. French divorce judges, who are under similar pressure to clear cases efficiently, also do their utmost to avoid dealing with litigants' time-consuming fault-based claims (Biland and Steinmetz 2017:314). If the plaintiff followed the judge's instructions to work out the terms of the divorce during the six-month statutory waiting period, which we will see in subsequent chapters often entails giving up property and child custody claims in exchange for the defendant's consent to divorce, judges can render relatively swift and uncontroversial decisions when the case returns for a second attempt.

> [E]ven when both sides keenly want to divorce and clearly express their desire to end their marriage, the court of first instance will often deny the divorce petition. This way of thinking about and trying divorce cases has already acquired inertia among judges in some courts. If it is the plaintiff's first divorce attempt, the defendant withholds consent, and there is no compelling evidence of the breakdown of mutual affection, a judge's basic predisposition is to deny the petition, which obviously obviates the need to collect and assess evidence about child custody and property division, and thus lightens judges' workload. (S. Guo 2018:113)

From judges' perspective, better yet is if the case goes away altogether and never returns, which happens more often than not (Chapter 6).

Bureaucratic efficiency, however, is only one of several institutional imperatives bearing on China's courts. Even if policy efforts aimed at optimizing the use of limited judicial resources succeed (Chapter 5), bureaucratic efficiency and capacity improvements in China's courts are not a sufficient condition of – and will not automatically translate into – more faithful implementation of China's domestic and global legal commitments. As we will see later in this chapter, judicial performance evaluation systems reward judges for case volume and efficiency and punish them for "social unrest." Judges are therefore incentivized to try the same case twice (to inflate case volume) by denying divorce petitions swiftly (to enhance efficiency), and thus to soothe the anger of defiant husbands unwilling to divorce and to defer or altogether avoid ruling on contentious matters such as property division and child custody that could potentially inflame violence between litigants or against judges themselves (to minimize "social unrest" and threats to their own personal safety). Hence my use of the word "twofer" to capture the "two for the price of one" quality of the benefits judges reap from denying first-attempt divorce petitions. In short, the technical ability to grant more divorce petitions, particularly to plaintiffs claiming domestic abuse, does not imply sufficient motivation on the part of judges to do so. Moreover, even if routinely granting first-time divorce petitions were sensible from a bureaucratic efficiency standpoint, doing so would be unthinkable from an ideological standpoint.

POLITICAL IDEOLOGY

What Lazarus-Black (2007) calls a "culture of reconciliation" in her study of why courts in Trinidad so rarely approve applications for personal protection orders submitted by domestic violence victims applies equally well to the Chinese context. Study after study of Chinese divorce refers to the enduring influence on judicial decision-making of the traditional cultural belief that "it is better to demolish ten temples than to destroy a single marriage" (宁拆十座庙, 不毁一桩婚; J. Guo 2018:28; Li 2003:7; Liu 2012:83; Ma 2006:23; Shi 2020:134; Xiong 2012:70; Xu 2016; Ye 2007:44; Zhou and Qiu 2018; W. Zhou 2018:28). China's contemporary political ideology of marital preservation taps into its traditional culture of marital reconciliation.

A biological metaphor of the family as the basic cell constituting the organism of society (Chen 2005a:155; Fincher 2014:23; Jiang 2009a:63; Li 2015; Liang 1982; Woo 2003:133; Zhang 1957) has long been part of the ideology (discussed in Chapter 2) that calls for preserving the family by opposing frivolous divorce. Indeed, since the time of Confucius, "the family was seen as a basic unit of society," and the stability of the family was therefore seen as beneficial to society as a whole (Baker 1979:10–11). Often characterized as a revival of Confucian ideology (Zhou 2017), China's renewed ideological emphasis on strengthening the family by restricting divorce also has strong roots in Marxist ideology (Jiang 2009a; Jiang and Zhu 2014:87; Liang 1982).[9] Ironically, it also bears a striking resemblance to American "family moralists" who, alarmed by rising divorce rates, promoted an ideology of "conservative family values" that gave rise to widespread US government policies and programs "promoting marriage and discouraging divorce" (Coltrane and Adams 2003).

According to legal scholars in Henan, "Xi Jinping champions the family as the basic cell of society and the first school in life. No matter what, we must attach importance to building up the family" (Henan Provincial Academy of Social Sciences Research Team 2017:10). China's Ministry of Civil Affairs has reportedly "warned of 'irrational divorces' and called for people to have a more responsible attitude towards marriage" (Zhou 2017). Parroting the party-state's ideological talking points, a legal scholar at China's Southwest University of Political Science and Law asserted, without supporting evidence, that "impulsive and irrational actions not only drove up the divorce rate, but also to some extent posed a new threat to social order" (Shi

---

[9] "Marx argued that in its essence marriage is indissoluble, though in reality it does sometimes die. Therefore divorce should be granted at times, but instead of being arbitrary, it must simply reflect the moribund state of the marriage. Thus in 1842 Marx was certainly no proponent of easy divorce and the abolition of the family" (Weikart 1994:658).

2020:140). A professor and Associate Dean of the Tsinghua University School of Law similarly proclaimed, "They may have quarreled about family affairs and they are divorcing in a fit of anger. After that, they may regret it. We need to prevent this kind of impulsive divorce" (Kuo 2020). According to the SPC's Du Wanhua (Du 2018:4), "China's continuously rising divorce rate over many years poses new challenges to harmonious and stable family construction." China's rapidly rising divorce rate is the backdrop against which Xi Jinping has made ideological calls for "civilized family construction," "core socialist values," "citizen moral construction," and a "harmonious society."

> Harmony and happiness in marriage and family are also the bedrock of national development, social progress, and the prosperity of the Chinese nationality. Since the 18th National Congress of the Chinese Communist Party [in 2012], Comrade Xi Jinping has put the construction of civilized families [家庭文明建设] at the core of the important tasks of the Party Central Committee. General Secretary Xi Jinping has strongly pointed out our need to attach importance to the construction of civilized families and to work hard to make millions upon millions of families the essential basis of the development of the Chinese nation, the progress of our nationality, and our harmonious society, and for families to become the point of departure for the people's dream. At the 19th National Congress of the Chinese Communist Party [in October 2017], he pointed out the need to integrate core socialist values into all aspects of social development and for them to become part of people's mentality, identity, and behavior. We will support action from all people, with officials taking the lead, starting with families and children. We will carry out a citizen moral construction campaign to advance public morality, professional ethics, family virtue, and personal integrity. We will encourage people to improve themselves, practice filial piety, and care for their family members. This fully reflects the high degree of importance the Party Central Committee attaches to civilized family construction and its care and concern for hundreds of millions of families.[10] (Du 2018:4)

If we were to strip out the China-specific and socialist language from this quotation, it would be nearly indistinguishable from the discourse of President George W. Bush and the Heritage Foundation justifying

[10] The last sentence is taken verbatim from Xi Jinping's December 12, 2016, speech at the inaugural meeting of the National Delegation for Civilized Families (Xinhua 2016). The term "the people's dream" (人民梦) refers to Xi Jinping's "Chinese dream" (中国梦) ideology of restoring China to its rightful place on the world stage (Z. Wang 2014).

marital counseling and divorce reduction programs for the purpose of promoting "strong marriage and stable families" (Catlett and Artis 2004).

Ideological discourse of this nature grew in prominence as a nation-wide "domestic relations trial reform" (家事审判改革), first introduced in 2016, ushered in new policy efforts aimed at preserving and reconciling marriages on the rocks through intensive mediation intervention on the part of social workers, psychologists, and female judges (Henan Provincial Academy of Social Sciences Research Team 2017; J. Jiang 2019:230; Li 2017; Shi 2020). One legal scholar describes China's "ideology of family justice reform" as "advocating the ethical concept of marriage and family that promotes civilisation and progress, giving full play to the family justice's role of diagnosis, repair, and treatment of marriage and family relations [sic]" (Shi 2020:136). Low fertility rates are an additional impetus not only for rescinding the one-child policy in 2016 but also for renewed official efforts to limit divorce (Myers and Ryan 2018) – as if prolonging unhappy marriages will promote childbearing. As mentioned earlier, courts in several provinces have even experimented with cooling-off periods for the explicit purpose of controlling rising divorce rates (Du 2018; J. Guo 2018; Shi 2020:140; J. Zhou 2018:35). In Henan Province, according to one report, under the banner of this reform, "Steadfastly 'urging reconciliation and avoiding break-up', and establishing 3–6 month 'cooling-off periods' for impulsive divorce cases with reconciliation potential, have helped 22,000 families on the verge of breakdown stay together" (Henan Provincial Academy of Social Sciences Research Team 2017:10).[11] In some ways cooling-off periods – particularly the one stipulated by Article 1077 of the 2020 Civil Code – are throw-backs to the old one-month approval period for Civil Affairs divorces prior to the 2003 Marriage Registration Regulations (J. Guo 2018:27; J. Zhou 2018:35).

Du Wanhua, the SPC's domestic relations trial reform czar, reaffirmed – using slightly different terminology – the legislative spirit of breakdownism when he underscored the need to separate "marriages in

---

[11] The SPC's 2018 Provisional Opinions on Further Deepening the Reform of the Methods and Work Mechanisms of Domestic Relations Trials subsequently clarified that cooling-off periods should not exceed three months (Article 40). In the 2020 Civil Code, however, provisions on cooling-off periods are limited to mutual-consent "divorces by agreement" processed by the Civil Affairs Administration.

crisis" from "marriages that have already died," and to restore marriages in crisis (Wang and Luo 2016:4).[12] Further to this point, "Only when a marriage is determined to be in crisis can judges identify the root cause of the marriage's disease and diagnose, treat, and heal the crisis" (J. Guo 2018:31). Du continued, "If the marriage is dead, the court will grant a divorce. Nowadays a huge number of divorce cases are spawned by marriage crises" (Wang and Luo 2016:4). Elsewhere Du again invoked a medical metaphor when calling for "bringing into full play the diagnostic and therapeutic function of domestic relations trials in order to provide emergency treatment to marriages that have not broken down and to families with problems" (Du 2018:5). He further underscored the imperative "to cultivate and practice core socialist values, to promote traditional Chinese family virtues … and to advance the harmonious and healthy development of society" (Du 2018:5). The key motivating objective of the domestic relations trial reform has been to repair marriages in crisis (Shandong Province Ji'nan Municipal Intermediate People's Court Research Team 2018:182; Wang and Luo 2016:4). According to an official who set up a "Happiness Class," "At a time when freedom of marriage and divorce are being advocated, impulsive and hasty marriages and divorces are on the rise. We are offering free guidance and psychological counseling for the couples careening into divorce without careful forethought" (Xinhua 2019). Du put the magnitude of the problem in perspective by pointing out that the category of marriage, family, and inheritance cases (of which divorce is a part) accounts for about one-third of all civil cases (Wang and Luo 2016:3). According to its proponents and spokespersons, the ideology of marital preservation promises not only to check divorce rates but also, in so doing, to protect the interests of children, women, and the elderly (Du 2018). Chapters 9–11 on the negative consequences of the divorce twofer suffered by battered women and their children suggest otherwise.

The contents of a "notice of cooling-off period" issued by the Chongqing Municipal Yubei District People's Court on May 9, 2020,

---

[12] Here Du quoted directly from the SPC's 2016 Opinions on Carrying Out Pilot Reform of the Methods and Work Mechanisms of Domestic Relations Trials: "On the basis of a diagnosis of the marital condition, marriages in crisis must be distinguished from marriages that have already died, the marital crisis must be defused, and the correct balance between protecting the freedom of marriage and maintaining family stability must be found." It reappears almost verbatim in the SPC's 2018 Provisional Opinions on Further Deepening the Reform of the Methods and Work Mechanisms of Domestic Relations Trials.

bring into high relief the ideological underpinnings of China's domestic relations trial reforms.

> "Falling in love is easy, marriage is difficult, marriage is a fine porcelain bowl that needs care and love from both sides [相爱容易, 婚姻不易, 婚姻是只细瓷碗, 需要双方的呵护和爱护]." From your first acquaintance, to romance, and ultimately to marital bliss, you built a family. You share a happy, beautiful past. Marital affection is the foundation of marriage's durability. Even if your mutual affection were stronger, you would inevitably encounter some bumps in the road. If there were two people even better for each other than you, they would still experience disagreements. A good marriage requires that both sides calmly accept their differences and embrace the other side's shortcomings. "Hand in hand, growing old together [执子之手, 与子偕老]" was your original intention as you approached marriage. Marriage is a long journey during which you will inevitably encounter setbacks. We urge you to calm down, carefully consider each other's efforts and hardships, empathize with and support each other, communicate with a positive attitude, resolve problems rationally and kindly, warm your children with patience and sincerity, cherish the person by your side, respect and trust one another, remain committed to your original intentions, and work together to create a better future!
>
> In order to restore your marital relations and maintain family and social stability to the greatest extent possible, and in accordance with the spirit of the [SPC's 2018] Provisional Opinions on Further Deepening the Reform of the Methods and Work Mechanisms of Domestic Relations Trials, you are hereby notified of the following provisions concerning your divorce dispute. (Cheng 2020)

The three provisions at the bottom of the notice concern: (1) the duration of the cooling-off period (i.e., one month), (2) the behavior required of the litigants during the cooling-off period (i.e., remaining cool-headed and rational, not raising the issue of divorce), and (3) additional items (i.e., the ability to extend the cooling-off period and/or withdraw the divorce petition) (Cheng 2020).

The first "notice of cooling-off period" issued by Sichuan Province's Anyue County People's Court in 2017 was similar in its abundance of legally irrelevant relationship advice. The judge presiding over the case deemed a cooling-off period appropriate in this case because "the plaintiff was less than entirely determined to divorce, the defendant was unwilling to divorce, and both sides had the potential to reconcile" (Sichuan Online 2017). The judge also emphasized that the purpose of cooling-off periods more generally is to prevent impulsive divorces, to protect the stability of marriage and family, and to rescue marriages on the brink (Li 2017). We will see in Chapters 7 and 8 that the language judges used in their holdings to deny divorce petitions is virtually identical to that in their notices of cooling-off periods. Both types of court decisions are bursting with hackneyed clichés written by paternalistic judges professing to know better than the plaintiffs themselves and imploring plaintiffs to treasure the toxic marriages they are desperate to exit. As if they have superior insight into the objective marital circumstances and best interests of plaintiffs seeking divorce, judges routinely assert their authority to invalidate plaintiffs' no-fault claims of irreconcilable differences and fault-based claims of statutory wrongdoing.

China's domestic relations trial reform is a contemporary extension of a deeper ideological legacy of institutionalized limits on the freedom of divorce (W. Chen 2013; Tsui 2001; Yi and Tong 1998). Earlier discourse about out-of-control "frivolous divorce" (or "rash" or "impulsive" divorce, 轻率离婚, 草率离婚, 轻易离婚; Diamant 2000b), "experimental divorce" (试离婚), "heat-of-passion divorce" (赌气离婚), and "abuse of the freedom of divorce" (滥用离婚自由; Chen 2005b; Fei 2010) persists in the form of discourse about the need for policy measures to control "impetuous divorce" (冲动性离婚; Li 2017; Ma 2018; J. Zhou 2018), which feeds an ostensibly broader phenomenon of "bogus lawsuits" (虚假诉讼; An 2015; Y. Zhang 2017; https://perma.cc/9DXY-B244). As we will see later in this chapter, such ideological discourse is not gender-neutral.

China's domestic relations trial reform also stems from and further supports China's broader ideology of "stability maintenance" (维稳; Han 2017; Lee and Zhang 2013; Yang 2017). Judges have been tasked with maintaining social stability in general (Zhang 2016a:23) and to do so by denying divorce petitions in particular. To support claims of a link between divorce and social stability, Du Wanhua has asserted that juvenile crime is driven by divorce, that 70–80% of juvenile offenders have divorced parents (Du 2018; Li 2017; M. Wang 2018; Wang and Luo 2016). According to a judge in Shanghai:

> The government believes that sustaining a marriage relationship means or equals maintaining social stability; and we have to carry out the Party's stability maintenance policy in work. Hence, China does not really have freedom of marriage – there is no freedom of divorce – even in metropolises like Shanghai. What if the divorce statistic reaches above 50%? How improper it would look, and how inharmonious it would appear. (J. Jiang 2019:239)

We will see in Chapters 7 and 8 the full extent to which political discourse about preserving and strengthening family harmony has penetrated China's courts. Judges have embraced and incorporated this political discourse into their decision-making (Li 2015a:173). Woven into the fabric of judges' reasoning and embroidered in high relief in their written decisions are threads of this political discourse about supporting family stability as a means of achieving the larger political goal of social stability.

Political ideology is not the only tool shaping judicial decision-making. Ideological signals from above exert direct pressure on judges and are also indirectly mediated by judicial performance evaluation systems.

JUDICIAL PERFORMANCE EVALUATION SYSTEMS

Judicial performance evaluation systems (variously 绩效考核体系, 绩效考评制度, and 案件质量评估体系), also known as judicial responsibility systems (法官责任制), serve to shape judicial behavior by delivering tangible rewards and punishments to judges according to their degree of compliance with prevailing political policies and ideologies. As civil servants without tenure, Chinese judges are highly responsive to incentive structures designed to support shifting political priorities. Their risk-averse practices are captured by the idiom "Seek not to do good work but rather to avoid blame" (不求有功, 但求无过; Li and Zhou 2018:64; Xiao, Ma, and Tuo 2014:63). In their efforts to minimize "incorrectly decided cases" (错案), judges' institutionalized practice of "seeking guidance from and reporting back to" (请示汇报) higher-level authorities responsible for evaluating their performance (Chen 2016a:214, 2016b:116; Tang 2016) has roots not only in the Mao era (Minzner 2009:75) but also parallels contemporary manifestations of the Soviet institutional norm of "telephone justice" (Hendley 2009, 2017; Ledeneva 2008). Judges' imperative to satisfy the demands of judicial responsibility systems (He 2009; Kinkel and Hurst 2015; Liebman 2015; Zhu 2016:194), which are institutional legacies of imperial China and the Mao era (Cui 2016; Minzner 2009), as well as of the Soviet Union (Solomon 2010, 2012), and which remain salient in contemporary Russian courts (Paneyakh 2014), compete with their incentives to uphold China's domestic laws and international legal commitments.

> Courts across China have established systems for quantifying judge performance assessment indicators. Performance is assessed primarily according to a judge's volume of closed cases, average closing times, mediation rates, appeal rates, rates of requests for judicial review, rates of reversing and remanding decisions for retrial, rates at which decisions are announced at the time of the trial, written decision approval rates, rates of petitioning caused by dissatisfaction with court decisions, rates by which parties abide by court decisions, and volume of research articles. This is the basis of rewards and punishments. Quantitative scores determine a judge's awards, promotions, economic compensation, and so on, and even influence a judge's reputation and image. (An 2015:179)

No different from their Soviet and Russian counterparts (Solomon 2015:169), Chinese judicial performance evaluation systems, since at least the 1990s, have emphasized moving caseloads (Zhu 2016:121n6). Although a reform to the system in 2014 ended some common practices, such as ranking entire courts, and introduced greater flexibility to accommodate local conditions (Chen 2016a:213–14; Xu, Huang, and Lu 2015:135), incentives that reward clearing dockets and that punish incidents of social unrest persist. Measures of social instability include incidents of petitioning and complaining to higher authorities about – and incidents of violence stemming from – court decisions (Liebman 2011a, 2014). In some courts, paralleling practices elsewhere in the state bureaucracy, an incorrectly decided case resulting in the "harmful social influence" of a litigant improperly petitioning to Beijing or the provincial capital, is a so-called "priority target with veto power" or "single item veto" (一票否决) that entirely wipes out a judge's accumulated merit points (Pan 2019:139; Yanhong Wang 2013:33; Z. Wang 2018; Yang 2017). Judges have even been criminally prosecuted for the crime of "abuse of power" (Article 168 of the Criminal Law) on the grounds of harming society by causing an unhappy litigant to petition repeatedly (Lou 2018:111). The slogan "six noes" (六无) captures judges' incentives to achieve the goal of no remands for retrial, no reversals, no petitioning by dissatisfied parties, no missed decision time limits, no legal or disciplinary infractions, and no negative media coverage (Y. Wang 2015).

Nothing will derail the career of a judge faster than an "extreme incident" (极端事件) that inflames public outrage fanned by media exposure.

> In the course their work, judges face immense risk, such as demotions and even terminations at the whim of superiors. As soon as a litigant

petitions in the complaints system or creates an incident that affects social stability, the judge will be investigated and even punished. The perennial possibility of an investigation of an incorrectly decided case is a Sword of Damocles hanging over the heads of judges. (C. Hu 2015:204)

Judges, no different from officials elsewhere in the state apparatus, make discretionary ad hoc concessions to litigants who pose credible threats of carrying out or inciting a quintessentially "extreme" incident such as petitioning, public protest, suicide, and murder. Judges complain that their courts have been hijacked by litigants who get what they want by threatening unrest (X. Li 2014:220). In the words of a judge from Fujian Province, one female defendant "screamed at me and climbed up to the courtroom window with the intention of committing suicide. We had to erect a safety net at the base of the building to protect her, and spent a long time pacifying her" (Cao 2018). Another judge in Anhui Province heeded a defendant's threat to drink the bottle of pesticide she clutched in her hand (Zhou and Qiu 2018).

The paramount importance of "maintaining social stability" has incentivized aggrieved citizens to threaten unrest while also incentivizing officials responsible for dealing with them to adopt populist strategies for redressing their grievances in arbitrary ways (Feng and He 2018; He 2014, 2017; Lee and Zhang 2013; Liebman 2011a, 2013, 2014; Zhang 2016a). The president of a basic-level court in Zhejiang's provincial capital of Hangzhou reported that "as litigants are inclined to use suicide, self-harm, fanatical and unruly petitioning, and other irrational methods of expressing their litigation demands, the pressure of maintaining stability in petitioning has grown" (https://perma.cc/M6G6-XCB7). The divorce twofer helps judges placate volatile defendants dead set against divorcing. According to a court official, "in divorce cases that harbor the threat of becoming complaints in the petitioning [信访] system, courts will typically not grant the divorce" (Hu 2019). Police responsible for responding to emergency domestic violence incidents fear disciplinary punishment following an "inharmonious event" in which an abuse victim, under pressure from her family, recants her allegations and files a complaint against the responding officer on the grounds that he broke up her family (J. Jiang 2019:234–35). Judges are sometimes reluctant to issue personal protection orders for the same reason (J. Jiang 2019:235).

In the context of divorce litigation, a plaintiff can sometimes get her way by threatening to commit suicide if her petition is *not* granted.

Meanwhile, a defendant who does not consent can sometimes get his way by threatening to murder the plaintiff if her petition *is* granted (Diamant 2000b:333, 336). Judges take such threats seriously because they are sometimes carried out (Chapter 9); judges have no way of knowing who is only bluffing (He 2017; Ng and He 2017a:130–31; J. Wang 2013:84). For this reason, social stability considerations compel judges to use the breakdownism test instrumentally and often unlawfully to deny divorce petitions not *despite* but *because* of domestic violence and the perceived potential for worse violence if a divorce is granted. One judge persuaded a plaintiff to reconcile with rather than to divorce her abusive husband: "He says he will kill you if you divorce him, and it seems he is serious. We cannot ensure your safety if we render a divorce decision. To tell you the truth, it is rather easy for us to render a divorce judgment. The reason why I bother to talk you into reconciliation is all for your good" (J. Wang 2013:84). A female plaintiff reported that, when she filed for divorce, a member of the court "staff frightened me that my husband would beat me more seriously if I didn't go back home immediately" (Wang, Qiao, and Yang 2013:35).

By both helping judges to clear cases efficiently and giving litigants additional time to negotiate and agree on the terms of the divorce in preparation for a subsequent attempt, the divorce twofer alleviates judges' workloads, boosts volume and efficiency measures, and reduces the probability of dissatisfaction, petitioning, and extreme incidents. This is why I call it a "twofer": by trying the same case twice, judges can get double credit while minimizing their professional liability. By denying a divorce petition, judges kick the can down the road for at least six months, and in so doing maximize their professional rewards and minimize their professional risks. In the words of a legal scholar and two judges, "To deny a divorce on the first attempt and grant it on the second attempt is safer and more reliable, and of great help raising a judge's individual performance evaluation scores" (Xiao, Ma, and Tuo 2014:63). The deputy director of a research office in a county court in Hunan Province put it this way: "Under the burden of 'many cases, few judges', petitioning and stability maintenance, performance evaluations, and other omnipresent pressures, judges are relatively cautious when they try first-attempt divorce petitions. By routinely denying divorces on the grounds of insufficient evidence, judges can close these cases quickly, avoid appeals, complaints, reversals, and other risks associated with judicial performance evaluation metrics" (Hu 2019).

Another judge in Guangxi agreed: "Denying first-attempt divorce petitions closes cases quickly, raises judicial efficiency, and cools off litigants, thereby lowering rates of complaints and appeals" (Xu 2016). He then elaborated:

> A divorce should be granted when one side files for divorce and mutual affection has indeed broken down. However, when the other side cites objective reasons such as "I'll have trouble finding another wife" or "the family will lose its backbone," does so with an unyielding attitude and maniacal personality, steadfastly refuses to divorce, and even displays extremist behavior and speech, intimidates the presiding judge, and so on, the judge will not dare decide the case lightly. (Xu 2016)

The architects of China's domestic relations trial reform hoped that marital preservation would promote social stability by promoting family stability. In theory, intensive intervention and cooling-off periods would nip conflicts in the bud before escalating into full-blown extreme incidents (Du 2018; J. Guo 2018; Hou 2018; Liu and Zheng 2018; Wang and Luo 2016; J. Zhou 2018). Ideally, the couple would reconcile. If reconciliation is beyond hope, however, reform measures were designed to help the couple divorce peacefully. According to a legal scholar, cooling-off periods are particularly well suited for situations such as "marriages that are dead beyond resuscitation in which one party, for example, acting emotionally and overly dramatically, threatens to commit suicide. In a case like this, the cooling-off period is not for reconciliation purposes but rather for psychological intervention, to let the litigant cool off and better exit the marriage" (M. Wang 2018). Another law professor similarly justified cooling-off periods: "If some litigants display extreme behavior before going to court, such as threatening to commit suicide, judges should not mediate but rather provide psychological aid" (Cao 2018).

Judges may be even more concerned about the threat of social unrest posed by male litigants. Regardless of its legal merits, a judge is unlikely to grant a divorce petition if he perceives a risk of violent retaliation against the plaintiff. According to Chen Min (陈敏), a leading voice in China's anti-domestic violence movement and author of the 2008 Guidelines, abusive defendants sometimes threaten their wives in court for precisely this reason. Most abusers deny their wives' allegations of domestic violence. Some, however, try to prevent divorces by deliberately threatening or even carrying out violence in full view of judges.

Consider an example of a divorce case involving domestic violence tried in a basic-level court. A woman filed for divorce the first time in 2014. The court affirmed that the male side "sometimes beat the female side, causing her physical and mental harm." Nonetheless, the court denied the divorce petition. In 2015 the woman filed for the second time. While they were waiting for the trial to begin, the male side beat the female side. The presiding judge had no choice but to reschedule the trial. Later, as the trial approached its conclusion, the male side suddenly banged the table with his fist and threatened to murder the female side if the divorce were granted. The judges once again denied the divorce petition. In 2016, after the Anti-Domestic Violence Law had already taken effect, the woman filed for the third time. While the judge was carrying out mediation, the male side once again expressed his determination to do everything to murder the female side if the court were to grant the divorce. In 2017, the court affirmed the male side's "domestic violence tendencies" but once again denied the divorce petition. (Chen 2018:8)

Chen concluded that the judge in this case "may have continuously denied the plaintiff's divorce petition in consideration of the possibility that the defendant would carry out his threats of violence if the divorce were granted." She further argued that a man's threat to murder his wife can be an *indirect* threat against the judge, particularly in a context in which "maintaining stability trumps everything" (Chen 2018:8).

JUDGES' SAFETY AND HEALTH

Litigants also *directly* threaten judges with violence. Judges take their personal safety into account when ruling on divorce petitions (Li 2015a:141). Judges who handle divorce cases say they live in a constant state of fear of attack (Zhou and Qiu 2018). In a survey of frontline judges in a basic-level court in Guangxi Province's city of Nanning, 99% of respondents reported having experienced – to varying degrees – abuse, intimidation, malicious accusations, and other threats to their personal safety and reputation. On several occasions, litigants carried weapons through the security check at the courthouse entrance (X. Li 2014:220).

In 2018, a disgruntled former litigant stormed into the courtroom of the judge who tried his divorce case. After he reportedly shouted something like, "Bullshit verdict!" ("判个××!"), the judge ordered him to leave and come back after the trial. Disobeying the judge's order, he toppled desks and threatened to kill the judge. The offender was reportedly infuriated because the judge approved his ex-wife's divorce petition. Ultimately, the judge had granted this divorce only on the third attempt (Chuncheng Evening News 2018). Perhaps the judge's reluctance to grant the divorce stemmed from the defendant's established history of violence. If female judges feel particularly vulnerable to such threats of physical violence, they may favor abusive husbands even if they are more sympathetic than male judges to abuse victims seeking divorce.

In a 2019 divorce case in Guangxi Province, the Rongan County People's Court notified the defendant by phone and WeChat message, instructing him to retrieve litigation materials in preparation for his trial. The defendant replied that he was too busy, and refused to follow court procedures. So the court sent hardcopies of the materials and his court summons to his officially registered residential address, and his father signed the delivery slip on his behalf. On the day of the trial, the court sent the defendant a text message reminder. The defendant replied with a threat: "I don't have time. Do whatever you want. Please tell her that when she gets together with someone else, she needs to return my bride price or else members of her family will absolutely die. If you harass me with any more texts, your family members will die sooner." After the trial was held with the defendant in absentia, the defendant sent several abusive and threatening text messages to the judge, including, "You guys at the court forced me onto the road of criminality" and "Prepare to collect corpses" (Rongan County People's Court 2019).

> A judge in a basic-level court recounted a divorce case she tried that involved domestic violence. The male side, adamantly opposed to the divorce, said to the judge, "I know where your daughter goes to school." Although she saw through his bluff, she also realized her work made her daughter's personal safety the target of the abuser's threats. In another example, on December 15, 2017, the public WeChat account of the municipal government of Putian in Fujian Province sent out a message with the headline, "sender of text messages threatening numerous judges is in a police detention center." According to a local court in the area, the detained person was a litigant in a divorce case several years earlier. Because his extremely serious domestic violence caused the breakdown of mutual affection, the presiding judges, on the basis of their determination of the facts, granted the divorce. Afterwards,

the person in detention continued violently harassing his ex-wife. In order to escape his harassment, stalking, intimidation, and beatings, his ex-wife had no choice but to flee. No longer able to control his ex-wife, he redirected his wrath towards the presiding judges. Over the years he continuously, in fits and starts, harassed and intimidated the judges in online posts until, on this particular occasion, he sent intimidating messages directly to the judges' cell phones and got himself locked up in detention. However, in practice, not all judges who are intimidated by litigants are able to receive the support and protection of local police. (Chen 2018:8)

Some litigants carry out their threats. According to one study, family disputes, particularly those in rural areas, are more likely than other kinds of disputes to precipitate violence against judges (Tian and Wang 2016:83). In the words of a former high-level SPC judge,

> improperly handled family disputes may give rise to extreme criminal cases and even the murder of judges. I frequently receive reports of such incidents from across China, many of which are suicides, homicides, assaults, familicides, and other such vicious incidents. In 2016 Ma Caiyun [马彩云], a judge in Beijing's Changping District People's Court, was murdered. In 2017 Fu Mingsheng [傅明生], a retired domestic relations judge from Guangxi Province's Luchuan County People's Court, was murdered. In each case the motive was a family dispute. (Du 2018:4)

Ma Caiyun died from gunshot wounds sustained in an attack by a male litigant aggrieved by the outcome of a divorce case she tried (Tian and Wang 2016:83). Fu Mingsheng was stabbed to death by a litigant upset by the outcome of a divorce case he had tried years earlier (Jin 2017). In 2000, Li Yuechen (李月臣), a judge in Shandong, was abducted and murdered with a cleaver and iron rod by a litigant who was unable to come to grips with his divorce verdict. In Gansu Province, five people were killed and 22 injured in 2006 when a bomb was detonated in the Yongle County People's Court for reasons related to a divorce case. In 2010, a litigant who was upset with the outcome of his divorce case killed four people, including himself, and injured another three with a handheld submachine gun in Hunan Province's Yongzhou Municipal Lingling District People's Court (He 2017:485n2; Tian and Wang 2016:83).

In August 2020, Hao Jian (郝剑), a judge in Heilongjiang Province's Harbin Municipal Shuangcheng District People's Court, granted a divorce to a woman who claimed her husband frequently carried out domestic violence. She submitted medical documentation of a perforated eardrum caused by a beating she received from her husband the previous month. The husband admitted to the allegations of wrongdoing and agreed to divorce. Dissatisfied with the judge's property division ruling, however, he appealed the decision. Before the Harbin Municipal Intermediate Court tried the case, the husband snuck a boning knife past security and into the original basic-level court and used it to stab Judge Hao once in the chest. He was already dead by the time paramedics arrived (Suo 2020; Zhao 2020).

Owing to their fear of violent retribution, judges are "exceptionally cautious" when handing divorce cases (J. Zhang 2018:110). In my collection of annual work reports from Zhejiang Province, 50 out of 87 basic-level courts specifically mentioned the problem of violence and threats of violence against judges. For example, in his 2009 work report, the president of the basic-level court in Zhejiang's city of Pinghu discussed

> Confronting challenges vis-à-vis stability maintenance. At the current time, some litigants, out of self-interest, make threats of violent disturbances, suicide, self-harm, and so on; attack, verbally assault, and physically injure judges; petition without cause, petition disruptively, and even make scenes in the courtroom in violent defiance of the law; and severely influence the smooth performance of trial and enforcement work. (https://perma.cc/Y75D-9D8U)

Similarly, the president of Zhejiang's Wuyi County People's Court reported in 2014 that "litigants have hurled invectives at, threatened, and even physically attacked judges, and in some instances have gone to their homes to make disturbances; handling cases is like walking on thin ice" (https://perma.cc/JCU6-HB3U). In his 2010 work report, the president of Henan's Provincial High Court, Zhang Liyong (张立勇), stated that "a small number of litigants have threatened, intimidated, insulted, and beaten judges, and have even used extreme methods of violence" (https://perma.cc/4FFZ-L9XE).

In Hunan Province's Hengyang County, Ning Shunhua's Sisyphean struggle to divorce her abusive husband, Chen Dinghua, stemmed in no small part from his thinly veiled threats against the court's judges. Between 2016 and 2020, she filed for divorce four times, and each time the Hengyang County People's Court denied her petition. According to one report, "Ning Shunhua said that Chen Dinghua, during almost every trial, openly stated his intent to pursue relentlessly whomever grants her divorce petition, exact revenge against society, produce a terrorist incident, etc." In the words of a member of the Hengyang Municipal Women's Federation, which intervened numerous times, "Her husband was unwilling to divorce and displayed extreme emotions….At one moment he would say he was calming down and a moment later he might once again threaten revenge" (Zhu 2021). Ning's lawyer said that "Chen once smashed his [the lawyer's] car and had made death threats to judges" (Feng 2021).

Between 2016 and 2021, Chen was held in administrative detention on six occasions for gambling, violence, and threats of violence. Between 2018 and 2020, the same court granted all three of Ning's applications for personal protection orders against Chen. On the day of their fourth divorce trial, Chen attacked Ning at the courthouse entrance, causing multiple injuries documented in a certified medical appraisal. Chen was put in administrative detention as a result, and two days later the court granted Ning's second application for a protection order (Feng 2021; Sohu.com 2021a; Zhu 2021). From the standpoint of the law, therefore, the judges should have affirmed Ning's fault-based grounds for divorce. Owing to the extra-judicial institutional pressures on courts I have thus far documented in this chapter, however, the judges did their utmost to disaffirm any grounds for divorce.

Ning's experience in divorce court illustrates additional themes of this book. After she filed her fifth divorce petition in March 2021, media coverage of her plight prompted the Hengyang County People's Court to issue a statement on the matter. In it, the court explained its rationale for denying all four of Ning's divorce petitions. "Chen Dinghua repeatedly expressed admission of his mistakes to Ning Shunhua and his determination to fix them as a way of seeking her forgiveness. Ning Shunhua expressed to the defendant by text messages and other means her willingness to give him more time and another chance. In the five years since her first divorce petition, Chen Dinghua, from beginning to end, fiercely pleaded his wish to reconcile" (Hengyang County Court 2021). In typical fashion, the court denied Ning's fourth divorce petition "in order to protect family stability and social harmony." It made light of Ning's complaints by chalking them up to poor relationship skills shared by both sides: "Husband and wife have hope for reconciliation provided that both sides correctly handle their marital and family problems, calmly and properly deal with their conflicts, effectively strengthen their communication, and engage in self-reflection to identify their shortcomings and correct them" (Sohu.com 2021a). As we will continue to see in Chapters 7 and 8, courts have commonly cited reconciliation potential in precisely this way as a pretext for sidelining documented claims of domestic violence, particularly when the defendant withheld consent to divorce.

In April 2021, the court finally granted Ning's fifth divorce petition, but – as with so many women seeking divorce – only after she waived her right to a share of the marital house and returned items of jewelry. Chen appealed the verdict, demanding that the court of second instance restore their marriage by reversing the original court of first instance's decision to grant the divorce. The court of second instance instead supported Chen's secondary request that, in the event it upheld the original divorce verdict, she return his bride price, and ordered Ning to compensate Chen ¥85,000 (Sohu.com 2021b).

Chinese judges' burdens of heavy dockets, performance evaluations, and their own and litigants' physical safety have reportedly taken a toll on their well-being in the form of burnout, mental health issues, including post-traumatic stress disorder, alcohol and drug use, and even suicide (Liu 2017:64; Zhou and Qiu 2018). Between 2008 and 2012, 156 judges across China died from illness related to work (often caused by overwork), accidents at work, and violent attacks by disgruntled litigants (Yuan 2013). In 2017, SPC President Zhou Qiang (周强) reported that 36 judges across China died of overwork in the previous year alone (https://perma.cc/3W35-XJWW). Judges have reported abysmally low levels of work satisfaction (C. Hu 2015). Not surprisingly, for these reasons courts have reportedly had trouble retaining judges (Fang 2015; X. Li 2014; X. Zhang 2014; Zheng, Ai, and Liu 2017:190). According to a large survey of judges, prosecutors, police officers, and lawyers, judges registered far and away the highest levels of work pressure. Moreover, judges identified performance evaluation systems as far and away their greatest source of pressure. Finally, compared to members of the other groups, judges identified attrition through resignation as a far more serious problem (Wu 2015). Crushing dockets and the risk of grave career repercussions from decisions that could potentially go awry have dampened judges' work enthusiasm, as reflected in another catchphrase, "three noes and one outflow" (三不一流失): judges have no courage, no ability, and no willingness to try cases, and they flow out of the court system (Y. Wang 2015).

To sum up so far, pressures from three endogenous institutional logics – limited judicial resources, political ideology, and performance evaluations – incentivize judges to deny first-attempt divorce petitions, particularly when they involve claims of domestic violence. Denying a first-attempt divorce petition is a rational strategy for both minimizing the risk of negative fallout and maximizing performance evaluations.

> Judges face case closing time limits, case closing rates, appeal rates, and other pressures from the judicial performance evaluation system. Under these kinds of work pressures, rational judges will do their utmost to minimize harmful risk, maximize case closing rates, and minimize appeal and complaint rates. Under the pressure of performance evaluations, and with the goal of maximizing self-protection and minimizing risk, judges deny first-instance divorce petitions. (J. Guo 2018:30)

The divorce twofer can only be understood as a consequence of norms and practices endogenous to the institutional environment in which China's courts are embedded. Although I have explained why judges routinely deny first-attempt divorce petitions, I have not explained why they might disproportionately deny the first-attempt divorce petitions of women. Routinely denying first-attempt divorce petitions is more than a rational strategy adopted by risk-averse, career-maximizing judges. Judicial decision-making also adheres to a cultural logic.

PATRIARCHY

The impact of the global diffusion of norms and laws promoting gender equality may be stymied by the persistence of countervailing local cultural schemas (Ridgeway 2011). Cultural categories of moral worthiness and deservingness can undermine women's efforts to get justice through the law (Lazarus-Black 2007:89–90; Michelson 2006:6–7; on "cultural categories of worth" more generally, see Steensland 2006). Divorced women in China belong to a stigmatized and socially disgraced cultural category of "outcasts" deemed "morally bankrupt" (Honig and Hershatter 1988:212–13, 224, 237–40; also see Buck 1931:907 and Mo 2017:391). Just as narratives about "frivolous lawsuits" helped justify a clampdown on tort litigation in the United States (Haltom and McCann 2004), narratives about "frivolous divorce" helped justify China's judicial clampdown on divorce in general and on female-initiated divorce in particular. A prevailing trope in Chinese narratives about "frivolous" and "impulsive" divorce is a woman recklessly rushing to divorce her husband only to harbor regrets after cooling off and regaining her composure (e.g., Chang 2017). Allegations of widespread "abuse of the freedom of divorce" are seemingly uniformly supported by anecdotes of "impetuous and capricious" (冲动任性) women initiating the litigation process (Ma 2018; Tian 2016:25; also see Honig and Hershatter 1988:212, 224). Narratives about a selfish generation of only-children – born in the 1980s and 1990s after the nationwide implementation of the one-child policy – fueling China's allegedly runaway divorce problem are supported by anecdotes of outrageously trivial arguments leading to female-initiated divorce, such as the wife who filed for divorce after her husband changed the Wi-Fi password and failed to share it with her, and the wife who filed for divorce because her husband failed to tear toilet paper on the perforations (Ma 2018:17).

This is hardly a uniquely Chinese phenomenon. Media narratives in the United States are likewise awash with "metaphors that blame women for frivolously wanting to end bad marriages and characterizing single and divorced mothers as short-sighted and self-serving" (Coltrane and Adams 2003:369). American judges thus invoke and reproduce shared, taken-for-granted cultural assumptions about gender when they *"unjustly discount women's personal trustworthiness"* (Epstein and Goodman 2019:405, emphasis in original).

Patriarchal cultural beliefs such as these help explain why women seeking help from China's courts bear the brunt of institutional pressures to maximize judicial efficiency. When "efficiency overrides due process" (效率压倒公平), litigation is biased in favor of men. When "efficiency takes priority over due process" (效率优先于公平), judges render decisions mechanically and mindlessly, "without the need to use their brains" (无需要动脑筋的), and in so doing bring gender stereotypes, implicit bias, and prejudice into play (Lin, Bu, and Li 2015:124). In an institutional context such as this, characterized as having undergone "judicial patriarchialization" (司法男权化), judges – the majority of whom are men – take men's claims more seriously than women's and are more likely to grant men's divorce petitions than women's (Lin, Bu, and Li 2015). Owing to the central role of prejudices and preconceptions in judicial decision-making (法官先入为主), the trial has been characterized as little more than a formalistic exercise (形式主义) of judges going through the motions (走过场) to render a predetermined judgment (先定后审; Li and Ye 2015). In the context of gender violence elsewhere in the world, stereotypes about women as unstable, unreasonable, emotional, hysterical, overly sensitive, flighty, and irrational undermine their credibility and thereby undermine gender equality in court (Epstein and Goodman 2019; Frohmann 1991; Goodmark 2005; Stanko 1982; Sweet 2019). Chinese judges are more likely to respond dismissively with impatience and annoyance to female litigants than to male litigants, often by interrupting with a raised voice, interjecting with belittling comments, pointing at them, striking the bench, and ignoring their questions (Bu, Li, and Lin 2015; Chen 2007; Li and Friedman 2016:161–62).

Chinese judges are on the lookout for litigants who try to game the system. They are suspicious of litigants who, with malicious intent, give false testimony, submit fake evidence, or use other deceptive methods to achieve their divorce goals (Dong and Ji 2016:89; Sun 2010). In particular, judges fear litigants make false claims about both domestic violence and the unknown whereabouts of their spouses. "Family harmony's influence on social harmony and the critical role of marital stability for social stability demand that judges exercise caution" and cast doubt on plaintiff's potentially exaggerated or even fabricated claims of defendants' unknown whereabouts (Xiong 2012:71).

Judges' suspicions about the integrity of litigants are not gender-neutral. With respect to domestic violence claims, judges commonly believe, either consciously or implicitly, that women exaggerate or fabricate their claims of marital violence in order to boost their chances of gaining child custody or to vent their frustrations and shame their husbands (Epstein and Goodman 2019; He and Ng 2013a; Jeffries 2016:6–7). Because judges perceive men's claims as more credible than women's (Sweet 2019), they tend to support seemingly homicidal men over seemingly suicidal women (He 2017).

Just as they harbor doubts about domestic violence claims, judges are likewise wary of claims of missing defendants. Plaintiffs, either on their own in opposition to their spouses or in cahoots with their spouses, may conceal to the court the whereabouts of their spouses and falsely claim they have tried unsuccessfully to make contact. In efforts to surmount obstructionism from a defendant who does not consent to divorce, and to deprive a defendant of marital property and child custody, a plaintiff may surreptitiously divorce under the false pretense of the defendant's unknown whereabouts (Tao and Lu 2012:66). Often the plaintiff alone orchestrates the exploitation of the public notice service of process system in this way. Married couples, however, may also be motivated by the shared benefits of a "fake divorce" mentioned in Chapter 2 and hatch a plot jointly to deceive judges (Tan and Wang 2011:116). In either case, litigants may provide fake addresses as decoys, give false testimony, arrange witnesses and coach them to lie, or falsify affidavits from villagers' committees (Xiong 2012:71). Not surprisingly, scholars have characterized the public notice method of serving defendants as a "legal fiction" (Zhao 2018) grounded in "deliberate fabrication" (Dong and Ji 2016:89). To the extent that judges' vigilance to combat litigation fraud and their skepticism of the veracity of plaintiffs' claims vary according to the gender of the plaintiff, we might expect judges to be warier of female plaintiffs and to give male plaintiffs greater benefit of the doubt.

Given the absence of defendants to challenge plaintiffs' claims, in absentia trials are less contentious and less complicated, and can therefore help judges clear their cases. For this reason, judges have an incentive to look the other way when plaintiffs claim not to know the whereabouts of their spouses. Scholars characterize judges' lax scrutiny of claims of missing spouses as judicial misuse and even abuse of the public notice method of serving defendants (Sun 2010; Y. Wang 2012:120). The same lax evidentiary standards that make them convenient to judges also invite their abuse – or at least the perception of their abuse – by litigants. We will see that judges' willingness to look the other way varies according to the gender of the plaintiff (Chapter 8).

One of China's oldest and most popular reality shows, *Legal Report* (今日说法), nationally broadcast daily on China Central Television, includes an illustrative episode about an unhappily married woman who disappeared without a trace. More than six years later, her husband learned she had married another man in a different city. In order to do so without committing the crime of bigamy, she had first obtained a public notice divorce from a court in the jurisdiction of her natal family by falsely claiming, with the support of fake evidence, that she and the original husband established their marital residence in her natal village, and that, as a migrant worker, he subsequently went missing (Zeng 2008:161). The surprise of discovering that one is no longer married has entered the popular vernacular as "unwittingly divorced" (被离婚; Y. Wang 2012; Zhao 2018).

To be sure, stories of male plaintiffs committing this sort of fraud are also in circulation, including the sensational case of billionaire Du Shuanghua (杜双华), whose wife filed for divorce a decade after he had already obtained a court divorce without her knowledge (Liu 2011; for additional examples of women who became unwittingly divorced, see Sun 2006:122–23 and Xu 2007:204). However, the well-known narrative of falsely claiming a defendant to be missing, sometimes with the support of fake evidence, in order to mislead the court into improperly using a public notice with the goal of acquiring most or the entirety of the marital estate, winning child custody, or expeditiously marrying a lover (Tan and Wang 2011:116; Y. Wang 2012:120; Zeng 2008:164), arguably carries greater cultural resonance when the plaintiff is a woman. Indeed, cultural stereotypes about duplicitous, wily, conniving women on the make and their ulterior motives to gain unfair advantage in property division and child custody undermine female litigants in US divorce trials (Epstein and Goodman 2019). Judges are more reluctant to grant in absentia divorces to women not only because they regard women's claims as less credible than men's, but also out of their fear of violent retribution exacted by men surprised to discover they are no longer married (S. Wang 2013:174n2).

When defendants are falsely purported to be missing, they are easily deprived of their civil litigation rights and marital rights, and are therefore easily deprived of substantive justice (Dong and Ji 2016:89–90; Xu 2007:204; Zeng 2008:162–63; Zhao 2018). However, just as female plaintiffs may be deemed less deserving of divorce than male plaintiffs, female defendants too may be deemed less deserving than male defendants of legal protections and procedural rights. Defendants may purposely conceal their own whereabouts in order to evade being served notice because they are already living with a new partner and hope to avoid criminal culpability and civil liability for unlawful cohabitation or bigamy (Ningbo Municipal Yinzhou District People's Court 2014:17). Owing to patriarchal cultural beliefs, this possibility may strike judges as more plausible when the allegedly missing defendant is a woman. Male plaintiffs may accrue advantage over otherwise similar female plaintiffs because women are given short shrift as both plaintiffs and as defendants.

Women tend to feature in moralistic narratives about frivolous and fake divorces. One such example tells the story of a woman from Feng County (a rural part of the municipality of Xuzhou in Jiangsu Province) who first conspired with her husband to process a fake divorce before filing a frivolous divorce petition. At the age of 16, after falling in love, she moved in with an 18-year-old man. The next year they had a baby girl. Only six years later, when their daughter approached school age and after they had reached the legal age of marriage (20 for women and 22 for men), did they register their marriage. Six days after registering their marriage, and after enrolling their daughter in school, they returned to the same marriage registration office to apply for a divorce. They had already resolved their daughter's school enrollment problem, and now wanted a baby boy. By giving birth to a baby boy out of wedlock they would be able to circumvent family planning policies and avoid a hefty fine for an "out-of-quota birth."[13] After carrying out their plan they remarried each other. Not long afterward, the husband became jealous after reading text messages on her phone. Unable to tolerate his suspicion that she was having an affair, she decided to scare him by filing for divorce in the Feng County People's Court. The court denied her request on the grounds that marital affection had not completely broken down and that reconciliation remained possible (Yu 2013). The moral of stories such as this is that courts, by denying meritless divorce petitions, promote family stability and, in so doing, bolster social stability and strengthen the nation.

SUMMARY AND CONCLUSIONS

Although China's divorce twofer has no legal basis, it dominates divorce litigation. The key to the puzzle of the routine denial of first-attempt divorce petitions in China's courts therefore lies with institutional pressures that countervail against the law. The institutional imperative for judges to uphold China's domestic laws and commitments to global legal norms is trumped by competing institutional imperatives to uphold the family, maintain social stability, and efficiently close cases.

Five sets of endogenous institutional norms and pressures at play in China's courts are reasons to expect that judges privilege both breakdownism over faultism and men over women. A political ideology emphasizing family harmony and marital preservation, heavy caseloads, performance evaluation systems that reward judicial efficiency and punish unrest, judges' perceptions of the possibility of violence carried out against court personnel by litigants accused of domestic violence, and patriarchal cultural values have compelled judges to ignore and subvert laws on the books intended to protect abuse victims, and are key forces behind the ubiquitous divorce twofer. Wide latitude to apply

---

[13] This story would be more plausible if the first-born child had been a son. Prior to the abolishment of the one-child policy in 2016, rural couples were generally allowed, without penalty, to try for a son if their first child was a girl (Kennedy and Shi 2019; Michelson 2010).

arbitrary, ad hoc, and inconsistent legal provisions concerning conditions of divorce and evidentiary standards (Chapter 2) allows judges to
yield to extralegal institutional pressures to deny divorce petitions in
general and the divorce petitions of women in particular. When judges
do grant divorce petitions, typically only after a failed first attempt,
the same extra-level institutional pressures animate their child custody
decisions (Chapter 10). We have seen from the secondary literature
reviewed so far in this book – and will continue to see from my original
empirical findings in the remainder of this book – egregious gender
injustice in the form of courts' brazen disregard for legal protections
to which women seeking to divorce their abusive husbands are legally
entitled.

CHAPTER FOUR

STUDYING JUDICIAL DECISION-MAKING
Court Decisions in Henan and Zhejiang

As part of broader government transparency initiatives, selected Chinese courts began publishing their decisions on public websites in the early 2000s, but in significant numbers beginning only in 2008 (Ma, Yu, and He 2016; Tang and Liu 2019; Yang and Chen 2014). Prior to the SPC's promulgation on July 1, 2013, of provisional rules requiring all courts to publish most of their decisions on the SPC's newly launched national website, China Judgements Online (中国裁判文书网, which went live on the same day),[1] provincial high courts regulated the online posting of decisions on their own websites under the guidance of the SPC (Ahl and Sprick 2018; Hou and Keith 2012; Liebman et al. 2020; Ma, Yu, and He 2016:200, 203; SPC 2013; Xu, Huang, and Wang 2014:88). Some provincial high courts maintained their online repositories even after the SPC centralized the dissemination of court decisions on its unified digital platform. The provincial repositories of Henan and Zhejiang are the sources of the court decisions I analyze in this book.

Scholars have raised concerns about the possibility of systematic selection bias in what courts have chosen to post online (Liebman et al. 2020; Ma, Yu, and He 2016; Yang, Tan, and He 2019). I heed their warnings against uncritically treating online court decisions as either true populations or random samples. By carefully benchmarking the characteristics of my Henan and Zhejiang samples, I show they are

---

[1] According to another report, the first 50 decisions were posted a few days earlier on June 28, 2013 (Yang and Chen 2014). The original URL for this website was www.court.gov.cn/zgcpwsw. Its replacement, https://wenshu.court.gov.cn/, was introduced in 2016.

well suited for studying adjudications in general and divorce adjudications in particular. By all measures, my samples of online divorce adjudications are at worst reasonably representative and at best spectacularly representative.

The sheer volume of China's online court decisions presents unprecedented research opportunities. Indeed, we can more readily study divorce adjudication outcomes in China than in perhaps any other part of the world, including the United States.[2] At the same time, however, the methodological challenges posed by such a colossal amount of text are daunting, to say the least. For this reason, few studies have drawn on more than relatively small samples of online court decisions. Until recently, most studies of online court decisions followed the same basic design: after collecting a sample of relevant decisions, often using keyword search terms, and sometimes from one or more courts in a specific city or province, the investigators read each decision and manually coded it according to characteristics of the litigants, legal representatives, case circumstances, outcomes, and so on (Chen and Yang 2016; Cheng and Gao 2019; He and Lin 2017; He and Su 2013; Y. Jiang 2019; Liebman 2015; Xia, Zhou, et al. 2019; J. Zhang 2018). Such a strategy, of course, is constrained by human limits to the number of court decisions that can be manually read and coded. By contrast, this book is the product of a computational (a.k.a. "big data") approach to automating the process of collecting and coding Chinese court decisions in order to analyze samples far too large to code manually. Some computational studies of court decisions have already appeared (Liebman et al. 2020; Xia, Cai, and Zhong 2019; Zhang and Zuo 2020), and many more are on the way.

But this is not a purely quantitative study. By letting us hear the personal voices of divorce litigants, qualitative case examples add a human dimension to the quantitative data. The individual experiences of litigants help us comprehend the tragic human toll of judicial decision-making patterns in the statistical results I report. Qualitative case examples provide a window into the real lives of divorce litigants. Knowing that a case example can represent thousands more like it also helps us grasp the scale of gender injustice in China's divorce courts.

I chose Henan and Zhejiang for several reasons. First, they are among the earliest and most prolific publishers of court decisions. Second,

---

[2] The University of Wisconsin's Court Record Data of divorce cases from 21 counties in Wisconsin is an unusual example of a large sample of US divorce cases (Cancian and Meyer 1998; Cancian et al. 2014).

their provincial high court websites, unlike China Judgements Online, were highly amenable to automated mass downloading of documents, thanks to sequentially numbered URLs. By contrast, not only has China Judgements Online incorporated sophisticated defenses against bulk downloading, but its court decisions are located at seemingly randomly generated alphanumeric URLs. Third, Henan and Zhejiang are large provinces that capture some of China's regional and socioeconomic diversity. For this reason, they provide analytical leverage in ways precluded by single-province research designs. A finding that observed differences between the two provinces in average caseloads per judge correspond to observed differences between the two provinces in adjudicated denial rates would support my argument that the former causes the latter (Chapter 6). At the same time, a finding that gender differences in divorce litigation outcomes are similar in the two provinces would support my argument about the pervasiveness of patriarchal cultural values and gender stereotypes and biases (Chapters 8, 10, and 11).

In what follows, I will first describe the provincial contexts represented in this study. Next I will provide background on court decisions in general and online collections of court decisions in particular. Then, after describing the characteristics of my two provincial samples, I will detail how I constructed my measures of judicial decision-making. Finally, I will assess the representativeness of the court decisions in my samples and describe my use of qualitative case examples.

HENAN AND ZHEJIANG

Reflecting their large sizes and locations in China's poorer agricultural heartland and more prosperous coastal Yangtze River Delta, respectively, Henan and Zhejiang taken together accounted for 11% of the national population in 2016 and represent a wide geographical and socioeconomic swath of the country. With crude divorce rates slightly below the national average (2.9 in Henan and 2.6 in Zhejiang compared with the national rate of 3.0 per 1,000 population), both provinces in 2016 together accounted for 10% of all divorces and 10% of all divorces granted specifically by court adjudication (Ministry of Civil Affairs of China, various years). In 2016, with a population of 95 million, Henan was the third most populous province behind Guangdong (110 million) and Shandong (99 million). Zhejiang's population (56 million) ranked it tenth in the country out of all 31 provincial-level units (provinces, autonomous regions, and centrally administered municipalities). In terms of per capita GDP, Henan (ranked 20th) was 25% lower – and Zhejiang (ranked fifth) 50% higher – than China as a whole. Similarly, in terms of urbanization, the share of Henan's population residing in urban areas (ranked 25th) was 9 percentage points below – and Zhejiang's (ranked 7th) 9 percentage points above – the national average of 56%. Reflecting the relative importance of agriculture in each province, the primary sector accounted for 11% of Henan's GDP but only 4% of Zhejiang's in 2016. Henan is a net sender of internal migrants, whereas Zhejiang is a net receiver of internal migrants (many hailing from Henan; Liu et al. 2014). In terms of the total value of international trade in 2016, Zhejiang ranked fourth behind Guangdong, Jiangsu, and Shanghai, whereas Henan ranked tenth (with imports and exports valued at only one-fifth of Zhejiang's). Zhejiang's rural per capita annual disposable income of ¥22,866 (ranked second) was roughly double Henan's ¥11,697 (ranked 18th).[3] Although the court fee for a divorce petition tried according to the simplified civil procedure was not substantial in absolute terms (¥150, or about US$23), it was equivalent to about five days' worth of rural per capita disposable income in Henan in 2016.

Mirroring Henan and Zhejiang's contrasting socioeconomic profiles are their contrasting profiles of judges. Although judges are a male-dominated profession in both provinces, women were better represented on the bench in Zhejiang (about one-third) than in Henan (about one-quarter) in 2013 (Henan Provincial Bureau of Statistics, various years; Zheng, Ai, and Liu 2017:181). In 2015, Zhejiang was ranked number one among all provinces and centrally administered cities in terms of judges' average caseload. Zhejiang's average caseload of 218 closed cases per judge was 2.2 times the national average and perhaps three times heavier than Henan's (Henan Provincial Bureau of Statistics, various years; Liu 2016; Yu and Meng 2016). The foregoing differences will help us make sense of regional variation in China's judicial clampdown on divorce (Chapter 6). At the same time, we will see uniform patterns of female disadvantage persist across these two otherwise different contexts (Chapters 8, 10, and 11).

Figures 4.1 and 4.2 depict the locations of all courts in Henan and Zhejiang, respectively. In China, leaving aside courts of special

---

[3] All uncited figures and rankings in this paragraph come from the National Bureau of Statistics (http://data.stats.gov.cn) and China Data Online (www.china-data-online.com).

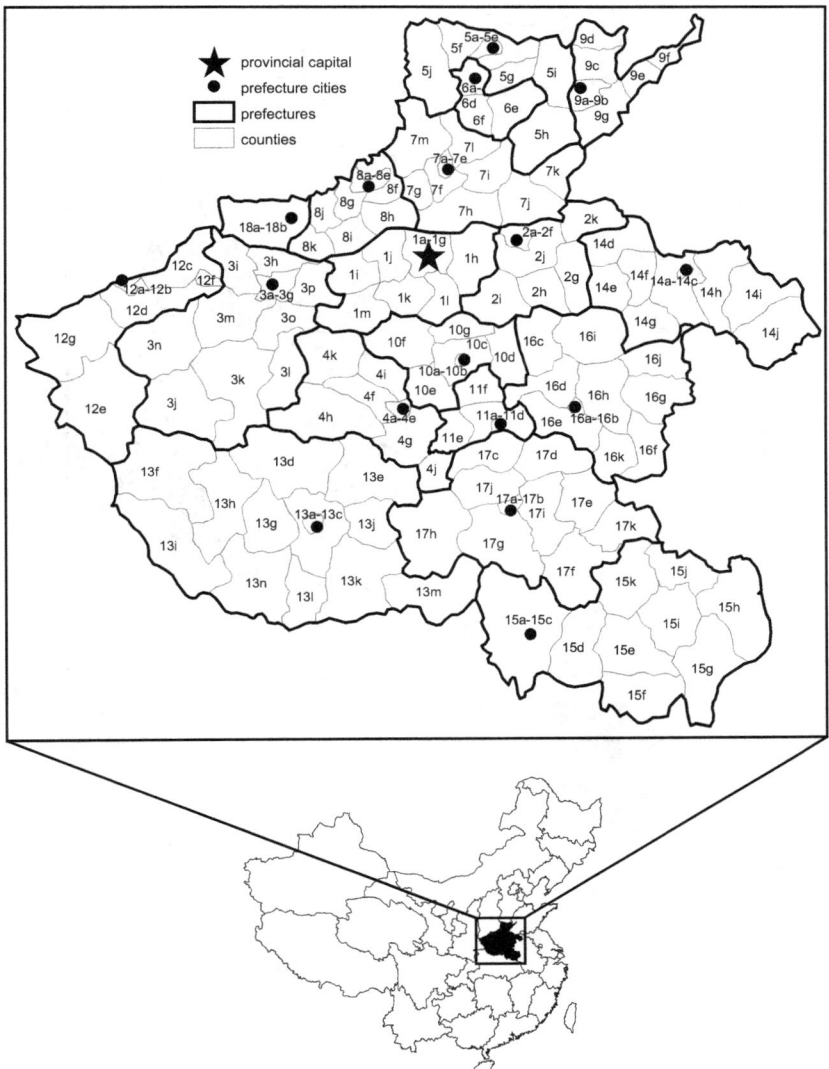

Figure 4.1 Locations of courts in Henan province
Note: Codes correspond to courts listed in the supplementary online material
available at https://decoupling-book.org/.

jurisdiction such as railway transportation and maritime courts, each
prefecture-level city and provincially administered city has one intermediate court, and each county, county-level city, and urban district
has one basic-level court. Henan's city of Luoyang, for example, has a

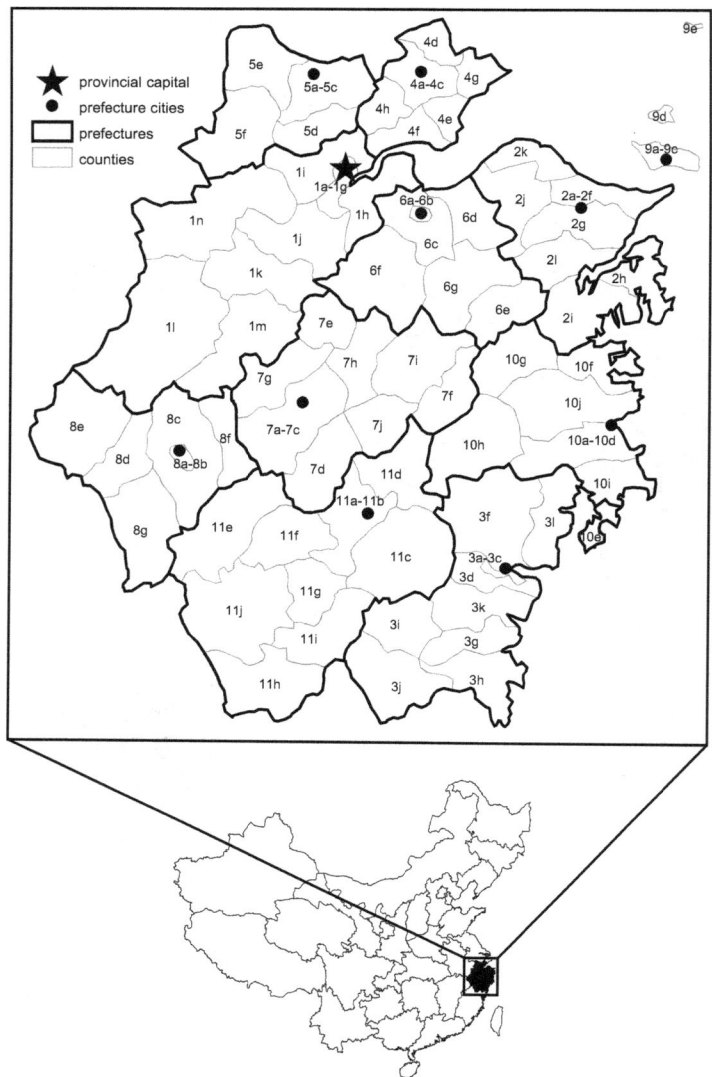

Figure 4.2 Locations of courts in Zhejiang province
Note: See note under Figure 4.1.

grand total of nine courts: one intermediate, one for each of its six districts, one for its hi-tech industry development zone, and one railway transportation court. Its intermediate court also has jurisdiction over an additional nine basic-level county and county-level city courts within the prefecture. All of Henan's 183 courts covering the 2009–2015 time period (including its three special courts) are represented in my sample of online court decisions. In addition to its provincial high court are 19 municipal intermediate courts (including one railway transport court) and 163 basic-level courts (including two railway transport courts). Of all 161 regular basic-level courts, 87 are in counties, 21 are in county-level cities, and 53 are in urban districts (belonging to 17 prefecture-level cities). Likewise, all of Zhejiang's 105 courts covering the 2009–2016 time period (including its two special courts) are in my sample. In addition to its provincial high court are 11 municipal intermediate courts and 93 basic-level courts (including one railway transportation court and one maritime court). Of all 91 regular basic-level courts, 34 are in counties, 19 are in county-level cities, and 38 are in urban districts (belonging to 11 prefecture-level cities). Court names corresponding to the location codes on the maps are available in the supplementary online material (https://decoupling-book.org/).

Among all decisions posted to China Judgements Online prior to 2016, more came from Zhejiang than from any other province. Henan was ranked fourth (Ma, Yu, and He 2016:208). At that time, both provinces had published fewer decisions on China Judgements Online than on their provincial websites. Henan's courts, initially slow to post their decisions on China Judgements Online, accelerated and completed the transition away from their provincial website in 2015. As I was finishing this book, Zhejiang still led the country in the number of cases posted to China Judgements Online, and Henan had moved up to third place. The contributions of China's provinces to China Judgements Online are generally commensurate with the volumes of cases processed by their courts. Henan and Zhejiang have each posted more court decisions than almost any other province because they have processed more cases than almost any other province in China. In 2017, Henan and Zhejiang trailed only Guangdong and Jiangsu in terms of concluded cases. At the same time, Zhejiang's case volume (and hence its contribution to China Judgements Online) has been disproportionate to its population. Case volumes in Zhejiang, Henan, Guangdong, Jiangsu, and Shandong were all similar even though Zhejiang's population was about half of the respective populations of Henan, Guangdong, and Shandong and about 70% that of Jiangsu (Yang, Tan, and He 2019:132). Thanks to the relatively large size and international character of its economy, Zhejiang's court caseloads have been relatively heavy compared to those of other parts of China (Chapter 5).

CHINESE COURT DECISIONS ONLINE

Civil court decisions contain the following basic contents, which generally appear in the following order: court name; decision type; case ID (案号); litigants and their legal representatives, including lawyers (当事人); dispute type; the plaintiff's legal complaint (诉称), which I usually refer to as either the plaintiff's statement or petition to the court, and which contains the plaintiff's claims and requested relief; evidence submitted by the plaintiff, including witness testimony; the defendant's statement (辩称), which is the defendant's response to the plaintiff's legal complaint; evidence submitted by the defendant, including witness testimony; the court's rulings on admitting or excluding pieces of evidence according to their authenticity and relevance; the court's holding(s) (理由), which in Chinese literally means "grounds," and refers to the court's legal reasoning and analysis behind its ruling(s); the court's decision(s) or verdict(s) on the matter(s) in dispute (裁判); court fees; the names and titles of decision-makers (the head judge, associate judge[s], assistant judge[s], and lay assessor[s]); the decision date; and the name of the court recorder (书记员). For additional descriptions of the format and contents of court decisions, see Hou and Keith (2012:73–76) and Liebman et al. (2020:184).

In this book, I generally refer to plaintiffs' legal complaints as "statements" or "petitions." They include requests, claims, reasons, and arguments, as well as supporting evidence. Defendants' statements include responses and supporting evidence. Judges affirm facts presented in litigants' statements, including marriage dates; names, sexes, and birth dates of children; and individual and marital assets. The plaintiff's legal complaint, the defendant's response, and matters of evidence are grouped together in a section called "facts" (事实). "Decision type" refers both to the court division (civil, criminal, administrative, or enforcement) and the type of document (adjudication, procedural ruling or order, mediation agreement, enforcement order, etc.). Litigants were always identified as either plaintiff or defendant and, in second-instance decisions, their original status in the first-instance trial. A litigant's information also includes, at best, name, sex, date of birth, ethnic group, level of education (only rarely), occupation (also rarely), and residential location (sometimes with a detailed address), and, at worst, only a surname. A surprisingly large number of court decisions even contain unredacted resident identity card (身份证) numbers. Information on representation often includes individual and firm/office names, from which the type of representation can be inferred (firm lawyer, legal aid lawyer, or legal worker). "Citizen representation" (公民代理) by a relative, friend, or colleague, for example, is also permitted but unusual. Sometimes personal information about a representative, such as sex and date of birth, is also included. Dispute type, usually the first sentence of the decision's main body, includes the nature of the legal complaint (e.g., debt collection, breach of contract, divorce, personal injury compensation). Judges typically explain their reasoning for excluding pieces of evidence. In their holdings, judges, citing relevant provisions in specific bodies of law, also explain the reasoning behind their judgments. On China Judgements Online, a title containing both the dispute type and decision type appears at the top of each court decision (e.g., "First-Instance Civil Adjudication in the Case of Plaintiff Pan Yanle and Defendant Zhang Dashuan's Divorce Dispute").[4]

Anyone who analyzes online court decisions must confront two kinds of information availability gaps: *document availability* in the form of the systematic nonpublication of certain types of court decisions and *content availability* in the form of the systematic suppression of certain pieces of information within the published decisions. With respect to the problem of document availability, mediations and withdrawals are systematically underrepresented in online collections of court decisions. Generally speaking, cases closed by judicial mediation are designated as mediation decisions (调解书), whereas judicial confirmations of private mediation agreements and case withdrawals are both designated as *caiding* decisions (裁定书). *Caiding* decisions are procedural rulings or orders that include approvals of plaintiffs' requests to withdraw their petitions, confirmations of litigants' private mediation agreements to render them legally binding, enforcement orders, dismissal orders, and transfer orders. According to the 2009 Measures of the Henan Provincial High Court on Posting Decisions Online, "*caiding* decisions are in principle not to be posted online" (Article 2). Henan's 2010 Detailed Rules on Posting Decisions Online were more emphatic by stipulating that "the court decisions of mediated and withdrawn cases are not to be posted online" (Article 5). Likewise, the 2011 Provisional Rules of the Zhejiang Provincial People's High Court

---

[4] Case titles were also available on the provincial high court website of Henan but not that of Zhejiang. Regardless, case titles are simply the concatenation of information contained elsewhere in the court decisions.

on Posting Decisions Online (hereafter the "2011 Provisional Rules") prohibited the online publication of cases closed by mediation or withdrawal (Article 4, Item 5 and Item 6, respectively).

In July 2013, when it launched China Judgements Online, the SPC clarified that mediations and withdrawals were generally not to be posted online; that court decisions involving death penalty review cases, state secrets, commercial secrets, and individual privacy were unequivocally not to be posted online; and that courts were to redact individual identifying information from court decisions before posting them online (SPC 2013; Xu, Huang, and Wang 2014:88). A few months later, when the SPC promulgated its 2013 Provisions of the SPC on People's Courts' Posting Decisions Online (hereafter the "2013 Provisions") for the purpose of unifying the regulation of the online publication of court decisions on its new centralized website, mediation agreements remained excluded (Article 4, Item 3), but *caiding* decisions were no longer off limits. The 2013 Provisions, which took effect on January 1, 2014, replaced earlier provisions of the same name issued by the SPC in 2010 (Tang 2018:91; Yang and Chen 2014). By stipulating that courts should post decisions on their own websites while the SPC builds a national website, the earlier provisions reflected a decentralized system. After the establishment of China Judgements Online, the 2013 Provisions cemented a centralized, unified national system, stipulated the responsibility of all courts to post their decisions there, and reflected a provision added to the 2012 Civil Procedure Law giving all citizens the right to search for and read nonexcluded court decisions (Liebman et al. 2020:180; Yang, Tan, and He 2019:140).

Zhejiang's 2011 Provisional Rules prohibited the online publication of court decisions on marital and family disputes (Article 4, Item 4). Because the SPC's 2013 Provisions contained no such restriction, it was removed from the 2014 Detailed Rules of the Zhejiang Provincial People's High Court on Posting Decisions Online (hereafter the "2014 Detailed Rules"). However, when it amended its 2013 Provisions in 2016 (hereafter the "2016 Provisions"), which took effect on October 1, 2016, the SPC did prohibit the online publication of all divorce decisions.

The extent to which courts complied with public disclosure rules can be seen in Figure 4.3. Let us first consider Henan in Panel A. Among its online court decisions made in 2009, 23% were *caiding* decisions. After the online publication of *caiding* decisions was prohibited in October 2009, their representation among all court decisions

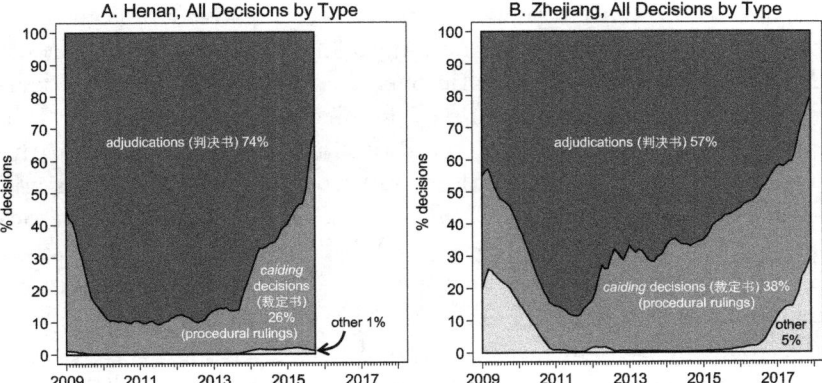

Figure 4.3 Composition of online court decisions
Source: Author's calculations from Henan and Zhejiang provincial high courts' online decisions.
Note: Henan *n* = 1,014,439 and Zhejiang *n* = 3,088,636 court decisions. Items in Panel A exceed 100% owing to rounding error. Smoothed with moving averages. The category of "other" types of decisions refers to mediation agreements (调解书), decisions (决定书), and notices (通知书). In Henan, "other" decision types consisted almost entirely of "notices." In Zhejiang, "other" decision types consisted almost entirely of mediation agreements in 2009 and 2010, but consisted almost entirely of "decisions" and "notices" in 2016 and 2017.

posted online dropped precipitously and hovered around 10% until the SPC lifted the prohibition in November 2013. At no point did Henan's courts post more than a handful of court decisions designated as mediations, which are cases concluded by judicial mediation. They did, however, post a few *caiding* decisions confirming the legal validity of private mediation agreements. The key takeaway from Panel A is that from 2010 to 2013, both *caiding* decisions and mediations were vastly underrepresented among all court decisions posted online. Whereas mediations and *caiding* decisions accounted for at least half of all of China's court decisions, they accounted for only around 10% of Henan's online court decisions during these four years.[5] Immediately after the 2013 Provisions were issued in November 2013, Henan's courts ramped up their online publication of *caiding* decisions. *Caiding* decisions as a share of all online court decisions more than doubled between 2013 and 2014, from 14% to 33% and grew to 46% by 2015.

---

[5] First, enforcement decisions, the vast majority of which are *caiding* decisions, accounted for over 20% of all court decisions. Second, first-instance civil mediations accounted for almost 20% all court decisions. Third, first-instance civil withdrawals accounted for 15% of all court decisions. See https://perma.cc/NZN9-E55J, https://perma.cc/EL9F-NEPQ, https://perma.cc/QR3S-6LYB, and https://perma.cc/NB2T-NUKJ.

Panel B shows that Zhejiang's courts were similarly responsive to changing rules from above. Among all of Zhejiang's online court decisions made in 2009, a little over one-quarter were *caiding* decisions, and almost one-quarter were mediation agreements. As a consequence of Zhejiang's 2011 Provisional Rules prohibiting the online publication of mediations and withdrawals, mediations and *caiding* decisions as a share of all court decisions declined dramatically from 49% in 2009 to 13% in 2011. Then, after the SPC issued its 2013 Provisions, *caiding* decisions as a share of all court decisions increased to 34% in 2014, 40% in 2015, 47% in 2016, and 45% in 2017. Zhejiang's courts also complied with the SPC's rules by not posting mediations. The "other" decisions emerging in 2017 consisted entirely of "decisions" (决定书) and "notices" (通知书). The patterns I have presented so far suggest that online court decisions are well suited neither for the study of mediation conducted by or brought to courts at any point in time nor for the study of withdrawals prior to 2014.

Turning now to the problem of content availability, Henan's 2009 and 2010 rules required the redaction of identifying information about witnesses and minors, but also required the full disclosure of litigants' names, sexes, and birthdates. By contrast, Zhejiang's 2011 Provisional Rules and 2014 Detailed Rules both required the redaction of all litigants' personal information such as names, sexes, addresses, resident identity card numbers, and bank account numbers. Zhejiang's rules thus went further than the SPC's requirement that litigants' names in only some types of cases, including family disputes, be redacted. Zhejiang's prohibition of the disclosure of all potentially identifying personal information, including litigant sex, remained in effect – and was generally followed by its courts – following the implementation of the SPC's 2013 Provisions. The almost complete omission of names and sexes of divorce litigants in Zhejiang's court decisions is a serious limitation to the study of gender differences in divorce litigation outcomes. Nonetheless, as we will see, enough courts published enough adjudicated divorce decisions containing litigant sex – or information sufficient to infer litigant sex – to support my empirical analyses.

The relatively few published *caiding* decisions approving plaintiffs' withdrawal requests contain only information about the litigants, their representatives, and statements such as this: "In the process of trying the plaintiff's divorce case against the defendant, the plaintiff submitted an application to the court on May 21, 2015, to withdraw the petition. The court approved the plaintiff's request." Published *caiding* decisions on withdrawals contain no information about claims, allegations, reasons, or evidence, and therefore are of limited empirical value. They cannot support a conclusive account of why, for example, women were more likely than men to withdraw their petitions (Chapter 6). Although we can hypothesize that women were disproportionately pressured by judges to do so, we cannot use published court decisions to test either this hypothesis or an alternative hypothesis – and popular narrative – that women's petitions are more "impulsive" than men's, that women are more likely than men to use divorce petitions as a tool to scare their husbands into improving their behavior, and that women are therefore less committed than men to follow through with their divorce petitions (Diamant 2000b:338). Similarly, given the scarcity of information in *caiding* decisions, we have no way to know whether the strongly negative association in the data between the participation of legal professionals and divorce petition withdrawals is a selection effect (plaintiffs who are determined to divorce hire legal professionals) or a treatment effect (legal professionals advise their clients not to withdraw their petitions).

Court decisions are not verbatim transcripts of everything every participant uttered throughout the litigation process. Because they omit ubiquitous informal behind-the-scenes negotiations, often brokered by judges (Chapter 10), court decisions contain significant blind spots that can be remedied only by ethnographic and interview research (He 2021; Li 2022).

To sum up, the composition of online court decisions is less reflective of the actual work of courts than of what courts were allowed to post. Collections of online court decisions include virtually no mediations and, prior to 2014, underrepresent withdrawals and other *caiding* decisions. As we will continue to see in this chapter, however, adjudications, the focus of this book, are generally well represented in online repositories of court decisions.

SAMPLE CHARACTERISTICS

The court decisions I analyze in this book were downloaded in bulk from the websites of the provincial high courts of Henan and Zhejiang: http://oldws.hncourt.gov.cn/ and www.zjsfgkw.cn/Document/JudgmentBook/, respectively.[6] Henan's decision dates range from February 26, 2000, to December 28, 2015, and Zhejiang's decision dates range from January 6, 2001, to December 31, 2017. In both provinces, the vast majority of decisions were made after 2008. For this reason, and because courts were required to stop posting divorce decisions online when the SPC's amended rules took effect on October 1, 2016, I limit all analyses of Henan's decisions to 2009–2015 and of Zhejiang's decisions to 2009–2016.

Decisions made after 2008 in my Henan sample total 1,014,439, of which 675,956 are civil decisions (67%) and 72,102 are adjudicated approvals and denials of first-instance divorce petitions.[7] Decisions made after 2008 in my Zhejiang sample total 3,088,636, of which 1,794,217 are civil decisions (72%) and 72,048 are adjudicated approvals and denials of first-instance divorce petitions. I flagged divorce cases by searching for the word "divorce" (离婚) in the titles or opening descriptions of decisions designated as adjudications (判决书).[8] I excluded post-divorce motions (离婚后). I removed duplicate cases from the Zhejiang sample of divorce decisions. There were no apparent duplicates in the Henan sample.

Panel A of Figure 4.4 shows the temporal distribution of adjudicated divorce decisions in the Henan and Zhejiang samples. Some of its peaks and valleys reflect compliance with rules about posting divorce decisions. Zhejiang's gaps in court decisions made in the second half of 2011 and most of 2012 may reflect its courts' compliance with the rule discussed above in the 2011 Provisional Rules prohibiting the

---

[6] The front pages of both of these websites have been archived at https://web.archive.org/. The URLs of the individual court decisions were http://oldws.hncourt.gov.cn/paperview.php?id=[decision ID#] and www.zjsfgkw.cn/document/JudgmentDetail/[decision ID#], for Henan and Zhejiang, respectively, where "[decision ID#]" refers to a unique numerical identifier. Alice Wang painstakingly downloaded the Henan decisions before they were taken offline in January 2018. The website has since been restored, but with only a tiny handful of the originally available decisions. Zuoyu Tian helped download the Zhejiang decisions before they were taken offline sometime in the middle of 2019. The SPC's 2016 Provisions requires each court to post on its website a URL to China Judgements Online (Article 2) in lieu of posting decisions to their provincial websites.

[7] The Henan Provincial High People's Court online library of court decisions was established in May 2008 and became inactive on December 31, 2015. During this time period, courts in Henan reportedly posted 1,142,514 court decisions to this provincial website and 924,651 court decisions to China Judgements Online (Henan Provincial High Court 2016:167).

[8] I identified divorce cases using titles of decisions in the Henan sample and opening descriptions of decisions in the Zhejiang sample. Court decisions posted to Zhejiang's provincial website do not contain case titles. No different from case titles, case descriptions summarize the nature of the legal matter and tend to end with "the case of" or "the matter of" (一案).

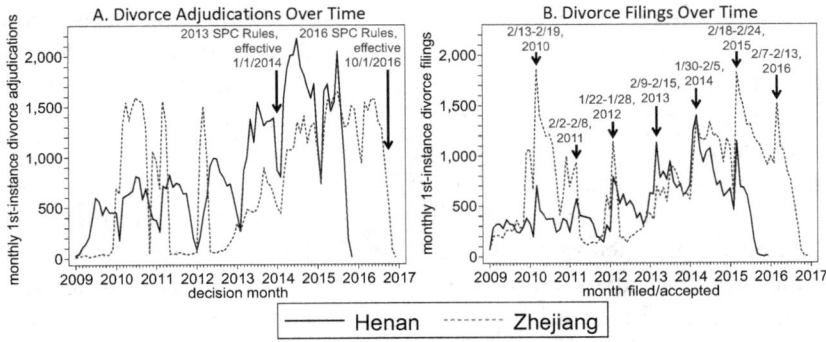

Figure 4.4 Decision dates and filing dates of online divorce adjudications
Source: Author's calculations from Henan and Zhejiang provincial high courts'
online decisions.
Note: Panel A depicts first-instance divorce petitions by the dates courts granted or
denied them (Henan n = 72,102 and Zhejiang n = 72,048). Panel B depicts first-
instance divorce petitions by the dates they were filed in court (Henan n = 42,764
and Zhejiang n = 68,866). Panel B contains fewer cases than Panel A because dates
of petition filings are often missing. Labeled dates with arrows in Panel B refer to
Spring Festival (Chinese lunar New Year) statutory holidays.

publication of marriage and family cases.[9] In the second half of 2013,
the launch of China Judgements Online and the 2013 Provisions
led to an immediate boost in the volume of posted decisions in both
provinces.

Panel A also shows that courts faithfully heeded the SPC's call in its
amended 2016 Provisions to stop posting divorce decisions effective
October 1 of the same year. The precipitous drop in Henan's volume of
online divorce decisions at the end of 2015 is simply a function of the
end of its high court's practice of uploading court decisions to its own
website and the beginning of its exclusive use of China Judgements
Online.[10] Zhejiang's high court, by contrast, continued to upload court
decisions to its own website before going offline in 2019. Although my

[9] I have no explanation for the dearth of Zhejiang's online divorce adjudications made in 2009.
In my Zhejiang collection of court decisions, divorce adjudications increased from only a few
hundred out of a total of about 127,000 court decisions in 2009 to over 14,000 out of a total of
about 174,000 court decisions in 2010. The same mysterious pattern can be found in Zhejiang's
court decisions posted on China Judgements Online.

[10] Only in 2013 did Henan's courts begin sending their decisions to China Judgements Online
in significant numbers. The vast majority of Henan's court decisions made prior to 2013 and
posted on its provincial high court's website were never posted on China Judgements Online.
Many, however, are available on an alternative online repository of court decisions, OpenLaw
(https://openlaw.cn/). Zhejiang's courts, by contrast, were simultaneously publishing their decisions on their provincial high court's website and China Judgements Online.

Zhejiang collection contains over 600,000 decisions of all types made in 2017, it contains only 19 decisions on divorce petitions made in the same year. China Judgements Online shows that Zhejiang's courts were more compliant than courts in most provinces. Nationwide, first-instance divorce adjudications published online dropped from 290,651 in 2015 and 253,371 in 2016 to 45,563 in 2017, and even further to 28,588 in 2018.[11] Although the SPC has prohibited courts from posting new divorce decisions since October 2016, some courts have continued to do so, albeit in much smaller numbers. Moreover, at the time I was finishing this book, divorce decisions did not appear to have been removed from China Judgements Online.

Annual dips in the production of decisions visible in Panel A correspond to annual surges in filings visible in Panel B. The ebbs and flows of divorce decision-making and divorce case filings are inversely related. The months in which courts decide the fewest divorce cases are January and February (Panel A) owing to the Spring Festival (Chinese lunar New Year) statutory holiday. By far the largest annual spikes in divorce filings occur during the month immediately following the Spring Festival break, the dates of which are indicated in Panel B. Divorce decision-making lulls during the holiday are immediately followed by divorce filing spikes. The annual Spring Festival travel rush (春节运) has become an annual divorce rush for migrant workers (Li 2015a:106). These annual divorce rushes are far less pronounced when Panel B is limited to urban courts, suggesting that they are driven by migrant workers. The limited ability of many migrant divorce-seekers to return home prolongs the divorce process (Chapter 9). Smaller spikes in July 2013 and 2014 follow the Dragon Boat Festival, another statutory holiday.

Table 4.1 summarizes key characteristics of my samples of divorce decisions, including the size and character of the jurisdictions of the basic-level courts that made them. It brings into high relief differences between Henan and Zhejiang. Henan is a more rural province than Zhejiang. Because the populations of county and county-level cities are predominantly rural, I refer to basic-level county and county-level city courts as "rural." Because the populations of urban districts are predominantly urban, I refer to basic-level urban district courts as "urban." In most respects, county-level cities resemble counties more than urban districts. Table 4.1 shows that, defined this way,

[11] I conducted this search on January 1, 2021.

rural courts handled 82–87% and 65–67% of all divorce cases I analyze from my Henan and Zhejiang samples, respectively. Most people and most adjudicated divorces are from rural areas. The rural character of divorce litigation also emerges from national judicial statistics. They show that family cases (divorce, inheritance, and other marriage and family) are overrepresented in People's Tribunals, which we know from Chapter 1 are predominantly rural. In the ten-year period spanning 2007 and 2016, 30–33% of all first-instance cases and 49–54% of all first-instance family cases were handled by People's Tribunals (SPC 2018).

TABLE 4.1 Distributions of cases, courts, and populations

	Rural courts	Urban courts	All courts	Population / basic-level courts / cases
Henan				
Population, 2014	76%	24%	100%	95,036,900
Basic-level courts	67%	33%	100%	161
Population % urban, 2014	37%	73%	45%	
Per capita GDP, 2014	¥34,505	¥44,098	¥36,803	
Average annual caseload per judge	60	73	65	26 basic-level courts
First-attempt divorce petitions				
Full sample	82%	18%	100%	57,502
With litigant sex	84%	16%	100%	54,200
Child custody decisions				
Full sample	86%	14%	100%	19,201
With litigant sex	87%	13%	100%	18,216
Zhejiang				
Population, 2014	62%	38%	100%	48,591,771
Basic-level courts	58%	42%	100%	91
Population % urban, 2014	21%	51%	33%	
Per capita GDP, 2014	¥60,432	¥157,606	¥97,071	
Average annual caseload per judge	181	224	200	70 basic-level courts
First-attempt divorce petitions				
Full sample	65%	35%	100%	51,573
With litigant sex	67%	33%	100%	8,626

TABLE 4.1 (*cont.*)

	Rural courts	Urban courts	All courts	Cases
Child custody decisions				
Full sample	66%	34%	100%	13,832
With litigant sex	67%	33%	100%	2,529

Source: Population and GDP data are from Henan Provincial Bureau of Statistics (2015) and Zhejiang Provincial Bureau of Statistics (2015). Court-level data on average judge caseloads – or on judges and caseloads necessary to calculate them – are from annual work reports and online introductions described in the "contextual and court-level variables" section of this chapter. Sample distributions are the author's calculations from Henan and Zhejiang provincial high courts' online decisions.

Note: Whereas Henan's population figures include all residents, Zhejiang's population figures are limited to people registered by public security organs. In Henan, "% urban" refers to the proportion of the population residing in cities and towns (城镇人口). In Zhejiang, "% urban" refers to the proportion of the population registered as nonagricultural (非农业人口). As described in this chapter, "average annual caseload per judge" refers generally to the mid-2010s and is presented in this table as averages of court-level averages. In 2014, US$1 was worth a little over RMB¥6. Zhejiang's population of 48.6 million refers to the officially registered population, and is therefore less than its 55.1 million residents in 2014.

According to "population % urban" figures in Table 4.1, Henan appears to be more urbanized than Zhejiang. As I will elaborate later in this chapter, this is a misleading artifact of differences between the two provinces in how urbanization is measured. Although this measure of urbanization is constructed differently in the two provinces, and therefore cannot be used for *inter*-provincial comparisons, it can be used for *intra*-provincial comparisons to validate my definition of "rural" and "urban" courts. In both provinces, courts I defined as "urban" were about twice as urbanized as courts I defined as "rural."

According to the share of the population residing in urban districts, Zhejiang (38%) was far more urbanized than Henan (24%) in 2014. Not surprisingly, per capita GDP levels were far higher in Zhejiang than in Henan and far higher in urban districts than in counties and county-level cities in both provinces. The distribution of basic-level courts generally mirrors the distribution of the population. In Henan, court concentration is greater than population concentration in urban areas because, on average, urban districts have smaller populations than counties and county-level cities.

Although Henan's population was about double Zhejiang's, its aggregate GDP was only about three-quarters that of Zhejiang in 2014. For this reason, differences were even greater between the two provinces in terms of per capita GDP. As we will see in greater detail in Chapters 5 and 6, Zhejiang's higher level of economic development translated into heavier caseloads for its judges.

Of all 72,102 first-instance adjudicated divorce decisions in the Henan sample, 57,502 appear to be judgments of first-attempt petitions and the remaining 14,600 appear to be judgments of subsequent divorce petitions following prior adjudicated denials or withdrawals. Similarly, of all 72,048 first-instance adjudicated divorce decisions in the Zhejiang sample, 51,573 appear to be judgments of first-attempt petitions and the remaining 20,475 appear to be judgments of subsequent divorce petitions filed after failed or aborted prior attempts. Removing decisions with missing data – most notably missing values of litigant sex – reduces the analytical samples of first-attempt adjudications to 54,200 in Henan and 8,626 in Zhejiang. My analyses of child custody determinations include granted divorce petitions regardless of how many attempts were necessary. In other words, whereas analyses of the decision to grant or deny a divorce petition are limited to adjudicated judgments of first-attempt divorce petitions, analyses of the decision to grant child custody to a plaintiff or a defendant (or both) encompass all granted first-instance divorce petitions that include child custody determinations. Hereafter, I refer to the sample of first-attempt divorce adjudications as the "main sample."

Table 4.2 affirms that online collections of court decisions are well suited for the study of adjudicated divorce outcomes. Looking at all years covered by the samples, online first-instance divorce adjudications account for 58% and 45% of the true population of first-instance divorce adjudications in Henan and Zhejiang, respectively.[12] Excluding years when courts uploaded relatively few decisions, online divorce adjudications as a proportion of all divorce adjudications are 69% in Henan (2012–2014) and 70% in Zhejiang (2010, 2014–2016). By any sampling standard these are remarkably high rates of representation if we have no reason to suspect systematic variation between published

---

[12] Excluding 2009 increases the representation of the Henan and Zhejiang samples to 60% and 52% respectively.

TABLE 4.2 Representation of online divorce cases, first-instance adjudications

	Henan			Zhejiang		
Year	Civil affairs yearbook	Online	Proportion online (%)	Civil affairs yearbook	Online	Proportion online (%)
2009	10,767	3,927	36	20,522	388	2
2010	12,542	6,937	55	19,711	14,150	72
2011	6,908	6,940	100	19,903	4,895	25
2012	11,026	7,905	72	19,187	4,496	23
2013	20,668	13,462	65	19,191	6,453	34
2014	28,021	20,023	71	19,225	12,762	66
2015	34,934	12,908	37	20,122	16,512	82
2016	–	–	–	20,892	12,392	59
Total	124,866	72,102	58	158,753	72,048	45

Source: Ministry of Civil Affairs of China, various years, and author's calculations from Henan and Zhejiang provincial high courts' online decisions. *Note*: "Civil affairs yearbook" refers to the officially published number of first-instance divorce petitions adjudicated by courts (divorces granted and divorces denied by adjudication). Henan's official 2011 figure of 6,908 divorce adjudications is likely an error.

and unpublished cases. In these years, disclosure rates of divorce adjudications in Henan and Zhejiang were higher than those in most provinces. A comparison of officially reported numbers of divorce adjudications and divorce adjudications posted on China Judgements Online shows overall disclosure rates of 61% in 2014 and 59% in 2015. In each year, about one-third of all provinces disclosed fewer than 40% of their divorce adjudications, while a few other provinces appear to have disclosed over 90% of their divorce petitions.[13] We should be confident that the conclusions I draw from my samples extend to the populations of divorce adjudications in Henan and Zhejiang to the extent that we are confident that unavailable decisions are not significantly and systematically different from those in my samples.[14]

[13] Details are available with the supplementary online materials at https://decoupling-book.org/.
[14] Table 4.2 also reflects a pattern we saw in Figure 2.1, namely the end of the "mediation surge" in 2012, a concomitantly dramatic increase in adjudications in Henan, and stable levels of adjudication over time in Zhejiang.

MEASURES

When writing their decisions, judges are required to adhere to a standardized template set by the SPC. As discussed earlier, online court decisions are divided into sections, including the court name, the parties (litigants and their legal representatives), the main body of the decision containing the litigants' statements, the evidence they submitted in support of their claims, the judges' determinations of the facts, the judges' holdings and final judgments, the judges' names, and the decision date. Online court decisions are simply HTML files containing otherwise unstructured GB18030-encoded text. Their sections are demarcated not by headings, much less by delimiters, but rather by content cues: commonly used words and phrases. Relevant information must be parsed from large quantities of raw text written with varying vocabularies and styles. Judges express the decision to deny a plaintiff's divorce request in a variety of ways. Plaintiffs make claims about domestic violence using a wide variety of words and expressions. Defendants express their unwillingness to divorce in different ways. Even the presentation of names, sexes, and birthdates of litigants is highly variable across court decisions. Dates are formatted in different ways. Numbers appear variously as Chinese and Arabic numerals. In short, court decisions are replete with inconsistencies and typos (Ma, Yu, and He 2016:199). Scholars must also be mindful of the existence of duplicates in online collections of court decisions (Yang, Tan, and He 2019:129).

The key sections from which I extracted and coded information are the following. The "parties" section includes selected information about the litigants and their advocates. The "facts" section includes litigants' claims as well as arguments they made and evidence they submitted to the court to support them. This section also includes the court's determination of the admissibility of the submitted evidence; the litigants' objections to, agreement with, and cross-examination of evidence; and the court's determination of the relevant facts of the case according to the litigants' statements, arguments, and admitted evidence. Where applicable, it also includes findings of the court's investigations, such as documents it requested from government agencies and witness testimony, sometimes from local authorities with knowledge of the matter in dispute. The "holdings" section contains the court's legal rationale for its ruling(s), including the legal sources on which they are based. The "decision" section contains the verdict(s). Finally, the "tail" section contains the names of the involved court personnel, their roles (associate judge, assistant judge, lay assessor, or clerk), and the date of the decision (Baidu 2020).[15]

The technical challenges posed by the task of rendering text into quantitative data were multiplied by the sheer volume of text. The main sections of text in the almost 150,000 court decisions in my two samples consist of 202 million Chinese characters, Latin letters, and Arabic numerals (95 million and 107 million in the Henan and Zhejiang samples, respectively). Applying conservative rules of thumb of 600 English words per 1,000 Chinese characters and 500 words of text per page, 202 million Chinese characters is over 240,000 pages of single-spaced English text.[16] If a 500-page ream of paper is 5 centimeters thick, then printing this much text would require a stack of paper 24 meters tall. Although hand-coding even a fraction of this much text would be hopelessly infeasible, the automated coding process nonetheless required a great deal of manual reading in order to develop and refine measures incrementally and iteratively through random audits – searching for errors by comparing quantitative codes with the original text from which they were derived. I hand-coded random samples and assessed the degree of consistency between the manual codes with the machine codes. Imperfection notwithstanding, they are highly accurate, reliable, and valid. Among 500 decisions I randomly selected from both samples, levels of agreement between hand codes and machine codes on all measures range from 78% to 100%, and are almost all well over 90%.[17] More details follow.

---

[15] Benjamin Liebman, Rachel Stern, and Alice Wang generously shared the Python "parsing script" they developed to extract these sections from Henan's court decisions. With minor modifications, I applied it to the court decisions I bulk downloaded from Zhejiang's provincial high court website. For more information about their parsing script, see Liebman et al. (2020:184). The search interface on China Judgements Online is obvious evidence that the SPC parses the court decisions on China Judgements Online in a similar way. It allows users to search for cases according to the contents of each of the foregoing sections, court name, case ID, date (or date range), type of case, type of decision, trial instance, judge name, lawyer name, law firm name, and so on. In its statistical reports, the SPC's China Judicial Big Data Research Institute (中国司法大数据研究院, http://data.court.gov.cn/) uses many of the same measures that I constructed for my analyses (e.g., Judicial Big Data Research Institute 2018). Parsed text, however, is not publicly accessible on, much less downloadable from, China Judgements Online. Several Chinese information technology companies have commercialized the data mining of online court decisions.

[16] Six hundred English words per 1,000 Chinese characters is the conservative end of the range quoted by professional translators (e.g., www.tianhengtranslations.com/word_count.htm).

[17] Among the measures I assessed, values of Cohen's kappa of interrater reliability range from .67 to 1.00, and are mostly well above .80. Values of Cohen's kappa for interrater reliability of at least .81 are considered "almost perfect" or "strong," and values between .61 and .80 are considered "substantial" or "moderate" (Landis and Koch 1977:165; McHugh 2012:279).

I took a keyword and keyphrase approach to constructing measures from the written court decisions. For the purpose of analyzing the decision to grant or deny a divorce petition (Chapters 6 and 8), I created a variable that limits the scope of analysis to first-attempt petitions. I also used this variable in analyses of the number of attempts and duration of time to win an adjudicated divorce (Chapter 9). Courts almost always cite in their decisions the case IDs of prior decisions pertaining to the dispute in question. I therefore coded as a subsequent-attempt divorce petition any first-instance divorce decision containing a reference to a previous civil case – either a specific civil case ID or a descriptive reference to a previous divorce litigation attempt. Descriptive references come from a wide array of words and phrases (e.g., 曾向本院起诉, 再次提出离婚, 再次诉至法院, 原告于[previous date]起诉要求离婚). I coded all remaining first-instance divorce decisions as first attempts. My analyses of child custody determinations include all divorces granted by adjudication regardless of how many attempts were necessary to get there.

Outcome Variables

The outcome measures I describe in this section correspond to the two sets of quantitative analyses at the heart of this book: the court ruling to grant or deny the petition and the court ruling to grant or deny child custody.

Grant or Deny the Divorce Petition. Adjudicated denials can be reliably identified by words and phrases in the "ruling" (裁判) section of court decisions, such as "deny" (不予支持 or 不予准许), "do not approve" (不准), and "reject" (驳回). Adjudicated approvals of divorce petitions can be identified by words and phrases, such as "approve" (准予 and 准许) and "dissolve" (解除), that do not satisfy the criteria for adjudicated denials.

Child Custody. In analyses of plaintiffs, the outcome is whether the court awarded child custody (yes or no) to the plaintiff. Likewise, in analyses of defendants, the outcome is whether the court awarded child custody to the defendant. I can also combine plaintiffs and defendants and consider whether the court awarded child custody to the mother or to the father. I machine-coded this dichotomous measure using combinations of words and phrases judges almost always used to record their decisions: "plaintiff" (原告), "defendant" (被告), "by" or "of" (由, used in "custody assumed by" or "under the care of"), "follow" or "go with" (随), "go back with" or "return to" (归), "custody"

(抚养), and "live" (生活, used in "live with"). Judges generally referred to plaintiffs and defendants as such. For purposes of coding this and other variables, I substituted the personal names of litigants with their corresponding roles of "plaintiff" and "defendant."[18]

In cases of only-children, child custody is a zero-sum game: it goes to either the plaintiff or the defendant. In cases of siblings, child custody could be granted solely to the plaintiff, solely to the defendant, or to both. My measure does not consider joint custody – a situation in which custody of one child is granted to both sides – because it was practically nonexistent. Indeed, the legal term "joint custody" (轮流抚养) appeared in only five child custody verdicts in the Henan sample and four in the Zhejiang sample. To assess the accuracy of this measure, I hand-coded 100 randomly selected decisions. To my amazement, my hand codes and the machine codes were in perfect (100%) agreement.

Explanatory Variables
The measures in this section support my efforts to answer the following questions. How prevalent are domestic violence allegations in divorce trials? Consistent with the faultism divorce standard, does a domestic violence allegation increase the probability of a ruling to dissolve the marriage? Consistent with the breakdownism standard, does a defendant's unwillingness to divorce increase the probability of a ruling to preserve the marriage? Which of these two standards matters more to judges? To what extent and in what ways do divorce outcomes vary by plaintiff sex? How do judges treat evidence? In what ways does case complexity – measured by the presence of marital property and/or minor children – influence judges' rulings? How important are claims of physical separation? What happens when a plaintiff "voluntarily" gives up property and/or child custody claims? Do these various sources of influence on judicial decision-making vary by plaintiff sex?

Domestic Violence
Similar to Luo's (2016:15n3) approach, I did not limit the definition of "domestic violence" to claims expressed by plaintiffs using this specific

---

[18] The following are typical examples of the sort of language judges use to assign child custody to defendants: "女孩李心甜由被告抚养"; "婚生长子陈某甲由被告抚养"; "女儿施乙归被告抚养"; "婚生女儿张某甲由被告抚养"; and "原、被告双方婚生子刘某2随被告陈某生活." Similarly, typical examples of language judges use to grant child custody to plaintiffs are "婚生女张某乙由原告抚养"; "原、被告之子由原告抚养"; "婚生子姚成成随原告共同生活并由其抚养"; "婚生女池某乙归原告抚养"; and "婚生子被告丙随原告生活."

term (家庭暴力) or its contraction (家暴). I included a variety of additional, often colloquial, expressions for physical and verbal abuse commonly used by plaintiffs (e.g., 打骂, 打伤, 殴打, 动手, 毒打, 大打出手, 拳打脚踢, and 拳脚相加).[19] Consistent with previous estimates about the prevalence of domestic violence reviewed in Chapter 1, the incidence of domestic violence allegations was about 30% overall and almost 40% among female plaintiffs in both samples; about 90% of plaintiffs in both samples who made domestic violence allegations were women (Chapter 7). Although it includes a small share of false positives caused by male plaintiffs who made allegations of violence inflicted by their wives' family members, this measure was generally very accurate. In my random audits, levels of agreement between hand codes and machine codes were 99% among 200 decisions from Henan (Cohen's kappa = .97) and 95% among 100 decisions from Zhejiang (Cohen's kappa = .89). Because marital rape lacks legal recognition in China (Fincher 2014:145; Honig and Hershatter 1988:277–78; Li 2015b:170), it appears relatively rarely in court decisions. It can sometimes be inferred when women refer euphemistically to involuntary or forced sex (Chapter 7).

Defendant Consent and Defendant Absenteeism
I defined a defendant's unwillingness to divorce using words and phrases such as "oppose," "disagree" with, or "object" to the divorce (不同意离婚, 不同意与原告离婚, 不同意解除, 不愿与原告离婚, 不想与原告离婚, and similar variants), "I request that the court reject the plaintiff's petition" (请求法院驳回, 请驳回, 希望法庭驳回, and similar variants), "I hope to reconcile with the plaintiff" (variants of 希望能和原告和好), and other relevant words and phrases. Defendants can only express consent or withhold consent if they participate in the litigation process, usually in person, in writing, or by proxy, but also occasionally by telephone. In order to assess the effect of consent, therefore, this variable also includes values for a defendant's failure to participate in court proceedings. I defined the absence

---

[19] I also include straightforward phrases such as "beat the plaintiff" (打了原告), provided the applicable phrase was not followed by "mother," "father," or "parents." Although both international and Chinese official legal definitions of domestic violence include violence against family members, I excluded from this measure explicit references to violence inflicted against plaintiffs' parents. Whenever possible, I also considered the possibility of false positives from text strings that are components of longer terms with a different meaning. For example, I ignored the string value of "动手" (raise a hand to strike) where it is part of the longer text string "动手术" (to have surgery).

of defendant participation using phrases such as "failed to appear in court" (未到庭), "failed to provide a defense" (未做答辩), "failed to submit a defense statement" (未提交答辩状), "in absentia trial" (缺席审理), "refused to appear in court without due cause after being served a court summons" (经本院传票传唤无正当理由拒不到庭), and other relevant variants. The presence of the word "public notice" (公告) differentiates in absentia public notice trials in which defendants were alleged to be missing from other in absentia trials in which defendants were served by regular means because they were not alleged to be missing. This measure thus includes four values: (1) "defendant in absentia: public notice," (2) "defendant in absentia: no public notice," (3) "defendant consented to divorce," and (4) "defendant withheld consent." By including absentee defendants in this measure of defendant consent, we can be confident that the value of "defendant consented to divorce" captures a documented expression of affirmative consent and therefore excludes a failure to withhold consent owing to failure to participate in court proceedings. In a random audit of 100 court decisions, hand codes and machine codes for this measure were in agreement 98% of the time (Cohen's kappa = .97).

As I discussed in Chapter 2, although divorces should be granted when defendants are declared missing (according to Article 32 of the Marriage Law), defendants whose whereabouts are alleged to be unknown are rarely declared missing. Defendants commonly failed to appear in court: they were no-shows in 35% and 29% of first-instance divorce adjudications in the Henan and Zhejiang samples, respectively. More specifically, "defendant in absentia: public notice" and "defendant in absentia: no public notice" accounted for 12% and 23% of Henan's main sample, respectively, and for 6% and 23% of Zhejiang's main sample, respectively. In only a few cases in each respective sample, however, were defendants formally declared missing (被宣告失踪). Even though, with court permission, plaintiffs can be represented in absentia in civil trials, this almost never happens in divorce cases. Defendants withheld consent in 50% and 56% of all first-attempt divorce adjudications in the Henan and Zhejiang samples, respectively, meaning they explicitly consented to divorce in 15% and 14% (Chapter 8, Table 8.6).

Litigant Sex
Personal details about litigants – including name, sex, date of birth, officially registered residential address, and ethnic group – are disclosed

in the vast majority of decisions in the Henan sample: 94% of all decisions on first-attempt petitions include litigant sex (54,200 out of 57,502). In the Zhejiang sample, by contrast, only 3% of first-attempt decisions disclosed litigant sex (1,534 out of 51,573). Similarly, litigant sex was disclosed in 95% of all child custody rulings in the Henan sample but in only 3% in the Zhejiang sample. Courts in Zhejiang took great care to redact the personal identifying information of litigants and their family members. The redaction of litigant names precludes gender guessing on the basis of given names (typically only surnames were retained).

I was, however, able to infer litigant sex (both plaintiffs and defendants) with near-perfect accuracy from almost 7,000 additional first-attempt decisions (and from more than 2,000 additional subsequent-attempt decisions) according to the content of text about three gendered topics: (1) bride price (彩礼), (2) dowry (嫁妆), and (3) wives' natal families (娘家). Because the bride price is paid by the husband's family, a litigant's statement concerning the plaintiff's payment of bride price or the plaintiff's request for the return of the bride price is a valid and reliable indication that the plaintiff is male. Because the dowry is paid by the wife's family, language in a court decision claiming or affirming the plaintiff's payment of the dowry or the plaintiff's request for its return is a valid and reliable indication that the plaintiff is female. Likewise, a statement concerning the plaintiff's receipt of – or obligation to return – the bride price or dowry indicates that the plaintiff is female or male, respectively. Finally, a litigant's statement concerning the plaintiff's return to "the wife's natal family" is a valid and reliable indication that the plaintiff is female.[20]

I assessed the reliability of this method of inferring litigant sex by comparing inferred sex with disclosed sex. The level of agreement between the two values of sex among the 474 litigants in the Zhejiang sample with both was 97% (Cohen's kappa = .95). Applying the same method of inferring sex to the Henan sample is a far better test of its accuracy. Thanks to high rates of disclosing litigant sex in Henan, its sample is an ideal source of "training data"

[20] When a plaintiff's sex was inferred using these rules, the defendant was assigned the opposite sex. I applied the same rules to defendants: when a defendant's sex was inferred using these rules, the plaintiff was assigned the opposite sex. The possibility of same-sex divorce is precluded by the absence of same-sex marriage in China. In hindsight, I could have incorporated additional words for dowry (陪嫁) and bride price (聘礼). I hasten to add, however, that they appear only rarely in the court decisions in my samples.

for machine coding litigant sex. The level of agreement between the two values of sex among the 27,434 litigants in the Henan sample with both was 96% (Cohen's kappa = .91). Plaintiff sex in my main Henan sample (n = 54,200) comes exclusively from the published court decisions because I would have gained only an additional 570 court decisions (1%) by inferring litigant sex in decisions that did not originally disclose it. Of all values of plaintiff sex in my main Zhejiang sample (n = 8,626), 83% were inferred.

Figure 4.5 shows that, consistent with previously published estimates reviewed in Chapter 1, women accounted for 66% and 67% of all plaintiffs in the main Henan and Zhejiang samples, respectively. While the gap persisted across levels of urbanization in both samples, Panel C also shows that it narrowed with urbanization in the Henan sample. Indeed, in the urban districts of the provincial capital of Zhengzhou, in which 4.6 million resided in 2014, almost 90% of whom were urban, plaintiffs filing for divorce for the first time were split evenly between women and men. Panel D shows that the gap narrowed to a much lesser extent in Zhejiang. Overall, female plaintiffs outnumbered male plaintiffs by a 2:1 ratio in both samples.

Civil Procedure

Information about judges reflects both the civil procedure (simplified or ordinary) and the composition of the collegial panel when the ordinary civil procedure was applied. A collegial panel of judges implies the application of the ordinary civil procedure. Measured this way, the ordinary civil procedure was applied in 59% and 17% of all first-attempt divorce adjudications in the Henan and Zhejiang samples, respectively. Over time, however, the two provinces began to converge in their embrace of the simplified civil procedure (Chapter 5).

The presence of a solo judge is redundant with language in a written decision indicating the use of the simplified procedure (适用简易程序). I validated my measure of the simplified civil procedure, coded according to whether the case was tried by a solo judge or a collegial panel, with a separate measure, coded according to the presence of terms for "simplified procedure" (简易程序) or "solo judge" (独任法官, 独任审理, or 独任审判) and the absence of the term "ordinary procedure" (普通程序) in the text of the court decisions. The two codes are identical in 98% of all decisions in each province's main sample. This measurement is further validated by the near-universal application of the ordinary civil procedure in public notice trials. As mentioned in

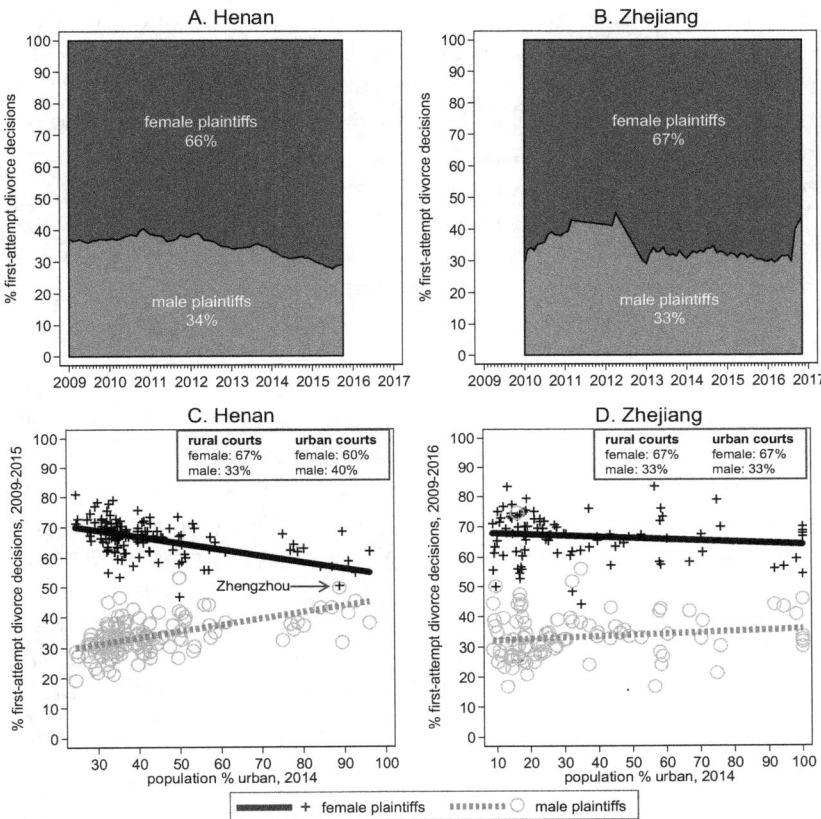

Figure 4.5 Gender composition of plaintiffs filing first-attempt divorce petitions

Source: Author's calculations from Henan and Zhejiang provincial high courts' online decisions; court work reports.

Note: n = 54,200 and n = 8,626 first-attempt adjudicated decisions (granted or denied) from Henan and Zhejiang, respectively. Panels A and B are smoothed with moving averages. Scatterplot points represent courts. Each court is represented twice, once for women and once for men. Panel C depicts 161 basic-level courts, including 88 county and 21 county-level city courts. Henan's 53 urban district courts are aggregated to their 17 prefecture-level cities. Kaifeng's Xiangfu District People's Court is represented twice because prior to December 2014 it was named the Kaifeng County People's Court. Thus, Panel C depicts 126 administrative units (88 + 21 + 17 = 126), once for women and once for men (252 points). Panel D depicts 91 basic-level courts (182 points). Panels C and D contain best-fit lines for female and male plaintiffs.

Chapter 2, courts are prohibited from applying the simplified procedure when the defendant's whereabouts are unknown. In both main samples, the ordinary civil procedure was applied in virtually every case (99%) coded as a public notice trial. Therefore, in order to avoid multicollinearity (i.e., in order to ensure that this variable is not redundant with the "defendant consent and absenteeism" measure discussed above), I assign a value of zero both to cases tried according to the simplified procedure and to public notice trials, and a value of one to all remaining cases tried according to the ordinary civil procedure.

Evidence

I used variants of phrases containing "plaintiff supplied" (原告提供) and "plaintiff submitted" (原告提交) in conjunction with evidence (证据) to measure whether or not plaintiffs submitted evidence. This code also incorporates language that describes, without the use of the word "evidence," plaintiffs' submission of relevant materials to support or prove their claims. Court decisions in Henan's main sample were far less likely than those in Zhejiang's main sample (50% and 82%, respectively) to indicate that the plaintiff submitted evidence. In my random audits, levels of agreement between hand codes and machine codes were 97% among 200 decisions from Henan (Cohen's kappa = .94) and 98% among 100 decisions from Zhejiang (Cohen's kappa = .92).

Children

I coded the presence of children using a variety of words and phrases for giving birth (e.g., 女儿, 生女, 生一女, 生下女, 儿子, 生男, 生一男, 生下子, 生下儿, 生子, 生儿, 婚生, 生育) while also doing my best to exclude those preceded by "did not" (e.g., 未生育). A different code for the presence of a child custody ruling automatically triggers a code for the presence of children. Although adoption is rare, it too is included in this measure. Inconsistently disclosed details about children prohibits distinguishing adult children from minors. Most first-attempt divorce adjudications involved children: about 80% in both samples. In my random audits, levels of agreement between hand codes and machine codes were 98% (Cohen's kappa = .92) among 200 decisions from Henan and 100 decisions from Zhejiang.

Property

I coded the apparent absence of marital property using variants of the statement, "there is no common property" (e.g., 无[or 没有]共同财产,

无[or 没有]夫妻共同财产, 无[or 没有]家庭共同财产, 无家庭财产, and 婚后无财产). Most first-attempt divorce adjudications involved marital property: 90% in both samples. In my random audits, levels of agreement between hand codes and machine codes were 99% among 200 decisions from Henan (Cohen's kappa = .96) and 99% among 100 decisions from Zhejiang (Cohen's kappa = .94).

Claim of Physical Separation

I identified claims of physical separations fairly broadly using phrases containing the word "separation" (e.g., 分居至今, 分居生活至今, 长期分居, 一直分居, and many similar variants) as well as the word "separation" alone (分居) in conjunction with a date or duration of time, as indicated by the presence of the word "year" (年) in close proximity. I also used terms that express the meaning of separation without using this specific word, such as not living together (e.g., 无共同生活, 没有在一起生活), also in conjunction with a date or duration of time. Of all divorce petitions in the main samples, 41% and 52% included claims of physical separation in the Henan and Zhejiang samples, respectively.

Plaintiff Gave Up Property or Child Custody

In her pathbreaking research on divorce and gender in rural China, Ke Li (2015a, 2015b) reports that women are often forced to bargain away marital property and child custody in exchange for their freedom. I identify instances of plaintiffs' giving up claims to property and child custody using expressions that appear in plaintiffs' statements, including "express my willingness to give up" (表示放弃), "voluntarily give up" (自愿放弃), "the plaintiff gives up" (原告放弃, 原告可放弃, or 原告均放弃), and many additional combinations of the word "give up" or "waive" in conjunction with "property" (财产) and "custody" (抚养). Concessions such as these were explicitly recorded in the decisions of only 7% and 3% of first-attempt divorce adjudications in the Henan and Zhejiang samples, respectively. Judges did not always document informal off-the-record sidebar negotiations in which they, together with defendants and lawyers, pressured women to concede their property and/or child custody claims (Chapter 10; Li 2022).

Number of Children and Their Sex Composition

All analyses of child custody orders are limited to eligible children, and thus exclude those who were 18 years of age or older at the time of the trial. For example, in a case of a couple with one 22-year-old daughter and one 13-year-old son, only the son would be included in the analysis. Chinese characters denoting the sex of the child used in judges' statements about which side was awarded custody are "子" and "男" for "son" (婚生子, 儿子, 男孩, etc.) and "女" for "daughter" (婚生女, 女孩, etc.). By counting each instance a son and each instance a daughter was assigned to a parent, I can, for each decision, easily calculate the number of children subject to a child custody order and their sex composition. By linking the sex of the child to the sex of the litigant, I can also easily code mothers and fathers who were respectively awarded custody of a son, of a daughter, of two daughters, of two sons, and of one son and one daughter. This variable includes seven values: (1) one daughter, (2) one son, (3) one of each, (4) two daughters, one son, (5) one daughter, two sons, (6) two or more daughters, and (7) two or more sons. Chapter 11 is devoted to analyses of the number and sex composition of children within families and their effects on child custody outcomes. In 100 randomly selected decisions, the level of agreement between hand-coded and machine-coded values is 94% (Cohen's kappa = .91).

Let me illustrate my coding method with a few concrete examples. First, "Daughter Zhang One X and Son Zhang Two X shall live with the defendant" (女儿张一×、男孩张二×随被告生活) is accurately machine-coded as custody of two children (one girl and one boy) assigned to the defendant (whom we know to be male). Second, in a typical example of a court splitting up siblings, "Custody of older daughter Jiang X Ling is granted to the plaintiff, custody of subsequent daughter Jiang X Tian is granted to the defendant" (原被告婚生长女江某玲由原告抚养, 次女江某天由被告抚养) is accurately machine-coded as each parent gaining custody of one daughter. Third, in another example of a court splitting up siblings, "Custody of son Zhou X One is granted to the defendant and custody of subsequent son Zhou X Two is granted to the plaintiff" (婚生长子周某乙由被告抚养, 婚生次子周某丙由原告抚养) is accurately machine-coded as each parent receiving custody of one son. Finally, "Daughter Ye X One shall live with the plaintiff and son Ye X Two shall live with the defendant" (婚生女儿叶某乙随原告生活, 儿子叶某丙随被告生活) is accurately machine-coded as custody of one daughter assigned to the plaintiff (whom we know to be female) and one son assigned to the defendant (whom we know to be male).

In order to simplify the presentation of multivariate regression results in Chapter 11, I collapsed all sex combinations of siblings into a single category. In the case of siblings, the same code is assigned to two girls, two boys, and one of each. Thus, I coded three values for the variable measuring the number and sex composition of children: (1) only-daughter, (2) only-son, and (3) siblings.

In compliance with a requirement in the 2013 Provisions to protect the privacy of minors, courts often redacted children's dates of birth. I therefore did not attempt to parse children's birthdates. In court decisions, birth order is sometimes denoted by characters for "older" or "first" (长, 大, etc.) and "younger" or "subsequent" (小, 次, 二, 2, etc.). Courts typically used words such as these only in cases of same-sex siblings in order to differentiate, say, two daughters (i.e., older daughter versus younger daughter). Mixed-sex siblings could be easily differentiated (i.e., daughter versus son) without birth order words. Because court decisions list children in chronological birth order (oldest to youngest), I was able to code the birth orders of some but not all of the litigants' children. Children over the age of 18 are not subject to child custody determination and are therefore excluded from child custody orders. Although birth order is not a central part of my analysis of child custody determinations, we will see that it brings son preference into high relief.

Claiming Child Custody

Judges recorded litigants' requests for child custody using terms such as "requested custody" (要求抚养), "live with me" (随我生活), "return to my custody" (归我抚养), and "under my custody" (由我抚养) appearing in plaintiffs' legal complaints and defendants' defense statements. Although litigants in these selected examples referred to themselves in the first person, many referred to themselves in the third person as "plaintiff" and "defendant." I coded four values: (1) plaintiff yes, defendant no, (2) both yes, (3) plaintiff no, defendant yes, and (4) neither. In most cases involving a child custody decision, custody was requested by either the plaintiff alone (43% and 41% in Henan and Zhejiang, respectively) or both sides (36% and 41%, respectively). This measure does not distinguish a request for two or more children (among siblings) from a request for only one child. In 100 randomly selected decisions, the level of agreement between hand-coded and machine-coded values is 81% (Cohen's kappa = .68). Coding errors are concentrated in the last two values. Limiting the assessment of accuracy to the first two values, which account for about 80% of all child custody decisions in my samples, increases the level of agreement between hand-coded and machine-coded values to 92% (Cohen's kappa = .83).

Physical Possession of a Child

Owing to the importance of the physical possession standard, the residential circumstances of the child is reported in about two-thirds of decisions made by rural courts and a somewhat lower proportion of decisions made by urban courts (see Table 11.1 in Chapter 11). I coded physical possession according to combinations of the words "plaintiff," "defendant," "currently" (现, 目前), "continuously" (一直), "long-term" (长期), "with" (跟), and "of" (由, used in "in the custody of") appearing in conjunction with either "plaintiff" or "defendant."[21] As I did for my measure of claiming child custody, I coded four values: (1) plaintiff yes, defendant no, (2) both sides, (3) plaintiff no, defendant yes, and (4) neither side or undisclosed. A code of two usually refers to parents in the same household or siblings who have already been split up by separated parents. Rarely does it mean both parents claimed to have physical possession of one or more children. Values of one and three include parents with sole possession of all children subject to a custody determination – an only-child or all siblings. A value of four includes cases in which the physical location of the child was either undisclosed or expressed using language not incorporated into my coding method.

I assessed the accuracy of the machine codes by comparing them to hand codes in 100 randomly selected decisions. Almost every error is confined to the fourth value. Overall, the level of agreement between hand-coded and machine-coded values is 78% (Cohen's kappa = .68). Excluding values of four, however, the level of agreement is 99% (Cohen's kappa = .97). Many values of four reflect truly undisclosed physical locations. But many also reflect alternative ways – beyond the scope of my coding method – in which judges conveyed information about children's physical locations.[22] For these reasons, the first three

[21] The following account for most instances of physical possession by defendants: 现由被告, 现跟被告, 现跟随被告, 现均随被告, 目前由被告, 长期随被告, and 一直跟随被告.

[22] A few examples of cases erroneously coded as "neither side or undisclosed" include "鉴于被告长期外出及本案的具体情况, 毛某甲由原告抚养为宜"; "近几年被告带领小孩在上海生活, 需要支出抚养、教育费"; "徐某乙自小就主要和祖父母一起生活"; "被告现外出无下落, 原、被告婚生一子刘占稳愿意跟随原告生活"; and "由于被告长年外出, 婚生两个子女现又均随其母生活."

values can be regarded as almost perfectly accurate, and the fourth value should be regarded as somewhat less accurate. In child custody cases in which physical possession was unambiguous, children were far more likely to be living with plaintiffs than to be living with defendants (Chapter 11).

Urbanization

Ignoring regional variation and instead, as scholars who apply macro-comparative cross-national research designs tend to do, treating China as internally homogeneous would be a mistake (Berkovitch and Gordon 2016). Perhaps the most salient social category shaping opportunity structures and life chances in China is household registration (*hukou*, 户口) status, which classifies people as either rural or urban. Because of the all-encompassing significance of its rural–urban divide, China is characterized as "one country, two societies" (Whyte 2010), a "two-class society" (Treiman 2012), and "caste-like" (Gong 1998). Although constraints on geographical mobility have relaxed over time, as evidenced by China's massive "floating" population of over 200 million migrants "living away from their places of *hukou*" (Y. Liu et al. 2014:50), most of whom are rural-to-urban migrants, a deep institutional chasm dividing China's rural and urban populations persists.

As discussed earlier, I classified courts dichotomously as either rural or urban according to the administrative status of the jurisdiction to which they belong. In some descriptive analyses, I treat urbanization as a continuous variable. China's National Bureau of Statistics reports national- and provincial-level urbanization as the proportion of the population residing in cities and towns (城镇人口). At the provincial level, using this measure, Zhejiang was far more urbanized than Henan in 2014 (65% versus 45%) (National Bureau of Statistics of China 2015:7). In Henan, as we saw earlier in Table 4.1, sub-provincial levels of urbanization in counties, county-level cities, and urban districts are reported using the same measure (Henan Provincial Bureau of Statistics 2015:871–73). In Zhejiang, however, this measure is available only for prefectures. The only measure of urbanization available for Zhejiang's counties, county-level cities, and urban districts is the proportion of the population registered by the public security administration as nonagricultural (非农业人口) for household registration (户籍) purposes (Zhejiang Provincial Bureau of Statistics 2015:46–48). Among Zhejiang's 11 prefectures, these two measures are correlated at $R = .58$ ($P = .06$). Because the "nonagricultural" population is considerably

137

smaller than the "urban" population, presumably because many people who belong to the "agricultural" population officially registered in villagers are actually residing in urban areas, we cannot compare urbanization levels between Henan and Zhejiang at the most granular sub-provincial level. In Table 4.1, what appears to be lower levels of urbanization in Zhejiang than in Henan is simply an artifact of measurement differences. Comparisons within provinces, of course, are perfectly valid.

While it generally holds up well, my method of classifying courts as rural and urban according to the administrative status of their jurisdictions is imperfect. To be sure, by definition, "urban" courts are far more urbanized than "rural" courts: in "rural" and "urban" courts, respectively, average levels of urbanization were 37% and 73% in Henan and 21% and 51% in Zhejiang (Table 4.1). However, Henan's Yima Municipal People's Court is classified as "rural" (because it is in a county-level city) even though 96% of its population were urban residents in 2014. On the flip side, in both provinces, several courts in urban districts in the outskirts of cities are classified as "urban" even though the populations they served were predominantly rural.[23]

Court decisions do not consistently disclose the residential locations of litigants. But the nearly 15,000 divorce decisions in my samples that do disclose at least counties or cities of residence, including the almost 4,000 that disclose detailed residential addresses, show that court locations reflect divorce litigants' officially registered residential locations. This should not be surprising given that plaintiffs, upon filing their petitions, are required to satisfy jurisdictional standing requirements. The Civil Procedure Law stipulates that court petitions should, under most circumstances, be filed in the defendant's place of residence (Article 21), which practically speaking usually means the defendant's place of *hukou* registration and which, in the case of divorce, is usually the same as the plaintiff's.

Recall that each county, county-level city, and urban district has one regular basic-level people's court. Plaintiffs who file for divorce are, by and large, tethered to the basic-level courts in the counties,

---

[23] The following *urban* districts had predominantly *rural* populations in 2014. In Henan, Shangqiu's Liangqiu and Liyang; Luohe's Wucheng and Zhaoling; and Kaifeng's Xiangfu. In Zhejiang, Taizhou's Luqiao and Huangyan; Wenzhou's Dongtou, Ouhai, and Longwan; Quzhou's Qujiang; and Jinhua's Jindong. Urban districts such as these – as well as counties and county-level cities – contain a mix of urban subdistrict offices (街道办事处) and rural townships and towns (乡镇). See Chapter 1 for more examples of urban districts with somewhat rural characteristics.

county-level cities, or urban districts of their officially registered residential addresses. Most plaintiffs and defendants – 94% and 97% in the Henan and Zhejiang samples, respectively – shared the same city or county. A smaller proportion – but still a majority – of plaintiffs and defendants shared the same address. Among plaintiffs and defendants whose detailed residential addresses were disclosed in the court decisions, 61% and 60% in the Henan and Zhejiang samples, respectively, lived together at the time of the adjudication. But even when they were physically separated, most plaintiffs and defendants – 85% and 79% in the Henan and Zhejiang samples, respectively – shared the same court jurisdiction. Finally, consistent with China's civil legal principle of privileging the defendant's jurisdiction, among the relatively few plaintiffs and defendants who lived in separate court jurisdictions, most plaintiffs – 84% and 91% in the Henan and Zhejiang samples, respectively – filed their first-attempt petitions in defendants' court jurisdictions. Overall, 99% and 98% of plaintiffs in the Henan and Zhejiang samples, respectively, filed their first-attempt petitions in courts with jurisdiction over defendants' residential locations.

We might expect gender inequality in divorce adjudication outcomes to be limited to or heightened in rural courts. According to the measure of judge sex I describe later in the chapter, male judges are overrepresented in rural areas. In both samples, the proportion of first-attempt decisions made by all-male collegial panels is much higher in rural courts than in urban courts. In Zhejiang, where the vast majority of first-attempt decisions are made by solo judges, the proportion of first-attempt decisions made by female solo judges is far smaller in rural courts than in urban courts. But even when controlling for judge characteristics, we might expect rural courts in general to be more conservative than urban courts (Ng and He 2017a) and in particular to uphold patriarchal values more strongly than urban courts. Rural judges may even consciously or unconsciously consider the relatively poor remarriage prospects of divorced men – caused by skewed sex ratios and a concomitant shortage of women in rural areas, and often called the "marriage squeeze" – when making their decisions (Jiang, Feldman, and Li 2014; Trent and South 2011).

Control Variables

Some of the measures in my multivariate analyses are in the background serving as control variables. The purpose of control variables is to approximate *ceteris paribus* conditions and thus to minimize the possibility an observed effect of one measure is actually an artifact of an omitted correlate. The following measures allow me to assess the effects of the explanatory variables discussed earlier among otherwise seemingly identical cases.

Female Judge Participation

Given that court decisions contain no information about judge sex, I inferred it from the judge's name using an open-source gender-guessing machine (J. Hu 2015).[24] Because some research identifies decision-making differences between female and male judges on otherwise seemingly identical cases (Boyd, Epstein, and Martin 2010), I not only differentiate female and male solo judges (simplified civil procedure) but also differentiate all-female, all-male, and mixed-sex collegial panels (ordinary civil procedure). Lay assessors are widely viewed as "lackeys" who submissively obey judges (X. He 2016). For this reason, I consider only the sex of judges in collegial panels. For example, I code as "all male" collegial panels with two male judges and one female lay assessor as well as collegial panels with one male judge and two female lay assessors. Given that court decisions contain no information about judge sex, I infer it from the judge's name. No clear patterns related to judge sex emerged from my empirical analyses of judicial decision-making. Even if we found judge sex to be associated with certain case outcomes, we would be unable to infer causality in the absence of information about how judges were assigned to cases (Boyd, Epstein, and Martin 2010; Sandefur 2015). For these reasons, variation by judge sex is not an empirical focus of this book. I include judge sex as a control variable in most multivariate regression analyses.

Legal Representation

Legal representation is an important control variable insofar as it is a proxy for a litigant's seriousness with and commitment to pursuing a particular outcome. Hiring a legal representative is more consistent with determined efforts to carry out a methodical plan – for plaintiffs, the plan to divorce – than with impulsiveness or bluffing. Any argument that a gender difference in the probability of an adjudicated denial is attributable to a gender difference in the probability of filing

---

[24] Sex codes produced by the gender-guessing machine are reasonably accurate. Among 71,310 litigants in the Henan sample whose names and sexes were both disclosed, the level of agreement with this gender-guesser was 86% (Cohen's kappa = .71). Results from an alternative gender-guesser are almost identical but slightly less accurate (Wudi 2014).

an impulsive divorce petition would therefore weaken considerably by the finding that a gender difference persists net of legal representation, unless we have good reasons to believe that plaintiffs who impulsively pursue divorce also impulsively retain legal representation. This control variable includes four values: a lawyer or legal worker represents (1) neither side, (2) only the plaintiff, (3) only the defendant, or (4) both sides. In the main samples, "neither side" was the largest category of legal representation in both Henan (49%) and Zhejiang (73%). Plaintiffs in both samples were far more likely than defendants to be represented by lawyers or legal workers (45% vs. 19% in Henan and 19% vs. 8% in Zhejiang).

Duration of Marriage
The date of marriage is a standard fact included in divorce decisions. Judges often refer to the duration of a marriage as an indication of the strength of mutual affection and a justification for denying divorce petitions. At the same time, judges may regard divorce petitions filed within only a few years of marriage as "impulsive divorces." Just as they typically redacted litigants' identifying personal information, courts in Zhejiang also often redacted marriage dates.[25] Marriage dates were either missing or unparsable in only 5% of the decisions in the Henan sample but in over 50% of the decisions in the Zhejiang sample. For this reason, I included a value of "missing" to this control variable in order to retain the full samples in the analysis. This control variable includes four values: (1) missing, (2) fewer than five years, (3) between five and 11 years, and (4) 12 or more years. Among first-instance divorce decisions from which this measure could be calculated, the largest duration of marriage category was fewer than five years.

Omitted Variables
Some measures that could have made it into my analyses proved unviable. One such measure is ethnicity. Among all first-attempt divorce adjudications, only about half from Henan and a measly 6% from Zhejiang contained information about litigant ethnicity. Almost all litigants whose ethnicities were disclosed were recorded as belonging to China's majority Han nationality (99% in Henan and 97% in Zhejiang). This pattern mirrors 2010 census data (99% in Henan and

---

[25] Zhejiang's 2011 Provisional Rules and 2014 Detailed Rules both require that courts redact all litigants' personal information, including names, sexes, addresses, identification numbers, and bank account numbers.

98% in Zhejiang; Henan Provincial Bureau of Statistics 2011; Zhejiang Provincial Bureau of Statistics 2015:73). Henan has three minority nationality autonomous districts and Zhejiang has one minority nationality autonomous county.[26] Although less than 1% of Henan's main sample consists of cases from the basic-level courts belonging to its three Hui autonomous districts, 24% of all 293 litigants in these cases with nonmissing ethnicities were recorded as belonging to the Hui minority nationality group (回族, one of China's Muslim minority nationalities). Likewise, although less than 1% of Zhejiang's main sample consists of cases from the basic-level court belonging to Jingning She Autonomous County (Lishui Municipal Jingning County People's Court), 77% of all 13 litigants in these cases with nonmissing ethnicities were recorded as belonging to the She minority nationality group (畲族). A lot of decisions in the main samples, however, do not include litigant ethnicity: this measure is missing in 45% of Henan's main sample and 75% of Zhejiang's main sample.

Litigant occupation was even more seldomly recorded in divorce decisions. When judges did record it, they tended to use crude categories, like "peasant" (农民), "employee" (职工 or 职员), and "small business owner" (个体工商户). For this reason, I did not attempt to measure occupation.[27]

Although People's Tribunals and their mobile courts decide a substantial share of divorce petitions, they are not identifiable in their written court decisions (Chapter 1). Because they cannot be distinguished from the basic-level courts to which they belong, I was unable to construct a measure that isolates these primarily rural outposts of China's basic-level courts.

Other measures slipped through the cracks in the course of my research, which was motivated primarily by the question of the extent to which courts – as they are supposed to do – grant divorces to battered women and deny child custody to abusers. Notwithstanding my empirical focus on domestic violence, it is not the only fault-based grounds for divorce stipulated by Article 32 of the Marriage Law. Bigamy, cohabitation with a third party, chronic gambling, drug use, and similar "bad habits" are also part of the faultism standard for

---

[26] Henan's Hui autonomous districts are Zhengzhou's Guancheng, Luoyang's Chanhe, and Kaifeng's Shunhe. Zhejiang's She autonomous county is Jingning, which belongs to the prefecture-level city of Lishui.

[27] Level of education and occupation appear to be more consistently disclosed in criminal decisions (Zhang and Zuo 2020).

divorce (Chapter 2). In this book, I make no attempt to estimate the prevalence of these other types of fault-based allegations or to assess how judges dealt with them.

Similarly, although judges sometimes indicate in their decisions previous divorces and remarriages, I made no effort to measure whether litigants had been previously divorced prior to their current marriage. In Chapter 9, I point out several cases in which couples divorced and remarried one another (复婚). More generally, judges often record whether the marriage in question was a remarriage (再婚) for either or both of the litigants.

Finally, this book includes no sustained analysis of property division as a divorce litigation outcome. From a measurement standpoint, property claims are extraordinarily complex (Palmer 2007:683–86). Beyond a prohibitive number of words and phrases required to measure the full range of contested items, including housing, vehicles, savings, investments, debt, dowries, bride prices, household items, and so on, was the similarly daunting task of identifying words and phrases necessary to measure how judges divided these motley components of marital estates.[28] Until scholars develop computational solutions to this problem, we will continue to rely on alternative research designs more amenable to the study of property division in divorce litigation (Davis 2010, 2014; Fincher 2014; He 2021; K. Li 2020, 2022; Zang 2020).

Contextual and Court-Level Variables

Information about courts, including case volumes and characteristics of judges, is not readily available in aggregated form from any published source. At the provincial level, it must be patched together on a piecemeal basis from provincial high court work reports and the few provincial statistical yearbooks that publish this information. An anonymous WeChat user did just this by painstakingly poring through hundreds of sources and compiling tables and a detailed appendix that cover 2008–2011 (Basic Level Legal Artisan 2016a, 2016b, 2016c; cited in Chen and Bai 2016).

---

[28] Housing includes all manner of types, sizes, and values. In rural areas, farmland, farming equipment, tools, and trees are also disputed. Some of the contents of housing that regularly appear in property claims include assorted types of furniture, household appliances, jewelry, bedding, carpets, and vehicles, as well as every imaginable kind of household and personal item, such as mattresses, mosquito nets, bamboo mats, washbasins, baskets, luggage, and computers, to name only a few examples.

Professor Rachel Stern generously shared 2014 caseloads for 73 courts in Henan (including 57 basic-level courts). The website of Henan's Provincial High People's Court contains URLs to every court in the province (www.hncourt.gov.cn/fyzx/). Each court website's "introduction to the court" (法院概况 or 法院简介) contains a brief description of the geographical, historical, demographic, and economic characteristics of its jurisdiction (in widely varying degrees of detail) as well as basic information about the court itself, including its history, judges, caseloads, and physical facilities. Useful information about judges is sometimes on a separate "introduction to judges" (法官简介) webpage. I downloaded and archived 262 such webpages in May 2019. At the time I finished writing this book, these webpages were still online, and many had been updated.

Zhejiang's Provincial High Court posted a treasure trove of information on its website before removing most of it in mid-2019. I downloaded and archived over 1,500 documents shortly before they were taken offline. Some are annual work reports. Some are annual summary tables of cases, from which I extracted 2012–2014 caseload numbers for 96 courts, 88 of which are basic-level courts. Some are even spreadsheets of judges' performance evaluations. In my analyses of variation in numbers of judges (Chapter 6), I calculated caseloads as the average of all available numbers for these three years. Finally, I downloaded the "introduction to the court" web profiles of 90 out of all 91 basic-level courts (only the Hangzhou Economic and Technological Development District People's Court is missing).[29]

In Chapter 6, I analyze variation in judge populations across all of China's 31 provinces and 150 of Henan and Zhejiang's basic-level courts. At the provincial level, numbers of judges come from Basic Level Legal Artisan (2016a). At the court level, judge counts in 92 of Henan's courts, including 82 basic-level courts, came from online court introductions dated 2008–2019. Also at the court level, judge counts in 78 of Zhejiang's courts, including 72 basic-level courts, came from a mix of undated court introductions downloaded in May 2019

[29] The former websites from which I scraped these materials are the following: www
.zjsfgkw.cn/Statistics/WorkStatement/ (annual court work reports); www.zjsfgkw.cn/Statistics/
DataCount/ (annual datasheets summarizing the work of courts); and http://zjsfgkw.cn/Judges/
CourtInfoDetail/ (descriptive introductions courts). The front pages of the first two of these
URLs are archived at https://web.archive.org/. At the time I finished writing this book, court
introductions and work reports were linked here: www.zjsfgkw.cn/col/col64/index.html.

and work reports dated 2010–2016.[30] Supplementary online material (available at https://decoupling-book.org/) includes court-level judge counts, concluded cases, and mean caseloads per judge.

In addition to collecting information about judges, I also collected information about lawyers and legal workers. I acquired official lawyer rosters from provincial lawyers associations. Henan's 2015 rosters contain the profiles of over 14,400 licensed lawyers.[31] Information on Henan's more than 4,000 legal workers in 2014 comes from a hardcopy roster of legal workers generously shared by Professor Ke Li (Henan Provincial Bureau of Justice 2014). In mid-2018, I scraped Zhejiang's online roster of over 17,000 licensed lawyers.[32] Finally, in early 2020, I collected the names and locations of over 2,700 legal workers in Zhejiang. I used some of this contextual information to benchmark the representativeness of my collections of online court decisions.

REPRESENTATIVENESS

Previous efforts to assess the representativeness of online court decisions have focused on overall disclosure rates and regional variation in disclosure rates. Scholars lament not only a sizeable numerical gap

---

[30] Court introductions vary in how they count judges. When multiple judge counts were reported, I privileged the most restrictive ones (e.g., frontline judges, quota judges, or judges occupying state personnel slots). Zhejiang's court work reports do not contain judge counts. Many of them do, however, contain average caseloads per judge. In reports containing multiple average caseloads per judge, I privileged average number of concluded cases per frontline judge. Judge counts can be easily inferred from information about closed cases and average caseloads per judge: dividing the number of concluded cases by average caseload per judge yields the number of judges. I hasten to point out that court-level judge populations were remarkably stable over time and appear to precede the implementation of a judge quota system described in Chapter 5 that drastically cut personnel slots allocated to judges. Eighteen basic-level courts in Zhejiang reported numbers of judges in both their court introductions (which I downloaded in May 2019) and at least one of their annual work reports for the years 2011–2015. Both sets of numbers were highly correlated ($r = .92$) and had similar means (58 in the former source and 53 in the latter source). Such a high degree of stability is unsurprising given that numbers of judges are determined primarily according to the size of the general population, an issue I will explore more deeply in Chapter 6. Scatterplots I present later in the chapter lend further confidence to my judge counts by showing they are highly correlated with estimated numbers of unique judges in my samples of court decisions. Of the 154 basic-level courts with judge counts (82 in Henan and 72 in Zhejiang), I excluded four from the analysis in Chapter 6 (one maritime court and three economic and technological development district courts).

[31] Before going offline in 2017, it was originally located at www.hnlawyer.org/index.php/Index-article-cctid-5-id-4691/, and remains archived at https://web.archive.org/.

[32] Zhejiang's online roster of licensed lawyers was located at http://lsgl.zjsft.gov.cn/zjlawyermanager/view/lawyers/LawyerOfficePageList/execute/lawofficeList.do, and remains archived at https://web.archive.org/. At the time I finished writing this book, it had relocated to http://lsgl.sft.zj.gov.cn/. I am grateful to Zuoyu Tian for his technical assistance. Earlier rosters of Zhejiang's licensed lawyers were available at www.zj.gov.cn/art/2013/6/3/art_28573_662.html, www.zj.gov.cn/art/2013/9/30/art_28573_73432.html, and www.zj.gov.cn/art/2016/9/30/art_28573_250575.html. The first two URLs are archived at https://web.archive.org/.

between what courts are supposed to publish and what they actually publish but also wild and poorly understood sources of variation between courts with respect to the magnitude of this gap (Liebman et al. 2020; Ma, Yu, and He 2016; Tang and Liu 2019; Yang, Tan, and He 2019). I already established that, from a numerical standpoint, the true population of divorce adjudications in Henan and Zhejiang is well represented in my collections of online divorce adjudications. We also know that adjudications more generally are much better represented than court decisions of all types taken together because courts have been prohibited from posting mediation agreements and, at some times and places, *caiding* decisions.

I will now assess the extent to which regional distributions of *all* online court decisions and some of their characteristics line up with corresponding population-level distributions. Annual work reports containing case volumes could be found from 40% of Henan's courts and the vast majority of Zhejiang's courts. Panels A and B of Figure 4.6 contain scatterplots of courts' online decisions by total concluded cases reported in their annual work reports. To be sure, we can identify some courts in the scatterplots that posted fewer decisions than others relative to their true caseloads. At the same time, however, they contain few outliers, and no obvious clusters of outliers. Panels A and B show that the number of decisions courts posted online correlates closely with the total number of cases they closed; the number of decisions courts posted online is highly commensurate with the number of decisions they made.[33]

Because court decisions contain the names of judges, we can compare the number of judges who appear in court decisions with the true number of judges. I treated each unique judge name appearing in all the decisions published by a court as a unique judge. This method of counting judges is, of course, imperfect. On the one hand, judges who moved between courts were double counted. Judges whose names appeared in two different ways in a court's decisions (owing to typos) were also double counted. On the other hand, two judges within a court who happened to share the same name were counted as only one judge. Nonetheless, according to Panels C and D, judge counts calculated according to this method correlate closely with judge counts reported in online court introductions and derived from court work reports.

---

[33] I was unable to limit Panels A and B to adjudications because court work reports seldom if ever disaggregate concluded cases by how they were concluded (i.e., by types of decisions).

146

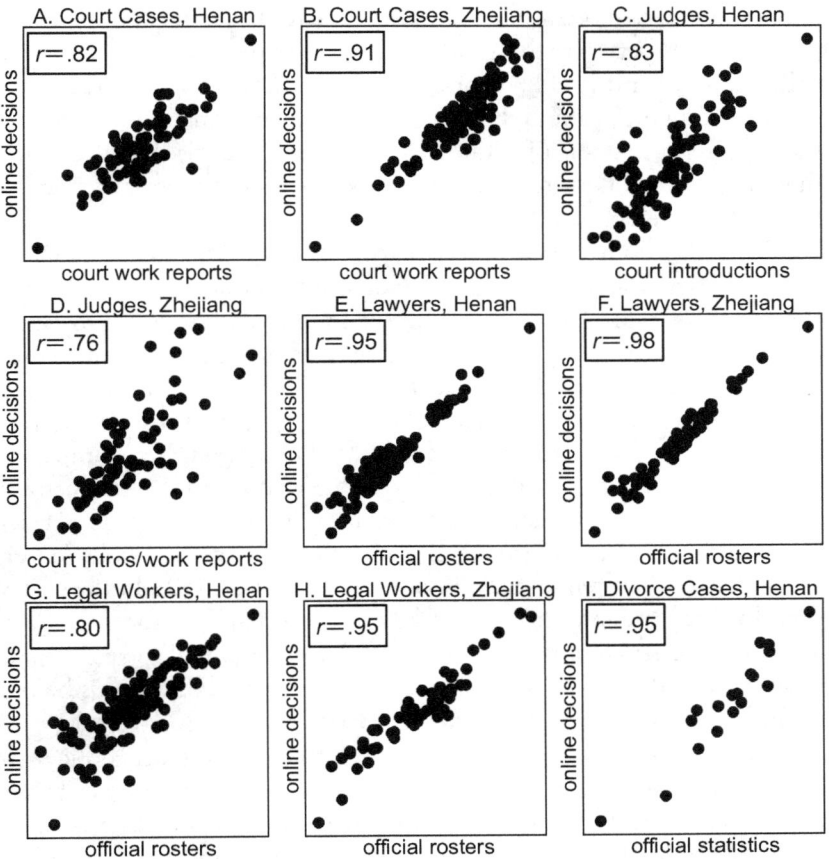

Figure 4.6 Consistency between sample and population counts
Source: Author's calculations from Henan and Zhejiang provincial high courts'
online decisions; other sources described in the section on "contextual and court-
level variables" earlier in the chapter.
Note: Panel A, 73 courts (2014); Panel B, 91 courts (2012–2014); Panel C, 82 basic-
level courts (various years); Panel D, 72 basic-level courts (various years); Panel E,
124 cities and counties (various years); Panel F, 64 cities and counties (various years);
Panel G, 125 cities and counties (various years); Panel H, 63 cities and counties
(various years); and Panel I, 18 prefectures (2014). Panel I "divorce cases" refers to
divorces granted by courts. The correlations in Panels A and B do not weaken after
removing intermediate courts (15 and 3 respectively).

I defined unique lawyers and legal workers the same way I defined
unique judges. Panels E, F, G, and H show that my estimates of unique
lawyers and legal workers appearing in court decisions were also highly
correlated with the true populations of licensed lawyers and legal workers.

Finally, and of more immediate relevance to the subject of this book, a comparison between the number of granted divorces in my Henan collection of online adjudications and the officially reported total number of divorces granted by Henan's courts reinforces confidence in the representativeness of online divorce adjudications. Panel I shows that these two sets of numbers are almost perfectly correlated across Henan's 18 prefectures.[34]

Although I do not incorporate it into my empirical analyses, age at marriage, which can be easily calculated by subtracting date of birth from date of marriage, provides another convenient benchmarking opportunity. China's trend in average age at marriage over time exhibits a peculiar pattern. The 1950 Marriage Law stipulated minimum marriage ages of 18 for women and 20 for men. In the early 1970s, during the "later, longer, fewer" (晚稀少) family planning campaign, age at marriage was raised to 23 for women and 25 for men in rural areas and to 25 for women and 28 for men in urban areas. This brief increase in the legal marriage age resulted in a conspicuous "later, longer, fewer" bump in actual age at marriage. The 1980 Marriage Law then lowered the marriage age to 20 for women and 22 for men. As a direct consequence of these policy shifts, women's average age at marriage increased from 20 to 23 between the early and late 1970s before declining in the early 1980s (Smil 1993:19; Xu 2019:208–09).

As we can see in Panel A of Figure 4.7, this idiosyncratic policy-induced bump appears in Henan's online divorce decisions. After leveling off in the late 1980s, marriage age once again rose in the 1990s (Xu 2019:209). This late-1980s plateau followed by a renewed increase in marriage age beginning in the 1990s also appears in Henan's online divorce decisions. These well-documented patterns are like a unique fingerprint of the impact of China's changing family laws over time. They reflect not data glitches but rather China's social history accurately captured in Henan's online divorce adjudications. Precisely following China's general pattern, age at marriage for women in the Henan sample increased from 20 in the early 1970s to 23 in the late 1970s before declining to 22 in the mid-1980s (Panel A).

The "later, longer, fewer" bump does not appear in Panel B constructed from Zhejiang's online divorce adjudications owing to a dearth of available cases in turn caused by a tendency of their courts not to

---

[34] To the best of my knowledge, divorce figures for Zhejiang disaggregated by region are unavailable anywhere.

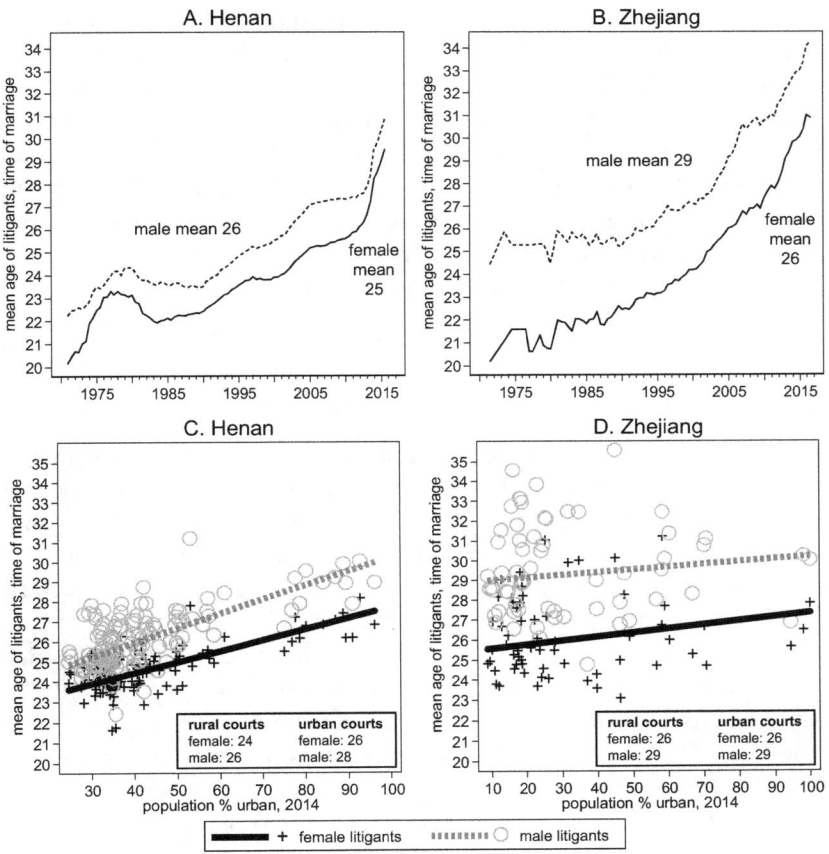

Figure 4.7 Mean age at marriage
Source: Author's calculations from Henan and Zhejiang provincial high courts'
online decisions; court work reports.
Note: n = 89,812 litigants from Henan and n = 1,432 litigants from Zhejiang.
Panels A and B are smoothed with moving averages. For more information on the
scatterplot points in Panel C, see the note under Figure 4.5. Panel D contains 124
scatterplot points (62 each for female and male litigants). Age at marriage is not
limited to first marriages.

disclose dates of birth. In terms of numbers of litigants married prior to
1985 in Figure 4.7 (among those in the samples with nonmissing ages
and marriage dates), Panel B contains far fewer than Panel A: 40 and
2,272, respectively. The marriage age trend of the remaining 1,420 litigants in Panel B who were married in 1985 or later, however, exhibits
the telltale plateau in age at marriage in the late-1980s followed by an
uptick beginning in the 1990s. China's post-1980s secular increase in

age at marriage reflects a worldwide pattern of delay in marriage associated with economic development, romantic ideals, and higher education (Xu 2019). The same forces explain not only the greater delay to marriage in urban areas compared to rural areas (in both Panels C and D) but also the greater delay to marriage in Zhejiang (Panel B) than in Henan (Panel A). The rural–urban gap was considerably greater in Henan than in Zhejiang. An increase in the level of urbanization from 30% to 90% was associated with an increase in women's average age at marriage from 24 to 27 in Henan (Panel C) and from 26 to 27 in Zhejiang (Panel D).

CASE EXAMPLES

This book is a quintessential example of mixed methods research. I combine the rigorousness of quantitative methods with the richness of qualitative methods. To do so, I illustrate and flesh out patterns that emerge from the quantitative data with qualitative case examples. I selected case examples in a couple of ways. First, while conducting random audits of my measures, I read a great number of decisions. In the course of doing so, I built a collection of illustrative cases. Second, I randomly selected decisions that satisfied certain criteria. In Chapter 9, for example, I analyze random samples of criminal domestic violence cases and present selected case examples to illustrate salient themes. Similarly, in Chapter 10 I present selected case examples from random samples of child custody decisions containing allegations of domestic violence.

Throughout this book I draw on 116 unique case examples, 112 of which are from my two samples and four of which (all criminal) are from outside my samples. Most (99) of the 112 case examples from my two samples are divorce cases. The remainder (13) are criminal cases. All but one criminal case appears in Chapter 9. They are distributed across much of each province. Sixty-one case examples from Henan are from 47 basic-level courts and three intermediate courts in 16 out of all 18 prefecture-level cities. Fifty-one case examples from Zhejiang are from 37 basic-level courts and two intermediate courts in all 11 prefecture-level cities. Only criminal case examples are from intermediate courts. Roughly mirroring the distribution of all divorce adjudications in the main samples, three-quarters of all divorce case examples, all of which are from basic-level courts, are from rural courts (78% and 71% in the Henan and Zhejiang samples, respectively).

In addition to these 116 case examples, I also refer readers to an additional 64 case examples – 39 from Henan and 25 from Zhejiang – available with the supplementary online material (https://decoupling-book.org/). I provide a URL to the full text of every case I cite. I did so not only to allow readers to verify my translations but also to assure them that I did not fabricate or embellish their contents. Many of them are simply beyond belief.

SUMMARY AND CONCLUSIONS

The SPC had a couple of key audiences in mind for its mass online disclosure of court decisions. First was the public. Public access to court decisions has been officially justified as a form of judicial transparency and a means of public supervision of the judiciary for the purpose of improving its levels of public trust and legitimacy (Ahl and Sprick 2018; Hou and Keith 2012; Liebman et al. 2020). Second was judges. Building on its tradition of publishing "standard cases" (典型案例) for the purpose of establishing best judicial practices, the SPC aimed to improve decision-making consistency and efficiency by enabling judges to search China Judgements Online for similar cases to use as reference benchmarks and by enabling court leaders to use it to identify and punish deviant judges (Ahl and Sprick 2018; Liebman et al. 2020). Even if lawyers were not an intended audience, they have undoubtedly benefitted from the ability of the online database to help them counsel their clients on realistic litigation prospects. Not surprisingly, a number of alternative commercial websites fashioned after LexisNexis and Westlaw have emerged with more powerful search interfaces catering to the needs of lawyers (He and Lin 2017; Liebman et al. 2020).

Finally, legal scholars, another incidental audience, have been champing at the bit to "web scrape" and analyze the millions of court decisions the SPC has made available on China Judgements Online. At the same time, however, scholarly enthusiasm to dig into online court decisions has been tempered by scholarly concerns about potential biases in the scope and contents of this mother lode of data on judicial decision-making (Liebman et al. 2020; Ma, Yu, and He 2016; Tang and Liu 2019). Since the beginning of 2014, an estimated 20% of court decisions have been prohibited from public disclosure. In other words, beginning in 2014, courts have been required to post about 80% of their decisions. Nonetheless, courts nationwide published only about 44% of the decisions they made in 2014. By 2017, courts' aggregate disclosure rate had increased to 60% (Yang, Tan, and He 2019:128–29).[35] Henan mirrored the national pattern with a 41% disclosure rate in 2014 among all its courts and an average disclosure rate of 54% in 2016 among selected courts (Liebman et al. 2020:185–86).

The overall gap between what Chinese courts were supposed to publish and what they actually published – also referred to as the "missingness problem" – has caused a certain amount of hand-wringing among scholars concerned about the possibility that published decisions are systematically different from unpublished decisions (Liebman et al. 2020; Tang and Liu 2019). This chapter should help allay such concerns. Owing to rules prohibiting the disclosure of certain kinds of cases, a sizeable share of unpublished court decisions is accounted for by withdrawals, other *caiding* decisions (most notably, enforcement cases), and mediations. Omitting these kinds of cases from the scope of analysis considerably increases disclosure rates. In 2014, courts in Henan and Zhejiang published more than 60% of their first-instance adjudications. In 2015, courts in Zhejiang probably published about 80% of their first-instance adjudications. In both years, about 75% of all first-instance adjudications nationwide were published on China Judgements Online.[36] As we saw, disclosure rates of first-instance divorce adjudications were even higher in some years (Table 4.2). Finally, geographical distributions of online court decisions and the "real world" they represent align closely in terms of all cases, divorce cases, judges, lawyers, and legal workers. Online court decisions appear to be appropriate for studying adjudications in general and divorce adjudications in particular, but not for studying mediations and *caiding* decisions.

Troubling pictures of egregious gender injustice painted by divorce adjudications disclosed online make it hard to imagine that courts systematically suppressed decisions that could conceivably undermine official efforts to strengthen public trust in the judiciary. A seemingly endless supply of online divorce decisions showing judges' routine and flagrant violations of China's domestic laws and international legal commitments suggests that courts were not terribly concerned about

---

[35] Tang and Liu (2019:22–23) report a 2014 nationwide disclosure rate of 42%. These estimates are limited to court decisions for which the full text was disclosed (文书公开) and exclude those for which only descriptive metadata were disclosed (信息公开).

[36] Details of these calculations are available with the supplementary online material at https://decoupling-book.org/.

censoring legally dubious and embarrassing content. If online court decisions have been curated in a way that underrepresents unsightly legal blemishes, the reality of gender injustice in China's divorce courts must be even grimmer than its appearance from the court decisions in my provincial samples.

But of course, for analytical purposes, the decisions themselves are only as good as the measures I use to analyze them. I have demonstrated in this chapter that my measures, albeit imperfect, are highly accurate. I will now begin to put these measures to work and show what we can learn from them.

CHAPTER FIVE

"MANY CASES, FEW JUDGES" AND THE VANISHING THREE-JUDGE TRIAL

For over two decades, Chinese judges have developed strategies for coping with increasingly oppressive caseloads. Since each court's allocation of judges is pegged to jurisdictional population more than to caseload, courts with acute shortages of judges have long been hamstrung with respect to appointing more. Courts disproportionately burdened with heavy caseloads therefore responded with innovative solutions. As a part of China's prosperous Jiangnan region (江南) of the Yangtze Delta, Zhejiang is one of China's most economically dynamic provinces. By contrast, Henan belongs to China's relatively poor agricultural interior (Chapter 4). Their caseloads reflect these contrasting levels of economic development. Zhejiang's courts have long been distinguished by their heavy dockets. Henan's court dockets, by contrast, have been relatively light in national perspective. Consequently, pressure on judges has been far greater in Zhejiang. Zhejiang was afflicted with the plight of "many cases, few judges" (案多人少) to a greater extent than and long before most provinces. Henan and Zhejiang represent opposite ends of the court caseload spectrum, and, as this chapter will show, the timing and vigor of their adaptive responses have differed accordingly. Zhejiang's early coping strategies, including its embrace of the divorce twofer (Chapter 6), were a bellwether for courts elsewhere as caseloads grew rapidly nationwide.

The correlation between the number of judges in courts and the number of residents in court jurisdictions has been nearly perfect. The problem for courts, of course, is that the most populous places in China do not have the heaviest caseloads. Because the supply of judges is not calibrated according to demand for litigation, the correlation between judges and caseloads is much weaker. For well over a decade, court officials in Zhejiang have complained that "the contradiction between the surging *demand* for judicial services and the inadequate *supply* of judicial resources is tremendous" (e.g., https://perma.cc/66HZ-TECW, emphasis added; also see https://perma.cc/575P-XV46). Courts in Zhejiang were forced to innovate earlier and more aggressively than those in Henan, but Henan's courts were catching up by 2015.

Initially, as courts became overwhelmed, judges found ways to cope within the confines of the traditional three-judge collegial panel. When a full collegial panel of three judges tried a case, only one tended to do the work while the others merely went through the motions or simply did not show up. Eventually, though, courts dispensed with the three-judge collegial panel. Courts often mobilized assistant judges – who lacked the full status of judges – and lay assessors to fill out collegial panels. Assistant judges even assumed full responsibility for trials. Additionally, simplified trial procedures were increasingly and indiscriminately applied. As court dockets became unmanageable in the late 2000s and early 2010s, the SPC, in an effort to ease judges' burden, encouraged and even mandated greater utilization of simplified procedures (civil and criminal) and greater participation of lay assessors. To a real extent, the SPC simply formalized what courts were already doing informally. Consequently, over time, the traditional three-judge collegial panel vanished.

In the remainder of this chapter, I will first introduce the problem of "many cases, few judges" in China's courts. I will then describe some of the informal and formal coping strategies courts developed in response. Finally, I will show that Zhejiang adopted them earlier and to a greater extent than Henan did. We will see in the next chapter that Zhejiang likewise adopted the divorce twofer earlier and to a greater extent than Henan did. This chapter thus sets the stage for the next chapter, which demonstrates that the divorce twofer belongs to a toolkit of judicial coping strategies.

CHINA'S CLOGGED COURTS

In January 2015, when he delivered his 2014 work report to the National People's Congress, SPC President Zhou Qiang stated, "caseloads in people's courts continue to rise rapidly, new types of cases increase, the pressure of handling cases grows heavier, the average annual caseload of frontline judges has exceeded 300 cases in some economically developed regions, cases are many and judges are few, and the problem of judge attrition is pronounced" (https://perma.cc/R6W5-JKRC). At the time, judges' caseloads were heavier in Zhejiang than in any other provincial-level administrative unit. Zhejiang's frontline judges averaged 187 cases per year, more than double the national average of 85 (https://perma.cc/Y5LB-EY9V), while those in Zhejiang's busiest basic-level courts averaged over 300.[1] Zhejiang had assumed this top spot in China as early as 2007 (https://perma.cc/YE6V-AHGX) and held it through 2017 (https://perma.cc/GR8M-ALCQ), after which it was edged out by Beijing (https://perma.cc/7B74-26TW).

An annual average of 300 cases would seem like a bed of roses to judges in many contexts around the world, including the United States (Chen and Bai 2016:34; Zhang 2016b). Given international variation in what judges do, there is no absolute caseload threshold that would qualify a court anywhere in the world as "clogged." This absence of a universal standard problematizes international comparisons. In China, however, the oppressiveness of 300 cases per year is incontrovertible. Prior to the nationwide conversion of assistant judges (助理审判员) into judges' clerks (法官助理) beginning in 2015, Chinese judges were responsible for the entire litigation process (Ng and He 2017a:34). They wrote and issued summons, prepared case dossiers, met with parties, analyzed evidence, conducted trials, and wrote decisions (Ye 2004:30; Zhengzhou Municipal Intermediate Court Research Group 2014). Dramatic growth in the volume of court cases, China's "litigation explosion," occurred while the population of judges barely budged (K. Chen 2019:108; W. Chen 2019; Fan and Jin 2012:98; Su 2010; Zheng 2018:130; Zuo 2018, 2020). Consequently, between 2011 and 2016, the average caseload per frontline judge increased from 79 to 113 nationwide, from 52 to 125 in Henan, and from 147 to 260 in Zhejiang (Basic Level Legal Artisan 2016a; Henan Provincial Bureau of Statistics, various years; https://perma.cc/EU2P-TVVE; https://perma.cc/H6CD-DLE9).[2]

---

[1] Zhejiang's basic-level courts that had exceeded 300 cases per frontline judge by 2014 include those belonging to Hangzhou's Binjiang District (https://perma.cc/3FHY-A88J), Hangzhou's Xiaoshan District (https://perma.cc/4MNT-LPKR), Hangzhou's Economic and Technological Development District (https://perma.cc/7WBM-PUAC), Wenzhou's Lucheng District (https://perma.cc/2X6U-RA73), Anji County (https://perma.cc/MRL4-PL2U), Cangnan County (https://perma.cc/L68D-C684), and Haiyan County (https://perma.cc/AU5A-YA5U). By 2017, Zhejiang as a whole had exceeded 300 cases per judge (https://perma.cc/GR8M-ALCQ).

[2] Because published figures are variously calculated using total judge counts and frontline judge counts, I adjusted some of the figures in this sentence by reducing counts of *all* judges to reasonable estimates of *frontline* judges according to the assumption that frontline judges accounted for 75% of all judges (Basic Level Legal Artisan 2016b).

This litigation explosion was driven first by economic development, which drove growth in the volume of cases in general and contract disputes in particular (Fan 2010:137; Zuo 2018:240–41). Second, court petitions ballooned following the implementation of the 2007 Measures of People's Courts on Collecting Litigation Fees that lowered barriers to court by cutting litigation fees by an average of 60% (Fan 2010:137; Jiang 2015:30). Procedural changes compounded the effects of this surge in caseloads. The revised 2012 Civil Procedure Law also burdened judges with new onerous pretrial and third-party claims procedures (Zhengzhou Municipal Intermediate Court Research Group 2014). In addition, court case filing reforms introduced in 2014 thwarted courts' ability to turn away cases by mandating that "cases must be filed and petitions must be tried" (有案必立、有诉必理; W. Chen 2019:18; Wang 2019b:141; Y. Zhang 2017:19). Just as observers feared, court dockets swelled by almost 30% in the first year following their implementation (Chinese Academy of Social Sciences Institute of Law Rule of Law Indicators Innovation Project Team 2017:95; C. Hu 2015:205n19; Zheng 2018:130). Judges also complained about new provisions in the amended 2014 Administrative Litigation Law (which took effect on January 1, 2015) requiring courts to accept all cases that satisfied legal requirements (e.g., https://perma .cc/24GD-PB36 and https://perma.cc/4XKT-GYMT). As a work report from a basic-level court in Zhejiang put it: "Due to the implementation of the case filing reform, the new Administrative Litigation Law, and related factors, cases have surged, judicial personnel must work evenings [白加黑] and weekends [5+2], and the bitter battle endures with no end in sight" (https://perma.cc/7TPK-4MJK; also see C. Hu 2015:198; X. Li 2014:219; Ng and He 2017a:38; L. Xu 2012:26).

Originating in the early days of China's legal reform (Meng 1982), the phrase "many cases, few judges" had become a prominent part of public and scholarly discourse by the late 2000s. One of its earliest appearances in the *People's Daily* – the primary print news outlet of the Chinese Communist Party – was in a 2002 article profiling Zhejiang's Yiwu Municipal People's Court, one of the busiest courts in the country. It reported that this basic-level court had used local government personnel slots (地方编制 or 事业编制) to hire more judges in an effort to alleviate the conflict between "many cases and few judges" (Chen 2002), thus suggesting that personnel slots allocated by the central government were woefully insufficient. "Many cases, few judges" appeared again a few months later in another *People's Daily* article about judges in Zhejiang's Huzhou Municipal Intermediate Court who, under the intense pressure of increasingly heavy workloads, were facing disciplinary measures for failing to meet statutory time limits for closing cases (Cai and Jiang 2002). The problems only deepened. In 2008 and 2009, three judges in Zhejiang's Yiwu Municipal People's Court successively won competitions for the most trials conducted in one day: over a dozen, over 20, and 35, respectively (Cai 2013:136). In 2010, this court had the distinction of closing more cases than any other court in the province (https://perma.cc/5S2Q-DEXN) – and therefore more cases than most courts in China. In 2011, Hangzhou's Xiaoshan District bumped it out of the top spot in Zhejiang (https://perma.cc/X2W2-3X4A) and held the position of busiest court in the province through 2015 (https://perma.cc/Q7W7-8XYK). Indeed, according to 2010–2014 data (available with supplementary online material at https://decoupling-book.org/), Yiwu had the second-most closed cases in the province behind Hangzhou's Xiaoshan District.

Oppressive caseloads were a major source of a "resignation boom" (离职潮) in basic-level courts (Chapter 3; also see Xue 2019:18). In 2011, SPC President Wang Shengjun reported that between 2008 and 2010, owing to low pay, weak professional protections, and heavy workloads, 8,781 judges in basic-level courts across China quit their jobs. Many judges reportedly suffered from poor physical and mental health, and some even collapsed at their work posts; 96 judges and bailiffs died for reasons related to their work, and another 466 judges and bailiffs suffered disabilities related to their work (Xinhua 2011). In his 2010 work report to the Provincial People's Congress delivered in January 2011, Henan's Provincial High Court President Zhang Liyong painted a local version of the national picture:

> At the current time, the primary difficulty in courts is this: the contradiction between many cases and few judges is presently extremely pronounced, the many frontline judges whose average caseloads exceed 100 cases experience chronic overwork, and many judges collapsed from exhaustion and illness at their posts. Between 2008 and 2010, 17 judges and five bailiffs died for work-related reasons. (https://perma.cc/4FFZ-L9XE)

In his 2014 work report delivered in January 2015, he reported that Li Yaqin (李亚钦), the president of the basic-level people's court of the city of Dengzhou, had died at work after years of exhausting overtime work (https://perma.cc/HR3T-76FK). As we are about to see, courts had a few tricks up their sleeves to deal with their heavy dockets.

INFORMAL INNOVATIVE RESPONSES TO CLOGGED COURTS

This section examines two strategies Chinese courts have used to cope with their increasingly heavy dockets. When judges try cases using the ordinary procedure, they are required to form collegial panels. Recall from Chapter 2 that solo judges are synonymous with the simplified procedure. Chinese judges, known for engaging in "symbolic or creative compliance," developed methods to comply with the letter if not the spirit of requirements such as this (Li, Kocken, and van Rooij 2016:62). First, because three-judge collegial panels consume scarce human resources, over time they came to exemplify "formal structure as myth and ceremony" (Meyer and Rowan 1977). Second, courts turned to assistant judges to lighten the load of associate judges.

Faking Collegial Panels

Fake collegial panels, in which judges and lay assessors showed up only to satisfy procedural requirements, were identified at least as early as the 1990s as a strategy for dealing with the problem of "many cases, few judges" (Cai and Cai 1998:31; Liu 2006:92). In order to relieve judges of the full service commitment of collegial panel participation, collegial panels became a formalistic and ritualistic charade known as "collegial in form, solo in practice" (形合实独) and "a panel but not collegial" (合而不议), in which the presiding judge assumed sole responsibility for trying the case despite being ceremonially accompanied by two panel members (Cai 2013:134; Jia et al. 2014; Huabin Li 2014:42; Shangqiu Municipal Intermediate Court Research Team 2017:65; Xu, Huang, and Lu 2011:141; Ye 2004:30; Zheng 2018:135n1). This phenomenon has also been characterized as "one judge tries the case, two judges accompany" (一人审，二人陪; S. Wang 2014:21) and the "solofication of the collegial panel" (合议制独任化; Jia et al. 2014; Yu 2009).

> Although a judge at a trial can be seen diligently reading a case dossier, in reality it may not be the dossier for the case being tried, but rather for a different case for which he assumes primary responsibility. Although he may be present for the full duration of the trial, his mind is elsewhere. Sometimes a judge who is present at the opening of the trial will get up and leave shortly thereafter, only to return for the conclusion. Sometimes a party will not ever see the other members of the collegial panel, meaning that not even the form or appearance of a collegial panel can be guaranteed. (W. Zhang 2012:89n1)

On the problem of fake collegial panels, a research team from Henan's Sanmenxia Intermediate Court wrote: "Many litigants reported that so-and-so judge was not at the trial, or that so-and-so judge sat for a while at the trial before leaving" (Jia et al. 2014). According to an assistant judge in a People's Tribunal attached to the Zhengzhou Municipal Huiji District Court,

> Most basic-level courts operate systems whereby cases are assigned to presiding judges who assume primary responsibility for their disposal, with the other members of the collegial panel passively going along. This kind of phenomenon of collegial panels existing in name only, of soloism being the actual practice, and of three names nonetheless getting signed on court decisions has become a growing problem. (Lü 2015)

Having not read the dossier before the trial and thus being unfamiliar with the details of the case, the other two judges on the collegial panel were mere accompaniments.

> Sometimes, after calling the court to order and introducing the members of the collegial panel, panel members will get up and exit the courtroom, leaving only the presiding judge to hear the case alone. Sometimes collegial panel members daydream and ignore the trial process, thinking only about their own affairs and occupying themselves with their own matters with a disinterested attitude. There are even some heads of collegial panels who do not bother notifying the other members of the panel, and, as an excuse, tell the litigants that the other panelists were unable to attend the trial and would instead deliberate together after the trial. In reality there are no collective deliberations, and the collegial panel has become a one-person show (独角戏). ... Oftentimes the head of the collegial panel writes the decision before calling a full-panel meeting to deliberate, during which the other panelists quickly skim the decision and express their agreement. This is a system of mutual backscratching: I will agree with your decision if you agree with mine. Sometimes the head of the panel will not even call a meeting, but will instead seek out the other panelists for the signatures on the decision. Some will not even seek out the other panelists, but will simply forge their signatures. (Lü 2015)

Courts also turned to lay assessors to populate collegial panels. Like the two secondary judges on three-judge collegial panels, lay assessors have also been characterized as window dressing and "lackeys." Although, formally speaking, lay assessors' votes and opinions count as much as those of judges, in practice they have little independent

160

voice (X. He 2016). The literal translation of the Chinese word for "lay assessor" is "accompanying adjudicator" (陪审员). They have been informally ridiculed as those who "accompany without adjudicating" (陪而不审; Cai 2013:133; Chen 2016a:218; Guo 2016; C. Wang 2012:80; Xu, Huang, and Lu 2011:140–41). Indeed, even when they were assigned to cases, trials were sometimes held in their absence (Cai 2013:134; Yu 2009:157). Regardless of whether collegial panels were formally composed of three judges or a mix of judges and lay assessors applying the ordinary procedure, they often operated in practice as if a single judge were applying the simplified procedure.

From an empirical standpoint, because my data derive from published court decisions, I am unable to measure the *actual* participation of members of collegial panels. I am therefore unable to assess differences between Henan and Zhejiang (or between courts within provinces) to the extent to which collegial panels were facades. I can, however, measure and assess variation with respect to the *nominal* participation of different kinds of decision-makers, including assistant judges and lay assessors.

Deputizing Assistant Judges

Prior to recent reforms, court recorders (书记员) could work their way up to the rank of assistant judge (助理审判员) and ultimately to associate judge (审判员; Q. Wang 2015:76; Wang 2019b:137; Weng 2020:115; Xue 2019:19; Zhang 2016a:19). Assistant judges were formally regarded as "judges-in-waiting" (候补法官, who can also be thought of as judge candidates, judge apprentices, or judges-in-training) and "judges-in-reserve" (法官后备人才). According to provisions in the 1995 Law on Judges, assistant judges were bona fide judges, provided they passed the national judges' examination, were formally appointed by the court's adjudication committee, and met other applicable qualifying standards. Although they lacked the status of fully qualified judges, they were nonetheless assigned to cases as if they were associate judges by courts taking advantage of a provision in the Organic Law of People's Courts.

Article 36 of the 2006 Organic Law of People's Courts stipulated that assistant judges were to *support* the work of associate judges and could also *temporarily* serve as full-fledged judges in a substitute function on the recommendation of the court president and the approval of the court's adjudication committee (Article 37 in the 1979 version and Article 34 in the original 1954 version; Weng 2020:116). The intent was to allow courts to deputize assistant judges to serve, on an ad interim basis only, as surrogate associate judges. They appear on court decisions with the title of "assistant judge" or "substitute judge" (代理审判员).

Courts' creative interpretation of this statutory provision allowed them to expand the ranks of frontline judges. As a judge in Hainan wrote: "When assistant judges are appointed to serve as judges, [in practice] they assume this role without limits; the word 'temporary' was long ago burned to ashes" (Q. Wang 2015:74). Another judge similarly characterized "the word 'temporary' as itself only 'temporary' when the appointment of assistant judges to handle cases on a temporary basis increasingly became the norm in the wake of growing caseloads" (Ye 2016:103). A legal scholar came to the same conclusion: "in judicial practice, [assistant] judges always served in a 'substitute' function and never in a 'support' function" (Xue 2019:19). Assistant judges were thus of great help to courts dealing with the crushing weight of their dockets (Chen 2016a:218–19, 2016b:122). This coping strategy was known informally as "repurposing judges" (借用法官; Fan 2010:142), and is reflected in the 2011 work report of a basic-level court in Zhejiang: "Attaching importance to the development of judges-in-reserve, five were formally appointed assistant judge and ten were provisionally appointed assistant judge in order to supplement further the force of frontline adjudicators" (https://perma.cc/8TE6-GAB4; also see https://perma.cc/SC4P-EDV3). In a 2009 work report of an intermediate court in Zhejiang, the definition of "frontline judge" explicitly includes "assistant judges" (https://perma.cc/9W2S-QCDL). This was a particularly common strategy among courts in economically developed areas such as Zhejiang and Shanghai with relatively heavy caseloads (Weng 2020:116–17).

Each collegial panel includes a head judge (审判长) appointed by the court president or division head. When a court president or division head participates in an ordinary procedure trial, they automatically becomes head judge of the collegial panel (Article 30 of the 2018 Organic Law of People's Courts and Article 41 of the 2012 Civil Procedure Law). Among members of collegial panels, only lay assessors were (and remain) ineligible to serve as head judges (Anyang Municipal Intermediate People's Court Research Team 2016:287). Courts commonly took advantage of an SPC opinion allowing assistant judges to serve as head judges on collegial panels (Q. Wang 2015:74–75; Weng 2020:116; Ye 2016:103).

We already know that assistant judges served on collegial panels with associate judges. A typical collegial panel consisted of one associate judge designated as head judge, another associate judge, and one assistant judge. A second typical configuration was a head judge plus two assistant judges. A third typical configuration was a head judge, one assistant judge, and one lay assessor. Assistant judges even served as head judges on collegial panels that included associate judges. When they did so, they perversely outranked associate judges (Q. Wang 2015:75). At the same time, assistant judges obviated the need for associate judge trial participation. In simplified procedure cases, assistant judges could conduct trials independently as solo judges. In ordinary procedure cases, assistant judges designated as head judges could lead two lay assessors, two assistant judges, or one of each on collegial panels. In each of the foregoing scenarios, cases could be handled in the absence of any associate judges. In short, assistant judges were a boon to clogged courts insofar as they conserved judicial resources by reducing trial work for associate judges in a variety of ways.

Before a new classification system of judge titles and ranks introduced in 2015 was mostly in place in 2018, court decisions contained the names and titles of participating head judges, associate judges, assistant judges, lay assessors, and court recorders. As we will see from my Henan-Zhejiang comparison later in this chapter, court decisions can be used to measure courts' degree of reliance on assistant judges through 2016 and, in most provinces, 2017. Courts stopped using the term "assistant judge" when it was scrubbed altogether from the 2017 version of the Law on Judges (which took effect January 1, 2018) and the 2018 version of the Organic Law of People's Courts (which took effect January 1, 2019). I will now turn to formal innovative responses from the SPC.

FORMAL INNOVATIVE RESPONSES TO CLOGGED COURTS

By the mid-2000s, collegial panels of decision-makers were decoupling from the work of judging. Although the SPC's 2009–2013 third five-year outline for court reform under the leadership of Wang Shengjun is known principally for *ideologically* promoting judicial populism (Liebman 2011b, 2014; Minzner 2011; Zhang 2016a), it also *pragmatically* promoted judicial efficiency (T. Zhang 2012). Specific measures called for or inspired by the outline include increasing the use of pretrial mediation – including "grand mediation" outside of court and case filing mediation inside of court – as a way to preempt trials; delaying judges' retirement or rehiring them after retirement; and adjusting performance evaluations to include efficiency targets (Lü 2015; Su 2010:180–81; L. Xu 2012:26; Xu, Huang, and Lu 2011:138; T. Zhang 2012:28–29; Zuo 2020). In this section I will focus on two specific efforts of the SPC to eliminate the charade of collegial panels by bringing formal procedural rules in line with courts' informal practices described in the previous section: first, the promotion of solo judging by expanding the scope of the simplified civil procedure and, second, the increase of lay assessor participation. I will then discuss how a quota system introduced by the SPC's 2014–2018 fourth five-year outline for court reform may have posed a setback to courts struggling to clear their dockets.

Expanding the Scope of the Simplified Procedure

The 1979 and 2006 versions of the Organic Law of People's Courts enshrined the principle of "the primary role of the collegial panel and the secondary role of the solo judge" (合议为主、独任为辅; K. Chen 2019:107; He et al. 2012). They stipulated that solo judging was to be limited to simple civil cases and minor criminal offenses. The simplified procedure was originally intended to be used sparingly in a supplementary capacity and within a narrow scope of application (Zheng 2018:133). According to an empirical study of the utilization of the simplified civil procedure in Zhejiang's city of Jinhua, as caseloads grew dramatically in the mid- to late 1990s, courts increasingly turned to it as a coping strategy that the authors characterized as an "abuse of the simplified procedure":

> Some courts, owing to "many cases, few judges," objectively face a conflict between their volume of trial work and their inadequate workforce of trial personnel, and thus use the simplified procedure when they have a lot of cases; some courts erroneously use the simplified procedure as a method of clearing a backlog of cases; and some courts, lacking proper understanding, use the simplified procedure as a means of increasing their work efficiency. (Zhu and Zou 2001:51)

The authors of an earlier study from which this specific passage was apparently plagiarized continued by writing: "For this reason, in judicial practice, many cases that should be tried according to the ordinary procedure are incorrectly tried according to the simplified procedure" (Cai and Cai 1998:33).

According to another study, "there is already consensus among legal scholars and practitioners on moderately expanding the scope of solo judging and limiting the use of collegial panels. ... These trends have undoubtedly reduced judicial costs and rationalized the allocation of courts' internal judicial resources. It has been enormously beneficial to relieving basic-level courts' problem of 'many cases and few judges'" (Chen 2016b:123; also see Cai 2013:131 and K. Chen 2019:106–07). This was particularly true in more economically developed regions such as Zhejiang, where the simplified procedure eclipsed the ordinary procedure as means of dealing with ballooning caseloads (L. Xu 2012:26; W. Zhang 2012:90). In Sichuan's provincial capital of Chengdu, eight frontline judges in a basic-level court each said that the simplified procedure cut their case disposal times in half (Zuo 2018:249n27).

This informal coping strategy from below became formalized and legitimized from above when the SPC made expanding the scope of the simplified procedure a cornerstone of its 2009–2013 third five-year outline for court reform (T. Zhang 2012:28). Under the SPC's guiding opinions on performance evaluations, which took effect nationwide in 2011, judges have been rewarded for high simplified procedure utilization rates (Kinkel and Hurst 2015:942; Shao 2015:39). A research team of legal scholars that authored a report on the revision of the Organic Law of People's Courts law recommended that the principle of the collegial panel's primacy be reversed, and that collegial panels instead be used to supplement solo judging (He et al. 2012). The drafters of the 2018 version of the Organic Law of People's Courts partially adopted this recommendation by giving equal status to solo judges and collegial panels.

Because many People's Tribunals do not even have enough judges to form collegial panels, they are often left with no choice but to "drag in lay assessors" (Lü 2015) or to apply the simplified procedure as a matter of necessity (L. Chen 2013; Yu and Gao 2015:23; Zhan 2013). The two People's Tribunals at the center of a study of divorce litigation in rural southwest China each had only two judges (Li 2015a:29). Among all 44 People's Tribunals in Henan's Luohe Municipality, the average number of judges was only 2.4 (X. Tang 2017:97). For this reason, the SPC's 2005 Resolutions on Comprehensively Strengthening the Work of People's Tribunals stipulates: "When conducting trials, People's Tribunals will generally apply the simplified procedure" (Resolution 10).

Official reform efforts to increase simplified procedure utilization rates in courts at all levels had been underway since the SPC's 1999–2003 first five-year outline for court reform. The SPC's 2004–2008 second five-year outline for court reform called for the creation of expedited procedures (速裁程序) – which were even more simplified than the simplified procedure – for small-claims debt cases (Zhao and Jie 2008:153). The SPC's 2003 Several Provisions Concerning the Application of the Simplified Procedure to Try Civil Cases clarified rules governing the use of the simplified procedure, including the ability of courts to dispense with the delivery of written summons in favor of faster, more flexible means of summoning litigants and the ability of litigants to choose the simplified procedure by voluntary agreement (T. Zhang 2012:26–27; Zhao and Jie 2008:154). These provisions, as well as additional ones on small-claims procedures, were incorporated into the 2012 version of the Civil Procedure Law (which took effect on January 1, 2013). By expanding the scope of the simplified procedure, they brought formal policy into closer alignment with informal practices (Xu, Lu, and Huang 2012:98; W. Yang 2014:170; T. Zhang 2012).

According to the 2012 Civil Procedure Law, the simplified civil procedure should be applied when "the facts are clear, rights and obligations are unambiguous, and the dispute minor" (Article 157); when both sides mutually agree to its application (Article 157); or when the financial value of the matter in dispute (标的额) is below a certain threshold and the case is therefore a small-claims suit (Article 162). Although Article 168 of the 1992 SPC Opinions on Several Issues Concerning the Application of the Civil Procedure Law provides guidance by defining each of these three qualifying standards, legal scholars nonetheless complain about the simplified procedure's ambiguity and the arbitrary nature of its application. In the absence of concrete standards by which to determine case complexity, the process of designating cases as simple or complex (简繁分流) has been widely characterized as arbitrary and subjective (Li and Ye 2015:105; Tang 1996:19; Zhu and Zou 2001:48).

> Any standards, regardless of how reasonable and carefully thought out they are, fail to qualify as standards if they lack sufficient clarity. … Just as everyone attaches a different meaning to "Hamlet," these standards have been cast aside, and the application of the simplified procedure has become enormously arbitrary and disorderly. Perhaps their original legislative intent was good. Perhaps they were intended to leave space for judges to investigate specific circumstances. However, unwarranted confidence in the quality, capacity, and moral character of China's judges, coupled with unawareness of uncontrolled practices on the ground, left openings for their abuse. (W. Yang 2014:170–71)

Courts have exploited these vague standards by applying the simplified procedure willy-nilly to heavy dockets (Pan 2019:127). In so doing, they have sometimes deprived litigants of their due process rights (Cai and Cai 1998; K. Chen 2019:105–07, 110; Tang 2016:144–45). Perhaps members of collegial panels provide a function comparable to that of lawyers in US lower courts. In the US context, lawyers' mere presence serves to hold judges to procedural rules. In the absence of lawyer participation, lower-court judges in the United States are more likely to break court rules by, for example, failing to authenticate evidence, failing to hold litigants to statutory burden of proof, and failing to swear in parties before they provide testimony (Sandefur 2015:925). In the Chinese context, when using the simplified procedure, judges have sometimes taken procedural shortcuts. In Zhejiang's city of Jinhua, for example, judges often did not give defendants the full 15 days to which they were entitled to respond to plaintiffs' legal complaints, and sometimes even scheduled trials on the very day they issued summons to involved parties. Likewise, although the Civil Procedure Law allows plaintiffs to submit their legal complaints orally in simple cases, some courts in Jinhua used plaintiffs' failure to submit written petitions as an excuse to reject their cases (Zhu and Zou 2001:48). Without other judges or lay assessors to hold them to procedural requirements, solo judges who conducted trials according to the simplified procedure sometimes did so with excessive informality, relying on their feelings (凭感觉; Cai and Cai 1998:33) and intuition (自由心证; Yang 2012:16) and in so doing brought into play their personal prejudices (个人的偏见; Chen 2015:11). One judge argued that the collegial panel helps prevent "judicial tyranny" (司法专横) and corruption (Lü 2015). Scholars have expressed concern that "solo judging lacks collaborative discussion and supervision" (S. Wang 2014:21), and therefore that "expanding the application of simplified procedure expands space for judges to exercise free discretion" (自由裁量; Zhao and Jie 2008:154). In the same vein, two lawyers asserted that "owing to a lack of institutionalized constraints and supervision, presiding judges and solo judges have a great deal of discretion, and discretion introduces arbitrariness" (Xu and Li 2011:36).

Other legal scholars made an open plea: "do not simplify or dispense with the ordinary procedure for the sake of a higher closing rate. Procedural reform is not the same as economic reform" (Zhao and Zhao 2011:70). That train left the station around 2013. The 2012

Civil Procedure Law and SPC judicial interpretations that pertain to it have turned the ordinary procedure into a relic.

> According to the SPC's rationale, first-instance cases in basic-level courts should, in principle, be tried by a solo judge. Only important, complicated, and difficult cases, or where the law otherwise prohibits solo judging [such as administrative litigation prior to mid-2017 and public notice trials], should be tried by collegial panels. This means solo judges have become the first-choice adjudicatory body in basic-level courts, and collegial panels have become a kind of exception. (Chen 2016a:215)

The system of solo judging "is a departure from the original intent of the collegial panel system, which was to realize justice through the equal and full participation of all panel members in order to bring their collective intelligence into full play and to prevent the influence of individual subjective bias" (Ding 2016:86). Supervision over solo judges was further weakened by judicial accountability reforms that streamlined courts' workflow in three ways: dispensing with the requirement that court presidents and division heads approve each court decision, abolishing trial judges' common practice of seeking guidance from court authorities, and reducing the influence of the court's adjudication committee in trial decisions (W. Chen 2019:19; UNDP 2014:15; Wang 2019b:133; Zhang 2016a:26). A corollary of improved judicial efficiency has been expanded autonomy for judges, which has been a double-edged sword. Cutting one way, it may have weakened political interference in judicial decision-making (Wang 2019a). Cutting the other way, however, judges have become even more cautious and risk-averse owing to a system of "lifetime responsibility" for incorrectly decided cases (终身负责制 and 错案责任倒查问责制) that accompanied the reforms (Song 2017; Xu, Huang, and Lu 2015). For both reasons, judges' relatively free rein in the courtroom may weaken due process for litigants.[3]

Thus, the simplified procedure not only helps ease judges' workloads by increasing judicial efficiency but also weakens supervisory checks

---

[3] A nondivorce case illustrates the costs to due process of judges' enormous discretion to determine what qualifies as important, complicated, and difficult (Chen 2016b:123). A middle-aged couple was sued by their daughter's ex-boyfriend for failing to repay a personal loan. The facts of the case were hotly contested because the defendants denied the existence of the loan, claiming instead that the plaintiff had forced them at knifepoint to sign a fake IOU. Although, for this reason, the case should have been ineligible for the simplified procedure, the judge nonetheless applied it and quickly ruled in favor of the plaintiff. After the filing deadline to appeal had passed, the defendants poisoned themselves to death at the courthouse entrance (Cai 2013:136).

on their rulings. We will see that because simplified procedure utilization rates were higher in divorce cases than in other kinds of civil cases, divorce litigants were disproportionately exposed to judges' biases, including their patriarchal cultural beliefs. Judges have regarded divorces as quintessentially simple cases. One judge characterized first-attempt divorce cases as those in which "the facts are especially clear and legal relationships are singular" (R. Tang 2014:79; also see Jiangsu Province Nantong Municipal Intermediate People's Court Research Team 2013:99; Tang 1996:19). In reality, of course, they involve contentious domestic violence, property division, and child custody claims, and are therefore anything but simple. Indeed, it is partly their contentious nature that makes judges so averse to grant first-attempt divorce petitions. The more contentious claims in a petition, the more likely judges were to deny it through the application of the simplified procedure (Chapter 8). In general, judges did not deny first-attempt divorce petitions because they regarded them as simple matters; they regarded them as simple matters because they were predisposed to deny them.

Most judges have regarded the choice of which civil procedure to apply as their prerogative. Even when litigants regard their disputes as serious and complex, judges often do not heed their explicit requests for the application of the ordinary procedure. Judges' impulse has been to apply the simplified procedure and to try cases alone, without collegial panels, and therefore sometimes without regard to the wishes of the involved parties (Cai 2013:136). By touting the half-price court fee associated with the simplified procedure (Chapter 2), judges may be able to mollify some plaintiffs. Indeed, courts have justified expanding the scope of the simplified procedure in terms of shortening times to outcomes – and hence of reducing litigants' "litigation fatigue" (诉累) – and in terms of reducing litigants' litigation costs (e.g., https://perma.cc/H6CD-DLE9; https://perma.cc/YN4X-MZ8C; https://perma.cc/82X2-2HV5). Nonetheless, because divorce cases involving domestic violence allegations, as well as those involving contested child custody or marital property claims, are often difficult and complex, many plaintiffs filing for divorce are unwilling to surrender their full due process rights. According to a judge in Jiangxi Province, many litigants are not only denied the opportunity to choose the civil procedure, but are also left in the dark concerning which procedure is chosen for them. Judges commonly try cases alone according to the simplified civil procedure without telling the involved litigants. Then, if a judge cannot finalize his ruling within the three-month deadline, he simply adds the names of additional judges to the court decision retroactively in order to switch over to the ordinary procedure (Liu 2014).

As we will see in Chapter 6, divorce cases were far more likely than other types of civil cases to be tried according to the simplified procedure. And as we will see in Chapter 8, case complexity paradoxically increased the likelihood of the use of the simplified procedure. Under the relentlessly growing weight of caseloads, "judges rushing around in haste have no time to listen patiently to litigants' testimony, and even incessantly interrupt and shut down litigants in order to conclude the case at hand in time for the next one on their schedule. This is why simplified procedure utilization rates are high" (Cai 2013:136). Courts have similarly expanded the scope of the simplified procedure in criminal litigation and, more recently, in administrative litigation.

Increasing Lay Assessor Participation

China's People's Lay Assessor System (人民陪审制), which can be traced back to the Chinese Communist Party's revolutionary base areas in the 1930s, was designed to strengthen "socialist judicial democracy" by serving as a means by which the masses can supervise the judiciary (Anyang Municipal Intermediate People's Court Research Team 2016:287; Fu 2018:94–95; L. Tang 2017:122; Zhang 2015). Lay assessors serve on collegial panels in first-instance trials conducted according to the ordinary procedure (Chapter 2). Lay assessor participation rates are one of many indicators included in courts' performance evaluation systems. Performance indicators are divided into three main categories: fairness, efficiency, and impact (Kinkel and Hurst 2015). Although lay assessor participation rates formally count as indicators of "fairness" in performance evaluation systems (Cai 2013:133; Fu 2018:101), they are widely recognized as serving in practice to enhance efficiency. Because lay assessors have the unique ability to occupy seats on collegial panels without occupying slots in the state personnel system for civil servants, they have become an important tool in efforts to alleviate judges' workloads (Zuo 2018:248–50), and their numbers and participation rates have grown rapidly since 2004 (Fan 2014:51; X. He 2016:734). In mid-2013, the SPC announced a plan to double the population of lay assessors (倍增计划) within two years to about 200,000 (He and Yu 2015:245; L. Tang 2017:126;

Xu, Huang, and Wang 2014:92). This target was achieved ahead of schedule when the number of lay assessors nationwide increased from 87,000 to 209,500 between 2013 and the end of 2014 (https://perma.cc/CZT7-ZHHC; https://perma.cc/6NR8-W4JT). Henan was reportedly the first province to meet this target, and actually quadrupled its pool of lay assessors within one year to over 30,000 (https://perma.cc/HR3T-76FK). Some courts have even recruited retired judges to serve as lay assessors and mediators (X. Li 2014:223; Y. Zhang 2017:22; Zhengzhou Municipal Intermediate Court Research Group 2014).

Introducing a Quota System to Standardize the Titles and Ranks of Judges

Beginning with the SPC's first five-year outline (1999–2003), "quota systems" (员额制) that imposed limits on numbers of judges, in part by eliminating the title of assistant judge, had been implemented in fits and starts as pilot programs in selected locations (Lin 2008; Weng 2020:109; Zhang 2019:115). Ultimately, as part of its fourth five-year outline for court reform (2014–2018), the SPC implemented a nationwide judicial appointment and classification system to standardize the titles, ranks, and corresponding responsibilities of court personnel (Q. Wang 2015; Wang 2019b; Zhang 2016a:26–28).

China likely had, and may still have, more judges than any other country (Zhang 2016b:59). SPC and government leaders diagnosed the problem of clogged courts not as a shortage of judges but rather as too many poorly qualified judges working inefficiently. Further expanding an already bloated corps of low-quality judges was an unpalatable solution (Q. Wang 2015:76), and adding more high-quality judges too expensive (Luo and Huang 2011:11). So rather than increasing the number of judges, the SPC did the opposite. Its goal was to professionalize the judiciary, to create an elite profession of specialized judges, to help China's body of judges "lose weight," and in so doing to improve the quality of judicial work and overcome low levels of public trust in courts (Liu 2019:105; Q. Wang 2015:76–77, 80; Zhang 2016a:18–19). In support of these goals, the SPC tried to retain and recruit the best legal talent by raising the salaries of judges who entered the "quota," which was possible in part thanks to the budgetary savings associated with denying entry to almost half of all judges (Fu 2018:93–94; Wang 2019b:133; Zhang and Ginsburg 2019:300).

Prior to the judge quota system reforms, the prevailing pathway into an associate judgeship was via a court recordership and assistant judgeship (Q. Wang 2015:76). Owing to spotty enforcement of qualification requirements, court recorders were often hired straight out of high school and worked their way up to assistant judge and then to associate judge (Zhang 2016a). In its work report, a basic-level court in Zhejiang described this process of promoting 15 clerks to assistant judge and putting them on the front lines in order to alleviate the "many cases, few judges" problem (https://perma.cc/YYK4-3VA2). Another Zhejiang work report describes the promotion of assistant judges to associate judge (https://perma.cc/R5KD-2TSR). In the court decisions in my samples, one can easily find clerks moving into assistant judgeships and assistant judges moving into associate judgeships. At the time, associate and assistant judges occupied around 60–70% of all state personnel slots allocated to courts (Song 2017:106). The SPC's new quota system drastically slashed their ranks by imposing a 39% cap on judges as a share of all slots in the state personnel system allocated by the central government to political and legal affairs positions (中央政法专项编制; Chen 2016a:215; Wang 2019b:136).

Most court leaders and associate judges, with the exception of some approaching retirement, entered the quota (Song 2017:111). Meanwhile, "assistant judge" as a title and rank was eliminated (Wang 2019b:137), and assistant judges were stripped of their authority to serve as solo judges or as members of collegial panels. Their status was reduced to "support staff" (辅助人员) and their title to "judges' clerk" (法官助理). Though they did not enter the quota as judges, most remained on the central government payroll as civil servants (Zhang 2019:112). Meanwhile, some former assistant judges and many newly recruited judges' clerks who were hired under contract employment systems (聘用制) or local government personnel systems were never considered part of the national civil service in the first place (Zhang 2019:117). Judges' clerks thus became a motley cohort of court personnel classified not only as civil servants, but also as ordinary staff (普通职员), temporary hires (临时用工人员), employees outside the state personnel system (编制外工作人员), and even contract workers (合同工). Judges' clerks under these various designations have been doing the same work despite differences in status, pay, benefits, and promotion opportunities (L. Wang 2016:66; Ye 2016:110).

Paradoxically, given that it so drastically reduced the number of judges, the judge quota system was also designed to increase judicial efficiency. First, as elsewhere in the world, judge's clerks in China, by providing clerical and administrative support to associate judges in preparation for and the disposition of cases, were intended to allow associate judges to focus their efforts more narrowly and productively on courtroom proceedings and rulings (Chen and Xu 2018; Weng 2020:115; Ye 2016:104). Second, because court presidents, vice-presidents, division heads, and other judges with administrative titles rarely did trial work prior to the reforms, a new requirement that *all* judges handle cases was intended to maintain a relatively stable number of *frontline* judges even while the total number of judges diminished (W. Chen 2019:18; Zhejiang Provincial High Court Research Team 2019; Zhou 2014).

China's population of judges had been consistently in the 190,000–210,000 range from the early 2000s until the judge quota system reforms (Qu and Fan 2019:25). In 2012, China had 195,028 judges (Chen and Bai 2016:46). By 2017, when the label for assistant judge changed to judge's clerk, the population of judges nationwide plummeted over 40% to approximately 120,000 (W. Chen 2019:18; Qu and Fan 2019:25; Xue 2019:18; Zheng 2018:131). In early 2019, judges numbered about 125,000 (People's Court Media Office 2019). A study of courts in Zhejiang, Chongqing, and Yunnan reports that quota system reforms reduced the number of judges there by over 60% (Wang 2019b).

Scholars generally agree that the judge quota system reforms exacerbated the problem of "many cases, few judges" (Chen and Bai 2016:25, 44; Hou 2017:52; Song 2017:106; Wang 2019b; Y. Wang 2017:76–77; Weng 2020:116). Judges' clerks, who had previously handled cases as frontline judges and expected opportunities for promotion to the rank of associate judge, found themselves relegated to positions of professional precarity (Wang 2016; Weng 2020; Zhang 2019; Zhejiang Provincial High Court Research Team 2019:58). These reforms dealt a major blow to the morale of court recorders and judges' clerks (Chen and Bai 2016:47; Hou 2017:52; Q. Wang 2015:78; Zhang 2019; Zhu 2020:65). With limited prospects for career mobility, many have quit their jobs and left the court system, further increasing the shortage of judicial personnel (Wang 2019b:137, 143; Zhang 2019:117).

The judge quota system reforms severed traditional career pathways to judgeships. Most assistant judges who became judges' clerks no longer formed a reserve of judges-in-waiting (Hou 2017:52). While a promotion pathway to associate judge remained for judges' clerks who retained the status of civil servant, for others it disappeared (Ye 2016:104). Meanwhile, prospects for career movement from court recorder to judge, for all practical purposes, died (Chen and Bai 2016:23–24, 46–47; Chen and Xu 2018:91; Weng 2020:115, 120; Xue 2019:19; Ye 2016:104). Critics add that, as well as fueling judicial attrition, the reforms have also narrowed the judicial recruitment pipeline by discouraging people from entering the profession (Fu 2018:96; Wang 2019b:137–38; Y. Wang 2017:71; Weng 2020; Zhang 2019:118). These challenges have been particularly acute for courts in the more economically developed parts of China that had come to rely on assistant judges to help clear their relatively heavy dockets (Hou 2017:52).

Beginning in 2016, courts in Jiangsu Province stopped using the terms "assistant judge" and "substitute judge" and started including the names of participating judges' clerks in their decisions. Most courts, however, continued to use the obsolete titles of judges in their decisions through the end of 2017 until the amended Law on Judges took effect on January 1, 2018. Assistant judges never faded from court decisions in my Henan and Zhejiang samples, which ended in December 2015 and December 2017, respectively. By the same token, judges' clerks appeared on no divorce decisions in either sample and on only a few dozen nondivorce decisions in my Zhejiang sample, all from 2017 (out of over 600,000 nondivorce decisions).

Given the timing of its implementation, therefore, the judge quota system has no direct bearing on the findings I present in this book. Why bother discussing it, then? First, it is a hugely consequential court reform in general and a formal innovative response to clogged courts in particular, and therefore germane to the subject of this chapter. Second, after the implementation of the judge quota system reforms, some courts in Zhejiang with desperate shortages of frontline judges have surreptitiously assigned trial work to judges' clerks – many of whom were former assistant judges – while covering their tracks by affixing on their decisions the names of bona fide judges in the quota (Wang 2019b:137; also see Zhang 2019:116). In other words, when *formal* innovations failed to alleviate – and even worsened – the enduring, intensifying problem of "many cases, few judges," some of China's most clogged courts responded with a new *informal* innovation: They directly contravened formal laws and rules governing the operation of courts by informally allowing judges' clerks to function as pre-reform frontline assistant judges (Q. Zhang 2018:63).

To be sure, formal innovative responses to clogged courts are not limited to those discussed in this section. The SPC has also introduced technological innovations to increase judicial efficiency. To much fan-fare, it has promoted the development of "smart courts" (智慧法院建设) that apply artificial intelligence to computer-assisted speech-to-text transcription and the automated production of recommended verdicts and sentences through the identification of similar cases (W. Chen 2019:20–21; Liebman et al. 2020; Zuo 2018:259; https://perma.cc/9DXY-B244; https://perma.cc/3W35-XJWW). Such developments are beyond the scope of this book, however.

THE VIEW FROM HENAN AND ZHEJIANG

In the United States, changes to federal civil procedure rules in the 1980s "to emphasize efficiency and conservation of judicial resources" and the proliferation of case management systems to help realize these priorities were associated with a decline in civil trials and an increase in summary judgments and motions to dismiss (Miller 2003:984). The upshot has been the "vanishing trial," a process by which the full trial has given way to streamlined judicial procedures that privilege efficiency over due process (Galanter 2004; also see Engstrom 2017). China's vanishing trial used to be a story about the rise of mediation and a corresponding decline in adjudication (Chapter 2; Fan 2008). The story began to change in the late 2000s, and did so particularly rapidly after the implementation of the 2012 Civil Procedure Law. In China, as we learned in the previous section, the rise of the simplified procedure, increased lay assessor participation, and a shrinking corps of judges, taken together, drove the story of the vanishing three-judge collegial panel. These measures to enhance judicial efficiency were facilitated by the nationwide establishment of specialized case management offices, which had been adopted by almost 40% of China's basic-level courts by the end of 2011 (Cai 2013:132) – the same year the SPC issued a judicial opinion on strengthening case management work (Xu, Lu, and Huang 2012:102–03) – and by almost 75% of all courts by the end of 2012 (Yuan and Ding 2012).

National judicial statistics permit a partial view of the vanishing three-judge collegial panel for China as a whole. In the ten years spanning 2007 and 2016, the proportion of cases processed by three-judge collegial panels precipitously declined from 26% to 7% with respect to *all* first-instance civil cases and from 22% to 4% with respect to first-instance *family* cases (SPC 2018). Among cases processed by means other than three-judge collegial panels, some were handled by collegial panels with lay assessors (applying the ordinary procedure) and some were handled by solo judges (applying the simplified procedure). Over the same ten-year period, the proportion of cases with lay assessor participation almost quintupled from 5% to 24% with respect to *all* first-instance civil cases and almost quadrupled from 4% to 15% with respect to first-instance *family* cases (SPC 2018).[4] The residual category of cases handled by solo judges applying the simplified civil procedure remained fairly stable over this time period, hovering in the 69–76% range for *all* first-instance civil cases and in the 73–81% range for first-instance *family* cases. Studies of individual courts show similarly stable simplified civil procedure utilization rates over time (e.g., Zuo 2018:249).

The foregoing patterns strongly support my story of a massive increase in lay assessor participation as a formal innovative response to clogged courts. Since lay assessors can only participate in trials conducted according to the ordinary procedure (because they must be part of collegial panels), the proportion of collegial panels in first-instance civil cases that included at least one lay assessor more than quintupled from 15% in 2007 to 78% in 2016 (SPC 2018). In contrast to my story of the expansion of the simplified procedure, however, the foregoing patterns show unexpected stability over time in simplified procedure utilization rates. The reason for this is a statistical artifact of the way the SPC and individual courts report judicial statistics. Official statistics on the application of the simplified procedure always combine case adjudications, mediations, and withdrawals. We therefore cannot disaggregate simplified procedure utilization rates by case disposal method. If we were able to isolate adjudicated cases, we would certainly see an increase in simplified civil procedure utilization rates and an even more conspicuously vanishing three-judge collegial panel because mediations and withdrawals have tended to be handled by solo judges applying the simplified civil procedure. In other words, if we were to remove mediations and withdrawals from the scope of analysis, we would certainly find an increase in the incidence of solo

---

[4] National judicial statistics on lay assessor participation and civil procedure type do not disaggregate family cases into more detailed case types, including divorce. Divorce, however, consistently accounted for about 80% of all concluded first-instance family cases between 2010 and 2016 (SPC 2018).

[5] Mediation agreements and withdrawals, far more than civil adjudications, have tended to be rendered and approved by solo judges applying the simplified civil procedure. Most first-instance civil cases have been closed by either mediation or withdrawal (Chapter 2), and mediations and withdrawals have been far more likely than adjudications to be presided over

judging in court trials.[5] Indeed, among all first-instance civil adjudications posted on China Judgements Online, the proportion in which the simplified procedure was applied more than doubled from 24% in 2009 to 52% in 2018.[6] As we will see shortly, I found the same pattern in my Henan sample. Zhejiang, by contrast, had already embraced the simplified procedure far earlier and to a much greater extent. Indeed, we need look no further than Henan and Zhejiang for evidence that the vanishing three-judge collegial panel was a function of the timing and severity of "many cases, few judges" problem.

Courts in Henan and Zhejiang have been at opposite ends of the caseload spectrum. In 2011, the number of judges per population in

by solo judges. Given that solo judges have been underrepresented in adjudications (relative to mediations and withdrawals), two coinciding and countervailing trends essentially canceled each other out: an increase in solo judging (which, once again, is the same as an increase in the utilization of the simplified procedure) and an increase in adjudications as a share of all first-instance civil cases (which we saw in Chapter 2). In other words, at precisely the same time that simplified procedure utilization rates (and hence solo judging) in adjudicated cases were increasing, adjudicated cases themselves as a proportion of all cases were also increasing. In official judicial statistics that combine case adjudications, mediations, and withdrawals, the latter trend surely offsets and obscures the prior trend because the scope of the simplified procedure is much smaller in adjudications than in either mediations or case withdrawals. Both of my provincial samples of first-instance civil court decisions show that withdrawals were far more likely than adjudications to have been handled by solo judges (57% versus 30% in Henan and 85% versus 63% in Zhejiang). Courts in Henan, like most courts in China, did not post mediation agreements (Chapter 4). Zhejiang's courts, however, did post a small share of its mediation agreements. Among the roughly 40,000 first-instance civil mediation agreements in my Zhejiang sample, about 90% were presided over by solo judges. The Civil Procedure Law allows mediation to be conducted by either a solo judge or a collegial panel (Article 86 in the 1991 version and Article 94 in the 2012 version). "In practice, in order to increase judicial efficiency, courts almost always have solo judges carry out mediation" (Meng 2012:86; also see X. Yang 2014). Withdrawals are no different because they are so often the result of mediation. According to the Civil Procedure Law, successful judicial mediation leads to either a written mediation agreement or a request from the plaintiff to withdraw the petition. According to an SPC judicial interpretation, withdrawals, unlike mediation agreements, are not final and irrevocable; a plaintiff who withdraws a petition may file the same first-instance petition again at a later date. From the perspective of a plaintiff, withdrawing a petition provides more options – and is therefore more advantageous and desirable – than accepting a mediation agreement, which is tantamount to surrendering the right to bring the case back to court (Zhao 2017:137). In the context of divorce litigation, however, this is a false choice because mediated reconciliations generally count as withdrawals and are exempt from written mediation agreements (Article 98, Item 1 of the Civil Procedure Law).

6   On December 19, 2019, I searched on China Judgements Online (https://wenshu.court .gov.cn/) for first-instance civil adjudications made by basic-level courts. I found 17,653,544 decisions satisfying these criteria dated between 2009 and 2018, of which 8,040,584 (46%) contained the term "applied the simplified procedure" (适用简易程序). Measured in this way, the simplified procedure utilization rate increased in each successive year: 24%, 25%, 28%, 33%, 35%, 42%, 42%, 45%, 47%, and 52%. This measure underestimates the true incidence of the simplified procedure because many court decisions do not explicitly indicate the type of procedure applied to the case. The most accurate measure, and the one I use with the decisions in my samples, is based on the composition of judges, for which there is no way to search on China Judgements Online.

these two provinces was identical: 14 judges per 100,000 residents, which was also the national figure. Meanwhile, Zhejiang's closed cases per population outnumbered Henan's by almost three to one (15.1 and 5.5 cases per 1,000 residents, respectively). Viewed another way, Zhejiang's courts closed 60% more cases than Henan's despite the fact that Henan's judges outnumbered Zhejiang's by over 76% (Basic Level Legal Artisan 2016a). Henan's judges remained far more numerous than Zhejiang's even after the implementation of the judge quota system.[7] In short, judges' caseloads have been far heavier in Zhejiang than in Henan, both in absolute terms and relative to the numbers of judges.

In his 2005 work report delivered to the National People's Congress in January 2006, SPC President Xiao Yang (肖扬) specifically singled out "basic-level courts in the east coast region" with respect to the "many cases, few judges contradiction" and in which "conditions of overwork are urgently awaiting improvement" (https://perma.cc/AHK2-NBTN). Exemplifying China's "east coast region" are Shanghai, Jiangsu, and Zhejiang, the coastal provincial-level units of the Yangtze Delta. In their annual work reports, basic-level courts in Zhejiang often parroted this sort of language from the SPC about caseload pressure. Many specifically noted the toll on judges' physical and mental health exacted by rapidly expanding caseloads (e.g., https://perma.cc/Y75D-9D8U; also see Chapter 3). Some extolled the spirit of heroism exhibited by court personnel who collapsed or died on the job from overwork (e.g., https://perma.cc/HYG9-XNAP; https://perma.cc/8LST-G28G).

I collected 479 work reports from 87 out of all 91 basic-level courts in Zhejiang. They cover the 2005–2016 time period, but almost all of them (96%) fall between 2008 and 2014. Only the four basic-level courts in the prefecture-level city of Zhoushan are not represented in this collection. At least one term for "judge attrition" (法官流失 or 人才流失) appeared in the work reports of 31 out of all 87 basic-level courts represented in my collection. Their heavier caseloads were an important reason for higher resignation rates in the more economically prosperous parts of China (Fang 2015). Compounding the problem

---

[7] By 2018, although the two provinces had converged in terms of numbers of cases (https://perma.cc/6U32-23L8; https://perma.cc/XX52-S9ER), and although judge populations had shrunk dramatically in both provinces, judges in Henan still outnumbered those in Zhejiang by about 50% (Henan Provincial Bureau of Statistics 2019: Table 25–20; https://perma.cc/XX52-S9ER).

of an unmanageable *quantity* of cases in these areas is the *quality* of those cases: commercial disputes are relatively complex, involve relatively high economic stakes, and are thus relatively labor-intensive and time-consuming for judges (Z. Tang 2014:45). Exacerbating these *push* factors driving judge attrition in China's wealthiest cities are *pull* factors in the form of higher-paying private sector jobs (Fan and Jin 2012:99; Kinkel 2015; Lü 2015; Song 2017:102–03; Wang 2019b).

Judges in Zhejiang were feeling more embattled and beleaguered than their counterparts in Henan. In both 2011 and 2015, Zhejiang's average judge caseload (110 and 218, respectively) was about triple Henan's (39 and 69, respectively; Basic Level Legal Artisan 2016a; Henan Provincial Bureau of Statistics, various years; https://perma.cc/F5JQ-35H6; https://perma.cc/7D85-PSBW).[8] In every year between 2014 and 2017, Zhejiang had a higher average number of closed cases per frontline judge than any other provincial-level unit in China: 187, 218, 260, and 315, at least double the national average in each year (https://perma.cc/Y5LB-EY9V; https://perma.cc/F5JQ-35H6; https://perma.cc/H6CD-DLE9; https://perma.cc/GR8M-ALCQ). The contents of their annual work reports reveal that Zhejiang's basic-level courts were universally concerned with the issue of heavy caseloads. Eighty-two out of 87 basic-level courts mentioned the specific term "many cases, few judges" (案多人少) in at least one of their work reports in my collection. Xiao Yang's specific term for "overwork" (超负荷工作) appeared in the work reports of 44 of 87 basic-level courts. "Average judge caseload" (variants of 法官人均结案) is another ubiquitous term in Zhejiang's work reports, appearing in 74 out of 87 basic-level courts. By contrast, out of 111 work reports from Henan, the term for "many cases, few judges" appeared in only two, only a few made reference to work pressure and personnel attrition, only one addressed average judge caseload, and none included the term Xiao Yang used for "overwork."[9]

---

[8] These comparisons are imperfect owing to inconsistent definitions of judges. The year 2011 figures include all judges. Henan's 2015 figure includes all judges, whereas Zhejiang's 2015 figure is limited to frontline judges. Assuming frontline judges account for 75% of all judges (Basic Level Legal Artisan 2016b), Henan's estimated average number of cases per frontline judge would be 92, which is still a far cry from Zhejiang's 218.

[9] I am grateful to Rachel Stern for sharing copies of 111 basic-level court work reports from Henan that pertain to the year 2014. Unlike Zhejiang's courts, Henan's have not systematically published the full text of court work reports presented to local people's congresses. Because most of the work reports in this collection are short media summaries, their use in a Henan-Zhejiang comparison is not entirely fair. Shorter media versions may omit issues and topics that appear in the unpublished full reports.

Henan and Zhejiang are a study in contrast both in the extent of the problem and in their pursuit of solutions. Dramatic differences between the two provinces in judge caseloads map onto corresponding differences in three empirically observable and measurable innovative responses, all of which were far more prevalent in Zhejiang than in Henan. First, courts put assistant judges to work on trials as an informal coping strategy. Second, courts' use of solo judging (i.e., the application of the simplified procedure) was initially an informal coping strategy that the SPC subsequently institutionalized. Third, lay assessor participation on collegial panels (which are limited to ordinary procedure trials) was another formal innovative response to clogged courts. The second and third of these innovative responses gave rise to the vanishing three-judge collegial panel.

Owing to their exceptionally heavy caseloads, Zhejiang's courts began dispensing with three-judge collegial panels earlier and more aggressively than Henan's courts. As early as 1999, Zhejiang's Daishan County People's Court touted its system of taking solo judging as the primary trial method (Xu and Jiang 2009:102). In 2004, a judge in Zhejiang's Provincial High Court wrote, "basic-level courts universally face the problem of too many cases and not enough judges, and in the vast majority of cases apply the simplified procedure to try them with solo judges" (Ye 2004:29). Some courts in Zhejiang called for increasing the application of the simplified procedure by limiting public notice trials because, as we know from Chapters 2 and 4, they must be conducted according to the ordinary civil procedure (e.g., https://perma.cc/AF38-8F7R). Indeed, as we will see in Chapter 8, public notice trials were far rarer in Zhejiang than in Henan. In their annual work reports, some courts in Zhejiang specifically complained about the issue of limited numbers of judges. For example, the 2009 work report of the Wenzhou Municipal Ouhai District People's Court states: "In recent years, the number of cases our court has received has increased at double-digit rates, while growth in the number of judges in state personnel slots for civil servants has been slow. The result has been ubiquitous overwork and extremely pronounced health problems among court personnel" (https://perma.cc/P8JJ-RPDQ).

The judge from Zhejiang continued by writing: "Even when collegial panels try cases, most of them have lay assessors. It is relatively rare to try cases with collegial panels composed purely of professional judges" (Ye 2004:29). Zhejiang's courts had already reached a lay assessor participation rate of 93% (in first-instance ordinary procedure cases) in 2013 when the rest of China's courts were ramping up their lay assessor participation rates under the SPC's national plan to double the number of lay assessors. At this time, Zhejiang's lay assessor participation rates were the highest in China (https://perma.cc/3KZL-R34P), 20 percentage points above the national average (Guo 2016:92n1). Indeed, Zhejiang's lay assessor participation rate had exceeded the national average by over 20 percentage points since at least 2009 (https://perma.cc/P2YE-9VFW). Zhejiang continued to lead the nation in lay assessor participation rates in 2015 and 2016 (https://perma.cc/3SNC-V8T4; https://perma.cc/H6CD-DLE9). By 2017, its lay assessor participation rate had reached an astonishing 97% (https://perma.cc/GR8M-ALCQ).

Zhejiang's courts had already adopted all three coping strategies, namely the use of assistant judges, solo judges, and lay assessors by 2009. Henan's courts, by contrast, tended to wait for signals and directives from above before adopting them. Figure 5.1 shows the sharp contrast between the two provinces in the extent and timing of their adoption of these three innovative responses to clogged courts. It depicts the composition of various configurations of decision-makers – head judges, associate judges, assistant judges, and lay assessors – participating in first-instance civil trials (Panels A and B) and all first-attempt divorce trials (Panels C and D) over time in both provinces. The top two layers of each panel in Figure 5.1 depict solo associate judges and solo assistant judges, respectively. Taken together, they depict simplified procedure utilization rates.

The four layers below solo judges depict various combinations of decision-makers on three-member collegial panels.[10] First, collegial panels with a "head judge + assistant judge + lay assessor" configuration consisted of precisely these three types of decision-makers. Second, a "collegial panel with lay assessor(s), no assistant judges" consisted of one head judge plus either one associate judge and one lay assessor or two lay assessors. Even when head judges of such collegial panels held

---

[10] Figure 5.1 excludes collegial panels consisting of more than three decision-makers because they were practically nonexistent. By cross-checking the names of head judges against the names of associate judges and assistant judges in other court decisions, we could infer the regular titles of some head judges. Many head judges in my samples of court decisions, however, appear solely in this role, suggesting that the role of head judge was, at least for some judges, "a permanent certified executive post" (Li 2010:110; also see Kinkel 2015:977 and Zheng, Ai, and Liu 2017: 179 on this point). Furthermore, judges who appear in some court decisions as head judges of collegial panels alternated between the various titles of assistant judge, associate judge, and head judge in other court decisions. Owing to these sources of uncertainty about the "real" titles of head judges, I preserved the titles of decision-makers as they appear in the published court decisions.

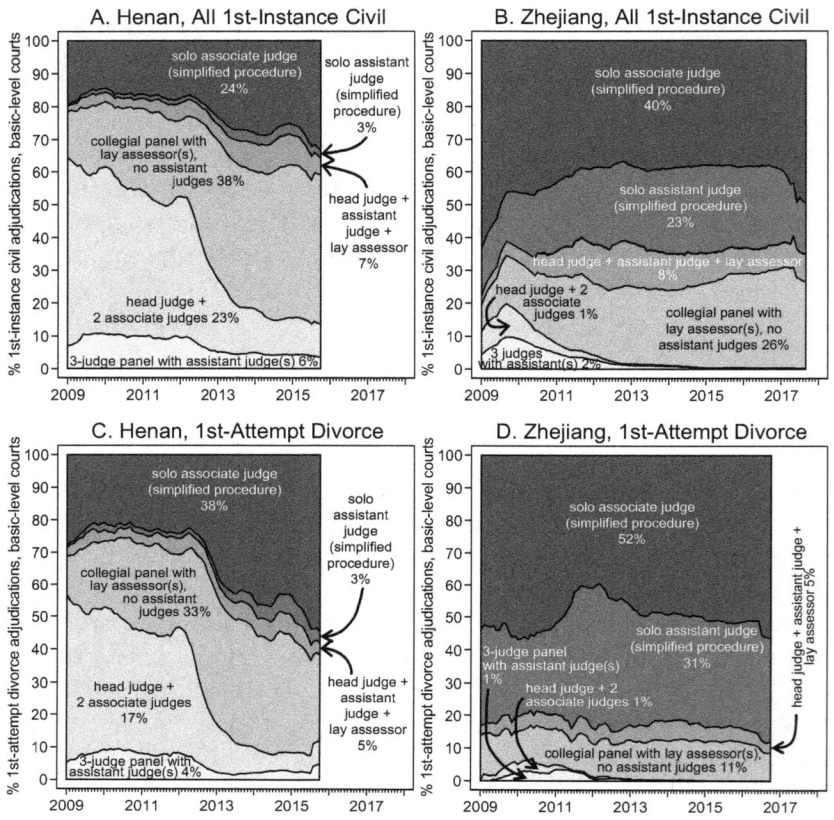

Figure 5.1 Composition of decision-makers assigned (and procedures applied) to civil cases
Source: Author's calculations from Henan and Zhejiang provincial high courts' online decisions.
Note: Panel A, n = 386,407; Panel B, n = 1,257,215; Panel C, n = 56,894; Panel D, n = 50,298. The sums of components do not always equal 100% due to rounding error. Smoothed with moving averages.

the regular title of assistant judge, which was relatively unusual, they were nonetheless vested with the full authority of a head judge, albeit temporarily. The same applies to head judges of, third, collegial panels composed of "head judge + 2 associate judges." Fourth, a "3-judge panel with assistant judge(s)" consisted of a head judge plus either one associate judge and one assistant judge or two assistant judges.

Figure 5.1 showcases the stark contrast between Henan and Zhejiang in the timing and intensity of their coping strategies. It reveals Zhejiang as an early and enthusiastic adopter of all three innovative responses to its unusually clogged courts and Henan as a more limited adopter only after innovative responses were sanctioned from above. First, compared to courts in Henan, courts in Zhejiang relied far more heavily on assistant judges as an informal coping strategy. In Henan, 3% of all first-instance civil adjudications were handled by solo assistant judges, a tiny fraction of Zhejiang's 23% (Panels A and B, respectively). In Henan, 15% of all first-instance civil adjudications were handled by either solo judges or collegial panels that included at least one assistant judge, less than half of Zhejiang's 33%.[11] Considering only simplified procedure cases, 10% were handled by assistant judges in Henan, less than a third of Zhejiang's 36% (Panels A and B, respectively).[12] Considering only ordinary procedure cases, assistant judges participated in 17% in Henan and 27% in Zhejiang (Panels A and B, respectively).[13] Among collegial panels with at least one assistant judge (i.e., within the category of "3-judge panel with assistant judge"), those in Henan were far less likely than those in Zhejiang to have two assistant judges (23% and 34% in Panels A and B, respectively). The foregoing differences between the two samples extend to first-attempt divorce trials (Panels C and D).

In order to put assistant judges to work on so many trials, courts in Zhejiang appointed and deputized considerably more assistant judges than courts in Henan did. I counted all unique names within each title of decision-maker (head judge, associate judge, assistant judge, and lay assessor) and within each court. They total about 32,000 in each provincial sample of first-instance civil adjudications. Of all unique names counted in this way in the Henan and Zhejiang samples, about 2,700 (9%) and 5,000 (15%) respectively, belong to assistant judges. Using this same crude method of counting unique judges, the ratio of associate judges to assistant judges in Zhejiang was less than half of that in Henan: associate judges outnumbered assistant judges in Henan and Zhejiang by ratios of 4.2:1 and 1.6:1, respectively.[14]

[11] In Henan (Panel A), all layers containing assistant judges (2.5%, 6.7%, and 6.0%) sum to 15.2%. In Zhejiang, (Panel B), all layers containing assistant judges (22.9%, 1.6%, and 8.3%) sum to 32.8%.
[12] In Henan (Panel A), 2.5% out of 26.3% (2.5% + 23.8% = 26.3%) represents 9.5%. In Zhejiang (Panel B), 22.9% out of 63.3% (22.9% + 40.4% = 63.3%) represents 36.2%.
[13] In Henan (Panel A), 12.7% (6.7% + 6.0%) out of 73.7% (6.7% + 38.3% + 22.7% + 6.0%) represents 17.2%. In Zhejiang (Panel B), 9.9% (8.3% + 1.6%) out of 36.6% (8.3% + 25.6% + 1.1% + 1.6%) represents 27.0%.
[14] According to data on the nearly 5,000 associate and assistant judges in Zhejiang in 2013, the ratio of associates to assistants was 1.9:1. By contrast, among all 308 associate and assistant

Second, and turning to formal coping strategies, Zhejiang's courts were similarly ahead of the curve in terms of their reliance on solo judges and the simplified procedure. We can easily see from the top two layers of all four panels in Figure 5.1 that solo judging was far more prevalent in Zhejiang than in Henan. Among first-instance civil adjudications, Henan's simplified procedure utilization rate (26%, Panel A) was less than half of Zhejiang's (63%, Panel B).[15] The magnitude of this gap persisted in first-attempt divorce adjudications (41% and 83% in Panels C and D, respectively).

As we can see in Panel A of Figure 5.1, Henan's courts followed suit by boosting their simplified procedure utilization rates, but only in 2013 after the amended Civil Procedure Law took effect. Between 2009 and 2012, the share of first-instance civil adjudications tried by solo judges increased modestly from 16% to 20%. Then, in 2013, it shot up to 30%, where it essentially plateaued (30% in 2014 and 33% in 2015). The same basic pattern emerges from first-attempt divorce adjudications, in which the simplified procedure utilization rate increased modestly from 23% to 27% between 2009 and 2012 before spiking to 46% in 2013, after which it continued to climb albeit at a slower rate to 50% in 2014 and 55% in 2015 (Panel C).

Third, lay assessor participation was more than twice as prevalent in Zhejiang than in Henan. In 2010, the proportion of all first-instance civil trials conducted by collegial panels composed of at least one lay assessor was 32% in my Henan sample (Panel A) and 67% in my Zhejiang sample (Panel B). By 2013, lay assessor participation had increased to 71% and 96% in each respective sample. By 2015, these estimates had increased to 78% and 99% in the two respective samples. In the three years spanning 2015 and 2017, practically every collegial panel that tried a first-instance civil case in my Zhejiang sample contained at least one lay assessor (Panel B). The same was true for first-attempt divorce cases (Panel D).

In addition to being more likely to contain *any* lay assessors, Zhejiang's collegial panels were also far more likely than Henan's to contain *two* lay assessors. Among all first-instance civil adjudications in my samples, the proportion of collegial panels with two lay assessors

judges in all courts in a "medium-size city" in Anhui Province, which, as a less developed interior province, more closely resembles Henan, the ratio of associates to assistants was 5.1:1 in 2014 (Zheng, Ai, and Liu 2017:180–81).

[15] In Henan, 23.8% (solo associate judge) + 2.5% (solo assistant judge) = 26.3%. In Zhejiang, 40.4% (solo associate judge) + 22.9% (solo assistant judge) = 63.3%.

in Henan (15%) was only about one-quarter of that in Zhejiang (59%). Within the category of "collegial panel with lay assessor(s), no assistant judges" depicted in Figure 5.1, the proportion of trials involving two lay assessors was 29% and 84% in the two respective samples. In my Henan and Zhejiang samples, the average number of lay assessors on collegial panels trying first-instance civil cases was 0.76 and 1.52, respectively. All of the preceding patterns extend to first-attempt divorce trials.

As a consequence of these patterns, the three-judge collegial panel became greatly diminished in Henan and, practically speaking, disappeared entirely in Zhejiang. In Henan, between 2009 and 2015, the proportion of first-instance civil adjudications in my sample handled by collegial panels composed of three judges – any combination of assistant and associate judges, as represented by the bottom two layers of each panel in Figure 5.1 – declined from 60% to 15%. This decline coincided with a commensurately dramatic increase in solo judging and lay assessor participation discussed earlier. In Zhejiang, the three-judge collegial panel was already a rarity in 2009, accounting for only 19% of first-instance civil adjudications in my sample. By 2014, it handled fewer than 1% – and by 2017 only 0.4% – of such cases in my sample as lay assessor participation in collegial panels became universal. As we can also see from the second-to-bottom layer of each panel in Figure 5.1, collegial panels composed of three associate judges went the way of the dodo bird in Zhejiang (Panels B and D) and were on the road to extinction in Henan, where they declined from 49% to 11% of all first-instance civil adjudications (Panel A) and from 44% to 5% in first-attempt divorce adjudications (Panel C) between 2009 and 2015.

By comparing the two sets of panels for each province in Figure 5.1, we can easily see that all three innovative responses were more prevalent among first-attempt divorce cases than in the larger category of first-instance civil cases of which they were a part. Courts treated divorce cases as relatively simple and unimportant, as less worthy of judicial resources than other kinds of civil disputes, and as an opportunity to put a dent in their dockets.

SUMMARY AND CONCLUSIONS

In this chapter I demonstrated that civil justice became increasingly perfunctory as a response to swelling caseloads. The SPC has been reluctant to expand the ranks of judges. As the volume of litigation mushroomed, the population of frontline judges handling cases remained stable and even declined after a judge quota reform imposed a hard cap on the number of judges a court could appoint. Aggravating the challenge of appointing judges in sufficient numbers has been the challenge of retaining judges. Insofar as judges could not be recruited in greater numbers and court cases multiplied relentlessly, judicial efficiency gains became the only way out of the problem of "many cases, few judges."

Desperate times called for desperate measures. Chinese judges are known for their pragmatism (Ng and He 2017a; T. Zhang 2012). Like overworked Russian justices of the peace (Hendley 2017:146–54) and US federal court judges (Robel 1990), Chinese judges have developed coping strategies to close cases and clear their dockets. They delegated trial work to assistant judges and lay assessors; they dispensed with the three-judge collegial panel and tried cases by collegial panels containing lay assessors or by solo judges. The vanishing three-judge panel was the confluence of informal coping strategies from below and formal policy signals from above. Some court officials have advocated for solo judges' application of the ordinary procedure (K. Chen 2019:110), which would likely be the final nail in the coffin of the three-judge collegial panel.

The efficiency gains for courts and judges have come at the expense of due process for litigants, particularly female litigants. In Chapter 6, I will show that justice became even more perfunctory in divorce litigation. China's clogged courts innovated not only by deputizing assistant judges, expanding the scope of the simplified procedure, and increasing lay assessor participation but also by clamping down on divorce. Doing so simultaneously helped judges satisfy additional imperatives: namely, to support higher-level political priorities and to minimize their own professional liability. The remainder of this book demonstrates that divorces have become collateral damage of courts' crushing dockets and that vulnerable women have in turn become collateral damage of the divorce twofer.

CHAPTER SIX

TRACING THE ORIGINS OF THE DIVORCE TWOFER TO HEAVY CASELOADS

The caseload pressure discussed in Chapter 5 weighs heavily in China's judicial clampdown on divorce. As a docket-shrinking machine, the divorce twofer has been embraced with particular vigor in regions with the heaviest dockets, as others have noted: "Under circumstances of 'many cases, few judges,' divorces vastly increased judges' workload and put stress on judicial resources. As they faced the enormous pressure of their dockets, many judges did their utmost to alleviate their backlogged cases, which precipitated the emergence of the 'two trial' [二次诉讼] norm" (He 2019:92; also see Liu 2012:84).

Thus far I have identified and summarized several explanations for the divorce twofer: limited judicial resources relative to caseloads, political ideology, performance evaluation criteria, and safety concerns. To empirically test the extent to which these endogenous institutional norms and pressures account for the decoupling of judicial practices from formal laws in China's divorce courts would require information on variation in both the explanation and the outcome. For example, evidence that variation in political ideology (the explanation) maps onto variation in rates at which courts granted divorce petitions (the outcome) would constitute empirical support for my argument. Variation could be temporal (over time) or geographical (over subnational units, such as provinces or courts). Even if we were to find, however, that changes over time in the character and strength of political ideology coincide with changes in judicial behavior, or that geographical variation in political ideology corresponds with variation in judicial behavior, such evidence might be only circumstantial. After all, many things change over time and vary by region. Further compounding the empirical challenge, measuring variation in political ideology, judicial performance evaluation systems, and judges' perceived safety threats from potentially violent divorce litigants would be difficult if not impossible.

By contrast, enough information on judges and their caseloads is available to assess the influence of "many cases, few judges" on the divorce twofer. This chapter provides empirical support for my paradoxical argument that the divorce twofer ultimately saves time and effort – at least for judges.

Routinizing six-month cooling-off periods on first attempts and granting divorces on second attempts (He 2009) confers multiple judicial benefits. First, the one-judge simplified civil procedure used to deny petitions consumes minimal human resources. Second, swiftly denying divorce petitions conserves time for other, more time-consuming types of cases that (unlike divorce) have a limit of one first-instance trial. Third, few petitioners returned to court after the statutory waiting period. Finally, judges devoted less time and wrote shorter decisions when they denied divorces than when they granted divorces or tried other types of cases.

The last section of this chapter shows that adjudicated denials were not the only way judges made cases disappear. Cases also disappeared when plaintiffs withdrew their petitions.

The cost of courts' imperative to maximize judicial efficiency has been disproportionately borne by women. Divorce litigation has been a casualty of clogged courts, and women in turn have been casualties of divorce litigation. We will see in this chapter that courts have sacrificed divorce cases in pursuit of judicial efficiency. We will also see that women's lawful rights and interests have been disproportionately sacrificed at the altar of efficiency by virtue of their overrepresentation among plaintiffs filing for divorce and their relatively high risk of facing pressure to withdraw their petitions.

In media narratives and scholarly accounts, the judicial clampdown on divorce reflects growing alarm on the part of China's leaders about rapidly rising divorce rates and courts' responsiveness to ideological calls for family harmony and marital preservation (Cao 2018; Kuo 2018; Shi 2020; Xinhua 2019). To be sure, China's ideological opposition to divorce has deep roots (Chapters 2 and 3). The empirical findings I present in this chapter, however, suggest the divorce twofer was initially driven by "many cases, few judges" as early as – and possibly earlier than – the late 1990s and early 2000s. The 18th National Congress of the Chinese Communist Party in 2012 saw Xi Jinping reintroduce a familiar political ideology promoting socialist family values (Chapter 3), which has further encouraged and provided convenient cover for China's judicial clampdown on divorce.

I have three primary tasks in this chapter. First, I provide evidence that the divorce twofer is part of courts' repertoire of coping strategies. Second, I demonstrate how the divorce twofer has helped judges clear their dockets. Third, I show that the divorce twofer is not limited to adjudicated denials of first-attempt petitions, but extends to petition withdrawals. Both methods of swiftly closing divorce cases have disproportionately targeted female plaintiffs.

THE DIVORCE TWOFER IS ANOTHER INNOVATIVE RESPONSE TO CLOGGED COURTS

China's judicial clampdown on divorce unfolded rapidly. The solid line in Panel A of Figure 6.1 shows that, between 1990 and 2006, the rate at which divorce petitions were denied in first-instance divorce adjudications was essentially flat at around 30% (that is, 70% of divorce petitions were granted). Denial rates climbed steeply after 2006, more than doubling to 62% by 2018.[1] The dashed line in Panel A represents divorce rates, which had begun climbing in 2003, when the Marriage Registration Regulations were amended to lower barriers to uncontested divorce (Chapter 1). As we can see, divorce adjudication outcomes almost perfectly tracked divorce rates. Panel B reconfigures the identical information in a couple of ways. First, rather than depicting the clampdown on divorce in terms of petition denial rates, it shows rates at which divorce petitions were granted. Second, it transforms the two time-series lines in Panel A into a scatterplot. Both panels show that, in the 13 years between 1990 and 2002, China's crude

---

[1] Although divorce outcomes in Panel A are limited to adjudications, the same upward trend would have emerged had I used official government data to depict *all* denied divorce petitions (petitions denied by both adjudication and mediation) plus divorce petitions subsequently withdrawn by plaintiffs as a proportion of *all* divorce petitions received by courts. Between 2007 and 2018, the proportion of *all* divorce petitions received by courts that did not result in divorce increased from 38% to 53% in China as a whole, from 40% to 61% in Henan, and from 47% to 50% in Zhejiang (Ministry of Civil Affairs of China, various years). The correlation between the overall rate at which *all* divorce petitions resulted in marital preservation and the rate at which *adjudicated* divorce petitions were denied was .94 between 1988 and 2018. As I discussed in Chapter 4, owing to a systematic underrepresentation of *mediations* and *withdrawals* in online collections of Chinese court decisions, online court decisions are suitable for studying *adjudicated* outcomes only.

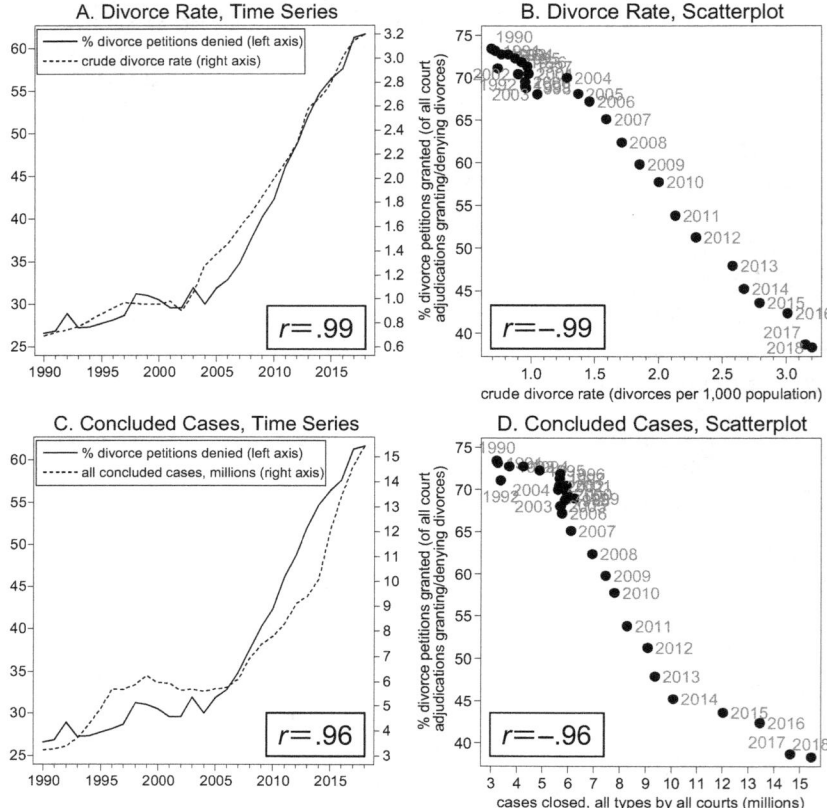

Figure 6.1 Time-series correlations of decisions to deny/grant divorce petitions
Source: Ministry of Civil Affairs of China, various years; SPC 2018; SPC statistical reports (http://gongbao.court.gov.cn/ArticleList.html?serial_no=sftj); CLY, various years.

Note: Divorce outcomes are limited to first-instance adjudicated decisions to grant or deny divorce petitions; mediations and withdrawals are excluded. The same patterns persist when the rate at which *adjudicated* petitions were denied is replaced with the rate at which *all* petitions were denied (i.e., including mediation and withdrawals).

divorce rate grew from 0.69 to 0.90 (per 1,000 population). Then, in the 16 years between 2003 and 2018, China's crude divorce rate tripled from 1.05 to 3.20. Given the near-perfect correlation between the two trends, attributing the judicial clampdown on divorce to rising divorce rates has certainly been tempting. Indeed, media reports (Cao 2018; Kuo 2018; Xinhua 2019) and published scholarship (Li 2015) alike suggest that growing alarm on the part of political leaders about rising divorce rates ultimately gave rise to the domestic relations trial reforms and its supporting ideological discourse concerning marital stability, household harmony, and civilized families (Chapter 3).

China's clogged courts were not a consequence of its rapidly rising divorce rates, which in turn were not the driving force behind the divorce twofer. The association between courts' clampdown on divorce and divorce rates is, at a minimum, indirect and, at most, a causal mirage. As we know from Chapter 2, only a small fraction of all divorces happen in court. Using official divorce statistics, we can easily disaggregate China's *total* crude divorce rate into two components: (1) a *court* crude divorce rate calculated from contested divorce disputes processed by courts and (2) a *Civil Affairs* crude divorce rate calculated from uncontested, voluntary, mutual-consent divorces processed by the Civil Affairs Administration (Chapter 1). China's total crude divorce rate has been driven exclusively by Civil Affairs divorces. The court divorce rate remained essentially flat in the 20 years between 1999 and 2018 at about 0.5 (per 1,000 population). The Civil Affairs divorce rate, however, grew from 0.4 to 2.7 over the same time period (Ministry of Civil Affairs of China, various years). Between 2004 and 2018, after the amendment of the Marriage Registration Regulations in 2003, only 22% of all divorces in China were processed by courts (Ministry of Civil Affairs of China, various years).[2]

The volume of divorce cases in China's courts has remained remarkably stable over time, and has thus shrunk as a share of all civil cases. In the 20 years between 1999 and 2018, the overall volume of concluded first-instance civil cases grew by 146% and the number of divorces granted by the Civil Affairs Administration grew by 698%. By contrast, in the same time period, the number of first-instance divorce cases concluded by courts grew by only 15%. As a consequence, concluded first-instance divorce cases as a share of all concluded civil cases shrank from 24% to 11% in the same time period (CLY, various years; Ministry of Civil Affairs of China, various years). As we saw in Chapter 3, the 2020 Civil Code shifted the cooling-off period from courts to the Civil Affairs Administration, possibly reflecting official recognition of a mismatch between where most divorces occur and where the clampdown on divorce has been applied.

---

[2] The patterns in Panels A and B of Figure 6.1 would remain identical if I were to replace total crude divorce rates with Civil Affairs crude divorce rates. However, if I were to replace total crude divorce rates with court crude divorce rates, the correlation would collapse (to $r = .26$ in Panel A and $r = -.26$ in Panel B).

Although divorce cases have not contributed to the *problem* of clogged courts, judges have exploited them as a *solution* for clogged courts. Courts have clamped down on divorce as a convenient means of lightening their dockets clogged by other kinds of cases, and have invoked ideological discourse about marital preservation to justify doing so (Chapter 7). If courts have been under ideological pressure to deny divorce petitions, judges in the most clogged courts have welcomed it the most. Denying a divorce petition takes little time, frees up judicial resources for cases that cannot be so easily swept aside, and is easily justified by China's enduring ideological call to "oppose frivolous divorce" and to "prevent the abuse of the freedom of divorce" (Chapters 2 and 3). In the typical ideological language of judges, they deny first-attempt divorce petitions to "prevent frivolous divorces that hot-headed couples will end up regretting" and because "a momentary argument or brief conflict may lead couples to rush to court blindly and impulsively, a court that carelessly grants divorces might summarily deny couples the opportunity to repair their marriages" (Jiang and Zhu 2014:86).

Panels A and B in Figure 6.1 therefore exemplify correlation without causation. Courts clamped down on divorce not because of rising divorce rates but rather because of rising caseloads, to which, as we just saw, divorce litigation contributed relatively little. Panels C and D in Figure 6.1 show that the correlation between first-instance adjudicated divorce outcomes and court caseloads is likewise almost perfect. Average caseload per judge would be an even better measure but is not consistently available during the period of analysis. Total caseloads, however, is a reasonable proxy measure for judges' workload given how stable the population of judges was (at about 200,000) over this time period.

Panel C shows that both the rate at which divorce petitions were denied and the volume of concluded cases began their rapid and sustained ascent after 2006. Once again, the identical trends are depicted in Panel D as a scatterplot after inverting divorce adjudication outcomes into rates at which divorce petitions were granted. Both panels show that the judicial clampdown on divorce noticeably intensified at the same time that caseloads grew particularly rapidly following the 2007 litigation fee reform (Chapter 5). Another conspicuous jump in caseloads corresponds with the 2015 case filing registration reform (Chapter 5).

Figure 6.1 depicts variation over time. I have argued so far that the association it shows between divorce rates and adjudicated divorce outcomes (Panels A and B) is causally spurious and that caseloads are a better explanation of the judicial clampdown on divorce (Panels C and D). Evidence from subnational variation strongly supports my central argument that the origins of China's divorce twofer can be traced back to "many cases, few judges." Courts that clamped down the hardest on divorce were precisely those with the heaviest dockets. Let us begin with a two-province comparison of Henan and Zhejiang before turning to analyses of variation among all 31 provincial-level units and 150 basic-level courts within Henan and Zhejiang.

We already know from Chapter 5 that judges' average caseloads were far heavier in Zhejiang than in Henan. Figure 6.2 shows that the judicial clampdown on divorce was also earlier and stronger in Zhejiang than in Henan. We can see in Panel A that Henan's clampdown closely tracked the national trend. In Henan, rates at which first-instance divorce adjudications resulted in granted divorces remained stable at around 74% between 1999 and 2006, modestly higher than the national average. Then, just as we saw in Figure 6.1, the clampdown on adjudicated divorce began in 2007. Until recently, Zhejiang's clampdown was one of the most extreme in China. Henan's clampdown intensified rapidly after 2011 and caught up to – and eventually surpassed – Zhejiang's. Average rates at which Henan's courts granted divorces dipped below the national average in 2012 and fell below Zhejiang's in 2016. By 2018, Henan was among the least divorce-friendly provinces in China in terms of adjudicated outcomes. By contrast, Zhejiang's courts had been unfriendly to divorce plaintiffs for at least a couple of decades. Zhejiang's clampdown had already been underway from the earliest point at which data are available. Zhejiang's courts granted divorces in only 57% of first-instance adjudications in 1999, and bottomed out at 36% in 2013. To put this in more concrete terms, of all plaintiffs whose divorce petitions were adjudicated between 2007 and 2018, the proportion who left court still married increased from 35% to 62% in China as a whole, from 32% to 69% in Henan, and from 56% to 61% in Zhejiang.

By benchmarking my sample of divorce adjudications posted online against all divorce adjudications, Figure 6.2 also lends further confidence to the representativeness of my two provincial samples (see Chapter 4). Panel B shows that granted divorces as a proportion of all adjudicated divorce petitions from 2013 to 2015 in my Henan sample (40%) closely approaches the proportion of granted divorces in the

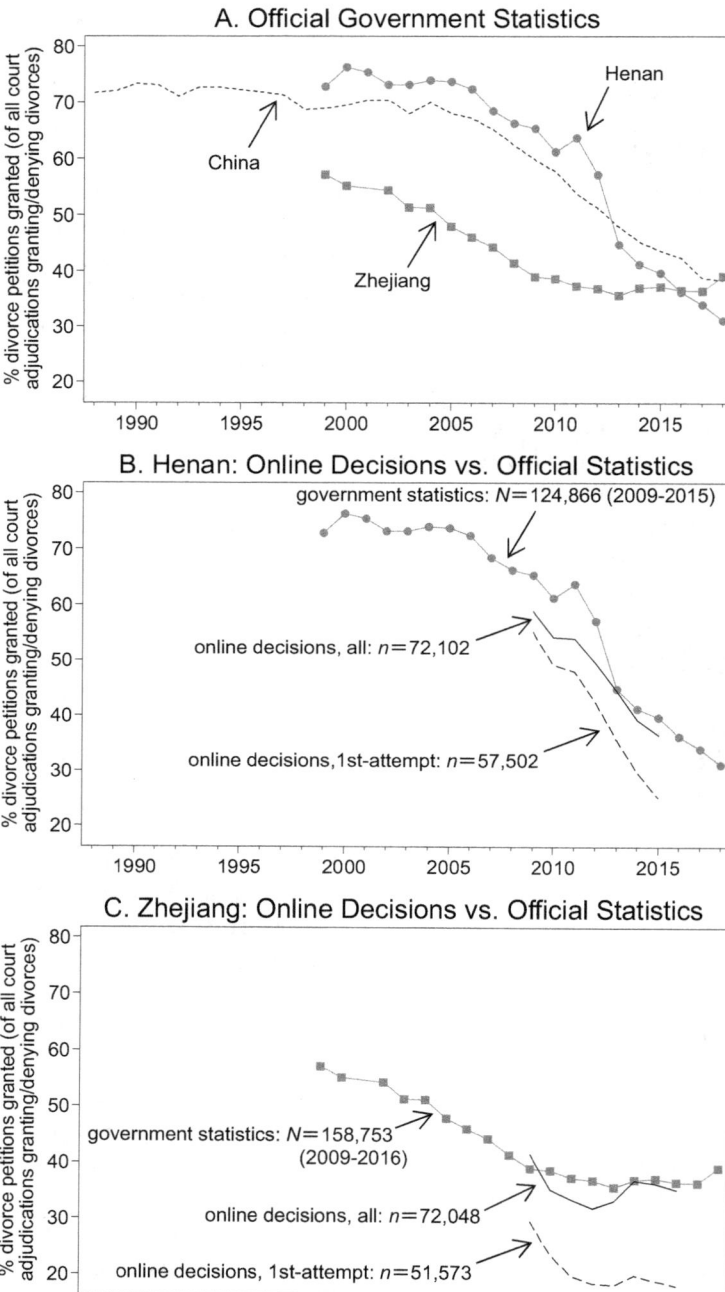

Figure 6.2 Proportion of divorce petitions (%) granted

Source: Ministry of Civil Affairs of China, various years; author's calculations from Henan and Zhejiang provincial high courts' online decisions.

Note: Data are limited to first-instance adjudicated decisions to grant or deny divorce petitions; mediations and withdrawals are excluded. Zhejiang's 2001 data point is omitted because it is undoubtedly erroneous. Data disaggregated by province are unavailable for years prior to 1999.

true population of divorce adjudications reported by the Ministry of Civil Affairs (41%). These three years account for 64% of all divorce adjudications in my Henan sample. Likewise, Panel C shows that the proportion of adjudicated divorce petitions approved by courts from 2014 to 2016 in my Zhejiang sample (36%) is similarly close to the approval rate in official sources (37%). These three years account for 58% of all divorce adjudications in my Zhejiang sample.

Finally, Panels B and C show that the clampdown disproportionately targeted first-attempt divorces – the key defining characteristic of the divorce twofer. Prospects for successfully divorcing on the first attempt (depicted by dashed lines) were relatively unlikely. Indeed, divorcing on the first try was increasingly an exercise in futility: among adjudicated first-attempt divorce petitions, only 25% were granted in Henan in 2015 (Panel B) and only 18% were granted in Zhejiang in 2016 (Panel C).

So far, the contrast I have shown between Henan and Zhejiang's courts both in the weight of their caseloads and in the extent of their clampdown on divorce supports the core argument of this chapter, namely that the latter is a consequence the former. The view from these two provinces, of course, offers only a limited vantage point. In the remainder of this section, I analyze more rigorously the effect of caseloads on the judicial clampdown on divorce at different levels of subnational variation. I zoom out and broaden the field of view to encompass all of China's 31 provincial-level units. I also zoom in to a view of 150 basic-level courts within Henan and Zhejiang. Subnational units at both levels afford a clear and consistent view of the strong relationship between judges' routine practice of denying first-attempt divorce petitions and the weight of their caseloads. We will see that the gaps between the two provinces in rates at which divorce petitions were granted are explained away by corresponding differences in average caseloads per judge.

In both sets of analyses of subnational variation, the volume of court cases was a function of general population size and economic conditions. The volume of court cases, in turn, influenced the size of the population of judges, albeit only secondarily. The population of judges was, above all, a function of the general population. By definition, the population of judges and the volume of court cases determined judges' average annual caseloads (cases per judge). Finally, judges' annual average caseload was strongly associated with judges' routine denial of first-attempt divorce petitions. In other words, the intensity of the judicial clampdown on divorce was a function of the weight of judges' average caseload, which in turn was a function of the number of judges and the number of court cases, which in turn were functions of population size and economic conditions. I will now present this sequence of empirical findings in greater detail.

Caseloads Were Strongly Associated with Both Population and Economic Conditions

Table 6.1 contains regression models predicting the annual volume of court cases at the provincial and court levels.[3] At the provincial level, Model 1 shows that Zhejiang closed 309,000 more cases than Henan did in 2011. At the court level, Model 1 shows that Zhejiang's courts on average closed almost 8,000 more cases than Henan's courts did. Model 2 introduces per capita GDP. When per capita GDP is held constant in Model 2, the gap between Zhejiang and Henan shrinks, suggesting that Zhejiang's heavier caseloads were a consequence of its more dynamic economic conditions (and that Henan's lighter caseloads were a consequence of its weaker economic conditions). Model 3 introduces population size. The huge boost it gives to R^2 values suggests that population is the more important determinant of caseload size. Its introduction also reopens the gap between Zhejiang and Henan (albeit only slightly in the court-level model). Given that Zhejiang's population is considerably smaller than Henan's, Model 3 tells us that the gap in case volumes between the two provinces would have been even greater if their populations had been the same size.[4] In all models, including separate ones for courts in Henan and Zhejiang (Models 4 and 5, respectively), both per capita GDP and population size significantly contributed to case volumes. Doubling per capita GDP (comparable to the difference between the two provinces) was associated with an increase of 157,435 cases at the provincial level and an increase of 2,073 cases at the court level.[5]

---

[3] Both sets of models include a dummy variable for Zhejiang. Because the omitted reference category in both sets of models is Henan, the coefficients for the Zhejiang dummy variables represent gaps between the two provinces. Owing to the small numbers of observations in the regression models, the magnitudes of the coefficients are as worthy of attention as their levels of statistical significance.

[4] When per capita GDP is omitted from Model 3, the gap between the two provinces becomes 630,000 cases at the provincial level and 8,450 cases at the court level.

[5] Because per capita GDP is log-transformed, the effect of a 100% increase in its value is interpreted as $227.13 \times \log(2) = 157.435$ (or 157,435 cases) in Model 3 at the provincial level and as $2.99 \times \log(2) = 2.073$ (or 2,073 cases) in Model 3 at the court level.

TABLE 6.1 Correlates of annual court case volume (1,000s of closed cases), unstandardized linear regression coefficients

	(1)	(2)	(3)	Henan (4)	Zhejiang (5)
Provinces, 2011					
Province					
Zhejiang (yes = 1)	309.14	122.75	455.85**		
Other (yes = 1) Cf.: Henan	−167.41	−222.21	203.17[+]		
Per capita GDP, logged		256.67*	227.13***		
Population, millions			7.94***		
Constant	515.97[+]	−2,118.28[+]	−2,560.53***		
R^2	.12	.29	.90		
N	31	31	31		
Courts, Henan and Zhejiang					
Zhejiang (yes = 1)	7.75***	5.97***	6.17***		
Per capita GDP, logged		2.29**	2.99***	1.85**	2.95***
Population, millions			13.46***	5.19***	15.87***
Constant	3.92***	−20.11*	−36.35***	−18.90**	−31.11***
R^2	.31	.37	.73	.57	.67
n	94	94	94	26	68

Source: See Chapter 4's "contextual and court-level variables" section; Henan Provincial Bureau of Statistics 2012; Zhejiang Provincial Bureau of Statistics 2015. *Note*: Provinces include autonomous regions and centrally administered cities (Beijing, Shanghai, Tianjin, and Chongqing). Court-level models are limited to basic-level courts. In court-level models, per capita GDP refers to 2014 values. Per capita GDP was not available for Wenzhou's Ouhai District in Zhejiang Province. In court-level models, closed cases refer to 2014 for Henan and to 2012–2014 for Zhejiang. See Chapter 4 for more information on measures. "Cf." denotes the omitted reference category.
[+] $P < .10$ * $P < .05$ ** $P < .01$ *** $P < .001$, two-tailed tests

These effects are unsurprising. More people means more litigation. More economic activity also means more litigation. First-instance civil cases have far outnumbered criminal and administrative cases, and have accounted for the vast majority of all cases in China's court system. Growth in the volume of civil cases has been driven by contract disputes in general and debt disputes in particular. In my collections of court decisions, contract disputes as a share of all first-instance cases were far more numerous in Zhejiang than in Henan (60% and 37%, respectively in 2014). Within the category of contract disputes, debt was by far the largest subcategory in both provincial collections.[6]

The Supply of Judges Was Only Weakly Associated with Caseloads
According to the SPC's 2002 Several Opinions Concerning Strengthening the Construction of the Profession of Judges, slots for judges in the state personnel system are supposed to be allocated "on the basis of a comprehensive consideration of China's circumstances, caseloads, land areas and population sizes of court jurisdictions, levels of economic development, and other factors" (Z. Tang 2014:45; Xu, Huang, and Lu 2015:133). This loose formula was reaffirmed in the SPC's 2004–2008 second five-year outline for court reform (Liu 2019:104) and added to the 2018 amended Organic Law of People's Courts (Article 46). In practice, however, judge quotas for courts have been determined primarily according to the number of people in their jurisdictions. To be sure, judge quotas have also been associated with caseloads, but largely because caseloads themselves have been associated with population size. Population size has been the primary determinant of the number of judges. For this reason, judges in China's more developed regions have been burdened with heavier per capita caseloads. Further compounding the problem, personnel slots for judges have been typically determined according to the officially registered population (户籍人口) and not according to the population of actual residents. Such a method punishes courts in more prosperous areas such as Zhejiang that receive migrants and rewards courts in less prosperous areas such as Henan that send migrants (Fan and Jin 2012:99).

Table 6.2 contains regression models predicting judge population. Model 1 shows that Zhejiang had 5,731 fewer judges than Henan at

---

[6] More details are provided in the supplementary online materials, available at https://decoupling-book.org/.

TABLE 6.2 Correlates of judge population, unstandardized linear regression coefficients

	(1)	(2)	(3)	Henan (4)	Zhejiang (5)
Provinces, 2011					
Province					
Zhejiang (yes = 1)	−5,731.00	−8,585.86**	−655.98		
Other (yes = 1)	−7,245.24*	−5,699.24**	−1,288.97		
Cf.: Henan					
Closed cases, 1,000s		9.23***	−2.83		
Population, millions			126.00***		
Per capita GDP, logged			1,028.92		
Constant	13,231.00***	8,466.20***	−7,695.65		
R^2	.17	.67	.88		
N	31	31	31		
Courts, Henan and Zhejiang					
Zhejiang (yes = 1)	−5.65	−28.79***	−15.49**		
Closed cases, 1,000s		2.99***	1.60**	7.17*	1.87***
Population, millions			38.24***	33.50	27.18**
Per capita GDP, logged			−0.54	−6.61	−1.34
Constant	63.85***	52.15***	38.17	83.30	35.25
R^2	.01	.48	.60	.63	.65
n	94	94	94	26	68

Source: See Table 6.1.
Note: Provincial judge counts are not limited to frontline judges but include all judges. Court-level judge counts refer to frontline judges wherever available. Also see note under Table 6.1.
+ P < .10 * P < .05 ** P < .01 *** P < .001, two-tailed tests

the provincial level and that Zhejiang's courts averaged 5.65 fewer judges than Henan's courts did. Model 2 introduces the volume of closed cases, which appears to be positively and strongly associated with the population of judges. Controlling for – i.e., holding constant – the volume of closed cases also widens differences between Henan and Zhejiang in numbers of judges at both provincial and court levels. Because caseloads have been so much heavier in Zhejiang than in Henan at both provincial and court levels, the coefficients in Model 2 tell us that Henan's judges would have outnumbered Zhejiang's by an even greater margin had the volume of cases been the same in the two provinces. In Model 3, the effect of general population size wipes out all other effects at the provincial level and greatly shrinks them at the court level. Because, as we saw from the previous analysis, population size is a key determinant of case volume, the former explains away the effect of the latter at the provincial level and attenuates the effect of the latter at the court level. Among courts that were otherwise seemingly identical in terms of population and economic conditions, an increase of 1,000 cases was associated with an average increase of only 1.6 judges. Courts averaged about 4,000 cases in Henan and about 11,500 cases in Zhejiang. According to Model 4, a caseload increase of 1,000 (or about 25%) would have added only about seven judges in Henan. According to Model 5, a caseload increase of 3,000 (or about 25%) would have added only about six judges in Zhejiang. In short, large differences in caseloads were associated with only small differences in numbers of judges.

The models indicate that Henan's larger population was the main reason why it had more judges than Zhejiang even though Zhejiang closed 60% more cases than Henan (825,110 versus 515,966). At the provincial level, population was the key determinant of personnel slots for judges. Population growth of 1 million people was associated with an extra 126 judges (Model 3). Put another way, for a province to gain an additional 1,000 judges, it would have needed a population increase of 8 million. At the level of the court, an additional population of 1 million was associated with an additional 38 judges (Model 3). Within the two provinces, however, a population difference of 1 million between court jurisdictions was quite rare. For this reason, we should instead interpret the effect in terms of a population increase of half a million, which would have yielded an average of 19 more judges. This is a substantively large effect given that, in both provincial samples, courts averaged about 60 judges and that court jurisdictions averaged about 600,000 people. A population increase of this amount was associated with an additional 17 judges in Henan (Model 4) and 14 judges in Zhejiang (Model 5).

In short, the supply of judges has had little to do with demand for their services. Judges have been allocated mechanically primarily according to population size, without due consideration of variation in caseloads among provinces and court jurisdictions with similar populations. Figure 6.3 depicts the sheer extent of the correlation between the judge counts and population size at both provincial and court levels: .93 at the provincial level (Panel A) and .78 at the court level (Panel B). Consistent with the regression results, correlations between the number of judges and caseloads were weaker: .74 at the provincial level and .51 at the court level (scatterplots omitted).

Henan and Zhejiang in 2011 illustrate the primacy of population size. At the provincial level (Panel A), Henan had the most judges in China because it was so populous (ranked third) even though its volume of closed cases was somewhat less remarkable (ranked seventh).

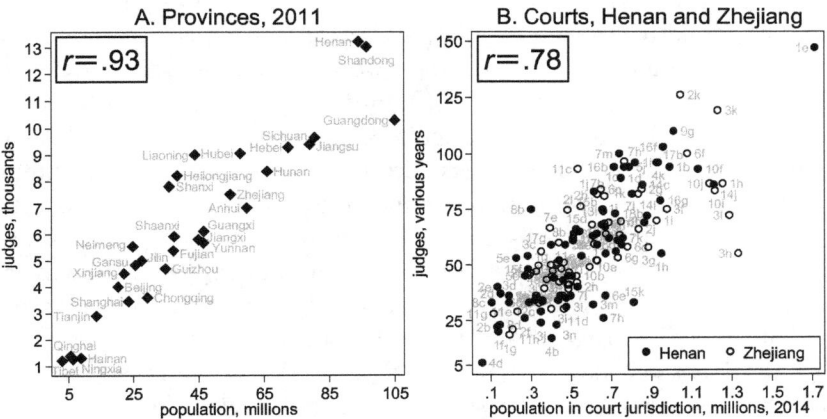

Figure 6.3 Association between judge population and general population
Source: Court work reports; Basic Level Legal Artisan 2016a, 2016b, 2016c; Henan Provincial Bureau of Statistics 2015; Zhejiang Provincial Bureau of Statistics 2015; author's calculations from Henan and Zhejiang provincial high courts' online decisions.
Note: Panel A, N = 31 provinces. Panel B, n = 150 basic-level courts (80 in Henan and 70 in Zhejiang). In Panel B, Henan r = .81, Zhejiang r = .74. On sources of numbers of judges, see Chapter 4. Court codes in Panel B are listed with their corresponding court names in supplementary online material at https://decoupling-book.org/. Panel B excludes courts of special jurisdiction and economic and technological development district courts.

Meanwhile, Zhejiang was in the middle of the pack in terms of judge counts (ranked 12th) because it was also in the middle of the pack in terms of population size (ranked tenth) even though its volume of closed cases was somewhat more remarkable (ranked fourth). Similarly, Sichuan had slightly more judges than Jiangsu because its population was slightly larger, even though Jiangsu's courts closed far more cases than Sichuan's. Finally, Chongqing had more judges than Shanghai because its population was larger even though Shanghai's courts closed far more cases than Chongqing's.

These provincial patterns extend to the court level (Panel B). Consider one of the busiest courts in Henan, Zhengzhou's Erqi District People's Court (1c). Other courts in Henan that closed fewer cases had more judges simply because they had larger populations.[7] Consider the busiest court in Zhejiang, Hangzhou's Xiaoshan District People's Court (1h), which also happened to be a relatively populous court jurisdiction. Other courts in Zhejiang with considerably lighter dockets nonetheless had similar numbers of judges because they were similarly populous.[8]

In areas such as Erqi and Xiaoshan with disproportionately heavy caseloads relative to their population sizes, an imbalance between cases and judges resulted in heavy average workloads. Judge-level caseloads by definition are determined by the number of judges and the number of cases. They are simply calculated as the number of closed cases divided by the number of judges. Critics have advocated for a system that better calibrates the supply of judges to the actual work of courts (Zhang 2016b:60). Across contexts of similar population size, similar numbers of judges despite wild variation and explosive growth in cases is the crux of the "many cases, few judges" problem. A widening imbalance between cases and judges has resulted in far heavier average caseloads per judge in Zhejiang than in Henan. Among all basic-level courts with available data, the average caseload per judge was 65 in Henan (26 courts) and 200 in Zhejiang (70 courts). The average volume of closed cases in Henan's basic-level courts (3,582 cases

---

[7] Examples of basic-level courts in Henan that had more judges than Erqi's because of the larger populations residing in their jurisdictions even though they closed fewer cases include Zhengzhou's Gongyi Municipal People's Court (1i), Zhoukou's Shenqiu County People's Court (16f), and Zhumadian's Yicheng District People's Court (17b).

[8] Examples of basic-level courts in Zhejiang whose numbers of judges were similar to Xiaoshan's because of their similarly large populations even though they closed far fewer cases include Municipal People's Courts in Ningbo's Cixi (2k), Wenzhou's Rui'an (3k), Shaoxing's Zhuji (6f), and Taizhou's Wenlin (10i) and Linhai (10j).

among 57 courts with available data in 2014) was only about one-third the average annual volume of closed cases in Zhejiang (10,334 cases among 87 courts with available data in 2012–2014). And yet, among the 150 basic-level courts depicted in Figure 6.3, the average number of judges per court was nearly identical in Henan and Zhejiang (57.4 and 57.8, respectively) because the average population in their jurisdictions was also nearly identical (575,754 and 592,746, respectively).[9] Numbers of judges and volumes of closed cases for all courts depicted in Panel B are available with the supplementary online material at https://decoupling-book.org/.

Table 6.3 contains models that are tautological insofar as the outcome (cases per judge) is defined by two regressors (closed cases and judge counts). The key point of Table 6.3 is to demonstrate that differences between Henan and Zhejiang in average cases per judge are attributable to differences in caseloads between the two provinces. At the provincial level, Model 1 shows that judges in Zhejiang handled an average of 71 more cases than judges in Henan did in 2011. At the court level, Model 1 shows the difference to be 132 a few years later. The introduction of judge counts in Model 2 did not change anything: on its own, the number of judges was unrelated to cases per judge and did not explain away any of the gaps between Henan and Zhejiang at either the provincial level or the court level. The insignificance – and even irrelevance – of judge counts is unsurprising given that they varied so little between areas with similar populations. Cases per judge were driven not by judge counts but rather by caseloads. When per capita GDP and population size – which we know from Table 6.1 are key determinants of caseloads – are introduced in Model 3, the gap between Henan and Zhejiang shrinks and the effect of judge count becomes statistically significantly negative. Among provinces and courts with seemingly identical populations and economic conditions, those with fewer judges have more cases per judge simply because per capita GDP and population size are proxies for caseloads. For the very same reason, the effect of per capita GDP shrinks dramatically and the effect of population disappears when caseloads are

---

[9] Crudely applying the rule of thumb that basic-level courts accounted for 80% of all judges yields an average of 72 judges per court in both provinces, which is practically identical to official figures of 72 in Henan and 73 in Zhejiang (Basic Level Legal Artisan 2016a, 2016b). Considering every basic-level court in the two provinces (with the exception of courts of special jurisdiction), 161 courts for Henan's 2015 population of 94.8 million and 91 courts for Zhejiang's 2015 population of 55.4 million means the average population size of a basic-level court jurisdiction was very similar in Henan and Zhejiang: 589,000 and 609,000, respectively.

TABLE 6.3 Correlates of cases per judge, unstandardized linear regression coefficients

	(1)	(2)	(3)	(4)	Henan (5)	Zhejiang (6)
Provinces, 2011						
Province						
Zhejiang (yes = 1)	71.00+	76.65+	31.33	−16.52		
Other (yes = 1)	17.77	24.91	2.94	−16.63		
Cf.: Henan						
Judges, 1,000s		.99		−7.45***		
Per capita GDP, logged			−9.21**	18.71*		
Population, millions			44.93***	0.09		
Closed cases, 1,000s			1.16***	0.11***		
Constant	39.00	25.95	−409.64***	−120.95		
R^2	.14	.15	.74	.85		
N	31	31	31	31		
Courts, Henan and Zhejiang						
Zhejiang (yes = 1)	132.47***	133.14***	94.59***	16.14+		
Judges		.12	−1.17***	−2.03***	−1.06***	−2.93***
Per capita GDP, logged			49.99***	17.94***	5.28	16.39**
Population, millions			137.23***	27.85	8.36	19.53
Closed cases, 1,000s				11.93***	13.02***	14.53***
Constant	65.00***	57.45**	−475.52***	−59.03	20.96	1.96
R^2	.50	.50	.71	.88	.88	.87
n	94	94	94	94	26	68

Source: See Table 6.1.

Note: Provincial judge counts used both as an independent variable and to calculate the dependent variable are not limited to frontline judges but include all judges. Court-level judge counts refer to frontline judges wherever available. Also see note under Table 6.1.

+ $P < .10$ * $P < .05$ ** $P < .01$ *** $P < .001$, two-tailed tests

added to Model 4.[10] At the same time, caseloads explain away the gap between Henan and Zhejiang in its entirety at the provincial level and almost entirely at the court level. Among provinces that were otherwise seemingly identical in terms of judge counts, population size, and economic conditions, a caseload increase of 300,000 cases (roughly the difference between Henan and Zhejiang in 2011) was associated with an average increase of 33 cases per judge (300 × .11 = 33; Model 4). Among courts that were otherwise seemingly identical in the same ways, an increase of 7,500 cases (roughly the average difference between courts in Henan and courts in Zhejiang included in the analysis) was associated with an average increase of 89 cases per judge (7.5 × 11.93 = 89; Model 4). The same patterns persisted in separate models for each province (Models 5 and 6). Next we will see that differences between Henan and Zhejiang in their use of the divorce twofer stemmed to a significant degree from differences in average caseloads per judge.

Judges' Tendency to Grant Divorces Was Negatively Associated with Their Caseloads

The final set of regression models presented in Table 6.4 strongly suggests that China's judicial clampdown on divorce was part of the mix of coping strategies courts adopted to deal with an acute imbalance between the supply of and demand for judges. Model 1 assesses the association between divorce rates and adjudicated divorce outcomes.[11] Although these were highly correlated over time at the national level (albeit only coincidentally, Figure 6.1), they were uncorrelated at the provincial level in 2011 (Table 6.4, Model 1). A change of 1 per-mille point in the crude divorce rate – a massive change given that the crude divorce rate was 2.1‰ in 2011 – was associated with a 1.1 percentage point increase in the rate at which courts granted divorce petitions. No subsequent model includes the provincial divorce rate because it remained irrelevant even when I did include it (details omitted). In short, regional variation in divorce rates does not map onto regional variation in the extent of the judicial clampdown on divorce.

---

[10] Whereas some scholars treat per capita GDP as a proxy for Chinese courts' bureaucratic capacity (Liebman et al. 2020; Tang and Liu 2019), the empirical patterns I report suggest precisely the opposite, namely that per capita GDP *weakens* courts' bureaucratic capacity insofar as it increases judges' average caseloads, in turn giving rise to the innovative responses documented in this and Chapter 5.

[11] Because divorce rates are not available at the level of the court jurisdiction, Model 1 is limited to the level of the province.

TABLE 6.4 Correlates of percentage of divorces granted (of adjudicated divorce petitions), unstandardized linear regression coefficients

	(1)	(2)	(3)	(4)	(5)	Henan (6)	Zhejiang (7)
Provinces, 2011							
Crude divorce rate (‰)	1.06						
Per capita GDP, logged		−16.95***		−15.71**	−4.71		
Province							
Zhejiang (yes = 1)			−26.40	−14.99	−4.46		
Other (yes = 1)			−5.12	−1.77	0.52		
Cf.: Henan							
Cases per judge, 100s					−26.07*		
Constant	55.75***	235.78***	63.72***	224.92***	122.23*		
R^2	.01	.33	.10	.36	.50		
N	31	31	31	31	31		
Courts, Henan and Zhejiang							
Per capita GDP, logged		−6.57***		−3.26+	−1.07	−2.81	0.04
Zhejiang (yes = 1)			−15.05***	−12.51***	−7.25+		
Cases per judge, 100s					−5.26*	−31.33+	−4.74*
Constant		98.92***	37.01***	71.23***	51.73***	86.88	30.89
R^2		.13	.23	.25	.29	.22	.10
n		94	94	94	94	26	68

Source: See Table 6.1. Court-level percentages of divorces granted (the outcome variable) at the court level are the author's calculations from Henan and Zhejiang provincial high courts' online decisions. For information about other measures, see Chapter 4.

Note: Crude divorce rate is not significant in any provincial-level model (details omitted). Divorce outcomes are limited to first-instance adjudicated decisions to grant or deny divorce petitions; mediations and withdrawals are excluded. In court-level models, divorce outcomes are limited to first-attempt adjudications. Official provincial data disaggregated by attempt are unavailable. Provincial judge counts used to calculate cases per judge are not limited to frontline judges but include all judges. Court-level judge counts refer to frontline judges wherever available. Also see note under Table 6.1. + $P < .10$ * $P < .05$ ** $P < .01$ *** $P < .001$, two-tailed tests

Model 2 shows that per capita GDP was strongly and negatively associated with courts' tendency to grant divorce petitions at both provincial and court levels. Model 3 shows the gap between Henan and Zhejiang in the rate at which divorce petitions were granted: 26 percentage points at the provincial level in 2011 (all first-instance petitions) and 15 percentage points at the court level in 2009–2016 (first-attempt petitions). Subsequent models show that both the effect of per capita GDP and the gap between the two provinces were attenuated by average caseloads per judge. In Model 4, the effects of per capita GDP and the dummy variable for Zhejiang are both attenuated by their mutual presence simply because Zhejiang's per capita GDP is so much higher than Henan's. The effects of both variables, however, are obliterated by the introduction of average cases per judge in Model 5. The introduction of average cases per judge in Model 5 explains away both the effect of per capita GDP and the gap between Henan and Zhejiang. These results tell us that the judicial clampdown in divorce would have been a lot more similar in Henan and Zhejiang had their average caseloads per judge been the same. In other words, an important reason why divorce was so much harder to obtain in Zhejiang's courts was because its judges were so much more overworked.

At the provincial level, an increase of 50 cases per judge was associated with a decrease of 13 percentage points in the rate at which divorce petitions were granted ($0.5 \times -26.07 = -13$). At the court level, an increase of 100 cases per judge was associated with a decrease of 5 percentage points in the rate at which divorce petitions were granted ($1 \times -5.26 = -5$). Because Henan's caseloads were so much lighter than Zhejiang's, there were no two courts in Henan that differed by 100 cases per judge. Differences of 30 between courts in Henan were more common. According to Model 6 (for Henan), an increase of 30 cases per judge was associated with a decrease of 9 percentage points in the rate at which divorce petitions were granted ($0.3 \times -31.33 = -9$). In Zhejiang, by contrast, differences of as much as 200 between courts were not uncommon. According to Model 7 (for Zhejiang), an increase of 200 cases per judge was associated with a decrease of 9 percentage points in the rate at which divorce petitions were granted ($2 \times -4.74 = -9$).

Figure 6.4 depicts the bivariate relationship between divorce petition grant rates and average caseloads per judge both among provincial-level units (Panel A) and courts (Panel B). Clearly visible in

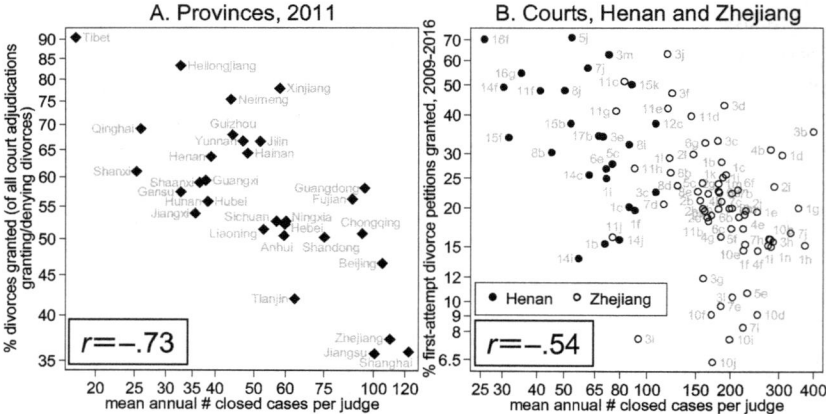

Figure 6.4 Association between percentage of divorces granted and cases per judge
Source: Court work reports; Basic Level Legal Artisan 2016a, 2016b, 2016c; author's calculations from Henan and Zhejiang provincial high courts' online decisions.
Note: Axes are scaled according to the natural logarithm of values. All data depicted in Panel A are from 2011. Panel B Y-axis data were aggregated from 2009 to 2016. Panel B X-axis data are from various years. On sources of closed cases per judge, see Chapter 4. Panel A N = 31. Panel B n = 95 basic-level courts (26 in Henan and 69 in Zhejiang). In Panel B, Henan r = −.47 (p = .02), Zhejiang r = −.29 (p = .02). Court codes in Panel B are listed with their corresponding court names in the supplementary online material at https://decoupling-book.org/. Panel B excludes courts of special jurisdiction and economic and technological development district courts.

Panel A is a cluster formed by Zhejiang, Jiangsu, and Shanghai with the lowest rates in the country at which courts granted divorce petitions. They were among China's provincial-level units – which also included Beijing, Chongqing, and Guangdong – with the heaviest caseloads per judge. These six places were the very same to top the list of heaviest caseloads per judge in 2019 (Sun 2019). But it was the three provincial-level units in the prosperous coastal Yangtze Delta region that formed a sort of judicial cabal by clamping down on divorce as a coping strategy. When all 31 provincial-level units are ranked according to rates at which they granted first-instance divorce petitions, Zhejiang, Jiangsu, and Shanghai occupied the bottom three spots in every year between 2002 and 2012 (Ministry of Civil Affairs of China, various years). They occupied the top three spots in a ranking of "the marketization level of each province from 2008 to 2014" (Tang and Liu 2019:21, 26). Consequently, their judges had the heaviest caseloads and dealt with them in part by denying a considerable majority of divorce petitions.[12] The orderly pattern depicted in Panel A gradually weakened after 2012 when courts across the country began to experience caseload spikes and as China's domestic relations trial reforms got underway (Chapter 3). As a consequence of both processes, courts began to converge in their treatment of first-attempt divorce petitions, thus forming the nationwide clampdown depicted in Figures 6.1 and 6.2. Zhejiang, Jiangsu, and Shanghai were all early adopters of the divorce twofer as an innovative response to heavy caseloads. Over time, many provinces, including Henan, expanded the three-province judicial cabal into a national one.

In Panel B, as in the regression results, the relationship between judges' average caseloads and the rate at which divorces were granted emerges across Henan and Zhejiang combined and within each province separately. Consider, for example, the contrast between two courts in Henan: Luoyang's Xigong District People's Court (3c) and Xinxiang's Fengqiu County People's Court (7j). They closed about the same number of cases in 2014 (3,700 cases). However, because the population of Fengqiu County was about double the population of Luoyang's Xigong District, Fengqiu's court had about twice as many judges as Xigong's. With an average caseload per judge almost double that of Fengqiu (107 versus 61), Xigong's rate of granting first-attempt divorce petitions (22.5%) was less than half of Fenqiu's (56.7%). Now consider the contrast between two courts in Zhejiang: Taizhou's Luqiao District People's Court (10d) and Wenzhou's Yongjia County People's Court (3f). Luqiao's court closed more cases (about 12,100) than Yongjia's (about 9,200). However, because Yongjia's population was about double Luqiao's, its court had considerably more judges than Luqiao's (about 75 and 48, respectively). Consequently, Luqiao's average caseload per judge (251) was double Yongjia's (123). Not surprisingly, therefore, Luqiao's rate of granting first-attempt divorce petitions (9.1%) was only a small fraction of Yongjia's (47.1%). The supplementary online material (available at https://decoupling-book.org/) contains

---

[12] Unlike provincial-level divorce statistics, which are published annually, provincial-level judicial statistics on closed cases, judge counts, assistant judge trial participation rates, simplified procedure utilization rates, and lay assessor participation rates are not systematically available. However, court decisions posted on China Judgements Online support my characterization of Zhejiang, Jiangsu, and Shanghai as a judicial cabal insofar as Shanghai and Jiangsu appear to be among the most enthusiastic adopters of all of Zhejiang's coping strategies discussed in Chapter 5, namely the use of assistant judges, the simplified procedure, and lay assessors. Details are available with the supplementary online material at https://decoupling-book.org/.

all numerical values in this paragraph as well as those available for every other court in the two-province sample.

We can also see in Panel B that variation *between* Henan and Zhejiang is greater than variation *within* each province. Some of the differences between the two provinces in average caseloads per judge could be an artifact of differences in how judge counts were reported. Henan's judge counts may have encompassed all court personnel bearing the title of judge, whereas Zhejiang's courts may have restricted counts to frontline judges who conducted trial work. Such reporting differences, which were certainly not universal, would account for only a small portion of the massive gap. More specifically, even if we make the false assumption that every judge count in Henan included *all* judges and every judge count in Zhejiang was limited to *frontline* judges, a reasonable upward adjustment to Zhejiang's judge counts would reduce the average caseload per judge in the sample from 197 to about 150, which is still more than double Henan's average caseload per judge of 65. To illustrate further, now consider two typical courts. The jurisdictions of Henan's Fengqiu County People's Court (7j) and Zhejiang's Shengzhou Municipal People's Court (6g) were of nearly identical population size in 2014 (733,147 and 731,200, respectively). For this reason, their judge counts were similar: 61 and 53, respectively. However, because Shengzhou's court closed more than four times as many cases as Fengqiu's, their average caseloads per judge were vastly different (162 and 61, respectively). Adjusting Shengzhou's frontline judge count upward would yield an estimated total judge count of 71. Even after making such an adjustment, Shengzhou's average caseload per judge would have still been double that of Fengqiu (121 and 61, respectively).[13] As we would expect, and as we can see in Figure 6.4,

---

[13] This adjustment assumes that frontline judges accounted for 75% of all judges (Basic Level Legal Artisan 2016b): 71 × .75 = 53. In this specific example, the judge count of Fengqiu's court (in Henan) included all 61 judges reported in 2012 (https://perma.cc/LHQ4-NFAD) while the judge count of Shengzhou's court (in Zhejiang) was derived from the average caseload of 162.1 per frontline judge in 2010 (https://perma.cc/F7HS-2A9X). As described in Chapter 4, I calculated Zhejiang's court-level caseloads as the average of all available figures from 2012 to 2014. Shengzhou's court closed 8,525 cases in 2012 and 8,724 cases in 2014, the average of which is 8,624.5 (as reported in the supplementary online material). I derived Shengzhou's judge count of 53 (also as reported in the supplementary online material) simply as 8,624.5 closed cases divided by 162.1 cases per judge. I applied the same procedure to derive judge counts for all courts in Zhejiang that did not report them in their "introduction to the court" web profiles (see Chapter 4). Although in this example I adjusted the Zhejiang court's frontline judge count upward to estimate its total judge count, I would have achieved the same result by adjusting the Henan court's total judge count downward to estimate its frontline judge count.

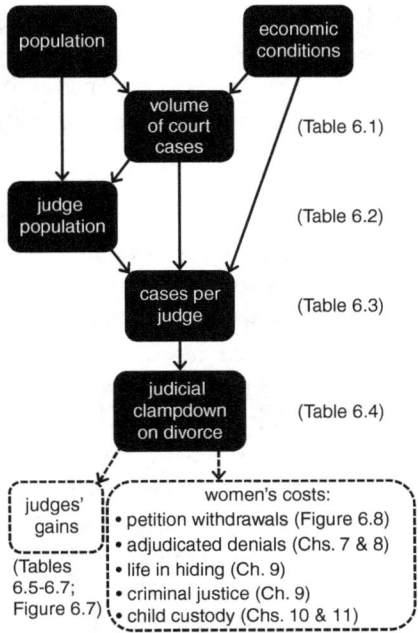

Figure 6.5 Path model of factors contributing to the judicial clampdown on divorce

Shengzhou's rate of granting first-attempt divorces (32.5%) was only a little over half that of Fengqiu (56.7%).

Figure 6.5 brings together in the form of a path model the key findings from the preceding series of regression analyses. It shows both the *direct* effect of average caseloads per judge and the *indirect* effects of judge counts, case counts, economic conditions, and general population size. And it tells us why Zhejiang's courts clamped down harder on divorce than Henan's courts did. Average caseloads per judge, a key determinant of the rate at which courts granted divorce petitions, were far heavier in Zhejiang than in Henan because courts in both provinces had similar numbers of judges even though Zhejiang's courts handled far more cases than Henan's courts did. Courts in both provinces had similar numbers of judges despite vastly different volumes of litigation because judge counts were determined primarily according to population size. Finally, Zhejiang's higher volume of civil litigation responsible for its heavier caseloads stemmed from its more dynamic economic conditions.

The remainder of this book is devoted primarily to the consequences of the divorce twofer – the dashed arrows stemming from the "judicial clampdown on divorce" box in Figure 6.5. The next section of this chapter follows the dashed arrow to the "judges' gains" box by demonstrating several concrete ways in which the divorce twofer helped judges clear their dockets. The last section of this chapter and all subsequent chapters follow the dashed arrow to the "women's costs" box.

THE DIVORCE TWOFER LIGHTENED JUDGES' WORKLOADS

To some degree, judges toiling under heavy caseloads welcomed divorce cases because they could get rid of them so quickly. We saw in Chapter 3 that divorce is the only type of case for which a do-over is permitted. Judges can easily brush off divorce cases, but no such leeway exists for nondivorce cases, which are generally allowed only one first-instance trial. A nondivorce case is rarely tried twice by a court of first instance, and usually only when a court of second instance remands it back for retrial. By contrast, adjudicated denials of first-instance divorce petitions could conceivably become "Groundhog Day" cases refiled and retried in perpetuity in basic-level courts. Casting aside divorce cases that could be refiled as soon as six months later has allowed judges to score points on their performance evaluations for efficiency and simplified procedure utilization while simultaneously allowing them to focus their efforts on more pressing cases ineligible for do-overs. The divorce twofer thus became an informal practice – an "unspoken rule," an "unwritten convention" (Chapter 3) – that in some areas was even codified into a quasi-formal procedure. I will show that judges benefitted from denying divorce petitions in two ways. First, most of the divorce petitions they denied never returned to court. Second, denying divorce petitions took far less time and effort than granting divorces. I will then demonstrate that routinely denying divorce petitions, which have been filed primarily by women, has allowed judges to turn their attention to nondivorce cases, which have been filed primarily by men. After all, judges who belong to civil divisions are responsible for handling every kind of civil case. They have privileged the kinds of cases that tend to be filed by men at the expense of divorce cases, which tend to be filed by women. As a result, judges and male litigants have been the winners and female plaintiffs have been the losers of the divorce twofer.

The Divorce Twofer Made Cases Disappear

Figures 6.6 and 6.7 depict as pyramids the outcomes of first-instance divorce filings in court. Unlike my earlier analyses of divorce outcomes, which were limited to adjudications, the pyramids also include petitions withdrawn by plaintiffs. I limit the pyramids to decisions made after 2013 because this is when Henan's courts consistently posted *caiding* decisions to grant plaintiffs' requests to withdraw petitions. Withdrawn petitions are vastly underrepresented in prior years (Chapter 4). Recall from Chapter 1 that mediation is the first step after a divorce petition is filed. The primary purpose of mediation at this stage is to achieve marital reconciliation, which, if successful, would typically result in a petition withdrawal. Some plaintiffs withdraw their petitions at the trial stage. Judges also engage in mediation for the purpose of hammering out the terms of a divorce. Of all first-instance divorce cases handled by courts in recent years, about one-third resulted in mediation agreements. Despite the prevalence of mediation agreements in divorce litigation, they are exceedingly scarce in my samples of court decisions because courts are prohibited from posting them online (Chapter 4). Mediations are therefore not included in the pyramids. Divorces were granted in the vast majority (about 90%) of cases concluded by mediation agreements in recent years; about two-thirds of all divorces granted by courts resulted in mediation agreements and not in adjudicated verdicts. Consequently, the absence of mediation agreements skews the appearance of the

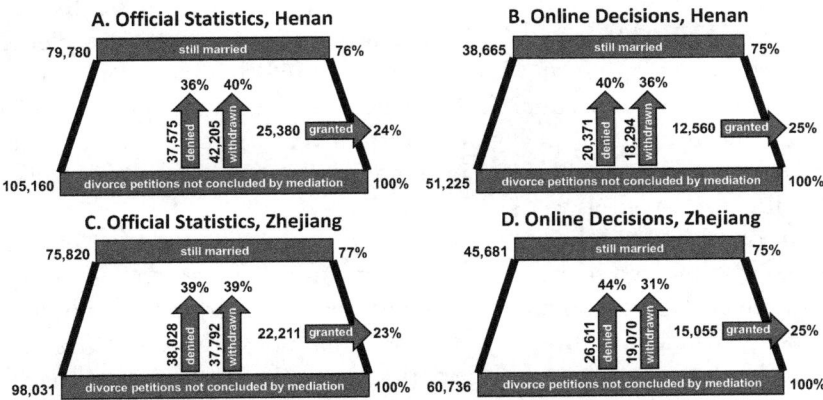

Figure 6.6 Outcomes of divorce petitions by source of data (official government statistics versus online decisions)
Source: Ministry of Civil Affairs of China, various years; author's calculations from Henan and Zhejiang provincial high courts' online decisions.
Note: Data are limited to first-instance decisions. Cases concluded by mediation agreements are excluded. Data are also limited to 2014–2015 for Henan and 2014–2016 for Zhejiang. Percentages do not always total 100% (and the sum of "denied" and "withdrawn" do not always equal "still married") owing to rounding error.

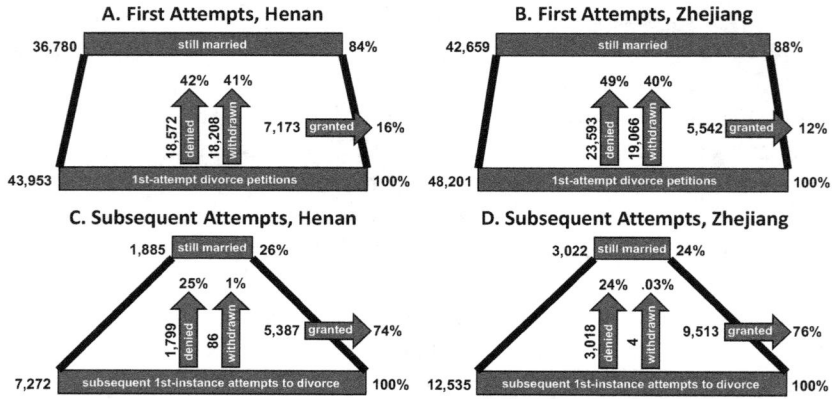

Figure 6.7 Outcomes of divorce petitions by attempt (first versus subsequent)
Source: Author's calculations from Henan and Zhejiang provincial high courts' online decisions.
Note: Data are limited to first-instance decisions. Cases concluded by mediation agreements are excluded. Data are also limited to 2014–2015 for Henan and 2014–2016 for Zhejiang. Percentages do not always total 100% (and the sum of "denied" and "withdrawn" do not always equal "still married") owing to rounding error.

pyramids in a few ways: the pyramids undercount both the total number of divorce petitions and the total number of granted divorces, and therefore misrepresent the overall rate at which courts granted divorce petitions. Had Henan's 56,142 mediations been included in Figure 6.6, the overall rate at which courts granted divorces would have appeared as 47% in Panel A. Likewise, had Zhejiang's 55,944 mediations been included in Figure 6.6, the overall rate at which courts granted divorces would have appeared as 48% in Panel C (Ministry of Civil Affairs, various years).

In other words, a little over half of all people who filed for divorce in court remained married after the conclusion of the process. As we can see in Figure 6.6, after excluding cases concluded by mediation agreements, about three-quarters of remaining divorce-seekers left court still married. Note the remarkable consistency between official statistics and the online court decisions in my samples – yet another indication of the representativeness of my data.

For all the reasons discussed earlier, judges would benefit from the divorce twofer even if every single petition they denied came back like a boomerang after the statutory six-month waiting period. Judges would benefit even more if only a portion of them returned. As it turns out, divorce courts were leaky. Only a small proportion of plaintiffs whose petitions were denied returned for another attempt. Some of them may have given up and stayed married, often but not always while physically separated. Others may have pursued "divorces by agreement" in the Civil Affairs Administration after "agreeing" to give up child custody, property claims, or both (see Chapter 9). According to one scholar, "the most important reason why women choose to divorce in the Civil Affairs Administration is because they want to get rid of their husbands and their insufferable marriages as quickly as possible. ... For many women, giving up their rights to economic compensation is the cost of freedom from an agonizing marriage" (Zhang 2011:78; for the same argument, see Li [2022] and Wang [2013:175]). To be sure, divorce cases also moved in the opposite direction. Many plaintiffs indicated in their divorce petitions that they filed for divorce in court only after their negotiations for an uncontested "divorce by agreement" in the Civil Affairs Administration had broken down. Women in both scenarios commonly discounted their claims to child custody and marital property as the price of divorce (see Chapter 10).

Official government statistics on divorce depicted in Figure 6.6 (Panels A and C) do not disaggregate first attempts from subsequent attempts. Because they include *all* divorce decisions, the pyramids in Figure 6.6 double-count a certain number of litigants who appear in both first-attempt and subsequent-attempt cases. They also include repeat players who are not double-counted. Some of the subsequent-attempt cases included in Figure 6.6 were spawned by prior cases that had been concluded prior to 2014. I can, of course, identify repeat players in my samples of court decisions. Among the cases represented by Panel B (for Henan) and Panel D (for Zhejiang), 14% and 21%, respectively, of the litigants were returnees.[14]

Figure 6.7 showcases the docket-shrinking property of the divorce twofer. Panels A and B depict first-attempt decisions and thus contain no repeat players. Panels C and D depict subsequent-attempt decisions and thus consist exclusively of repeat players. Figure 6.7 thus disaggregates the pyramids in Figure 6.6 (Panels B and D) constructed from

---

[14] The story of leaky courts persists after limiting the scope of analysis to adjudications (i.e., excluding petition withdrawals): in the Henan and Zhejiang samples, 22% and 30%, respectively, of litigants were returnees. Zhejiang's higher proportion of repeat players makes sense given the much higher rates at which its courts denied divorce petitions prior to 2013. Although the two provinces had converged by 2016 in terms of rates at which divorce petitions were denied, litigants sometimes waited two or more years after a first-attempt denial before filing a new first-instance divorce petition (Chapter 9).

my samples of court decisions.[15] Subsequent attempts are not limited to second attempts. Some plaintiffs succeeded or gave up after three or even more attempts.

Two noteworthy patterns emerge from Figure 6.7. First, plaintiffs tended to remain married in first-attempt adjudications and to accomplish their mission to divorce in subsequent-attempt adjudications. This, of course, is a defining characteristic of the divorce twofer.[16] According to a study of divorce cases in a basic-level court in Zhejiang's provincial capital of Hangzhou, 81% of plaintiffs who returned after a failed first attempt were successful on the second attempt (Liu 2012:81; Zhang 2013). Second, courts are sieves for divorce cases. Among the first-attempt petitions judges denied, most never returned to court. Courts would not be leaking divorce cases if, in Figure 6.7, the bottom bars representing subsequent-attempt divorce cases (Panels C and D) were equal to the top bars representing all the first-attempt divorce cases in which litigants failed to divorce and thus remained married (Panels A and B). Even if we exclude petitions withdrawn by plaintiffs, the number of returnees (7,186 in Henan and 12,531 in Zhejiang) pales in comparison to the number of plaintiffs whose petitions had been denied in first-attempt adjudications (18,572 in Henan and 23,593 in Zhejiang). These numbers make sense only if a sizeable share of petitioners never returned to court.[17] Indeed, according to a

---

[15] In Figure 6.7, the sum of Henan's first-attempt petitions (43,953, Panel A) and subsequent first-instance petitions (7,272, Panel C) is equal to all of its first-instance petitions in Figure 6.6 (51,225, Panel B). Likewise, the sum of Zhejiang's first-attempt petitions (48,201, Panel B) and subsequent first-instance petitions (12,535, Panel D) is equal to all of its first-instance petitions in Figure 6.6 (60,736, Panel D).

[16] Withdrawn petitions were almost all coded as first-attempt petitions because *caiding* decisions are so brief and thus almost never contain information about the nature or history of the disputes (Chapter 4). Generally speaking, whether a plaintiff who withdrew her petition did so on the first attempt or a subsequent attempt is impossible to ascertain. Surely, however, plaintiffs who filed for divorce again were highly motivated to dissolve their marriages and therefore highly unlikely to withdraw their petitions. In any event, the story of the divorce twofer does not change after excluding withdrawn petitions from the pyramids in Figure 6.7: the proportion of first- and subsequent-attempt divorce petitions granted would have been 28% and 75% respectively in Henan and 19% and 73%, respectively, in Zhejiang.

[17] Given a lag time of sometimes several years between first-attempt adjudicated denials and subsequent-attempt decisions, an increase in the volume of court divorce filings over time in Henan could account for some but certainly far from all of Henan's disappearing divorce cases. Zhejiang's court divorce filings, by contrast, remained almost perfectly stable in the decade between 2009 and 2018 (Ministry of Civil Affairs of China, various years). Another similarly implausible alternative explanation for what appears to be disappearing divorce cases would be courts' overwhelming tendency to dispose of second-attempt divorce petitions by mediation. Since courts generally do not publish mediation agreements, I have no way to assess this possibility. For it to be plausible, however, rates at which courts disposed of subsequent-attempt divorce petitions by mediation would have needed to be about double the rates at which

study of divorce cases in a basic-level court in Zhejiang's provincial capital of Hangzhou, only 22% of plaintiffs whose first-attempt petitions were denied returned to file a second first-instance petition (Liu 2012:81; Zhang 2013).

Table 6.5 shows once again that courts denied the majority of first-attempt divorce petitions and granted the majority of subsequent-attempt divorce petitions.[18] More importantly, it shows the uniquely low rates at which first-attempt divorce petitions were granted, not only compared to subsequent-attempt divorce petitions, but also compared to other types of civil cases. Successful first-attempt divorce cases were truly exceptional. Courts in both provinces granted plaintiffs' petitions in first-attempt divorce cases at rates that were less than half of the win rates enjoyed by plaintiffs in every other type of case except administrative litigation.[19]

First-attempt divorce trials were also exceptional in their sparing use of collegial panels. As low-hanging fruit for quick-and-easy adjudicated denials using the simplified procedure, first-attempt divorce petitions have helped courts to economize on scarce judicial resources. Simplified procedure utilization rates in Table 6.5 suggest that, among all the types of cases they handled, courts devoted the fewest judicial resources to first-attempt divorce cases. By contrast, contract disputes in both provinces were much more likely to be tried according to the ordinary civil procedure. Compared to how they treated divorce cases, courts attached

---

they disposed of all divorce petitions by mediation. A study of 1,202 divorce cases in Yunnan Province that includes both adjudications and mediations shows not only that first-attempt petitions outnumbered subsequent-attempt petitions by a ratio of 8.5:1 but also that judges were far less likely to close cases by mediation on subsequent attempts (W. Zhou 2018:6, 12).

18   I adhered to the classification system used in official judicial statistics (SPC 2018). "Contracts" includes all subcategories belonging to the larger categories of "contracts, management without cause, and unfair advantage" (合同、无因管理、不当得利纠纷) and "labor and personnel" (劳动争议、人事争议). "Torts and other rights" likewise includes all subcategories belonging to the larger categories of "tort liability" (侵权责任纠纷), "personal dignity rights" (人格权), "property ownership rights" (物权纠纷), "civil disputes related to corporations, securities, insurance, bills of exchange, etc." (与公司、证券、保险、票据等有关的民事纠纷), and "intellectual property rights and competition" (知识产权与竞争纠纷). Discrepancies between Figure 6.7 and Table 6.5 in rates at which divorce petitions were granted are attributable to (1) the exclusion of withdrawn petition from Table 6.5 and (2) the greater temporal scope of Table 6.5.

19   "Petition granted" in a divorce case refers only to whether the divorce was granted, and does not consider whether other claims, such as child custody, property division, or civil damages, were awarded. In other types of civil cases, as well as in administrative litigation cases, "petitions granted" refers to whether any claim was granted, and thus includes partial wins. Insofar as a court can award another claim in a divorce case only if it first grants a divorce, the meaning of "petition granted" is roughly comparable across categories. In the criminal context, "petition granted" refers to a conviction (a nonacquittal).

TABLE 6.5 Application of the simplified procedure and plaintiff win rates by case type, first-instance adjudications

Case type	% Petitions granted	% Simplified procedure	Cases
Henan (2009–2015)			
Divorce, first attempts	37	39	55,179
Divorce, subsequent attempts	76	27	14,198
Other marriage and family	91	29	17,866
Contracts	93	24	187,165
Torts and other rights-related	95	19	110,714
Criminal	99	41	193,944
Administrative litigation	37	0.2	9,103
Total	89	30	588,169
Zhejiang (2009–2017)			
Divorce, first attempts	20	83	50,207
Divorce, subsequent attempts	73	74	19,914
Other marriage and family	89	76	12,059
Contracts	97	60	1,060,004
Torts and other rights-related	93	80	133,058
Criminal	99	62	231,148
Administrative litigation	38	1	11,509
Total	94	62	1,517,899

Source: Author's calculations from Henan and Zhejiang provincial high courts' online decisions.
Note: "% petitions granted" refers to the plaintiff win rate. For divorce cases, only a granted divorce counts as a win. Other claims in divorce petitions, such as child custody, property division, or civil damages, are not considered. For nondivorce civil cases and administrative litigation cases, any awarded claim counts as a granted petition. In other words, partial wins count as wins. In the criminal context, it refers to guilty verdicts (nonacquittals).

far more importance to contract disputes. As we will see shortly, contract disputes happened to be filed overwhelmingly by men, whereas, as we already know, divorces were filed overwhelmingly by women.

Subsequent-attempt divorce trials more closely resembled the civil trials of other types of cases in terms of both win rates and the use of the simplified procedure. Note also that in Table 6.5 administrative litigation cases were practically never tried according to the simplified procedure. The original 1989 Administrative Litigation Law required the use of collegial panels (Article 46). Only after the amended version of the law took effect on July 1, 2017, at the very end of the period of analysis, were solo judges permitted to apply the simplified procedure in administrative litigation cases (Article 83).

The Divorce Twofer Reduced Judge Effort

The divorce twofer was a docket-shrinking machine not only by making cases disappear. By allowing judges to deny so many first-instance divorce petitions in a relatively perfunctory manner, the divorce twofer also reduced the effort they put into first-instance divorce trials, and thus freed up time and effort for them to deal with other kinds of cases they deemed more important.

Table 6.6 contains mean and median durations of time from when civil cases were filed to when judges rendered adjudicated verdicts. Note the generally high degree of consistency between means and medians, suggesting that time distributions are not overly skewed one way or the other. I disaggregate times to close cases by type of procedure (ordinary versus simplified) because of Zhejiang's dramatically higher simplified procedure utilization rates (Chapter 5). Overall case closing times were slower in Henan (in the "total" column) only because its simplified procedure utilization rates were so much lower. Across the two provincial samples, case closing times among cases of the same type tried according to the same procedure were generally similar.

Thanks to the divorce twofer, judges in both provinces closed first-attempt divorce cases faster than they closed any other type of civil case (according to means/medians in the "total" column). Once again, Zhejiang's relatively enthusiastic embrace of the divorce twofer is evident in its remarkably swift adjudicated denials. The mean/median time from initial case filing to adjudicated denial using the simplified procedure was 52/51 days in Henan and 37/33 days in Zhejiang. Among all first-attempt divorce cases tried according to the ordinary procedure, decisions to deny petitions were about 20 days faster in Henan and, strangely, a few days slower in Zhejiang than decisions to grant petitions.[20] Compared to divorces granted using the ordinary procedure, first-attempt denials using the simplified procedure cut the duration of time to an adjudicated decision by over one-half (about

---

[20] Given how seldom judges in Zhejiang tried civil cases using the ordinary civil procedure, the slightly longer time judges spent on each divorce denial (compared to each petition they granted) using the ordinary procedure did not come close to offsetting the substantially shorter time they spent on each divorce denial (compared to each petition they granted) using the simplified procedure.

TABLE 6.6 Time to decision (mean/median days) by case type, first-instance civil adjudications

Civil case type	Ordinary procedure		Simplified procedure		Total
	Granted	Denied	Granted	Denied	
Henan (2009–2015)					
Divorce, first attempts	113/114	**93/90**	59/58	**52/51**	81/72
(n)	(7,071)	(8,679)	(1,993)	(10,110)	(27,853)
Divorce, subsequent attempts	107/109	105/105	57/57	59/58	91/85
(n)	(3,945)	(1,114)	(1,553)	(793)	(7,405)
Other marriage and family	103/104	106/104	59/59	59/60	88/80
(n)	(4,844)	(518)	(2,638)	(288)	(8,288)
Contracts	104/103	118/121	56/55	74/68	89/81
(n)	(50,175)	(3,463)	(25,703)	(1,338)	(80,679)
Torts and other rights-related	109/109	116/119	62/61	68/70	96/89
(n)	(28,633)	(1,337)	(11,095)	(339)	(41,404)
Total	106/106	102/100	58/57	56/53	89/82
(n)	(94,668)	(15,111)	(42,982)	(12,868)	(165,629)
Zhejiang (2009–2017)					
Divorce, first attempts	114/111	**117/116**	51/45	**37/33**	51/38
(n)	(3,657)	(3,552)	(5,084)	(34,517)	(46,810)
Divorce, subsequent attempts	119/117	120/122	49/43	45/40	64/51
(n)	(3,777)	(495)	(9,395)	(4,590)	(18,257)
Other marriage and family	128/129	141/149	58/52	61/56	70/62
(n)	(1,507)	(125)	(7,208)	(1,021)	(9,861)
Contracts	121/119	136/142	47/40	71/70	74/64
(n)	(329,097)	(4,100)	(568,157)	(18,476)	(919,830)
Torts and other rights-related	126/134	135/143	67/61	72/71	76/68
(n)	(12,915)	(1,303)	(85,535)	(5,202)	(104,955)
Total	121/119	128/130	50/42	51/43	73/62
(n)	(350,953)	(9,575)	(675,379)	(63,806)	(1,099,713)

Source: Author's calculations from Henan and Zhejiang provincial high courts' online decisions.

Note: A large number of cases are omitted from this table owing to missing filing dates. Dates could be reliably extracted from only a portion of all decisions. See note under Table 6.5 for the definition of "granted" and "denied."

60 days) in Henan and by two-thirds (about 80 days) in Zhejiang. Finally, among all first-attempt divorce cases tried according to the simplified procedure, the mean/median amount of time saved by denying petitions compared to granting them was one week per case in Henan and about two weeks per case in Zhejiang.

The aggregate time savings from the divorce twofer has therefore been immense in both provinces. Multiplying mean or median savings in time gained from denying first-attempt divorce petitions by the volume of adjudicated denials of first-attempt divorce petitions in the two samples yields millions of days in total time savings. Of course, the time necessary to adjudicate subsequent-attempt divorce petitions spawned by first-attempt denials must be subtracted from this amount of time savings. However, as we know, most first-attempt adjudicated denials never come back. Those that do return are generally both less burdensome, and thus benefit judges' volume and efficiency scores, and are at lower risk of leading to social unrest or "extreme incidents" that would hurt judges' performance evaluations (Chapter 3).

To any estimate of the divorce twofer's total net time savings must be added the amount of time additional judges and lay assessors – whose efforts were spared by the solo judges who single-handedly denied first-attempt divorce petitions using the simplified procedure – would have otherwise spent as members of collegial panels in trials granting first-attempt divorces. Needless to say, judges' labor accounts for only a small portion of the duration of time from case filing to adjudicated decision. We do not know the true time savings gained by the divorce twofer, because we do not know how much time judges actually devoted to cases. We know only when cases were filed and when decisions were finalized; the court decisions do not reveal exactly how judges allocated their time in the interim. Surely, though, the divorce twofer benefitted judges not only by conserving a real measure of their scarce supply of time and effort but also by increasing their simplified procedure utilization rates, shortening their case closing times, and thereby boosting their performance evaluation scores.

The relative brevity of judges' written decisions in first-attempt divorce adjudications further suggests that the amount of time and effort saved was substantial. Table 6.7 contains mean/median numbers of characters – almost all Chinese, of course, but also some Latin letters, Arabic numerals, and symbols – per court decision. I disaggregate length of court decision by type of procedure for the same reason I disaggregated time to decision in the previous analysis. The written

TABLE 6.7 Length of written decisions (mean/median characters) by case type, first-instance civil adjudications

Civil case type	Ordinary procedure		Simplified procedure		Total
	Granted	Denied	Granted	Denied	
Henan (2009–2015)					
Divorce, first attempts	1,181/1,043	935/860	1,247/1,152	908/849	1,021/915
(n)	(16,222)	(17,618)	(3,978)	(17,361)	(55,179)
Divorce, subsequent attempts	1,462/1,291	1,222/1,100	1,435/1,314	1,140/1,063	1,392/1,241
(n)	(8,177)	(2,195)	(2,592)	(1,234)	(14,198)
Other marriage and family	1,642/1,382	1,759/1,491	1,387/1,257	1,421/1,257	1,576/1,341
(n)	(11,451)	(1,162)	(4,785)	(468)	(17,866)
Contracts	1,916/1,564	2,471/2,098	1,422/1,239	1,711/1,573	1,837/1,506
(n)	(131,534)	(11,393)	(41,951)	(2,287)	(187,165)
Torts and other rights-related	3,102/2,846	2,309/1,975	2,598/2,438	1,660/1,485	2,971/2,725
(n)	(85,654)	(4,490)	(19,962)	(608)	(110,714)
Total	2,243/1,859	1,620/1,161	1,731/1,455	1,036/896	2,017/1,616
(n)	(253,038)	(36,858)	(73,268)	(21,958)	(385,122)

Zhejiang (2009–2017)					
Divorce, first attempts	1,308/1,109	1,107/1,035	1,635/1,379	1,149/1,069	1,213/1,090
(n)	(4,606)	(4,091)	(5,447)	(36,063)	(50,207)
Divorce, subsequent attempts	1,721/1,384	1,551/1,337	1,765/1,525	1,440/1,316	1,670/1,430
(n)	(4,649)	(605)	(9,844)	(4,816)	(19,914)
Other marriage and family	3,152/2,259	3,695/3,251	2,182/1,830	2,342/1,980	2,440/1,927
(n)	(2,606)	(271)	(8,081)	(1,101)	(12,059)
Contracts	1,902/1,411	4,258/3,581	1,698/1,372	2,978/2,533	1,823/1,406
(n)	(417,877)	(8,398)	(613,259)	(20,470)	(1,060,004)
Torts and other rights-related	4,001/3,585	4,588/3,965	3,205/2,995	3,089/2,781	3,375/3,089
(n)	(24,386)	(2,812)	(99,897)	(5,963)	(133,058)
Total	2,014/1,450	3,408/2,701	1,908/1,504	1,905/1,358	1,965/1,481
(n)	(454,124)	(16,177)	(736,528)	(68,413)	(1,275,242)

Source: Author's calculations from Henan and Zhejiang provincial high courts' online decisions.

decisions of cases closed using the ordinary procedure were generally longer than those of cases closed using the simplified procedure. Regardless of how judges ruled and which procedure they used, their first-attempt divorce decisions were shorter than those of any other type of civil case. In particular, their decisions to *deny* first-attempt divorce petitions were shorter than their decisions in any other type of case. In both provinces, written decisions that denied first-attempt divorce petitions were generally about 20–30% shorter than those that granted first-attempt divorces. Not only were adjudicated denials shorter in length, but, as we will see in Chapter 7, they also contained a considerable amount of recycled and rehashed boilerplate text justifying marital preservation in therapeutic, moral, and ideological terms. Although subsequent-attempt divorce decisions were longer than first-attempt divorce decisions, much of the text they contained was redundant. Because many of the facts do not change – or require only minor revisions – between attempts, judges simply copy and paste portions of their first-attempt decisions into their subsequent-attempt decisions.

The Divorce Twofer Disproportionately Impacted Women

When judges sacrificed divorce cases in response to their heavy caseloads, they did not do so in a gender-neutral manner. Women were disproportionate casualties of the divorce twofer. Table 6.8 shows female representation among plaintiffs and defendants by case type. Among plaintiffs, women were concentrated in divorce cases. In Henan, divorce cases accounted for 17% of all plaintiffs but for 29% of all female plaintiffs in first-instance civil adjudications. In Zhejiang, divorce cases accounted for 5% of all plaintiffs but for 11% of all female plaintiffs in first-instance civil adjudications. Women also went to court in large numbers as both plaintiffs and defendants in "other marriage and family cases," which consisted primarily of disputes related to child custody, inheritance, eldercare, adoption, and relationship breakups among unmarried couples (e.g., betrothal gifts among couples who called off their marriage engagement as well as property division and child custody among cohabiting couples who split up). Commensurate with their overrepresentation among plaintiffs filing for divorce, women were underrepresented among plaintiffs filing for relief in contract, tort, and administrative disputes. These patterns provide further evidence that judges attached greater importance to and took more seriously cases filed by men than cases filed by women.

TABLE 6.8 Female litigants by case type, first-instance adjudications

Case type	Plaintiffs			% Female	Defendants	
	% Female	Plaintiffs	Decisions		Defendants	Cases
Henan (2009–2015)						
Divorce, first attempts	**66**	52,196	52,150	**34**	52,145	52,106
Divorce, subsequent attempts	67	13,402	13,386	33	13,379	13,372
Other marriage and family	43	22,814	16,610	48	27,602	16,612
Contracts	23	143,597	118,569	21	228,155	132,763
Torts and other rights-related	39	158,084	95,171	13	131,187	86,638
Criminal	–	–	–	8	251,385	182,073
Administrative litigation	31	13,527	6,915	–	–	–
Total	38	403,620	302,801	17	703,853	483,564
Zhejiang (2009–2017)						
Divorce, first attempts	**67**	8,476	8,476	**33**	8,506	8,477
Divorce, subsequent attempts	69	3,474	3,459	31	3,491	3,480
Other marriage and family	57	2,547	1,625	47	3,432	1,659
Contracts	25	190,519	160,067	32	402,694	226,152
Torts and other rights-related	42	37,803	22,869	19	31,317	20,890
Criminal	–	–	–	11	83,689	58,655
Administrative litigation	31	5,134	2,702	–	–	–
Total	30	247,953	199,198	28	533,129	319,313

Source: Author's calculations from Henan and Zhejiang provincial high courts' online decisions.
Note: Litigant sex is limited to reported values in all case types except divorce. In divorce cases, reported values of litigant sex are supplemented with a highly reliable method of inferring litigant sex detailed in Chapter 4. Most discrepancies between numbers of plaintiffs, defendants, and decisions are accounted for by organizational litigants (e.g., plaintiffs in contract disputes that are companies or rural credit cooperatives). Some, but relatively few, are also caused by parsing errors or errors in the court decisions. Whereas divorces include only one plaintiff and one defendant, other types of cases often include multiple plaintiffs and multiple defendants.

Drawing on and reinforcing cultural stereotypes, judges could more easily justify the divorce twofer by characterizing the divorce petitions of women as "frivolous" and "impulsive," and therefore without legal merit.

Moreover, the divorce twofer disproportionately impacted *rural* women. Not only were divorce cases concentrated in rural courts, but women's representation among plaintiffs filing for divorce was greater in rural areas than in urban areas (Chapter 4). Because contract disputes were overrepresented in urban courts, judges in rural courts dealt with women seeking divorce on a more regular basis than their urban counterparts did. As we will see throughout this book, women's vastly poorer outcomes in rural courts likely stemmed at least in part from the greater durability of patriarchal cultural beliefs in rural areas.

PETITION WITHDRAWALS WERE PART OF THE DIVORCE TWOFER

Petition withdrawals benefitted judges in the same way adjudicated denials did. The pyramids in Figures 6.6 and 6.7 depict two judicial pathways to marital preservation: adjudicated denials and withdrawn petitions. Both pathways helped judges swiftly clear their dockets and gain points on their performance evaluations (Kinkel and Hurst 2015:57). As discussed earlier, a third pathway, mediated denials, was extremely rare by the mid-2010s. Petition withdrawals, like adjudicated denials, conserved judicial resources and expedited case closing times. But petition withdrawals also offered additional benefits to judges.

From the standpoint of judges, withdrawn petitions have been even more desirable than adjudicated denials for at least four reasons. First, they were far more likely to be presided over by a solo judge, and thus greatly reduced workloads. Second, they further shortened case closing times because petition withdrawals can be closed without any consideration whatsoever of substantive legal matters (X. Wang 2016:52). Third, owing to the previous reason, the decisions judges wrote to approve them were extremely short, typically only a few sentences (Chapter 4). When plaintiffs did not show up for their trials, judges – who regarded them as having voluntarily waived their right to a trial despite receiving a court summons – handled their cases as petition withdrawals in accordance with the Civil Procedure Law (Article 143). Far more often, however, judges wrote in their decisions simply that the plaintiff had requested to drop the case, sometimes adding that the plaintiff's request was "voluntary." Fourth, owing to the foregoing reasons, performance evaluation systems reward withdrawals more than adjudicated denials. At the same time, because they do not include holdings on the litigants' legal claims, petition withdrawals cannot count against judges as "incorrectly decided" cases (X. Wang 2016:52).

Given judges' incentives to maximize withdrawn petitions, many withdrawals were neither voluntary nor initiated by plaintiffs; these must be understood as adjudicated denials by another name, and therefore as part of the divorce twofer. As we know from Chapter 2, courts are required to attempt to achieve mediated reconciliation. When a judge's persuasive efforts are successful, the plaintiff withdraws her divorce petition, and the couple goes home ostensibly reconciled. Victims of domestic violence are often coerced and intimidated into "voluntarily" dropping their cases (Chen and Duan 2012:34). Courts are not the only organizations responsible for mediating marital conflict. Local police as well as mass organizations such as villagers' committees and urban residents' committees also routinely conduct mediation for the purpose of achieving marital reconciliation and preventing divorces. Such mediation efforts, however, often serve to reinforce the coercive control of abusive husbands (Chen 2009; Han 2017).

In private, abusive husbands sometimes threaten even worse violence – including death – if their wives file for divorce. Consider, for example, the husband who beat his wife, breaking her ribs, for questioning him about his habit of patronizing prostitutes. "As soon as she raised the issue of divorce, he grabbed a knife and roared, 'In life your body belongs to the Shi family, in death your ghost belongs to the Shi family!' From this point on, although he continued to beat her black and blue on a regular basis, she dared not utter the word divorce again" (Li 2003:3). After abused women filed for divorce, their husbands often threatened the same consequences unless they withdrew their divorce petitions. In court, however, wife-beaters were often on their best behavior, apologizing for their wrongdoing, begging for another chance, and promising to be better husbands. Judges often gaslighted female plaintiffs by downplaying their claims of violence and commending their husbands' apparent commitment to self-improvement and reconciliation (Chapter 7). Even when abusive husbands made threats of violence in court, judges nonetheless encouraged wives to drop their petitions in consideration of the safety of both the wives and the judges (He 2017; also see Diamant [2000b:336] and Chapter 3).

They may have tried to comfort plaintiffs by pointing out that, according to the Measures of People's Courts on Collecting Litigation Fees, the court fee for a petition withdrawal was only half that of an adjudicated denial decided by a collegial panel, which would be a possible or even likely alternative outcome. Judges have thus colluded with perpetrators of domestic violence by exerting pressure on female plaintiffs to withdraw their petitions (Li 2022).

To summarize, abusive husbands who used intimidation tactics to end their wives' pursuit of divorce found support from judges with a vested interest in maximizing petition withdrawals. Despite the nonvoluntary nature of many withdrawn divorce petitions, judges often explicitly – and dishonestly – indicated in their written decisions that "the plaintiff's voluntarily application to withdraw the lawsuit is lawful and hereby approved by the court." Variations of this sort of language include "the plaintiff voluntarily applied to withdraw the petition" and "the plaintiff's withdrawal of the petition is voluntary and does not contravene the law."

Domestic violence is invisible in *caiding* decisions because they contain no information about the nature of plaintiffs' legal complaints. In their subsequent-attempt divorce petitions, however, plaintiffs sometimes characterized their prior withdrawals as less than voluntary. In female plaintiffs' portrayals of their prior petition withdrawals, judges acted to support male defendants' efforts to intimidate their wives into withdrawing their petitions.

Each of the following cases refers to a prior case that had been handled by the court as a withdrawn petition. Some of the plaintiffs, fearing for their lives, were no-shows in court. Although the plaintiffs in these cases had never requested to withdraw their petitions, the courts' presumption – supported entirely by the law – was that their failure to appear in court was tantamount to withdrawing their petitions. Other plaintiffs, compelled by abusive husbands, dropped their cases before they even went to trial. Because judges "regarded withdrawn lawsuits as having never happened in the first place" (X. Wang 2016:52), they sometimes denied subsequent-attempt divorce petitions as if they were first-attempt divorce petitions. The following examples foreshadow many themes of this book. They illustrate judges' tendency to affirm reconciliation potential and to disaffirm the breakdown of mutual affection (Chapter 7). They illustrate judges' tendency to ignore evidence of domestic violence (Chapters 7 and 8). They illustrate the formation of a population of female abuse victims forced into hiding for their own safety, whom I call "marital violence refugees" (Chapter 9). And they illustrate judges' tendency to grant child custody to abusive husbands whose children were left in their sole physical custody after their wives fled to safety (Chapters 10 and 11).

In my first example, the defendant successfully intimidated the plaintiff into withdrawing her petition. In her subsequent-attempt petition, she claimed that the domestic violence began when, after exchanging one sentence with a guy at work, her husband suspected they were having an affair. He not only beat her, but also choked her and forced her to drink poison. She stated that only by begging for her life was she spared. After this, all she had to do was exchange words with someone of the opposite sex for her husband to suspect they were having improper relations. She claimed that her husband's jealousy and suspicion precipitated numerous beatings, which ultimately made her unable to live in her marital home. Forced to leave, she moved to the county seat (the urban area of Henan's Song County), where her husband found her and beat her again. At this point she no longer dared return home, and started drifting from place to place (流浪) for the next seven years. The court affirmed the plaintiff's testimony by writing:

> In August 2003, the defendant beat the plaintiff when he suspected she was having secret relations with someone else, after which the plaintiff moved back to her natal family. The defendant's numerous efforts, with the help of family and friends, to bring her back home were fruitless. Since then, the plaintiff has been a migrant worker, and has continuously lived apart from the defendant. In October 2004, the defendant organized a group of friends and family to find the plaintiff in the urban center of Song County, and beat her again when they found her.

In the same year she filed for divorce. "Out of fear of encountering the defendant and getting viciously beaten by him, the plaintiff lacked the courage to appear in court for her trial. In the end the court disposed of the case as a petition withdrawal." The court granted the divorce but awarded child custody to the defendant (Decision #843766, Song County People's Court, Henan Province, July 12, 2011).[21]

Another court granted a plaintiff's second divorce petition after she had "voluntarily" withdrawn her prior petition under the defendant's threats of violence. As she put it (in the third person): "In 2006, the plaintiff filed for divorce with the Yancheng Court. Owing to the defendant's threats, the plaintiff later withdrew her petition. After

---

[21] Case ID (2011)嵩城民初字第100号, archived at https://perma.cc/UKL4-BY7U.

doing so, the defendant not only failed to change his ways, but the conflicts intensified." The court granted this – the plaintiff's second – divorce petition (Decision #867215, Luohe Municipal Yancheng District People's Court, Henan Province, November 22, 2011).[22]

Another plaintiff described the reason for her so-called petition withdrawal.

> In the fall of 2012, the defendant, in a fit of anger, beat me with a knife in one hand and a chair in the other hand. When his own mother tried to stop him, he kicked her, causing her to sustain a bone fracture. I previously filed for divorce in 2012, on the 17th day of the first month of the lunar calendar. Under duress from the defendant's threats, I dared not appear in court. The court disposed of the case as a petition withdrawal.

The plaintiff supported her allegations with audio recordings. The defendant did not appear in court, and the court denied the plaintiff's divorce request (Decision #1163699, Fangcheng County People's Court, Henan Province, May 15, 2014).[23]

A plaintiff from elsewhere in Henan recounted a similar experience (referring to herself in the third person). "In 1994, the plaintiff filed for divorce, but under duress from the defendant's threats dared not appear in court. In order to escape the defendant's domestic violence, the plaintiff left home in 2010, and both sides have been physically separated ever since." The court denied the plaintiff's divorce request on the grounds that the foundation of marital affection was solid owing to over 20 years of marriage, that conflicts over minor life issues do not rise to the level of the breakdown of mutual affection, and that they still had reconciliation potential if they invested more effort and care into their marriage (Decision #1075264, Xinyang Municipal Shihe District People's Court, Henan Province, October 21, 2013).[24]

In the words of another plaintiff, owing to her husband's domestic violence,

> I lost confidence in life. The tears washing my face all day blur my vision. On several occasions I considered suicide, but when I thought

---

[22] Case ID (2011)郾民初字第1560号, archived at https://perma.cc/CU4K-FJNC. Decision #1115124 (Zhengzhou Municipal Guancheng Hui District People's Court, Henan Province, January 24, 2014) is similar: Case ID (2013)管民初字第2072号, archived at https://perma.cc/9GKQ-8REJ.

[23] Case ID (2014)方拐民初字第47号, archived at https://perma.cc/9TJN-EFR3.

[24] Case ID (2013)信浉民初字第1615号, archived at https://perma.cc/8QB8-R2QT.

of my septuagenarian mother and my young children, I decided instead to use the legal arsenal to protect my rights. In November 2010, in pursuit of my freedom, I filed for divorce in court. While the case was pending, the defendant showed up and caused a ruckus several times at my natal family's home. Under duress from his threats, I had no choice but to withdraw my petition. After withdrawing my petition, the defendant intensified his cruelty and almost killed me with his domestic violence.

On her second litigation attempt, she submitted photographic evidence of an injury caused by domestic violence and testimony from two people who witnessed the defendant hitting and threatening her. The court refused to admit the photographic evidence on the grounds that it could not prove the cause of the injury, and refused to admit the witness testimony on the grounds that it could not be corroborated. Citing the plaintiff's lack of evidence supporting her claim of the breakdown of mutual affection and "the definite marital foundation of both sides thanks to their over 20 years of marriage and three children they had while living together," the court denied the plaintiff's divorce petition (Decision #1029697, Xun County People's Court, Henan Province, August 29, 2013).[25]

In its ruling on a plaintiff's second divorce petition, another court referred to its successful achievement of "mediated reconciliation" on the prior attempt. The plaintiff's version of events, however, was quite different.

> After marrying, the defendant frequently carried out domestic violence against the plaintiff. Time and again, the plaintiff put up with it, and the defendant's temper only got worse. His tendency to beat the plaintiff broke her heart. When they were both migrant workers in Guangdong, the plaintiff, unable to tolerate the defendant's abuse, called the police for help, and they became physically separated as a result. During their separation, they were unable to agree on the terms of a divorce. After the plaintiff filed for divorce with the Taikang County People's Court, the defendant verbally threatened the safety of the plaintiff and her family. Under duress from his threats, the plaintiff withdrew her petition. The defendant showed no contrition or willingness to change. Viewing this marriage as beyond salvageable, the plaintiff once again left the defendant, and they remain physically separated. Domestic violence has caused the breakdown of mutual affection.

---

[25] Case ID (2013)浚民初字第675号, archived at https://perma.cc/YV6E-PECK.

Citing a lack of evidence to support the plaintiff's claims, the court denied the plaintiff's second petition and called on husband and wife to build mutual understanding, respect, and compassion, and to cherish their marriage (Decision #1297014, Taikang County People's Court, Henan Province, September 4, 2014).[26]

If courts colluded with abusive husbands by turning a blind eye to their threats of violent retaliation against their divorce-seeking wives and by persuading female plaintiffs to withdraw their petitions, we should expect to find that women were more likely than men to drop their lawsuits. Although the pyramids in Figure 6.7 combine both female and male plaintiffs, we have good reasons to expect that their shapes vary by plaintiff sex. Chapter 8 is devoted to analyzing rates at which judges granted first-attempt divorce petitions. It assesses the extent to which and explains why judges, in first-attempt divorce trials, were less likely to grant women's petitions than they were to grant men's petitions. In the remainder of this chapter, I will assess differences between female and male plaintiffs in rates at which plaintiffs withdrew petitions. My assessment is limited to the Henan sample because only a miniscule number of *caiding* decisions in the Zhejiang sample report litigant sex, and the information they contain is too skimpy to infer litigant sex using the method described in Chapter 4.

We can see from Panel A of Figure 6.7 that the petition withdrawal rate was 41% among all first-attempt divorce petitions in the Henan sample closed in 2014 and 2015. Disaggregating by plaintiff sex, the rates were 42% and 38% for female and male plaintiffs, respectively (a highly statistically significant difference of 4 percentage points). Figure 6.8 temporally extends the analysis to the entire 2009–2015 period of time and depicts variation by court context. The lines in Panel A of Figure 6.8 (for female and male plaintiffs) do not represent changes over time in withdrawal rates. Rather, they represent changes in the disclosure of *caiding* decisions approving petition withdrawals. They correspond closely with Figure 4.3, which shows that Henan's courts posted *caiding* decisions online before provincial regulations prohibited them from doing so in 2010, and then resumed posting them in late 2014 after the SPC authorized them to do so (Chapter 4).

---

[26] Case ID (2014)太民初字第1333号, archived at https://perma.cc/P76N-7YHP.

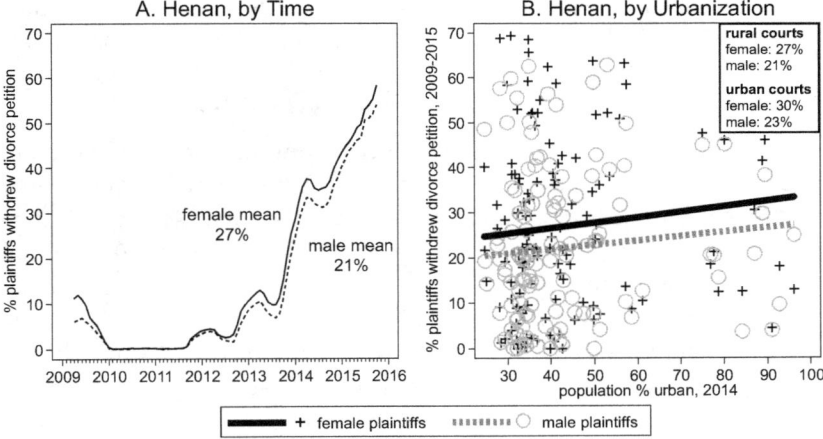

Figure 6.8 Proportion of plaintiffs (%) withdrawing divorce petitions
Source: Author's calculations from online decisions posted by the Henan provincial high court.
Note: n = 72,711 first-attempt divorce adjudications and *caiding* decisions by 161 basic-level courts. Panel A is smoothed with moving averages. For more information on the scatterplot points in Panel B, see the note under Figure 4.5. Panel B contains best-fit lines for female and male plaintiffs.

In Figure 6.8, we are concerned not with withdrawal rates per se (which we know are inaccurate, particularly prior to 2014) but rather with differences in withdrawal rates by plaintiff sex. Panel A shows that withdrawal rates between 2009 and 2015 averaged 27% for women and 21% for men (a highly statistically significant difference of 6 percentage points). Panel B shows that this gap persisted across rural and urban courts.

SUMMARY AND CONCLUSIONS

This chapter provides one explanation for why, over time, courts became increasingly loath to grant divorces. Mounting caseloads, not rising divorce rates, drove the judicial clampdown on divorce. As they toiled under ever-heavier dockets, judges increasingly turned to and benefitted from the divorce twofer. As part of a larger judicial toolkit of coping strategies (Chapter 5), the divorce twofer has helped make the work of judges more manageable. As a judge in Anhui explained,

> we're simply too busy. The case filing system has caused cases to pour into courts in huge numbers while the quota system has caused a reduction

in the number of presiding judges. As a result, judges are all dealing with huge backlogs of cases that must meet trial deadlines. Barely able to scratch the surface of cases, judges save the most trouble by denying first-attempt divorce petitions. (Zhou and Qiu 2018)

The divorce twofer has helped courts economize on scarce human resources in part because the simplified procedure, which requires only one judge, has been applied at higher rates in first-attempt divorce trials than in any other type of first-instance civil trial. Additional benefits judges have enjoyed from denying first-attempt divorce petitions include briefer written decisions and shorter times to finalize and issue them. Judges were able to write these decisions quickly not only because they were so short, but also because, as we will see in Chapter 8, they reused so much generic text, much of it grounded in political ideology. As judges put it, by preserving marriages, they were protecting family harmony and, in so doing, maintaining social stability.

From the standpoint of judges, perhaps best of all was the extent to which the divorce twofer served to shrink dockets by virtue of the small share of plaintiffs who returned for a second attempt after an unsuccessful first attempt – following either an adjudicated denial or a petition withdrawal. Efficiency increases for judges were associated with efficiency declines for litigants. We will see in Chapter 9 that swift denials of divorce petitions resulted in substantial delays for plaintiffs.

Compared to plaintiffs who filed for divorce in parts of China with less per capita litigation, those in Zhejiang have been punished for no reason other than being in Zhejiang. Their divorce prospects were dimmer simply because judges have been allocated to courts principally according to the populations of their jurisdictions and only secondarily according to their caseloads. For this reason, courts in the Yangtze Delta areas of Zhejiang, Jiangsu, and Shanghai, which were afflicted most severely by the problem of "many cases, few judges," have clamped down on divorce harder than courts almost everywhere else in China.

Meanwhile, women everywhere have disproportionately borne the cost of the divorce twofer. Women were both overrepresented among plaintiffs filing for divorce and more likely than men to withdraw their petitions. As we will see in Chapter 8, their divorce petitions were also more likely than men's to be denied. Denying divorce petitions and facilitating petition withdrawals are not the only ways courts have harmed female divorce-seekers. Courts have also harmed women when granting divorces. Promulgated in 2011, the SPC's third Judicial Interpretation of Several Issues Concerning the Application of the Marriage Law stipulated conditions under which housing no longer counted as joint marital property. Real estate titled to only one spouse and either purchased in its entirety prior to marriage or purchased after marriage with the assistance of the parents of that spouse became redefined as individual property (Fincher 2014:47–48; Zang 2020:1216). Legal scholars have decried this new rule for its practical effect of dispossessing women of property and shoring up the patriarchal family (Yang 2011). Taisu Zhang (2012:37–41) argues that the harm it inflicted on women was an unintended consequence of the SPC's primary intent to enhance judicial efficiency by simplifying the determination of property ownership, and thus to help courts cope with the problem of "many cases, few judges." When granting divorces, courts' child custody determinations have also harmed women (Chapters 10 and 11).

Although I have shown that China's divorce courts are leaky, I have no way of systematically tracking and ascertaining the fates of the large share of adjudicated denials and petition withdrawals that did not return as subsequent-attempt petitions. Perhaps some divorce petitions were indeed frivolous, and for this reason did not reappear in court. Judges would surely be tempted to take the small proportion of repeat players as proof that the divorce twofer, by giving impulsive plaintiffs a chance to cool off, saves marriages. Undoubtedly some couples did reconcile. Undoubtedly some plaintiffs turned to the Civil Affairs Administration after "voluntarily agreeing" to waive claims to child custody, property, or both. Finally, undoubtedly some couples failed to reconcile but remained married – either living under the same roof or physically separated – only because plaintiffs were unable to find a way to divorce. The prevalence of these outcomes is an empirical blind spot of my research.

A second empirical blind spot concerns divorce petition withdrawals. *Caiding* decisions are devoid of any information concerning litigants' claims and supporting evidence necessary to support an explanation for why women were at significantly higher risk than men of withdrawing their lawsuits. While this gender difference is consistent with my argument that women often withdrew their divorce petitions under the duress of their abusive husbands, we cannot entirely rule out that women were less serious than men about following through with their lawsuits. This alternative explanation is the public narrative, grounded in gender stereotypes, about irrationally suspicious women filing for divorce frivolously as a scare tactic to keep their husbands in line (Chapter 3), and is difficult to square with the Sisyphean determination – so prominently on display in each subsequent chapter of this book – of so many women to divorce their abusive husbands.

CHAPTER SEVEN

HOW JUDGES GASLIGHT DOMESTIC VIOLENCE VICTIMS IN DIVORCE TRIALS

Chapter 6 empirically demonstrates the benefits to judges of deny-ing first-attempt divorce petitions. In this chapter, we will see the full extent to which hell-bent judges did not let anything – not even domestic violence – stand in their way of reaping those benefits. Their rulings were often legally preposterous but institutionally sensible. They were legally preposterous because they so flagrantly flouted basic tenets of Chinese family law (Chapter 2). At the same time, however, they were institutionally sensible owing to countervailing institutional forces reviewed in Chapter 3: a political ideology that ascribes the real-ization of social harmony and stability maintenance to the strength and health of the family; performance evaluation systems that reward judicial efficiency and punish social unrest; and the cultural logic of patriarchy that diminishes the moral worth of women and the credibil-ity of their legal claims. Preceding chapters lead us to expect that law is not the sole or most important influence on Chinese judicial deci-sion-making in general and in divorce trials in particular. Qualitative findings I present in this chapter bear out our expectation that the institutional logics driving judges' divorce decisions have at least as much to do with extralegal forces as with the law itself.

Studies of intimate partner violence and policy responses focus not only on the direct perpetrators, primarily husbands and boyfriends, but also on the judges who discount and thereby enable it (Epstein and Goodman 2019; Lazarus-Black 2007). The empirical focus of this chapter is judges' holdings in adjudicated divorce cases. A holding

(理由) refers to the section of a written court decision containing the court's grounds or rationale for its verdict (判决).

I have two tasks in this chapter. First, I establish the pervasiveness of domestic violence allegations in divorce trials. Second, I qualitatively document the strategies judges deployed to circumvent fault-based divorce standards and reap the professional benefits of the divorce twofer. Judges downplayed the seriousness of abuse. They denied that spousal battery rose to the level of domestic violence. They tried to convince women of their abusers' love and remorse. They portrayed abuse as isolated incidents from which regretful perpetrators grew to be better people. They negated the legal culpability of abusers. They recast domestic violence as ordinary family disagreements caused by poor communication skills. And they offered relationship advice to abuse victims.

In their divorce petitions, plaintiffs often supported with evidence their fault-based claims that marital affection had already broken down beyond repair owing to domestic violence. Judges overwhelmingly quashed such claims, responding along the lines of, "Oh, he didn't break the law, he just got a little upset. You're overreacting. You may think your marriage is dead, but it is merely wounded. You can rebuild a happy marriage if you just try a little harder." Holdings such as these – universally issued by every basic-level court in Henan and Zhejiang – are equal parts farce and travesty.

Judges' rhetorical strategies were the very essence of gaslighting (Sweet 2019). Abusers commonly turned the tables on their victims. They reframed and redefined domestic violence as just a normal part of marriage. They claimed their victims' injuries were deliberately staged or accidentally self-inflicted. By supporting abusers' (mis)representations of reality, "institutional authorities sometimes become unknowing colluders in gaslighting tactics, setting women up for further violence and loss of credibility" (Sweet 2019:867). Profoundly at odds with the legal meaning of domestic violence and female abuse victims' own understandings of what brought them to court were the revisionist, gaslighting narratives of their husbands, their family members, and judges.

JUDGES COMMONLY FACED DOMESTIC VIOLENCE ALLEGATIONS AND ROUTINELY IGNORED THEM

Let me first establish the sheer prevalence of domestic violence allegations before demonstrating their unimportance to judges. My measure of domestic violence claims detailed in Chapter 4 is consistent with previous estimates cited in Chapter 1: about 30% of all plaintiffs (most of whom were women) and almost 40% of female plaintiffs alleged domestic violence. As Figure 7.1 shows, rates at which female plaintiffs in my samples made claims of domestic violence – 38% in Henan and 39% in Zhejiang – are consistent with previously published estimates. Figure 7.1 also shows that allegations of abuse were consistent across rural and urban courts, although male plaintiffs' likelihood of making abuse claims appeared to increase slightly with urbanization. Given that women accounted for two-thirds of all plaintiffs in both samples, these estimates, if accurate, mean that a full one-quarter of all first-attempt divorce petitions were filed by women making domestic violence allegations.

Also consistent with previously published estimates, 90% and 87% of plaintiffs in the Henan and Zhejiang samples, respectively, who made abuse claims were women (Chen and Duan 2012:29–30; Htun and Weldon 2018:49; Li 2015b:168, 171; Runge 2015:32; Zhao and Zhang 2017:193–94). My estimates of roughly 10% of domestic violence claims made by male plaintiffs in both samples were probably inflated owing to at least two sources of false-positives. First, my measure undoubtedly captured some domestic violence allegations made by female defendants in cases filed by men. Second, my measure also captured some instances of male plaintiffs alleging that they had been beaten by in-laws (e.g., Decision #270158, Shangqiu Municipal Liangyuan District People's Court, Henan Province, July 10, 2009, and Decision #107262, Shangcheng County People's Court, Henan Province, August 6, 2009).[1] Estimates of the incidence of domestic violence claims among female plaintiffs were self-evidently less prone to such false-positives.

My next task was to compare how plaintiffs and judges talked about domestic violence. Female divorce-seekers presented allegations of domestic violence in gruesome detail and meticulously documented them with evidence. They reported all manner of weapons used against them, including cleavers, fruit knives, daggers, single-blade knives, folding knives, switchblade knives, long knives, machetes,

---

[1] Case ID (2009)商梁民初字第325号, archived at https://perma.cc/HVU2-GE7R, and Case ID (2009)商民初字第187号, archived at https://perma.cc/THT3-3NYZ. Neither of these two examples is a first-attempt petition; both are second-attempt petitions. Although the plaintiff in the second example alleged that his wife strangled him with a rope, he also alleged that her brothers beat him. They nonetheless illustrate a measurement limitation in my analysis of first-attempt divorce adjudications.

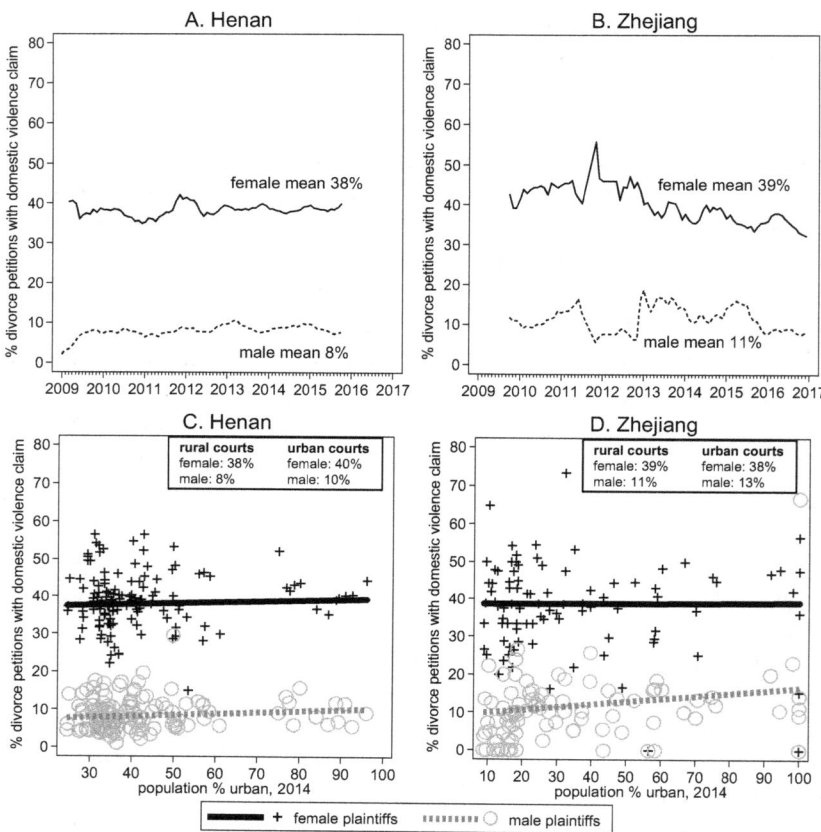

Figure 7.1 Proportion of plaintiffs (%) making domestic violence allegations
Source: Author's calculations from Henan and Zhejiang provincial high courts'
online decisions.
Note: n = 54,200 and n = 8,626 first-attempt adjudicated decisions (granted or
denied) from Henan and Zhejiang, respectively. All sex differences are statistically
significant (χ^2, P < .001). Panels A and B are smoothed with moving averages. For
more information on scatterplot points, see the note under Figure 4.5.

scissors, sickles, hatchets, axes, pickaxes, trowels, hammers, shovels,
pipes, rods, benches, folding stools, and so on. They reported getting
stabbed, cut, and hacked. They reported being choked, strangled,
suffocated, and burned. They reported bone fractures, ruptured eardrums, broken noses, and concussions. They reported sexual violence.
Women rarely used the word for "rape" (强奸), much less the terms
"sexual violence" (性暴力) and "sexual maltreatment" (性虐待).

They more often used various euphemisms for unwanted sexual intercourse (强迫性交, 强行发生性关系) or even euphemistic references to sex (e.g., "marital life," 夫妻生活) in which duress must be inferred by context. Copious alcohol consumption emerged as a perennial theme in domestic violence allegations. They recounted thoughts of suicide and failed suicide attempts, and even instances of being goaded by their husbands to commit suicide. Beyond reporting the occurrence of physical violence, they also reported threats of violence and even of murder, not just against themselves but also against their family members. And they documented their allegations with police reports, hospital records, photographs, transcripts of text messages, and apology letters.

Table 7.1 contains the same estimates of the incidence of plaintiffs' domestic violence allegations ("made domestic violence claim") that we already saw in Figure 7.1. I also considered a more extended set of words and terms that plaintiffs used in association with allegations of domestic violence. In Table 7.1, "any violence words" refers to the incidence of selected words and terms used by plaintiffs in divorce petitions containing allegations of domestic violence. They are not limited to words and terms with overt meanings of violence but also include those with bearings on and connotations of violence. "Violence words" consist of the following 57 Chinese words and terms: "battery" (暴力, 家暴, 殴打, 动手, 打骂, 非打即骂, 毒打, 大打出手, 拳打脚踢, 拳脚, 暴躁, 粗暴); "maltreatment" (虐待); "injury," "contusion," "bruises," "bone fracture," "choke," "knife" (打伤, 受伤, 骨折, 挫伤, 遍体鳞伤, 掐, 脖子, 刀); "torture," "suffering" (折磨); "temper" (脾气); "verbal abuse" (谩骂, 辱骂, 侮辱); "threats" (扬言, 威胁); "suicide" (自杀); "aggravation," "intensification," "escalation" (变本加厉); "forced" (被迫, 强行); "alcohol intoxication" (喝酒, 酒后, 酗酒, 嗜酒); "odious habits," "incorrigible" (恶习, 恶劣, 屡教); "terror" (恐惧, 恐吓); "endure," "intolerable" (忍让, 忍受, 忍气吞声, 忍无可忍); "medical treatment" (住院, 医院, 治疗, 医疗费, 医药费); "sought police help" (报警, 派出所, 公安局); "machismo," "patriarchal" (大男子, 重男轻女); and "promised to change" (保证书, 承诺). The first nine words and terms on this list are those that are also used in my measure of domestic violence allegations (see Chapter 4). In the Henan and Zhejiang samples, 42% and 52%, respectively, of plaintiffs' petitions contained at least one of these violence words. Gender gaps in both the incidence of violence words and the incidence of domestic violence allegations were identical.

TABLE 7.1 Proportion of plaintiffs' petitions and judges' holdings (%) containing domestic violence language

	All plaintiffs	By plaintiff sex		Gender difference
		Female	Male	
Plaintiffs' allegations				
Made domestic violence claim				
Henan (n = 54,200)	28	38	8	30*
Zhejiang (n = 8,626)	30	39	11	27*
Used any violence words				
Henan (n = 54,200)	42	52	22	30*
Zhejiang (n = 8,626)	52	61	34	27*
Judges' holdings, any violence words				
Among all cases				
Henan (n = 54,200)	9	10	6	4*
Zhejiang (n = 8,626)	9	11	7	4*
Among cases in which plaintiff made domestic violence claim				
Henan (n = 15,182)	18	18	17	1
Zhejiang (n = 2,562)	18	18	20	−2

Source: Author's calculations from Henan and Zhejiang provincial high courts' online decisions.
Note: Limited to first-attempt adjudications. Slight discrepancies between numbers in the "gender difference" columns and numbers from which they were derived in the "by plaintiff sex" are due to rounding error.
* $P < .001$, χ^2 test.

Despite the prevalence of violence words in plaintiffs' legal complaints petitions, they were conspicuously absent from judges' holdings. Violence words appeared in 52% and 61% of female plaintiffs' divorce petitions in the Henan and Zhejiang samples, respectively. At the same time, they appeared in only 10% and 11% of judges' holdings in cases filed by women in the two respective samples. Even when plaintiffs made domestic violence claims, judges refrained from using violence words in their holdings. Among all cases in which plaintiffs made allegations of domestic violence (100% of which, by definition, contain violence words), judges used violence words in only 18% of their holdings. In short, judges seldom acknowledged, much less validated, plaintiffs' claims of domestic violence. They addressed violence in fewer than one in five domestic violence cases. Of all first-attempt divorce petitions containing domestic violence claims, judges granted fewer than 2% on this basis.[2] As we will see, when judges did address domestic violence claims, they invalidated them. If everything we knew about domestic violence in China came from judges' divorce holdings, we would come away with the impression that it was exceedingly rare, even among China's most acrimonious marriages, and that marital discord was largely a matter of ordinary misunderstandings between well-intentioned spouses who were capable of reconciling and whose marriages should therefore be preserved. Silence and misrepresentations of domestic violence were central judicial gaslighting strategies.

Plaintiffs in divorce trials generally did not fit the profile of hapless, passive victim (Li 2015a:147). On the contrary, initiating divorce proceedings reflects self-advocacy and agency. Many litigants knew and asserted their legal rights. Undoubtedly, some litigants acquired legal knowledge from "little experts" – divorcees who shared knowledge gained from experience (Gallagher 2006).[3] In particular, plaintiffs frequently invoked language from the SPC's 1989 Fourteen Articles, which calls on judges to "conduct a comprehensive analysis of the marriage's foundation, postmarital affection, grounds for divorce, the current state of marital relations, reconciliation potential, and other aspects when determining whether marital affection has indeed broken down." Many plaintiffs, even those without legal representation, cited chapter and verse of the Fourteen Articles by claiming a weak "marital foundation" and a lack of "reconciliation potential" in their efforts to persuade judges that mutual affection had broken down. The term "marital foundation" (婚姻基础) in the Fourteen Articles refers to how well the couple knew each other and to the strength of their relationship before marrying. Plaintiffs commonly used this term when claiming they "did not know each other well before marrying" (婚前缺乏了解), "married in haste" (草率结婚), came to know the true nature of their spouses only after it was too late, and thus "failed to build marital affection after marriage" (婚后未建立起夫妻感情), which in

---

[2] To be more specific, judges granted divorces and included the word "domestic violence" in their holdings in fewer than 2% of all first-attempt divorce cases in which plaintiffs made domestic violence allegations. Some judges acknowledged but disaffirmed plaintiffs' domestic violence claims when they granted divorces on other grounds. Therefore, the true proportion of divorce petitions granted on fault-based grounds of domestic violence is even smaller.

[3] Although Gallagher developed the concept of "little experts" in the context of labor disputes, surely it is similarly applicable to the divorce litigation context.

turn made it "difficult to live together" (难以共同生活). Each one of these expressions appears in Article 2 as grounds for affirming the breakdown of mutual affection. "Reconciliation potential" (和好的可能) refers to the future possibility of repairing marital damage and restoring marital harmony. To underscore the futility of reconciliation, plaintiffs often asserted that their marriage "existed in name only and was dead in reality" (名存实亡). Plaintiffs also made claims of specific durations of marital separation in their efforts to persuade judges that they satisfied the physical separation test stipulated by the Fourteen Articles (Article 7). Most notably, plaintiffs claimed to have met the breakdownism standard insofar as reconciliation potential had been shattered by the defendant's domestic violence. Plaintiffs spoke the language of faultism in their efforts to establish the breakdown of mutual affection. Their claims that mutual affection had broken down were often grounded in defendant wrongdoing.

We will see in this chapter that plaintiffs' legal knowledge and agency were largely for naught. Defendants and judges invoked the same legal language in the Fourteen Articles to support the opposite conclusion: a "relatively good marital foundation" and the existence of "reconciliation potential." While plaintiffs also frequently referred to various types of wrongdoing stipulated in Article 32 of the 2001 Marriage Law (infidelity tantamount to unlawful cohabitation or even bigamy, gambling, domestic violence) and submitted appropriate evidence in support of their fault-based claims, judges were fixated on the breakdownism standard. As we saw in Chapter 2, *legally* speaking, statutory wrongdoing automatically establishes the breakdown of mutual affection: the SPC, in a 2001 judicial interpretation that carries the force of law, declared that "a divorce request should not be denied when a litigant has committed wrongdoing" (Jiang 2009b:18). *Practically* speaking, however, judges overwhelmingly privileged their analysis of the quality of the marital foundation and reconciliation potential over domestic violence allegations. The Fourteen Articles, by requiring judges to analyze the reasons for marital discord and the potential for reconciliation, calls on judges to act like marriage counselors. We will see that judges went beyond making diagnostic assessments by routinely offering marital advice when they denied divorce petitions.

In the remainder of this chapter I present qualitative case examples showcasing judges' repertoire of gaslighting strategies. I organize into seven sections the various discursive strategies deployed to sideline and neutralize domestic violence allegations.

JUDGES ALMOST UNIFORMLY APPLIED THE BREAKDOWNISM STANDARD

Ultimately, the breakdown of mutual affection is the standard that mattered most to judges. The following represents tens of thousands of court decisions in my samples containing nearly identical language: "Mutual affection is the foundation of marriage, and the statutory standard by which the People's Court grants and denies divorces is whether or not mutual affection has indeed broken down" (Decision #939023, Xingyang Municipal People's Court, Henan Province, January 13, 2013).[4] Some judges even proclaimed in their holdings that breakdownism is the only relevant legal test: "The court holds that whether or not marital affection has completely broken down is the sole standard by which to weigh the decision to grant or deny a divorce" (Decision #2393036, Zhuji Municipal People's Court, Zhejiang Province, October 14, 2011).[5]

> Supplementary case examples set #7–1 is online at: https://decoupling-book.org/.

A key task for judges, then, was to reconcile an irreconcilable legal contradiction: the presence of domestic violence in the absence of the breakdown of mutual affection. A defendant's lack of consent was often the only evidence judges needed to deny divorce petitions according to the breakdownism standard (Xu 2007:204). Holdings such as this were commonplace: "The defendant's unwillingness to divorce shows that marital relations between the plaintiff and defendant have not completely broken down" (Decision #1644365, Zhongmu County People's Court, Henan Province, August 7, 2015).[6] Judges sometimes even used procreation as evidence of mutual affection. A holding that "the couple has been married for X years and has a child" was the common basis of an adjudicated denial.

> The plaintiff and defendant have lawful marital relations that should be protected by law. After marrying they had two children, which shows that they built definite mutual affection when living together. At this

---

[4] Case ID (2012)荥民一初字第378号, archived at https://perma.cc/UZV7-28SJ.
[5] Case ID (2012)绍诸牌民初字第74号, archived at https://perma.cc/Q36H-4GV8.
[6] Case ID (2015)牟民初字第1954号, archived at https://perma.cc/BLC2-EKNH.

time the plaintiff requests a divorce, but she did not submit evidence proving that mutual affection has indeed broken down. For this reason, the court denies support of her petition. (Decision #4796484, Cangnan County People's Court, Zhejiang Province, July 13, 2016)[7]

Even in cases involving compelling allegations of domestic violence, judges frequently justified denying petitions for the sake of the children, as if prolonged exposure to violence somehow promoted "the healthy upbringing of children," a common refrain in judges' holdings.

Even when judges did not use the specific term "mutual affection," such as in the following examples of adjudicated denials, they nonetheless applied the breakdownism test using a similar language.

> Plaintiff Fang and Defendant Wang freely and willingly registered their marriage and had a son. Their marital foundation is relatively good. Post-marital conflict between husband and wife is minor. Their disagreements are over trivial matters. Defendant Wang pledged to correct his violent temper. Husband and wife have the potential to reconcile provided they improve their communication and show mutual understanding, forgiveness, and tolerance. (Decision #2354904, Kaihua County People's Court, Zhejiang Province, June 28, 2010)[8]

Supplementary case examples set #7–2 is online at: https:// decoupling-book.org/.

When judges were hard-pressed to hold that marital affection had not broken down, they could always deny a divorce petition on the basis of political ideology and socialist morality. This was another strategy they deployed to square the legal circle.

JUDGES PRIVILEGED POLITICAL IDEOLOGY AND SOCIALIST MORALITY OVER THE LAW

On the rare occasions that judges invoked fault-based language in their holdings, it was almost always to invalidate plaintiffs' claims of wrongdoing. Judges often avoided addressing plaintiffs' fault-based claims altogether by couching their adjudicated denials in ideologically resonant

---

[7] Case ID (2016)浙0327民初6240号, archived at https://perma.cc/73AX-6CD4.
[8] Case ID (2010)衢开民初字第340号, archived at https://perma.cc/HDX8-QH62.

246

words and terms such as "harmony," "stability," "civilized," and "frivolous divorce" (also see Ahl 2020:178). The following examples are excerpts from holdings in cases involving plaintiffs' allegations of wrongdoing.

> Family is the cell of society, and family harmony is a precondition of social harmony. Although the freedom of marriage in the Marriage Law includes the freedom of divorce, once marriage is established family obligations must be assumed. For this reason, the law does not permit frivolous divorce. (Decision #497630, Xixia County People's Court, Henan Province, February 10, 2011)[9]

> The court holds that the family is the cell of society, and that marital and family stability have a direct bearing on social stability as a whole. (Decision #2286486, Quzhou Municipal Kecheng District People's Court, Zhejiang Province, February 28, 2011)[10]

> In order to preserve the stability of socialist marriage and family, the court denies support of the plaintiff's request. (Decision #4586310, Quzhou Municipal Qujiang District People's Court, Zhejiang Province, July 18, 2016)[11]

> The defendant does not consent to divorce and still desires to preserve the marriage, which proves that there is still reconciliation potential. For this reason, in order to protect family harmony and stability, and in consideration of the healthy upbringing of minors, the court denies support of the plaintiff's divorce petition. (Decision #1631871, Luohe Municipal Yancheng District People's Court, Henan Province, August 7, 2015)[12]

The last example illustrates not only the salience of political ideology but also judges' tendency to use of defendants' unwillingness to divorce as evidence that mutual affection had not broken down.

Supplementary case examples set #7–3 is online at: https:// decoupling-book.org/

As we saw in Chapter 6 (Table 6.5), judges denied the majority of divorce petitions on the first attempt but granted the majority of subsequent divorce petitions. Sometimes, however, plaintiffs required

[9] Case ID (2010)西丹民初字第74号, archived at https://perma.cc/B2PJ-M2HR.
[10] Case ID (2011)衢柯巡民初字第34号, archived at https://perma.cc/TQP3-CMCT.
[11] Case ID (2016)浙0803民初1432号, archived at https://perma.cc/G69T-GYER.
[12] Case ID (2015)郾民初字第01206号, archived at https://perma.cc/2TZ9-9YGZ.

three or four attempts – as we saw at the beginning of Chapter 1 – or even five attempts – as we saw with the case of Ning Shunhua in Chapter 3 – before judges finally granted their divorce petitions. Indeed, sometimes judges will deny petitions seemingly without limits. In its decision to deny a plaintiff's fifth divorce petition, Henan's Qingfeng County People's Court wrote that "the number of divorce petitions filed is not a measure of whether or not mutual affection has broken down. Defendant Yao X has believed all along that marital affection is very good and that husband and wife can continue to live together. For this reason, marital affection has not reached the point that it has indeed broken down" (Decision #987756, May 16, 2013).[13]

As they heeded the political call to preserve marriages, judges sometimes made moral arguments of no legal relevance. On her second divorce attempt, the plaintiff, just as she had done the first time, claimed her husband frequently "beat her black and blue" (打得青紫不断). In particular, she alleged that on May 28, 2014, her husband beat her ruthlessly (死命打), after which she called 110 for help (the equivalent of 911 in the United States) and the next day sought assistance from the All-China Women's Federation. She went on to claim that on July 8, 2014, the defendant almost choked her to death, and that he released her throat only when she bit his hand. She submitted medical documentation as evidence. The defendant challenged the evidence by arguing that it failed to prove he caused the injury in question, and that she was the one who started it in the first place when she rubbed food in his face. Similar to the contents of the "notice of cooling-off period" cited in Chapter 3, the court's holding in this case invoked a moralistic appeal of no legal relevance intended persuade the litigants to stay together.

> There is an old saying: Each marriage is the destiny of a union in this life formed over three previous lifetimes [凡为夫妻之因, 前世三生结缘, 始配今生夫妇]. Husband and wife, affectionately face to face, inseparable lovers and friends, beautifully united, with profound conjugal love, are of two bodies and one heart. ... And yet you came to court to divorce while others look on and sigh with lament! ... Life is not a dress rehearsal; every day is a live broadcast. If life were like a video game that you can lose and restart from the beginning, what do you think life would become? Time that passes is never returned. Each day that goes by cannot be recovered. For this reason, you must cherish

---

[13] Case ID (2012)清民初字第3620号, archived at https://perma.cc/ZR8Z-D8JY.

every moment. You must also treasure each other, communicate with sincerity, love each other, and jointly nourish with care this precious gift of a family. (Decision #4538954, Chun'an County People's Court, Zhejiang Province, May 20, 2016)[14]

JUDGES GAVE MORE CREDENCE TO DEFENDANTS' DENIALS THAN TO PLAINTIFFS' ALLEGATIONS

As we saw in Chapter 2, SPC rules allow judges to apply a "preponderance of evidence" standard when adjudicating between two versions of events. In my sample of tens of thousands of divorce cases involving claims of domestic violence, however, one judge did so. In this solitary case, the litigants made typical statements. The plaintiff alleged that her husband had beaten her, covered her body in bruises, bitten her arm, and kicked her stomach when she was pregnant. In addition to petitioning for marital dissolution, she also claimed civil damages for emotional distress. As evidence, she submitted a copy of a "pledge letter" in which her husband admitted beating her as well as six photographs documenting the injuries she sustained. To support his denial of her allegations, the defendant argued that the events precipitating her calls for emergency police assistance were not domestic violence but "merely mutual acts of domestic quarreling," and submitted police reports from two such calls in support of his version of events. Applying the "preponderance of evidence" standard (Chapter 2), the court held:

> In this case, although the defendant denied carrying out domestic violence and denied causing the injuries in the photographs submitted by the plaintiff, police reports of the plaintiff's emergency calls establish that physical conflict occurred on September 28, 2013 and that the defendant both beat the plaintiff causing a head injury and bit and injured the plaintiff's right arm on June 16, 2014. In light of the hidden nature of domestic violence, the unwillingness of outsiders to intervene, and a desire to prevent others from finding out, these events are consistent with the informal ways domestic conflicts are handled after they are reported to the police. The court holds that the probability is relatively high that the injuries depicted in the photographs submitted by

---

14 Case ID (2015)杭淳威民初字第75号, archived at https://perma.cc/KG4S-ZP9X. The plaintiff repeated the same claims she had made on her first attempt in the same court in front of the same presiding judge: Decision #3541419, September 25, 2014, Case ID (2014)杭淳威民初字第97号, archived at https://perma.cc/C8TB-2R5X.

the plaintiff were caused by the defendant. Moreover, the defendant's pledge letter shows that he beat the plaintiff once again on October 23, 2013 and admitted inflicting all kinds of suffering on the plaintiff when she was pregnant, resulting in serious physical and psychological harm. (Decision #3521129, Hangzhou Municipal Jianggan District People's Court, Zhejiang Province, May 12, 2015)[15]

Although the litigants' statements were typical, the court's ruling was atypical in several respects. First, the court granted the divorce on the first attempt, albeit perhaps in part because the defendant consented to divorce. Second, the court awarded civil damages. Wrongdoing is a precondition of civil damages, and judges rarely affirmed the occurrence of domestic violence (which would privilege faultism standards for granting divorce over their preferred breakdownism standards for denying divorce). Judges can only grant civil damages according to Article 46 of the Marriage Law if they first affirm the occurrence of one of four faults: (1) bigamy, (2) cohabitation with a third party, (3) domestic violence, and (4) maltreatment or desertion of a family member.

Rarely, however, did litigants request "compensation for emotional distress" (精神损害抚慰金, 精神损害赔偿金, and similar terms) or other types of damages despite their legal right to do so. In the full Henan sample, I found only 3,247 requests for civil damages from plaintiffs and 1,545 from defendants (4.5% and 2.1% of all 72,102 adjudications, respectively). In the full Zhejiang sample, I found only 1,003 requests from plaintiffs and 687 from defendants (1.4% and 1.0% of all 72,048 adjudications, respectively). Of all of these 6,482 claims for civil damages I was able to identify in both samples (4.5% of all 144,150 adjudications), only 294 were awarded with some amount of compensation (4.5% of all requests, and 0.2% of all adjudications). Moreover, only between one-third and one-half of plaintiffs' requests for civil damages were associated with domestic violence allegations. Even when courts granted divorces, they were exceedingly unlikely to recognize the few claims of plaintiffs who both made allegations of domestic violence and requested civil damages: they awarded civil damages in only 5.8% and 14.9% of such cases in the Henan and Zhejiang samples, respectively. The rarity of both claims for and awards of civil damages in my samples mirrors findings in previous research (Bu, Li,

[15] Case ID (2015)杭江民初字第375号, archived at https://perma.cc/DT96-QSQ2.

and Lin 2015:13; Chen, Shi, and Zhang 2016; Deng 2017:111–12; Li 2015b; Lin, Bu, and Li 2015:125). Plaintiffs are reluctant to claim civil damages in part because they know that, owing to the divorce twofer, they will likely leave court without a divorce and face the possibility of retaliation from their abusive husbands (Deng 2017:113).

Third, the judge in this case, by ruling that the evidence favored the plaintiff's claims more than the defendant's claims, chose to believe the plaintiff's claims. From the standpoint of the law, judges are supposed to give women the benefit of the doubt in "he said, she said" scenarios. In domestic violence cases, they are supposed to relax ordinary evidentiary standards by applying the "preponderance of evidence" rule – precisely as this judge did. Judges typically ignored plaintiffs' allegations, however, even when they were supported by evidence. Chinese courts have seemingly limitless discretion with respect both to admitting and excluding evidence and to affirming and disaffirming litigants' claims. Judges could and did deny divorces willy-nilly regardless of the quantity and quality of evidence supporting claims of defendant wrongdoing.

One court decision in the Zhejiang sample provides an example of a widespread phenomenon of judges' misusing or ignoring the applicable laws and SPC interpretations (including opinions and guidelines) I reviewed in Chapter 2. The plaintiff's allegations in this case were as follows. During an argument over their daughter's school tuition in August 2009, the defendant beat the plaintiff, causing her to suffer a dislocated atlanto-axial joint (between the first and second cervical vertebrae of the neck) and as a result to spend eight days in the hospital. On November 13, 2009, the defendant intimidated the plaintiff by threatening in text messages, among other things, to use sulfuric acid to mutilate her. On March 1, 2010, the defendant beat the plaintiff at her workplace before a crowd. To support these claims, the plaintiff submitted two photographs documenting the March 1, 2010, injury; two sets of hospital records; an incident report from the local police substation documenting the threatening text messages; a "pledge letter" dated March 3, 2010, written under the urging of the local police substation and the villagers' committee in which the defendant promised to stop beating the plaintiff; and a statement from the village mediation committee documenting multiple mediation efforts that were precipitated by marital tensions, conducted over the previous few years, and ultimately proved unsuccessful. The defendant simply stated, "I do not consent to divorce, the plaintiff's statements are false, and I wish to reconcile with the plaintiff." In response to the plaintiff's evidence, the defendant confirmed writing the pledge letter but disavowed its contents ("I wrote what the village leader told me to write"); had no objections to the police incident report and one set of hospital records; professed ignorance about the second set of hospital records; and denied causing the injury in the photographs. In its holding, the court affirmed every piece of evidence, even stating that the photographs showed bruising on the plaintiff's right hand and that the hospital records dated March 1, 2010 established that the plaintiff's left shoulder had been injured by a forcible blow inflicted by "another person's fist" within one hour of the medical examination. Although the court did not exclude any of the submitted evidence, it nonetheless did not explicitly state that the documented injuries had been caused by the defendant. The court stated that the plaintiff's evidence only proved "the occurrence of several incidents of conflict" and poor results of mediation conducted by the police substation and villagers' committee, but failed to prove the breakdown of mutual affection, particularly in light of the defendant's opposition to the divorce request and hope for reconciliation. Declaring that reconciliation remained possible, the court denied the plaintiff's divorce petition (Decision #2333373, Anji County People's Court, Zhejiang Province, April 16, 2010).[16]

Another woman alleged that her husband frequently raped her. She told the court that for several years she had slept in a separate room, and that, under his mother's urging, her husband had on many occasions broken in and forced himself on her while his mother watched. She recounted another time when her mother-in-law and sister-in-law attacked and choked her. She testified that on one morning, her husband and mother-in-law broke into her room, at which point he held her down on the bed, forcibly removed her clothes, beat her, and "committed a brutal act" that left bruises on her body and for which there was forensic documentation. In support of her allegations, she submitted a copy of a "pledge letter" written by the defendant proving that he beat her. In his defense, her husband denied all her allegations, arguing that she fabricated them in an effort to get away with

---

[16] Case ID (2010)湖安良民初字第22号, archived at https://perma.cc/94HQ-3DQC.

her unspecified "betrayal." Without pursuing additional evidence, the court ruled as follows:

> Husband and wife should be mutually loyal and respectful. Although plaintiff and defendant were not acquainted for long before marrying, no fundamental conflicts have arisen after marrying. Moreover, they have already given birth to a son and a daughter, and have retroactively registered their marriage. In the past two years, the defendant has been unable to deal correctly with marital affection and family conflict. Both sides have fought over trifles, bringing harm to their marital affection. Both sides should diligently reflect on and learn from their experiences, and, taking the interests of family harmony and the physical and psychological health of their children as the starting point, forgive, accommodate, and respect each other, and together build a harmonious, happy family. In the course of the trial, the plaintiff failed to submit evidence that mutual affection has broken down, the defendant did not consent to divorce, and the defendant expressed his hope to live happily with the plaintiff. The court is therefore unable to affirm the breakdown of mutual affection. In order to protect the stability of marriage and the physical and psychological wellbeing of children, the court, in accordance with Article 32 of the Marriage Law, hereby denies to grant a divorce between plaintiff Luo X and defendant Ding X. (Decision #1150780, Shangcheng County People's Court, Henan Province, April 8, 2014)[17]

A defendant was likely to deny a plaintiff's claim that he caused her injury, and the court was likely to side with him by ruling that the plaintiff's evidence proved only that an injury occurred but not who caused it. When plaintiffs supported their allegations of domestic violence with photographic evidence of injuries, courts often supported defendants' objections that the submitted evidence failed to establish the cause of an injury. As a typical example, a plaintiff described an incident in which the defendant battered her to the point that "my body was covered in blood and sustained soft tissue injuries in several places." She supported her claim with a diagnostic report from a local hospital, a letter from the local police substation, and a photograph. To support his counterclaim that the plaintiff caused her own injuries by hitting herself, the defendant submitted a CD (光盘), the contents of which were undisclosed. The court held that

---

[17] Case ID (2013)商民初字第940号, archived at https://perma.cc/H5JH-R9BS.

although marital affection has been harmed by conflicts, anger, and physical and verbal fighting over trifling matters, the breakdown of mutual affection has not reached the level stipulated by the Marriage Law. Furthermore, because the defendant is unwilling to divorce and strongly desires reconciliation, the plaintiff and defendant should have an opportunity to reconcile. The court therefore denies the plaintiff's divorce petition. (Decision #1025781, Fugou County People's Court, Henan Province, September 3, 2013)[18]

> Supplementary case examples set #7–4 is online at: https://decoupling-book.org/.

Defendants often counterclaimed that the alleged injuries were self-inflicted (Fincher 2014:152). In the following example, the court affirmed that an injury had in fact occurred, but, after the defendant denied causing it, failed to affirm the defendant's responsibility for the injury, and ultimately denied the plaintiff's divorce petition. It illustrates judges' tendency to support defendants' denials of domestic violence allegations.

> In support of her claims, the plaintiff provided five photographs showing injuries to prove the defendant's frequent violence. Defendant's statement: Mutual affection with the plaintiff is very good and I do not consent to divorce. Only two of the five photographs provided by the plaintiff depict the plaintiff, and the other three are of someone else. Furthermore, I did not cause the plaintiff's injuries. Rather, she caused them herself by falling down the stairs. (Decision #958199, Qingfeng County People's Court, Henan Province, April 6, 2013)[19]

> Supplementary case examples set #7–5 is online at: https://decoupling-book.org/.

On her third attempt to divorce in court, a female plaintiff testified that her husband's violence intensified after she withdrew her first divorce petition following a court-mediated reconciliation. As she explained, she had given him an opportunity to fulfill his promise to

---

[18] Case ID (2013)扶民初字第659号, archived at https://perma.cc/RD4U-EF5W.
[19] Case ID (2013)清民初字第572号, archived at https://perma.cc/L9QC-YAEE.

stop beating her for six months, at which point she would be eligible to file a new divorce petition. She described how he choked her; how he dragged her out of bed by her feet and down the stairs; how he attacked her with a knife; how she called the police after he smashed a new bed she bought; and how, in front of the police, he declared his intention to murder her entire family. To support her claims, she submitted six photographs. He objected to all of them for different reasons. He said one photograph depicted an injury that was the result not of his beating her but rather of getting struck by the bed when – as he admitted – he flipped it over. Because it found that the photographs "cannot prove the defendant carried out domestic violence against the plaintiff," the court excluded them from evidence. As Chinese courts so often did in similar cases, the court denied the plaintiff's petition on the grounds that the couple's relatively long acquaintanceship before marriage and their relatively solid marital foundation made reconciliation still possible, provided they put family and child first, strengthened understanding and trust, and paid attention to managing and controlling their emotions. In this case, the total duration of time from her first divorce attempt to the actual divorce was two-and-a-half years (Decision #4521359, Hangzhou Municipal Yuhang District People's Court, Zhejiang Province, June 17, 2016).[20]

Another plaintiff, like so many subjected to the divorce twofer, testified that marital affection did not improve after the court denied her first divorce petition. She specifically alleged that her husband had beaten her and that she had reported him to the police on more than one occasion in the time since the previous trial. She had filed her first divorce petition the year before, and claimed to have suffered a broken rib during one of her husband's many instances of abuse. To support her claims, she submitted a copy of a police report. The defendant counterclaimed that her injury was not the result of his beating but rather the result of his pulling her back to safety when she rushed up to the fourth floor to jump off the building. The court denied the plaintiff's petition for divorce after holding that the litigants had built significant marital affection through their over ten years of marriage and birth of a son, and after insisting that they could reconcile – if only they corrected their shortcomings, empathized with and trusted each other, and gave greater consideration to family and child. In this case,

---

[20] Case ID (2016)浙0110民初6798号, archived at https://perma.cc/UPE2-VL5C.

the total duration of time from her first divorce attempt to the actual divorce was over one-and-a-half years (Decision #4643900, Yongkang Municipal People's Court, Zhejiang Province, August 8, 2016).[21]

JUDGES DENIED THE VALIDITY OF PLAINTIFFS' EVIDENCE ON BEHALF OF ABSENTEE DEFENDANTS

Even when defendants did not deny plaintiffs' allegations of domestic violence, judges sometimes did so on their behalf. In both of the following examples, the defendant failed to participate in trial proceedings. Luckily for them, the judges acted – in a manner of speaking – as their advocates.

> [The defendant] often beats me without provocation. Domestic violence is a constant. In recent years the defendant's beatings have intensified, and the defendant has tried to desert me by forcing me out of the home. When drunk, the defendant becomes wild and curses and beats me, and has even wielded a knife to kill me. At around 7 pm on the lunar calendar's 20th day of the 12th month of 2009 … the defendant went after me with a knife to my parents' home and tried to hack me to death. Thankfully someone pulled me away and I escaped injury. At around 11 pm on August 8, 2010 the defendant refused my offer of ¥20,000 in exchange for a divorce and held a knife to my neck. The blade cut my skin leaving a wound 2 cm in length. For this reason, living together is impossible, and mutual affection has completely broken down. … The plaintiff submitted the following pieces of evidence: … (4) photographs proving the fact of the injury caused by the defendant's attempt to kill the plaintiff. … The defendant made no statement of defense and submitted no evidence. … The court holds that … the plaintiff's fourth item of evidence shows only that the plaintiff was injured but cannot prove that the defendant caused the injury, and the court therefore considers it inadmissible. … Although in recent years trifles of life have caused some conflict and impacted marital affection, mutual affection has not broken down. Furthermore, the plaintiff failed to submit evidence proving that marital affection has indeed broken down. (Decision #2463687, Cangnan County People's Court, Zhejiang Province, September 30, 2010)[22]

The next example illustrates how judges even denied the validity of evidence supporting plaintiffs' claims of physical separation. It also

---

[21] Case ID (2016)浙0784民初4589号, archived at https://perma.cc/R7MB-VP98.
[22] Case ID (2010)温苍民初字第1186号, archived at https://perma.cc/CZ59-SL6X.

foreshadows my discussion in Chapter 9 of the relationship between domestic violence and labor migration.

> In the beginning of 2011, the defendant suspected I was carrying on with another man. Holding a knife, he threatened and beat me. I had no choice but to leave home and go to [the city of] Xinxiang to work. After a while I missed my children and returned to visit them. At that time the defendant beat me again. He also prohibited our children from calling me mother. Later on someone introduced me to a job in [the provincial capital of] Zhengzhou. The defendant's actions have caused tremendous physical and psychological harm to me. ... The defendant did not make a statement. In support of her claims, the plaintiff submitted the following pieces of evidence: ... (2) a housing rental lease signed by the plaintiff and Yin X on May 30, 2011 and an affidavit signed by Yin X on April 20, 2013, both for the purpose of proving that marital relations have broken down according to the defendant and plaintiff's continuous physical separation since May 30, 2011, which meets the two-year requirement. ... The defendant submitted no evidence. ... From its review of the evidence, the court finds that ... the plaintiff's second set of evidence proves only that a tenant-landlord relationship exists between the plaintiff and Yin X, but proves neither that the plaintiff and defendant are living apart nor that mutual affection has broken down. Furthermore, Yin X did not testify in court. These pieces of evidence are therefore inadmissible. ... The court holds that if both sides let bygones be bygones and mutually respect one another, they can certainly form a harmonious and civilized family. For this reason, the court denies support of the plaintiff's petition. (Decision #988853, Huixian Municipal People's Court, Henan Province, June 5, 2013)[23]

Supplementary case examples set #7–6 is online at: https://decoupling-book.org/.

JUDGES TRIVIALIZED VIOLENCE

Trivializing abuse as "failing to rise to the level of domestic violence" allowed judges to reconcile invoking breakdownism to deny a divorce request after affirming the occurrence of physical abuse. Remarkably, they did so even when defendants openly admitted to beating their wives. In one case, the female plaintiff provided photographs and

---

[23] Case ID (2013)辉民初字第1037号, archived at https://perma.cc/AV3L-J26U.

medical records of seven days of inpatient hospital treatment for an injury sustained by the defendant's domestic violence. The defendant admitted beating her and causing the injury, but after adding that "the incident happened for a reason," he said he did not consent to the divorce. The court concluded that "although in the course of living together husband and wife have become angry about household chores and other minor life matters, and beatings have occurred as a result, they have been rare and do not constitute domestic violence, and therefore do not prove that mutual affection has indeed broken down" (Decision #952495, Nanzhao County People's Court, Henan Province, February 28, 2013).[24]

In her statement to the court, a plaintiff claimed that "the defendant on many occasions physically injured me. For the sake of my son, I repeatedly tolerated his abuse, but endured serious domestic violence as a consequence." Although the defendant admitted beating and cursing the plaintiff, he denied committing domestic violence. Moreover, he said he beat her because she played too much mahjong and was unfaithful. In its holding, the court wrote:

> Although the defendant occasionally beat and cursed the plaintiff, there is no evidence that his acts of beating and berating the plaintiff were frequent and persistent or that they caused serious consequences, and they therefore do not constitute domestic violence. Furthermore, the plaintiff failed to provide evidence of other statutory conditions of the breakdown of mutual affection. The court therefore denies support of the plaintiff's petition to divorce the defendant. (Decision #3737154, Zhoushan Municipal Putuo District People's Court, Zhejiang Province, May 5, 2015)[25]

The foregoing case illustrates judges' discretionary application of an SPC judicial interpretation that includes "frequency and persistence" in its definition of domestic violence (Chapter 2). Judges even denied divorce petitions after affirming the occurrence of domestic battery. In one case, the court denied the plaintiff's second divorce petition even though it affirmed her claim that her husband injured her head when he beat her in 2010, three years after it denied her first divorce petition. In light of the defendant's continued unwillingness to divorce, his repeated pleas for forgiveness, and "considering that marital conflict

---

[24] Case ID (2012)南召民初字第1071号, archived at https://perma.cc/9LVA-UEEZ.
[25] Case ID (2015)舟普六民初字第36号, archived at https://perma.cc/2B8F-G3Z2.

caused by everyday domestic issues is unavoidable, the court is unable to establish the existence of the odious habit of recurrent domestic violence" (Decision #824784, Zhengzhou Municipal Zhongyuan District People's Court, Henan Province, July 11, 2012).[26]

Another plaintiff recounted the following history of injuries. In 2008, she was hospitalized after the defendant caused a concussion and chest hemorrhaging. In 2012, she was hospitalized again after the defendant cut her with the glass lining of a hot water thermos and smashed a beer bottle over her head, causing a cerebral hematoma. In 2013, she was hospitalized for 13 days with a broken nose, a fractured eye socket, an ear contusion, and head and chest wounds. To support her allegations, she submitted as evidence police and hospital documentation. In his defense, the defendant stated: "I do not consent to divorce, marital relations are good. Both sides occasionally argue and fight, but afterwards we're as good as new." The court, in an epic understatement, held: "In recent years, some conflict has emerged over family trifles. Last year the defendant was on the extreme side of contentious, but mutual affection has not declined to the level of complete breakdown" (Decision #2859679, Longquan Municipal People's Court, Zhejiang Province, March 5, 2014).[27]

In hundreds of decisions in my samples, courts trivialized claims of physical abuse, often supported by medical and police documentation, by reducing it to "unavoidable friction" (variations of 有些摩擦在所难免). My samples are replete with examples of courts' normalization of abuse. In one case, the plaintiff claimed that the defendant ruptured both of her eardrums and threatened to stab her and her whole family to death, and that she reported him to the police, who "took him away." In his statement, the defendant simply said, "I do not consent to divorce, affection between me and the plaintiff has not declined to the point of breaking down." In its holding, the court stated that "squabbling over family trifles is unavoidable in marriage" (Decision #1194815, Miyang County People's Court, Henan Province, June 23, 2014).[28]

Similar to judges elsewhere in the world (Jeffries 2016:8), Chinese judges reframed and redefined domestic violence as mere "pushing and shoving" and as mutual fighting (Fincher 2014:145) in order to

---

[26] Case ID (2012)中民一初字第1456号, archived at https://perma.cc/E52Y-69X7. For a similar case, see Merry (2009:89–90).

[27] Case ID (2014)丽龙民初字第63号, archived at https://perma.cc/5WA3-9XQN.

[28] Case ID (2014)泌民初字第218号, archived at https://perma.cc/5GT2-ZS6T.

undermine plaintiffs' efforts to establish fault-based grounds for the breakdown of mutual affection.

> Plaintiff's statement: … moreover the defendant has committed severe domestic violence, which I have reported to the police numerous times. However, the defendant has not changed one bit. Despite writing countless pledge letters, the defendant has never respected any of the promises they contain. At the end of 2012, I filed for divorce in court, and the case was concluded by mediated reconciliation. However, the defendant failed to atone for past mistakes. On the contrary, domestic violence against me intensified. … In September 2015 I filed for divorce again in court, and for various reasons the court denied my petition. But the current situation has not improved the least bit. The defendant carries out even more domestic violence against me. For this reason, I am filing for divorce. … The plaintiff submitted the following supporting evidence: … (2) 18 text messages proving that the defendant committed domestic violence; (3) one pledge letter proving that mutual affection has broken down and that the defendant has committed domestic violence; (4) one court mediation decision and one court adjudication decision proving that the plaintiff had already filed two divorce petitions in court and that this is the third time filing for divorce, which also proves that mutual affection has broken down; … (6) one personal safety protection order application proving that I am a domestic violence victim; (7) 20 WeChat messages proving that the defendant's threatening behavior constitutes domestic violence; and (8) police visit receipts and appraisal notices proving the defendant's actions against me and my family constitute domestic violence. Defendant's statement: … I object to the plaintiff's allegations of domestic violence. I believe that knocking and bumping [磕磕碰碰] into each other is a normal part of marital life. … The court holds that whether mutual affection has broken down is the basis of deciding whether to grant a divorce. Quarrels over family trifles are a normal phenomenon in marital life and difficult to avoid. The plaintiff filed for divorce once again after the court denied the plaintiff's previous petition on November 11, 2015, but the plaintiff has still failed to provide evidence sufficient to prove that mutual affection has broken down, that the defendant committed domestic violence, gambled, used drugs, or has another odious habit, or that the plaintiff and defendant have been physically separated for at least two years. (Decision #4683589, Quzhou Municipal Qujiang District People's Court, Zhejiang Province, August 19, 2016)[29]

---

[29] Case ID (2016)浙0803民初01430号, archived at https://perma.cc/UJ5J-HRKJ.

Supplementary case examples set #7–7 is online at: https://decoupling-book.org/.

Courts often affirmed plaintiffs' evidence of domestic violence while simultaneously denying the breakdown of mutual affection. In her legal complaint, a plaintiff described her husband as "petty" (小心眼) and then claimed he frequently read her cell phone messages and forbade her from interacting with other men. According to the plaintiff's statement, her loss of personal freedom was the reason for their many fights, including one after which she was hospitalized with a broken nose and bruised right eye. On the basis of medical documentation submitted by the plaintiff and witness testimony, the court affirmed her claim of domestic violence as factual. The defendant failed to appear in court or to submit a written defense statement. In its ruling to deny the plaintiff's divorce petition, the court wrote:

> The plaintiff believes that… the defendant committed domestic violence against the plaintiff, causing the complete breakdown of mutual affection. Although the court holds as factual the defendant's injury of the plaintiff on April 27, 2010, it also holds that it was an occasional act of violence caused by trifles of life, does not constitute an act of recurrent violence, and therefore does not fall within the scope of domestic violence as stipulated by the Marriage Law. (Decision #2348792, Sanmen County People's Court, Zhejiang Province, June 17, 2010)[30]

Judges also held that marital affection and reconciliation potential persisted owing to abusive defendants' love for their wives and commitment to rectifying their errors. Judges discursively transformed what plaintiffs understood as intolerable and unlawful abuse constituting grounds for divorce into innocent misunderstandings and mistakes on the part of caring husbands, and in so doing gaslighted plaintiffs by calling into question their sense of reality (Sweet 2019). In response to a plaintiff's request for a divorce on the grounds of "the defendant's ceaseless physical abuse and domestic violence," the defendant responded by stating, "I was not calm enough, truly did beat her, and regret what I did; no matter what, it is wrong to hit people, and I admit my mistake." In its holding, the court declared: "The defendant is sincere about repenting, mending his ways, and putting an absolute

---

[30] Case ID (2010)台三健民初字第99号, archived at https://perma.cc/HL6T-DRE4.

end to heated behavior. ... The plaintiff's grounds for divorce do not meet the statutory requirement stipulated by the Marriage Law that mutual affection has broken down, and the court therefore denies support of the plaintiff's petition" (Decision #1575160, Luohe Municipal Shaoling District People's Court, Henan Province, July 28, 2015).[31]

Supplementary case examples set #7–8 is online at: https://decoupling-book.org/.

JUDGES IGNORED POLICE WARNINGS

With respect to legal responses to domestic violence, Zhejiang's city of Wenzhou was an early bird in a couple of respects. First, according to one report, in 2006, it issued China's first anti-domestic violence government order, the Provisions of the Municipality of Wenzhou on Preventing and Combatting Domestic Violence. Second, at the end of 2013 it created a domestic violence warning system governed by the Measures of the Municipality of Wenzhou for the Implementation of a Domestic Violence Warning System (Zhou 2013).[32] Jiangsu had already taken the lead on domestic violence warning systems earlier in the same year (Tan 2016). Zhejiang's cities of Jiaxing and Lin'an followed suit within a few years (https://perma.cc/6XTQ-AY8A; https://perma.cc/XTV6-AXP7). Under these systems, police authorities issue written warnings (家庭暴力告诫书) for "minor incidents, such as face slapping, that do not constitute criminal battery." These written warnings were also intended to serve as evidence in divorce trials (Zhou 2013). Indeed, they were incorporated into the 2015 Anti-Domestic Violence Law, which stipulates that judges can use them to affirm the occurrence of domestic violence (Article 20). In the first two years of this system, Wenzhou issued 471 domestic violence warnings (J. Liu 2016). In 2017, these systems went province-wide with the Measures

---

[31] Case ID (2015)召民二初字232号, archived at https://perma.cc/YMH3-ECQG.

[32] In fact, the municipal government of Hunan's provincial capital of Changsha had already issued Several Provisions on Preventing and Combatting Domestic Violence in 1996 (H. Zhang 2012:44–45; H. Zhang 2014:229). Henan issued its provincial Decisions on Preventing and Combatting Domestic Violence in 2006 and Regulations on Preventing and Combatting Domestic Violence in 2018 (Equality 2020). Zhejiang issued its provincial Regulations on Preventing and Combatting Domestic Violence in September 2010 (Chen and Duan 2012:37n2).

of the Province of Zhejiang for the Implementation of a Domestic Violence Warning System. Article 13 in both versions is clear: "In divorce trials involving domestic violence, people's courts may use domestic violence warnings as evidence to affirm domestic violence as a factual occurrence."

In practice, however, very few domestic violence warnings ended up as evidence in trials – either civil or criminal. Even when divorce-seekers did submit domestic violence warnings in support of their fault-based claims, judges still found ways to deny their divorce petitions. Forced to accept occurrences of domestic violence as facts, judges would (mis)characterize them as insufficiently serious or too "minor" to satisfy statutory faultism standards.

One plaintiff submitted a domestic violence warning documenting a head injury with red swelling caused by the defendant. The husband challenged the evidence by stating, "it was because of a dispute that occurred when the plaintiff insulted me." Despite affirming the admissibility of the evidence, the court denied the plaintiff's petition for divorce under the pretext of insufficient evidence of the breakdown of mutual affection. In its holding, the court wrote: "Although the defendant carried out a minor act of domestic violence, he did not commit another such act after the Public Security Bureau issued its warning" (Decision #3936527, Wenzhou Municipal Longwan District People's Court, Zhejiang Province, November 17, 2015).[33]

Another judge, before denying the plaintiff's petition for divorce, held that the evidence was inadmissible for the following reason:

> The domestic violence warning simply recorded a fight between the two sides that led to an injury to the plaintiff's scalp, which, according to the plaintiff's testimony, required only three stitches. Moreover, because the plaintiff was unable to provide additional corroborating evidence, the allegations could not be affirmed as factual. ... The plaintiff claimed that the defendant committed a serious instance of domestic violence but failed to submit evidence proving it. (Decision #3854541, Cangnan County People's Court, Zhejiang Province, September 18, 2015)[34]

In each of these cases, the presiding judge recast what should have been a legally unambiguous occurrence of domestic violence as, respectively, "a minor act" and "a fight between the two sides" falling short

---

[33] Case ID (2015)温龙开民初字第373号, archived at https://perma.cc/5ZUB-S9Y3.
[34] Case ID (2015)温苍龙民初字第608号, archived at https://perma.cc/7LGM-VBZW.

of "a serious incident of domestic violence." By redefining domestic violence as relatively harmless and/or mutual fighting, judges denied divorces to plaintiffs legally deserving of divorce.

One court even went so far as to hold that a domestic violence warning "could not fully and effectively prove the occurrence of domestic violence as a factual matter," and that it therefore "did not affirm a link between this piece of evidence and the plaintiff's claim of domestic violence." For these reasons, the court denied the plaintiff's divorce petition (Decision #4554804, Tiantai County People's Court, Zhejiang Province, June 17, 2016).[35]

On June 19, 2016, less than a month after a plaintiff withdrew her divorce petition on May 23, 2016, her husband received a domestic violence warning. She filed for divorce once again two days later, on June 21, 2016. Recall that the Civil Procedure Law provides for an exception to the six-month statutory waiting period on the basis of "new developments" or "new reasons" (Chapter 3). Although the plaintiff claimed that the incident precipitating the domestic violence warning constituted a "new development," the court disagreed, holding that domestic fights had long been a fixture of their marriage, and refused to hear the case. Whereas domestic violence claims are usually an inconvenient obstacle courts ignore or clear out of the way in order to deny divorce petitions, in this case the court used recurrent violence to its advantage as an expedient means of making the case go away for at least a few more months (Decision #4591750, Chun'an County People's Court, Zhejiang Province, July 21, 2016).[36]

Supplementary case examples set #7–9 is online at: https:// decoupling-book.org/.

As we have seen, defendants' unwillingness to divorce provides the ideal pretext for courts to deny the breakdown of mutual affection. Instead of granting divorce petitions on the grounds of fault-based evidence of domestic violence, judges routinely swept aside domestic violence allegations when defendants were unwilling to divorce or affirmatively expressed their desire to reconcile. By privileging breakdownism over faultism, judges took abusive defendants' contrition and

[35] Case ID (2016)浙1023民初2366号, archived at https://perma.cc/W87S-UTYP.
[36] Case ID (2016)浙0127民初2588号, archived at https://perma.cc/T7FF-YFLX.

wish to stay together as evidence of reconciliation potential and therefore as grounds for denying divorce petitions.

JUDGES MISUSED PLEDGE LETTERS

Abusers, sometimes at the behest of authorities, made written apologies for beating their spouses and written promises to stop their wrongdoing. They often broke those promises. A court decision granting a woman's application for a personal protection order against her husband documents an incident in which, under the belief that she was at her older sister's home, he attacked her brother-in-law with a knife only six days after promising in a pledge letter never to beat her again (Decision #4545264, Qingtian County People's Court, Zhejiang Province, June 1, 2016).[37]

In divorce trials, judges' regularly misused defendants' promises and apologies. Judges even turned such evidence against plaintiffs, in violation of the 2008 Guidelines. When plaintiffs submitted pledge letters as evidence of the *breakdown* of mutual affection, judges sometimes treated them as evidence of the *existence* of mutual affection. Hundreds of decisions in my samples contain court holdings with language such as: "After getting married, the defendant physically abused the plaintiff. However, the defendant issued a pledge letter, which the plaintiff accepted, expressing the defendant's enthusiastic commitment to drug rehabilitation. This shows the defendant's recognition of his mistakes and desire to restore this marriage" (Decision #2874358, Anji County People's Court, Zhejiang Province, May 6, 2014).[38] Although the 2008 Guidelines clearly stipulate that courts should accept pledge letters containing relevant content as evidence of domestic violence, they often failed to do so (e.g., Decision #4865420, Lanxi Municipal People's Court, Zhejiang Province, October 24, 2016).[39]

My final qualitative example in this chapter brings together a number of themes. First, despite an abundance of evidence documenting the defendant's history of domestic violence, including a personal protection order, a public security administrative punishment decision, a pledge letter, and the defendant's self-incriminating testimony, the

---

[37] Case ID (2016)浙1121民保令00001号, archived at https://perma.cc/Y377-DX3V.
[38] Case ID (2014)湖安民初字第387号, archived at https://perma.cc/755Q-NAEW.
[39] Case ID (2016)浙0781民初5298号, archived at https://perma.cc/WSM2-Z3WR.

judge ruled against the plaintiff. Second, the court misused the defendant's pledge letter. Rather than using it for the plaintiff's intended purpose of proving domestic violence and establishing grounds for divorce, the court used it as evidence of the defendant's contrition, the possibility of marital reconciliation, and the absence of the breakdown of mutual affection. Third, the court appeared to apply the criteria of frequent and persistent to the definition of domestic violence in its holding to disaffirm the plaintiff's allegations.

After the plaintiff initially filed for divorce in 2005, the court's attempt to achieve mediated reconciliation succeeded when she withdrew her petition in order to give him a second chance. She filed again in December 2015. In March 2016, the court once again attempted to mediate, this time unsuccessfully. The court then approved the plaintiff's request for a personal protection order. In response to the plaintiff's harrowing and thoroughly documented testimony of chronic abuse causing "serious injuries," "tremendous anxiety and psychological darkness," and "psychological trauma," the defendant admitted to his violence. "I admit smashing the window on the front door of the plaintiff's family home, but I did it because I couldn't get in. On November 16, 2015, at about 6:00 pm I slapped the plaintiff four times." Regarding the medical documentation and photos the plaintiff submitted, the defendant stated, "I do not object to their authenticity. The photos are from when I hit her on the evening of November 22, 2015. The situation as described is factual. However, I did not beat her more than once. Only multiple beatings qualify as domestic violence." The defendant added,

> I only hit the plaintiff once on November 22, 2015, because she pulled a disappearing act, and even transferred her cell phone number. I told her that since she came home we should try to get along. But she refused to talk to me. All she said was that she had already filed for divorce, and that if I had any questions I should ask her lawyer. I asked her eight times if she was sure she wanted to do this. When she said she was sure, I hit her. This is the best way to deal with her.

In its holding, the court even affirmed that

> the defendant slapped the plaintiff five times and punched her head once. The plaintiff reported the incident to the police. On November 23 the plaintiff admitted herself to the Hangzhou X Hospital for treatment. The hospital diagnosed an internal head injury and multiple external head contusions. ... On January 19, 2016, the Yuhang District Branch of the Hangzhou Municipal Public Security Bureau issued an

administrative punishment decision to the defendant stating that …
the defendant had beaten the plaintiff with an open hand and closed
fist, causing a minor injury to the right side of the plaintiff's face.

And yet the court denied her second-attempt petition. Judges appeared
to be willing to affirm the occurrence of domestic *battery*, which did
not legally imply the breakdown of mutual affection, while being careful not to affirm the occurrence of domestic *violence*, which would have
legally implied the breakdown of mutual affection.

> Although the plaintiff believes the defendant repeatedly beat her and
> her family members, the evidence she submitted as well as the evidence
> the court collected on her behalf only proves that the defendant beat
> her on November 22, 2015. Regarding the alleged incidents of January
> 19, February 5, and February 14, 2016, there are corresponding police
> reports and notes. Because the police did not resolve these incidents, the
> evidence only proves that the plaintiff and her parents, owing to alter-
> cations with the defendant, repeatedly sought police help, but not that
> the defendant repeatedly beat and abused them. Because the evidence
> at hand does not prove that marital affection has indeed broken down,
> there is insufficient evidence to support the plaintiff's petition, and
> the court denies support of it. The defendant stated that the reason he
> beat the plaintiff on November 22, 2015 was because he wanted to talk
> things over with the plaintiff. However, the plaintiff had already filed for
> divorce and did not want to talk things over. Even if the defendant beat
> the plaintiff because he did not want to divorce, the use of violent means
> to save a marriage is not rational, appropriate, or lawful. On the contrary,
> it is detrimental to the improvement of marital affection. In his pledge
> letter, the defendant addressed this by promising never again to beat the
> plaintiff, and that he would work hard and take care of his family. From
> this day forward the defendant should avoid the occurrence of events
> like these, control his feelings, and show greater care and concern for the
> plaintiff and her family. If the plaintiff and defendant strengthen under-
> standing and trust, are more considerate and tolerant of each other, put
> the interests of their family and children first, their marriage can still be
> reconciled. (Decision #4387302, Hangzhou Municipal Yuhang District
> People's Court, Zhejiang Province, April 1, 2016)[40]

Supplementary case examples set #7–10 is online at: https://
decoupling-book.org/.

---

[40] Case ID (2015)杭余塘民初字第715号, archived at https://perma.cc/F77W-B5KY.

To judges, pledge letters were simply one more tool to support the pretense that reconciliation was possible, and were thus a convenient pretext for denying divorce petitions.

SUMMARY AND CONCLUSIONS

In this chapter, I have let plaintiffs and judges do most of the talking. I provided qualitative examples illustrating judges' highly discretionary application of China's legal standards for divorce. They reveal judges' seemingly boundless determination to deny divorce petitions, regardless of the facts presented to them. According to China's own laws and judicial interpretations, judges had a solid legal basis for granting the plaintiff's divorce request in most if not all of the case examples I presented. In each case, they could have granted the divorce according to China's faultism standards by affirming the plaintiff's evidence of domestic abuse or according to China's breakdownism standards by affirming the plaintiff's claim that mutual affection had indeed broken down. In the context of domestic violence, these competing standards overlap insofar as establishing fault automatically establishes the breakdown of mutual affection. According to China's Law on Judges, their formal professional duties and responsibilities include upholding the law and protecting the due process rights of litigants. Judges, however, are also tasked with protecting state interests (Article 10, Item 4 in the 2019 version). Judges' routine denial of divorce petitions reflects their greater loyalty to prevailing political priorities such as marital preservation and social stability – and their responsiveness to institutional incentives intended to maintain this loyalty – than to the legal needs of vulnerable women. Judges are also required to maintain neutrality vis-à-vis litigants (Zhu 2016:223). As we have seen, however, they tended to support husbands' denials of domestic violence allegations despite ironclad evidence and despite sources of law calling on them to give abuse victims the benefit of the doubt in cases with inconclusive evidence.

This chapter has shown how judges constructed an alternate reality in which domestic violence was merely run-of-the-mill bickering common to healthy marriages. By ignoring, downplaying, and turning on its head evidence of domestic violence, judges' rhetorical strategies bear the quintessential hallmarks of gaslighting (Sweet 2019). Judges discursively transformed domestic violence into ordinary tensions that can be overcome with a modicum of determination on the part of both husband and wife. In so doing, judges represented domestic violence victims as irrational, hotheaded, and overly emotional, blind to their loving husbands' hopes for a future together; as irresponsible mothers dead set on depriving their children of the intact families necessary for their healthy upbringing; as obstacles to marital reconciliation; and thus as unpatriotic for failing to do their part to strengthen the nation by strengthening family relations.

In this chapter, I have zoomed in on selected case examples illuminating the role of domestic violence (or more precisely, the lack thereof) on judges' holdings and verdicts. In the next chapter, I will zoom out to a view of all the first-attempt divorce adjudications in my samples.

CHAPTER EIGHT

DIVORCE DENIALS

Judicial Discourse and Judicial Decision-Making

Chapter 7 contains findings from a qualitative analysis of selected examples of judges' treatment of domestic violence allegations. We saw that judges normalized abuse by discounting its severity. We also saw that they discounted and turned on its head evidence women submitted in support of their abuse claims. My approach of thoroughly reading, one by one, the full text of – and *qualitatively* drawing out salient themes across – selected court decisions fruitfully illuminated the rhetorical strategies by which judges invalidated women's allegations of domestic violence. This approach does not, however, support an assessment of how widely these themes were shared in the full corpus of over 100,000 first-attempt divorce adjudications in my two samples. Nor can it sustain an assessment of the extent to which factors such as plaintiff sex and domestic violence allegations were associated with case outcomes.

In this chapter, I *quantitatively* demonstrate the ubiquity of judges' gaslighting strategies and their gendered consequences, to rule out the possibility that the case examples in Chapter 7 are cherry-picked outliers. This chapter is broadly divided into two parts. The first part is devoted to an analysis of judicial discourse. I focus on how courts justified their decisions to deny divorce petitions in general and to ignore domestic violence allegations in particular. We will see that they did so less on legal grounds and more on ideological, moral, and therapeutic grounds. We will also see that the gaslighting strategies I identified in Chapter 7 pervade the samples and that judges did not apply them equally by plaintiff sex. Judicial discourse was gendered insofar as judges directed it toward women more than toward men. The second part is devoted to an analysis of judicial decision-making: (1) the extent and nature of gender inequality in case outcomes, and (2) the effect of domestic violence allegations on case outcomes. I will also show sizeable gender gaps in plaintiffs' adjudication outcomes and in some of their determinants. Women's claims were deemed less credible and were thus taken less seriously than men's. Most of these problems were concentrated in rural courts, which account for the majority of divorce adjudications. We saw in Chapters 5 and 6 that divorce cases have been casualties of courts' relentless pursuit of efficiency. In this chapter we will see that women are casualties in the divorce litigation process.

Because China's endogenous legal test of breakdownism dominated judicial discourse and supported judges' holdings to deny divorce petitions even in cases involving statutory wrongdoing, plaintiffs' domestic violence claims did not improve their chances of obtaining a divorce on the first try. If judges had been more willing to decide divorce cases according to fault-based standards, the opposite pattern would have emerged – namely, female plaintiffs would have had higher success rates than male plaintiffs – simply by virtue of the sheer prevalence of domestic violence allegations made by female divorce-seekers.

What I report in this chapter is limited to first-attempt divorce petitions for two reasons. First, as we saw in Chapter 6, courts denied most first-attempt petitions and granted most subsequent-attempt petitions.[1] Second, as we also saw in Chapter 6, divorce courts were leaky: first-attempt adjudicated denials far outnumbered subsequent-attempt

---

[1] I excluded from all analyses in this chapter cases filed after prior divorce litigation attempts that resulted in either adjudicated denials or withdrawals. According to legal scholars (X. Wang 2016:52) and a great deal of anecdotal legal advice posted online by lawyers, courts tend to treat first-attempt case filings as if they never happened after plaintiffs withdraw their petitions. For this reason, one might expect a court to treat a second-attempt divorce petition filed following the withdrawal of a first-attempt petition like a new first-attempt petition and therefore to be less inclined to grant it compared to a second-attempt petition filed following an adjudicated denial. The court decisions in my provincial samples only partially support this expectation. While second-attempt divorce petitions were significantly more likely to be granted when the first-attempt petition was denied than when it was withdrawn, courts in both scenarios were nonetheless highly inclined to grant divorces. In other words, although subsequent-attempt divorce litigation outcomes differed depending on whether the prior petition had been denied or withdrawn (on subsequent litigation attempts, prior denials were more advantageous than prior withdrawals), both sets of outcomes were far more similar to one another than they were to the outcomes of first-attempt trials; both sets of outcomes stood in sharp contrast to the outcomes of first-attempt trials. Whereas courts granted only a minority of first-attempt divorce petitions (Chapter 6), they granted the clear majority (over 70% in both samples) of divorce petitions that followed both first-attempt denials and first-attempt withdrawals. These patterns support my argument in Chapter 6 that withdrawals were part of the divorce twofer and, in many cases, an adjudicated denial by another name.

petitions. Because they were so routinely denied, first-attempt divorce petitions were more consequential than subsequent attempts. Relatively few plaintiffs whose petitions were denied on the first attempt returned. When China's multiple legal divorce standards clashed and breakdownism prevailed over faultism, battered women were often subjected to further violence or forced into hiding as they awaited the next opportunity to file for divorce – the central topic of Chapter 9. When they did return to court after an adjudicated denial, plaintiffs' subsequent-attempt petitions were usually granted. For these reasons, first-attempt divorce petitions are where most of the action has been and where the stakes have been highest. We will see in Chapter 9 that the outcomes of initial divorce attempts were hugely consequential for the physical security of abused women.

JUDICIAL DISCOURSE

In her study of disputes in American lower courts, Merry (1990) identified two prevalent types of nonlegal discourse: moral and therapeutic. She found that judges invoked moral discourse in marital cases, for example, to redefine the legal problem of domestic violence as a moral problem of failing in the social role of husband. Chinese judges did the same thing. Their moral discourse was also conspicuously ideological. Chinese judges invoked the language of socialist morality to urge disputants, in their political role as citizens, to fulfill their obligation to support nation-building priorities.

The qualitative case examples I presented in Chapter 7 also bring into high relief Chinese judges' use of therapeutic discourse. In American lower courts, judges' use of therapeutic discourse excused wrongdoing, such as marital abuse, by attributing it to individual illness or psychological weakness (Merry 1990:114–15). In China, judges' therapeutic discourse similarly rationalized domestic violence as a matter of poor communication skills or weak trust, and thus eliminated abusers' legal culpability by redefining it as a fixable, shared problem between spouses.

Chinese divorce litigation boils down to a discursive battle between plaintiffs and judges over whether mutual affection has broken down. Unsurprisingly, much of the lexical material fueling this battle derives from the SPC's 1989 Several Concrete Opinions on How to Determine in Divorce Trials Whether Marital Affection Has Indeed Broken Down, to which this book refers by its nickname, the Fourteen

Articles (Chapter 2). Plaintiffs borrowed the language of the Fourteen Articles by claiming mutual affection had broken down and reconciliation was hopeless. They referred to officially stipulated grounds for affirming the breakdown of mutual affection that were both no-fault, such as a weak marital foundation or physical separation, and fault-based, such as abuse, bigamy, gambling, indolence, or other "odious habits."

Judges pushed back by using the same language to invalidate plaintiffs' claims. They most commonly did so in two ways, as we have seen. First, they held that plaintiffs failed to prove their claims with admissible evidence. Second, focusing on the key condition of "the possibility of reconciliation" (有无和好的可能) stipulated throughout the Fourteen Articles, they held that plaintiffs' assessments were wrong, that their marriages could be restored, and that reconciliation was still very much possible. In judges' holdings, reconciliation potential as legal grounds for denying a divorce petition almost always outweighed wrongdoing as legal grounds for granting it. Even when a plaintiff could prove domestic violence, the court often held that it had not damaged the marriage beyond repair, and that the breakdown of mutual affection could therefore not be affirmed. In so doing, judges upheld the enduring ideological principle of "opposition to frivolous divorce."

In their adjudicated denials, judges almost invariably offered relationship advice. This tendency long predated China's domestic relations trial reforms introduced in 2016, when marital reconciliation became a focus of national policies designed to stem explosive divorce rates (Chapter 3). The official rationale for providing marital counseling, of course, was to help the couple reconcile and thus to contribute to social stability maintenance. An unofficial purpose was to help the court reconcile a glaring and ubiquitous contradiction: on the one hand, its holding that the possibility of marital reconciliation was very much alive, which it used to *disaffirm* the breakdown of mutual affection, and, on the other hand, compelling allegations of the defendant's wrongdoing, which the court could and should have used to *affirm* the breakdown of mutual affection. When a court provided relationship advice, which it did in almost every adjudicated denial, it did so to express confidence that the marital problems in the plaintiff's legal complaint – even if they constituted statutory wrongdoing that automatically established grounds for the breakdown of mutual affection – could be overcome, and thus that marital affection had not broken down. Although judges who forcibly preserved marriages by ignoring or making light of statutory wrongdoing un-equivocally flouted abuse victims' legal right to a divorce, judges' emphasis on marital reconciliation was simultaneously in line with long-established judicial norms and practices. After all, ever since the Marriage Law was introduced in 1950, mediation with the aim of rec-onciliation has been a bedrock practice at every step on the road to divorce (Chapter 1).

As we saw in Chapter 7, judges acted like marriage counselors and therapists. Recall the case example in which the judges chastised the litigants for treating their marriage as a video game and urged them to "treasure each other, communicate with sincerity, love each other, and jointly nourish with care this precious gift of a family." When they de-nied divorce petitions, judges almost unfailingly provided advice such as, "Divorce is not the only way of resolving marital conflict" (e.g., Decision #2830590, Jiaxing Municipal Nanhu District People's Court, Zhejiang Province, March 13, 2014).[2] Also recall from Chapter 7 the paternalistic words of wisdom judges imparted in other case examples in support of their holdings that reconciliation remained possible, such as "improve [your] communication and show mutual understanding, forgiveness, and tolerance," "forgive, accommodate, and respect each other," "forgive, accommodate, and trust each other," and "strengthen [your] communication skills, forgive each other, and cherish family." Beyond justifying their optimism about reconciliation prospects and their determination that marital discord had not reached the point of the breakdown of mutual affection, therapeutic discourse such as this did not pertain to any formal source of law.

For the purpose of assessing the degree of importance judges attached to allegations of domestic violence, I quantitatively analyzed the lexi-cons of judges' holdings by counting words, terms, and expressions in judges' holdings. Holdings are devoted to judges' legal reasoning be-hind their decisions, and they almost always begin with the phrase, "The court holds that" (本院认为). We already know from Chapter 6 that divorce decisions as a whole were considerably shorter than those of any other type of civil case. Mean/median numbers of characters in the holdings sections of first-attempt divorce decisions were 199/157 in Henan and 179/158 in Zhejiang.

I identified key themes in judges' gaslighting strategies by measuring the prevalence of salient vocabulary (based on my qualitative analysis

---

[2] Case ID (2014)嘉南民初字第225号, archived at https://perma.cc/2JVS-4VZA.

of Chapter 7's case examples). I also identified the most commonly used words in judges' holdings. I ranked words according to the frequencies in which judges invoked them in two sets of holdings: (1) adjudicated denials of first-attempt petitions (24,896 and 29,790 holdings in the Henan and Zhejiang samples, respectively) and (2) first-attempt cases involving domestic violence allegations (16,102 and 13,122 holdings in the Henan and Zhejiang samples, respectively). Most first-attempt divorce adjudications in which plaintiffs alleged domestic violence resulted in denials (72% in Henan and 86% in Zhejiang). For this reason, domestic violence cases accounted for a sizeable share of all adjudicated denials of first-attempt petitions (32% in Henan and 28% in Zhejiang). In order to rule out the possibility that lexical similarities between these two sets of holdings are an artifact of overlap between these two categories of cases, I first removed every holding in the set of domestic violence cases from the set of adjudicated denials, thus ensuring that no holding was double-counted.

Before ranking words according to their usage by judges, I segmented all the text into words because there is no white space between Chinese words. I used the Stanford Word Segmenter to segment the text of holdings according to the Penn Chinese Treebank standard (Chang, Tseng, and Galen 2018). I then used KH Coder to count word frequencies (Higuchi 2020). Not every word in sets of holdings I analyzed was a candidate for counting and ranking. Words on a list of meaningless "stop-words" were excluded.[3]

I use word frequencies to analyze and compare the vocabularies in judges' holdings, not only between divorce case types (adjudicated denials versus cases with domestic violence allegations) but also between provinces (Henan versus Zhejiang). If, as Chapter 7 suggests, judges' first priority is clearing their dockets and supporting political priorities, then we should expect to find a high degree of linguistic similarity across provinces and across all denied divorce cases, including those without domestic violence allegations, reflecting a blanket approach. If, on the other hand, judges' first priority is treating domestic violence allegations seriously and protecting the legal rights of plaintiffs, then we should expect to find divergent vocabularies across both sets of holdings, reflecting case-by-case judicial decision-making. By the

---

[3] I am grateful to Zuoyu Tian for his assistance building the list of stop-words. Examples of stop-words excluded from the topic model are common subjects and objects ("I," "you," "he," "she," etc.), prepositions, articles, and so on. Stop-words also include ubiquitous but meaningless nouns such as "plaintiff" (原告), "defendant" (被告), and "court" (本院 and 人民法院).

same token, if judges did not routinely gaslight plaintiffs who made allegations of domestic violence, then we might also find lexical variation between the two provinces.

Word frequencies are useful for identifying salient words in a corpus of documents that are simply too large for conventional qualitative analysis. I will focus on the top 50 most frequently used words. Lists of salient words such as these are commonly referred to as "bags of words" because they contain no information about their syntactic organization. For this reason, I apply hierarchical clustering methods to these word lists in order to identify clusters of words that judges tend to use together in stock phrases. Word rankings in conjunction with hierarchical clustering thus bring specific characteristics of judges' gaslighting strategies into sharper focus.

Lexicons of Adjudicated Denials
The contents of divorce holdings exhibited astonishingly little variation, regardless of whether a plaintiff made a domestic violence allegation. Whether the trial was held in Henan or Zhejiang likewise made little, if any, difference. Judges drew from an extremely limited pool of stock words and phrases that referred overwhelmingly to breakdownism and rarely to faultism. They rendered their holdings mechanically, in highly standardized and scripted boilerplate.

In both provincial samples of first-attempt divorce decisions, plaintiffs used the word for "mutual affection" (感情) in 83% of their legal complaints. In both Henan and Zhejiang, only the words "marry" and "divorce" appeared in more legal complaints. Judges used the word for "mutual affection" even more frequently: it appeared in 93–94% of their holdings in the two samples. Whereas plaintiffs used it to claim that mutual affection had broken down, judges used it to hold the opposite. Defendants who were unwilling to divorce also challenged plaintiffs' claims that marital affection had broken down. All participants in divorce litigation spoke the language of breakdownism. As we saw in Chapter 7, plaintiffs also spoke the language of faultism in their efforts to establish the breakdown of mutual affection.

By contrast, rarely did judges refer to fault-based standards of wrongdoing. Judges used terms such as "violence" (暴力), "odious habit" (恶习), "fault" (过错), and "Article 46" (四十六) or "46," the provision in the Marriage Law on civil damages for wrongdoing, in their holdings in only 4% of first-attempt decisions in each of the two samples.[4] On the rare occasions judges used the language of wrong-doing, they did so only to say that it was not tantamount to the breakdown of mutual affection. Meanwhile, judges grounded their decisions in political and ideological discourse by using words such as "harmonious" (和谐 and 和睦), "stability" (稳定), and "civilized" (文明) in 25% and 13% of holdings in my Henan and Zhejiang samples, respectively. These politically salient words are similarly represented in subsamples of holdings involving allegations of domestic violence.

Before scrutinizing judges' language at a more granular level, we can draw a couple of preliminary conclusions from this simple exercise. First, even in cases that involved wrongdoing, judges were averse to applying fault-based legal standards. They tended to apply the breakdownism standard in a one-size-fits-all manner. Second, we can also see that, within this general pattern that applies to Henan and Zhejiang alike, ideological discourse was almost twice as prevalent in Henan as it was in Zhejiang. Judges used political slogans as grounds for denying divorce petitions. Variations of "for the sake of maintaining harmonious and civilized marital and family relations" (维护和睦文明的婚姻家庭关系), "for the benefit of marital and family stability and of social harmony" (为有利于婚姻家庭稳定和社会和谐), and "in order to maintain family harmony and social stability" (维护家庭和谐、社会稳定) are prevalent throughout holdings in both samples, but somewhat more so in holdings from Henan.

Figure 8.1 depicts word clouds of the top 50 most frequent words across the two provinces in two types of holdings: (1) adjudicated denials and (2) cases involving allegations of domestic violence.[5] If every word were unique, there would be 200 words across all four word clouds (50 per word cloud). In fact, there are only 73 unique words because there is so much redundancy between holdings for adjudicated denials of cases without domestic violence allegations (Panels A and B) and holdings for domestic violence cases (Panels C and D). Clearly, judges attached little importance to domestic violence allegations. To judges, there was nothing about cases involving domestic violence allegations that merited their special attention or consideration. Redundancy between holdings from Henan (Panels A and C) and Zhejiang (Panels

---

[4] Article 46 of the 2001 Marriage Law subsequently became Article 1091 in the Civil Code, which took effect on January 1, 2021.

[5] Again, these are mutually exclusive sets of holdings because I removed all domestic violence cases from the set of all adjudicated denials.

Figure 8.1 Word clouds of top 50 most frequently used words in judges' holdings
Source: Author's calculations from Henan and Zhejiang provincial high courts' online decisions.
Note: Limited to first-attempt adjudications. Words were scaled according to their frequencies in holdings. Their placement locations were optimized according to their sizes. For this reason, although Chinese words and their English translations are scaled identically, they are not located in the same places in their respective word clouds. Every adjudicated first-attempt divorce decision in my samples is included, except granted divorce petitions that did not contain domestic violence allegations. Court decisions are not used in more than one word cloud; each court decision is used in only one word cloud.

B and D) also underscores the extent to which domestic violence was similarly unimportant to judges in both provinces.

All four word clouds share a common set of 35 words. Panels A and C of Figure 8.1 each contains seven unique words found in no other word cloud; Panel B contains three unique words; and Panel D contains only two unique words. Word clouds from the same province share even more in common. Henan's two word clouds share 41 words, Zhejiang's 45 words. Because some domestic violence cases led to actual divorces (28% and 14% in Henan and Zhejiang, respectively), the word clouds for domestic violence cases contain unique words pertaining to granting divorces. With respect to Henan, Panel C contains nine such words (in italics) that do not appear in Panel A: *granting* (予以) the divorce petition on the basis of the Marriage Law's provision (Article 32), *stipulating* (规定) that divorce should be granted when *mediation* (调解) fails or when a physical *separation* (分居) test is satisfied, and thus also ruling on the disposition of *pre-marital* (婚前) *property* (财产), *custody* (抚养) of a *child* (孩子), and *child support payments* (抚养费). Similarly, in Zhejiang, Panel D contains five such words (in italics) that do not appear in Panel B: after *affirming* (认定) that mutual affection has indeed broken down and *granting* (予以) the divorce, some *claims* (主张) such as child custody (抚养) could be *dealt with* (处理), but other claims (typically concerning property) could not be dealt with (不予处理) or must be *dealt with* through separate litigation (另案处理 or 另行处理).

Although the word clouds for domestic violence cases contain words associated with granted divorces, their tiny sizes reflect their relatively rare usage owing to high denial rates. Notably absent are words associated with wrongdoing in general and domestic violence in particular, a point to which I will return later.

For reference purposes, Table 8.1 contains all 73 unique words across both provinces and case types. The first page of the table contains the 35 words shared by all four word clouds.

To support their holdings, judges cited Article 32 of the Marriage Law in 94% and 98% of their adjudications in the Henan and Zhejiang samples, respectively. Indeed, this was the sole legal provision judges cited in 32% and 44% of all holdings in the Henan and Zhejiang samples, respectively. Article 32 contains 12 words in the word clouds, three of which are particularly prominent: "marital" (夫妻), "affection" (感情), and "breakdown" (破裂). These three words account for only 4% of all 73 unique words but for 21% of all word frequencies in the

TABLE 8.1 Unique Chinese words in word clouds

English translation	Original Chinese	# Clouds	Denials Henan (Fig 8.1A)	Zhejiang (Fig 8.1B)	Domestic violence Henan (Fig 8.1C)	Zhejiang (Fig 8.1D)
1. marital	夫妻	4	✔	✔	✔	✔
2. affection	感情	4	✔	✔	✔	✔
3. both sides	双方	4	✔	✔	✔	✔
4. divorce	离婚	4	✔	✔	✔	✔
5. breakdown	破裂	4	✔	✔	✔	✔
6. live	生活	4	✔	✔	✔	✔
7. deny	不予	4	✔	✔	✔	✔
8. evidence	证据	4	✔	✔	✔	✔
9. support	支持	4	✔	✔	✔	✔
10. family	家庭	4	✔	✔	✔	✔
11. marriage	婚姻	4	✔	✔	✔	✔
12. request	请求	4	✔	✔	✔	✔
13. demand	要求	4	✔	✔	✔	✔
14. together	共同	4	✔	✔	✔	✔
15. marry	结婚	4	✔	✔	✔	✔
16. postmarital	婚后	4	✔	✔	✔	✔
17. litigation	诉讼	4	✔	✔	✔	✔
18. relations	关系	4	✔	✔	✔	✔
19. prove	证明	4	✔	✔	✔	✔
20. reconcile	和好	4	✔	✔	✔	✔
21. foundation	基础	4	✔	✔	✔	✔
22. supply	提供	4	✔	✔	✔	✔
23. conflict	矛盾	4	✔	✔	✔	✔
24. has indeed	确已	4	✔	✔	✔	✔
25. possibility	可能	4	✔	✔	✔	✔
26. trifles	琐事	4	✔	✔	✔	✔
27. communication	沟通	4	✔	✔	✔	✔
28. definite	一定	4	✔	✔	✔	✔
29. mutual	相互	4	✔	✔	✔	✔
30. register	登记	4	✔	✔	✔	✔
31. give birth	生育	4	✔	✔	✔	✔
32. children	子女	4	✔	✔	✔	✔
33. build	建立	4	✔	✔	✔	✔
34. occur	发生	4	✔	✔	✔	✔
35. fact	事实	4	✔	✔	✔	✔

English translation	Original Chinese	# Clouds	Denials		Domestic violence	
			Henan (Fig 8.1A)	Zhejiang (Fig 8.1B)	Henan (Fig 8.1C)	Zhejiang (Fig 8.1D)
36. completely	彻底	3	✔	✔	✔	✗
37. grant	予以	2	✗	✗	✔	✔
38. cherish	珍惜	2	✗	✔	✗	✔
39. claim	主张	3	✔	✗	✔	✔
40. rapport	互谅	3	✔	✔	✗	✔
41. custody	抚养	2	✗	✗	✔	✔
42. lawful	合法	2	✗	✔	✗	✔
43. produce	产生	2	✗	✔	✗	✔
44. grounds	理由	2	✗	✔	✗	✔
45. romance	恋爱	2	✗	✔	✗	✔
46. law	法律	2	✗	✔	✗	✔
47. compromise	互让	2	✔	✔	✗	✗
48. according to law	依法	2	✗	✔	✗	✔
49. submit	提交	2	✔	✗	✔	✗
50. angry	生气	2	✔	✗	✔	✗
51. ought to	应当	2	✔	✗	✔	✗
52. insufficient	不足	2	✗	✔	✗	✔
53. strengthen	加强	2	✗	✔	✗	✔
54. time	时间	2	✔	✗	✔	✗
55. property	财产	1	✗	✗	✔	✗
56. premarital	婚前	1	✗	✗	✔	✗
57. child	孩子	1	✗	✗	✔	✗
58. good	较好	1	✗	✔	✗	✗
59. voluntary	自愿	1	✗	✔	✗	✗
60. separate	分居	1	✗	✗	✔	✗
61. stipulate	规定	1	✗	✗	✔	✗
62. deal with	处理	1	✗	✗	✗	✔
63. child support	抚养费	1	✗	✗	✔	✗
64. bring forward	提出	1	✔	✗	✗	✗
65. freely	自由	1	✗	✔	✗	✗
66. affirm	认定	1	✗	✗	✗	✔
67. mediation	调解	1	✗	✗	✔	✗
68. litigant	当事人	1	✔	✗	✗	✗
69. withhold consent	不同意	1	✔	✗	✗	✗
70. maintain	维护	1	✔	✗	✗	✗
71. harmony	和睦	1	✔	✗	✗	✗
72. valid	有效	1	✔	✗	✗	✗
73. stability	稳定	1	✔	✗	✗	✗

Source: Author's calculations from Henan and Zhejiang provincial high courts' online decisions.
Note: Words are ranked according to their share of all words in all four word clouds combined.

281

four word clouds; at least one of them appeared in 95–96% of holdings in each provincial sample of first-attempt divorce adjudications. At least one of these three words was in the vast majority of holdings to grant divorces (94% and 91% in the Henan and Zhejiang samples, respectively) and almost universally found in holdings to deny divorces (98% in each sample).

Article 32 contains an additional nine words in the word clouds: "has indeed" (确已), "family" (or "domestic," 家庭), "demand" (which can also mean "request," 要求), "bring forward" (提出), "divorce" (离婚), "litigation" (诉讼), "ought to" (应当), "mediation" (调解), and "separation" (分居). Elsewhere in the Marriage Law are 30 additional words in the word clouds, the most prominent of which are "both sides" (双方), "live" (or "living," "life," 生活), "marriage" (婚姻), "request" (or "petition," 请求), "together" (or "joint," "common" 共同), "marry" (结婚), and "postmarital" (婚后). Some of these words – such as "marital," "affection," "breakdown," "marry," and "family" – were more likely to be used in holdings to deny divorces. Others – such as "divorce," "live," and "together" – were more likely to be used in holdings to grant divorces. The words "live" and "together," for example, appeared in holdings to grant divorces when they referred to joint property, joint debt, child custody, and future living expenses.

Although Article 32 also contains the term "domestic violence" (家庭暴力) as grounds for affirming the breakdown of mutual affection, the language of violence rarely appears in judges' holdings. As we have seen, it is conspicuously absent even in cases involving allegations of domestic violence. Violence words are therefore also conspicuously absent in all the word clouds, even those constructed from holdings of cases involving allegations of domestic violence. The word "violence" (暴力) appears in only 2% of the holdings in each provincial sample of first-attempt divorce adjudications, and in only 5% and 8% of holdings in cases involving allegations of domestic violence in the Henan and Zhejiang samples, respectively. The contracted form of "domestic violence" (家暴) appears in fewer than 70 out all the nearly 150,000 holdings in both samples of first-instance divorce adjudications. We also saw in Chapter 7 that judges' holdings are largely devoid of other words related to domestic violence, such as "beat," "hit," "punch," "kick," and so on. Finally, when judges did use violence words, they often did so in the process of invalidating plaintiffs' claims of abuse on evidentiary grounds or on the grounds that the incidents were not serious enough to constitute domestic violence.

A Typology of Judicial Discourse in Adjudicated Denials

While Marriage Law words in general and Article 32 words in particular formed the core of judges' lexicon of adjudicated denials, they were similarly central to holdings to grant divorces. Words associated with Article 32 were therefore not uniquely constitutive of the language of adjudicated denials. Because they were not deployed specifically for the purpose of denying divorce petitions, they did not define a distinct discourse of adjudicated denial. Other words, however, did form four discourses strongly associated with adjudicated denials of divorce petitions: (1) ideological words, (2) Fourteen Articles words, (3) other therapeutic words, and (4) evidentiary words. I will discuss each in turn.

First, in contrast to the Marriage Law words I just described, ideological words were deployed for the specific purpose of denying divorce petitions and do define a distinct discourse of adjudicated denial. I already showed that four words with political valence in China – "stability," "civilized," and two synonyms for "harmonious" – appeared in a lot of holdings, particularly in the Henan sample. Of these four ideologically salient words, only "stability" (稳定) and one of the words for "harmony" (和睦) were among the top 50 most frequently used words in any word cloud: They both appear in Panel A of Figure 8.1 for adjudicated denials. Judges were far more likely to use these words when denying divorces than when granting divorces. Judges often riffed on the ideological language of socialist morality by holding that divorce would be to the detriment of family unity and *harmony*; that litigants should stay together and work earnestly to protect *harmonious* and *civilized* marital and family relations; that for the sake of family and social *harmony* and *stability*, the litigants should try to reconcile; and so on.

China's ongoing domestic relations trial reforms have renewed the supply of this discursive grist for the mill of adjudicated denials. We previously saw that judges parroted ideological discourse by holding that "the family is the cell of society" (also see Fincher 2014:23–24). Divorce decisions are not merely legal matters but also political matters. The following adjudicated denial is a case in point:

> The plaintiff claimed that "the defendant spends the entire day glued to online video games and carried out severe domestic violence against the plaintiff, resulting in their failure to develop marital affection." Although the plaintiff submitted police and medical documentation, and although during the trial the defendant admitted physically fighting with the plaintiff owing to family conflict, the plaintiff must submit

valid evidence to prove that it constitutes domestic violence. … At the same time, the family is societal, and plays a huge role maintaining equal, harmonious, and civilized marital and family relations as well as social stability. This is the unshirkable duty of every family member. (Decision #1077421, Zhengzhou Municipal Erqi District People's Court, Henan Province, November 18, 2013)[6]

This example also anticipates my discussion in the following pages about the importance of judges' evidentiary discourse, which they used to invalidate plaintiffs' legally valid evidence.

Second, the SPC's 1989 judicial interpretation, known as the Fourteen Articles, is a major source of vocabulary in judges' discourse of adjudicated denial. Each italicized word and phrase in the rest of this paragraph appears in the Fourteen Articles. Because the Fourteen Articles stipulates that *inadequate premarital acquaintanceship* constitutes grounds for affirming the *breakdown of mutual affection*, plaintiffs often claimed not to know the nature of the person they married until it was too late, whereas judges held that both sides had established a solid *premarital acquaintanceship*. Likewise, because the Fourteen Articles calls for consideration of the *marital foundation* when determining the state of *mutual affection* and *marital relations*, plaintiffs claimed a weak *foundation*, whereas judges claimed a solid *foundation*. Because the Fourteen Articles stipulates as grounds for divorce *difficulty living together* owing to wrongdoing – including *maltreatment* – and failure to *establish* or *build marital affection*, plaintiffs claimed that *living together* was impossible, whereas judges held that the litigants had already *built* definite *marital affection* in their years *living together*. Finally, because the Fourteen Articles stipulates that *marital affection* should be determined according to *reconciliation potential*, plaintiffs claimed the *impossibility of reconciliation*, whereas judges held that *reconciliation remained possible*.

Some of these italicized words and terms – most notably, "marital," "affection," "breakdown," and "both sides" – also appear in the Marriage Law. But others – most notably, "establish" or "build" (建立), "foundation" (基础), "reconcile" (和好), and "possibility" (可能) – are unique to the Fourteen Articles. Judges put the words "reconcile" and "possibility" together to form "reconciliation potential." These words and expressions should be familiar from the

---

[6] Case ID (2013)二七民一初字第2676号, archived at https://perma.cc/NBX3-HGJE.

case examples in Chapter 7. Although the Marriage Law stipulates that the breakdown of mutual affection is grounds for divorce, it contains no legal test to help judges determine "whether mutual affection has indeed broken down" (part of the title of the Fourteen Articles). For this reason, these three words and terms intended to help judges assess the strength of mutual affection – namely "build," "foundation," and "reconciliation potential" – unique to the Fourteen Articles appeared in the clear majority of adjudicated denials in my samples.

Several courts in Zhejiang were particularly fond of quoting the Fourteen Articles almost verbatim: "After conducting a comprehensive analysis of the marriage's foundation, postmarital affection, grounds for divorce, the current state of marital relations, and other aspects, the court's holding is to confirm that marital affection between plaintiff and defendant has not completely broken down and that reconciliation is possible" (e.g., Decision #3417261, Yiwu Municipal People's Court, Zhejiang Province, March 26, 2015).[7] When judges used the word "foundation" in a manner consistent with the Fourteen Articles, namely to refer to the foundation of marital affection, they sometimes added ideological words to the discursive mix. Another court in Zhejiang, for example, frequently held that "Marital and family relations should be constructed on a foundation of civilization, equality, and harmony" (e.g., Decision #3592860, Huzhou Municipal Wuxing District People's Court, Zhejiang Province, June 4, 2015).[8]

Judges sometimes used the word "foundation" to deny divorce petitions in an exclusively ideological manner inconsistent with the Fourteen Articles. Chapter 7 cites one of several holdings in my samples asserting that "the maintenance of marital life, and family stability is the foundation of social stability." Henan's Taikang County People's Court invoked this statement in 86 of its holdings in my Henan sample. Other courts similarly held that "harmonious and stable families are the foundation of a harmonious society" (e.g., Decision #1305470,

---

[7] Case ID (2015)金义民初字第243号, archived at https://perma.cc/7VLR-MK4L. The Fourteen Articles calls on judges to "conduct a comprehensive analysis of the marriage's foundation, postmarital affection, grounds for divorce, the current state of marital relations, reconciliation potential, and other aspects when determining whether marital affection has indeed broken down." In addition to the Yiwu Municipal People's Court, urban district courts in Ningbo, Taizhou, Shaoxing, and Jinhua as well as the Yuhuan County People's Court were similarly fond of paraphrasing the same passage to deny divorce petitions.
[8] Case ID (2015)湖吴民初字第550号, archived at https://perma.cc/3ACE-UT87.

Qi County People's Court, Henan Province, October 31, 2014)[9] and "the family is the cell of society; harmonious and civilized marital and family relations are the foundation of a harmonious and civilized society" (e.g., Decision #1353450, Xia County People's Court, Henan Province, January 13, 2015).[10] Notwithstanding some variation in usage, judges tended to invoke the word "foundation" in the context of the "marital foundation" as stipulated by the Fourteen Articles.

Because they were so frequently used by judges to deny divorce petitions in both provinces, the words "build," "foundation," "reconcile," and "possibility" are in all four word clouds. Judges' reliance on the Fourteen Articles helps us understand the basis of their impulse to privilege breakdownism over faultism. Both the 1989 Fourteen Articles and the 2001 Marriage Law provide fault-based grounds on which judges *may* affirm the breakdown of mutual affection. Neither source of law, however, stipulates that judges *must* affirm the breakdown of mutual affection when they affirm wrongdoing. Meanwhile, judges roundly ignored a separate source of law – the 2001 Interpretations of the SPC on Several Issues Regarding the Application of the Marriage Law – requiring them to grant divorces when a faultism test is satisfied (Article 22; Jiang 2009b:18). Indeed, I found only ten cases (out of almost 150,000 first-instance divorce adjudications) in which judges explicitly cited this provision. (They granted the divorce in all ten of them.) Judges routinely affirmed the occurrence of domestic violence but nonetheless denied the divorce petition by holding that mutual affection had not broken down and that reconciliation remained possible. In essence, judges rendered adjudicated denials as if the SPC never issued its judicial interpretation in 2001 requiring them to privilege faultism over breakdownism.

Judges also contorted facts and evidence to ensure that faultism tests were not satisfied in the first place. As we saw in Chapter 7, judges routinely held that plaintiffs' allegations of domestic violence did not meet the legal definition of domestic violence. Even in the face of overwhelming evidence of domestic violence, including confessions by defendants, judges routinely – and inexplicably – held that plaintiffs' allegations could not be proven. Normalizing domestic violence by reducing them to the mere family trifles and petty squabbling that (they asserted) were unavoidable and intrinsic features of marriage

---

[9] Case ID (2014)杞民初字第1502号, archived at https://perma.cc/SJ5X-WM4M.
[10] Case ID (2014)陕民初字第1159号, archived at https://perma.cc/4KBL-67SH.

was one of judges' gaslighting strategies for privileging breakdownism over faultism. Contriving an inability to affirm wrongdoing, as judges so often did, helped them skirt the SPC's 2001 judicial interpretation requiring them to grant divorces when they did affirm wrongdoing.

The ease and efficiency of denying a divorce petition simply by holding – on the ostensible basis of a *comprehensive analysis* of the *current state of marital relations* – that *reconciliation is possible* because husband and wife *built* a solid *marital foundation* helps explain the enduring allure to judges of the Fourteen Articles. And yet, despite its profound influence, judges cited the Fourteen Articles by name in less than 1% of their holdings in all first-attempt divorce adjudications in my samples.

Third, judges' therapeutic discourse emerged from the vocabulary they used in their relationship advice to litigants. To be sure, judges also used Fourteen Articles vocabulary therapeutically. When they held that *reconciliation* remained *possible*, they expressed hope and encouragement to litigants, urging them to invest time and effort into strengthening the *marital foundation* they had already *built* in their years of life together.

Most of the words that formed their therapeutic discourse, however, are altogether outside the scope of the law. Judges normalized abuse by diminishing it to ordinary *conflict* (矛盾, literally meaning "contradiction") and family *trifles* (琐事) that, with commitment and effort, could be overcome. They held that couples could overcome this minor and unavoidable friction by virtue of having already built a *definite* (一定) marital foundation. Although, as judges so often held, marital problems had *occurred* (发生), reconciliation was possible if both sides improved their *communication* (沟通) and worked to cultivate greater *mutual* (相互) understanding, care, and consideration. Each of these six italicized words appears in all four word clouds in Figure 8.1.

An additional ten words that helped form judges' therapeutic discourse appear in at least one of the word clouds. The fact that both wife and husband registered their marriage *voluntarily* (自愿) after *freely* (自由) forming a *romance* (恋爱) was proof, according to judges, that the couple had built a *good* (较好) foundation of mutual affection. Although marital life inevitably *produced* (产生) some conflict, judges urged both sides to *strengthen* (加强) their communication skills, build mutual understanding and rapport (互谅), accommodate one another and *compromise* (互让), *cherish* (珍惜) their families, and *maintain* (维护) family harmony and stability for the sake of social harmony and stability. Therapeutic discourse accompanied the vast majority of adjudicated denials.

Fourth, judges grounded their adjudicated denials in evidentiary discourse. They held that plaintiffs failed to *prove* (证明) their claims because they failed to *supply* (提供) valid *evidence* (证据). Each of these three italicized words appears in all four word clouds. Judges also held that the evidence plaintiffs did *submit* (提交) was *insufficient* (不足) to support their claims. Judges' frequent use of evidentiary discourse to deny divorce petitions is also reflected in a legal provision they were fond of citing: Article 64 of the Civil Procedure Law, which stipulates that "litigants are responsible for supplying evidence to support their claims." This specific provision was cited in 33% and 12% of all first-attempt adjudicated denials in the Henan and Zhejiang samples, respectively, more than double the rate at which it was cited in first-attempt adjudicated approvals. Judges invoked this provision as a legal pretext for denying divorce petitions.

Even when plaintiffs did submit evidence, judges often held that it was circumstantial or otherwise insufficient to support their claims, as we saw in Chapter 7. Moreover, judges' use of evidentiary discourse to deny divorce petitions belied judicial rules and interpretations issued by the SPC obliging them to relax this provision, shift the burden of proof to the defendant, and adopt an alternative "preponderance of evidence" standard in domestic violence cases (Chapter 2). This alternative standard – namely, Article 73 of the 2001 Several Provisions of the SPC Concerning Civil Procedure Evidence – appeared in only two out of the nearly 150,000 first-instance adjudicated divorce decisions in my samples. Judges almost always applied conventional standards of evidence to domestic violence cases as if the SPC had never issued special instructions for the purpose of extending the benefit of the doubt to vulnerable abuse victims.

So far I have identified the words and terms judges used most frequently in two sets of holdings: (1) adjudicated denials of cases that do not involve domestic violence allegations and (2) all adjudicated decisions (both to deny and to grant divorces) in cases that do involve domestic violence allegations. Vocabularies in these two sets of holdings were strikingly similar both because judges tended to deny the divorce petitions of plaintiffs who made domestic violence allegations and because judges' gaslighting strategies were similar in cases that did and did not involve domestic violence allegations. Table 8.2 summarizes the key words and terms in each of the four judicial discourses of

TABLE 8.2 Typology of judicial discourse in holdings to deny divorce petitions

Discourse type	Component words and terms
Ideological	Harmony (和睦, 和谐), stability (稳定), civilized (文明)
Fourteen Articles	Reconciliation potential, possibility of reconciling (和好可能, 和好的可能), build (建立), foundation (基础), comprehensive analysis (综合分析)
Other therapeutic	Trifles (琐事), conflict (矛盾), occur (发生), produce (产生), cherish (珍惜), rapport (互谅), compromise (互让), mutual (相互), maintain (维护), good (较好), strengthen (加强), communication (沟通), definite (一定), freely (自由), romance (恋爱), voluntary (自愿)
Evidentiary	Evidence (证据), prove (证明), insufficient (不足), submit (提交), supply (提供)

Note: With the exception of "civilized" and "comprehensive analysis," every word and term in this table appears in at least one dendrogram in Figure 8.2. The words "reconcile" and "build" were counted only if they were positive (i.e., I excluded variations of "lack of reconciliation potential" [无和好可能] and "failure to build" [未建立]).

adjudicated denial. Frequency distributions of words, which are reflected in the word clouds in Figure 8.1, tell how often judges used them in their holdings but tell us little about their contextual meanings. So far I have provided only selected examples of context for the words that formed four types of judicial discourse in holdings to deny divorce petitions. I will now present results from a hierarchical cluster analysis (HCA) of the 50 most frequently used words in each sample of holdings.

Patterns of Judicial Discourse in Adjudicated Denials
By identifying words that tended to be used in tandem and thus to cluster together, HCA is a useful tool for contextualizing words and teasing out discursive patterns in the entire corpus of holdings. I limit the scope of the HCA to domestic violence cases because one of my key tasks in this chapter is to assess the influence of plaintiffs' domestic violence allegations on judges' holdings and verdicts.

Let us now take a closer look at how judges used the words depicted in the word clouds for first-attempt divorce adjudications involving allegations of domestic violence. Figure 8.2 contains two dendrograms – one for each province – depicting average conditional probabilities of the co-appearance of words and clusters of words within individual holdings. That is, the unit of analysis is the holding; the results of the HCA show the words judges tended to use together in the same holding. The holdings I used to construct the word clouds in Panels C and D of Figure 8.1 are the same ones I used in the HCA. Like the word clouds, each dendrogram contains the 50 most frequently used words in its corresponding provincial sample of holdings. The words in Panels A and B of Figure 8.2 are thus the same as those in Panels C and D of Figure 8.1, respectively. Both dendrograms share 38 words in common (denoted by a heavier font). Every pairwise combination of words in each dendrogram exists in its corresponding sample of holdings. Put another way, every possible pair of words in a dendrogram can be found within at least some of the holdings from which it was constructed. Although all clusters in each dendrogram are therefore connected to one another, I removed weaker links in order to facilitate the identification of word clusters. More specifically, I removed links connecting clusters of words whose average conditional probability of co-appearance in the holdings was 0.2 or less. As I present findings from the HCA, I will illustrate key discursive patterns with examples both of phrases and sentences judges commonly constructed with words in the dendrograms and of synonyms judges commonly used in lieu of words in the dendrograms.

We already know that well over 90% of holdings in first-attempt divorce cases contained the word "affection." We can see in Figure 8.2 that this word almost always appeared together with the words "marital" and "breakdown" in both provincial samples (Cluster 1a). This is hardly surprising given that these three words appear together in both the Fourteen Articles and Article 32 of the Marriage Law. Nor should we be surprised that the words "deny" and "support" clustered together in both samples of holdings (Cluster 1b), given that judges tended to rule to "*deny support* of the plaintiff's divorce petition." Judges' holdings to deny divorce petitions often referenced plaintiffs' legal complaints: the court *denies support* of "the plaintiff's *litigation request demanding a divorce*" (原告要求离婚的诉讼请求). For this reason, the words "demand," "request," and "litigation" clustered together in both Henan (Cluster 1c) and Zhejiang (Cluster 1d).

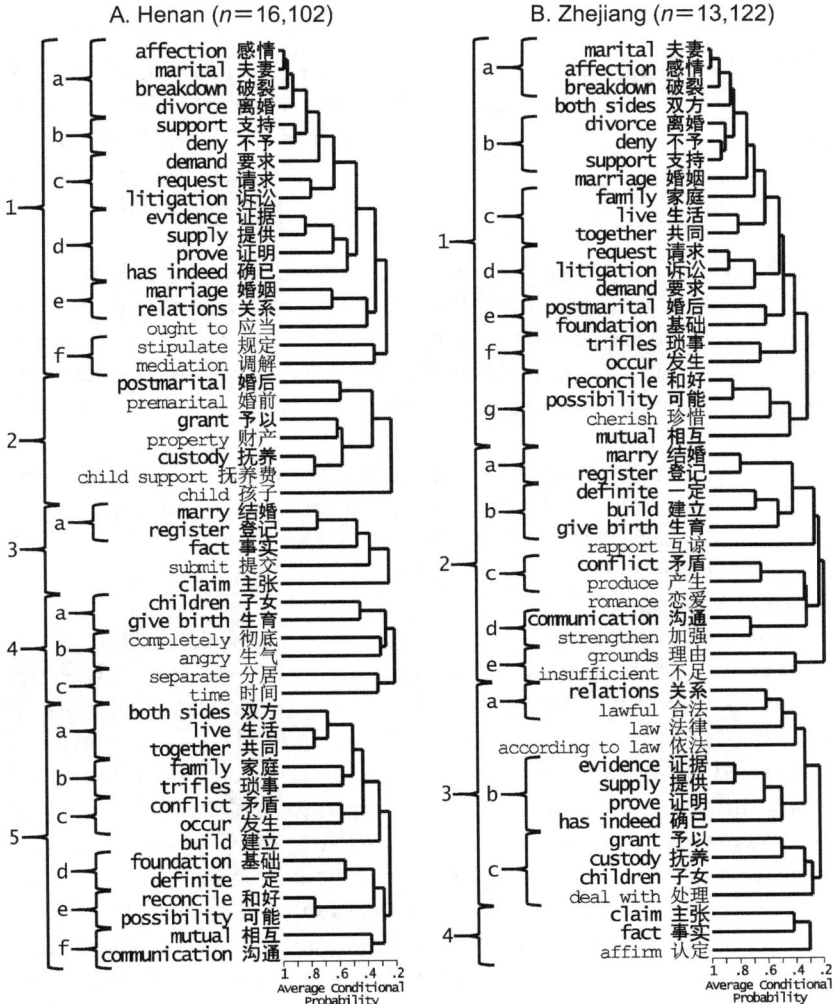

Figure 8.2 Hierarchical cluster analysis of top 50 words in domestic violence cases

Source: Author's calculations from Henan and Zhejiang provincial high courts' online decisions.

Note: Limited to first-attempt adjudications. The words in these dendrograms in Panels A and B are identical to those depicted in Panels C and D of Figure 8.1, respectively, because they were derived from holdings in first-attempt divorce decisions containing allegations of domestic violence. Major clusters are numbered and minor clusters are lettered. Words common to both dendrograms are in a heavier font (38 words); unique words are in a lighter font (24 words in total, 12 words per dendrogram). Words are clustered using the farthest neighbor (or complete linkage) method according to Kulczynski's similarity measure of the average conditional probability that Word B is present in a court decision given that Word A is present in the same court decision.

The dendrograms also contain clusters of words judges used to grant divorces. They are less prominent, however, because judges so rarely granted first-attempt divorce petitions even in cases involving allegations of domestic violence. Henan's Cluster 2 and Zhejiang's Cluster 3c contain the word "grant" as well as words associated with property division and child custody.

Given that the breakdownism test requires determining whether "mutual affection has indeed broken down," we also know that the word "has indeed" was inextricably linked to the words "breakdown" and "marital affection" in both the Marriage Law and the Fourteen Articles. In judges' holdings, however, "has indeed" was more closely linked to evidentiary discourse. "Has indeed" was closely linked to "evidence," "supply," and "prove" in both Henan (Cluster 1d) and Zhejiang (Cluster 3b). Many if not most adjudicated denials contain variations of a boilerplate sentence along the lines of: "The plaintiff failed to supply evidence proving her claim that mutual affection has indeed broken down."

In Henan, judges tended to use the Fourteen Articles word "foundation" in conjunction with the word "definite" (Cluster 5d). They frequently held that litigants possessed a "definite marital foundation" (一定的婚姻基础 or 一定的感情基础). This word cluster was strongly associated with another Fourteen Articles word cluster (Cluster 5e) containing the words "reconcile" and "possibility." Judges often held that reconciliation was possible because the marriage rested on a solid foundation. Judges expressed their optimistic prognosis for reconciliation using a variety of synonyms for "reconcile" (e.g., 可调和, 重归于好, 如初, 重新, 修复, 恢复, 有望). As we continue to review judges' flimsy determinations of the existence of mutual affection and reconciliation potential, bear in mind that each case in the HCA involves an allegation of domestic violence.

In Zhejiang's holdings, the words "definite" and "build" were part of a cluster of words that also included "give birth" (Cluster 2b). In addition to the word "build" (which can also be translated as "establish") that appears in the Fourteen Articles, judges also used a few synonyms (e.g., 构建, 共建, 组建) to refer to building happy families, building a harmonious society, and so on. This cluster in turn was connected to another cluster that included "marry" and "register" (Cluster 2a). When judges affirmed the validity of the marriage by holding that it was lawfully registered, they did so not only to establish the court's standing. Insofar as marrying under duress constitutes grounds for divorce according to the Fourteen Articles (Article 6), judges used these words to hold that litigants had registered their marriages on their own volition. Judges also regarded voluntary marriage registration as proof that a couple had "built definite marital affection" (e.g., 应视为已建立一定的夫妻感情). Applying the same logic, judges regarded childbirth as additional proof of marital affection. My samples of holdings are full of statements such as "Plaintiff and defendant, having voluntarily registered their marriage and given birth to a son and a daughter, should have a definite foundation of mutual affection."

Judges in Henan, too, used childbirth as evidence that marital affection had not broken down. Consider the words in Cluster 4. Judges held that occasional *anger* and arguing over family trifles was unavoidable, and that *giving birth* was evidence that marital affection was once strong and could therefore be rebuilt. As judges often put it, *anger* had led to physical *separation* but had not caused mutual affection to break down *completely*. They often added that the *time* duration of *separation* was relatively short and thus did not satisfy the minimum two-year requirement. Judges also used defendants' unwillingness to divorce as evidence of marital affection. Although the term "withhold consent" is not among the 50 most frequently used words in the holdings of domestic violence cases, it is in the word cloud in Panel A of Figure 8.1. Judges sometimes cited the "earnest" (诚恳) "wishes" (愿望) of defendants – even those who had committed domestic violence – to reconcile as evidence of the couple's marital affection and reconciliation potential. Judges similarly cited abusive defendants' "remorse" (悔改, 后悔) for their wrongdoing, promises to "rectify" themselves (改正, 改造, 改错, 改善), and hopes for another chance to reconcile as grounds for denying divorces. As we saw in Chapter 7, judges sometimes used defendants' apology letters as grounds for their adjudicated denials. Judges also used the words "child" and "children" to justify denying divorces "for the sake of the healthy upbringing of children."

Zhejiang's Cluster 1 contains Fourteen Articles words. The word "foundation" is most closely linked to the word "postmarital" (Cluster 1e). Sentences in which judges used both words include the following few examples: both the marital *foundation* and *postmarital* affection are good; both the premarital *foundation* and *postmarital* affection are good; although the marital *foundation* is good, disputes that emerged in their *postmarital* life together have not been properly handled; both sides built a good premarital *foundation*, their *postmarital* life together has been long, and they gave birth to a daughter; and plaintiff and defendant possess a good *foundation* for their marriage, and in their *postmarital* life together have built definite marital affection. Judges used a variety of synonyms for "good" when describing the quality of the marital foundation (e.g., 一般, 尚好, 尚可).

In both Henan and Zhejiang, Fourteen Articles words were closely linked to therapeutic words. In Henan, the Fourteen Articles words "build," "foundation," "reconcile," and "possibility" belong to a cluster of words that also includes the therapeutic words "both sides," "live," "together," "family," "trifles," "conflict," "occur," "mutual," and "communication" (Cluster 5). One of Zhejiang's corresponding clusters that includes "foundation," "reconcile," and "possibility" also includes "both sides," "live," "together," "family," "trifles," "occur," and "cherish" (Cluster 1). Zhejiang's Cluster 2 also contains the Fourteen Articles word "build" as well as the therapeutic words "rapport," "conflict," "produce," "communication," and "strengthen."

Judges held that marital conflict "occurred" as a result of – or was "produced" by – "family trifles" (家庭琐事), and was thus a normal and even inevitable part of marriage. While "conflict" was their word of choice in this context, they had a repertoire of synonyms (e.g., 冲突) and words that similarly expressed marital discord, including "estrangement" or "grown apart" (隔阂) and "argument" or "dispute" (争执, 吵架, 纠纷, 分歧, 吵闹, 争议, 争吵). A common synonym for "trifle" was "friction" (摩擦). Judges also used synonyms for "occur" and "produce" in this context (e.g., 造成, 导致). When they trivialized and normalized domestic violence, judges often held that "occasional" (时有, 偶尔) "rifts" (裂痕) did not rise to the "level" (地步) of "major" (大的) or "fundamental" (根本性, 原则性) marital problems. Some judges responded to allegations of domestic violence by holding that "opposition to frivolous divorce is a fundamental spirit of China's Marriage Law" (Decision #3128494, Quzhou Municipal Kecheng District People's Court, Zhejiang Province, October 30, 2014).[11] And they held that litigants' marital issues were not serious enough to cause the breakdown of mutual affection and that plaintiffs had either failed to submit evidence in support of their claims otherwise or had submitted evidence that was "insufficient" (不足, 不充分) to prove their claims.

---

[11] Case ID (2014)衢柯巡民初字第00317号, archived at https://perma.cc/97EC-WQTF.

Judges' acknowledgment of marital discord was the premise of their relationship advice. They held that marital damage could be mended – and even that documented domestic violence could be prevented in the future – if both sides "worked harder" (加强, 多加, 增强, 增进, 努力, 尽到, 坚持, 进一步) on their relationship skills. They advised litigants to fix their "shortcomings" (不足之处, 缺点), deal with conflict "correctly" (正确, 妥善), and "improve" themselves (改正, 改造, 改错, 改善). As judges so often explained in their holdings, litigants could overcome the "personality" (性格) differences at the root of their marital discord "provided" (只要) they learned to build "rapport and mutual understanding" (互谅, 体谅, 理解, 融洽); "compromise" or "give and take" (互让); "love, respect, and tolerate each other" (互敬, 互爱, 尊重, 宽容, 包容); "show care, affection, and consideration for one another" (关爱, 爱护, 呵护, 照顾, 体贴); "trust each other" (信任, 互信); "communicate" more regularly and effectively (沟通, 交流); be "honest, sincere, and loyal" (忠诚, 以诚相待); act "rationally" (理性) and with a "sense of responsibility" (责任感, 责任心); and "help and support each other" (互助, 扶助, 帮助, 扶持, 持家).[12] Finally, judges also explained that their holdings to deny divorce petitions were for the purpose of providing an "opportunity" (机会) for litigants to "cool off" (冷静) and "reflect on" (思考, 考虑) their commitment to their families. Judges advised litigants to adjust their attitudes and to "cherish" (珍惜, 珍视) and to feel blessed to have their "happy" (美满, 美好, 幸福), "perfect" (完美), "complete" (完整), and "precious and hard-earned" (来之不易) families. We have seen variations of a common cliché in judges' holdings: "If you cherish what you have you can restore marital harmony."

Clearly, the top 50 words in each set of holdings are a fraction of the rich vocabulary judges used to deny divorce petitions. Ideological words are absent from both dendrograms in Figure 8.2 because they were not among the top 50 most frequently used words in either sample. This does not mean that ideological discourse was unimportant. As we saw at the outset of this section and can see again in Table 8.3, ideological words appeared in the holdings of 25% and 13% of all first-attempt adjudications in the Henan and Zhejiang samples, respectively. The other three types of judicial discourse were simply more prevalent. Indeed,

---

[12] Some of these separate words typically appear as combined words in judges' holdings (e.g., 互谅互让 and 互敬互爱).

therapeutic words that appear in at least one word cloud in Figure 8.1 dominated judges' holdings. At least one of the 16 words comprising therapeutic discourse appeared in 75% and 83% of holdings in the Henan and Zhejiang samples, respectively. Each of the remaining two judicial discourses of adjudicated denials – Fourteen Articles discourse and evidentiary discourse – also appeared in the majority of holdings in first-attempt divorce adjudications in both samples. Finally, Table 8.3 shows that whereas judges' ideological discourse was more prevalent in

TABLE 8.3 Proportion of judges' holdings (%) containing types of words, by plaintiff claim of domestic violence

	All decisions	By plaintiff domestic violence claim		Domestic violence claim difference
		Yes	No	
Any ideological words				
Henan	25	27	24	3
Zhejiang	13	15	13	2
Any Fourteen Articles words				
Henan	54	57	53	4
Zhejiang	69	73	68	5
Any other therapeutic words				
Henan	75	80	73	7
Zhejiang	83	89	81	8
Any evidentiary words				
Henan	61	67	58	9
Zhejiang	60	67	58	9
Any of the above categories				
Henan	93	96	92	4
Zhejiang	93	97	92	5

Source: Author's calculations from Henan and Zhejiang provincial high courts' online decisions.
Note: Limited to first-attempt adjudications. Categories of words correspond to the typology of judicial discourse in Table 8.2. Henan $n = 57,502$ and Zhejiang $n = 51,573$ adjudications of first-attempt divorce petitions. All differences are statistically significant ($P < .001$, χ^2 tests).

the Henan sample than in the Zhejiang sample, Fourteen Articles discourse and therapeutic discourse were more prevalent in the Zhejiang sample than in the Henan sample.

Perhaps the most disconcerting pattern in Table 8.3 is that domestic violence allegations did not reduce judges' use of any of these types of judicial discourse. On the contrary, judges responded to domestic violence claims with even greater usage of these types of judicial discourse. Domestic violence claims also triggered evidentiary discourse. More often than not, domestic violence claims were invalidated on evidentiary grounds, as we have seen. Next I will show that judges were much more likely to invoke any of the four judicial discourses when the plaintiff was a woman than when the plaintiff was a man.

Gendered Exposure to Judicial Discourses of Adjudicated Denial

Table 8.4 contains two sets of comparisons of the prevalence of judicial discourses: (1) female versus male plaintiffs and (2) divorces denied versus divorces granted. With respect to the first comparison, all four types of judicial discourse in both provincial samples were more prevalent in judges' holdings when the plaintiff was a woman. Given that domestic violence allegations so greatly increased the incidence of evidentiary discourse, we should not be surprised that the gender gap was greatest there: 7 and 6 percentage points in the Henan and Zhejiang samples, respectively. Judges' disproportionate use of therapeutic discourse in cases filed by women was also pronounced: a gap of 3 and 5 percentage points in the two respective samples.

With respect to the second comparison, Table 8.4 brings into sharp relief the concentration of all four types of judicial discourse in adjudicated denials. All four types of judicial discourse represent the language judges tended to use to deny divorce petitions. In both samples, judges' use of these discourses was vastly more likely in adjudicated denials than in holdings to grant divorces. The degree to which these judicial discourses were concentrated in adjudicated denials is truly striking. Differences in the Henan and Zhejiang samples were 21 and 8 percentage points, respectively, in the use of ideological words, 25 and 33 percentage points, respectively, in the use of Fourteen Articles words, 21 and 36 percentage points, respectively, in the use of other therapeutic words, and 40 and 44 percentage points, respectively, in the use of evidentiary words. The incidence of these judicial discourses in adjudicated denials was generally about double their incidence in holdings to grant divorces.

297

TABLE 8.4 Proportion of judges' holdings (%) containing types of words, by plaintiff sex and outcome

	All decisions	By plaintiff sex			All outcomes	By outcome		
		Female	Male	Gender difference		Denied	Granted	Outcome difference
Any ideological words								
Henan	25	25	24	1**	25	32	12	21**
Zhejiang	14	14	13	2*	13	15	7	8**
Any Fourteen Articles words								
Henan	53	54	52	2**	54	63	38	25**
Zhejiang	71	71	70	2	69	76	43	33**
Any other therapeutic words								
Henan	75	76	73	3**	75	83	62	21**
Zhejiang	85	87	82	5**	83	90	55	36**
Any evidentiary words								
Henan	61	63	56	7**	61	75	35	40**
Zhejiang	63	65	59	6**	60	69	25	44**
Any of the above categories								
Henan	93	94	92	2**	93	99	84	15**
Zhejiang	95	96	93	2**	93	97	78	19**

Source: Author's calculations from Henan and Zhejiang provincial high courts' online decisions.

Note: Limited to first-attempt adjudications. Categories of words correspond to the typology of judicial discourse in Table 8.2. For cross-tabulations by plaintiff sex, Henan n = 54,200 and Zhejiang n = 8,626 adjudications of first-attempt divorce petitions. For cross-tabulations by outcome, Henan n = 57,502 and Zhejiang n = 51,573 adjudications of first-attempt divorce petitions. Slight discrepancies between numbers in the "gender difference" and "outcome difference" columns and numbers from which they were derived in the "by plaintiff sex" and "by outcome" columns, respectively, are due to rounding error.

* P < .05 ** P < .001, χ^2 test

If women were at greater exposure to these four judicial discourses, and if these four judicial discourses were associated with adjudicated denials, then perhaps women's greater risk of having their petitions denied explains why they were more exposed to these four judicial discourses. In other words, perhaps judges were more likely to invoke a judicial discourse of denial in cases filed by women simply because they were more likely to deny the divorce petitions of women. If this is true, then female and male plaintiffs who won their cases should have been similarly or identically exposed to these judicial discourses. Likewise, female and male plaintiffs who lost their cases should have had essentially the same level of exposure to these judicial discourses.

We can easily test this possibility with regression analysis. If women's greater exposure to judicial discourses of denial was simply a function of their greater likelihood to lose their cases, then controlling for the outcome should erase gender differences in exposure to the four judicial discourses. The results presented in Table 8.5 entirely support this expectation. The regression models in Table 8.5 also allow for a comparison of gender gaps between rural and urban courts. Rural courts are those in counties and county-level cities, and urban courts are those in urban districts (Chapter 4).

To facilitate the interpretation of the regression models in Table 8.5, I converted regression coefficients into average marginal effects (AMEs), which are interpreted simply as changes in the probability of a given outcome associated with changes in a given explanatory variable. For example, in Model 1 for Henan's rural courts, changing the plaintiff from male to female is associated with a .03 increase in the probability that at least one ideological word appeared in the holding. Zhejiang's corresponding AME was identical. AMEs for female plaintiffs in models for judges' use of Fourteen Articles words in rural courts (Model 3) were identical or nearly so. The magnitude of AMEs for female plaintiffs was even greater in models for the appearance of other therapeutic words and evidentiary words in rural courts' holdings (Model 5).

Note, however, that AMEs for female plaintiffs are only positive and statistically significant (at the conventional level of $P < .05$) in models for rural courts. Female plaintiffs in urban courts, by contrast, were no more exposed than male plaintiffs to these four judicial discourses (with the possible exception of therapeutic discourse in Zhejiang, where the AME is only marginally statistically significant).

TABLE 8.5 Average marginal effects on the appearance of word types in judges' holdings, calculated from logistic regression models

	Any ideological words		Any Fourteen Articles words		Any other therapeutic words		Any evidentiary words	
	(1)	(2)	(3)	(4)	(5)	(6)	(7)	(8)
Henan (n = 54,200)								
Rural courts (n = 45,353)								
Female plaintiff	.03***	.004	.03***	.01	.04***	.02***	.06***	.01**
Adjudicated denial		.19***		.21***		.19***		.41***
McKelvey & Zavoina pseudo-R^2	.61	.64	.26	.31	.15	.20	.17	.34
Urban courts (n = 8,847)								
Female plaintiff	−.01	−.01	−.03**	−.03*	−.01	−.005	.01	.02*
Adjudicated denial		.26***		.23***		.24***		.29***
McKelvey & Zavoina pseudo-R^2	.42	.50	.16	.22	.23	.33	.26	.34
Zhejiang (n = 8,626)								
Rural courts (n = 5,753)								
Female plaintiff	.03***	.02*	.04***	−.004	.07***	.02**	.06***	.003
Adjudicated denial		.06***		.32***		.33***		.39***
McKelvey & Zavoina pseudo-R^2	.75	.74	.23	.31	.54	.59	.26	.38
Urban courts (n = 2,873)								
Female plaintiff	.01	.01	.01	−.01	.03+	.01	.02	.01
Adjudicated denial		.11***		.35***		.31***		.30***
McKelvey & Zavoina pseudo-R^2	.48	.50	.49	.54	.21	.43	.27	.36

Source: Author's calculations from Henan and Zhejiang provincial high courts' online decisions.

Note: Limited to first-attempt adjudications. Categories of words correspond to the typology of judicial discourse in Table 8.2. All models include court fixed effects (court dummies) and year of decision. Significance tests are based on standard errors calculated using the delta method and are adjusted for nonindependence between decisions clustered within courts (108 rural courts and 53 urban courts in Henan; 53 rural courts and 38 urban courts in Zhejiang).

+ $P < .10$ * $P < .05$ ** $P < .01$ *** $P < .001$, two-tailed tests

Once the verdict to grant or deny the divorce petition is introduced into the models for rural courts, the effect of plaintiff sex almost or entirely disappears. The interpretation of this pattern is clear: what originally appeared to be a gender difference in exposure to judicial discourses of denials was actually the effect of a gender difference in adjudicated denials. Judges were more likely to use judicial discourses of denials in their holdings when the plaintiff was a woman because they were more likely to deny the divorce petitions of women. At the same time, this pattern is limited to rural courts. In urban courts, by contrast, for the simple reason that judges were equally likely to deny the divorce petitions of female and male plaintiffs, judges were also equally likely to infantilize female and male plaintiffs with holdings ordering them to stay together for the sake of society, the nation, their children, and their own happiness. Women were disproportionately targeted with judicial discourses of adjudicated denial only because they were disproportionately targeted for adjudicated denial. Judges were more likely to gaslight women because they were more likely to deny their divorce petitions.

JUDICIAL DECISION-MAKING

So far we have seen astonishingly little variation in judges' holdings. In their crusade to deny divorce petitions, they mindlessly applied boilerplate holdings of little bearing on the specific circumstances of the cases at hand. Holdings were often so general that they could apply to almost any case after filling in a few blanks with the litigants' names, their children, pertinent dates, the thrust of the plaintiff's legal complaint, and so on. Judges' holdings to deny divorce petitions shared a remarkably limited lexicon of words and terms grounded in political ideology, relationship advice, and cherry-picked legal provisions on reconciliation potential (in the Fourteen Articles) and evidence that should not apply to cases involving allegations of domestic violence. Copying and pasting boilerplate text helped judges realize one of the key benefits of the divorce twofer, which is to clear their dockets by expeditiously denying divorce petitions. This section is devoted to documenting the reason why judges were more likely to apply this strategy in cases filed by women than in cases filed by men: judges were much more likely to deny a divorce petition if it was filed by a woman than if it was filed by a man. I will begin with descriptive patterns before turning to regression analysis results.

Descriptive Correlates of Adjudicated Denials

Reading and manually coding even a small fraction of documents in a corpus of this size is infeasible. Chapter 4 documents my methods of machine-coding the contents of court decisions into measures that I use to analyze divorce verdicts in the remainder of this chapter. My dependent variable – my object of inquiry, the outcome I try to explain – consists of verdicts in first-attempt divorce trials. There are only two possible outcomes in this analysis of judicial decision-making: a granted or denied divorce petition.

China's judicial clampdown on adjudicated divorce has been achieved in no small part on the backs on women. Figure 8.3 disaggregates by plaintiff sex the long-dash lines in Figure 6.2 (Panels B and C) depicting China's judicial clampdown on divorce. Panels A and B of Figure 8.3 show a wide gap between female and male plaintiffs in the probability of an adjudicated denial. The overall gender gaps were 11–12 percentage points in the two samples. In Henan, the gender gap widened over time from 2 percentage points in 2009 to 13 percentage points in 2015. Among first-attempt divorce adjudications, the probability of a denial increased from 43% to 66% for men and from 45% to 78% for women (Panel A). As we saw in Figure 6.2, trends were flatter in Zhejiang, particularly after 2009. Zhejiang's gender gap remained stable at 12–13 percentage points from 2010 to 2016 (Panel B). By 2015, Henan's denial rates had almost caught up with Zhejiang's. In 2015, 75% and 78% of adjudicated first-attempt divorce petitions were quashed in the Henan and Zhejiang samples, respectively. Meanwhile, in the same year, among female plaintiffs, denials accounted for 78% and 82% of all first-attempt adjudications in the two respective samples.

In short, women's divorce requests were far more likely than men's to be denied on the first attempt. Women's disproportionate burden was compounded by five factors. First, as we can also see in Figure 8.3, the gap between female and male plaintiffs in first-attempt divorce denial rates was widest in rural areas where most divorce petitions were filed. In the two samples, the average gender gap (the female denial rate minus the male denial rate) was 14–15 percentage points in rural courts, which we know contained the majority of both people and divorce petitions. Figure 8.3 also shows that urbanization not only shrank the gender gap, but also, at least in the case of Henan, reversed it. No different from the gender gap in exposure to judicial discourses of denial discussed in the previous section, the gender gap in adjudicated

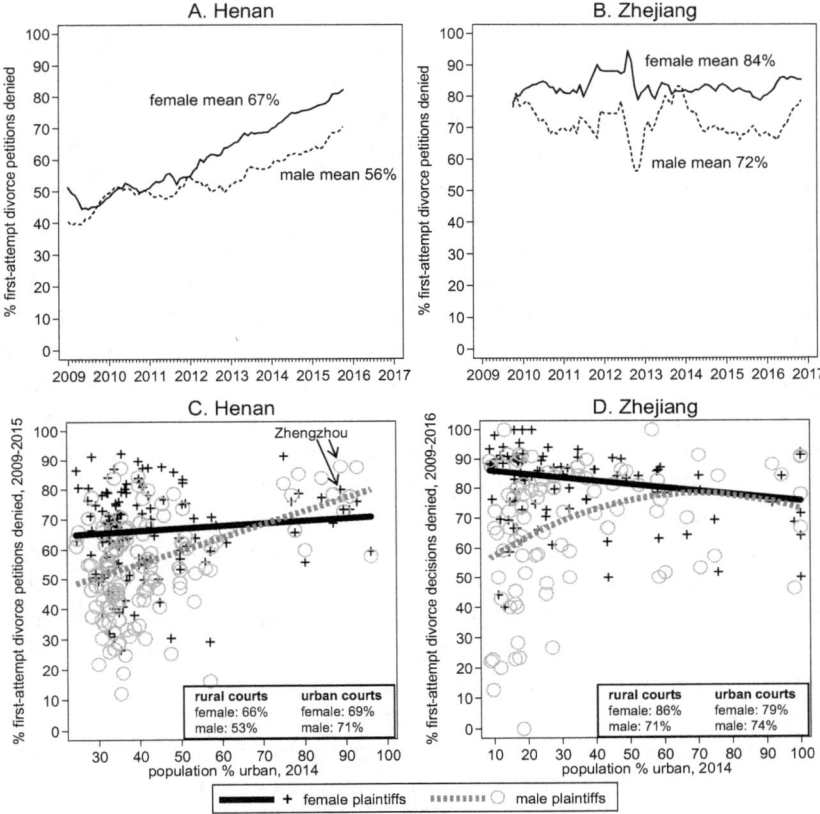

Figure 8.3 Proportion of first-attempt divorce petitions (%) denied
Source: Author's calculations from Henan and Zhejiang provincial high courts'
online decisions.
Note: n = 54,200 and n = 8,626 first-attempt adjudicated decisions (granted or
denied) from Henan and Zhejiang, respectively. All sex differences are statistically
significant (χ^2, $P < .01$). Panels A and B are smoothed with moving averages. For
more information on scatterplot points, see the note under Figure 4.5.

outcomes appears also to have been largely a rural phenomenon. In
urban courts, the average gender gap flipped to −3 percentage points
in Henan and shrank to 5 percentage points in Zhejiang.[13] Consider

---

[13] The discrepancy between the Henan's gender gap of 14 percentage points and the numbers
presented in Panel C for rural courts (66 − 53 = 13) is due to rounding error: 66.19 − 52.52
= 13.67. Similarly, the discrepancy between Henan's gender gap of −3 percentage points and
the numbers presented in Panel C for urban courts (69 − 71 = −2) is due to rounding error:
68.75 − 71.49 = −2.74.

Henan's provincial capital of Zhengzhou, labeled in Panel C. In Zhengzhou's seven district courts, which together supplied 953 decisions, female plaintiffs were more likely than male plaintiffs to win the divorces they sought. The rate at which divorce petitions were denied was 80% and 88% among female and male plaintiffs, respectively. The positive impact of urbanization, however, was relatively limited, as only 16% and 33% of first-attempt divorce adjudications in the Henan and Zhejiang samples, respectively, were filed in urban courts.

Second, Table 8.6 reproduces what we already saw in Figure 7.1, namely that women were disproportionately exposed to marital violence. Table 8.6 presents descriptive characteristics of key explanatory variables in the regression analysis later in the chapter. In both samples, female plaintiffs made allegations of domestic violence in almost 40% of their petitions. The remarkable discursive similarities we saw between judges' holdings in adjudicated denials and judges' holdings in domestic violence cases suggests that allegations of domestic violence did not sway judges to grant divorces. Indeed, because domestic violence allegations increased the likelihood that judges invoked a judicial discourse associated with adjudicated denials, we should not be surprised to discover that domestic violence allegations were also positively associated with adjudicated denials.

Third, the improbability of obtaining an adjudicated divorce on the first attempt disproportionately impacted women in part because male defendants were more likely than female defendants to withhold consent. Table 8.6 shows that cases in which the defendant withheld consent represent by far the largest category of the "defendant consent and absenteeism" variable and account for at least one-half of all first-attempt divorce trials in each sample. Within this category, public notice trials were far rarer in Zhejiang than in Henan, perhaps because they reduce judicial efficiency by virtue of the requirement that they be conducted according to the ordinary civil procedure (Chapters 2 and 5). Meanwhile, defendants in only a small proportion of cases (15% and 14% in the Henan and Zhejiang samples, respectively) consented to divorce. Table 8.6 also shows that female plaintiffs were more likely than male plaintiffs to face defendant obstructionism and less likely than male plaintiffs to have defendant consent. We know that judges used defendants' unwillingness to divorce as evidence of mutual affection and thus as grounds for denying divorce petitions. We also know that judges fear provoking the violent wrath of disgruntled male defendants.

TABLE 8.6 Frequency distributions (%) of main variables in regression models

| | Henan (n = 54,200) | | | | Zhejiang (n = 8,626) | | | |
| | All plaintiffs | By plaintiff sex | | Gender difference | All plaintiffs | By plaintiff sex | | Gender difference |
		Female	Male			Female	Male	
Sex composition of plaintiffs	100	66	34		100	67	33	
Court verdict								
Divorce denied	63	67	56	10***	80	84	72	12***
Divorce granted	37	33	44	-10***	20	17	28	-12***
Total	100	100	100		100	101	100	
Domestic violence								
Apparent plaintiff claim	28	38	8	30***	30	39	11	27***
No apparent plaintiff claim	72	62	92	-30***	70	61	89	-27***
Total	100	100	100		100	100	100	
Defendant consent and absenteeism								
Defendant in absentia								
Public notice	12	9	19	-10***	6	4	10	-6***
No public notice	23	24	20	4***	23	24	22	2*
Defendant consented to divorce	15	15	16	-2***	14	14	15	-1+
Defendant withheld consent	50	52	45	7***	56	58	53	5***
Total	100	100	100		99	100	100	
Civil procedure								
Ordinary civil procedure	47	47	47	-0.2	8	6	11	-5***
Simplified civil procedure	53	53	53	0.2	92	94	89	5***
Total	100	100	100		100	100	100	
Plaintiff submitted evidence								
Apparently yes	50	50	49	1***	82	83	80	3***
Apparently no	50	50	51	-1***	18	17	20	-3***
Total	100	100	100		100	100	100	

TABLE 8.6 (cont.)

	Henan (n = 54,200)				Zhejiang (n = 8,626)			
	All plaintiffs	By plaintiff sex		Gender difference	All plaintiffs	By plaintiff sex		Gender difference
		Female	Male			Female	Male	
Case complexity								
Both children and marital property	74	76	69	7***	72	76	65	11***
Children no, marital property yes	16	14	21	-7***	18	15	25	-10***
Children yes, marital property no	7	8	7	1***	6	7	6	1
Neither	3	2	4	-1***	3	2	4	-2***
Total	100	100	101		99	100	100	
Physical separation claim								
Apparently yes	41	41	42	-1**	52	53	50	2*
Apparently no	59	59	58	1**	48	47	50	-2*
Total	100	100	100		100	100	100	
Plaintiff gave up property or child custody								
Apparently yes	7	7	5	2***	3	3	3	0.1
Apparently no	93	93	95	-2***	97	97	97	-0.1
Total	100	100	100		100	100	100	

Source: Author's calculations from Henan and Zhejiang provincial high courts' online decisions.

Note: Limited to first-attempt adjudications. The numbers of observations here and in Table 6.5 ("first attempts") are different because this table is limited to the subsample of observations with disclosed litigant sex and nonmissing values of covariates included in the logistic regression models. Ordinary civil procedure cases exclude public notice trials in order to prevent redundancy between the two variables; public notice trials, by definition, use the ordinary civil procedure. Totals do not always equal 100% owing to rounding error. Slight discrepancies between numbers in the "gender difference" column and numbers from which they were derived in the "by plaintiff sex" columns are also due to rounding error.

+ P < .10 * P < .05 ** P < .01 *** P < .001, χ² test

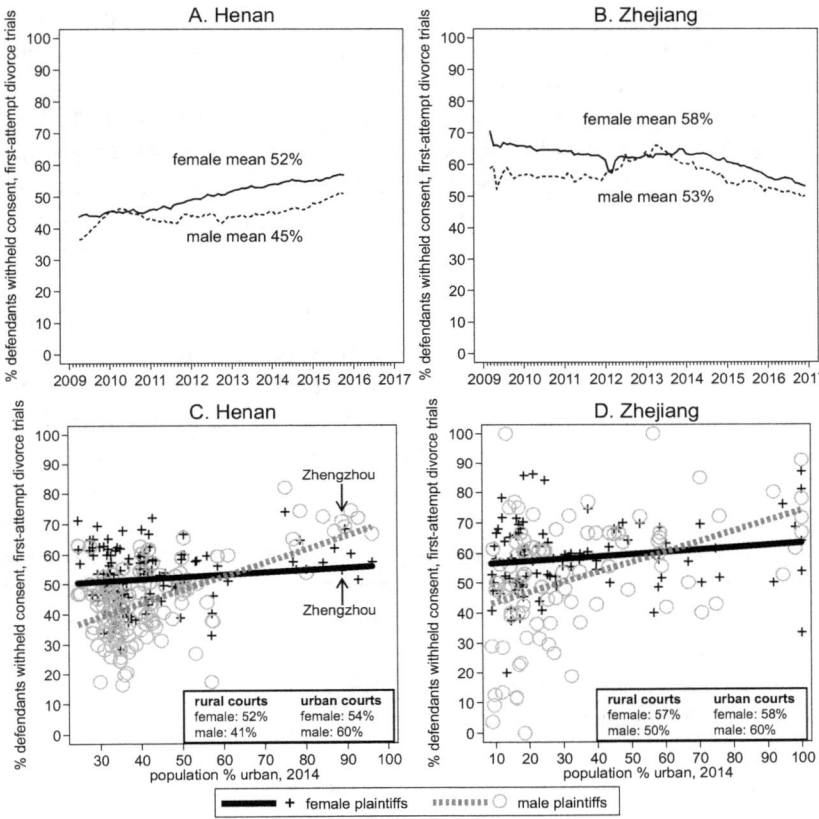

Figure 8.4 Proportion of defendants (%) who withheld consent to divorce
Source: Author's calculations from Henan and Zhejiang provincial high courts'
online decisions.
Note: Lines for females and males refer to plaintiffs. Lines for female plaintiffs are
interpreted as the proportion of defendants who withheld consent to divorce when
the plaintiff was female. $n = 54,200$ and $n = 8,626$ first-attempt adjudicated decisions
(granted or denied) from Henan and Zhejiang, respectively. With the exception
of urban courts in Zhejiang, all sex differences are statistically significant (χ^2, $P <$
.001). Panels A and B are smoothed with moving averages. For more information on
scatterplot points, see the note under Figure 4.5.

Figure 8.4 shows that the gender gap in defendant obstructionism
remained fairly stable over time. It also shows how defendant obstructionism varied by urbanization. Female plaintiffs' disadvantage was another exclusively rural phenomenon in both samples. Whereas female
plaintiffs were more likely than male plaintiffs to face defendant

obstructionism in rural areas, the opposite was true in urban areas (although the small difference in Zhejiang's urban courts was not statistically significant). Once again, Henan's capital of Zhengzhou is illustrative of urban courts more generally: whereas the husbands of 55% of female plaintiffs withheld consent, the wives of 71% of male plaintiffs withheld consent. On the whole, female plaintiffs' advantage in urban courts such as those in Zhengzhou was far overshadowed by their disadvantage in rural courts, where the vast majority of divorce adjudications occurred.

Fourth, as we can also see in Table 8.6, female plaintiffs were less than half as likely as male plaintiffs to have public notice trials. Because, as we will see, judges were relatively inclined to grant divorces when defendants were unable or chose not to participate in first-attempt trials, women's lower chances of success in their attempts to divorce are explained in part by men's vast overrepresentation among plaintiffs in public notice trials.[14]

Figure 8.5 depicts patterns with respect to courts' utilization of the ordinary procedure. Note that Henan's time trend – its turn away from the ordinary procedure in favor of the simplified civil procedure beginning in 2012 – reflects what we already saw in Figure 5.1. Zhejiang's far greater aversion to the ordinary procedure also reflects what we saw in Figure 5.1. Figure 8.5 disaggregates the application of the ordinary civil procedure according to plaintiff sex. Men who filed for divorce were much more likely than women to have their cases tried according to the ordinary civil procedure. This gender gap narrowed or altogether disappeared with urbanization; like other gender gaps, it was primarily a rural phenomenon.

As mentioned in Chapter 4, the ordinary civil procedure was much more common when the defendant was in absentia because its application is legally mandated in public notice trials. Courts applied the ordinary civil procedure in practically 100% of public notice trials, as required by the SPC. Because my measure for civil procedure and my measure for defendant consent and absenteeism are therefore partially

---

[14] Data limitations prohibit an assessment of the extent to which this overrepresentation is endogenous to courts. It could be a function of men's greater likelihood to claim missing spouses, courts' greater likelihood to accept the missing spouse claims of male plaintiffs, or a combination of both. Regardless of its origins, this overrepresentation disadvantages female plaintiffs relative to male plaintiffs. Although, as I discussed in Chapter 2, the Marriage Law stipulates that a formal missing person declaration by a court constitutes statutory grounds for divorce, my samples of court decisions reveal that this almost never happens, undoubtedly because, as also discussed earlier, courts can enjoy all the conveniences of a public notice trial without the hassle of making a formal missing person declaration.

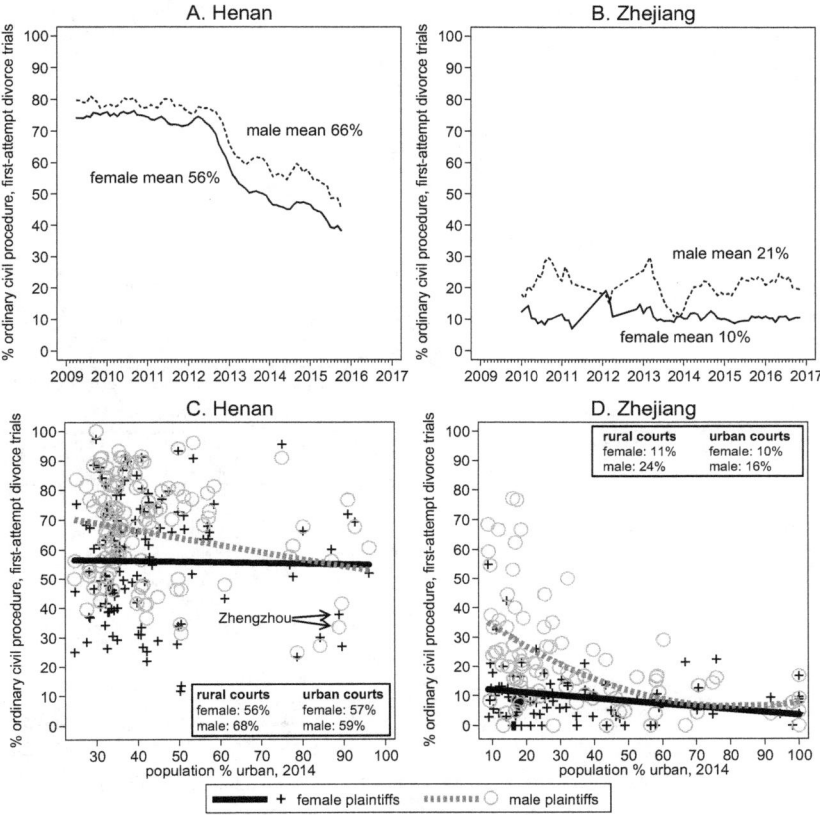

Figure 8.5 Ordinary civil procedure utilization rate (%) in first-attempt divorce trials
Source: Author's calculations from Henan and Zhejiang provincial high courts' online decisions.
Note: n = 54,200 and n = 8,626 first-attempt adjudicated decisions (granted or denied) from Henan and Zhejiang, respectively. With the exception of urban courts in Henan, all sex differences are statistically significant (χ^2, P < .001). Panels A and B are smoothed with moving averages. For more information on scatterplot points, see the note under Figure 4.5.

redundant (i.e., we already know the type of civil procedure that courts used in public notice trials), in the regression analyses later in the chapter I removed all public notice trials from the measure of the ordinary civil procedure in order to prevent multicollinearity.

The gender gap in courts' use of the ordinary civil procedure was partially an artifact of a gender gap in defendant absenteeism. In other words, gender gaps in public notice trials depicted in Figure 8.6 mirror gender gaps in courts' application of the ordinary civil procedure in

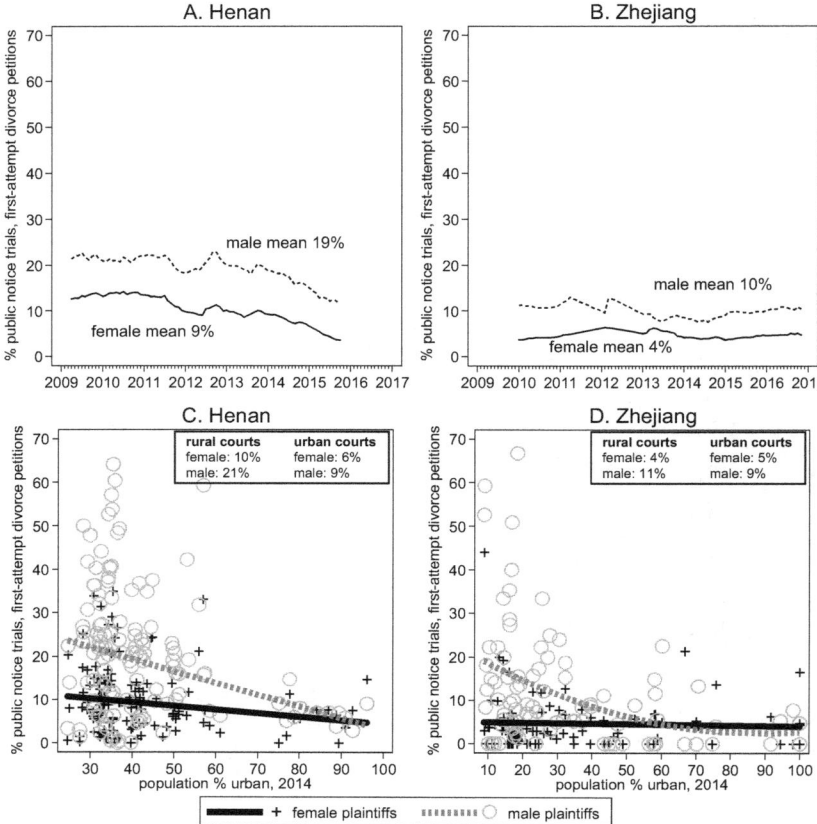

Figure 8.6 Public notice trials (%) among all first-attempt divorce trials
Source: Author's calculations from Henan and Zhejiang provincial high courts'
online decisions.
Note: n = 54,200 and n = 8,626 first-attempt adjudicated decisions (granted or
denied) from Henan and Zhejiang, respectively. All sex differences are statistically
significant (χ^2, P < .001). Panels A and B are smoothed with moving averages. For
more information on scatterplot points, see the note under Figure 4.5.

Figure 8.5. To some extent, female plaintiffs were less likely to have their
cases tried according to the ordinary civil procedure *because* they were
less likely to have public notice trials. Indeed, as we can see in Table 8.6,
once we remove public notice trials from my measure of ordinary civil
procedure, the gender gap narrowed (Zhejiang) or disappeared (Henan).
The wives of male plaintiffs were a lot more likely than the husbands
of female plaintiffs to be summoned by public notice and absent from

their trials. And this is an important reason why male plaintiffs were more likely than female plaintiffs to have their cases tried according to the ordinary civil procedure. Once again, this gender gap with respect to public notice trials was limited almost entirely to rural courts.

Altogether, about one-third of plaintiffs in each sample did not face defendants in their first-attempt trials. A far greater share of defendants was AWOL in Henan than in Zhejiang undoubtedly because Zhejiang is far more urbanized than Henan. We can see in Figure 8.6 that defendants whose whereabouts were allegedly unknown or who opted out of court proceedings for other reasons were overrepresented in rural areas. In the rural courts in my samples, 35–40% of first-attempt trials were held without the participation of defendants (including but not limited to public notice trials), compared with only 25–30% in the urban courts in my samples.

Fifth, the foregoing dynamics that militated against women's efforts to divorce were multiplied by women's disproportionate representation among first-attempt divorce petitioners in court. Table 8.6 shows that, as previously reported in Chapter 4 (Figure 4.5), and consistent with previously published estimates reported in Chapter 2, women accounted for 66% and 67% of all plaintiffs filing first-attempt divorce petitions in the Henan and Zhejiang samples, respectively.

The remaining variables in Table 8.6 also pertain to divorce verdicts. Female plaintiffs were more likely than male plaintiffs to submit evidence in support of their legal complaints. As we will see, whether judges treated women's evidence as seriously as men's evidence is another matter. The cases of female plaintiffs were more likely than those of male plaintiffs to involve both children and marital property. Judges' aversion to ruling on complex and contentious matters such as these may have therefore contributed to female plaintiffs' higher risk of adjudicated denial. Physical separation of at least two years is statutory grounds for divorce that should reduce the probability of an adjudicated denial. Over 40% of cases in Henan and a little over half of cases in Zhejiang involved claims of physical separation. Finally, plaintiffs sometimes gave up claims to property or child custody as a means of obtaining defendants' consent to divorce and thus of boosting their chances of obtaining a divorce verdict. Women were more likely than men to make this sort of concession in Henan but not in Zhejiang. Plaintiffs' concessions on property or child custody were concentrated in cases in which the divorce was granted. In Henan, almost one out of five female plaintiffs – but only about one out of 10 male plaintiffs – whose divorce petitions were granted had "voluntarily" given up property or child custody claims. The same pattern, albeit a more muted one, emerges from the Zhejiang sample.

Descriptive characteristics of additional variables not included in Table 8.6 are available elsewhere (Michelson 2019c). Let us now turn to a multivariate assessment of the relative importance of domestic violence allegations as grounds for granting divorces (faultism) and defendants' unwillingness to divorce as grounds for denying divorces (breakdownism).

Multivariate Correlates of Adjudicated Denials

I use AMEs to assess the impact of plaintiff sex, domestic violence (faultism), and defendant consent (breakdownism) on courts' verdicts, net of control variables included in the regression models. A marginal effect – also known as a first difference – is the difference between the predicted probabilities for each group. An AME is the average of all marginal effects computed for each observation in the sample. The interpretation of AMEs is highly intuitive. An AME can be interpreted as the effect of a variable (say, of changing the value of plaintiff sex from male to female) on the probability the outcome of interest occurs, holding all remaining variables at observed values (Long and Freese 2014:242–46; Mize 2019:85–87).[15] An AME of .05 for "female plaintiff" thus means that the probability a court denied a divorce petition was .05 higher for women who filed for divorce than for men who filed for divorce. The difference between two AMEs is known as a second difference.

I will proceed in two steps. In the first step, I will present overall AMEs for plaintiff sex, domestic violence (faultism), and defendant consent (breakdownism). Comparing the magnitudes of these effects allows me to conduct two empirical assessments: (1) the magnitudes of and reasons for gender differences in adjudicated outcomes of divorce trials and (2) the importance judges attached to the faultism and breakdownism standards for granting divorces. In the second step, I will present AMEs for domestic violence (faultism), defendant consent (breakdownism), in absentia trials (defendant absenteeism), and other explanatory factors that vary by plaintiff sex. For example, comparing

---

[15] Marginal effects at the mean (MEMs) are calculated while holding all remaining variables at sample means. AMEs are generally the preferred choice (Long and Freese 2014:245–46; Mize 2019). I replicated all analyses using both methods; results are highly robust.

the effects of defendant consent by plaintiff sex allows me to test whether defendant consent interacted with plaintiff sex.[16] Recall from Chapter 4 that I combined defendant consent and defendant absenteeism into a single variable in order to isolate affirmative consent (and affirmatively withholding consent) from failure to withhold consent by virtue of being an absentee defendant and not participating in the litigation process.

I include fixed effects for the court that adjudicated the case in order to account for unobserved heterogeneity across contexts. Because basic-level court jurisdictions correspond to rural counties and urban districts, court fixed effects (court dummy variables) serve the function of controlling for unobserved characteristics of both courts and the contexts in which they are embedded. For example, court fixed effects control for court-level variation in caseloads, an issue at the heart of Chapters 5 and 6. Court locations also reflect and therefore control for the social origins of divorce litigants. Divorce litigants who hailed from rural areas were overwhelmingly at the mercy of rural courts. As we saw in Chapter 4, migrants from rural areas rarely filed their divorces in urban courts. Rural courts tended to serve rural residents, and urban courts tended to serve urban residents.

The models also include additional control variables. Control variables are essential in order to minimize the possibility that an observed effect is an artifact of an omitted correlate. In order to assess the effects of the variables of central interest among otherwise similar cases, I control for the year of the decision, whether or not the plaintiff submitted evidence, whether or not the plaintiff gave up marital property or child custody, a physical separation claim, the participation of one or more female judges, the civil procedure adopted (ordinary or simplified), marital duration, marital property, children, and the participation of legal counsel. We will see that some of these control variables are important in their own right. Details on the construction of all measures are in Chapter 4.

---

[16] Regression models presented in this section include interactions between plaintiff sex and all explanatory and control variables. I test interaction effects by testing the equality of AMEs (i.e., by testing whether second differences are statistically significant; Long and Freese 2014:285). In regression models for categorical outcomes, group differences cannot be reliably assessed by testing the statistical significance of the coefficients of interaction terms (Allison 1999; Long and Mustillo 2021). Current methodological best practices call instead for testing interaction effects – that is, testing differences between groups in the effect of a covariate on the probability of experiencing a given outcome – by testing whether first differences (one for each group) are equal (Long and Mustillo 2021; Mize 2019).

Table 8.7 contains AMEs estimated from models of judges' decisions to deny first-attempt divorces in the Henan and Zhejiang samples. In Model 1, which controls only for decision year and court, the AMEs for the gender gap in the probability of an adjudicated denial – average female predicted probabilities minus average male predicted probabilities – are .09 in Henan and .11 in Zhejiang. Model 2 adds claims of domestic violence. In both Henan and Zhejiang, a claim of domestic violence increased the probability of a first-attempt adjudicated denial by .09 and .04 in the Henan and Zhejiang samples, respectively. Model 2 also shows that the highly statistically significant gender gap is reduced by controlling for claims of domestic violence. As we will see, this effect of domestic violence in Model 2 is largely an artifact of (1) an overrepresentation of domestic violence claims in cases in which defendants withheld consent (because judges rarely granted divorces in such cases) and (2) an underrepresentation of domestic violence claims in public notice trials (because judges were reasonably likely to grant divorces in such cases). In short, defendant consent and defendant absenteeism are driving what appears to be an effect of domestic violence.

When "defendant consent and absenteeism" is introduced in Model 3, the gender gap shrinks yet again, suggesting that some of the gender gap in the probability of an adjudicated denial on the first attempt was due to female plaintiffs' greater exposure to domestic violence and spousal obstructionism, and to the more limited use of public notice trials for their cases. Indeed, defendant consent and absenteeism accounts for the majority of the gender gap in the Henan sample. Just as striking is the sheer magnitude of the effect of defendant consent and absenteeism. Recall from Chapter 2 that statutory grounds for the breakdown of mutual affection can be established relatively straightforwardly both in public notice trials and when the defendant consents. Regression results show that only under these two circumstances was a court reasonably likely to grant a plaintiff's divorce request. In the full model (Model 4), a spouse's unwillingness to divorce increased the probability of an adjudicated denial by .51 and .47 in the Henan and Zhejiang samples, respectively. The effect of defendants' withholding consent was greater than the effect of plaintiffs' domestic violence allegations on divorce outcomes by dozens of orders of magnitude. Similarly, in absentia trials in which defendants were not served by public notice (because they were not alleged to be missing) increased the probability of an adjudicated denial by .27 and .35 in the Henan

TABLE 8.7 Average marginal effects on adjudicated denials, calculated from logistic regression models

	All basic-level courts				Rural	Urban
	(1)	(2)	(3)	(4)	(5)	(6)
Henan						
Female plaintiff	.09***	.07***	.03***	.03***	.04***	-.01
Plaintiff domestic violence claim		.09***	.02***	.01*	.02***	-.01
Defendant consent and absenteeism						
Defendant in absentia						
Public notice			-.06**	-.11***	-.10***	-.16***
No public notice			.25***	.27***	.26***	.32***
Defendant withheld consent			.57***	.51***	.50***	.54***
Cf.: Defendant consented to divorce						
Ordinary civil procedure				-.09***	-.09***	-.10***
Plaintiff submitted evidence				-.05***	-.04***	-.07***
Case complexity						
Children no, marital property yes				-.06***	-.06***	-.03*
Children yes, marital property no				-.15***	-.14***	-.18***
Neither				-.20***	-.20***	-.20***
Cf.: Both						
Physical separation claim				-.10***	-.11***	-.08***
Plaintiff gave up property or child custody				-.32***	-.33***	-.27***
Additional controls	No	No	No	Yes	Yes	Yes
McKelvey & Zavoina pseudo-R²	.20	.21	.53	.63	.64	.62
n (first-attempt trials)	54,200	54,200	54,200	54,200	45,353	8,847

TABLE 8.7 (cont.)

	All basic-level courts				Rural	Urban
	(1)	(2)	(3)	(4)	(5)	(6)
Zhejiang						
Female plaintiff	.11***	.10***	.08***	.06***	.08***	.01
Plaintiff domestic violence claim		.04***	.01	.01	.01	.01
Defendant consent and absenteeism						
Defendant in absentia						
Public notice			.07+	.07+	.09+	.05
No public notice			.30***	.35***	.36***	.32***
Defendant withheld consent			.49***	.47***	.46***	.49***
Cf.: Defendant consented to divorce						
Ordinary civil procedure				−.21***	−.19***	−.27***
Plaintiff submitted evidence				−.02+	−.02*	−.01
Case complexity						
Children no, marital property yes				−.04***	−.04**	−.03+
Children yes, marital property no				−.09***	−.08**	−.12***
Neither				−.13***	−.13*	−.15**
Cf.: Both						
Physical separation claim				−.08***	−.08***	−.07***
Plaintiff gave up property or child custody				−.23***	−.26***	−.18**
Additional controls	No	No	No	Yes	Yes	Yes
McKelvey & Zavoina pseudo-R^2	.14	.15	.42	.50	.52	.49
n (first-attempt trials)	8,626	8,626	8,626	8,626	5,753	2,873

Source: Author's calculations from Henan and Zhejiang provincial high courts' online decisions.
Note: All models include court fixed effects (court dummies) and year of decision. Significance tests are based on standard errors calculated using the delta method and are adjusted for nonindependence between decisions clustered within courts (161 and 91 in the Henan and Zhejiang samples, respectively). "Cf." denotes the omitted reference category. In order to prevent multicollinearity, "ordinary civil procedure," excludes public notice trials (which by definition entails the application of the ordinary civil procedure).
+ P < .10 * P < .05 ** P < .01 *** P < .001, two-tailed tests

and Zhejiang samples, respectively. The relatively minor importance of faultism standards and the major importance of breakdownism standards are also reflected in the minor change in pseudo-R^2 values between Model 1 and Model 2 and the major change in pseudo-R^2 values between Model 2 and Model 3.[17]

In both samples, defendant consent and absenteeism substantially reduced the effect of making a domestic violence claim. When controlling for plaintiff sex, defendant consent, and defendant absenteeism in Model 3, the effect of an apparent domestic violence allegation approached irrelevance in both samples (.02 in Henan and .01 in Zhejiang). Note that with the introduction of additional variables in subsequent models, the effect of a claim of domestic violence almost entirely disappeared (although its effect of .01 remained statistically significant in the Henan sample). Defendant consent and absenteeism explained away most of the effect of domestic violence claims for two reasons: (1) defendants who did not consent to divorce were disproportionately accused of perpetrating domestic violence and (2) plaintiffs were relatively unlikely to make claims of domestic violence in public notice trials. One obvious interpretation is that abusers also tended to be obstructionists. However, given limitations in the data, we cannot entirely rule out an alternative possibility that abuse claims were endogenous to spousal consent: some plaintiffs may have made abuse claims because their spouses were unwilling to divorce. Similarly, although it seems highly plausible that plaintiffs were at much lower risk of domestic violence when their spouses were missing, we cannot entirely rule out an alternative possibility that missing spouses obviated plaintiffs' perceived need to make abuse claims.

We now have clues that help explain why male plaintiffs were more likely than female plaintiffs to succeed in their efforts to divorce on the first attempt. Women's sizeable disadvantage in the probability of obtaining an adjudicated divorce stemmed from a triple whammy of gender differences in the incidence of domestic violence, defendant obstructionism (in the form of withholding consent), and missing defendants. We also know that these costs were further amplified by a huge overrepresentation of women among plaintiffs who filed for divorce in court.

---

[17] This pattern is mirrored by various pseudo-R^2 formulas, including adjusted count and McFadden's (for a discussion of competing pseudo-R^2's, see Long and Freese [2014:126–31]).

The average marginal effect of a claim of abuse in the full model (Model 4) was tiny in both samples, and below the threshold of statistical significance in the Zhejiang sample. Meanwhile, the effect of defendant consent and absenteeism remained immense: it alone contributed more to pseudo-R^2 values than did all remaining control variables combined, including the court dummies. The effect of defendant consent and absenteeism towers above that of everything else in the model.

Female plaintiffs' disadvantage persisted in Model 4 net of controls. Even among plaintiffs who were otherwise similar in terms of defendant consent, defendant absenteeism, domestic violence claims, and an array of controls, women were still less likely than men to obtain an adjudicated divorce on the first attempt. I disaggregated rural and urban verdicts by applying the same model separately to rural (Model 5) and urban courts (Model 6). Separately modeling rural and urban court decisions shows that women's net disadvantage was limited to rural areas in both provinces. We already saw descriptive findings showing that urbanization reduced and erased gender differences in verdicts as well as in two of their key determinants, namely defendant consent and defendant absenteeism. Model 5 shows that, net of controls, the probability of an adjudicated denial in a rural court was statistically significantly higher for female plaintiffs than for male plaintiffs in both provinces (by .04 in Henan and .08 in Zhejiang). Model 6, by contrast, shows no gender difference whatsoever in urban courts in either province. The absence of a gender difference in urban courts is not a function of control variables, as the effect of plaintiff sex remained statistically insignificant even after stripping them out to create an urban-only version of Model 1. For this reason, had Model 1 been limited to urban courts, the AMEs for female plaintiffs would have been much smaller and statistically insignificant in both provinces (details omitted).

We already know that public notice trials, which must be held using the ordinary civil procedure, were associated with relatively low adjudicated denial rates. Regression results also show that the application of the ordinary civil procedure outside the scope of public notice trials reduced the probability of an adjudicated denial by .09 in Henan and by .21 in Zhejiang compared to when judges applied the simplified civil procedure. Which civil procedure judges used was generally a good predictor of its verdict. Judges tended to reserve the ordinary civil procedure for when they granted divorces.

Not surprisingly, courts were less likely to deny the divorce petitions of plaintiffs who reportedly submitted evidence in support of their petitions. Compared to plaintiffs who apparently did not submit evidence, the probability of an adjudicated denial among those who apparently did submit evidence was .05 and .02 lower in the Henan and Zhejiang samples, respectively.

In both provinces, cases that involved both children and property were much more likely than cases that involved only one or the other, or neither, to result in an adjudicated denial. In other words, cases that involved marital property but no children, children but no marital property, or neither, were much less likely than cases that involved both marital property and children to result in an adjudicated denial. Ruling on property division and child custody can be both time-consuming and fraught. In their efforts to maximize judicial efficiency and minimize the possibility of complaints, petitioning, and other "extreme incidents" antithetical to the political imperative of maintaining social stability, judges shied away from granting divorces in relatively complex cases, including those involving domestic violence claims. Moreover, as we have seen in both Chapter 7 and this chapter, judges used children as evidence of mutual affection and thus as grounds for denying divorce petitions.

Owing to their disinclination to grant divorces in cases involving marital property and children, judges' likelihood of applying the simplified civil procedure perversely increased commensurately with case complexity. Although judges are supposed to use the simplified civil procedure only when "the facts are clear, rights and obligations are unambiguous, and the dispute minor" (see Chapter 5), they tended to do precisely the opposite. In Henan, 34% of lower-complexity cases involving neither marital property nor children, 37–39% of cases involving one but not the other, and 42% of higher-complexity cases involving both marital property and children were tried according to the simplified civil procedure. In Zhejiang, simplified civil procedure utilization rates also increased with case complexity: 65% in lower-complexity cases, 76% in cases involving one item but not the other, and 85% in higher-complexity cases involving both items. Judges averse to wading into the thicket of property division and child custody determinations fast-tracked for adjudicated denial cases involving such matters by designating them as "minor disputes" in which "the facts are clear" in order to apply the simplified civil procedure. In so doing, as we saw in Chapter 5, they deprived litigants of their due process rights. By contrast, lower-complexity cases that did not involve marital property, children, or both were more likely to be tried according to the ordinary civil procedure, because judges were more willing to grant divorces when they could do so without the hassle and risk of ruling on such matters. Domestic violence allegations, which are often complex from an evidentiary standpoint, were similarly associated with higher simplified procedure utilization rates.

Claims of physical separation reduced the probability of an adjudicated denial by .10 in Henan and by .08 in Zhejiang, which comes as no surprise given that physical separation constitutes grounds for divorce in both the Fourteen Articles and the Marriage Law. Nonetheless, a physical separation claim far from guaranteed a successful divorce. Judges were often unconvinced that litigants met the statutory minimum separation period or that separation was the result of the breakdown of mutual affection.

Because withholding consent had the practical effect of preserving a marriage or at least prolonging a divorce petition, defendants weaponized consent by withholding it until plaintiffs made concessions on the terms of the divorce. Even when defendants wanted out of their marriages, they often strategically withheld consent in order to gain an advantage vis-à-vis property division and child custody. Such a tactic forced some plaintiffs to exchange their legal rights for their freedom (Li 2022). When plaintiffs gave up their rights, defendant consent magically increased. As we can see in Table 8.6, 50% and 56% of defendants in the Henan and Zhejiang samples, respectively, withheld consent. By contrast, in cases in which the plaintiff gave up property or child custody, only 26% and 44% of defendants in each respective sample withheld consent. Not surprisingly, therefore, abandoning a claim on marital property, child custody, or both dramatically reduced the probability of an adjudicated denial by .32 in Henan and .23 in Zhejiang.

Such concessions were also captured by my case complexity measure. Rather than explicitly stating that they forwent a claim to marital assets (variations of "the plaintiff gives up" identified in Chapter 4), plaintiffs could simply claim that there was no marital estate to contest (variations of "there is no common property" also identified in Chapter 4). Either way increased plaintiffs' chances of winning their bid for divorce.

Gender Gaps in Adjudicated Denials

My final empirical task in this chapter is to assess conditions under which playing fields were relatively even and uneven between female and male plaintiffs. Table 8.8 goes beyond the contents of Table 8.7 by presenting predicted probabilities from which AMEs in Table 8.7, Model 4, were calculated. In Table 8.7, the AME of .01 for making a domestic violence claim in Model 4 for Henan corresponds to the overall difference in Table 8.8 between plaintiffs in Henan who made claims of domestic violence (.64) and those who did not (.63). Table 8.8 further shows that this slightly positive effect of making a claim of domestic violence is limited to female plaintiffs in the Henan sample. Among female plaintiffs in Henan, the difference between those who made claims of domestic violence (.66) and those who did not (.63) is statistically significant. A claim of domestic violence had no effect among female plaintiffs in Zhejiang or among male plaintiffs in either sample. Let us now consider gender gaps among plaintiffs who made allegations of domestic violence before turning to gender gaps among plaintiffs who shared other characteristics.

In Henan, claims of domestic violence widened the gender gap considerably. Whereas the gender gap was only .02 among plaintiffs who did not make such a claim, it was a much wider .06 among plaintiffs who did make such a claim. The difference between these two gender gaps (a test of second difference) is statistically significant. Thus, the effect of making a claim of domestic violence was greater for female plaintiffs than for male plaintiffs. The obvious interpretation of this pattern is that judges treated men's domestic violence claims more seriously than women's domestic violence claims; they more readily dismissed women's domestic violence claims as unimportant or fabricated. In the Zhejiang sample, by contrast, domestic violence claims were equally irrelevant to women and men alike.

In Table 8.8, we see once again that plaintiffs' divorce prospects were highest when they passed the breakdownism test with either a public notice trial or defendant consent. The overall predicted probability of an adjudicated denial in a public notice trial (.23 in Henan and .53 in Zhejiang) was far less than the overall probability (.63 in Henan and .80 in Zhejiang). In Henan, plaintiffs' chances of getting denied were even lower in this type of trial (.23) than in trials in which the defendant expressed consent to divorce (.34). By contrast, when defendants failed to participate in court proceedings for other reasons,

TABLE 8.8 Average predicted probabilities of adjudicated denials

	All plaintiffs	By plaintiff sex		Gender difference
		Female	Male	
Henan (n = 54,200 first-attempt trials)				
Overall	.63	.64	.61	.03***
Plaintiff claim of domestic violence				
a. Yes	.64[b]	.66[b]	.60	.06***[b]
b. No	.63[a]	.63[a]	.61	.02***[a]
Defendant consent and absenteeism				
a. Defendant in absentia: public notice	.23[b, c, d]	.26[b, c, d]	.16[b, c, d]	.09***Λ[b, c, d]
b. Defendant in absentia: no public notice	.61[a, c, d]	.66[a, c, d]	.50[a, c, d]	.16***[a, c, d]
c. Defendant consented to divorce	.34[a, b, d]	.33[a, b, d]	.35[a, b, d]	−.02[+a, b]
d. Defendant withheld consent	.85[a, b, c]	.84[a, b, c]	.86[a, b, c]	−.02***[a, b]
Evidence				
a. No apparent evidence from plaintiff	.65[b]	.66[b]	.64[b]	.02***[b]
b. Plaintiff supplied evidence	.61[a]	.62[a]	.58[a]	.05***Λ[a]
Case complexity				
a. Both children and apparent marital property	.66[b, c, d]	.67[b, c, d]	.64[a, b, d]	.03***
b. No apparent children, apparent marital property	.60[a, c, d]	.61[a, c, d]	.57[a, c, d]	.05***Λ[d]
c. Yes children, no apparent marital property	.51[a, b, d]	.51[a, b, d]	.49[a, b]	.02[+]
d. Neither children nor apparent marital property	.46[a, b, c]	.45[a, b, c]	.46[a, b]	−.003Λ[b]

Zhejiang (n = 8,626 first-attempt trials)

Overall	.80	.82	.76	.06***
Plaintiff claim of domestic violence				
a. Yes	.80	.83	.77	.06*
b. No	.79	.82	.76	.06***
Defendant consent and absenteeism				
a. Defendant in absentia: public notice	.53[b, d]	.61[b, d]	.37[b, d]	.23***^c, d
b. Defendant in absentia: no public notice	.80[a, c, d]	.86[a, c, d]	.69[a, c, d]	.16***^c, d
c. Defendant consented to divorce	.45[b, d]	.46[b, d]	.44[b, d]	.03^a, b
d. Defendant withheld consent	.93[a, b, c]	.93[a, b, c]	.93[a, b, c]	.002[a, b]
Evidence				
a. No apparent evidence from plaintiff	.81	.82	.80[b]	.02[b]
b. Plaintiff supplied evidence	.79	.82	.75[a]	.07***[a]
Case complexity				
a. Both children and apparent marital property	.81[b, c, d]	.84[b, c, d]	.79[b, c, d]	.05***
b. No apparent children, apparent marital property	.78[a, c, d]	.81[a, d]	.73[a, d]	.08***
c. Yes children, no apparent marital property	.72[a, b]	.76[a]	.66[a]	.09^
d. Neither children nor apparent marital property	.68[a, b]	.70[a, b]	.65[a, b]	.05

Source: Author's calculations from Henan and Zhejiang provincial high courts' online decisions.

Note: All contents of this table are postestimation calculations from the same models used to make the postestimation calculations of AMEs in Table 8.7, Model 4. A caret (^) denotes a slight discrepancy due to rounding error between an AME (in the "gender difference" column) and the corresponding predicted probabilities from which it was calculated (in the "by plaintiff sex" columns). Likewise, differences between predicted probabilities in this table are not always identical to corresponding AMEs in Table 8.7 owing to rounding error. Superscript letters correspond to other categories of the same variable. Known as contrasts, they denote the statistical significance (at $P < .05$) of differences between variable categories (first differences). In the "gender difference" column, they denote the statistical significance (at $P < .05$) of gender gaps (second differences) across different variable categories. On contrasts, see Long and Freese (2014:252) and Mize (2019:106).

+ $P < .10$ * $P < .05$ ** $P < .01$ *** $P < .001$, two-tailed tests

overall predicted outcomes were about the same as in all trials taken together. Public notice trials and mutual consent were by far the most realistic pathways to divorce in terms of likelihood of success. They were also the least common pathways, together accounting for only 28% and 20% of first-attempt divorce trials in the Henan and Zhejiang samples, respectively.

Although plaintiffs as a whole benefitted from in absentia trials only when an allegedly missing defendant was served by public notice (thus satisfying the breakdownism standard), male plaintiffs enjoyed a large and statistically significant advantage over female plaintiffs when defendants failed to participate in court proceedings for any reason. Gender differences in the probability of a divorce on the first attempt, ranging from .09 to .23, were massive and statistically significant in both samples when defendants were AWOL, regardless of how the court served the defendant. Indeed, among male plaintiffs in the Henan sample, divorce approached a forgone conclusion (.84) in public notice trials. Tests of second difference show that, among all in absentia trials, public notice trials narrowed the gender gap in Henan (.16 versus .09, a statistically significant difference) and widened the gender gap in Zhejiang (.16 versus .23, a statistically insignificant difference).

Women's severe disadvantage in the context of in absentia trials – both as plaintiffs and as defendants – is consistent with patriarchal cultural beliefs about women as less credible and less deserving than men. My empirical findings suggest that judges, who themselves were mostly men, took claims about missing spouses more seriously and treated them as more credible when they were made by male plaintiffs. The court decisions in my samples reflect cultural narratives not only about female plaintiffs making false claims of domestic violence in illicit efforts to abscond with marital property and child custody (Epstein and Goodman 2019), but also about female plaintiffs who, for the same reasons, falsely conceal the whereabouts of their husbands. The court decisions may further reflect judges' implicit belief that missing female defendants, particularly those they suspected were in illicit extramarital relationships, were less deserving than male defendants of the legal protections and due process rights they lost when they were absent from trials. In short, judges were far more inclined to protect husbands than to protect wives from getting "unwittingly divorced" (Chapter 3).

Courts were also relatively inclined to grant divorces to plaintiffs when defendants expressed their consent. In neither sample were female plaintiffs disadvantaged when both sides agreed to part ways. In the Zhejiang sample, mutual consent put women at a small but statistically insignificant disadvantage (.03). Quite the contrary in the Henan sample, where courts were more inclined to grant divorces to female plaintiffs than to male plaintiffs in the context of mutual consent, albeit to only a small (−.02) and marginally statistically significant extent.

Finally, an adjudicated divorce was highly improbable in the absence of spousal consent. According to Model 4, the average predicted probability of an adjudicated denial when the defendant withheld consent was .85 in Henan and .93 in Zhejiang. In other words, the probability of obtaining a unilateral divorce among plaintiffs whose spouses withheld consent was only .15 in Henan and .07 in Zhejiang. In the context of defendants who withheld consent to divorce, female and male plaintiffs were on a playing field that was similarly harsh to everyone. Adjudicated unilateral divorce prospects were slim for female and male plaintiffs alike on the first attempt. The chances of female and male plaintiffs seeking unilateral divorces in Zhejiang were identical. However, female plaintiffs in Henan had a small (−.02) but statistically significant advantage over male plaintiffs when defendants withheld consent.

Judges likewise treated evidence submitted by male plaintiffs more seriously than evidence submitted by female plaintiffs. Although female plaintiffs were more likely than male plaintiffs to submit evidence (Table 8.6), the probability a court denied a divorce to a female plaintiff who submitted evidence was .05 and .07 greater than it was for a male plaintiff who submitted evidence in the Henan and Zhejiang samples, respectively. By contrast, the probabilities of adjudicated denials were more similar for female and male plaintiffs who did not appear to support their claims with evidence (gender gaps of only .02 in both samples). These patterns suggest that plaintiffs' failure to submit evidence levelled the playing field and that their submission of evidence widened the gender gap in adjudicated divorce outcomes in both samples. Judges attached greater weight to evidence submitted by male plaintiffs and discounted evidence submitted by female plaintiffs. Evidence benefitted male plaintiffs far more than it benefitted female plaintiffs, strongly suggesting that courts treated men's claims more seriously than women's.

Finally, with respect to case complexity, the gender gap in the probability of obtaining an adjudicated divorce was relatively wide in cases that involved marital property but did not involve children. In both samples, female and male plaintiffs were more similarly likely to obtain an adjudicated divorce in cases involving both children and marital assets as well as in cases involving neither children nor marital assets. Male plaintiffs' significant advantage over female plaintiffs in cases involving marital assets but no children suggests that property division was more contentious than child custody and that courts protected the financial interests of male litigants (both plaintiffs and defendants) more than they protected the financial interests of female litigants (both plaintiffs and defendants). Previous research shows that judges, in their property division rulings in divorce cases, favored men over women (Li 2015b). Although an analysis of courts' rulings on property division is beyond the scope of this book, my findings nonetheless reveal that female plaintiffs were significantly less likely than male plaintiffs to be granted divorces in cases involving marital property. Judges, consciously or unconsciously, were more likely to deny divorce requests when they were made by women who threatened the integrity of marital estates, over which men tend to exercise control, particularly in rural areas. Insofar as judges in both Henan and Zhejiang, when deciding cases involving marital assets but not involving children, were more likely to preserve the marriage if the plaintiff was a woman, they acted, wittingly or unwittingly, to preserve the assets – such as housing and farmland – owned, controlled, or used by men and their families.

SUMMARY AND CONCLUSIONS

The evidence in this chapter is unambiguous: In the Chinese context of divorce litigation, breakdownism was king and faultism was of practical irrelevance. Consistent with poignant anecdotal evidence of Chinese courts' general failure to grant divorces on the basis of domestic violence (Fincher 2014), plaintiffs' claims of abuse clearly did not improve their chances of getting divorced in court. This is precisely what we would expect if judges privileged breakdownism over faultism. Judges in both provinces responded to domestic violence allegations in the same way they responded to other legal complaints they deemed "frivolous": they were similarly likely to deny them on ideological grounds, on evidentiary grounds, and, above all, on breakdownism grounds by holding that mutual affection had not broken down. Indeed, claims of abuse appear to have been counterproductive. An allegation of domestic violence perversely increased the likelihood of an adjudicated denial, particularly in rural Henan.

Judges heeded ideological calls to prevent frivolous divorce, preserve marriages, and reduce social instability. China's breakdownism divorce standard, applied by judges in support of the national political priority of preserving marriages and clamping down on frivolous divorces, overwhelmingly trumped other circumstances, including marital violence, that, strictly according to China's domestic laws and international commitments, could – and should – fully support judges' rulings to dissolve marriages. The breakdownism test enabled judges' routine denial of first-attempt divorce petitions even when they contained well-supported allegations of domestic violence. Although the essential nature of judging is to rule on contentious disputes, judges avoided entering the fray for fear of fallout from "extreme incidents" caused by male defendants whom they perceived as potentially violent. Judges' fear of the potential harm to social stability posed by documented wife-beaters may help explain why plaintiffs' domestic violence allegations perversely increased the likelihood of an adjudicated denial. Stability maintenance was not judges' only source of pressure. Also under enormous pressure to close cases, they saved time, enhanced their work productivity, and improved their efficiency scores by disregarding and trivializing domestic violence claims. Finally, cultural forces led them to look askance at domestic violence claims as potentially exaggerated or fabricated.

Although divorce litigation was rife with allegations of domestic violence, they had no discernable effect on the character of judicial discourse in court holdings. Regardless of domestic violence claims, judges fixated on couples' reconciliation potential, a key test stipulated by the Fourteen Articles for determining whether mutual affection broke down. By doing so, they flouted a separate SPC judicial interpretation requiring them to grant divorces when fault-based grounds could be established. Judges infantilized plaintiffs by attributing their marital strife to poor relationship skills. In their holdings, judges asserted their judgments of what was morally appropriate as much as – if not more than – what was legally appropriate. As if judges knew what was best for the personal lives of litigants, and as if the patriotic duty of litigants to reconcile trumped their legal right to divorce, judges challenged plaintiffs' claims, assessments, evidence, and wishes, instead promoting socialist values to justify and obscure their legally dubious holdings to deny divorce petitions that satisfied fault-based standards. Judges gaslighted plaintiffs by characterizing domestic violence as minor conflict produced by family trifles with husbands who loved them. And they offered paternalistic and patronizing relationship advice which, they assured abuse victims, would help prevent future conflict from escalating to violence.

Much if not most of the judicial discourse in judges' holdings was disconnected from the law. Ideological and therapeutic discourses were pervasive. Although the similarly pervasive Fourteen Articles and evidentiary discourses were, by definition, rooted in the law, judges turned the law on its head, deployed these discourses to advance their professional needs and political priorities (which of course were intertwined), and in so doing undermined the lawful divorce rights of plaintiffs. Judges tended to invoke the Fourteen Articles to affirm reconciliation potential and thus to preserve rather than to dissolve marriages. By the same token, they tended to invoke rules of evidence to disaffirm rather than to affirm plaintiffs' claims.

Compared to male plaintiffs, female plaintiffs were at greater risk of exposure to these judicial discourses because they were at greater risk of adjudicated denial on the first try. Notwithstanding strong legal bases in China for granting divorces on fault-based grounds, judges handled cases involving domestic claims essentially the same as they handled any other divorce case. No matter how egregious or well-supported an abuse allegation may have been, judges adhered to their boilerplate script proclaiming that the plaintiff had failed to prove the breakdown of mutual affection, that marital conflict was only minor, that the defendant was eager to reconcile, that reconciliation was therefore possible, and that marital preservation was in the national interest. In the face of documented accounts of horrific violence, judges hardly skipped a beat as they waxed ideological, moral, and therapeutic platitudes for the purpose of justifying their adjudicated denials.

Courts carefully rationed scarce judicial resources and tended to devote collegial panels only to divorce petitions which, if granted, struck judges as unlikely to lead to appeals, complaints, or "extreme incidents," and which were filed by plaintiffs who seemed deserving of divorce and whose claims seemed credible to judges. Courts routinely denied first-attempt divorces in part because they preferred to let litigants work out contentious child custody and property division matters on their own and to return for a second attempt after coming to an agreement on the terms of the divorce (He 2009). For this reason, plaintiffs deemed uncredible and undeserving – in no small measure on the basis of cultural stereotypes – and plaintiffs with contentious and untied loose ends were fast-tracked to adjudicated denials using the simplified procedure. The perverse upshot is that courts turned upside down (admittedly vague) legal standards concerning the determination of civil procedure. In practice, the ordinary procedure was reserved for the most straightforward cases, such as childless couples with no marital property, and flagged for adjudicated approval. The simplified procedure was used for more complex cases, such as those with children, property, claims of domestic violence, or the perceived potential for "extreme incidents" of violence, and flagged for adjudicated denial.

My empirical findings show that mutual consent and public notice trials, key statutory conditions of the breakdown of mutual affection, were the only realistic pathways to divorce on the first attempt. Domestic violence, a competing fault-based statutory condition, did not move the needle toward divorce. Victims of domestic violence, mostly women, were revictimized by judges who ignored their claims. Although breakdownism prevailed over faultism by a massive margin, judges did not apply the breakdownism standard equally. Judges showed a far greater inclination to affirm the breakdown of mutual affection on the basis of a missing defendant when the plaintiff was a man. Women's overall disadvantage in getting a divorce on the first attempt was attributable in part to their specific disadvantage in trials in which defendants were missing or refused to participate. Male litigants – both plaintiffs and defendants alike – enjoyed preferential treatment from judges in in absentia trials. Judges were far more reluctant to grant the divorce requests of female plaintiffs in the absence of their husbands than they were to grant the divorce petitions of male plaintiffs in the absence of their wives.

Women had worse outcomes than men both as plaintiffs and as defendants. As plaintiffs, wives were less likely than husbands to get divorced on the first try. Their greater exposure to spousal obstructionism required them to make concessions on property division and child custody in exchange for their freedom. As defendants, wives were more likely than husbands to get "unwittingly divorced" in public notice trials, in which they were often deprived of due process rights, property rights, and child custody rights.

These findings emerged with remarkable consistency from both Henan and Zhejiang. At the same time, most gender disparities were confined to rural courts in both provinces. Women's experiences were far less grim in urban courts. To be sure, rural and urban courts were similarly likely to brush off female divorce-seekers who suffered domestic violence. However, gender differences in the probability of spousal obstructionism, the probability of a public notice trial, and, most importantly, the probability of an adjudicated denial were almost entirely limited to rural courts.

In Chapter 9, we will see that the result of denying divorces in the name of harmony can be anything but harmonious. Indeed, an adjudicated denial can be tantamount to a death sentence – to either plaintiff or defendant. Judges' fear of extreme incidents of violence – directed toward plaintiffs or even the judges themselves – was one of many factors behind their tendency to deny the divorce petitions of abuse victims. Such is the inscrutable logic by which marital preservation promotes social stability. We will see that, in their efforts to prevent such incidents from occurring, judges in fact enabled them, by prolonging women's exposure to their abusive husbands. Judges aggravated the physical security risks of abuse victims by routinely denying their first-attempt divorce petitions. China's ideological call to maintain social stability by preserving marriages is dubious on its face. Chapter 9 suggests it is also dubious in light of relevant empirical evidence. The experiences of domestic violence victims in China's criminal justice system suggest that greater and more effective intervention by public authorities – including court intervention in the form of dissolving abusive marriages – would more effectively protect abuse victims and promote social stability.

CHAPTER NINE

FIGHT OR FLIGHT

Consequences of the Judicial Clampdown on Divorce

In this chapter, we shift our attention from divorce cases to criminal cases. China's judicial clampdown on divorce has diverted marital disputes into the criminal justice system. When judges failed to protect battered women, domestic violence sometimes escalated to criminal battery or homicide. Consequently, some women seeking relief in civil court ended up as victims in criminal court after their husbands harmed or murdered them, or as defendants when, in response to chronic abuse, they took matters into their own hands. So far, China's criminal courts appear not to recognize domestic violence as a sufficiently mitigating factor to merit acquittal in homicide cases. Nonetheless, reforms introduced in 2015 have clearly turned the tide toward leniency in sentencing.

Women abused by their husbands often pursued help before filing for divorce. They were aware of their legal rights and did their best to advance them by seeking the help of relevant public authorities, including public security organs, villagers' committees, residents' committees, work units, and branches of the All-China Women's Federation. Court decisions I present in this chapter are consistent with previous studies documenting public authorities' reluctance to intervene in "private domestic matters" as well as families' pressure to stay with abusive spouses (Fincher 2014; Han 2017; Lin et al. 2021; Liu and Chan 1999). The All-China Women's Federation gave false hope by routinely advising battered women to file for divorce without also advising them of the Sisyphean nature of Chinese divorce litigation. In their court petitions, women often reported that police failed to intervene adequately – or at all. In a representative divorce case, the female plaintiff who made a domestic violence allegation stated that "the police wouldn't take my incident report on the grounds that it was a domestic dispute [家庭纠纷]" (Decision #1573098, Yucheng County People's Court, Henan Province, June 25, 2015; also see Zheng 2015:161).[1] Others reported that police intervention was limited to a brief mediation session that ended after their husbands expressed a requisite measure of contrition. Sometimes police officers or villagers' committee members, in the course of carrying out mediation, likewise seemed content to have resolved the problem after making the husband apologize or write a pledge letter (Zheng 2015:161). Women who, for good reason, lack confidence in the commitment and ability of police to stop their husbands' abuse may fear reporting domestic violence to the police at all. In the words of one abuse victim, "When he smashed things and verbally threatened me, I didn't always report it to the police out of fear that he would retaliate" (Decision #4387302, Hangzhou Municipal Yuhang District People's Court, Zhejiang Province, April 1, 2016; also see Fincher 2014:140).[2]

Many women testified that their families had also pressured them to stay with abusers. Owing to the pervasiveness of family persuasion and mediation aimed at marital reconciliation, and not wanting their parents to lose face or worry, some women reported that they feared telling their natal family members about the abuse they suffered (also see Zheng 2015:165, 168). In surveys of survivors of intimate partner violence in China, the majority of respondents reported seeking no help at all (Hu et al. 2020; Wang, Fang, and Li 2013:35–36).

Even if they know where to seek help and want to escape, battered women often fear doing so. One plaintiff stated to the court that whenever her husband "found something even slightly against his liking, he would curse and beat the plaintiff. For this reason, the plaintiff tried to leave him many times. Under the pressure of the defendant's threats, however, she resigned herself to continuing to live together with the defendant." Her husband denied the allegations and expressed unwillingness to divorce. The court, asserting that husband and wife could still reconcile if they treasured marital affection, denied the plaintiff's divorce petition (Decision #2365494, Rui'an County People's Court,

---

[1] Case ID (2015)虞民初字第1226号, archived at https://perma.cc/ZF4K-VTHV.
[2] Case ID (2015)杭余塘民初字第715号, archived at https://perma.cc/F77W-B5KY.

Zhejiang Province, August 5, 2010).[3] Inadequate intervention from public authorities, including courts' reluctance to grant divorces, heightens the risk of prolonged domestic violence and thus motivates some victims to resort to desperate measures of self-help.

> The majority of women threatened by domestic violence do not dare file for divorce in court. The minority of abused women who do initiate divorce litigation will be forced to remain exposed to domestic violence if they did not collect relevant evidence because judges will find its occurrence difficult to affirm. This kind of situation may cause physical injury and even death, or generate criminal acts of "combatting violence with violence" [以暴制暴]. (Li and Jia 2019:62)[4]

Recall from Chapter 2 that the drafters of the 1980 Marriage Law feared that a clampdown on divorce could result in homicides. We will see in this chapter that their fears have been realized.

What do abused women do when all their efforts to escape domestic violence fail? Some seek relief by way of "fight or flight." At a literal level, the hormonal fight or flight response is a well-documented involuntary clinical reaction triggered by the traumatic stress of domestic violence (Walker 2017:325). At another level, it represents the pragmatic choices and coping strategies of women attempting to survive (Zheng 2015). When they receive no protection through official channels, sometimes they take flight and escape their abusers; sometimes they fight and kill their abusers.

Marital abuse can be terminated in several ways. One way is to mobilize the force of law by petitioning for divorce or requesting intervention from other public authorities. A second way is to take flight; in China, women often finance their flight from abuse through migrant labor force participation. A third way to terminate abuse is to terminate the victim; abusers sometimes kill their victims. A fourth way is to terminate the abuser; victims sometimes kill their abusers. The evidence I present throughout this book points to the near futility of the first way. In this chapter, a mix of quantitative findings and case examples reveals the too common consequences of that failure. I will begin by demonstrating that the divorce twofer prolonged abused women's exposure to violence when courts denied their first-attempt divorce petitions.

---

[3] Case ID (2010)温瑞民初字第00120号, archived at https://perma.cc/Q7H6-83A7.
[4] For the 1985 case of a woman who "met violence with violence" and murdered her husband, see Honig and Hershatter (1988:296).

LEAVING ABUSIVE MEN IS DANGEROUS

Staying with abusive men is dangerous. Leaving abusive men is also dangerous. Some women stay with their abusers when, in their assessment, the risks of leaving outweigh the risks of staying. In the United States, women's risk of getting murdered is greatest when they leave their abusive partners (Walker 2017:Chapter 12). Domestic abusers everywhere want the subjects of their abuse to get the message, "If I can't have you, no one will" (Walker 2017:114, 306). In China, too, abusive men's threats to murder their wives – such as, "If you don't kill me first, I'll make sure you die a horrific death" and "If you dare try to divorce me, I'll murder your entire family" – are pervasive (X. Wang 2017:25). In this section I show that they sometimes put their threats into action.

A criminal case in Zhejiang documents how close a woman came to losing her life when she insisted on divorcing her husband, Li Fufa.[5] When discussing the practicalities of their divorce, including household debt, Li pinned his wife down on the sofa and started stabbing her face with a knife. At this moment his mother-in-law happened to enter the home. When she rushed into the living room and pulled the husband off, he stabbed her hand. His wife seized the opportunity to flee. Li chased and caught her outside a restaurant, where many people witnessed him continue to stab her face and neck. His mother-in-law once again pulled Li off, allowing the wife to escape. According to a forensic pathology report, Li's wife sustained a traumatic tracheal rupture, a traumatic transection of the thyroid, a laryngeal nerve injury, and multiple injuries to the left and right jaw as well as to the back of the skull. Li was sentenced to 11 years in prison for attempted homicide (Decision #3236920, Yiwu Municipal People's Court, Zhejiang Province, November 28, 2014).[6]

In a similar case, a man with the surname Zeng nearly killed his wife who was trying to divorce him. When Zeng was stabbing his wife in the head, chest, and other areas, his mother-in-law tackled him, allowing his father-in-law to disarm him, at which point his wife escaped and notified the police. She suffered a punctured tongue, an arm laceration, and a radial nerve rupture. The court gave Zeng an eight-year prison sentence for attempted homicide. To foreshadow

---

[5] Criminal court decisions usually report defendants' names in full but only the surnames of victims.
[6] Case ID (2014)金义刑初字第2591号, archived at https://perma.cc/TV7J-T63G.

my discussion later in this chapter about the role of compensation in criminal sentencing, the court attributed its lenient sentence to the wife's expression of forgiveness of Zeng offered in exchange for the compensation (of an unspecified amount) she received from his family (Decision #2638685, Ningbo Municipal, Yinzhou District People's Court, Zhejiang Province, December 30, 2013).[7]

Supplementary case examples set #9–1 is online at: https:// decoupling-book.org/.

Many women do not survive attacks like these. Such was the fate of one woman who returned to her natal family after what the court euphemistically described as "arguing and fighting over trifles." In his testimony, Li Suzhen admitted hitting his wife. He made several trips to her natal home to persuade her to return home with him. On his final rebuffed effort, she declared her desire to divorce him. As Li put it, "I was furious. I thought, if we couldn't be together, she should die, I should die, and that would be the end of it. I ran into her family's kitchen, grabbed a cleaver, and cut her neck with great force." She bled to death after he severed her left neck artery and vein. Li was sentenced to life in prison. In the course of the trial, Li compensated her family with ¥230,000 and received a forgiveness letter from her parents in return, which may have spared him from a death sentence. Criminal reconciliation of this nature is a topic to which I will come later in this chapter (Decision #1184232, Puyang Municipal Intermediate People's Court, Henan Province, March 5, 2014).[8]

Supplementary case examples set #9–2 is online at: https:// decoupling-book.org/.

Tragically, the foregoing criminal case examples are merely the tip of the iceberg. My samples contain hundreds more. According to official reports, about 10% of all homicides in China are related to domestic violence (Palmer 2017:290; Zheng 2015:162). A crude – and conservative – method I developed to identify criminal cases involving murders of spouses produces an identical estimate in the Henan sample

---

[7] Case ID (2013)甬鄞刑初字第1732号, archived at https://perma.cc/N8X2-KGB7.
[8] Case ID (2013)濮中刑一初字第18号, archived at https://perma.cc/2KG8-N272.

(10%) and a modestly lower estimate in the Zhejiang samples (8%). The criminal cases in this section are part of a larger pool of at least several hundred cases of spousal murder and over 1,500 cases of spousal battery in my two provincial samples.[9] Later in this chapter I will analyze the full pool in more detail. But first I will show that the divorce twofer, by extending the divorce process, ipso facto also extends the time during which abused women are forced to remain with their husbands. When courts routinely deny their divorce petitions, the dangers of their situations are prolonged.

DIVORCE DENIALS PROLONG DANGERS TO WOMEN

Since courts began increasing their suppression of first-petition divorces, the population of divorce-seekers awaiting relief has swelled. The duration of time from first filing until divorce can be calculated in two ways: (1) by searching for first-attempt filing dates in the text of subsequent-attempt decisions and (2) by linking first-attempt and subsequent-attempt court decisions. In so doing, we learn that mean/median time to an adjudicated *denial* on the first attempt was 70/62 days and 45/35 days in the Henan and Zhejiang samples, respectively. When the divorce was *granted* on a subsequent attempt, total mean/median time was 410/408 days and 391/362 days in the two samples, respectively (beginning from the time when the initial petition was filed). Thus, simply subtracting the former values from the latter values, the mean/median delay to divorce caused by first-attempt adjudicated denials was 340/346 days and 346/327 days in the Henan and Zhejiang samples, respectively.[10] Given what we know from Chapter 6 about judges' preference for applying the simplified civil procedure in adjudicated denials, the mean/median delay to a divorce might be more realistically estimated as the time from an adjudicated denial using the simplified procedure to time to granting a divorce using the ordinary

---

[9] I identified cases of "homicides" (故意杀人罪) and "intentional injury" (故意伤害罪, what I sometimes call "criminal battery") involving spouses by searching for three types of patterns in my samples of court decisions: (1) variations of keywords for "marital affection" (夫妻感情), "marital relations" (夫妻关系), and "marital conflict" (夫妻矛盾, 夫妻吵架, and 夫妻打架); (2) references to "wife" or "husband" as victim; and (3) references to "the wife of" or "the husband of" the defendant. This method yields a crude and conservative estimate of fewer than 900 cases of criminal domestic battery and homicide over about one decade in the Zhejiang sample, which is only about half of the 1,700 cases of criminal domestic violence reported elsewhere for Zhejiang in the three years spanning 2008 and 2010 (J. Jiang 2019:229).

[10] In an earlier publication, I mistakenly reported time to all adjudicated outcomes rather than time to adjudicated divorce. The correct numbers I report here deviate only slightly from those I previously reported (Michelson 2019a:355).

procedure: 380/381 days in Henan and 434/441 days in Zhejiang. By all measures, mean and median delays to divorce caused by the divorce twofer range from almost one year to over one year in both samples. If many plaintiffs can return to their home jurisdictions to file for divorce only once per year for the Spring Festival national holiday, as we saw in Chapter 4, we should not be surprised that the statutory six-month waiting period often becomes a one-year waiting period in practice.

If courts are more likely to deny first-attempt divorce petitions filed by women, as Chapter 8 proved, then it can only be true that the delay to freedom is longer for women than for men. Another way to view gender disparities in denials of and delays to divorce is to compare the number of attempts required to obtain an adjudicated divorce. Table 9.1 contains all court decisions from both samples in which divorce petitions were granted and in which plaintiff sex is known. It shows differences between women and men in the likelihood of requiring only one attempt to do so among plaintiffs who successfully obtained an adjudicated divorce.

TABLE 9.1 Proportion of plaintiffs (%) granted divorce, by number of attempts until divorce granted

	All plaintiffs	By plaintiff sex		Gender difference
		Female	Male	
Henan (2009–2015)				
Rural courts				
Granted on first attempt	66	61	74	−13
Granted on subsequent attempt	34	39	26	13
All granted divorces	100	100	100	
n	26,363	16,903	9,460	
Urban courts				
Granted on first attempt	64	63	65	−1
Granted on subsequent attempt	36	37	35	1
All granted divorces	100	100	100	
n	4,185	2,643	1,542	
All basic-level courts				
Granted on first attempt	65	61	73	−11
Granted on subsequent attempt	35	39	27	11
All granted divorces	100	100	100	
n	30,548	19,546	11,002	

TABLE 9.1 (*cont.*)

| | All plaintiffs | By plaintiff sex | | Gender difference |
		Female	Male	
Zhejiang (2009–2016)				
Rural courts				
Granted on first attempt	39	31	52	−21
Granted on subsequent attempt	61	69	48	21
All granted divorces	100	100	100	
n	2,820	1,766	1,054	
Urban courts				
Granted on first attempt	45	42	51	−9
Granted on subsequent attempt	55	58	49	9
All granted divorces	100	100	100	
n	1,425	938	487	
All basic-level courts				
Granted on first attempt	41	35	52	−17
Granted on subsequent attempt	59	65	48	17
All granted divorces	100	100	100	
n	4,245	2,704	1,541	

Source: Author's calculations from Henan and Zhejiang provincial high courts' online decisions.
Note: The analysis is limited to divorces successfully obtained through adjudication (denied divorce petitions are excluded). Slight discrepancies between numbers in the "gender difference" column and numbers from which they were derived in the "by plaintiff sex" columns are due to rounding error. With the exception of urban courts in Henan, all sex differences are statistically significant (χ^2, $P < .01$).

The first pattern to emerge from Table 9.1 is a familiar one: the divorce twofer was more prevalent in Zhejiang than in Henan. Of those who successfully divorced, the majority in Henan did so on the first attempt, whereas the majority in Zhejiang required at least two attempts. Differences between the two provinces narrowed over time as the judicial clampdown on divorce intensified in Henan and remained stable in Zhejiang (Chapter 6). Prior to 2012, 75% of divorces granted by adjudication in the Henan sample required only one attempt. By 2015, this proportion had declined to 53%; almost half of all divorces granted by adjudication in Henan had been previously denied. Second, in both provinces women required more attempts than men. The probability of success on the first attempt was 11 and 17 percentage points greater for men than for women in the Henan and Zhejiang samples, respectively. In both provinces, gender disparities were greatest in rural areas, where divorces were concentrated. In rural courts, differences between men and women in the probability of success on the first attempt were 13 and 21 percentage points in Henan and Zhejiang, respectively. Meanwhile, in urban courts, gender gaps were a substantially narrower 1 and 9 percentage points, respectively. In short, rural women were the most impacted by the divorce twofer.

Table 9.2 builds on this analysis by considering specific durations of time required to obtain an adjudicated divorce. It contains fewer court decisions than Table 9.1 owing to a large number of missing filing dates. The first thing we notice is that few divorces granted by adjudication were finalized within three months of initial filing. Among plaintiffs whose petitions were granted within three months, gender differences range from nil to relatively small, with women enjoying

TABLE 9.2 Proportion of plaintiffs (%) granted divorce, by duration of time from initial filing to granted divorce

	All plaintiffs	By plaintiff sex		Gender difference
		Female	Male	
Henan (2009–2015)				
Rural courts				
Three months	26	28	22	5**
Six months	63	58	71	−13**
One year	72	70	77	−8**
Two years	96	96	96	−1
n	14,491	9,540	4,951	
Urban courts				
Three months	26	29	21	8**
Six months	60	59	60	−0.1
One year	68	68	69	−0.2
Two years	96	96	95	1
n	2,181	1,409	772	
All basic-level courts				
Three months	26	28	22	6**
Six months	62	58	69	−11**
One year	72	70	76	−7**
Two years	96	96	96	−0.2
n	16,672	10,949	5,723	

TABLE 9.2 (*cont.*)

	All plaintiffs	By plaintiff sex		Gender difference
		Female	Male	
Zhejiang (2009–2016)				
Rural courts				
Three months	31	30	32	−2
Six months	46	40	58	−19**
One year	71	67	76	−9**
Two years	95	95	95	−0.04
n	2,525	1,594	931	
Urban courts				
Three months	37	39	33	6*
Six months	52	50	55	−5
One year	72	72	73	−1
Two years	94	94	94	−0.4
n	1,267	833	434	
All basic-level courts				
Three months	33	33	32	0.4
Six months	48	43	57	−14**
One year	71	69	75	−6**
Two years	95	95	95	−0.2
n	3,792	2,427	1,365	

Source: Author's calculations from Henan and Zhejiang provincial high courts' online decisions.
Note: The analysis is limited to divorces successfully obtained through adjudication (denied divorce petitions are excluded). Slight discrepancies between numbers in the "gender difference" column and numbers from which they were derived in the "by plaintiff sex" columns are due to rounding error.
* $P < .05$ ** $P < .001$, χ^2 tests

the advantage, particularly in urban courts. Of all divorces granted by adjudication in both provinces, the vast majority (94–96%) were finalized within two years of initial filing, regardless of plaintiff sex. Among plaintiffs whose divorce petitions were ultimately granted by adjudication, 38% and 52% were still married six months after initially filing for divorce in Henan and Zhejiang, respectively. Over time this gap shrank as the two provinces converged in their embrace of the divorce twofer; by 2015, 48% of plaintiffs in Henan were still married at the six-month mark. Gender disparities are only pronounced at this stage in rural courts, where the probability of a successful divorce within six months was 13 and 19 percentage points greater for men in Henan and Zhejiang, respectively. Gender disparities at the point of one year after initial filing are entirely consistent with but less pronounced than those at the point of six months after initial filing.

Table 9.3 brings together the previous two analyses – namely, of the number of attempts necessary to divorce and of the duration of time

TABLE 9.3 Correlates of time (days) from initial filing to granted divorce, unstandardized linear regression coefficients (means)/quantile regression coefficients (medians)

	(1)	(2)	(3)
Henan (2009–2015)			
Rural courts			
Female plaintiff	24***/7***	30***/10***	−12***/−5***
Ordinary civil procedure		73***/70***	68***/62***
Granted on subsequent attempt			303***/304***
Constant	370***/368***	303***/321***	82***/76***
R^2	.11/.08	.13/.09	.54/.53
n	14,491	14,491	14,491
Urban courts			
Female plaintiff	−12/−8	−6/−3	−3/−5
Ordinary civil procedure		90***/71***	77***/66***
Granted on subsequent attempt			308***/307***
Constant	354***/349***	271***/351***	47**/59
R^2	.12/.10	.15/.11	.54/.53
n	2,181	2,181	2,181
All basic-level courts			
Female plaintiff	19***/6**	25***/8***	−11***/−5***
Ordinary civil procedure		75***/70***	69***/63***
Granted on subsequent attempt			304***/305***
Constant	371***/368***	300***/350***	82***/79**
R^2	.11/.09	.13/.09	.54/.53
n	16,672	16,672	16,672

TABLE 9.3 (*cont.*)

	(1)	(2)	(3)
Zhejiang (2009–2016)			
Rural courts			
Female plaintiff	43***/45***	53***/55***	1/2
Ordinary civil procedure		80***/77***	90***/82***
Granted on subsequent attempt			317***/297***
Constant	354***/315***	314***/312***	127***/88***
R^2	.09/.08	.12/.09	.53/.52
n	2,525	2,525	2,525
Urban courts			
Female plaintiff	6/−3	21/12	−2/2
Ordinary civil procedure		119***/89***	115***/91***
Granted on subsequent attempt			330***/300***
Constant	306***/340***	256***/223	−7/15
R^2	.05/.03	.09/.05	.55/.54
n	1,267	1,267	1,267
All basic-level courts			
Female plaintiff	31**/33**	43***/39***	−.2/1
Ordinary civil procedure		92***/80***	98***/84***
Granted on subsequent attempt			322***/298***
Constant	376***/341***	335***/334***	138***/87***
R^2	.08/.06	.10/.07	.54/.53
n	3,792	3,792	3,792

Source: Author's calculations from Henan and Zhejiang provincial high courts' online decisions.

Note: Since male plaintiffs are the omitted reference group, a negative number means shorter times for women and a positive number means longer times for women. Ordinary civil procedure refers to the final trial in which the divorce was granted by adjudication. All models include court and year fixed effects. Significance tests in linear regression models are based on standard errors adjusted for nonindependence between decisions clustered within courts (161 and 90 in the Henan and Zhejiang samples, respectively). $^+ P < .10 * P < .05 ** P < .01 *** P < .001$, two-tailed tests from initial filing to divorce – into a regression analysis. It reveals that women's longer delays to divorce are explained almost entirely by their greater susceptibility to the divorce twofer. In Model 1, the baseline model without controls, we see that women's mean/median time to divorce exceeded that of men by 19/6 days in Henan and 31/33 days in Zhejiang. Model 1 also shows that the gender gap was limited to rural courts, where women's mean/median time to divorce was 24/7 days longer than men's in Henan and 43/45 days longer than men's in Zhejiang.

The type of civil procedure applied to the trial (ordinary vs. simplified) is added to Model 2. We know from Chapter 2 that the ordinary procedure slows down trials, and from Chapter 6 that this is the main reason why judges prefer to apply the simplified procedure. Not surprisingly, therefore, Model 2 shows that the application of the ordinary civil procedure delayed adjudicated divorce by between two and three months in both provinces in rural and urban courts alike.

Adding the civil procedure variable to Model 2 widened the gender gap in rural courts. We learned in Chapter 8 that male plaintiffs in rural courts were more than twice as likely to have their divorce petitions heard in public notice trials. For this reason, women – particularly rural women – were less likely to have the ordinary civil procedure applied to their divorce petitions. Owing to the SPC requirement that public notice trials be conducted according to the ordinary civil procedure (Chapter 4), delays associated with the ordinary civil procedure are partly a function of the 60-day public notice period (Chapter 2). Among plaintiffs, women's relatively long delays to divorce were therefore mitigated by their relatively greater exposure to the simplified civil procedure, which, in turn, was partly a result of their relatively smaller exposure to public notice trials. In other words, the gender gap in time from initial filing to successful divorce would have been even wider had the ordinary civil procedure been applied at identical rates to the trials of female and male plaintiffs. In Model 2, among plaintiffs with identical levels of exposure to the ordinary civil procedure, women's mean/median time to divorce was 25/8 days longer than men's in Henan and 43/39 days longer than men's in Zhejiang. Also in Model 2, the gender gap remains limited to rural courts: 30/10 days in Henan and 53/55 days in Zhejiang.

When my measure for the divorce twofer ("granted on subsequent attempt") is added to Model 3, the gender gap disappears completely in Zhejiang and even reverses direction in Henan. The interpretation of this pattern is simple: rural women's longer delays to adjudicated divorce were the direct consequence of their greater likelihood of experiencing the divorce twofer. They were far more likely than men to have refiled for divorce after an adjudicated denial. Rural women experienced relatively long delays to adjudicated divorce because rural courts were much more likely to deny their first-attempt petitions and thus to force them to refile after the statutory six-month waiting period. Many, however, appear not to have returned to court (Chapter 6). Among women whose initial petitions were denied, some may have sought to divorce outside the court system, and others may have abandoned their quests for divorce altogether.[11]

Because adjudicated denials delay the divorce process, the divorce twofer elevates dangers to women's physical safety, particularly in rural areas. Courts' routine denial of first-attempt divorce petitions fuels the expansion of a population of frustrated and often vulnerable plaintiffs awaiting divorce, among whom women are vastly overrepresented. If female plaintiffs are more likely than male plaintiffs to be victims of domestic violence, which we know is true, then it must also be true that the divorce twofer prolongs women's exposure to domestic violence. Even if plaintiffs who return to court for another attempt are guaranteed a divorce, the mean and median delay of over one year introduced by the divorce twofer helps enable the continuation of violence. This epitomizes the principle that justice delayed is justice denied. Judges delay justice by denying divorce petitions and deny justice by delaying divorces. The next case example illustrates a homicide committed after a divorce twofer involving domestic violence.

A woman, surnamed Yu, filed her second divorce petition in May 2010. She claimed that her husband, Wang Jinya, frequently argued with and beat her over family trifles. Although online repositories of court decisions do not contain the court's denial of Yu's original divorce

---

[11] After the first attempt, courts in my samples were actually more likely to grant adjudicated divorces to female plaintiffs than to male plaintiffs. Among subsequent-attempt decisions, the probabilities of adjudicated divorces granted to female and male plaintiffs, respectively, were .82 and .68 (n = 13,743) in Henan and .77 and .73 (n = 3,447) in Zhejiang (gender differences in both samples are statistically significant). This, however, may be a Pyrrhic victory for women insofar as subsequent attempts are so far outnumbered by first attempts (Chapter 6). Moreover, the right-censored nature of the court decisions (plaintiffs may or may not return to court after the end of the period of observation) problematizes any effort to interpret the meaning and significance of women's apparent advantage on a subsequent attempt following a first-attempt adjudicated denial. Published court decisions are poorly suited for the systematic analysis of what happens to litigants after first-attempt adjudicated denials.

petition in 2007, her statement to the court on her subsequent attempt in 2010 – namely, that "in the time since then, the defendant has failed to rectify himself" – suggests she had made the same allegations the first time.[12] The court granted the divorce on June 13, 2010, almost three years after denying her prior petition. On June 23, 2010, when Yu was collecting her belongings, he tried to persuade her to move back in. When she refused, he murdered her by bludgeoning her head with a wooden hammer, after which he stabbed and cut her neck with a knife, and once again bludgeoned her head with a copper rod. According to the forensic pathology report, the knife wounds severed her trachea and esophagus, as well as an artery and a vein on the right side of her neck, causing massive blood loss, and the blunt force trauma from the hammer and rod crushed her skull. When their landlord heard Yu's scream for help and knocked on the door, Wang said nothing was going on, that he and his ex-wife were simply having a chat. Later, after the landlord heard a loud banging noise, he knocked on the door again. When no one answered, he called the police, who entered the premises and discovered Wang hanging from the ceiling. They rushed him to the hospital, where he was saved. One of their three children testified that Wang's regular abuse was the reason why Yu had filed for divorce. The court held that Wang's actions were consistent with domestic violence and sentenced him to death (Decision #5012675, Ninghai County People's Court, Zhejiang Province, December 21, 2010).[13]

Effective intervention from any number of sources might have saved Yu's life. Yu's divorce was needlessly – and, arguably, unlawfully – prolonged. To at least some degree, courts have blood on their hands. We have no way of knowing the extent to which the court's adjudicated denial of Yu's initial petition was responsible for her subsequent murder. However, had the authorities believed her allegations and taken them seriously the first time, the court may have granted her divorce years earlier than it did and reduced opportunities for Wang to kill her. After noting Wenzhou's pioneering anti-domestic violence work (see Chapter 7), a judge from Zhejiang made the flabbergasting assertion that legal intervention to protect women like Yu is beyond the scope of public authorities: "If, after a divorce, a domestic abuser seeks to

---

[12] As we know, plaintiffs, in their efforts to convince judges of the impossibility of reconciliation, often claim that their husbands' behavior failed to improve during the six-month statutory waiting period following an adjudicated denial (Chapter 7).

[13] Case ID (2010)浙甬刑一初字第220号, archived at https://perma.cc/8733-9QB7. The divorce decision from the same court that led to this murder is Decision #2350347, Case ID (2010)甬宁民初字第00772号, archived at https://perma.cc/Y92G-E9U4.

commit revenge or a violent attack, it would be difficult to prevent. This would no longer be a legal matter."[14]

> Supplementary case examples set #9–3 is online at: https:// decoupling-book.org/.

As we saw in Chapter 7, in their efforts to deny divorce petitions, courts trivialized and negated women's domestic violence allegations. In so doing, courts simultaneously evaded their responsibility to refer criminal domestic violence cases to procurators. According to both the 2015 Opinions Concerning the Handling of Criminal Domestic Violence Cases in Accordance with the Law and the 2015 Anti-Domestic Violence Law, judges are supposed to transfer to the procuracy cases in which they discover domestic violence that constitutes a criminal offense. They are also supposed to inform victims of their right to initiate private criminal prosecution (provided by Article 112 in the Criminal Procedure Law; R. Zhang 2017:52). The Criminal Law also includes all kinds of provisions that could serve as the basis for criminally prosecuting domestic violence, such as maltreatment and desertion, assault and battery, rape, and homicide (e.g., Articles 17, 95, 234, 235, 236, 237, 260). Finally, the Marriage Law stipulates that public security organs, upon the request of domestic violence victims, should carry out administrative punishment of offenders (Article 43). It also stipulates that domestic violence victims have the right to initiate private criminal prosecution, at which point public security organs should conduct criminal investigations and the procuracy should initiate criminal prosecutions (Article 45). From judges' perspective, notifying procurators of criminal wrongdoing they discover in divorce litigation would validate plaintiffs' domestic violence claims, oblige judges to grant divorces on fault-based grounds, and thus undermine the professional benefits of the divorce twofer. Judges are reluctant to issue personal protection orders for the same reason (J. Jiang 2019:235).

Police, too, appeared to take a hands-off approach to domestic violence. The court decisions in my samples show that many women sought police help, but few received it. Thousands of divorce petitions in my samples contain both allegations of domestic violence and reported instances (often documented) of calls made to police

---

[14] Susan Finder generously shared this quotation from her personal interview, October 9, 2018.

for help. According to their testimony, police often failed to provide adequate intervention – or to intervene at all – after women called 110 or reported domestic violence in other ways. Tens of thousands of court decisions – both civil and criminal – in my samples contain references to public security administrative punishment decisions. Rarely, however, do they pertain to domestic violence. Fewer than 200 divorce petitions in my samples contain both allegations of domestic violence and references to public security administrative punishment decisions, which can be and are used as evidence of wrongdoing. Even among the roughly 2,000 criminal cases I found in my samples involving intentional injury and murder between spouses, references to public security administrative punishment decisions are few and far between, also numbering fewer than 200. The most common types of criminal case involving administrative punishment are drunk driving resulting in injury or death – which is classified as the offense of "dangerous driving" (危险驾驶) – and theft (盗窃).

When courts deny divorce petitions, and in so doing prolong women's exposure to their abusive husbands, women face difficult, high-stakes choices. Some may pursue divorce in the Civil Affairs Administration. However, the procedural requirement of mutual consent to divorce and mutual agreement on all terms of the divorce gives enormous bargaining leverage to the spouse who did not initiate the divorce. Consequently, when courts deny their divorce petitions, women often give up child custody and marital assets in exchange for freedom from their abusive husbands (Li 2022). Other women resign themselves to staying married rather than risking destitution, the loss of their children, and the potentially deadly consequences of leaving their abusive husbands. Battered women aware of the hidden rule of the divorce twofer understand that filing for divorce will likely fail on the first attempt and result in violent retaliation from their husbands (Deng 2017:113).

When courts fail to provide relief, some women seek protection from other public authorities. Study after study, however, shows inadequate intervention on the part of police, civil government agencies, local residents' and villagers' committees, and government-operated nongovernmental organizations such as the All-China Women's Federation (Chen 2018; Cheng and Gao 2019; Fincher 2014; Guo 2019; H. Zhang 2014:232; Zheng 2015). Indeed, according to the author of one study of domestic violence victims, "all the women to whom I talked have sought help from the police and All Women's Federation [sic], but to no avail. In their words, 'The police and the All

Women's Federation [sic] are dog's fart (gou pi),' meaning that they are useless" (Zheng 2015:172).

> After women experience domestic violence, the majority will instinct-ively seek the help of social organizations or state organs with public authority, such as the local police, the local branch of the All-Women's Federation, the Civil Affairs Bureau, the local villagers' or residents' committee, unions, and similar organizations, and some will even go to court to apply for personal protection orders. For a variety of rea-sons, however, the aforementioned organizations will ordinarily regard the reported situations as common family conflicts and only carry out mediation. The effectiveness of personal protection orders is very limited, which causes some women to resort to filing for divorce in court. However, courts often treat domestic violence cases the same way they treat ordinary family disputes. For this reason, courts will treat the divorce petitions of abused women the same way they treat ordinary family disputes and first carry out mediation. The premise of mediation is that both sides share responsibility for the conflict. However, abused women cannot be blamed for the abuse they receive. Moreover, whereas mediation requires that both sides compromise, abused women have had their basic physical rights violated and therefore fundamentally have nothing to concede. (Cheng and Gao 2019:13)

As a result, many women take measures to protect themselves. Prominent among women's self-protection strategies is flight.

FLIGHT: FLEEING ABUSERS

My samples show that abuse victims who returned to court after the statutory six-month waiting period often claimed worsening violence (also see Xu 2007:204). As they awaited their next opportunity to divorce, many abuse victims often became marital violence refugees. One plaintiff indicated the following in her statement to the court:

> After I gave birth to my second daughter, the defendant's cruelty towards me intensified. Oftentimes, upon returning home after being out all day, the defendant would beat and curse me. In order to escape this torture, I filed for divorce. In Case ID (2003)民民初字第827号, the Minquan County People's Court denied my petition for divorce. I then fled with my older daughter and begged for food in order to survive. (Decision #422754, Minquan County People's Court, Henan Province, July 20, 2010)[15]

---

[15] Case ID (2010)民民初字第440号, archived at https://perma.cc/RWN3-CWYG.

In this case, the duration of the first attempt (from case filing to adjudicated denial) was 50 days, but the total duration of time between original first-attempt case filing and adjudicated divorce was 2,492 days: almost seven years.

Another plaintiff stated to the court: "In the time since suffering a beating by the defendant in 2007, I have been in hiding, afraid to return home, for over three years. In early 2010 my divorce petition was denied by the Song County People's Court, after which I have still not dared to return home" (Decision #562570, Song County People's Court, Henan Province, April 1, 2011).[16] The litigation took over one year, but the overall process of divorcing lasted three or four years.

In her statement to the court, a woman claimed that after her first filing for divorce in 2009, her husband and his family prevented her from participating in the trial by physically blocking and verbally threatening her before dragging her back home, where they beat her. The court subsequently denied her second divorce petition three years later. On her third attempt in 2014, she testified that "currently I am raising our children elsewhere by myself, doing my utmost to avoid him, and living in a constant state of fear. At this point we have already been physically separated for five years." Although the plaintiff did everything right by both satisfying the statutory physical separation requirement and submitting as evidence a copy of her husband's "pledge letter" in which he admitted carrying out domestic violence, the court ignored her claim of physical separation and ruled the pledge letter inadmissible after the defendant recanted its contents. The basis of the court's decision to deny her divorce petition was that "plaintiff and defendant have been married for 14 years and have a son and a daughter. Conflicts in their everyday life are difficult to avoid but not fundamentally insurmountable. Plaintiff and defendant should cherish the marital affection they have already established. They are capable of reconciling if, from this point forward, they improve their communication skills" (Decision #1168173, Changge Municipal People's Court, Henan Province, February 8, 2014).[17]

One decision contains the story of a woman who, after the Lankao County People's Court denied her initial divorce petition in December 2011, "had no choice but to escape the reality of my situation by getting a job outside my place of residence. I never imagined my suffering

---

[16] Case ID (2011)嵩城民初字第54号, archived at https://perma.cc/3WCP-T5WV.
[17] Case ID (2013)长民初字第01711号, archived at https://perma.cc/ALB6-LYLT.

would not lessen after I fled, much less that it would gradually deepen over time. My current state of mental health is on the verge of collapse" (Decision #890371, Lankao County People's Court, Henan Province, November 7, 2012).[18] In another second-attempt divorce petition, the plaintiff submitted police records of nine requests for police help in support of her claim of intensifying violence following the court's denial of the first-attempt petition. The court denied the petition after affirming that the evidence proved only that calls to the police were made as a consequence of "disputes," but not that domestic violence occurred (Decision #4405727, Changxing County People's Court, Zhejiang Province, November 24, 2015).[19]

When defendants contested plaintiffs' claims of uninterrupted separation, or if plaintiffs returned briefly for planting and harvesting crops in efforts to maintain claims to farmland, judges not infrequently held that plaintiffs failed the applicable statutory physical separation test and, on this basis, denied their second-attempt divorce petitions.

> On June 3, 2012, owing to some trivial matter, the defendant hurled a bench towards my body. Luckily I ducked and escaped harm. One week later, the defendant attacked me and my younger sister using the same method. For this reason, I filed reports with police substations in both Wuzhen [Town] and Wutong [Subdistrict Office]. At the end of the same year, the defendant once again violently beat me, and also spread threats outside the home about wanting to beat me to death, causing me to dare not live at home and forcing me to live outside the home to this day. In addition, the defendant maliciously slandered my reputation by spreading rumors. On December 25, 2013, the defendant filed for divorce at the Tongxiang County People's Court on the grounds of breakdown of mutual affection. [In its holding, the court affirmed that the decision of this prior petition shows the plaintiff's consent to the defendant's divorce request.] On March 10, 2014, the defendant withdrew his petition. Since then, marital affection not only did not improve, but on the contrary worsened. Harboring a deep grudge, the defendant threated to kill me. The defendant came to my residence and smashed a hole in the glass and screen of the entrance door. After this happened I called the police.

The defendant in this case denied committing any act of domestic violence. The defendant further claimed that the plaintiff had occasionally

---

[18] Case ID (2012)兰民初字第2803号, archived at https://perma.cc/X2QW-XJEM.
[19] Case ID (2015)湖长太民初字第259号, archived at https://perma.cc/4GK9-D25L. I use a female pronoun even though the plaintiff's sex is not disclosed.

returned home during the alleged period of physical estrangement. The court, citing the plaintiff's double failure to prove that domestic violence caused the breakdown of mutual affection and to meet the two-year separation test, denied her divorce petition (Decision #3525299, Tongxiang County People's Court, Zhejiang Province, December 9, 2014).[20]

When women flee marital violence, their default destination is often their natal families. Because their husbands can so easily find them there, however, this poses risks not only to themselves but also to their family members. For this reason, many abused women go into hiding. They frequently participate in labor migration in order to escape their abusers, to support themselves, and to accumulate money necessary to finance the divorce (K. Li 2015a:101–6). China's migrant labor force thus includes marital violence refugees as well as women hoping to satisfy the one-year physical separation test before their next divorce attempt.

Themes shared by the following examples of women's flight from marital violence include husbands' jealousy and control, and wives' efforts to free themselves and earn a livelihood through migrant labor force participation. These examples also show, however, that their husbands often find them. I will begin with the applicant's statement in one of the very few protection orders in my samples of court decisions.

> If the applicant had any contact with another person, the respondent would get suspicious and punch and kick the applicant. In order to escape the respondent and maintain a livelihood, the applicant struck out on her own as a migrant worker. The respondent immediately travelled to the applicant's new abode and workplace, and created unprovoked disturbances. He carried out domestic violence in front of her landlord and coworkers. Most intolerable to the applicant was the respondent's suspicious heart. Whenever he went to the applicant's rental home, he would search her cell phone. On October 9, 2016, the respondent once again went to her rental home and carried out domestic violence, hitting and injuring her face, chest, and other parts of her body. (Decision # 4828890, Songyang County People's Court, Zhejiang Province, October 27, 2016)[21]

The defendant in the next example similarly hunted down his wife after she fled to her parents' home and then to Guangdong Province, a common destination for migrant workers from Henan.

---

20 Case ID (2014)嘉桐乌民初字第441号, archived at https://perma.cc/DHC5-5N7U.
21 Case ID (2016)浙1124民保令3号, archived at https://perma.cc/2HY4-VNV2.

One day in the fall of 1997, we had an argument over some trifle. That night, the defendant demanded to have sex with me. When I refused, he argued with me some more, and then started punching my body. I had no choice but to return to my natal family. Afterwards the defendant went there to take me back. In the spring of 2000, in order to escape the defendant, I was forced to migrate to Guangdong Province to work. When, in 2003, the defendant learned I was in Guangdong, he went there too. In 2005, when I returned to Tianguan [Town] to open a hair salon, the defendant stayed in Guangdong. In September 2008, after returning, the defendant went to my hair salon and threw a hissy fit. That night he tried to force me to have sex. When I refused, he intimidated me with a knife. I was so angry I started a hunger strike. The defendant wrote a pledge letter promising not to harass me again. Who knew that a couple of weeks later, when he tried once again to have sex with me and I refused, he would beat me again. Since then I have not seen the defendant.

The court denied the plaintiff's divorce request on the grounds that they had bought a house together – supposed proof of the strength of their marital foundation – and that the defendant exhibited contrition by recognizing his mistakes (Decision #338557, Xixia County People's Court, Henan Province, June 28, 2010).[22]

Supplementary case examples set #9–4 is online at: https://decoupling-book.org/.

In some ways, the women whose stories are captured in these court decisions are the lucky ones. Taking flight may have increased their chances of survival. The women whose stories appear in the next section were less fortunate.

FIGHT: KILLING ABUSERS

For almost two decades, Chen Min has provided expert testimony in criminal trials on behalf of women prosecuted for murdering their abusive husbands, including two in my Zhejiang sample. In the 2003 trial of Liu Shuanxia (variously 刘栓霞 and 刘拴霞), who, after over a decade of chronic and increasingly frequent beatings, killed her abusive husband by adding rat poison to his noodles two days after he attacked

---

[22] Case ID (2010)西丹民初字第61号, archived at https://perma.cc/5HD4-7BC6.

her with an axe, Chen provided the first expert witness testimony on "battered woman syndrome" (受虐妇女综合征 and 受虐妇女综合症) in China.

Although Lenore Walker is hardly the sole voice on why abused women stay with and sometimes kill their abusers, her theory of "battered woman syndrome" (Walker 2017) not only remains the dominant explanation in general (Rothenberg 2002, 2003), but has also exerted considerable influence in scholarly and advocacy circles in China (Chen and Yang 2016; Li and Jia 2019; Liu and Liu 2020; X. Wang 2015; Xing 2013; Yun 2019) and on Chen Min's work in particular (Chen 2004). At the time of the trial, Chen worked at the China Law Society. As a graduate student at the University of British Columbia in the late 1990s, Chen studied Canada's landmark 1990 Supreme Court ruling, R. v Lavallee, which acquitted Angelique Lyn Lavallee even though it found she had murdered her abusive boyfriend. In so doing, the court formally recognized the existence of battered woman syndrome, legitimated self-defense on the part of women who satisfy its defining characteristics, and permitted the admission of expert testimony in cases involving battered women in Canada's legal system (Shaffer 1990). After returning to China in 1999, Chen devoted herself to the pursuit of legal recognition for battered woman syndrome in Chinese courts (Pan 2018). In courts elsewhere, including Australia, New Zealand, and the United States, battered woman syndrome is accepted as a type of post-traumatic stress disorder experienced by women subjected to their abusers' coercive control, jealousy, possessiveness, violence, and death threats, and as a potential trigger of lethal self-defense (Rothenberg 2002, 2003; Sheehy, Stubbs, and Tolmie 2012; Walker 2017:49, Chapter 12). So far, however, Chen's quest remains elusive.

Returning to the trial of Liu Shuanxia, Hebei Province's Ningjin County People's Court failed to accept Chen's justifiable self-defense argument, much less the concept of battered woman syndrome she introduced, but did recognize domestic violence as a mitigating circumstance that warranted leniency. Liu was sentenced to 12 years in prison (Liu and Liu 2020:46; Sohu.com 2003; Sprick 2018:295; X. Wang 2017:17–18; Yun 2019:81n19).

Although this trial included the first expert witness testimony of its kind, it does not represent the first attempt to mount a battered woman syndrome defense in a Chinese murder trial. Liu Wei (刘巍) and Liu Xiuzhen (刘秀珍) made the first such attempt in 2000 as lawyers working on behalf of Peking University's Center for Women's Law Studies and Legal Services. The defendant's husband in this case had inflicted horrific abuse on her for years. She had a dozen or so scars on her face, chest, and other areas from cigarette burns caused by her husband. On one occasion he pushed her into a pot of boiling water before cutting her face with a broken beer bottle. The hot water scalding was so severe she received inpatient hospital treatment for one month. Throughout the trial, the prosecution repeatedly characterized the husband's violence as "mutual fighting" (打架). Perhaps because she murdered not only her husband but also the prostitute who was in bed with him (in their marital bed after he ordered his wife to get out of it and sleep somewhere else), she was sentenced to death. Liu Wei participated in the second-instance trial, in which she introduced the concept of battered woman syndrome. The court of second instance changed the sentence to death with a two-year reprieve (Li 2003:3; Yun 2019:80–81), which automatically becomes a life sentence if the defendant exhibits good behavior.

After joining the SPC's China Institute of Applied Jurisprudence in 2007, Chen authored the 2008 Guidelines, which served as an important basis for the subsequent 2015 Anti-Domestic Violence Law (Pan 2018). The 2008 Guidelines also helped set the stage for the participation of expert witnesses in criminal domestic violence cases. In 2012, four courts, including intermediate courts in Zhejiang Province's Wenzhou (Chen's hometown) and Anhui Province's Ma'anshan, began to admit expert witness testimony on a pilot basis (Liu and Shi 2016; C. Wang 2016). In 2013, Chen published a book for judges trying cases involving domestic violence (M. Chen 2013).

Until the early 2010s, battered women who killed their husbands were routinely sentenced to life in prison and sometimes even immediately executed (Chen and Yang 2016:22; Xing 2013:25; Zheng 2015:163). The year 2015 was a turning point (Chen and Yang 2016:20; Liu and Liu 2020:44). Much like the 2015 Anti-Domestic Violence Law, the 2015 Opinions of the SPC Concerning the Handling of Criminal Domestic Violence Cases in Accordance with the Law (hereafter, the "2015 Opinions") brought together relevant provisions scattered across a number of bodies of laws and clarified their relevance to the determination of criminal offenses and criminal sentencing related to domestic violence. Although the concept of justifiable self-defense (正当防卫 and 防卫过当) was already part of China's Criminal Law, the 2015 Opinions clarified its application in the context of domestic violence (Cheng and Gao 2019:13; Guo 2019:240; X. Wang 2015:87). In particular, Articles 19 and 20 in the 2015 Opinions offer clear guidance on the application of provisions on mitigated punishment or clemency (减轻或者免除处罚) – which were also already in the Criminal Law (including Article 20) – in cases involving wrongdoing by the victim giving rise to the injury or murder at issue. At the same time, in 2014 and 2015, the SPC issued "model cases" to provide guidance to judges in criminal trials involving domestic violence (D'Attoma 2019).

Also occurring in 2015, the retrial of Li Yan (李彦) received considerable attention from scholars and journalists around the world (J. Jiang 2019:241–42; Palmer 2017:291–92; Tan 2016:315; Tatlow 2015; Zhao and Zhang 2017:202; Zheng 2015:162–63). In the course of suffering gruesome and recurrent abuse over her marriage of less than two years, Li had sought help from public authorities – including the police, the All-China Women's Federation, a hospital, and the local justice department – to no avail when they each "advised her to just 'bear it.'" Li testified that her husband "grabbed her hair and hit her head against the wall, stubbed out cigarettes on her face and legs, and locked her outside on cold nights. … Often after beating her, he abused her sexually, she said." In 2010, when her husband beat her with an air rifle and threatened to kill her with it, she "grabbed the weapon and slammed the barrel against his head twice, killing him, she told the police at the time." She then dismembered his corpse (Tatlow 2015; also see Palmer 2017:291–92). In her first-instance trial in 2011, the Ziyang Municipal Intermediate People's Court in Sichuan Province – no different from how divorce courts in Henan and Zhejiang so often deal with allegations and evidence of domestic violence (Chapters 7 and 8) – affirmed Li's injuries but held that she was unable to prove that they had been caused by her husband (J. Jiang 2019:246n13). The court sentenced her to death with immediate execution. All death sentences must be reviewed by the SPC. In this case, the SPC did not approve the lower court's death sentence and instructed the Sichuan Provincial High Court to retry the case. In her 2014 retrial, which was concluded in April 2015, the court – perhaps under pressure from domestic and international outcries of support for Li, and perhaps anticipating the sea change about to be catalyzed by the 2015 Opinions – changed her sentence to death with a two-year reprieve, which, practically speaking, amounts to a life sentence (J. Jiang 2019:241; Palmer 2017:290; Tan 2016:315; Tatlow 2015).

Although most domestic homicides are husbands killing their wives, a sizeable proportion of all women in Chinese prisons are there for killing their husbands (Chen 2014; Li 2003; Li and Jia 2019:61–62; Xing 2013; Zheng 2015:162). According to one estimate, over half of all violent crimes committed by women were in response to domestic violence (Li and Jia 2019: 62, 69). According to another estimate, there were about 140 criminal domestic violence cases per year between 2014 and 2018 in China, of which about 20 were wives who murdered or attempted to murder their husbands (Cheng and Gao 2019:11). This estimate is consistent with another of about one or two cases per month of women murdering their abusive husbands in China (Li and Jia 2019:66). Cases of women who kill (or try to kill) their husbands are concentrated in rural areas (Cheng and Gao 2019:12; Li and Jia 2019:62). These estimates imply that Henan and Zhejiang taken together, with about 11% of China's population, should have experienced about two cases per year of women murdering and attempting to murder their abusive husbands.[23]

Owing to limitations in their methods of searching for relevant cases, however, the authors of these studies vastly underestimated the incidence of criminal domestic violence cases. In my two provincial samples of court decisions, I found about 55 cases of women who murdered their (sometimes former) intimate partners, of whom about 43 were abusers. Most of the victims in these cases were husbands, but a few were ex-spouses and nonspousal intimate partners. Added to these are an estimated ten or so attempted homicides, yielding a grand total of about 53 cases of women murdering or attempting to murder their abusive husbands between 2009 and 2015 in Henan and between 2009 and 2017 in Zhejiang.[24] This is a substantial undercount owing to imperfections in the methods I applied. Moreover, even if I were able to identify every relevant case in my samples, I would still underestimate the true number because my samples are not comprehensive; courts do not publish all of their decisions. Finally, murder-suicides do not appear in the court decisions because there is no defendant to prosecute. For obvious reasons, suicide – which is on the minds of

---

[23] A study of media coverage of domestic violence homicides found that 213 men and 839 women were murdered by family members from March 2016 (when the Anti-Domestic Violence Law took effect) through the end of 2019 (Equality 2020).

[24] I derived these estimates by extrapolating from a sample of 200 court decisions (100 from each provincial sample) that I read and coded out of a total of 451 court decisions (279 from Henan and 172 from Zhejiang) that satisfy my crude criteria (discussed earlier) for homicides or attempted homicides involving spouses.

many abuse victims and carried out in nontrivial numbers (Fincher 2014:159; Zheng 2015) – is generally not recorded in a court decision unless it is unsuccessful. According to my rough and highly conservative estimates, Henan and Zhejiang alone had about seven cases per year, which implies about 70 per year nationwide if these two provinces are representative of China as a whole.

My samples reveal several salient patterns. First, among those who killed their intimate partners, men far outnumbered women. More specifically, women murdered by their male intimate partners outnumbered men murdered by their female intimate partners by a ratio of 2.9:1 (2.2:1 in Henan and 4.3:1 in Zhejiang). This imbalance is almost identical to the 2.8:1 ratio of female to male intimate partner homicide victims in the United States. Corresponding ratios elsewhere in the world range from 1.3:1 in Japan, 1.5:1 in France, and 2.3:1 in the Netherlands on the low end of the spectrum to 3.0:1 in Hong Kong, 3.9:1 in Canada, 4.2:1 in Taiwan, 4.4:1 in England and Wales, 4.5:1 in Germany, and 15.7:1 in India (Stöckl et al. 2013:Appendix).

Second, men who murdered their wives tended to do so out of jealousy and possessiveness, whereas women who murdered their husbands did so typically to escape chronic violence. The most important factor associated with cases of men murdering their wives was divorce. In about half of all such homicides, female victims were trying to divorce or had already divorced their husbands. In over one-third of all such homicides, male offenders suspected their wives were cheating on them. Both motives were far more prevalent among male defendants. Not surprisingly, in each provincial sample, cases of men murdering their wives' (alleged) lovers outnumbered cases of women murdering their husbands' (alleged) lovers by a ratio of almost 2:1.

In sharp contrast, by far the most important factor among female homicide offenders was domestic violence. Indeed, this was the only salient factor in cases of women killing their husbands. As noted earlier, about 80% (roughly 43 out of 55) of all cases of women who murdered their intimate partners alleged chronic abuse.

Third, defense lawyers almost never argued for acquittal. They instead tended to argue for leniency (McConville et al. 2011; Zuo and Ma 2013). Leniency in sentencing did indeed become conspicuous beginning in 2015. Comparing sentencing patterns between 2009–2014 and 2015–2017, the proportion of intimate partner homicides resulting in life sentences dropped precipitously from 57% to 35%, respectively, and the proportion resulting in fixed-term prison sentences increased commensurately. Leniency toward female defendants was even more conspicuous. According to the Criminal Law, the statutory minimum sentence for intentional homicide is ten years. Only when "circumstances are relatively minor" can sentences be mitigated. Sentences lighter than ten years are therefore, by definition, lenient (Article 232). Among women prosecuted for murdering their abusers, the proportion given lenient prison sentences of less than ten years increased between the two time periods from 9% to 46%, and the proportion given prison sentences ranging from ten years to life dropped commensurately from 91% to 54%. Again, all sentencing patterns I present come from first-instance trials and do not reflect subsequent decisions to change original sentences.

Despite a clear uptick in leniency beginning in 2015, criminal sentencing of women who murdered their abusive husbands continued to exhibit tremendous variation (Chen and Yang 2016:20). Indeed, the proportion of such women in my samples sentenced to life in prison remained stable at about one-third in both time periods. One study of women who murdered their abusive husbands found that "similar cases were not decided similarly" (同案不同判), that sentences ranged from three years in prison to death with two-year reprieves, leaned toward the harsh end of the spectrum, and almost never included probation even though judges have that option (Li and Jia 2019:65–67). Another study of criminal sentencing of women who murdered their abusive husbands and ex-husbands found the most lenient sentence to be a suspended three-year prison term with three years of probation (Xing 2013:25).

Owing to such enormous variation in sentencing, many women who murdered their abusive husbands received harsh sentences. Take, for example, the case of a woman who, in response to her husband's long-term and frequent domestic violence, and after family members talked her out of divorcing him, murdered him by serving him a dish of shredded radish laced with rat poison (tetramine). She then bought gasoline and attempted to incinerate his corpse in the family's pigsty before packing the remains in a bag and throwing it into a well. Explicitly taking the victim's wrongdoing and the victim's family's forgiveness into consideration, the court characterized her life sentence as "lenient" (从轻处罚, Decision #759786, Zhumadian Municipal Intermediate People's Court, Henan Province, March 15, 2011).[25]

---

[25] Case ID (2011)驻刑二初字第12号, archived at https://perma.cc/PQ6S-R6V6.

Other women received far more lenient sentences. Consider the homicide case of Xu Ping. In its decision, the court affirmed that while "both sides exchanged blows after arguing" (发生争吵, 后相互厮打), Xu's husband knocked her to the floor, after which she grabbed a fruit knife. As he moved to dodge the knife, Xu, in panic and confusion, stabbed her husband in the chest, puncturing his heart. Although the court recorded no information about a history of domestic violence and affirmed that the stabbing was intentional, it also affirmed that the defendant was at fault for causing the victim's death and that her actions constituted justifiable self-defense in light of the fact that she wielded a knife only because her husband was beating her. After stabbing her husband, Xu cried for help and, together with a neighbor, rushed him to the town hospital, where he was declared dead. Village authorities and village residents vouched for Xu's good character and beseeched the court to extend mercy with a lenient sentence. Although the court rejected her defense lawyers' request for probation, it affirmed Xu's justifiable self-defense and gave her a relatively lenient sentence of three years in prison (Decision #809501, Guangshan County People's Court, Henan Province, June 14, 2012).[26]

Supplementary case examples set #9–5 is online at: https://decoupling-book.org/.

Courts, however, do not consistently affirm justifiable self-defense in criminal domestic violence trials. In 2013, for example, the Xi'an Municipal Intermediate People's Court in Shaanxi Province found Wang Taoping guilty of intentional injury (not murder) and sentenced her to life in prison for beating her husband to death with a scale weight, cutting board, and hot water thermos. The court held that both sides were at fault for violence in their marriage and that her lawyers failed to provide evidence that she suffered from battered woman syndrome (Yun 2019:78). In cases like this, courts extend leniency (as the court in this case characterized Wang's life sentence) not on the basis of justifiable self-defense, but rather according to the defendant's cooperative attitude, confession, admission of guilt, risk to society, and payment of compensation to the victim's family.[27]

[26] Case ID (2012)光刑初字第65号, archived at https://perma.cc/7G3H-9H6C.
[27] Case ID (2014)陕刑三终字第00045号, archived at https://perma.cc/QJD5-98BL.

Courts affirmed justifiable self-defense in criminal domestic violence cases only sparingly. To the best of my knowledge, they have never invoked – much less affirmed – battered woman syndrome. Indeed, the term appears in only two court decisions I found on China Judgements Online (one from Shaanxi just discussed, and the other from Sichuan discussed next). In both cases, the term was introduced by lawyers. Not a single decision in my Henan and Zhejiang samples contains this term.

Between 2015 and 2017, Chen Min provided expert witness testimony in a number of homicide trials across China on behalf of battered women (Rong 2020:47). In the five court decisions I could find that contain Chen Min's expert witness testimony, two of which are in my Zhejiang sample, not once did she utter the term "battered woman syndrome." In a 2016 trial in which Chen testified, however, the defendant's lawyers did use the term.

Yang Shengmei had been battered by her ex-husband since they were married in 1989. They divorced in 2004 but continued to live together. In 2015, they argued about his intention to sell property; Yang wanted their daughters to inherit it. One day, when preparing his lunch, she added rat poison (tetramine) to his alcohol and food. When local medical personnel were unable to diagnose his symptoms, they recommended he be transferred to a different hospital. Fearing getting caught, Yang instead moved him back home, where he died. Together with two accomplices, she dismembered the corpse and scattered the pieces throughout the area before turning herself in. Perhaps because the 2015 Opinions calls for leniency in cases of "serious domestic violence" in which the victim, in self-defense, intentionally murders or harms the perpetrator, the procurators argued that "the 'degree of domestic violence' can only be affirmed as 'ordinary domestic violence,' and does not justify Yang Shengmei's murder of Li X." They recommended a sentence within the range of "death, life imprisonment, or fixed-term imprisonment of not less than ten years" in accordance with Article 232 of the Criminal Law. Yang's lawyers countered by arguing that her ex-husband's domestic violence rose to the level of "serious" owing to his history of committing domestic violence in public areas, choking her, and committing domestic violence in front of their children. They further argued that Yang's behavior possessed the hallmarks of battered woman syndrome insofar she killed in self-defense with the sole goal of freeing herself from the control of domestic violence. In her testimony, Chen Min explained the psychology of battered women like Yang, who kill their abusers, why battered women like Yang often choose poisoning as their method of murder, and why battered women like Yang dismember and dispose of the corpse after killing their abusers. Accepting Yang's lawyers' argument that the circumstances of her crime were "relatively minor" and merited leniency, the court sentenced her to ten years in prison (Guang'an Municipal Intermediate People's Court, Sichuan Province, April 27, 2016; also cited in Song 2016).[28]

Although Chen has refrained from using the term "battered woman syndrome" in her expert witness testimony to courts across China, she has nonetheless introduced some of its key elements. In each case, she represented the murder as reasonable and justified by making some or all of the following points. Domestic violence is a means of asserting control. Owing to abusers' coercive control, victims often stay with them. Victims may be financially unable to leave or believe that tolerating domestic violence, compared to leaving, is less dangerous to themselves and their family members. Victims of domestic violence murder their abusers in self-defense when outside intervention is lacking or fails, they reach the limit of their ability to endure abuse, and they fear for their own life or the lives of their family members. When victims of domestic violence kill their abusers, they often choose methods that minimize the risk of a violent counterattack. Victims sometimes dismember parts or the entirety of the corpse in order to hide or render unrecognizable the parts that elicit fear. Finally, victims of domestic violence who kill their abusers pose no risk to society.

Chen also testified in the 2016 homicide trial of Guo Qinjuan in Yunnan Province. In this case, Guo's husband had routinely beaten her and threatened her safety. He had been forcibly detained by police in a drug detoxification center. He had also undergone public security administrative punishment for stabbing her father with a switchblade knife. Over the years, Guo had sought help from relatives and friends, the All-China Women's Federation, and local justice authorities. She had reported her husband to the police. She had even filed for divorce in court citing domestic violence as the cause. She ultimately withdrew her divorce petition. Nothing, however, stopped her husband's abusive behavior. The court affirmed the following events precipitating the murder. Guo was eating dinner with her parents when her husband stormed in, demanding money. During the ensuing altercation, he

---

[28] Case ID (2016)川16刑初7号, archived at https://perma.cc/JPY6-3VEK.

threatened to murder the whole family, dragged Guo's mother by her hair into the courtyard, pushed her down, and brandished a switchblade knife. When Guo intervened, he knocked her down. Guo then grabbed a wooden club from behind the courtyard gate. When he turned away, she seized her chance to attack, hitting him on the head until he collapsed and died. Guo called the police to report the crime and waited for them to arrive. According to Chen's expert testimony,

> carrying out violence is not the goal but is rather a means of exercising control. It happens whenever the victim disobeys or objects. The result of violence is the victim's obedience, the victim's fear of doing anything the offender does not want her to do. ... Even when victims are subjected to extremely serious violence, they may choose to endure it because they believe preserving the marriage is safer than leaving or because they lack the financial means to leave. However, when the offender threatens to murder the victim's parents, she may choose to murder the offender after concluding that doing so is the only way to protect her family. ... Owing both to differences in physical strength and to psychological terror, victims often wait until offenders are unprepared.

After Chen testified, Guo's defense lawyers made the following sentencing recommendation:

> Acquitting Guo Qinjuan will help realize the positive social impact of law. The victim's family has said that the defendant may go unpunished and has requested that the prosecution withdraw its case. Villagers also believe the defendant should be released and allowed to raise her child and take care of her aging parents. These are the sincere reactions and wishes of society's masses for Guo Qinjuan after she beat her husband to death.

The court held that Guo deserved leniency because her husband was so clearly at fault for the events precipitating his death, she reported her crime, she waited for the police to arrive, she provided a confession, she displayed repentance, and she posed no public safety threat, and furthermore because the victim's family forwent all claims for civil damages, submitted a forgiveness letter on its own initiative, and requested the court treat her leniently. During the pretrial police investigation, ten family members of the victim signed the forgiveness letter pleading on behalf of Guo for mercy and no prison time. Over 100 residents of Guo's village signed a petition requesting leniency. She received a suspended three-year prison term with five years of probation.

Guo's case is unusual in at least two respects, namely, the extent to which the court accepted her defense lawyers' arguments and the leniency of her sentence. First, the court came tantalizingly close to recognizing battered woman syndrome. In response to the defense lawyers' claim that "her actions were the reasonable self-defensive responses of a battered woman [受暴妇女] and belong to battered women's special type of self-defense," the court held that "her actions reflect the resistance of a battered woman, have the nature of self-defense, were specifically directed at the other side, and the harms they pose to society are different from those of other homicide cases. The defense's argument for mercy should be adopted" (Chuxiong Yi Autonomous Prefecture Intermediate People's Court, Yunnan Province, November 7, 2016).[29]

Second, Guo's case is an exceedingly rare example of a sentence of probation. Indeed, I was unable to find a single homicide case involving spouses in my Henan and Zhejiang samples that resulted in a probation sentence, much less an acquittal. As we saw in Chapter 6, acquittal rates were close to zero among all criminal cases (Table 6.5). By contrast, in a study of 113 cases of women who murdered their intimate partners in Australia, Canada, and New Zealand, acquittals account for 20% (Sheehy et al. 2012). As mentioned earlier, Chinese defense lawyers tend to argue for lenient punishments rather than acquittals (McConville et al. 2011; Zuo and Ma 2013). Moreover, procuratorial performance evaluation systems that reward convictions and punish acquittals incentivize procurators to withdraw cases they fear they might lose (McConville et al. 2011:196).

In other ways, however, Guo's case illuminates several themes widely shared by court cases involving domestic violence victims. First, accounts of their experiences with domestic violence are virtually identical among both plaintiffs seeking divorce in civil court and defendants facing charges of homicide in criminal court. Second, her divorce petition withdrawal was probably involuntary. As we saw in Chapter 6, when abused women withdrew their divorce petitions, they often did so under duress.

Third, her lawyers' argument for an acquittal ("Acquitting Guo Qinjuan will help realize the positive social impact of law") included a thinly veiled appeal to Chinese judges' general concern about the potential for public backlash against court decisions widely perceived as unfair. In this context, the term "social impact" (社会效果) refers to

---

[29] Case ID (2016)云23刑初15号, archived at https://perma.cc/6X49-3NCU.

"whether judicial decisions have resulted in [or could result in] social or mass instability" (Kinkel and Hurst 2015:942). The judges' holding that "over 100 of Guo Qinjuan's fellow villagers actively petitioned for leniency, which confirms that granting probation to Guo Qinjuan will have no major harmful influence on the residential community" could be a tacit acknowledgement of their concern about the potential for discontent or even unrest in the village – or higher-level collective petitioning by villagers – if Guo were imprisoned or executed. Similarly, in the Liu Shuanxia case discussed earlier, the court may have been swayed by a collective plea for leniency it received from her entire village (Sprick 2018:295; X. Wang 2017:10, 17). As we know, judges lose points on their performance evaluations for making decisions that harm social stability. Under pressure to maintain social stability, judges do consider public sentiment when ruling on criminal cases (J. He 2016:81–95; Miao 2013).

Supplementary case examples set #9–6 is online at: https:// decoupling-book.org/.

The iconic Deng Yujiao case is a case in point. Procurators, under enormous pressure from overwhelming public sympathy for Deng, who, apparently in self-defense, murdered a county government official whom she alleged was trying to rape her, lowered their original charge of murder to intentional injury. Deng's acquittal of the lesser charge is often used to illustrate courts' responsiveness to public opinion as they carry out their political mandate to maintain social stability (Lei and Zhou 2015:559; Sprick 2018:283; Zhang 2016a:24–25).

Fourth, abusers threaten to harm and kill not only their intimate partners, but also the family members of their intimate partners (Walker 2017:306–7; Zheng 2015). Documented examples include: "If you dare go to the KTV club I'll break your legs," "If you dare commit suicide I'll force your mother to marry your younger sister to me, and if your mother doesn't agree I'll murder your whole family," and "If you dare leave me, I'll make sure your family line is exterminated!" (Chen 2018:6). (Chapter 7 contains a number of similar threats against women and their families.)

Fifth, a lot of women who murdered their abusive husbands had previously sought help from public authorities. Murder was a last, desperate resort. When battered women seek help from local police, villagers' committees or urban residents' committees, the Civil Affairs Administration, and court, they hope that any one of them will stop their husbands' violent behavior, as stipulated by the Marriage Law (Article 43, a provision omitted from the 2020 Civil Code). Public authorities often fail to provide or facilitate effective domestic violence intervention. In one study of criminal prosecutions of women who injured or murdered their abusive husbands, a sizeable proportion had previously sought help – to no avail – from various official sources, including divorce courts (Cheng and Gao 2019:12).

> When abused women seek the help of police because of domestic violence, their requests are not handled with adequate care and attention, and when they then resort to divorce litigation, they often face obstructionism from their husbands who withhold consent to divorce. Failure to get relief through channels of public authority causes women, left with no other choice, to fight back by murdering their husbands. (Guo 2019:240)

As we saw in Chapters 7 and 8, no matter how egregious a husband's abuse is, and no matter how well his wife documents it with evidence, he can effectively block his wife's divorce petition simply by withholding consent.

As a consequence, the judicial clampdown on divorce also endangers men. The following case underscores the safety risks to both women and men when abuse victims stay with their abusers. The couple in this case married, divorced, and remarried. Situations like this are not altogether uncommon; victims and their abusers sometimes remarry each other after they divorce (Li 2003:4; also see the case of Xue Aihua in the next section of this chapter). The defendant had filed for a new divorce only a week before the incident for which she was criminally charged and in which she used a hammer to attack her husband. In his testimony to the court, he stated:

> I pulled her hair, slapped her, and used a cleaver and hammer to intimidate her. Afterwards, when I held the door shut with both of my hands in order to prevent her from leaving, she hit me on back of my head with the hammer, causing me to fall unconscious to the floor. What happened next is unclear to me. When I regained consciousness I was in bed, and there was blood on my head and blood on my mouth. My throat and crotch were extremely painful. An ambulance took me to the hospital. Our relationship is quite bad, and we frequently argue. I often beat and curse her, and she has reported me to the police on many occasions.

The procurator accused her of using the hammer to hit his head, face, chest, scrotum, and testicles. Rejecting her defense lawyer's claim of justifiable self-defense, the court sentenced her to two years in prison (Decision #4685540, Yuyao Municipal People's Court, Zhejiang Province, August 31, 2016).[30]

Some men do not survive similar attacks. Consider, for example, the case of Zhang Dianru. She killed her husband after seeking the help of police, who did not intervene but rather advised her to hide. The defense team made the following statement to the court on Zhang's behalf:

> After extreme and prolonged abuse, the defendant exhausted the sources of help of which she was aware. When she sought police help, public security personnel told her to hide out at a hotel. When she asked her husband for a divorce, he refused. Having lost her ability to work, she was subjected to the victim's economic control. When she went to the All-China Women's Federation for help, she was told to go to court and file for divorce. She was unable to file for divorce owing to her lack of both common legal knowledge and money. When she asked relatives for help, the answer she received was "put up with it."

Zhang had previously sustained an injury, after jumping off a cliff in a suicide attempt, that resulted in her inability to work. On the night of the murder, the victim came home drunk, argued with Zhang, and threatened to murder her older brother. When he fell asleep, she gathered tools to use as murder weapons. As in most murder cases I studied, she used common household items. First she hit the victim on the head with a scale weight, a hammer, and a wrench. His cause of death was severe open head trauma. She then stabbed him over 40 times in the chest and abdominal areas. Finally, when she thought about the times he raped her, she cut off his external reproductive organs before calling the police to turn herself in. In her expert testimony to the court, Chen Min explained:

> Owing both to differences in physical strength and to psychological terror, victims often wait until offenders are unprepared, such as when they are asleep, drunk, or otherwise physically incapacitated. They may poison offenders or attack them with clubs, rods, or knives. When a victim attacks an offender, she wants to make sure he is dead in order to prevent him from murdering her in revenge. ... Some (former) victims will dispose of parts of (former) offenders' corpses by cutting off organs

[30] Case ID (2016)浙0281刑初169号, archived at https://perma.cc/L4CS-KYHR.

that caused victims to feel particularly fearful. Cutting off a reproductive organ represents the victim's experience of sexual violence. The victim sees the dead offender's reproductive organ as a source of her suffering and a symbol of her pain and humiliation.

Although the court rejected the defense lawyer's argument for probation, it showed leniency by giving Zhang a mitigated prison sentence of eight years in consideration of her cooperation, remorse, and lack of risk to society. Also playing a role in the court's lenient sentence was the forgiveness letter furnished by her parents-in-law after Zhang said she was unable to pay compensation. The court nonetheless ordered Zhang to compensate her parents-in-law ¥40,000 (Chuxiong Yi Autonomous Prefecture Intermediate People's Court, Yunnan Province, May 6, 2016; also cited in Liu and Shi 2016).[31]

> Supplementary case examples set #9–7 is online at: https:// decoupling-book.org/.

Over time, and particularly since 2015, criminal courts – in sharp contrast to divorce courts – in China have taken an increasingly empathetic, compassionate, and merciful stance toward female victims of domestic violence, albeit falling short of acquittal. This trend is partly a function of new laws and legal guidelines reviewed in this section, as well as a function of China's more general "kill fewer, kill cautiously" shift away from capital punishment in criminal sentencing that began in the mid-2000s (Miao 2013; Trevaskes 2008, 2010). Finally, as we will see next, it is to some degree a function of courts' mandate to maintain social stability.

LENIENCY IN CRIMINAL DOMESTIC VIOLENCE CASES

We have seen that courts, in their written decisions, indicated that they extended leniency to defendants who surrendered to the police, gave full confessions, cooperated throughout the investigation, displayed sincere remorse, and so on. Most of these conditions for leniency are written into the Criminal Law's provisions on sentencing (e.g., Articles 62, 63, 67, and 78). We have also seen that courts

---

[31] Case ID (2015)楚中刑初字第114号, archived at https://perma.cc/UUV5-X4B9.

sometimes – but far from consistently – affirmed justifiable self-defense as the basis for leniency.

In the homicide case of Yao Shuangxia, the court attributed its lenient sentence to the following: the crime occurred at home, the victim bore fault for triggering the crime, Yao was a first-time offender, she reported the crime on her own accord, she surrendered to the police, and she confessed to her crime. Yao described the events culminating in her murder of her husband.

> After getting married in 1997, Xi X [her husband] often beat me. I was afraid my family would be angry so I never told them. Beginning in 2003, I heard gossip at the factory about a female co-worker named Li X who regularly visited my home. I was afraid to ask [my husband] about this. At the end of 2003 I went to my mother-in-law's home to give birth to my daughter. When I returned to work in 2004, Li X was living in my home [with my husband], and stayed there until 2006. In 2007, I moved back into my home. At this point Xi X had an alcohol addiction. He drank daily. Each day he drank at least six or seven bottles of beer. He would also finish a bottle of liquor in three days. Whenever he drank he beat me. On Chinese New Year's Eve in 2012 we returned to [Xi X's parents' home in] Beihou [Village] for the Spring Festival. That night my daughter asked if she could sleep with me, and I agreed. Xi X, our daughter, and I all shared a bed. Xi X, probably unhappy about this, got me up in the middle of the night to make him a bowl of noodles. When I served him his noodles, he said I did a bad job making them. He then held me against the floor and beat me. My crying woke up our daughter. When I saw my daughter had woken up, I stopped crying. After I carried her to my mother-in-law, I went to the storage room and grabbed a bottle of pesticide to kill myself. However, since there wasn't enough left in the bottle to kill me, and drinking it without killing myself would only cause trouble for my family, I didn't drink it. ... On the night of the first day of the New Year, I slept on the sofa in the living room. Xi X insisted I sleep in the bedroom, and dragged me by my feet into the bedroom and kicked and beat me for a while. My in-laws heard the abuse and separated us. The next day I returned to my natal home. On the fifth day of the New Year, Xi X came to retrieve me. Not wanting to anger my mother, I went home with Xi X. At 8 pm on February 28, 2013, I went to the factory with Xi X to start my shift. At around 10 pm, Xi X found me and asked me to get him a bottle of beer. I took one out of the work cabinet for him. After he finished drinking it, he asked for another. As I reached to hand him another bottle, it slipped out of my hand and shattered on the floor, immediately triggering Xi X's abuse. After he finished drinking another bottle of beer, he told me to go home

with him. At the time, the factory gate was already locked. Xi X called someone to open the gate and we left. When we returned home he wanted more beer. He opened a bottle and poured it into a teapot. Then he wanted liquor. He poured himself half a cup. As the two of us lay on the bed, he drank beer and liquor. After drinking, he beat me for a while and made me pour him more to drink. Xi X drank and read in bed while I poured his drinks. When I tried to sleep, Xi X hit me in the face, causing my face to swell up. In between beatings, he used a cigarette lighter to burn my face. This continued until 9 am, when Xi X wanted to have sex with me again. When he was done, I used toilet paper to wipe him. Xi X continued to read on his cell phone. I poured him more beer. Xi X continued to drink and read until about 11 am. After drinking a total of four bottles of beer and about 100–200 ml of liquor, he fell asleep. I got out of bed and got dressed. As I sat on the sofa in the living room and looked at Xi X, I felt increasingly angry. As I thought about how Xi X drank and beat me every day, and how impossible life had become, I wanted to choke Xi X and then die together with him. I found a black cell phone charging cable. After adjusting Xi X's head, I wrapped the cable around the back of his neck, crossed both ends of the cable over each other in front of his neck, and pulled with both hands as hard as I could. Then the cable snapped. Xi X opened his eyes, glared at me, and reached out for my hair. I squeezed his neck with my bare hands while I straddled his body. One of Xi X's hands remained under the blanket, and the other hand flailed in the direction of my hands. I clutched his neck with all my might and did not release my grip. After a while Xi X stopped moving, and I released my hands. When I got up I noticed a foul smell. I lifted up the blanket and saw a big wet spot. Xi X had defecated in his underpants. Because his body was still warm, and I was afraid he would wake up and discover feces in his underpants, I removed his striped underpants, used toilet paper to wipe off the feces, and put on a pair of brown underpants. I also dressed him in thermal underpants and a thermal undershirt. I removed the soiled blanket and covered him with a smaller one. I put his dirty underpants and dirty toilet paper in a red plastic bag and threw it in the outside trash. When I returned home I expected Xi X to wake up, but his body became colder and colder. I started to think he was dead. I didn't know what to do. I called my father's sister, who told me to stay at the scene and call the police. I then called my son's school and asked his teacher to tell my son to contact my father's sister after school. After that I called the police to turn myself in.

Forensic evidence such as the victim's elevated blood alcohol level and semen collected from Yao's body corroborated her testimony.

Moreover, several witnesses, including relatives and co-workers, cor-roborated Yao's allegations of her husband's domestic violence, infi-delity, and alcohol abuse. Her mother also testified that, following the Spring Festival incident, Yao wanted a divorce, but that family members had intervened. Although the court did not affirm justifi-able self-defense, it came close by affirming that "unbearable domestic violence and psychological torture inflicted by the victim caused the defendant to murder him." Likewise, although the court rejected the defense lawyer's argument that the circumstances of her crime were "relatively minor," it accepted the argument that the murder victim was at grave fault. For these reasons, and in light of the defendant's cooperation, the court sentenced the defendant to eight years in prison. Because it was only a tiny fraction of the ¥821,359 her in-laws requested in the civil lawsuit they attached to the criminal prosecu-tion, the court's order that Yao compensate them ¥17,115 for funeral expenses was probably at most only a marginal factor in the leniency of her sentence (Decision #1059225, Zhengzhou Municipal Intermediate People's Court, Henan Province, November 8, 2013).[32]

Beyond this specific case, however, compensation for civil damages plays an important role in criminal sentencing. Since the mid-2000s, the SPC has promoted criminal reconciliation as part of China's broader stability maintenance agenda. The theory behind what has been dubbed "blood money" (Ng and He 2017b) and "cash for clem-ency" (Trevaskes 2015) is that the criminal offender's payment of com-pensation to the victim's family can nip two potential sources of social unrest in the bud. In exchange for compensation, the victim's fam-ily makes a formal expression of forgiveness and the court spares the offender's life. Criminal reconciliation practices were thus designed to placate the anger of the *victim's* family members with compensa-tion and thus to reduce the likelihood they will protest or petition in response to what they perceive as an unjust ruling not to execute the offender. By the same token, by preempting the anger of the *offender's* family that might otherwise be caused by a death sentence, leniency serves to reduce the likelihood the other side will protest or petition the court decision (Liebman 2015:214–15). Compensation is some-times ordered by courts in their rulings on petitions for civil damages attached to criminal cases (刑事附带民事诉讼) – what McConville et al. (2011) call "incidental civil action" in criminal litigation. Courts

---

[32] Case ID (2013)郑刑一初字第41号, archived at https://perma.cc/FS22-4YRK.

also recognize compensation agreements reached privately or through mediation outside the court system.

Criminal reconciliation has been formalized through "standard cases" (典型案例) issued by the SPC as models to establish best practices in criminal sentencing (Trevaskes 2015). Beyond standard cases, the 2010 Provisional Guiding Opinions of the SPC on Criminal Sentencing (which in 2017 became the Guiding Opinions of the SPC on Sentencing for Common Crimes) stipulates that compensating the victim's economic losses can mitigate prison sentences by up 30% (Article 9) and that forgiveness from the victim or the victim's family can mitigate prison sentences by up to 20% (Article 10; Xing 2013:27). The payment of compensation from the offender or the offender's immediate family in exchange for both forgiveness from the victim's family and sentencing leniency from the court has become an institutionalized practice in China's criminal courts (Liebman 2015:180–85). Criminal reconciliation has even become part of judicial performance evaluation systems (Yanhong Wang 2013:33). According to one study, victims' families submitted "forgiveness letters" (谅解书) to the court in 80% of cases of women who murdered their husbands. Some of these letters were jointly signed by local residents (Li and Jia 2019:64, 67). In some cases, the parents of murder victims kneeled in front of the judges begging for leniency (Xing 2013:27).

In my samples of homicide cases involving spouses, women's sentences were far more lenient than men's. Whereas 13% of men convicted of murder received death sentences (most of which were suspended), not a single woman was sentenced to death. Likewise, 55% of male defendants and 39% of female defendants received life sentences. Finally, the remaining 32% of men and 61% of women received prison sentences ranging from two to 15 years. Among defendants who received fixed-term prison sentences, women (19%) were three times more likely than men (6%) to receive mitigated sentences of less than ten years for the "relatively minor circumstances" of their cases (according to Article 232 of the Criminal Law). Female and male defendants in the criminal domestic violence cases in my samples were almost equally likely to receive forgiveness (41% and 39%, respectively). Sentencing disparities between women and men therefore cannot be attributed to differences in the likelihood of receiving forgiveness. Courts' greater leniency toward female defendants seems to have more to do with judges' greater likelihood of finding them to be more cooperative, their risk to society to be smaller, the criminal circumstances of their cases to be less serious, and their criminal acts more likely to constitute justifiable self-defense.

Forgiveness was associated with leniency for both female and male defendants. However, forgiveness in the absence of compensation was relatively rare for male defendants. Men convicted of murder tended to buy forgiveness from their victims' families and thus to buy leniency from courts. Perhaps because they had greater financial wherewithal to pay compensation, men were twice as likely as women to compensate their victims' families (35% and 18%, respectively). Among male defendants, 76% received forgiveness when they provided compensation compared to only 19% when they did not. Women's lower incidence of paying compensation, however, did not reduce their likelihood of receiving forgiveness. Indeed, in contrast to male defendants who tended to receive forgiveness in exchange for compensation, female defendants tended to receive forgiveness without compensation.

Some husbands who murdered or attempted to murder their wives were given remarkably lenient sentences after paying compensation. A man in the city of Wenzhou named Yu Qing made a murder-suicide plan after his wife insisted on a divorce despite his numerous efforts to talk her out of it. After his final effort failed, he choked her to death before slitting his own throat and wrists. His suicide attempt failed when he was discovered and rushed to the hospital. In court, Yu's defense lawyer argued for leniency on the basis of reasonable suspicion that his wife was having an affair and therefore bore a certain responsibility for her own murder. He further argued that the character of maliciousness in murders like this one is inherently different from that in ordinary murders and that the reason he chose to murder her and kill himself was because "he loved her too much." In consideration of the victim's family's expression of forgiveness in exchange for ¥170,000 in compensation, the court gave him a lenient prison sentence of 15 years (Decision #4848656, Wenzhou Municipal Intermediate People's Court, Zhejiang Province, September 28, 2016).[33]

Supplementary case examples set #9–8 is online at: https://decoupling-book.org/.

---

[33] Case ID (2016)浙03刑初73号, archived at https://perma.cc/U4YL-2JXG.

Some women also compensated their victims' families. Wu Jinrong had been subjected to over a decade of marital violence in her second marriage. On one occasion, her husband beat her so hard she permanently lost hearing in one ear. According to the court, "on a regular basis, after getting drunk, he physically injured her, insulted her dignity, psychologically threatened her, smashed and burned household objects, and committed other forms of domestic violence." One night, after coming home drunk, he entered her daughter-in-law's bedroom (the wife of the son from her first marriage) and smacked her grandson until he woke up. After her daughter-in-law protested, he began to break objects in the living room and, wielding a cleaver, threatened to harm family members. The defendant, recalling many similar incidents, killed him by bludgeoning his head with a hoe and a shovel. Both village authorities and the court initiated mediation between the defendant and the victim's family. In exchange for financial compensation of ¥50,000 and a minivan, the victim's family expressed its forgiveness. Although the court rejected the defense lawyers' request for probation, it showed leniency by giving her a mitigated prison sentence of five years (Decision #821646, Nanyang Municipal Wancheng District People's Court, Henan Province, July 3, 2012).[34]

Cases like this, however, are unusual. Relatively few women who killed their husbands provided compensation, and the payment of compensation had little effect on their sentences. Women who killed their husbands were far more likely than their male counterparts to receive forgiveness without compensation. Victims' families and the public were naturally inclined to extend their empathy, sympathy, and forgiveness to women who murdered their abusers. By contrast, forgiveness of men who murdered their wives tended to be financially induced.

The case of Xue Aihua exemplifies one of the hallmarks of abusive men: "pathological jealousy" that is "a cornerstone to homicidal rage" (Walker 2017:307). Xue murdered her husband by chopping his face, head, and neck with an axe, resulting in hemorrhagic shock from a ruptured jugular vein. Owing to his chronic abuse, Xue had previously divorced him, after which – under the husband's coercion – they remarried. She had started working at a cotton mill with the help of her sister-in-law, who also worked there. Prior to this she stayed mostly at home doing farm work. Her husband, owing to his jealousy, was in

---

[34] Case ID (2012)南宛刑初字第90号, archived at https://perma.cc/FE74-TELX.

the habit of checking in on her at work. She stated in her testimony to the court that, on the day before the murder, he

> went to the factory and beat me because he didn't trust me and suspected I was sleeping with my male colleagues ... . So he hit me, choked me, and, holding me against a machine, punched my head, face, and mouth, giving me a fat lip. That night when I was eating dinner he made me call his sister to ask her to submit my resignation for me. Before I had a chance to say more than a few words he started cursing me, saying that a woman like me only brought shame and that he wanted to murder my whole family. When my sister-in-law overheard this she asked me to pass the phone to him, and they then argued over the phone. I went to bed. When he entered the bedroom he demanded that I tell him about my attempts to seduce men, and that if I refused he would use gasoline to burn me to death and torture me to death. When he finished ranting, he tugged me by my hair and punched my head with his fist. My husband often beat me. Recently the beatings increased in frequency. He threatened to torture me to death, to use gasoline to burn me to death, and to bury me alive.[35] It made me angry, but I was also very afraid he would harm me. Because I was previously married to someone else, he was repulsed by the fact that I wasn't a virgin when he married me, and frequently suspected I was messing around with other men. ... Sometimes when I spent a long time buying groceries he'd say, "that took a while, did you get together with so-and-so?" Sometimes when I worked late he'd say, "did you turn off the machine and run somewhere to get together with so-and-so?" When the bank account was off by ¥500–600, he would say I spent the money on hotel rooms with men. He wouldn't let me wear a bra. After he said bras were to seduce men, he beat me. He wouldn't let me speak to other men. He wouldn't let me comb my hair or brush my teeth because he said they were to seduce men. If I wanted to buy clothes I needed his approval. He wouldn't let me buy clothes with flowers because he said they were to seduce men. He wouldn't let me

---

[35] Lhamo (拉姆), a popular live streamer from an ethnically Tibetan county in Sichuan Province, was burned to death by her ex-husband in 2020. Like Xue Aihua, Lhamo had remarried her abusive husband under duress. She originally divorced him in the Civil Affairs Administration after he choked her and beat her with a wooden bench, breaking her arm. After the divorce, she returned to her natal home to recuperate. Soon afterward, her ex-husband showed up to express his remorse and beg her to remarry him. When she refused, he put a knife to the neck of one of their two children before taking both of their children to the river and threatening to jump unless she remarried him. After they remarried, he continued to beat her. Though she sought police help on numerous occasions, the police failed to intervene. She turned to the local branch of the All-China Women's Federation, which was similarly unhelpful. When she divorced her husband for the second time, this time in court, the court granted custody of both children to her husband even though he had continuously threatened to murder the children unless she returned to him (BBC 2020; Chen 2020; Hou 2020). As we will see in Chapter 10, courts routinely grant child custody to wife-beaters.

grow my hair long because he said it was to seduce men. Whenever I cut my hair he would say I was commemorating another man. He often told me, "I don't see anything good about you, I see only flaws; how unfortunate I was to find someone like you."[36]

Xue's ten-year-old son, mother, sister-in-law, husband's nephew, and brother-in-law all corroborated her testimony and vouched for her good character. Her oldest daughter testified that her father

> had a suspicious heart and frequently suspected she [Xue] was involved with other men. If she exchanged words with a man by the front door, he would hurl curses at her out of suspicion. A few years ago she started working at a factory that is only 100 meters from our house. She got off work at 8:00, and if she were to return home at 8:30 he would demand to know what she had done in the intervening half an hour.

Xue's testimony about the murder itself was as follows:

> At around 6:40 am, I got up to make breakfast. He was still lying in bed with our son. When I thought about his suspicion, his physical abuse, and his anger over all these years, I got the idea of hacking him to death with an axe. I first turned off the main power switch to the house. I then took out the axe from the black suitcase in the east room and walked next to the bed on which they lay. He saw me standing next to him and, thinking there was a power failure, handed me a flashlight. I took the flashlight with one hand. When he started glaring at me, I suddenly filled with anger, lifted up the axe, and aimed for his head. He reached out to hit me. I lifted the axe and chopped a few more times. As I hacked him with the axe, I asked, "Are you going to hit me? Get up and hit me! All these years I never once wronged you, and all you did was beat me … ." My son then pulled me away and took the axe. I saw he [the victim] was bleeding out, and heard the sound of blood dripping onto the floor. When I saw he was motionless and believed he was dead, I took my son out of the bedroom and into the kitchen, where I called my sister-in-law to tell her I hacked her brother to death. I asked her to come look after the boy so I could turn myself in to the police.

In her testimony, the sister-in-law recounted the defendant's answer to her question of why she hacked him to death. She said she only wanted

---

[36] According to Walker, "Based on our data, this jealousy is most often unfounded; the abused women in our research were not that interested in another sexual relationship. However, the batterers' need to control their women leads them to be suspicious and intrusive" (Walker 2017:307). Walker reports that an escalation of violence over time is also a predictor of homicide carried out by one side against the other (Walker 2017:308).

to hack his eyes so he could no longer beat her, but once she started hacking, she lost control of herself.

In its holding, the court cited provisions in the 2015 Opinions on mitigating circumstances and justifiable self-defense in intentional homicide. Also citing the victim's family's forgiveness and request for leniency as well as Xue's remorse, the court sentenced her to five years in prison (Decision #1401817, Xinye County People's Court, Henan Province, April 24, 2015).[37] This is the only court decision in my Henan sample that cites the 2015 Opinions. My Zhejiang sample likewise contains only one decision that cites the 2015 Opinions. Indeed, according to a keyword search on China Judgements Online, the 2015 Opinions have been cited in fewer than 100 court decisions (as of June 2020). Perhaps because the contents of the 2015 Opinions are largely derivative of other bodies of law, judges and lawyers have chosen to cite the original sources of their contents. Or perhaps judges and lawyers apply its provisions without citing it by name.

Abused women sometimes fear divorce owing to their economic dependence on their abusers (Cheng and Gao 2019:12; Zheng 2015:176), that is, owing to the economic control of their abusers. Over the years, Yao Rongxiang's philandering husband had doused her with scalding water, hit her head against the floor, hit her with a steel pipe, and hit her with a beer bottle. One night he announced his decision to divorce her and split custody of their four children. In despair at the prospect of having no means to raise her children, Yao concluded that she no longer had a reason to live. She waited until he was sound asleep before bludgeoning his head with a threaded steel pipe and then cutting his neck with a cleaver. He died on the scene from a craniocerebral injury and massive blood loss. Yao stated that her original plan was to commit suicide, but, after thinking about her children, she decided instead to surrender to the police. In their testimony to the court, the victim's parents expressed their forgiveness, requested a lenient sentence, and withdrew their original request for civil damages. In her expert testimony to the court, Chen Min stated:

> At its core, domestic violence is control. Violence itself is not the end but rather a means of achieving control over the victim. Even when the offender forces the victim to divorce, he is doing so to control the victim, to make the victim obey him. Victims who can no longer

---

[37] Case ID (2015)新刑初字第00117号, archived at https://perma.cc/5UL7-JGJP. This case was reported in the media (Zhao 2015).

endure chronic domestic violence often commit suicide or murder the offenders. In order to avoid aggravated attacks, female victims will use extreme methods to kill offenders when offenders have temporarily lost their ability to fight back. Female victims who inflict harm ordinarily direct such behavior against offenders. After offenders die, the female victims who killed them pose no risk of harm to anyone else.

In the only decision in my Zhejiang sample to cite the 2015 Opinions, the court sentenced the defendant to five years in prison (Decision #3431222, Wenzhou Municipal Intermediate People's Court, Zhejiang Province, March 5, 2015; also cited in Chen and Yang [2016:21]).[38]

In addition to illuminating the influence of forgiveness on sentencing, this final example also foreshadows a finding I present in Chapter 10. When couples with minor children do get divorced, siblinged children tend to be split between their parents, often according to arrangements determined by the father.

SUMMARY AND CONCLUSIONS

As we know, a failed initial divorce petition granted on a subsequent attempt is the divorce twofer's primary defining characteristic. Insofar as almost everyone who seeks a divorce can eventually get one, some observers might wonder what the harm is in waiting. Perhaps, skeptics might contend, the primary harm is merely inconvenience, which might be more than offset by the benefits some couples enjoy by reconciling after an adjudicated denial.

This book documents the manifold harms of the divorce twofer. If the divorce twofer provides any benefits, they are monopolized by judges in the form of gains to their work efficiency and performance evaluation scores (Chapters 3, 5, and 6). From the standpoint of families, the social and personal harms of the divorce twofer clearly outweigh their benefits. We have seen that a lot of adjudicated denials never return to court (Chapter 6). Perhaps divorce-seekers let down by courts ended up pursuing mutual-consent "divorces by agreement" in the Civil Affairs Administration. Given that abusers, simply by withholding their consent, could activate the divorce twofer in court (Chapters 8 and 9) and prevent Civil Affairs divorces outside the court

---

[38] Case ID (2015)浙温刑初字第4号, archived at https://perma.cc/BAE2-BWWR. This case also received media attention (Yao 2015; Zou 2015).

system, women desperate to divorce grievously sacrificed property and child custody in exchange for their husband's consent (Li 2022). We will see the prevalence of precisely this trade-off in the context of child custody determinations in Chapter 10. Unable to make the financial sacrifices their husbands demand and unwilling to give up custody of their children, some women resigned themselves to staying married.

This chapter documents the mortal harms associated with the divorce twofer: its grave physical security and public health implications. An official justification for the divorce twofer is that it introduces a de facto cooling-off period designed to de-escalate conflicts (Chapter 3). Among battered women who eventually obtained an adjudicated divorce, the divorce twofer typically protracted their exposure to domestic violence by one year or more. Indeed, domestic violence often intensified between divorce attempts. Delays caused by the divorce twofer have swelled the ranks of marital violence refugees who take flight from their abusive husbands. After participating in labor migration, often as an escape route from domestic violence, some women resign themselves to remaining married but separated owing to the logistical difficulties of returning to their residential court jurisdictions to file for divorce and participate in trial proceedings (K. Li 2015a:98). The divorce twofer thus puts many women in a sort of divorce purgatory.

This is primarily a rural story. Divorce petitions were concentrated in rural courts. Likewise, the gender gaps in delays to divorce were limited to rural courts. Finally, most of the case examples in this chapter are from rural areas.

Among women who did not or could not take flight, delays caused by the divorce twofer may have done more to prolong and intensify marital abuse than to cool it off. As a consequence, some women unable to take flight may have felt compelled to fight. Judges were delusional if they truly believed they were saving marriages by denying divorces. They professed concern that *granting* divorces to battered plaintiffs would generate instability and even murders. Even if their concerns were partially valid, the opposite was undoubtedly equally or more valid: *denying* divorces to abuse victims generated murders and suicides, the very essence of instability. Judges more faithfully fulfilled their *ideological* mandate to rescue marriages by denying divorces than their *legal* mandate to rescue abuse victims by granting divorces.

Granting divorces the first time would certainly save lives. To be sure, we cannot blame the divorce twofer for all incidents of violence that follow in the wake of adjudicated denials of divorce petitions. After all, men also beat and kill their ex-wives. Public authorities, however, are undoubtedly less reluctant to intervene in violent incidents between two people who are not married to each other. If an abuser were no longer married to his victim, public authorities would have even flimsier excuses for not intervening. If police were as willing to arrest and punish wife-beaters as they were to arrest and punish drunk drivers, the likely consequence would be fewer men killing their wives and fewer women killing their husbands.

Policies and practices that prevent divorces have done less to create harmonious families than to prolong marital misery and violence. Recall from Chapter 2 that one impetus for the introduction of the breakdownism standard in the 1980 Marriage Law was to prevent homicides that might otherwise result from forcibly preserving acrimonious marriages. By turning the breakdownism standard on its head and using it to deny divorce petitions, courts have transformed civil cases into criminal cases in a way the original drafters of the breakdownism standard feared. Recall also from Chapter 3 that Chinese government leaders have justified the divorce twofer by invoking a widespread claim that divorce contributes to juvenile crime. If juvenile crime is driven as much by marital *conflict* as by marital *dissolution* (Amato 2000; Amato and Cheadle 2008), then China's judicial clampdown on divorce, by forcibly preserving unhappy marriages, may contribute more than divorce itself to juvenile crime, another source of criminal cases.

A considerable number of eminently preventable criminal cases have stemmed from the poor outcomes of women's prior help-seeking efforts. Women are at risk of *sustaining* harm when they seek to divorce their abusive husbands. Women are also at risk of *inflicting* harm on their abusers when their help-seeking efforts are stymied. In trials of women charged with killing their abusive husbands, criminal courts have steadfastly eschewed the concept of battered woman syndrome, and have therefore been averse to acquit – or even to sentence to probation in lieu of prison time – the very women they affirmed to be victims of domestic violence. Nonetheless, I have shown in this chapter that China's criminal courts have taken domestic violence increasingly seriously, particularly beginning in 2015. Indeed, domestic violence appears to be taken far more seriously in criminal courts than in divorce courts. China's criminal courts experienced a watershed in 2015, when they started more fully and consistently recognizing domestic violence as a mitigating factor in murder trials of women who killed their husbands. China's divorce courts experienced no corresponding watershed. On the contrary, China's judicial clampdown on divorce intensified after 2015 (Chapter 6).

When women take flight to escape their abusive husbands, they often have little choice but to leave their children at home. As we will see next, judges tend to grant custody to the parent with physical possession of the child even when the child's living arrangement is the direct consequence of domestic violence.

CHAPTER TEN

POSSESSION IS NINE-TENTHS OF THE LAW
Why Wife-Beaters Gain Child Custody

In 2013, a female plaintiff filed her third divorce petition with a basic-level court in Henan. She had withdrawn her first petition in 2011, and the court denied her second petition in 2012. She claimed that only after getting married did she discover her husband's dark side and violent temper. She stated that her husband treated her and their young daughter as his "punching bags" (出气筒) and that she had tried many times, to no avail, to persuade him to change his ways. She also claimed to have called the police on numerous occasions about his abuse. She added that the defendant had even severely beaten their daughter when she was only nine or ten years old, and when she intervened he beat her "black and blue" (打得遍体鳞伤) too, after which husband and wife spent most of their time apart. The defendant denied the allegations and expressed unwillingness to divorce. Moreover, he said, their daughter had always been living with him under his and his parents' care. Without investigating the plaintiff's domestic violence allegations, the court granted custody to the defendant according to the principle of protecting the rights and interests of children. In its holding, the court explained that their daughter had always been in the physical possession of her father and paternal grandparents. According to the court, because their daughter was accustomed to her environment, preserving the current situation would be in her best interests (Decision #1160567, Luoyang Municipal Jianxi District People's Court, Henan Province, December 9, 2013).[1]

---

[1] Case ID (2013)涧民四初字第225号, archived at https://perma.cc/UDY6-VNH4.

As nonsensical – and even as perverse – as it appears both on its face and vis-à-vis the "best interests of the child" principle cited by the court, rulings such as this are utterly typical in China's rural courts. Although China's family laws were designed to protect women and children, and to weaken if not eradicate the patriarchal family, courts in practice have done more to serve than to challenge rural China's patriarchal order (Li 2022). Courts supported patriarchal prerogatives by ignoring women's domestic violence allegations and by granting child custody to the parent with physical possession of the child. Paradoxically, domestic violence *reduced* victims' chances of winning child custody.

Among the reasons is simply that children in rural areas overwhelmingly live with their fathers or their paternal grandparents. In one common scenario, they live with one or both parents in or near their paternal grandparents' home. In a second common scenario, they are among China's more than 60 million "left-behind children" who tend to live in villages with their paternal grandparents while their parents participate in labor migration. In a third common scenario explored in Chapter 9, their mothers fled (or were pushed out by) abusive husbands and reluctantly left their children behind, becoming what I have termed "domestic violence refugees." In a fourth scenario, children were "snatched" away by their fathers. Because judges tend to apply a physical possession standard in their child custody determinations, fathers in all four scenarios enjoy an enormous advantage. Judges' child custody orders are thus entirely consistent with the adage, "Possession is nine-tenths of the law." On that basis they routinely grant child custody to fathers who, according to relevant laws and official guidelines, have no business raising them.

As in custody determination proceedings elsewhere in the world, where courts engage in "secondary victimization of abused mothers" (Rivera, Sullivan, and Zeoli 2012) and where women suffer additional "institutional abuse at the hands of the family court" (Bemiller 2008), abused women in China who left their husbands were further victimized by courts when they were denied custody of their children. Courts in China and elsewhere undermine women's rights by discounting the credibility of their allegations and their moral worthiness of justice and due process (Epstein and Goodman 2019). I demonstrate in this chapter that, beyond these reasons common to different contexts, Chinese judicial decision-making is further shaped by patriarchal practices and beliefs, most notably patrilocality and patrilineality, which remain pervasive in rural areas, and by heavy caseloads that incentivize judges to follow the most expeditious path.

Child custody spans two chapters. I first illustrate key themes that emerged from my qualitative analysis of selected examples before presenting quantitative patterns of child custody determinations in my full collection of court decisions.

LAWS ON THE BOOKS CONCERNING CHILD CUSTODY

China's ratification in 1992 of the United Nations International Convention on the Rights of the Child affirmed its domestic legal commitments to the protection of children against violence already enshrined in the Constitution; the Law on Protecting the Rights and Interests of Women, also known as the Law on Protecting Women and Children; the Law on Protecting Minors; the Criminal Law; and the General Principles of the Civil Law (R. Zhang 2017:50; also see Chapter 2). While none of these bodies of law explicitly addresses child custody, they and the Marriage Law do contain provisions on violence against women and children that can nonetheless be used in child custody determinations (Su 2018:54; R. Zhang 2017:50). Likewise, the 2015 Anti-Domestic Violence Law is silent on child custody per se, but can – and should – support judges' consideration of domestic violence as a factor determining the best interests of the child (D'Attoma 2019).

The 2008 Guidelines (see Chapter 2), by explicitly stipulating that domestic violence offenders are unfit to serve as custodial parents (Article 63; Liu 2013:79n1), are consistent with global best practices of treating spousal abuse and child abuse as part of a common syndrome that puts children's personal safety at risk (Jeffries 2016). They also itemize the numerous harms to children caused by exposure to domestic violence, such as difficulty focusing, diminished academic achievement, truancy, weakened self-esteem, distrust of others, use of violence to solve problems, and so on (Article 13; R. Zhang 2017:49). By doing so they are consistent with the current scholarly consensus on the harms to children of directly witnessing or indirect exposure to domestic violence (Jeffries 2016; Y. Jiang 2019:19; Walker 2017: 155–56; R. Zhang 2017:48).

Notwithstanding China's embrace of relevant global legal norms on paper, judges tend to turn elsewhere for justification of their child custody orders. Legal standards concerning the determination of child custody come primarily from the SPC's 1993 Several Concrete Opinions Concerning Handling Child Custody Matters in Divorce Trials (hereafter "the 1993 Opinions") and the 2001 Marriage Law. According to the 1993 Opinions, courts, when determining child custody, should "proceed from the position of the best interests of children's physical and mental health and the protection of their lawful rights and interests in conjunction with a consideration of the concrete circumstances of parents' abilities and means to raise children" (Preamble). The most salient provisions in the 1993 Opinions include: (1) custody of children less than two years old should be granted to mothers, with exceptions for illness and other circumstances that privilege fathers (Article 1, the "infant standard");[2] (2) the means to support children in terms of financial security, housing, time, and so on (Preamble, the "financial means standard"); (3) parents with serious chronic infectious diseases or other serious illnesses should not be granted child custody (Article 3, Item 4, the "illness standard"); (4) when the custody of a child who is at least ten years old is contested, the opinions of that child should be considered (Article 5, the "child's opinion standard"); and, most importantly, (5) custody should be granted to the parent with whom the child has been living for a relatively long period of time when a change in the environment would be of obvious harm to the child (Article 3, Item 2, the "physical possession standard"). The only provision in the Marriage Law specifically pertaining to child custody is consistent with the "infant standard" in the 1993 Opinions: custody of nursing babies should be granted to mothers (Article 36). It also stipulates that parents who are not granted custody enjoy visitation rights (探望权, Article 38). Joint legal custody (协议轮流抚养) is a possibility provided by the 1993 Opinions (Article 6), but only if both sides can come to an agreement on relevant terms and if the court agrees that it serves the interests of the child.

Nowhere in the 1993 Opinions or 2001 Marriage Law is a "domestic violence standard." Nonetheless, as previously mentioned, with the strong support of other laws and official guidelines, judges can and should consider domestic violence as a factor in the assessment of a child's health and safety – the very crux of the child's best interests

---

[2] What I call the "infant standard" is generally known in Europe and the United States as the "tender years doctrine" (Artis 2004).

(R. Zhang 2017:49–52). Owing to multiple and conflicting standards for determining "best interests," however, judges enjoy enormous latitude on which standard to apply (Su 2018:54; R. Zhang 2017:50). When a father who perpetrated domestic violence has physical possession of a child, does his established history of violence trump the "current situation" in the determination of the child's best interests and thus tilt the balance in favor of the mother? How do judges treat litigants whom they deem to have failed the "illness standard" owing to a serious injury or mental illness caused by domestic violence? Similarly, how do judges treat litigants whom they deem to have failed the "financial means standard" as a consequence of giving up stable work and housing in order to escape domestic violence? The 2008 Guidelines explicitly address scenarios such as these, and call on judges to privilege the safety of children by granting custody to victims even if their life situation is somewhat financially precarious. For example, they stipulate that judges, when assessing parents' financial means to raise their children, should consider victims' *potential* abilities as well as victims' abilities *prior* to marriage or *prior* to the abuse (Article 64).

As we will see, however, judges generally ignore the 2008 Guidelines because they are for reference purposes and cannot be used as the legal basis of court rulings (Y. Jiang 2019:20). Judges instead tend to apply the "physical possession standard" when they award child custody to fathers who, on the basis of other circumstances, including domestic violence, should be disqualified from serving as legal custodians on the basis of competing legal standards.

According to the 1993 Opinions, parents who are not granted child support and who have stable income should make child support payments in the amount of 20–30% of monthly gross income (Article 7). When the plaintiff is awarded child custody, the defendant's whereabouts are unknown, and the defendant's income is unknown, child support payments are calculated as 20–30% of the average annual income for the local area (divided by 12 to arrive at a monthly payment) (Dong and Ji 2016:92–93). In practice, courts often use 25% – the midpoint of this range – as the income divisor, and sometimes order annual payments (monthly payments multiplied by 12) or even one-time lump sum payments (monthly payments multiplied by the number of months until the child turns 18). I do not analyze child support orders in this book.

WHAT WE KNOW ABOUT THE LAW IN ACTION CONCERNING CHILD CUSTODY

From the limited empirical research on differences between mothers and fathers in the likelihood of receiving child custody rights, we can piece together a blurry picture of fathers' advantage in rural areas and mothers' advantage in urban areas. A study of 114 child custody decisions from courts of all types across China reveals fathers' overall advantage (Y. Jiang 2019:19). In another study of 512 child custody decisions made by three basic-level courts in Hainan Province – two rural and one urban – judges were far more likely to grant child custody to fathers (Hu 2016; Hu and Shen 2016). A similarly stark paternal advantage emerges from an analysis of 281 child custody decisions made by a basic-level county court in rural Chongqing (Chen and Zhang 2015). In contrast, a study of courts in more developed urban areas appears to tell the opposite story. According to findings from an analysis of 405 child custody decisions from courts in five cities in southern Jiangsu Province, one of the most prosperous parts of China, mothers enjoyed a considerable advantage (Zhao 2019). This picture of a contrast between rural and urban courts, however, is muddied by an anomalous study of 182 child custody decisions made by three rural basic-level courts in Jilin Province. Here mothers enjoyed an overwhelming advantage, which the authors attribute to mothers' greater inclination to petition for child custody (Hongxiang Li 2014; Li, Wang, and Zheng 2016). The findings I present later in Chapter 11 from a collection of child custody decisions several dozen orders of magnitude larger than these small samples – and from hundreds rather than only one or a few courts – paint a clear picture of a sizeable advantage to fathers in rural courts and of a similarly sizeable advantage to mothers in urban courts.

Turning to the question of the legal standards judges apply to custody determinations, previous research shows that courts tend to grant custody of infants to their mothers (Chen and Zhang 2015; Zhao and Ding 2016). Although the "infant standard" seems cut and dried, judges have some room to make exceptions, thanks to a catch-all "other circumstances" provision that can be used to disqualify mothers from raising their infant or nursing children. When it comes to older children, however, the "physical possession standard" seems to dominate child custody determinations. This was the clear finding of a study of basic-level courts in Nanjing's urban districts (Zhao and

Ding 2016), a study of a basic-level county court in rural Chongqing (Chen and Zhang 2015), and a study of 300 child custody disputes across China (Xia 2020). Judges typically disregard other legally relevant circumstances, including domestic violence. The author of a study of child custody decisions from Beijing in 2016 and 2017 found that "under most circumstances, domestic violence was not a factor in the determination of child custody. … Even in cases involving domestic violence, the primary factors courts took into consideration were preserving the current situation and the opinions of children ten years of age and older" (Su 2018:54). At the same time, however, another study found that courts rarely solicited the opinions of qualified children (Chen and Zhang 2015:29). Prior research also suggests that, more generally, the impact of the 2015 Anti-Domestic Violence Law has been limited at best, even beyond the realm of child custody (Y. Jiang 2019).

Child custody is not always disputed. Litigants often reach an agreement on child custody, obviating the need for judges to adjudicate. However, such agreements are not always entirely voluntary. A great deal of informal bargaining occurs in the litigation process, often at the behest – or at least with the support – of the court. Indeed, by instructing courts to make child custody rulings only when the parents cannot come to a mutual agreement on their own, Article 36 of the Marriage Law incentivizes judges to orchestrate child custody agreements, which they often bring about by applying pressure through mediation. In his study of rural courts, Zhu Suli (2016:200) asserts that judges "use discretionary measures to force the party who is more eager for a divorce to make greater concession [sic] on property division or in some other aspect." Here, of course, "some other aspect" includes child custody. In the trial process, judges do not passively hear arguments and weigh evidence; whenever possible, they actively broker deals between litigants (Ng and He 2017a:40).

When abusive husbands withhold consent to divorce, women, in desperation, often "agree" to give up child custody in exchange for their freedom (Li 2015a, 2015b). Even when their husbands consent to divorce, women may still find themselves under enormous pressure from courts, their husbands' families, and sometimes even their natal families to drop their child custody claims (Li 2022; Tan 2017). In a process Ke Li aptly characterizes as "collusion," legal advocates sometimes persuade their female clients to give up child custody and marital property, and in so doing help judges and abusive husbands more than the clients they ostensibly represent (Li 2022). According to one study:

> Owing to the vestiges of the feudal ideology of 'carrying forward the ancestral line through sons' [传宗接代], even if a court does grant custody of a son to his mother, the male side may not accept defeat, and may resort to abuse and violence against the female side; the female side may concede child custody to the male side in order to get out of the marriage as quickly as possible. (Tan 2017:270)

All the foregoing types of concessions, which are typically recorded by judges as "voluntary" (自愿), are tantamount to coercion.

Given the importance of physical possession in the determination of child custody, some men resort to other extreme measures to enhance their bargaining power in court. As one observer puts it,

> Children who have been snatched in divorce battles have become objects that at any moment can be transformed into "things" to be hidden and to serve as bargaining chips [谈判的筹码]. They lose their basic personal freedoms, their original lives and educational environments are crudely upended, and they are forced into separation from their mothers or siblings; they are like "hostages." (R. Zhang 2017:49)

As we will see, abuse victims who flee for their lives and leave their children behind are at a severe disadvantage with respect to child custody because the children are left in the exclusive physical possession of their husbands and parents-in-law. Further aggravating their victims' plight, abusers may take advantage of the opportunity to hide marital assets and deprive their wives of their lawful property rights (Fincher 2014; Wu 2014:101–2).

Several reports on divorce litigation in China address the problem of parents "snatching" their own children (Fincher 2014:161–62; Thomas 2016). The logic of child-snatching is twofold. First, given that courts so rarely grant joint custody, child custody is almost always a zero-sum game in only-child families, and can even be so in multi-child families. Second, as discussed earlier, courts tend to privilege the parent with physical possession of the child. According to one estimate, "children are forcefully snatched" (抢孩) or "hidden" (藏匿) by a parent in as many as 60% of cases involving child custody disputes (Zhang 2017:47n2). Fathers who win custody, sometimes as a direct consequence of child-snatching, often block mothers from physical access to – or even communication with – their own children (Thomas 2016; Zhang 2017:48). Even when courts do grant child custody to mothers, they rarely enforce their judgments (Fincher 2014:145; Li 2015b:165; Palmer 2007:684n28; Tan 2017:270; Zeng 2013:242). Physical possession is therefore tantamount to de facto custody that courts often subsequently formalize in their rulings. Likewise, courts rarely enforce visitation rights provided by the Marriage Law to parents without legal custody (Li, Wang, and Zheng 2016:19; Ni 2014:214).

Consistent with research outside China showing that abusive men use child custody as a way to continue to exert control (Bemiller 2008:247; Jeffries 2016; Rivera, Sullivan, and Zeoli 2012:235), one study even reports instances of men harming their children as a method of exacting revenge against their wives, or to lure their wives back home (R. Zhang 2017:48). To some judges, violence against children is a red line that precludes any chance of child custody. However, husbands beating their wives is another matter. Like some judges elsewhere in the world (Bemiller 2008; Jeffries 2016; Walker 2017:114), Chinese judges may believe a wife-beater can be a good father, or at least that documented violence against a spouse does not appreciably increase safety risks to a child. In the words of a Chinese judge:

> If one side inflicts severe violence against a child, all bets are off when it comes to child custody; I will not grant child custody to him. In cases where there is domestic violence but the victim is not a child, however, I will take the domestic violence behavior into consideration as a strike against the offender's bid for child custody, but will not deprive him of child custody rights solely on this basis; I will make my determination according to the concrete circumstances of the case. (R. Zhang 2017:48)

The same study includes additional evidence that judges are not averse to granting child custody to perpetrators of domestic violence. In a court in Hunan Province, a 43-year-old female plaintiff filed for divorce as a last resort after her husband committed "extremely serious" domestic violence that caused liver and kidney hematomas. The court granted custody of their daughter to the plaintiff and custody of their son to the defendant (R. Zhang 2017:48n4).

EXPLAINING WHY PHYSICAL POSSESSION IS THE DOMINANT CHILD CUSTODY STANDARD

Judges disregard domestic violence for a variety of reasons. They may assume women exaggerate or fabricate domestic violence claims to gain child custody or unfair advantage in some other respect; a woman's domestic violence claim can therefore backfire by diminishing her personal credibility (Bemiller 2008; Epstein and Goodman 2019; He and Ng 2013a; Jeffries 2016; Perrin 2017; Rathus et al. 2019). They may also normalize or trivialize abuse as ordinary marital friction that does not rise to the level of domestic violence (Epstein and Goodman 2019; J. Jiang 2019; Li 2015b).

Judges all over the world choose from a menu of competing legal standards. In Australia, Canada, Ireland, New Zealand, the United Kingdom, and the United States, for example, judges often grant joint custody of children to abusive husbands when, in their assessment, the best interests of the child are served by co-parenting more than they are jeopardized by domestic violence – owing in part to the success of the "fathers' rights" movement. Judges operate under the misguided belief that spousal abuse poses negligible risks to children, that bad husbands can be good parents, and that domestic violence inflicted against spouses is therefore of limited relevance to custody determinations (Bemiller 2008; Jeffries 2016).

As we will see, there is no apparent need for a fathers' rights movement in China; fathers already have the courts' full attention, particularly in rural areas where men enjoy considerable advantages in divorce litigation. In China, two key reasons explain why judges downplay and ignore domestic violence when determining child custody. First, judges support durable patriarchal values and practices, most notably patrilocality and patrilineality. In so doing, they endorse and enforce some of the very *cultural* rules of patriarchy that have been denounced and prohibited by the *legal* rules of China's party-state. Second, judges' tendency to preserve the status quo also reflects their imperative to maximize judicial efficiency and social stability. Under the dual pressure of crushing dockets and stability maintenance mandates, the physical possession standard helps judges close divorce cases efficiently while minimizing contentiousness.

Judges Privileged Patriarchy over the Safety of Women and Children

Perhaps judges tend to apply the physical possession standard because doing so preserves what they view, either consciously or unconsciously, as the normatively proper patriarchal order. As we will see, the majority of child custody decisions are made by courts that serve predominantly rural populations. In rural China, owing to the overwhelming practice of patrilocality and village exogamy, wives typically come from outside the village, move into the husband's village, and reside in or near the husband's home (Chen 2005; Gruijters and Ermisch 2019). As perennial outsiders, wives might never enjoy recognition as full-fledged members of their marital families or even of their marital villages. Often knowing nobody when they arrive (Baker 1979:42), their limited social support – particularly relative to that of their husbands – puts them at a disadvantage in many domains, including divorce litigation (Li 2016). According to tradition, only after fulfilling her primary obligation to produce a son does a rural woman enjoy some measure of status and security in her husband's home (Baker 1979:47).

> [T]he birth of a son was of the greatest importance to a family, not only in order to provide for the parents in their old age, but also in connection with ancestor worship. A daughter being of no help in either direction, her birth was not a matter of such joy or importance. All families therefore, did their utmost either to beget a son or, if that were impossible, to adopt one. (Baker 1979:3)

A rural woman's plight may be compounded by the legendarily fraught relationship between daughters-in-law and mothers-in-law. Rural patrilocality often means that women cannot avoid tyrannical mothers-in-law (Baker 1979:43), a theme that emerged in many court decisions I analyzed for this chapter.

Patriarchy is manifested in various ways. In some parts of rural China, "many couples get pregnant first and then get married; if the female side does not get pregnant after cohabitating for a period of time, she faces the risk of desertion" (Hu and Shen 2016:127). Reflecting entrenched son preference in rural China, one plaintiff reported that "the defendant's attitude towards me diametrically changed after I gave birth to a girl [in 2010]; when it came to the question of whether I would have another child, he and his parents incessantly harangued me" (Decision #2611439, Shaoxing Municipal Yuecheng District People's Court, Zhejiang Province, December 6, 2013).[3] In the samples of court decisions I analyze in this book, hundreds of plaintiffs seeking divorce reported to be in arranged marriages, which had been outlawed by Article 1 of the 1950 Marriage Law. Despite campaigns in the early 1950s to enforce the Marriage Law for the official purpose of eradicating arranged marriage, bigamy, bride-buying, and other

---

[3] Case ID (2013)绍越民初字第4064号, archived at https://perma.cc/3LZS-URYT.

"feudal" practices that oppressed women (Deng 2016:187; Diamant 2000a, 2000b), China's family laws have symbolically promoted gender equality while serving in practice to reproduce patriarchy (Davis 2010, 2014; Friedman 2006; He and Ng 2013a, 2013b; Johnson 1983; Li 2022; Palmer 2017; Stacey 1983; Wolf 1985).

One report chronicles the saga of a female plaintiff who filed for divorce in a basic-level court in a rural district belonging to the city of Xuzhou. She described how, over a period of five years, her husband's affection turned cold after she failed to get pregnant. They constantly fought about her apparent barrenness. In his words, "Isn't it true that men in the countryside marry women in order to have children?" She shot back, "He should think about his older age and realize that eight or nine times out of ten it's the man's problem when a woman doesn't get pregnant." After years of conflict, she filed for divorce and exclaimed in her statement to the court, "Liu Xin'an [the defendant] married me only for the sake of continuing his family's ancestral line [传宗接代]. I was unable to get pregnant, and now he wants another woman to have his child!" (Tian 2016:26). Even if the plaintiff's fears were unfounded in this particular case, they were probably not unreasonable: "In the absence of a son, some men, influenced by the cultural importance of the continuum of descent, will use unscrupulous physical methods and shack up with another woman as a scheme to produce a son who will continue to 'burn incense' for the family [男孩续'香火']" (Ye 2007:43).[4] Although the plaintiff in this moralistic story was ultimately able to avert divorce and live happily ever after,[5] her case illuminates the powerful patriarchal forces that valorize sons to the point of vastly reducing mothers' chances of gaining custody of sons.

So-called skipped-generation (隔代) households form when rural parents join China's over 220 million migrant workers and leave their children behind in the care of grandparents (Duan et al. 2013). According to data from the 2010 population census, China's 61 million left-behind children accounted for 22% of all children and

---

[4] Burning incense refers to ancestor worship. On this and the continuum of descent, see Baker (1979).

[5] The article in which this case was featured was written for a public audience and published in a popular magazine. The presiding judge ordered a six-month cooling-off period on the grounds that the petition was frivolous, impulsive, and an abuse of the freedom of divorce. In the fifth month, just as the cooling-off period was about to expire, the plaintiff became pregnant at the age of 43. With the help of the court's marriage counseling, her husband once again displayed love and affection, and she called off the divorce. Later she gave birth to fraternal twins, one boy and one girl (Tian 2016:26–27).

38% of all rural children nationwide (All China Women's Federation Research Team 2013). Between 2000 and 2005, China's population of left-behind children almost tripled from 20 to 59 million (Duan et al. 2013). Their population increased again to over 90 million in 2016 before dropping back down to about 70 million in 2018 following central government policies to incentivize parents to stay in their villages (Geng and Wang 2018). In 2010, the majority of all left-behind children – an estimated 57% – were in the care of their grandparents. Among children left behind by both parents, an estimated 70% were in the care of their grandparents (Duan et al. 2013:43).[6] All evidence points to paternal grandparents as the default custodians of China's left-behind children. Maternal grandparents, by contrast, play a much smaller role (Bai et al. 2018; Chen, Liu, and Mair 2011; Hou 2019; Li 2018; Lu 2017; Zeng et al. 2013). When migrant workers divorce, their minor children are likely living with or otherwise under the care of paternal grandparents. Rural fathers therefore derive an immense advantage in divorce litigation from judges' tendency to preserve the status quo by granting child custody to the parent with physical possession.

Fathers gain additional advantage from skewed sex ratios in rural China, where boys far outnumber girls. With limited chances to bear a son under China's family planning policies, many rural parents did not leave things to chance. Son preference reflects both enduring patriarchal cultural forces and pragmatic old-age security considerations, and was realized by the widespread practice of sex-selective abortion. Rural sex ratios at birth became highly distorted as a result (for a review of the literature on this issue, see Michelson 2010:191–92). As we shall see in Chapter 11, courts often match child and parent sex when determining child custody. For this reason, all else being equal, mothers' chances of winning child custody in rural China are further reduced by the greater supply of sons relative to daughters.

The upshot is that sons are coveted and vigilantly guarded by their fathers' families. "In rural China, men continue to occupy a dominant position; women have no right to speak, and no property rights. … The ideology of the 'continuum of descent' remains relatively widespread in the countryside, and men will do everything in their power to fight for child custody" (Zeng 2013:242). To many rural women, therefore, making a claim for child custody, particularly of a son, may seem futile.

---

[6] The remaining left-behind children were under the care of other people or lived independently.

Under patrilocality, even when mother and father are living with a child under the same roof, the roof is understood to be the father's. According to prevailing *legal* rules, mother and father have equal claims to custody of a child in the physical possession of both parents. Prevailing *cultural* rules, however, dictate that the father and his family enjoy exclusive rights to the child. "In the countryside, many people take for granted as obvious that, after a couple divorces, custody of their children, particularly sons, should be granted to fathers. For this reason, women find it difficult to assert and protect their child custody rights" (Fan 2017:145).

The authors of one study identify three primary reasons, all rooted in patriarchy, why rural courts tend to privilege fathers:

> First, influenced by the "continuum of descent" ideology, when husbands and wives divorce, the husband's family always wants to maintain custody of the children, particularly of sons. ... Second, the majority of basic-level court personnel are deeply influenced by this traditional ideology. This phenomenon is further heightened by a lack of gender consciousness in society. Third, some mothers fear that raising minor children will affect their ability to form a new family (Hu and Shen 2016:126–27).

Even if mothers themselves do not endorse the third reason, judicial authorities may use it to rationalize denying – or to pressure mothers to waive – their child custody claims, as seen in the following interaction between a woman seeking divorce in rural China and her legal representative.

> [D]ivorced women are further depreciated on the marriage market if they bring children from previous relationships into new ones. Adding insult to injury, the children would become "*tuoyouping* [拖油瓶, literally an 'oil bottle in tow']," a derogative term for those who follow divorced mothers into remarriages. In line with this cultural logic, the legal worker announced: "you'll be better off letting him [the husband] raise the kid." (Li 2015b:164)

Elsewhere in the world, women's remarriage prospects are indeed diminished by having children in tow (de Graaf and Kalmijn 2003; Di Nallo 2019).

Authors of several studies have similarly argued that judges' child custody determinations are influenced by patriarchy because judges themselves have internalized patriarchal values and thus endorse the cultural importance of the family lineage (Chen and Zhang 2015:28–29;

Hu and Shen 2016:129; Li 2015b:164). Women accounted for fewer than one-third of China's judges in 2013 (Zheng et al. 2017:177). Meanwhile, as we have seen, approximately two-thirds of plaintiffs seeking divorce are women. Some research even suggests that female and male judges are similarly supportive of patriarchal cultural norms, similarly (un)sympathetic of female litigants and (in)credulous of their legal complaints, and therefore similarly biased in favor of male litigants (Bu et al. 2015:11). Perhaps female judges are more sympathetic than male judges to the plight of female litigants but are also more fearful than male judges of threats to their personal safety posed by potentially violent male litigants.

Even if their decisions are not motivated by patriarchal cultural beliefs, judges may fear retaliation from husbands, particularly those with established histories of violence. In the wake of several high-profile murders of judges by men or their family members disgruntled by a divorce outcome, judges' tendency to favor fathers is therefore also shaped by a consideration of their own safety more than of children's safety (Chapter 3).

Judges' Privileged Efficiency over the Safety of Women and Children

Court reforms over the past decade have been guided by the dual imperative to enhance judicial efficiency and minimize social unrest (Chapters 3, 5, and 6). Determining child custody on the basis of the child's physical location helps judges close divorce cases quickly and reduces the likelihood of appeals, complaints, and petitioning by disgruntled litigants – for which judges are penalized on their performance evaluations (Chapter 3). Setting aside the infant standard, which judges tend to apply by default in custody disputes involving children less than two years old, the physical possession standard is usually less fraught than other competing standards. In custody disputes involving children at least two years of age, judges can render a quick ruling after merely ascertaining the child's recent and ongoing living arrangements. Insofar as litigants generally agree on the child's physical location as a simple factual matter, the application of the physical possession standard obviates the need for judges to undertake potentially contentious and time-consuming fact-finding investigations, assessments of evidence, and witness interviews. For similar reasons, French divorce judges tend to uphold "*de facto* situations" (Biland and Steinmetz 2017:303, 314).

Chinese legal standards pertaining to child custody provide little in the way of concrete clarity and guidance (Su 2018:54; R. Zhang 2017:50). Legal ambiguity demands the exercise of judicial discretion in the determination of the nature and extent of abuse necessary to disqualify a wife-beater; the material resources necessary to meet the financial means standard; and whether an ailment is sufficiently serious to meet the illness standard. Because vague standards invite contestation, judges are averse to apply them. Establishing the validity of marital abuse allegations can be onerous in terms of time and evidentiary requirements. And even though the 2008 Guidelines call on judges to relax evidentiary standards and to believe women's oral statements (Chapter 2), judges are loath to affirm domestic violence claims lest an angry husband carry out an "extreme incident" of retaliation against his wife – for which the judge would be held liable and punished – or possibly even against the judge (Chapter 3). Likewise, determining the material fitness of a parent through the application of the financial means standard and the physical fitness of a parent through the application of the illness standard are, from the perspective of judges, similarly undesirable, risky propositions.

The physical possession standard, by contrast, is relatively unambiguous. Given the relatively clear-cut nature of the child's living arrangements, litigants will likely see little reason or recourse for challenging the fairness of a ruling against their favor made on this basis. A judge merely needs to ask, "Where has the child been living?" If both parties agree on the answer, which in rural areas is most likely to be the home of the child's father or his family, the judge can simply hold: "According to the law, it would be in the child's best interests to stay there." In short, the physical possession standard can be a divorce judge's best friend and a female litigant's worst enemy. Judges' overreliance on the physical possession standard streamlines their work often at the expense of both women's due process rights and children's safety.

CASE EXAMPLES ILLUSTRATING JUDGES' DISREGARD FOR DOMESTIC VIOLENCE WHEN DETERMINING CHILD CUSTODY

The cases I analyze in this chapter come from a larger collection of 33,033 child custody decisions – 19,201 from Henan and 13,832 from Zhejiang – made by every one of the 252 basic-level courts in both provinces. I analyze cases primarily but not exclusively from rural courts because, as we know, this is where most divorce litigation occurs. I selected cases for qualitative analysis in three steps. First, I identified the over 8,500 decisions in both provincial collections of child custody decisions that contain plaintiff allegations of domestic violence. Second, among these decisions, I randomly selected 100 from each province (200 total). Third, I read through them in search of salient examples of prominent themes, focusing on cases in which the child custody claims of female plaintiffs were denied. As I analyzed the case examples, I organized them according to the key themes they illustrate. Each theme relates to a strategy or set of strategies judges used to sideline domestic violence allegations. Each subsection corresponds to a theme. I selected 25 case examples, 14 from Henan and 11 from Zhejiang.

Some of the cases I present will appear extreme or anomalous at best and outrageously implausible at worst. Truth can indeed be stranger than fiction. The case examples were not hard to find; I barely scratched the surface. Let us assume that within my collection of 8,500 child custody decisions containing plaintiff allegations of domestic violence, every 200 randomly selected cases contain 25 stories similar to those I selected for this chapter. If so, my collection as a whole could contain over 1,000 more horrifying case examples. This puts the sheer scale and human toll of gender injustice in China's courts into perspective.

Not surprisingly, given that about 90% of all plaintiffs who made domestic violence allegations were women, the plaintiff was female in each case example. Moreover, the plaintiff petitioned for child custody in every case example but one. Among all 25 case examples, 10 involved only-daughters, 12 involved only-sons, and 3 involved siblinged children (one daughter and one son in all 3 cases). The court awarded child custody to the plaintiff in only 4 cases, 1 of which involved an only daughter and 2 of which involved siblinged children who were split up between the parents. In 1 case of siblings split up between the parents, custody of the daughter was granted to the mother and custody of the son was granted to the father. In the other case in which the court split up custody of siblings, custody of the son was granted to the mother because he was only four years old. In 3 of the 4 cases in which the plaintiff was awarded child custody, she already had physical possession of the child. I present 19 out of all 25 case examples in this chapter. The remainder are available online as supplementary case examples.

I will begin with a representative case:

> The court affirms the following facts: ... .Plaintiff and defendant became acquainted in June 2007, and started living together after their relationship became romantic. In May 2008 they held a wedding ceremony according to rural customs, and their son was born on November 24, 2008. On May 6, 2009, they registered their marriage at the Luohe Municipal Yancheng District Civil Affairs Bureau. Prior to getting married, the two sides lacked mutual understanding, and the defendant beat and cursed the plaintiff over minor matters. In 2011, when the plaintiff filed for divorce, this court denied her petition. Both plaintiff and defendant are migrant workers, and their son lives with the defendant's parents when they are away.

This solitary case encapsulates several themes animating court-adjudicated divorce cases in China. First, it palpably illustrates the influence of patriarchy. Like many marriages in rural areas, this one was registered retroactively. As discussed earlier, many rural couples wait until pregnancy before holding a wedding ceremony. Second, domestic violence claims are pervasive in divorce petitions filed by women seeking to divorce their husbands in China's courts. Third, in accordance with the judicial norm of the divorce twofer, courts typically deny first-attempt divorce petitions and grant petitions on subsequent attempts. Fourth, owing to dominant rural norms of patrilocality and patrilineality, wives usually move into the husband's village, or even into the in-law's home, and experience weak and marginal status as perennial outsiders – just as they have for centuries (Baker 1979:2; F. Chen 2005; Gruijters and Ermisch 2019). Indeed, in my randomly selected examples, I encountered no cases of matrilocal families (上门女婿). Fifth, under the same norms, children, particularly sons, are widely regarded as the exclusive descendants of their paternal lines. Sixth, rural China's left-behind children are typically in the care of their paternal grandparents.

Continuing with the case, the court's holding amply illustrates the tension between judges' mandate to follow the law and their impulse to ignore and subvert it:

> Proceeding from the position of the best interests of children's physical and mental health and the protection of their lawful rights and interests, and given the actual circumstances of the son, Ying Ningtong, who is currently living with the defendant's parents, an endeavor to avoid a sudden change in his living environment, and the defendant's request for custody, the son Ying Ningtong should continue to live with the defendant.

This was the basis of the court's decision to grant child custody to the man it had just confirmed to have beaten his wife (Decision #1113605, Luohe Municipal Yancheng District People's Court, Henan Province, January 15, 2014).[7] As we will continue to see, child custody determinations are fraught with contradictions. Indeed, "feudal" patriarchal norms such as these often upheld by rural courts are explicitly condemned by Chinese law.

Judges Ignored the Violence Precipitating Mothers' Separation from Their Children

When a Chinese woman is abused by her husband, she will often "endure violence" rather than pursue divorce. At some point, whether she files for divorce or not, she is likely to seek refuge with and help from her natal family (Liu and Chan 1999; Wang, Fang, and Li 2013:36, 67). Sometimes these women take their children with them. Often, however, under duress, they leave their children behind. When this happens, judges focus narrowly on the specific question of physical possession and disregard the circumstances under which children came to be in the physical possession of their abusive fathers in the first place. In most cases, the abuse that precipitated the departure of women from their marital homes and their concomitantly precarious circumstances are treated as irrelevant. Indeed, these common consequences of domestic violence are sometimes used against women insofar as courts cite them as justification for denying child custody to abuse victims. Even when they affirm women's allegations of domestic violence, courts rarely, if ever, consider the legal relevance of marital abuse to an assessment of children's safety in the determination of their best interests.

One female plaintiff claimed her husband frequently beat her, and that he had even beaten her during pregnancy. After she fled to her natal family, he reached out to her and, through the help of the villagers' committee, wrote a pledge letter in which he admitted his mistakes and promised to make amends. According to the plaintiff, he failed to keep his promise and continued beating her. Their oldest son was already more than 18 years old and not subject to a child custody order. The plaintiff requested custody of their younger son. The defendant did not challenge the plaintiff's allegations. His

---

defense statement was short and simple: he agreed to divorce and requested custody of their second son. The court held that "Because the second son Wen X is currently living with the defendant, and since a change to his environment would be harmful to his upbringing, custody is therefore granted to the defendant, and the plaintiff will make child support payments according to the applicable formula" (Decision #1425781, Puyang County People's Court, Henan Province, April 23, 2015).[8]

Sometimes a husband will show up at the parental home of his estranged wife and beat her there. In one illustrative case, a plaintiff claimed that when her husband got drunk, he would punch and kick her (拳打脚踢), and had caused her physical injury doing so. She submitted several pieces of written witness testimony not only that he frequently beat her, but also that he went to her natal family to beat her there. The court accepted and affirmed the objectivity and relevance of the evidence and permitted it to be used in support of her claims. Although the court affirmed the plaintiff's claims of marital abuse, and although the defendant failed to appear in court or to submit a written response to the plaintiff's claims, the court granted custody of their daughter to the defendant because she was currently living with him and thus "in order not to change the life to which she was accustomed" (Decision #1189402, Zhecheng County People's Court, Henan Province, June 16, 2014).[9]

Sometimes husbands even beat their parents-in-law. In an in absentia trial, the defendant failed to respond to the plaintiff's claims that he not only regularly beat her but also on one occasion beat her and her mother simultaneously. For this reason, as the plaintiff explained, she was forced to leave the marital home and dared not return. In its holding, the court stated that "after the plaintiff left, the son, Yang X, was continually under the care of the defendant's parents; since a change to his environment would be harmful to his upbringing, custody is therefore granted to the defendant; the plaintiff will pay commensurate child support payments" (Decision #488815, Yuzhou Municipal People's Court, Henan Province, December 23, 2010).[10]

Even in cases in which the child may be in the physical possession of mothers, courts often consider the child the rightful property of

---

[8] Case ID (2015)濮民初字第183号, archived at https://perma.cc/C3FE-TB4T.
[9] Case ID (2014)柘民初字第189号, archived at https://perma.cc/2MUR-SB77.
[10] Case ID (2010)禹民一初字第2924号, archived at https://perma.cc/AAN6-6GQE.

the father. In one such case, a female plaintiff explained to the court that her husband had deceived her by luring her into marriage, after which he regularly beat her without provocation. He had written several pledge letters admitting his mistakes and promising to mend his ways. According to the plaintiff's statement, he resumed his old violent habits in short order each time. A quintessential divorce twofer, this was her second divorce petition. She felt she had no choice but to escape her situation by returning to her natal family. Although she had taken their young son with her, she ultimately returned to her marital home in an effort to reconcile. When the beatings resumed, she left again with her son, this time for good, and "with a broken heart." The court inexplicably granted custody to the defendant according to the "actual circumstances of the case," and ordered the plaintiff to pay child support (Decision #1211839, Jiaozuo Municipal Shanyang District People's Court, Henan Province, August 5, 2014).[11]

The lack of stable income may prevent courts from granting child custody to female domestic violence victims, but not from ordering them to pay child support. Courts can and do consider a woman too poor to assume custody but not too poor to pay child support. For example, a female plaintiff from a rural area claimed that her husband ruthlessly and ferociously beat her. She escaped his clutches two years prior to filing for divorce, left her young daughter behind, and dared not return home. The court granted custody to the father on the grounds that the plaintiff lacked a stable job and stable income. The court then ordered the plaintiff to pay child support (Decision #271720, Lushi County People's Court, Henan Province, December 29, 2009).[12]

In another example of what I have called a marital violence refugee, a plaintiff claimed that both her husband and mother-in-law frequently beat and cursed her and that her husband had carried out long-term physical violence and verbal abuse. She further claimed to have become a migrant worker in order to escape domestic violence. The court had denied her first divorce petition the year before. This time the court granted the divorce but denied her claim for child custody on the grounds that her son had been living with her husband's family and that her job stitching together sugar sacks did not provide her with sufficient means to assume child custody. The court nonetheless

---

[11] Case ID (2014)山民三初字第00194号, archived at https://perma.cc/7GQ2-G79S.
[12] Case ID (2009)卢民一初字第616号, archived at https://perma.cc/5PEM-3J2C.

ordered her to pay child support (Decision #3400274, Lanxi Municipal People's Court, Zhejiang Province, March 6, 2015).[13]

Judges in one case explicitly and bluntly endorsed the patriarchal family. In its decision to grant child custody to the male defendant, the court held: "Both plaintiff and defendant have made child custody claims. Given that their conditions for raising children are essentially equivalent, and in consideration both of the circumstances of the case and of local customary practice [当地习惯], custody of their son is granted to the defendant." The court may have responded with particular sympathy to the defendant's assertion that, owing to his residence in an isolated mountain village, his remarriage prospects were nil (Decision #2359853, Pingyang County People's Court, Zhejiang Province, August 2, 2010).[14] A different court made a similar ruling: "Both plaintiff and defendant requested custody of their son. In consideration of their family circumstances, the principle of the best interests of the child, local customary practice [当地风俗], and other factors, custody of their son should be granted to the defendant" (Decision #1070232, Xin County People's Court, Henan Province, October 8, 2013).[15]

To be sure, courts do not altogether ignore marital abuse. Indeed, courts affirmed plaintiffs' claims of abuse in almost every example in this section. In many instances, defendants even confirmed the plaintiff's allegations of abuse. However, judges rarely affirm abuse with the status of domestic violence. Affirming that a defendant beat a plaintiff is not the same as affirming the occurrence of domestic violence. Judges likewise often affirm injuries without affirming plaintiffs' claims that they were caused by domestic violence (Chapter 7). In one study, half of all claims of domestic violence were based solely on oral statements (Y. Jiang 2019:16–17). Even when plaintiffs do submit documentation in support of their claims, judges often refuse to admit it as evidence (Y. Jiang 2019). Judges tend to ignore the preponderance of evidence standard discussed in Chapter 2 as well as a provision in the 2008 Guidelines specifically calling on them to relax evidentiary standards, to use their common sense (自由心证), and to grant child custody to abuse victims when they determine, on the basis of

---

[13] Case ID (2015)金兰马民初字第31号, archived at https://perma.cc/L6MY-TWGY.

[14] Case ID (2010)温平水民初字第210号, archived at https://perma.cc/FD4R-XTGR. The language of the court's holding is similar to that in Article 4 of the 1993 Opinions. On men's remarriage challenges following divorce owing to a shortage of rural women, see Attané et al. (2019).

[15] Case ID (2013)新民初字第441号, archived at https://perma.cc/U3EP-U5TF.

compelling indirect evidence, a high probability of domestic violence even when they cannot directly affirm its occurrence (Article 63).

Consider this example. In support of her claim of severe physical and emotional harm caused by the defendant's domestic violence, the plaintiff submitted a CT report produced by the Lianshi Town Hospital. The court excluded this piece of evidence after the defendant objected to its admission on the grounds that it proved only that the plaintiff sustained an injury but not that the defendant caused the injury. The court then granted custody of their daughter to the defendant on the grounds that she had been continuously living with the defendant and his parents (Decision #4600907, Huzhou Municipal Nanxun District People's Court, Zhejiang Province, July 4, 2016).[16]

Judges Legitimated Child-Snatching by Fathers and Their Families

In the foregoing examples, judges treated violence as irrelevant to child custody determinations. Physical possession trumped other considerations, including the safety of the child. Just as they are uninterested in the circumstances under which mothers leave their children behind, judges are similarly unconcerned about the circumstances under which children enter the physical possession of fathers. As a result, they even reward fathers for abducting and hiding their children.

In one case, the plaintiff requested custody of her daughter. On the basis of its assessment of the litigants' statements and the results of its investigation, the court affirmed the following facts:

> Their daughter Yang Wenyuan was born on May 10, 2000. After getting married, the male side frequently drank to excess and, after getting drunk, carried out domestic violence against the female side. On July 8, 2007, once again after drinking, the male side beat the female side, after which the female side resolved to divorce him. Under the persuasion of relatives and others, the defendant wrote a pledge in which he promised to cease his heavy drinking and violence against the plaintiff. During the 2008 Spring Festival, they once again both got upset and at this point began their physical separation. While the trial was taking place, the defendant took their daughter Yang Wenyuan to live with him in the city of Kunming [the provincial capital of Yunnan].

With the help of the defendant's sister, the court was able to reach the defendant on the phone in Kunming. He stated, "I will consent to

---

[16] Case ID (2016)浙0503民初1017号, archived at https://perma.cc/6R7V-D2JR.

the divorce provided I get custody of my daughter." In its holding, the court then justified its decision to grant child custody to the defendant by writing, "their daughter is currently living with the male side and, furthermore, the plaintiff indicated that she gave up her child custody claim" (Decision #219113, Nanzhao County People's Court, Henan Province, August 20, 2009).[17]

As we will see next, the plaintiff's apparent change of heart has the markings of a concession yielded in exchange for divorce. No sooner did the defendant demand custody as a condition of divorce than the plaintiff dropped her claim for child custody. The plaintiff appeared to have exchanged child custody for her freedom.

Judges Were Complicit in Women's Bargaining Away Legal Rights in Exchange for Freedom from Marital Abuse

Judges are highly unlikely to grant plaintiffs' divorce petitions when defendants are unwilling to divorce, particularly on the first attempt (Chapters 7 and 8). For this reason, defendants wield bargaining leverage over the terms of the divorce. Statements such as this are common: "I will consent to the divorce if custody of both children and ownership of the house are granted to me" (Decision #808997, Luohe Municipal Yuanhui District People's Court, Henan Province, June 28, 2012).[18]

Judges and litigants' legal advocates sometimes try to persuade victims of domestic violence to withdraw their claims for child custody and property division (Li 2022). When these pressure tactics occur in pre-trial mediation, they may be invisible in the written court decisions. When they occur in the course of the trial, however, they can sometimes be inferred. Judges may record mid-trial concessions as claims that are withdrawn, added, or amended by litigants in the course of the trial. When they contravene plaintiffs' original requests as expressed in their statements to the court, we can interpret them in one of two ways. First, they could reflect a negotiating strategy on the part of plaintiffs, whereby they petition for something they do not particularly want with the intent of subsequently offering it in exchange for something they do particularly want. Second, they could reflect efforts – by or under the auspices of courts – to bully plaintiffs into giving up something they genuinely wanted. Even in cases in which

---

[17] Case ID (2009)南召皇民初字第18号, archived at https://perma.cc/TS6X-SXPU.
[18] Case ID (2012)源民初字第297号, archived at https://perma.cc/7YC7-NBJ7.

the first interpretation is correct, courts are nonetheless responsible for putting children at risk by granting child custody to fathers with established records of violence.

After litigants present their claims and arguments to the court, they sometimes change their minds. This is often noted by judges in their written decisions in passages that begin with the phrase, "in the course of the trial" (庭审中).[19] Sometimes litigants negotiate on their own, and sometimes they respond to pressure from judges to compromise and make concessions. Only when judges explicitly indicate their mediation efforts (e.g., "through mediation" 经调解) can we differentiate between these two scenarios. Regardless of whether litigants bargain amongst themselves or judges broker deals, negotiations occur under the auspices – and subject to the approval – of the court.

If her husband refuses to divorce, a female plaintiff might need to give up child custody in exchange for her freedom. If she wants child custody, she will likely need to give up something – perhaps child support or marital assets, including the dowry and the bride price – in exchange for her husband's consent to divorce. We can easily infer from one court decision that, in the middle the trial, the female plaintiff gave up child support from the defendant in exchange for child custody (Decision #1363347, Tanghe County People's Court, Henan Province, March 11, 2015).[20] In another such case, the plaintiff stated to the court that she had taken her son to live temporarily with her parents after her husband beat her. The following month, when her husband arrived to try to take their son back home with him, a physical altercation ensued between the defendant, the plaintiff, and her father. The plaintiff alleged that, in the process, the defendant broke a bone in her hand. She also claimed that local police investigated and documented the incident. In her statement to the court, the plaintiff requested custody of their son and a one-time child-support payment of ¥60,000 from the defendant. The defendant, however, withheld consent to divorce unless the court granted custody of their son to him. In the course of the trial, quite possibly as a result of judicial mediation, "the plaintiff voluntarily withdrew her claim for child support," softening the blow to the defendant of both the divorce itself and of losing custody of his son (Decision #2293399, Linhai Municipal

---

[19] Alternative phrases with the equivalent meaning include 本案诉讼中, 在审理中, and 在审理过程中.

[20] Case ID (2015)唐民一初字第93号, archived at https://perma.cc/S4LH-S28P.

People's Court, Zhejiang Province, March 18, 2010).[21] From the contents of the court decision, we can only speculate about whether the court pressured the plaintiff to forgo child support or she decided on her own accord to make this concession. Either scenario underscores the considerable leverage defendants wield simply by withholding consent to divorce and demanding child custody.

Women waive property claims for the same reasons. In a similar case, a plaintiff seeking to divorce her husband, who she claimed had beaten her four times and prompted her to call the police numerous times, thoroughly documented her claims with medical and police records. She requested custody of the older daughter but not of the younger son. The defendant, however, refused to divorce and demanded custody of both children if the court granted the divorce against his will. In the middle of the trial, the plaintiff suddenly "voluntarily gave up all claims to marital assets." In the end, the court granted the plaintiff's petitions for divorce and custody of the daughter (Decision #655594, Shenqiu County People's Court, Henan Province, August 22, 2011).[22]

Whether the plaintiff made her concessions at the behest of the court or on her own is less important than the enormous sacrifices she made to achieve the divorce. "Wins" such as these come at a considerable cost. Although they have every legal right to child custody and marital property, women often end up losing one or both to men who have committed statutory wrongdoing and present safety risks to their children. Even if plaintiffs' concessions in cases like this are genuinely voluntary, they fly in the face of an arsenal of laws, judicial opinions, and official guidelines fully supporting – and even demanding – that judges protect the health and safety of children by keeping them out of the custody of abusive parents.

Supplementary case examples set #10–1 is online at: https:// decoupling-book.org/.

Judges Cherry-Picked Children's Opinions

On the rare occasions that judges solicited the opinions of children, they did so to justify preserving the status quo. As mentioned earlier, the opinion of the child is one standard that judges may use to determine

---

[21] Case ID (2010)台临民初字第414号, archived at https://perma.cc/CC2F-8D48.
[22] Case ID (2011)沈民初字第294号, archived at https://perma.cc/4YRR-849V.

child custody. At the same time, however, the 2008 Guidelines advise judges to discount or altogether disregard the child's opinion in cases involving domestic violence. Article 65 stipulates that children cannot accurately assess their own best interests (Item 1). It also stipulates that children remain emotionally attached to abusive parents they simultaneously fear and resent. It makes explicit reference to the Stockholm Syndrome as a reason why children may express a wish to live with an abusive parent (Item 2). The following female abuse victim's account lends credence to concerns about the safety risks to children, and to the need for caution when they express a willingness to live with their abusive fathers.

> When we were divorcing, my son expressed his willingness to live with his paternal grandparents and father only because he knew they wouldn't allow him to live with me. We've been divorced for over one year. In the beginning his father wouldn't allow him to see me or to take my phone calls. This year he said he wanted to be with me, and I spoke about this with his paternal grandparents. His father seemed to be treating him a little better. But ten days ago my son and his father got into a fight, and his father swung a chair at him and missed. … His father cursed at him: "You're going to give me a hard time? You think I'll let you give me a hard time? I sure didn't let your mother give me a hard time!" … I'm worried about my son. I told him not to provoke his father, and that his grandparents would protect him if his father beats him. (R. Zhang 2017:48)

In the next case, marital violence that had been previously punished by the public security administration gave no pause to the judge. A plaintiff claimed to the court that her husband had beaten her many times over a period of years, and that she had reported him to the police. No longer able to endure his violence, she left him, and thus her son, behind. To support her claims, she submitted photographs, a hospital medical history booklet, and a CT report as evidence. In his defense, the defendant stated that in one incident he beat her only because they got into a fight after he "joked" that she was an "unvirtuous woman" (不守妇道), and that the local police substation had already dealt with the matter. The court acquired from the police substation copies of a public security administrative punishment decision and interrogation notes related to this incident. The defendant did not object to the medical documentation submitted by the plaintiff, and even confirmed the facts of the violent incident as stated by the plaintiff, but clarified to the court that "normally I did not beat the plaintiff." The police had punished the defendant with two days of administrative detention and a fine of ¥200. The court granted custody to the defendant on the basis of the son's opinion and in order to avoid a change to his living environment (Decision #4533679, Cangnan County People's Court, Zhejiang Province, May 12, 2016).[23] Even if the son's opinion was sincere, and even if doing so respected the child's opinion, the judge's decision to keep him in the custody of a violent offender is antithetical to the spirit and letter of China's family laws.

Indeed, it seems no behavior is out of bounds; nothing seems to disqualify a father from gaining child custody. In this next case, judges disregarded the opinion of a child with compelling safety concerns. A plaintiff's divorce request was finally granted on the sixth attempt. According to the plaintiff, the defendant erupted into a rage at least four or five times per month for trivial reasons or no reason at all. Among the numerous egregious transgressions allegedly committed by the defendant was his abuse of their daughter. According to the plaintiff, he regularly beat and berated her. When, on June 8, 2009, the defendant threatened to stab their daughter to death, the plaintiff picked her up early from school and reported the incident to the police.[24] The plaintiff claimed that she and her daughter were equally fearful for her safety, and that her daughter supported the divorce and wanted to live with her mother. In support of her claims, the plaintiff

---

[23] Case ID (2016)浙0327民初1768号, archived at https://perma.cc/TP4L-W382.

[24] In a criminal case outside the scope of my random sample of child custody decisions, an abusive husband murdered his son who was left in his care after his wife fled with their two daughters. In 2007, after the wheat harvest, the defendant got drunk and abused – physically and verbally – his wife and children. For this reason, his wife ran away with their two daughters. She left their seven-year-old son at home. The defendant searched in vain for his wife and daughters. In April 2008, after getting drunk again, he took out his frustrations on his son. The defendant stated to the court, "My son was hungry, and pestered me to get him something to eat, so I took him to get a steamed bun in the village, but I couldn't find any. I was mad, and bought a bottle of beer. After returning home I drank half of it. My son was still crying and fussing, demanding that I get him something to eat. I thought of how my wife left with our daughters without a care for our son. The more I thought about it the angrier I got. I was upset. I thought, your mother doesn't want you, you're starving, what's the point of living? I'll kill my son and then kill myself. I got a hoe from the courtyard and held it over my son's head. I don't know if I chopped his head three or four times. Blood was all over the floor." A forensic autopsy report indicated the cause of death was an open craniocerebral injury. The defendant then jumped off a railway bridge in a suicide attempt. When that failed, he tried to smash his head with a rock. A local police officer took him away before he could further harm himself. He stated that he had drunk 100–150 ml of hard liquor in the morning, and about the same amount in the early afternoon before drinking half of the bottle of beer he purchased when he was out in search of food for his son. The court sentenced him to life in prison. Decision #75449, Zhumadian Municipal Intermediate People's Court, Henan Province, May 27, 2009, Case ID (2009)驻刑少初字第10号, archived at https://perma.cc/9LV3-ND7C.

submitted an affidavit from their villagers' committee and several police reports documenting the defendant's death threats as well as a statement from their daughter indicating her wish to live with the plaintiff if the divorce were granted. Although the defendant objected to the child's statement, alleging that it was coerced by the plaintiff, the court affirmed it as factual and objective. The court finally granted the plaintiff's divorce request, but denied her claim for child custody: "Because the plaintiff has been living away from her family on a long-term basis, their daughter has been primarily under the care of the defendant and others. Throughout the litigation process, the defendant repeatedly expressed that 'I want to raise my daughter.' Furthermore, the plaintiff expressed that she can relinquish custody rights" (Decision #3000083, Haiyan County People's Court, Zhejiang Province, April 11, 2014).[25] Once again, the plaintiff's change of heart inserted into the court's holding smacks of pressure applied to the plaintiff to withdraw her petition for child custody. The contrast with the previous case is noteworthy. In the previous case, the son's opinion was deemed credible and accepted when it served the convenience of the court, whereas in this case the daughter's opinion was ignored and deemed unreliable when it was inconvenient to the court and contradicted the father's wishes. In both cases, the courts' decisions jeopardized the safety of children.

Not even a rape conviction convinced a judge to remove a child from the defendant's home. After a plaintiff claimed her husband frequently carried out domestic violence, she requested custody of both of her children, one daughter and one son, who at the time were being raised by her husband's parents. The defendant, claiming his wife had engaged in improper relations with another man, declared that he would agree to divorce only if his wife's lover were to assume criminal liability. The irony of his ultimatum stemmed from his own criminal liability. Although he was currently serving a prison sentence of three years and eight months for the crime of rape, he appeared in person for the trial. The defendant's parents beseeched the court to allow them to raise the children until his release from prison. The litigants' daughter, who was more than ten years old, submitted a written statement expressing her desire to continue living with her father in the home of her paternal grandparents. The court did not solicit the opinion of their son because he was less than ten years old. The court granted custody of both children to the defendant, ordered the plaintiff to pay child support, and allowed the defendant's parents to serve as temporary surrogate custodians while he served his prison sentence (Decision #1541542, Puyang County People's Court, Henan Province, June 17, 2015).[26]

Judges Disregarded Risks to Children

The well-being of children is not an apparent concern of courts. Nowhere in any decision I read did judges indicate any concern that men who abuse their wives might endanger their children. Without any sense of dissonance or contradiction, judges say in the same breath that a man is abusive and dangerous to his wife but fit to serve as the primary custodian of a child. One wonders whether judges who write holdings such as the following truly believe that abusive husbands pose no risk of harm to their children. The judges in one case held that

> the defendant repeatedly beat and injured the plaintiff. This is the direct cause of the deterioration of marital affection. For this reason, the defendant is at fault. The plaintiff had no choice but to file for divorce, and the plaintiff and defendant's marital affection can be regarded as having irretrievably broken down. The court therefore approves the request to divorce. The plaintiff and defendant's daughter, He X, has been continuously living with the defendant. From the perspective of the best interests of the child, the defendant is more fit to assume custody of He X. (Decision #334543, Xichuan County People's Court, Henan Province, July 19, 2010)[27]

Supplementary case examples set #10–2 is online at: https://decoupling-book.org/.

SUMMARY AND CONCLUSIONS

Consistent with global legal norms, Chinese law stipulates that child custody should be determined according to the best interests of the child. Chinese law, however, is also vague on the details. Without clear standards on "best interests," judges are given enormous latitude to cherry-pick legal provisions that facilitate expeditious decision-making.

---

[26] Case ID (2015)濮民初字第915号, archived at https://perma.cc/QG24-N874.
[27] Case ID (2010)淅香民初字第07号, archived at https://perma.cc/5X29-QRUT.

Judges routinely privilege the status quo over the safety of children. Even in egregious cases of violence carried out by fathers, typically against their wives, but sometimes even against their children, judges have little hesitation to grant child custody to the father. To judges, no behavior seems to be sufficiently beyond the pale to disqualify a father from assuming legal custody of a child.

Judges were gun-shy about ruling on contentious matters, including domestic violence, for several reasons. As judges faced growing pressure to close their cases, determining child custody according to the current living situation of the child was one of many prevailing legal standards, and was arguably the most convenient to judges insofar as its application obviated the need to investigate contentious claims and to assess relevant evidence. Judges also wanted to avoid upsetting violent husbands for fear of "extreme incidents" of retribution directed against their wives or the judges themselves (Chapter 3). When making a child custody determination, a Chinese court was therefore likely to affirm and uphold the child's current living situation regardless of whether doing so undermined the interests of mother and child or contradicted competing legal standards that would more effectively protect the interests – including the health and safety – of mother and child.

A refrain commonly recorded in court decisions expressed by women seeking to divorce their husbands was that it was "for the sake of the child(ren)" that they waited as long as they did (often years) before finally leaving their abusive husbands. At one level, it simply means that mothers suffered protracted misery in order to provide for their children's needs as best as they possibly could. At another level, it means mothers may have stayed in intolerable marriages knowing that leaving would have been tantamount to forfeiting custody rights and losing their children.

Although China's Marriage Law was officially heralded as "revolutionizing the family" by upending patriarchal norms (Diamant 2000b), previous research as well as findings I present here show that rural courts in practice have served to validate and reproduce patriarchal norms. In opposition to China's socialist ideology of gender equality and arsenal of laws intended to protect it, judges, consciously or unconsciously, have served to uphold China's rural patriarchal order. As we will see in Chapter 11, courts supported the cultural imperative in many rural areas of preserving the family line through sons. Women's child custody prospects were determined to a large extent by both the number and sex composition of children.

411

CHAPTER ELEVEN

QUANTITATIVE PATTERNS IN CHILD CUSTODY DETERMINATIONS

Sons to Fathers, Daughters to Mothers, Abusers Rewarded, Victims Punished

Qualitative case examples illuminate patterns less visible in the quantitative data. We saw in the previous chapter, for example, that litigants sometimes amended, negotiated, and conceded their initial child custody claims. Such processes are more difficult to study quantitatively, and indeed are often altogether invisible in the written court decisions. However, quantitative analysis is the only means by which to paint a macroscopic picture of key patterns of judicial decision-making in huge and representative samples such as mine. Furthermore, some patterns emerge with clarity only from large-scale quantitative analyses. For example, the influence of the number and sex composition of children is difficult to tease out of a few qualitative examples but is striking in the full sample of child custody determinations.

Findings I present in this chapter confirm much of what we learned in the previous chapter. In particular, they reaffirm judges' tendency to privilege defendants' physical possession of children over plaintiffs' claims of domestic violence. They also showcase additional extra-legal considerations that previous studies have found influence child custody determinations. Judges commonly split up siblings out of a sense of fairness to the parents and because fathers sometimes only pursue custody of their sons, which in turn allows or compels courts to grant custody of daughters to their mothers. Evidence of fathers' "demand for sons" has also been found in the United States (Dahl and Moretti 2008). When siblings do stick together, they are much more likely to go to the father than to the mother (Chen and Zhang 2015:28). Although it is an option available to judges, joint legal custody is exceedingly rare (Hu and Shen 2016; Shandong Province Ji'nan Municipal Intermediate People's Court Research Team 2018:184). Both siblings and only-children are often assigned to the parent matching their biological sex (Chen and Zhang 2015; Lang 2016; Zhao and Ding 2016). When granting custody of daughters to mothers, courts sometimes do so "in consideration of the biological characteristics of girls" (Zhao and Ding 2016:28–29). As one judge put it: "In a context of only-children and son preference, most families of fathers will not fight for custody of only-daughters, which causes courts to grant to mothers custody of 91.2% of only-daughters [in this particular sample of cases], which in turn causes them to feel abandoned" (Lang 2016:31). We will see that women's child custody prospects were indeed determined to a large extent by both the number and sex composition of their children.

We will also see that these problems have been concentrated in rural areas, and that women's outcomes in urban courts have been far better. According to one study, "in rural areas, the belief that men are superior to women is relatively influential, particularly among fathers and their families, who are therefore unenthusiastic about winning custody of daughters but regard winning custody of sons as relatively important" (Ni 2014:214). In another study, rural courts upheld the traditional norm of "sons stay with the husband's family" (子留夫家; Chen and Zhang 2015:28–29).

Before turning to my empirical findings, let me briefly describe my analytical approach. I am ultimately interested in explaining variation with respect to one outcome: whether a court awarded child custody to a litigant. I will present findings from both descriptive bivariate analyses and multivariate regression analyses. In some analyses, I assess outcomes for plaintiffs and defendants simultaneously (taking as the unit of analysis the *litigant*, of which there are two per divorce case: one plaintiff and one defendant). However, given that both plaintiff and defendant in the same case can receive custody, most of the analyses take a plaintiff-oriented and then a defendant-oriented view (taking the *case* as the unit of analysis, from the perspective of either the plaintiff or the defendant only). In other words, I examine whether plaintiffs gained custody (which, in cases involving siblinged children, did not exclude defendants from also receiving custody) and then I examine whether defendants gained custody (again with plaintiffs also receiving custody in some cases). Differences between plaintiffs and defendants merit analysis. Moreover, mother–father differences emerge with greater clarity after looking at outcomes for plaintiffs and then for defendants. Assessing which parents received custody without attention to whether they were plaintiffs or defendants sometimes obscures differences between mothers and fathers simply because plaintiffs enjoyed an advantage over defendants and because mothers were overrepresented among plaintiffs.[1]

If all child custody orders were zero-sum (i.e., if custody of all children were granted to one side only), models for plaintiff outcomes would be inversely identical to models for defendant outcomes. Likewise, if the scope of analysis were limited to couples with only-children (custody of whom, in the absence of joint legal custody, was granted to one side only), models for plaintiff outcomes and models for defendant outcomes would also be inversely identical. Because the majority of couples in China have only one child, models for plaintiff outcomes and models for defendant outcomes are inversely *similar*. They are not inversely *identical*, however, because child custody is positive-sum for many couples with siblinged children, who are often split up with each parent receiving custody.

My multivariate analytical strategy is the same in this chapter as in Chapter 8. After estimating regression models, I use average marginal effects (AMEs) to assess the impact of litigant sex, domestic violence, and the physical possession of children on courts' child custody orders, net of control variables included in the models. An AME can be interpreted as the effect of a change in a variable (e.g., a change in the composition of children from one girl to one boy) on the probability the outcome of interest occurs, holding all remaining variables at observed values (Long and Freese 2014:242–46; Mize 2019:85–87). The regression models include interactions between litigant sex and all other explanatory and control variables. Models in this chapter contain the same control variables as models in Chapter 8. Whether a court is rural or urban is a good indicator of both the social origins of its litigants (Chapters 2 and 4) and the size and composition of its docket (Chapter 6). As before,

---

[1] In descriptive bivariate analyses that combine plaintiffs and defendants, gaps between mothers and fathers are suppressed by the concentration of mothers among plaintiffs, who enjoy a considerable advantage over defendants. Combining plaintiffs and defendants in the multivariate regression analysis would complicate assessments of the effects of domestic violence on child custody outcomes. In order to test whether domestic violence affects mothers and fathers differently, I would need to add a three-way interaction term for litigant sex (mother versus father), litigant role (plaintiff versus defendant), and domestic violence allegations (no versus yes for plaintiff's claim of domestic violence).

therefore, I include fixed effects for the court that adjudicated the case in order to account for unobserved heterogeneity across contexts.

FATHERS ENJOYED AN ADVANTAGE IN RURAL COURTS

From both the qualitative case examples and my review of previous research in Chapter 10, we have reason to expect that judges, when awarding child custody, cared more about which parent had physical possession than about domestic violence allegations. To the extent this is true, and insofar as patrilocal and patrilineal practices endemic to rural areas privilege fathers with respect to the physical possession standard, we also have reason to expect that fathers enjoyed an advantage in child custody determinations in rural courts. Let us now see whether these expectations hold up.

Variables of explanatory interest and their descriptive characteristics are shown in Table 11.1. I described in Chapter 4 my measurement methods for all variables.

TABLE 11.1 Frequency distributions (%) of main variables in regression models

	Henan		Zhejiang	
	Rural	Urban	Rural	Urban
Plaintiff awarded child custody				
No	27	29	33	34
Yes	73	71	67	66
Total	100	100	100	100
Defendant awarded child custody				
No	54	59	59	61
Yes	46	41	41	39
Total	100	100	100	100
Litigant sex				
Plaintiff mother	67	66	67	70
Plaintiff father	33	34	33	30
Total	100	100	100	100
Defendant consent to divorce				
Defendant in absentia				
Public notice	22	13	11	11
No public notice	27	21	31	21
Defendant consented	28	42	31	39
Defendant withheld consent	23	24	26	29
Total	100	100	99	100

TABLE 11.1 (*cont.*)

	Henan		Zhejiang	
	Rural	Urban	Rural	Urban
Child custody claims				
Plaintiff yes, defendant no	42	45	41	39
Both sides	36	35	40	45
Plaintiff no, defendant yes	13	11	13	14
Neither side or undisclosed	9	8	5	3
Total	100	99	99	101
Physical possession of child(ren)				
Plaintiff yes, defendant no	37	25	39	34
Both sides	6	3	4	3
Plaintiff no, defendant yes	23	15	21	17
Neither side or undisclosed	34	57	35	45
Total	100	100	99	99
Composition of children				
One girl only	32	39	41	42
One boy only	39	42	47	45
Siblings	30	20	12	13
Total	101	101	100	100
Domestic violence				
Apparent plaintiff claim	26	31	31	33
No apparent plaintiff claim	74	69	69	67
Total	100	100	100	100
n	15,837	2,379	1,683	846

Note: Totals do not always equal 100% owing to rounding error.

Tables 11.2 and 11.3 contain AMEs calculated from logistic regression models. Table 11.2 contains models for rural courts and Table 11.3 contains models for urban courts. Each table contains models that take the litigant as the unit of analysis. Each model considers *either* plaintiffs or defendants, but not both simultaneously. Once again, models for plaintiffs' outcomes are inversely *similar* to models for defendants' outcomes because most cases are zero-sum: a win for the plaintiff is a loss for the defendant, and vice versa. They are not inversely *identical*, however, because some cases are positive-sum: when siblings are divided between mothers and fathers – which happens more often than not – a win for the plaintiff is also a win for the defendant.

An AME in these tables is interpreted as the effect of a change in a given explanatory variable on the probability a litigant will be awarded child custody. Since each variable in my models is categorical (as opposed to continuous), AMEs are interpreted as differences vis-à-vis omitted reference groups. For example, an AME for "female plaintiff" refers to the average difference between female plaintiffs and the omitted reference group of male plaintiffs, all else being equal. Similarly, an AME for "one girl only" refers to the average difference between plaintiffs with only-daughters and plaintiffs with only-sons (the omitted reference group), all else being equal.[2] Let me illustrate how this works with rural Henan's models for plaintiff outcomes in Table 11.2. According to Model 1 for plaintiff outcomes, the predicted probabilities of gaining child custody are .688 for mothers and .804 for fathers: .688 − .804 = −.116, which is the AME of −.12 for "female plaintiff." According to Model 4 for plaintiff outcomes, which contains the full set of control variables, the predicted probabilities of gaining child custody are .729 for mothers and .731 for fathers: .729 − .731 = −.002, which is the AME for "female plaintiff." Thus, by the time we reach Model 4, after incrementally adding control variables, the gap between female and male plaintiffs has vanished. The control variables added to intervening models level the playing field between mothers and fathers. In other words, mothers and fathers who had the same values of the newly added variables also had the same probability of receiving child custody. The mother–father gap in the probability of receiving child custody was associated with corresponding mother–father gaps in the intervening control variables. Mothers and fathers had unequal probabilities of receiving child custody because they were unequal in some other respect. I will focus on factors that account for mothers' disadvantage in rural courts.

The same pattern of fathers' large advantage in Model 1 shrinking with the addition of control variables in subsequent models – often to the point of disappearing entirely – persists across all analyses of *rural* courts (Table 11.2). This pattern does not extend to *urban* courts,

---

[2] Throughout all analyses, what I refer to as only-daughter or only-son couples were in fact couples with only one son or only one daughter subject to a child custody determination. Most of these children were truly only-daughters and only-sons, but some had older siblings at least 18 years of age who were not subject to child custody determinations.

417

TABLE 11.2 Average marginal effects on receiving child custody, rural courts, calculated from logistic regression models

	Henan (n = 15,837)				Zhejiang (n = 1,683)			
	(1)	(2)	(3)	(4)	(1)	(2)	(3)	(4)
Child custody to plaintiff								
Female plaintiff	-.12***	-.03**	.001	-.002	-.07*	.05**	.02+	.02
Plaintiff domestic violence claim	-.10***	-.03***	-.01	-.01+	-.11***	-.03*	-.02	-.01
Composition of children								
One girl only	.12***	.08***	.05***	.05***	.09***	.05**	.04**	.05***
Siblings	.29***	.29***	.24***	.25***	.20***	.18***	.17***	.17***
Cf.: One boy only								
Defendant consent to divorce								
Defendant in absentia								
Public notice		.11***	.10***	.11***		.04	.05+	.05+
No public notice		.03**	.04***	.04***		.03	.05*	.05*
Defendant withheld consent		-.05***	-.01**	-.01*		.02	.03*	.03+
Cf.: Defendant consented								
Child custody claims								
Plaintiff only		.28***	.10***	.10***		.43***	.26***	.25***
Defendant only		-.31***	-.11***	-.11***		-.50***	-.39***	-.41***
Neither side or undisclosed		.13***	.04***	.04***		.14+	.07	.09+
Cf.: Both sides								
Physical possession of child								
Plaintiff only			.18***	.18***			.29***	.28***
Defendant only			-.41***	-.40***			-.24***	-.26***
Neither side or undisclosed			-.02+	-.02+			.05	.04
Cf.: Both sides								
Additional controls	No	No	No	Yes	No	No	No	Yes
McKelvey & Zavoina pseudo-R²	.23	.54	.74	.75	.20	.71	.84	.85

	(1)	(2)	(3)	(4)	(5)	(6)	(7)	(8)
Child custody to defendant								
Female defendant	-.17***	-.05***	-.02**	-.03***	-.10**	.03⁺	.002	.002
Plaintiff domestic violence claim	.14***	.04***	.01⁺	.02*	.13***	.05*	.03*	.02
Composition of children								
One girl only	-.12***	-.08***	-.06***	-.05***	-.09***	-.05***	-.04**	-.04**
Siblings	.30***	.23***	.21***	.20***	.36***	.22***	.19***	.18***
Cf.: One boy only								
Defendant consent to divorce								
Defendant in absentia								
Public notice		-.16***	-.14***	-.16***		-.03	-.04	-.04
No public notice		-.02	-.03**	-.03***		-.03	-.04*	-.04*
Defendant withheld consent		.07***	.03***	.03***		.003	-.005	.0002
Cf.: Defendant consented								
Child custody claims								
Defendant only		.26***	.12***	.11***		.41***	.39***	.39***
Plaintiff only		-.40***	-.16***	-.16***		-.50***	-.28***	-.28***
Neither side or undisclosed		-.18***	-.08***	-.08***		-.17*	-.10⁺	-.11*
Cf.: Both sides								
Physical possession of child								
Defendant only			.23***	.22***			.24***	.26***
Plaintiff only			-.39***	-.39***			-.28***	-.28***
Neither side or undisclosed			-.12***	-.13***			-.05	-.05
Cf.: Both sides								
Additional controls	No	No	No	Yes	No	No	No	Yes
McKelvey & Zavoina pseudo-R^2	.31	.44	.77	.78	.28	.74	.84	.86

Source: Author's calculations from Henan and Zhejiang provincial high courts' online decisions.
Note: All models include court fixed effects (court dummies) and year of decision. Significance tests are based on standard errors calculated using the delta method and are adjusted for nonindependence between decisions clustered within courts (109 and 52 in the Henan and Zhejiang samples, respectively). "Cf." denotes the omitted reference category.
⁺ $P < .10$ * $P < .05$ ** $P < .01$ *** $P < .001$, two-tailed tests

TABLE 11.3 Average marginal effects on receiving child custody, urban courts, calculated from logistic regression models

	Henan (n = 2,379)				Zhejiang (n = 846)			
	(1)	(2)	(3)	(4)	(1)	(2)	(3)	(4)
Child custody to plaintiff								
Female plaintiff	.08*	.11***	.08***	.07***	.15**	.14***	.10***	.09***
Plaintiff domestic violence claim	-.12***	-.05***	-.03*	-.02*	-.09**	.002	.01	.02
Composition of children								
One girl only	.07**	.04*	.02	.02	.04	.03	.04	.03
Siblings	.24***	.21***	.18***	.19***	.02	.11**	.10**	.10**
Cf.: One boy only								
Defendant consent to divorce								
Defendant in absentia								
Public notice		.21***	.19***	.18***		.15***	.13***	.17***
No public notice		.09**	.09***	.09***		-.01	.01	.05
Defendant withheld consent		-.06*	-.02	-.01		-.02	-.002	.02
Cf.: Defendant consented								
Child custody claims								
Plaintiff only		.22***	.12***	.11***		.42***	.34***	.32***
Defendant only		-.38***	-.27***	-.27***		-.45***	-.37***	-.36***
Neither side or undisclosed		.03	-.001	-.01		.06	.08	.02
Cf.: Both sides								
Physical possession of child								
Plaintiff only			.27***	.26***			.16*	.20**
Defendant only			-.35***	-.36***			-.28**	-.26**
Neither side or undisclosed			.05	.03			-.01	.01
Cf.: Both sides								
Additional controls	No	No	No	Yes	No	No	No	Yes
McKelvey & Zavoina pseudo-R^2	.58	.68	.78	.79	.28	.73	.81	.88

	(1)	(2)	(3)	(4)	(5)	(6)	(7)	(8)
Child custody to defendant								
Female defendant	.07+	.11***	.09***	.08***	.12**	.11***	.07**	.05**
Plaintiff domestic violence claim	.17***	.09***	.06**	.06**	.07*	-.002	-.01	-.01
Composition of children								
One girl only	-.07**	-.04**	-.02	-.02	-.04	-.02	-.03	-.02
Siblings	.31***	.29***	.27***	.26***	.32***	.17***	.16***	.19***
Cf.: One boy only								
Defendant consent to divorce								
Defendant in absentia								
Public notice	-.24***	-.22***	-.23***			-.06	-.05	-.08*
No public notice	-.07*	-.07***	-.07***			.04	.03	-.004
Defendant withheld consent	.06*	.03	.01			.02	.01	-.01
Cf.: Defendant consented								
Child custody claims								
Defendant only		.34***	.26***	.26***	.26***	.39***	.32***	.31***
Plaintiff only		-.31***	-.19***	-.17***	-.17***	-.50***	-.39***	-.34***
Neither side or undisclosed		-.04	-.01	-.01	-.01	-.12	-.12	-.03
Cf.: Both sides								
Physical possession of child								
Defendant only				.20***	.22***		.20*	.14
Plaintiff only				-.44***	-.43***		-.28***	-.37***
Neither side or undisclosed				-.16**	-.15*		-.07	-.15
Cf.: Both sides								
Additional controls	No	No	No	Yes	No	No	No	Yes
McKelvey & Zavoina pseudo-R^2	.37	.61	.75	.77	.31	.71	.82	.92

Source: Author's calculations from Henan and Zhejiang provincial high courts' online decisions.

Note: See note for Table 11.2. Child custody decisions are from 52 and 38 courts in the Henan and Zhejiang samples, respectively. + $P < .10$ * $P < .05$ ** $P < .01$ *** $P < .001$, two-tailed tests however. In urban courts, by contrast, mothers enjoyed an advantage that persisted with the addition of control variables. Looking at Table 11.3, and taking plaintiffs in urban courts as an example, mothers enjoyed an advantage of .08 in Model 1 (the AME was calculated from predicted probabilities of .730 [for mothers] − .650 [for fathers] = .080). The extent of mothers' advantage remained virtually unchanged with the addition of the full set of controls in Model 4. The same pattern of mothers' advantage in Model 1 persisting with the addition of control variables in subsequent models persists across all analyses of urban courts – plaintiffs and defendants in both Henan and Zhejiang (Table 11.3).

Figure 11.1 depicts variation in the probability of gaining child custody by litigant sex (mothers versus fathers), litigant role (plaintiffs versus defendants), and urbanization without any controls. It therefore reflects the same mother–father gaps captured by all renditions of Model 1 in Tables 11.2 and 11.3. Three key takeaways emerge from Figure 11.1. First, in rural areas, where divorce trials were concentrated in both provinces, courts were much more likely to grant child custody to fathers than to mothers. Rural courts ruled in favor of men by a massive margin. The opposite is true in urban areas. Reflecting how the advantages of mothers and fathers flip between rural and urban courts, mothers' and fathers' lines (representing average probabilities of gaining child custody) cross over with urbanization in both provinces. Second, rural fathers' advantage is larger in Henan than in Zhejiang, and urban mothers' advantage is larger in Zhejiang than in Henan. Third, plaintiffs everywhere enjoyed an enormous advantage over defendants. Recall that, owing to differences between Henan and Zhejiang in how sub-provincial urbanization is measured, we can use urbanization to compare courts *within* but not *between* provinces.

In what follows, I will focus on rural courts for two reasons. First, rural courts were more influential than urban courts in the overall landscape of child custody determinations. Second, the regression models identify clear reasons for fathers' advantage in rural courts. We can identify factors that attenuated (and altogether eliminated) the mother–father gaps on the rural end of the urbanization spectrum in Figure 11.1. By contrast, mothers' advantage persisted net of controls in urban courts. In urban courts, mothers did better than fathers regardless of the ways in which mothers and fathers otherwise differed. Nothing in the regression models attenuates mothers' advantage in urban courts. The story of urban courts is therefore a relatively simple

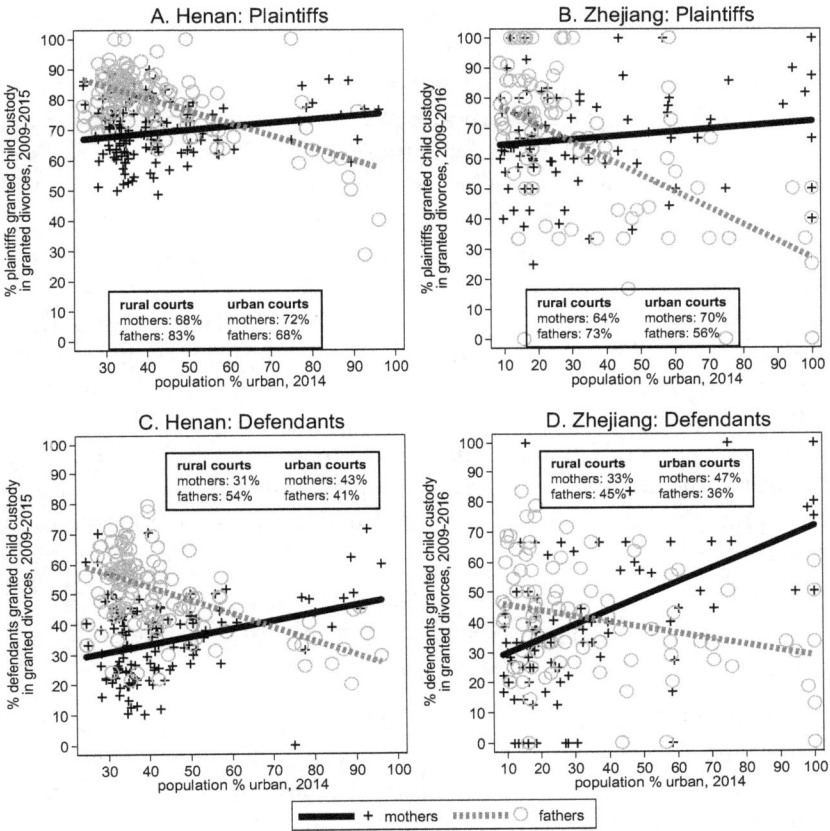

Figure 11.1 Proportion of litigants (%) awarded child custody
Source: Author's calculations from Henan and Zhejiang provincial high courts'
online decisions.
Note: n = 18,216 for Henan and n = 2,529 for Zhejiang. With the exception of
urban courts in Panel C, all sex differences are statistically significant (χ^2, $P < .05$).
For more information on Henan's scatterplot points, see the note under Figure 4.5.
Panels B and D contain 177 scatterplot points each: 87 basic-level courts for female
litigants and 90 basic-level courts for male litigants. Each panel contains best-fit lines
for mothers and fathers.

one. Moreover, because they handled far fewer child custody disputes
than rural courts did, urban courts had a smaller overall impact in
terms of numbers of divorce litigants and their children.

I will proceed by identifying and discussing the effects of various case
characteristics on child custody outcomes in general and on mother–
father gaps in child custody outcomes in particular. I will identify what

matters and what does not matter to judges, including the impact of domestic violence allegations. In all analyses, plaintiffs' domestic violence allegations hurt plaintiffs and rewarded defendants. For example, among *plaintiffs* in Henan's rural courts, the probability of receiving child custody was .10 lower among those who made claims of domestic violence than among those who did not make such claims (Table 11.2, Model 1). Among *defendants* in Henan's rural courts, by contrast, the probability of receiving child custody was .14 greater among those who were accused of abusing their spouses than among those who were not accused of such behavior (Table 11.2, Model 1). These effects shrink and sometimes disappear with the addition of control variables in subsequent models. The same patterns extend to urban courts (Table 11.3). After explaining why rural courts privileged fathers, I will then explain why, in Henan and Zhejiang alike, and in both rural and urban courts, plaintiffs (mostly mothers) were hurt by the domestic violence allegations they made and why defendants (mostly fathers) benefitted from abusing their spouses.

FATHERS ENJOYED ADVANTAGES FROM WITHHOLDING CONSENT AND PUBLIC NOTICE TRIALS

In Tables 11.2 and 11.3, Model 2 adds defendants' consent and litigants' requests for child custody. By comparing Models 1 and 2 in Table 11.2, we can see that controlling for these two variables dramatically shrinks inequality between mothers and fathers in Henan's rural courts, and reverses it in Zhejiang's rural courts. We can see in Table 11.2 that, by withholding consent to divorce, a defendant in a rural court in Henan reduced a plaintiff's probability of gaining child custody by .05 and increased his own probability of gaining child custody by .07. This pattern extends to Henan's urban courts (Table 11.3) but to neither type of court in Zhejiang (Tables 11.2 and 11.3).

Recall that, in order to avoid conflating a defendant's affirmative consent with his failure to withhold consent, my measure of defendant consent to divorce includes whether the defendant participated in trial proceedings or was in absentia (Chapter 4). Unsurprisingly, judges tended to favor plaintiffs when defendants failed to participate in trial proceedings. Across both samples, and in rural and urban courts alike, public notice trials helped plaintiffs and hurt defendants (although the effects are not always statistically significant in the Zhejiang sample). Defendants' failure to participate for other reasons exerts the same effect, but less strongly and only in the Henan sample. Moreover, fathers gained an advantage from this tendency of judges to favor plaintiffs when defendants were in absentia. Let me explain.

In rural courts, defendant consent to divorce accounts for a portion of – and thus partly mediates – fathers' advantage in gaining child custody for two reasons. First, male defendants were far more likely than female defendants to withhold consent to divorce. As we know, withholding consent to divorce is an important source of leverage in child custody disputes, and men were more likely than women to exert it. As I reported in Chapters 4 and 8, female plaintiffs were far more likely than male plaintiffs to face defendant obstructionism of this nature. Second, in rural courts, female defendants were far more likely than male defendants to be served by public notice and thus to fail to participate in trial proceedings. Public notice trials (trials held without defendant participation after public notice service of process failures) were particularly common in Henan's rural courts, where they were almost twice as likely among male plaintiffs (32%) as among female plaintiffs (17%). Even though public notice trials were less common in other contexts, male plaintiffs were more likely to have public notice trials in rural and urban courts in both provinces. The upshot is that, in rural courts, judges were more likely to award child custody to male plaintiffs than to female plaintiffs in part because public notice trials, which were more common for male plaintiffs, practically preclude the possibility of a contested child custody claim. A defendant who fails to participate in trial proceedings will not request child custody, greatly advantaging the plaintiff. As we will see next, "ask, and ye shall receive": whether a litigant requests custody is a critical determinant of judges' child custody orders.

FATHERS ENJOYED AN ADVANTAGE FROM REQUESTING CHILD CUSTODY

Table 11.4 shows that mothers were far less likely to contest custody of sons than of daughters. As we have seen, daughters are less desirable to fathers in general and to fathers in rural areas in particular. In a context of entrenched son preference, many mothers appear to have abandoned hope of gaining custody of a son. Patterns of child custody requests in Table 11.4 reflect the importance of sons to the rural patriarchal family. In only-daughter couples, a request for child custody is, by definition, a request for custody of a daughter; in only-son couples, a request for child custody is, by definition, a request for custody of a son. By contrast, in couples with siblinged children, a child custody request could be for one or more of the children. Among couples with two children, for example, a child custody request could mean a request for custody of two children (two sons, two daughters, or one of each) or a request for one child (one of two sons, one of two daughters, the daughter of mixed-sex siblings, or the son of mixed-sex siblings). I am unable to differentiate between these various scenarios among couples with siblinged children owing to tremendous variation in how they are documented in the court decisions. Nonetheless, given that the majority of couples with more than one child less than 18 years old had at least one son (which we will see in greater detail below), and given the clarity of patterns of requests for custody of only-daughters and only-sons, Table 11.4 leaves no doubt that, in all contexts, fathers were more likely to request custody of sons than of daughters and that, also in all contexts, mothers were more likely to request custody of daughters than of sons. Compared to sons, daughters were less important to fathers.

One possibility is that son preference among fathers was mirrored by daughter preference among mothers. Another possibility is that mothers chose to request custody of daughters strategically, as the most realistic option. Perhaps mothers tried to avoid making requests that, in their estimation, could arouse the ire of their husbands, provoke contentious courtroom battles, and thus compromise their litigation goals. If a male defendant digs in his heels when a female plaintiff requests custody of a son, and if neither side is amenable to compromise, the court may be inclined to deny the entire divorce petition. A third and related possibility is that judges, motivated both to close cases quickly and to minimize the risk of violent retribution from angry husbands, applied pressure on mothers to give up their requests for custody of their children in general and of their sons in particular. A fourth possibility is that, to some mothers, particularly those in rural areas, the very notion of taking a son, especially an only-son, from his father is pure whimsy, culturally nonsensical, and a breach of prevailing patriarchal norms.

Table 11.4 also shows that, in rural courts, mothers were less likely than fathers to request child custody at all.[3] The opposite was true in

---

[3] Note that in Table 11.4, mothers and fathers in Zhejiang's rural courts appear to request child custody at similar rates only because this table combines plaintiffs and defendants. When plaintiffs and defendants are disaggregated in Zhejiang's rural courts, we find that fathers were significantly more likely than mothers to request child custody: 86% and 79%, respectively, among plaintiffs and 60% and 40%, respectively, among defendants.

TABLE 11.4 Proportion of litigants (%) requesting child custody

	Henan			Zhejiang		
	Mothers	Fathers	n	Mothers	Fathers	n
Overall						
Rural courts	61	67***	31,674	66	68	3,366
Urban courts	66	61***	4,758	75	67***	1,692
All basic-level courts	62	66***	36,432	69	68	5,058
By composition of children						
Rural courts						
One girl only	67	56***	9,990	68	63+	1,382
One boy only	51	68***	12,214	60	68***	1,574
Siblings	68	75***	9,470	81	86	410
Urban courts						
One girl only	68	56***	1,844	75	61***	708
One boy only	60	62	1,984	72	70	760
Siblings	73	69	930	81	79	224
All basic-level courts						
One girl only	67	56***	11,834	70	62***	2,090
One boy only	52	68***	14,198	64	69*	2,334
Siblings	68	75***	10,400	81	83	634

Note: This table combines plaintiffs and defendants. Ns therefore refers to the number of individual litigants, not to the number of cases (which, of course, is equal to the number of couples). Because the numbers of fathers and mothers are identical, their respective numbers can be calculated simply by dividing Ns in half.
+ $P < .10$ * $P < .05$ ** $P < .01$ *** $P < .001$, χ^2 test

urban courts, where mothers were more likely than fathers to request child custody. Mothers' smaller incidence of requesting child custody in rural courts stems in part from their greater incidence of being in absentia as defendants. In order to be sure the effect of requesting child custody is not an artifact of the defendant's failure to participate in trial proceedings, Model 2 (in Tables 11.2 and 11.3) controls for in absentia trials (as part of my measure for "defendant consent to divorce").

The effects of requesting child custody are larger and more consistent than the effects of defendant consent to divorce. In rural courts, mothers were less likely than fathers to receive custody of a child of any sex in part because they were less likely than fathers to ask for it. Some rural women may worry that a child will reduce their remarriage prospects. In some divorce cases, women had already formed new partnerships. In some cases, women were under pressure to forfeit child custody in exchange for their freedom. Finally, to some rural women, challenging the patriarchal prerogatives of their husbands' families would be counterproductive or altogether incomprehensible. In rural and urban courts alike, asking for child custody dramatically improved litigants' chances of gaining it, and failing to do so had an equally dramatic effect in the opposite direction. In Table 11.2, the AMEs for female plaintiffs and defendants (which capture the extent and direction of inequality between mothers and fathers) shrink between Models 1 and 2 in part because mothers were less likely than fathers to request child custody in rural courts. Table 11.3 shows that in urban courts, by contrast, where mothers were more likely than fathers to request child custody, mothers' advantage persisted.

Whether a litigant requested child custody was also a function of physical possession. Litigants whose children were already living with them were more likely than litigants whose children were living with their estranged spouses to request legal custody.

FATHERS ENJOYED AN ADVANTAGE FROM PHYSICAL POSSESSION OF CHILDREN

Model 3 (in Tables 11.2 and 11.3) adds physical possession, which almost completely explains away the gap between mothers and fathers in rural courts. In rural courts, fathers' advantage in child custody orders shrinks or disappears among plaintiffs and defendants alike in both provinces (Table 11.2, Model 3). The reason is simple: fathers were significantly more likely than mothers to have physical possession of children. Rural patrilocality emerges in high relief from Figure 11.2, which depicts variation in the probability of physical possession of a child by litigant sex (mothers versus fathers), litigant role (plaintiffs versus defendants), and urbanization. In areas served by rural courts, children were more likely to be living with their fathers than with their mothers; in rural courts in both provinces, mothers were less likely than fathers to have physical possession of their children. The rural gap is particularly noteworthy in Henan; rural fathers' advantage was smaller in Zhejiang than in Henan. And whereas in Henan the mother–father gap narrowed and disappeared with urbanization, in Zhejiang's urban courts, mothers' likelihood of having physical possession of a child surpassed that of fathers.

428

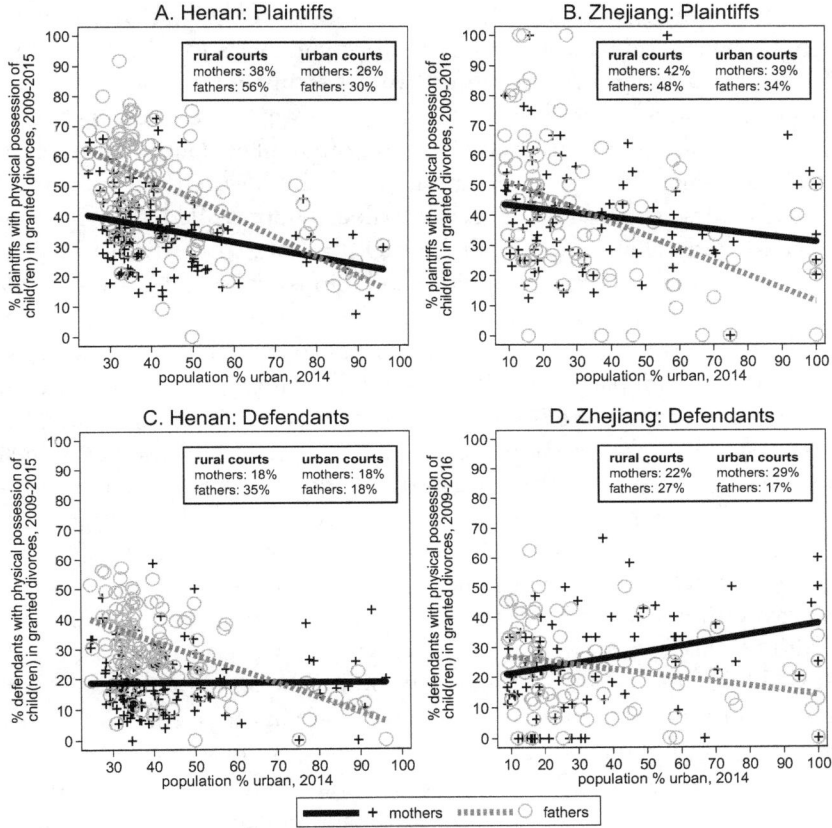

Figure 11.2 Proportion of litigants (%) with physical possession of a child
Source: Author's calculations from Henan and Zhejiang provincial high courts'
online decisions.
Note: n = 18,216 for Henan and n = 2,529 for Zhejiang. With the exception of urban
courts in Panels B and C, all sex differences are statistically significant (χ^2, $P < .05$).
For more information on Henan's scatterplot points, see the note under Figure 4.5.
Panels B and D contain 177 scatterplot points each: 87 basic-level courts for female
litigants and 90 basic-level courts for male litigants. Each panel contains best-fit lines
for mothers and fathers.

Child custody outcomes (in Figure 11.1) clearly correspond to physical possession patterns (in Figure 11.2). While Figures 11.1 and 11.2
certainly suggest that physical possession influences child custody outcomes, multivariate regression analysis will help us assess more definitively the extent to which mother–father inequality in physical possession explains mother–father inequality in child custody determinations.

Many litigants without physical possession of their children challenged their estranged spouses by petitioning courts for child custody. Some, however, did not. Mothers were less likely to contest fathers' physical possession of children than fathers were to contest mothers' physical possession of children.[4] Litigants often asked courts to formalize the status quo. The current location of the child, which litigants often asked courts to preserve, reflects patrilocal norms. Table 11.5 shows that in both Henan and Zhejiang, in rural and urban courts alike, only-daughters were far more likely to be in the physical possession of their mothers. It also shows that the opposite was true for only-sons and siblings (most of whom include sons) in rural Henan. Although the same general pattern applies to rural Zhejiang, differences between mothers and fathers are not statistically significant. In urban courts, by contrast, physical possession of only-sons and multiple children was less gendered in both provinces, and even favored mothers in Zhejiang.

The limitations of my measure of requests for child custody also apply to this measure. Among couples with siblinged children, physical possession reflects one of a number of possibilities, including custody of two children (two sons, two daughters, or one of each) or of one child (one of two sons, one of two daughters, the daughter of mixed-sex siblings, or the son of mixed-sex siblings). I could not reliably or comprehensively distinguish between these various scenarios for the same reason I could not do so with my measure of requests for child custody. Nonetheless, Table 11.5 shows that, in all contexts, mothers were more likely to have physical possession of daughters than of sons and that, in rural areas, fathers were more likely to have physical possession of sons than of daughters.

An additional limitation of this measure is its high proportion of missing values (coded as "neither side or undisclosed"). Rates of physical possession in Figure 11.2 and Table 11.5 are therefore underestimates. Rates at which children were already split up by parents who had separated are also underestimates. Of all couples with siblinged

---

[4] When both sides participated in trial proceedings, the proportion of mothers and fathers requesting child custody when they did not already have physical possession of a child (or when physical possession was not disclosed) was 66% and 77%, respectively, among plaintiffs and 53% and 59%, respectively, among defendants in Henan's rural courts; 75% and 81%, respectively, among plaintiffs and 50% and 56%, respectively, among defendants in Henan's urban courts; 71% and 78%, respectively, among plaintiffs and 46% and 64%, respectively, among defendants in Zhejiang's rural courts; 73% and 83%, respectively, among plaintiffs and 61% and 62%, respectively, among defendants in Zhejiang's urban courts. With the exception of defendants in Zhejiang's urban courts, all differences between mothers and fathers are statistically significant ($P < .05$, χ^2 tests).

TABLE 11.5 Proportion of litigants (%) with physical possession of a child

	Henan			Zhejiang		
	Mothers	Fathers	n	Mothers	Fathers	n
Overall						
Rural courts	31	42***	31,674	35	34	3,366
Urban courts	23	22	4,758	36	22***	1,692
All basic-level courts	30	39***	36,432	36	30***	5,058
By composition of children						
Rural courts						
One girl only	42	32***	9,990	39	30***	1,382
One boy only	24	48***	12,214	32	36	1,574
Siblings	30	43***	9,470	35	39	410
Urban courts						
One girl only	28	19***	1,844	38	20***	708
One boy only	23	24	1,984	36	23***	760
Siblings	17	23*	930	30	29	224
All basic-level courts						
One girl only	39	30***	11,834	39	27***	2,090
One boy only	24	45***	14,198	33	32	2,334
Siblings	29	41***	10,400	33	36	634

Note: As discussed in Chapter 4, many court decisions in the samples do not disclose the living arrangements of children. For this reason, the figures in this table undercount the physical locations of children. Comparisons between mothers and fathers are still valid provided the degree to which physical possession is undercounted does not systematically vary by litigant sex. See the note under Table 11.4.
* $P < .05$ ** $P < .01$ *** $P < .001$, χ^2 test

children in the Henan and Zhejiang samples, I could identify 16% and 14%, respectively, who had split them apart prior to the divorce trial. Excluding decisions from which I could not ascertain the physical locations of children (often because they were undisclosed), the proportion of siblings split apart by their parents was in the range of 25–30% in both samples.[5]

[5] Examples of siblings split apart by their parents include Decision #1022822, Minquan County People's Court, Henan Province, August 30, 2013 (Case ID (2013)民民初字第813号, archived at https://perma.cc/H7MF-DD7N); Decision #1345612, Weishi County People's Court, Henan Province, September 18, 2014 (Case ID (2014)尉民初字第1169号, archived at https://perma .cc/7RS3-UVXN); Decision #1570725, Taiqian County People's Court, Henan Province, July 10, 2015 (Case ID (2015)台民初字第00828号, archived at https://perma.cc/9LRA-FDAX); and Decision #4417391, Wencheng County People's Court, Zhejiang Province, May 5, 2016 (Case ID (2016)浙0328民初741号, archived at https://perma.cc/R3BJ-PKRJ).

The introduction of physical possession in Model 3 (in Tables 11.2 and 11.3) greatly weakens the effect of requesting child custody in rural and urban courts in both provinces because, as we have seen, litigants who requested child custody often already had physical possession of the child. In rural areas, fathers were more likely than mothers to have physical possession of children, ergo they were more likely to request custody, ergo they were more likely to gain custody. The opposite was true in urban areas. In other words, rural women were less likely than rural men and urban women to request child custody in part because they were less likely to have physical possession of their children.[6]

These patterns persist with the addition of control variables in Model 4. In Henan's rural courts, the predicted probability a plaintiff with exclusive physical possession was awarded child custody was a whopping .96 compared to .78 for a plaintiff who shared physical possession of their child or children (the corresponding AME of .18 in Table 11.2, Model 4 is simply the difference between these predicted probabilities: .96 − .78 = .18). Meanwhile, when the defendant had sole physical possession of the child or children, a plaintiff's predicted probability of gaining child custody was only .38 (.38 − .78 = −.40, which is the corresponding AME in Table 11.2, Model 4). In Zhejiang's rural courts, a plaintiff with physical possession of a child enjoyed a similar advantage gaining child custody: a predicted probability of .91 compared to .63 for a plaintiff whose spouse also had physical possession of the child or children (.91 − .63 = .28, which is the corresponding AME in Table 11.2, Model 4). Finally, the predicted probability a plaintiff in rural Zhejiang gained child custody when the defendant had sole physical possession of the child or children was .37 (.37 − .63 = −.26, the value of the corresponding AME in Table 11.2, Model 4).

The story of urban courts stands in stark contrast. Nothing explains away mothers' advantage in urban courts (Table 11.3).

Let us take stock of the empirical findings I have presented so far. Courts greatly favored fathers over mothers in rural areas, and mothers over fathers in urban areas. In rural courts, fathers benefitted from female defendants who were both more likely than male defendants to

---

[6] Note that in Table 11.5 mothers and fathers in Zhejiang's rural courts appear to have physical possession of children at similar rates only because this table combines plaintiffs and defendants. When plaintiffs and defendants are disaggregated, as they are in Figure 11.2, we find that fathers were significantly more likely than mothers to have physical possession of children: 48% and 42%, respectively among plaintiffs and 27% and 22%, respectively, among defendants.

be in absentia and less likely than male defendants to withhold consent to divorce. Fathers in rural courts also gained some of their advantage from mothers' lower rates of petitioning for child custody. Finally, fathers' advantage gaining child custody from rural courts stemmed to a large extent from their correspondingly greater likelihood to have physical possession of their children.

FATHERS ENJOYED AN ADVANTAGE FROM DOMESTIC VIOLENCE

In the samples of child custody decisions, the proportion of all plaintiffs who made claims of domestic violence was 26% and 32% in Henan and Zhejiang, respectively. Consistent with Figure 7.1, the incidence of plaintiffs' allegations of domestic violence was slightly higher in urban areas than in rural areas. Most claims of domestic violence were made by women: 90% in Henan and 83% in Zhejiang. Thus, the proportion of female plaintiffs who made claims of domestic violence was 35% and 39% in the Henan and Zhejiang samples, respectively.

Plaintiffs who made domestic violence allegations had worse outcomes than those who did not, and defendants who were accused of domestic violence had better outcomes than those who were not. These effects are reflected in every version of Model 1 in Tables 11.2 and 11.3. Model 2 introduces defendant consent to divorce and requests for child custody. When these variables are added to the model, they attenuate the effect of plaintiff domestic violence allegations for plaintiffs and defendants alike in rural and urban courts in both provinces (Tables 11.2 and 11.3, Model 2). When defendants failed to participate in trial proceedings, plaintiffs were less likely to make claims of domestic violence, perhaps because there was less of a need to do so when the plaintiff's request for child custody was uncontested. After all, as we can see from the AMEs in Model 2 (Tables 11.2 and 11.3), a defendant's absence from trial proceedings greatly increased the likelihood that a court awarded child custody to the plaintiff. In short, the effect of domestic violence is partly mediated by the effects of defendant consent to divorce.

The effect of domestic violence is similarly mediated by the effects of requests for child custody. Put more plainly, plaintiffs who made allegations of domestic violence were less likely than those who did not make such allegations to request child custody. For this reason, what appears to be the effect of domestic violence is in part the effect of requesting child custody. Finally, as we have seen, an important reason why litigants did not request child custody is because they did not have physical possession of the child. In short, the regression models tell a story that can be summarized in the form of a path model: domestic violence→physical possession of child→request for child custody→child custody order. Let me elaborate.

Several of the qualitative examples I presented in Chapter 10 paint a grim picture in which domestic violence was the key reason why litigants did not have physical possession of their children in the first place. The quantitative data reveal the pervasiveness of this problem. In all contexts, domestic violence dramatically reduced the probability that women had physical possession of their children. Among plaintiffs in Henan who did and who did not make domestic violence claims, the proportion with physical possession of a child was 31% and 45%, respectively. Similarly, among plaintiffs in Zhejiang, the respective proportions were 35% and 44%. For this reason, when physical possession is added to Model 3 in Tables 11.2 and 11.3, the effect of domestic violence allegations shrinks yet again everywhere except in Zhejiang's urban courts. We can infer from these findings that physical possession of children is an important reason why in prior models the effect of plaintiffs' domestic violence allegations was negative for plaintiffs and positive for defendants. Thus, the effect of domestic violence is driven in part by inequality between abuse victims and abuse offenders with respect to the physical possession of children. When plaintiffs and defendants were equally likely to have physical possession of children (Model 3), the effect of domestic violence was much smaller or altogether absent. When their victims escaped, often without their children, perpetrators held an advantage with respect to child custody simply by having sole physical possession of their children. These patterns persist after adding all remaining control variables to Model 4.

Taken together, the regression models tell a story (depicted in the path model earlier) in which domestic violence reduced the probability of physical possession of children, which in turn reduced the probability of requesting child custody, which in turn reduced the probability of being awarded child custody. Leveling the playing field between abuse victims and abuse perpetrators with respect to physical possession washed out the negative effect of domestic violence. At the same time, however, plaintiffs' domestic violence allegations failed to improve their custody outcomes. Among plaintiffs and defendants who were equally likely to have physical possession of children, were equally likely to request child custody, and were otherwise seemingly identical (Model 4), domestic violence still failed to increase victims' or decrease perpetrators' chances of winning custody. Simply put, domestic violence was of no importance and made no difference to judges.

FATHERS ENJOYED AN ADVANTAGE FROM SONS, MOTHERS ENJOYED AN ADVANTAGE FROM DAUGHTERS

In contrast to the hit-or-miss nature of information about the physical possession of children and the motley assortment of ways it appears when courts do record it in their decisions, courts recorded child custody decisions in an almost uniform manner. I could therefore reliably and comprehensively identify and disaggregate siblings in courts' child custody orders. When a court granted custody of at least one child among siblings to a litigant, I was able to distinguish the full array of possibilities for that particular litigant: custody of all children among same-sex siblings, custody of all children among mixed-sex siblings, custody of one daughter among same-sex siblings, custody of one daughter among mixed-sex siblings, custody of one son among same-sex siblings, custody of one son among mixed-sex siblings, and so on. Recall how rarely courts granted joint legal custody. For this reason, in no instances were both parents coded as simultaneously receiving custody of an only-child. We can likewise be confident that when both parents are coded as receiving custody of siblings, the codes reflect courts' tendency to split siblings apart and do not imply joint legal custody.

Indeed, courts split siblings apart in over half of all child custody determinations involving siblings: 62% of the time in Henan and 51% of the time in Zhejiang. This happened more often in rural courts than in urban courts: 62% and 56%, respectively, in Henan, and 59% and 36%, respectively, in Zhejiang. Even twins were divided. In the handful of child custody determinations involving twins (about two dozen in the Henan sample and about a dozen in the Zhejiang sample), courts almost always split them apart. In one illustrative case, the twins were in the physical possession of the defendant's parents. The twins' mother, the plaintiff, made two requests: custody of one of the twins and the return of her dowry. In the course of the trial, she bargained away her dowry. This compromise – achieved when the plaintiff "voluntarily" forfeited her property rights, possibly in order to secure her right to child custody – spared the court the hassle of dealing with the marital estate. In its verdict, the court ordered custody of one twin to each parent and made no ruling on property division (Decision #224435, Linzhou Municipal People's Court, Henan Province, October 19, 2009).[7] Of course, we have no way of knowing whether the defendant obeyed the court order. Given that courts so rarely enforce their decisions, the plaintiff would have ended up with nothing except her freedom in the not unlikely event the defendant failed to comply with the court order.

No law suggests – much less requires – that judges split up siblings. In one case, the judge invoked a generic "principle of fairness" (公平原则) as a rationale (Decision #1229092, Weishi County People's Court, Henan Province, September 9, 2014).[8] In a similar case, when a male defendant withheld consent to divorce unless he was awarded custody of both children, the court granted the daughter to the plaintiff and the son to the defendant as a matter of fairness (Decision #1547183, Nanshao County People's Court, Henan Province, December 26, 2013).[9] The female plaintiff in my final example, owing to her husband's affair with another woman in the village, sought a divorce and ¥10,000 in damages for emotional distress. Her husband admitted to the affair and claimed he had broken it off. As an expression of his resolve to walk the straight and narrow, he had chopped off part of his finger – and the court affirmed both his act and motivation as factual. He then insisted on custody of both children as a condition of agreeing to divorce. Following the principle of fairness, the court gave custody of their son to him and custody of their daughter to the plaintiff (Decision #777658, Puyang County People's Court, Henan Province, December 15, 2011).[10]

Son preference emerges in high relief from Table 11.6. In both samples, only-son couples far outnumbered only-daughter couples. Indeed, in both provinces, couples with at least one son outnumbered couples with at least one daughter by a sizeable margin. In Henan, the proportions of couples with only-daughters and only-sons were 33% and 39%, respectively. In Zhejiang, the proportions were 40% and 48%, respectively. Child custody determinations, on average, involved a lot more children in Henan than in Zhejiang, since couples in Zhejiang

---

[7] Case ID (2009)林民郊初字第153号, archived at https://perma.cc/HQ5D-RUAN.
[8] Case ID (2014)尉民初字第1171号, archived at https://perma.cc/522R-VMN2.
[9] Case ID (2013)南召民初字第1164号, archived at https://perma.cc/LG5Y-HXWQ.
[10] Case ID (2011)濮民初字第1976号, archived at https://perma.cc/GHE5-T5XR.

TABLE 11.6. Proportion of couples (%) with children of various sex compositions

	Henan			Zhejiang		
	Rural courts	Urban courts	All basic-level courts	Rural courts	Urban courts	All basic-level courts
All compositions						
One daughter only	32	39	33	40	40	40
One son only	38	42	39	48	47	48
Siblings, both sexes	22	14	21	8	6	7
Siblings, two daughters	3	2	3	3	3	3
Siblings, two sons	4	4	4	2	3	3
Total	99	101	100	101	99	101
Combinations						
Any siblings	30	20	29	13	12	13
At least one daughter	57	55	57	50	49	50
At least one son	65	59	64	58	56	57
n (couples divorcing)	16,539	2,662	19,201	9,152	4,680	13,832

Note: Totals do not always sum to 100% owing to rounding error. Likewise, discrepancies between combined categories and their component parts are due to rounding error. Because this table includes decisions in which litigant sex is either not disclosed and cannot be inferred, Ns are greater in this table than in subsequent analyses that include litigant sex. All differences between rural and urban courts are statistically significant in both samples ($P < .001$, χ^2 tests).

were more likely to have only-children. The proportion of couples with more than one child less than 18 years old ("any siblings") in Henan (29%) was more than double that in Zhejiang (13%).

In both provinces, son preference was endemic to rural areas more than to urban areas. In rural courts, as Table 11.6 shows, the overall proportion of couples with at least one son (64% in Henan and 57% in Zhejiang) was greater than the overall proportion of couples with at least one daughter (57% in Henan and 50% in Zhejiang). Table 11.6 also shows that the extent to which couples with sons outnumbered couples with daughters was greater in rural areas than in urban areas (although in the Zhejiang sample son preference was only slightly stronger in rural areas than in urban areas).

Before its abolishment in 2016, China's so-called one-child policy allowed couples to have a second child under certain circumstances. For example, in support of rural patriarchal norms, rural couples were generally allowed to have a second child if the firstborn was a daughter. Even when they already had a son, two daughters, or one of each, many rural couples paid a fine after retroactively registering an "above-quota" or "out-of-plan" birth, or attempted to avoid a fine by hiding an unauthorized child (Kennedy and Shi 2019; Michelson 2010).

Table 11.6 shows that, consistent with China's family planning policies, couples were far more likely to limit fertility to one child after having a son than after having a daughter. Couples who started with a daughter were more likely than couples who started with a son to have a second child, often in efforts to bear a son. An overrepresentation of boys among only-children and relatively balanced sex ratios among siblings are telltale signs of a tendency to keep trying for a son after a firstborn girl. Sex ratios provide more direct evidence of this tendency. In both samples, the sex ratios of younger siblings were far more skewed than the sex ratios of older siblings. Sex ratios of boys to girls among the oldest children – including only-children – subject to child custody orders were 1.09:1 in Henan and 1.12:1 in Zhejiang. Younger siblings, by contrast, were much more likely to be boys than girls. Among younger siblings (higher-parity children), ratios of boys to girls were 1.64:1 in Henan and 1.34:1 in Zhejiang. The overall sex ratios and parity-specific sex ratios of children found in my samples of court decisions generally mirror those of young children in the Chinese population (Michelson 2010). Son preference in rural areas is responsible for such a high degree of overrepresentation of boys among younger siblings.

Some scholars, however, argue that China's sex ratio imbalance is in large part a statistical artifact of an overrepresentation of girls among unregistered children (Kennedy and Shi 2019). Of course, I am unable to assess the extent to which girls are "statistically missing" from (or "statistically invisible" in) court decisions. Perhaps some litigants did not disclose their unregistered children to courts. After all, a child custody claim should be supported by proof of parenthood in the form of a household registration booklet or birth certificate. I encountered only a small handful of court decisions in which children were described as "unregistered" (e.g., 未上户口). Even if it does inflate sex ratios, a failure to disclose unauthorized girls reinforces their liminal legal status, particularly if courts are complicit by looking the other way in their efforts to close cases, and is itself an indication of son preference.

Table 11.7 contains proportions of mothers and fathers receiving child custody by the number of children (only-children versus siblings) and urbanization (rural courts versus urban courts). It reaffirms two patterns we have already observed in both Figure 11.1 and the regression models in Tables 11.2 and 11.3, namely that mothers were less likely than fathers to be awarded child custody in rural courts and more likely than fathers to be awarded child custody in urban courts.[11] It also shows a consequence of courts' tendency to split siblings apart: litigants with siblinged children were vastly more likely than litigants with only-children to gain child custody. Custody of only-children is almost always a zero-sum game owing to the almost total irrelevance of joint legal custody. For this reason, the respective proportions of mothers and fathers receiving custody of only-children always sum to 100%. If siblings were never split up, the respective proportions of mothers and fathers receiving custody of siblinged children would likewise always sum to 100%. Because siblings were so commonly divided between parents, sums of proportions of mothers and fathers receiving custody of siblinged children were far in excess of 100% (and typically in excess of 150%). Table 11.7 also shows that, when siblings did stay

---

[11] Note that in Table 11.7 mothers and fathers in Zhejiang appear to have been equally likely to gain child custody from rural courts (54%) only because it combines plaintiffs and defendants. When plaintiffs and defendants are disaggregated, as they are in Figure 11.1, we find that mothers were significantly less likely than fathers to be awarded child custody: 64% and 73%, respectively among plaintiffs and 33% and 45%, respectively, among defendants. A similarly large difference in Zhejiang's rural courts between mothers and fathers with respect to receiving custody of only-children is obscured by combining plaintiffs and defendants.

TABLE 11.7 Proportion of litigants (%) awarded child custody

	Henan			Zhejiang		
	Mothers	Fathers	n	Mothers	Fathers	n
Couples with one child						
Rural courts	47	53***	22,204	51	49	2,956
Urban courts	57	43***	3,828	62	38***	1,468
All basic-level courts	48	52***	26,032	54	46***	4,424
Couples with siblinged children						
Rural courts	77	85***	9,470	75	83*	410
Urban courts	79	77	930	72	62+	224
All basic-level courts	77	84***	10,400	74	76	634
Couples with any children						
Rural courts	56	63***	31,674	54	54	3,366
Urban courts	62	50***	4,758	63	42***	1,692
All basic-level courts	57	62***	36,432	57	50***	5,058

Note: See the note under Table 11.4.
$^+ P < .10$ * $P < .05$ ** $P < .01$ *** $P < .001$, χ^2 test

together, they were more likely to go to fathers than to mothers in rural areas in both Henan and Zhejiang. Among couples with siblinged children divorcing in rural courts, the proportions of mothers and fathers granted custody of no children was 23% and 15% respectively in Henan and 25% and 17%, respectively, in Zhejiang. As striking as these patterns are, however, they obscure enormous variation according to the sex composition of children.

Table 11.8 contains litigants' probabilities of receiving child custody by litigant sex, the number of children, and the sex composition of children. The sheer extent to which courts matched parent and child sex emerges with remarkable clarity. In Henan and Zhejiang, in both rural and urban courts, mothers were far more likely than fathers to receive custody of a daughter when there was only one daughter up for grabs. When there was more than one girl in the family, mothers and fathers were similarly likely to receive custody of a daughter because courts tended to split them up. Meanwhile, fathers were far more likely than mothers to receive custody of a son when there was only one available. An additional son greatly boosted mothers' chances of receiving custody of a son because courts tended to split them up, although fathers remained advantaged in Henan's rural courts even in cases involving more than one son.

TABLE 11.8 Proportion of litigants (%) awarded custody of daughters and sons

	Henan			Zhejiang		
	Mothers	Fathers	n	Mothers	Fathers	n
Granted custody of any daughter						
Rural courts						
One girl only	60	40***	9,990	56	44***	1,396
One girl, one boy	69	31***	6,148	63	37***	188
One girl, two boys	67	33***	300	58	42	24
Two or more girls	93	93	954	98	96	94
Two girls, one boy	88	87	508	89	94	36
Any siblings with girls	73	43***	8,060	75	61**	356
Urban courts						
One girl only	66	34***	1,844	68	32***	708
One girl, one boy	70	30***	508	61	39+	66
One girl, two boys	62	38*	78	–	–	–
Two or more girls	96	96	110	97	100	68
Two girls, one boy	100	67*	30	100	100	12
Any siblings with girls	74	44***	758	79	74	152
All basic-level courts						
One girl only	61	39***	11,834	60	40***	2,104
One girl, one boy	69	31***	6,656	62	38***	254
One girl, two boys	66	34***	378	58	42	24
Two or more girls	93	93	1,064	98	98	162
Two girls, one boy	89	86	538	92	96	48
Any siblings with girls	73	43***	8,818	76	65**	508

TABLE 11.8 (*cont.*)

	Henan			Zhejiang		
	Mothers	Fathers	n	Mothers	Fathers	n
Granted custody of any son						
Rural courts						
One boy only	36	64***	12,220	46	54***	1,580
One boy, one girl	22	78***	6,148	28	72***	188
One boy, two girls	20	80***	508	28	72**	36
Two or more boys	86	94***	1,418	93	93	84
Two boys, one girl	78	88*	300	92	100	24
Any siblings with boys	35	81***	8,524	49	80***	346
Urban courts						
One boy only	50	50	1,984	56	44***	760
One boy, one girl	26	74***	508	45	55	66
One boy, two girls	47	53	30	67	33	12
Two or more boys	94	90	172	92	97	72
Two boys, one girl	69	79	78	–	–	–
Any siblings with boys	47	78***	820	71	74	156
All basic-level courts						
One boy only	38	62***	14,204	49	51	2,340
One boy, one girl	22	78***	6,656	32	68***	254
One boy, two girls	22	78***	538	38	62+	48
Two or more boys	87	93***	1,590	92	95	156
Two boys, one girl	76	86*	378	92	100	24
Any siblings with boys	36	81***	9,344	56	78***	502

Note: See the note under Table 11.4. "Any siblings with girls" refers to any combination of siblings that includes at least one girl. "Any siblings with boys" refers to any combination of siblings that includes at least one boy. Ns of "any siblings" do not equal the sum of listed sibling combinations because they include a small number of additional combinations of siblings not included in the table (e.g., two boys, two girls).

+ $P < .10$ * $P < .05$ ** $P < .01$ *** $P < .001$, χ^2 test

Most striking of all in Tables 11.7 and 11.8 is how much more poorly mothers in rural courts fared in the absence of either a daughter or multiple children. Among only-son couples in rural courts, the proportion of mothers awarded child custody was 36% in Henan and 46% in Zhejiang (Table 11.8). In urban courts, mothers of only-sons did as well or better than fathers of only-sons (Table 11.8). Mothers of only-daughters did even better. Among only-daughter couples in rural courts, the proportion of mothers awarded child custody was 60% in Henan and 56% in Zhejiang (Table 11.8). In urban courts, mothers of only-daughters were awarded child custody 66% and 68% of the time, respectively (Table 11.8). Among couples with more than one child in rural courts (regardless of the children's sex composition), the proportion of mothers awarded child custody was 77% in Henan and 75% in Zhejiang (Table 11.7).

The same patterns – the boost from daughters and multiple children to mothers' chances of receiving child custody – emerge from the regression models in Tables 11.2 and 11.3. In Model 1, for both rural and urban courts, plaintiffs benefitted from only-daughters, and defendants were hurt by only-daughters because most plaintiffs were women and most defendants were men (Tables 11.2 and 11.3). In every model, plaintiffs and defendants alike benefitted tremendously from multiple children because courts tended to split them up. After adding requests for child custody to Model 2, the effects of only-daughters (positive for plaintiffs and negative for defendants) shrink across the board (in all version of Model 2 in Tables 11.2 and 11.3). Thus, the regression models tell another story summarized in the following path model: sex of child/sex of parent→physical possession of child→request for child custody→child custody order. I will elaborate.

The effects of the composition of children are partly mediated by the effects of requests for child custody, which, as we know, are partly mediated by the effects of the physical possession of children. In simpler terms, as previously discussed, mothers were more likely than fathers to request custody of daughters because they were more likely than fathers to have physical possession of daughters (this pattern extends to both rural and urban courts). By the same token, fathers were more likely than mothers to request custody of sons because they were more likely than mothers to have physical possession of sons (this pattern is limited to rural courts). Because the physical possession of children is so highly gendered, its addition to Model 3 further shrinks the effect of only-daughters (for plaintiffs and defendants alike everywhere except

443

Zhejiang's urban courts). In other words, Model 3, by equalizing litigants' physical possession of children, shrinks the gap between those with only-daughters and only-sons. Thus, plaintiffs' advantage securing custody of only-daughters can be attributed in part to plaintiffs' greater likelihood to have physical possession of only-daughters (because plaintiffs were mostly women). Likewise, defendants' advantage securing custody of only-sons can be attributed in part to defendants' greater likelihood to have physical possession of only-sons (because defendants were mostly men).

In many, if not most, cases, courts simply preserved the status quo by applying the physical possession standard. As we saw, judges attached no importance whatsoever to plaintiffs' domestic violence allegations. At the same time, however, the highly gendered nature of child custody orders – the degree to which courts matched parent and child sex – is not only a story about courts' preserving the current situation established by the divorcing couple. Courts did more than formalize presorted gender matches made by the parents. Courts were also active agents of gender sorting. Courts themselves reproduced patriarchal norms by granting custody of daughters to mothers and of sons to fathers even when mothers and fathers were equally likely to request child custody and equally likely to have physical possession of children.

The regression models in Tables 11.2 and 11.3 show overall effects on litigants' probabilities of receiving child custody – mothers and fathers taken together. They do not show whether the various effects they depict differ between mothers and fathers. In regression parlance, they do not show interaction effects. Table 11.9 contains predicted probabilities, calculated from Model 4 in Tables 11.2 and 11.3, that support tests of interactions between litigant sex and child sex. Note that differences between "one girl only" and "one boy only" in Table 11.9 correspond to AMEs for "one girl only" in Model 4 in Tables 11.2 and 11.3. For example, the AME of .05 for "one girl only" (vis-à-vis the omitted reference group of "one boy only") among plaintiffs in Henan's rural courts (Table 11.2, Model 4) corresponds to .675 − .626 = .049 in Table 11.9 (in the "all litigants" column).[12] Likewise, the AME of −.05 for "one girl only" among defendants in Henan's rural

---

[12] The discrepancy of .01 between .67 − .63 = .04 in Table 11.9 and the AME of .05 in Table 11.2 is due to rounding error. The predicted probabilities reported in Table 11.9 are actually .6745 (which rounds down to .67) and .6257 (which rounds up to .63).

courts (Table 11.2, Model 4) corresponds to .36 − .41 = −.05 in Table 11.9 (in the "all litigants" column).

By showing whether the effects of the number and sex composition of children differed between mothers and fathers, Table 11.9 is similar to Table 11.8. Unlike Table 11.8, however, Table 11.9 allows us to assess whether the effects of the number and sex composition of children differed between mothers and fathers who were otherwise seemingly identical (i.e., after adding a full set of control variables).[13] Whereas Table 11.8 contains raw, descriptive probabilities, Table 11.9 contains postestimation predicted probabilities calculated from Model 4 in Tables 11.2 and 11.3.

Two patterns jump out of Table 11.9. First, control variables greatly shrink the effects of the number and sex composition of children. For example, in couples with only-daughters in Henan's rural courts, mothers' overall advantage was .20 (60% − 40% = 20% in Table 11.8). After adding controls, mothers' advantage shrank to .07 among plaintiffs and .06 among defendants (Table 11.9). Had I calculated the contents of Table 11.9 according to Model 1 in Tables 11.2 and 11.3 (i.e., before controlling for requests for child custody and physical possession of children), mothers' and fathers' gender-specific advantages and disadvantages would have been far greater. Second, even net of controls, among mothers and fathers whose requests for child custody and physical possession of children were seemingly identical, courts favored mothers over fathers when determining the custody of only-girls and favored fathers over mothers when determining the custody of only-boys. Among plaintiffs and defendants in rural and urban courts in Henan and Zhejiang (i.e., in every analysis), mothers were advantaged by only-daughters. Mothers' gender-specific advantage was statistically significant everywhere except Zhejiang's rural courts. Net of controls, fathers were advantaged by only-sons only in Henan's rural courts.

Differences between mothers and fathers (in the "mother–father differences" column in Table 11.9) are first differences, which are gaps between two groups in the probability the outcome of interest occurs. Differences between first differences are second differences. Mother–father differences did in fact differ between only-daughter couples and only-son couples to a statistically significant extent everywhere except Zhejiang's rural courts. Tests of second differences in Table 11.9 tell us that, net of controls, gaps between mothers and fathers in the

---

[13] For details on my methods and procedures, see Long and Freese (2014:285), Long and Mustillo (2021), and Mize (2019).

TABLE 11.9 Average predicted probabilities of courts' granting child custody

	All litigants	By parent type		Mother-Father differences
		Mothers	Fathers	
Henan				
Rural courts (n = 15,837)				
Plaintiffs				
a. One girl only*	.67[b, c]	.69[b, c]	.62[b, c]	.07***[b, c]
b. One boy only	.63[a, c]	.60[a, c]	.69[a, c]	−.08***[∧a, c]
c. Siblings	.87[a, b]	.88[a, b]	.85[a, b]	.02[+∧a, b]
Defendants				
a. One girl only*	.36[b, c]	.40[b, c]	.34[b, c]	.06***[b, c]
b. One boy only	.41[a, c]	.34[a, c]	.43[a, c]	−.09***[a]
c. Siblings	.61[a, b]	.56[a, b]	.63[a, b]	−.07***[a]
Urban courts (n = 2,379)				
Plaintiffs				
a. One girl only	.67[c]	.73[b, c]	.57[b, c]	.16***[b, c]
b. One boy only	.65[c]	.66[a, c]	.65[a, c]	.004[∧a]
c. Siblings	.85[a, b]	.86[a, b]	.82[a, b]	.04[a]
Defendants				
a. One girl only	.35[c]	.47[b, c]	.29[b, c]	.19***[∧b, c]
b. One boy only	.36[c]	.38[a, c]	.35[a, c]	.03[a]
c. Siblings	.62[a, b]	.63[a, b]	.62[a, b]	.01[a]

Zhejiang
Rural courts (n = 1,683)
  Plaintiffs

a. One girl only	.66[b,c]	.67[b,c]	.64[c]	.04^
b. One boy only	.62[a,c]	.62[a,c]	.61[c]	.01
c. Siblings	.79[a,b]	.79[a,b]	.77[a,b]	.03^

  Defendants

a. One girl only	.36[b,c]	.39[c]	.36[b,c]	.03[c]
b. One boy only	.40[a,c]	.41[c]	.41[a,c]	−.002
c. Siblings	.57[a,b]	.54[a,b]	.62[a,b]	−.08[+a]

Urban courts (n = 846)
  Plaintiffs

a. One girl only	.66	.72[b]	.53[b]	.19***[b]
b. One boy only	.63[c]	.63[a,c]	.64[a]	−.002[^,c]
c. Siblings	.73[b]	.78[b]	.63	.14*[^]

  Defendants

a. One girl only	.34[c]	.44[b]	.29[b,c]	.16***[^,b]
b. One boy only	.36[c]	.33[a,c]	.36[a,c]	−.03[a]
c. Siblings	.55[a,b]	.57[b]	.53[a,b]	.04

Note: All contents of this table are postestimation calculations from the same models used to make the postestimation calculations of AMEs in Table 11.2 (rural courts) and Table 11.3 (urban courts), Model 4. A caret (^) denotes a slight discrepancy due to rounding error between an AME (in the "mother–father differences" column) and the corresponding predicted probabilities from which it was calculated (in the "mother" and "father" columns). Likewise, differences between predicted probabilities in this table are not always identical to corresponding AMEs in Table 11.2 (rural courts) and Table 11.3 (urban courts) owing to rounding error. Superscript letters correspond to other categories of the same variable. Known as contrasts, they denote the statistical significance (at P < .05) of differences between variable categories (first differences). In the "mother–father differences" column, they also denote the statistical significance (at P < .05) of mother–father gaps (second differences) across different variable categories. On contrasts, see Long and Freese (2014:252) and Mize (2019:106).

+ P < .10 * P < .05 ** P < .01 *** P < .001, two-tailed tests likelihood of gaining custody of only-daughters (which favored mothers) was, in most analyses, statistically significantly different from the gap between mothers and fathers in gaining custody of only-sons (which favored fathers).

OTHER EFFECTS

In my presentation of results from analyses of child custody determinations, I have focused attention on what mattered most to judges: the physical possession of children, litigant sex, and the number and sex composition of children. I have also drawn attention to something unequivocally unimportant to judges: domestic violence allegations. My analyses include additional control variables I have not yet discussed. I simply note here that the effects of the other variables included in Model 4 paled in comparison to the effects I thoroughly discussed. For example, on the whole, the participation of female judges did not improve mothers' chances of gaining child custody. Similarly, generally speaking, mothers with legal representation fared no better than mothers without legal representation. Other variables added to Model 4 had similarly inconsequential effects on child custody outcomes. After all, AMEs in Model 3 and Model 4 are virtually identical.

SUMMARY AND CONCLUSIONS

Chapter 8 demonstrated, on the basis of an analysis of over 60,000 court decisions in my Henan and Zhejiang samples, that, far more often than not, courts denied the first-attempt divorce petitions of domestic violence victims. A plaintiff's claim of domestic violence, even when fully documented by admissible evidence, failed to increase even slightly the court's probability of granting her divorce request. In Chapter 9, we saw that victims of marital abuse who were denied the divorces they requested were forced either to return home with their abusers or live elsewhere, often at the cost of separation from their children. My analyses of child custody determinations in both this chapter and Chapter 10 reveal that domestic violence allegations were similarly unimportant to Chinese judges when they made child custody determinations. Just as domestic violence claims did not increase the likelihood that courts granted women's divorce requests (Chapter 8), they likewise did not increase the likelihood that courts granted child custody to marital abuse victims.

On the contrary, men were rewarded with child custody for beating their wives, because courts by and large preserved the status quo by granting custody to the parent who had physical possession of the child. When women left their abusive husbands, they were sometimes fleeing for their lives. With life and limb at risk, women sometimes left everything – including their children – behind. Owing to the importance judges attached to physical possession in their child custody orders, doing so perversely undermined their chances of winning child custody, and perversely put the health and safety of children at risk.

The over 20,000 child custody determinations I analyzed in this chapter bring into high relief judges' impulse to preserve the status quo. In rural areas, which accounted for the majority of all child custody determinations, the status quo was a patriarchal one insofar as fathers were more likely than mothers to have physical possession of children in general and of sons in particular. Although a litigant's request for child custody was another major source of influence on the court's decision, many litigants requested child custody only when they already had physical possession of a child. Some litigants' child custody requests were motivated by their desire to preserve and formalize such highly gendered de facto custody arrangements. Consistent with the logic of patriarchy and the title of this chapter, rural courts tended to grant custody of only-sons to fathers. The likelihood of receiving custody of an only-son from a rural court was far lower among mothers. In rural areas, mothers' best chances for child custody came from multiple children and from only-daughters. In cases involving siblings, courts frequently split them up between the parents. In cases of mixed-sex siblings, courts typically granted custody of sons to fathers and custody of daughters to mothers.

To be sure, some litigants without physical possession of a child did contest the status quo by petitioning for custody of a child living with the other parent. Many, however, resigned themselves to – and thus did not contest – the living arrangements of their children at the time of the trial. Courts even pressured mothers to withdraw their requests for child custody, particularly when the child was already in the physical possession of the father. In rural areas, mothers desperate to escape miserable marriages not infrequently conceded custody of children, particularly of sons, in court-brokered compromises that favored fathers in terms of child custody and property division. Owing to both the cultural importance of patrilineality and pragmatic old-age security considerations in a context of patrilocality, rural fathers generally care more about sons than daughters. And owing to endemic son preference in rural China, when couples separate prior to divorcing, sons often stay with fathers, and daughters often follow mothers. In short, there are several mechanisms behind the strong association between litigants' child custody requests and their physical possession of children. Much of the time courts passively affirmed and formalized the preexisting living arrangements of children. When parents had similar claims on children, courts were active agents of patriarchy by staunchly supporting the prerogatives of fathers, particularly in rural Henan.

In sum, judges, through their decision-making behavior, supported the very patriarchal norms which China's family laws were designed to dismantle. More than serving to protect women from patriarchy, courts operated in the service of patriarchy. Courts did less to stand up to patriarchy and more to preserve it. On the whole, Chinese family law has significantly failed to penetrate the rural patriarchal order.

Fathers' advantages in child custody determinations were limited to rural areas, which accounted for a sizeable majority of all child custody determinations. Urban courts, by contrast, favored mothers over fathers. Women's better outcomes in urban courts may have less to do with courts per se – e.g., the social values of judges – and more to do with weaker patriarchal control over residential arrangements, to which courts tended to defer in their child custody orders. In rural areas, children were more likely to be in the physical possession of their fathers than of their mothers owing primarily to the norm of patrilocal marriage, whereby women marry into their husband's families, and the entrenched tradition of patrilineality, whereby lines of descent are carried forward through sons. As neolocal residence becomes more common and newly married couples increasingly establish homes apart from their parents in rural areas, and as rural old-age pension support strengthens, the rural family's patriarchal grip on sons should weaken and mothers' prospects of gaining child custody in contested divorce cases should improve. Until either that happens or courts take the rights of women and the best interests of children more seriously, divorced mothers without daughters or siblinged children will continue to find themselves at a severe disadvantage in child custody determinations in China's rural courts.

One limitation of my analysis is the absence of a measure for infant or nursing children. Information about the ages (or years of birth) of children is spotty at best. Decisions referring to children "under the age of two" (e.g., 未满两周岁, 不满两周岁, and 不到满两周岁) or "of nursing age" (e.g., 在哺乳期) were few in number, less than 5% in both samples. However, if judges tended to grant custody of infant and nursing children to their mothers, empirical results I have presented in this chapter indicating an overall disadvantage to mothers would be conservative. Imagine that, all else being equal, courts were equally likely to grant custody of children more than two years old to mothers and fathers. If this were true, and if judges tended to apply the infant standard, then mothers would have enjoyed an overall advantage in the probability of winning custody of a child of any age. For this reason, my empirical findings indicating an overall advantage to fathers likely understate the true extent of gender differences in child custody determinations.

CHAPTER TWELVE

CONCLUSIONS

Assessing the Impact of Law by Observing Judicial Behavior

China's laws are consistent with global legal norms that allow and even oblige courts to support unilateral divorce petitions from plaintiffs claiming to be victims of domestic violence. China's laws also include a competing and highly subjective legal standard – the breakdown of mutual affection – that Chinese judges routinely apply largely according to mutual consent and the lack thereof. Pressure from clogged courts, a political ideology hostile to divorce, and performance evaluation systems that reward judges for volume and efficiency and punish them for social unrest and "extreme incidents" compel judges to deny divorce petitions. The breakdownism divorce standard provides convenient support and justification for judges to do so. By routinely denying divorce petitions when plaintiffs file them for the first time, judges extend a judicial process of a few months into a litigation repeat that typically drags on for over a year. When plaintiffs return to court for another try, judges tend to grant their refiled petitions. This routine practice, which I call the divorce twofer because it rewards judges in several ways, prolongs abused women's exposure to the source of their abuse. Some women stay with their abusers until the divorce is finalized and child custody and property division are resolved. Some women escape by participating in labor migration or otherwise going into hiding. Women who leave their children behind in the process of fleeing abuse often, as a consequence, lose their claims for child custody.

In their struggle to divorce, women have often sacrificed child custody and marital property in exchange for their husbands' consent to divorce. Over 40 years ago, Mnookin and Kornhauser (1979) argued that courts in the United States, in a process they called "bargaining in the shadow of the law," set the terms for out-of-court negotiations in divorce disputes. Even though courts account for only a small share of all divorces in China, they cast a long shadow over the entire landscape of divorce. Judges have rarely granted divorce petitions when defendants withheld consent. Simply by withholding consent, spouses – even abusive spouses – have mostly thwarted first-attempt divorce petitions. In the Civil Affairs Administration, where most divorces are processed, mutual consent is a sine qua non of divorce. Spouses of divorce-seekers therefore wield enormous leverage over the terms of divorce in both forums simply by withholding consent. Defendants, most of whom are men, use their consent as a bargaining chip. Plaintiffs, most of whom are women, must then use marital property and child custody as bargaining chips. Once they secure their spouses' consent to the divorce itself and to all terms of the divorce, often at great cost, divorce-seekers can go either to the Civil Affairs Administration or to court. Perhaps for this reason, and because Civil Affairs divorces are quicker, easier, and cheaper, most divorce-seekers whose first-attempt petitions were denied in court do not return to court for another try. If divorce litigation were less restrictive and judges attached less importance to mutual consent, fewer women would settle for raw deals in the Civil Affairs system.

Divorce-seekers' bleak prospects of success in China's courts has extended seamlessly to victims of domestic violence. Simply put, domestic violence has been unimportant to judges. The inherent legal ambiguity and flexibility of the breakdownism divorce standard has helped judges sideline the legal relevance of domestic violence allegations. As a forum of last resort for victims of marital abuse, courts have generally done less to protect vulnerable women than to empower and enable their abusers.

Women's outcomes have been worse than men's in other respects, too. Gender bias animates every stage of the litigation process. Among plaintiffs filing for divorce, women have been less successful than men at ending their marriages on the first try. Women, often under duress, have been more likely than men to withdraw with petitions. Courts have been more likely to issue adjudicated denials to female plaintiffs than to male plaintiffs. When they do grant divorces, courts have been more likely to grant child custody to fathers than to mothers. By subverting laws designed to deliver gender justice, courts are themselves a mechanism of gender injustice.

In this book, I set out to document and explain decoupling in China's divorce courts. "Decoupling" refers not only to the efforts of divorce-seekers to decouple from their spouses. It also refers to a yawning and widening gap between, on the one hand, China's judicial practices and, on the other hand, its domestic laws and international legal commitments. Working in the long tradition of gap studies in the field of law and society (Gould and Barclay 2012), I have sought to understand the gap in China between the law on the books that supports divorce and the law in action that restricts divorce.

Although it is not supported by any law, the divorce twofer, as a highly institutionalized practice, has assumed a law-like and policy-like quality. Throughout this book I have referred to as "endogenous" the salient institutional forces competing with and undermining the exogenous force of law. The law in action is endogenously shaped in a couple of respects. First, judges' incentives to *deny* first-attempt divorce petitions are rooted in now-familiar local institutional influences on judicial decision-making that compete with and neutralize its domestic laws and international legal commitments calling on judges to *grant* first-attempt divorce petitions. Second, law is endogenous to organizational prerogatives and practices. As Lauren Edelman's (2016) legal endogeneity theory would lead us to expect, legal ambiguity gives China's basic-level courts "wide latitude to construct the meaning of law and compliance with law" (p. 14) and enables Chinese judges to interpret and apply the law in ways that are at odds with the law on the books. In contrast to views of law as "an exogenous, coercive, downward force on organizations" (Edelman 2016:41), legal endogeneity theory views law as endogenously created by the very organizations subject to its control.

Michael Lipsky's ([1980] 2010) classic theory of street-level bureaucracy provides a complementary framework for explaining how and why Chinese judges created bottom-up legal and policy substitutes for the top-down domestic laws and international legal commitments they sidelined and subverted. Just as legal ambiguity is at the center of Edelman's (2016) explanation for "the gap between ideal and actual" (p. 104), space for discretionary judgment is at the center of Lipsky's (2010) explanation for "the gap between the realities of practice and service ideals" (p. xvi), "the gap between policy as written and policy as performed" (p. xvii), and "the gap between public promises and performance" (p. 214).

CHINESE JUDGES AS STREET-LEVEL BUREAUCRATS

Street-level bureaucracies are public service agencies composed of a sizeable share of street-level bureaucrats, the key defining characteristics of whom include direct interaction with citizens seeking public services and a high degree of discretion in how they carry out their work (Lipsky 2010:3). As such, street-level bureaucrats are "frontline workers" serving as gatekeepers to state resources, services, and opportunities (Lipsky 2010; Maynard-Moody and Portillo 2010). Street-level bureaucracies include "the schools, police and welfare departments, lower courts, legal services offices, and other agencies whose workers interact with and have wide discretion over the dispensation of benefits or the allocation of public sanctions" (p. xi). Lipsky focuses on police officers, teachers, and social workers, but explicitly extends the scope of his theory to "judges, public lawyers and other court officers, and many other public employees who grant access to government programs and provide services within them" (p. 3).

As a consequence of their considerable discretion to interpret and implement rules, the individual decisions of street-level bureaucrats "become, or add up to, agency policy" (p. 3). By redefining law and policy, street-level bureaucrats decouple their decision-making from the judicial ideal. In a practical sense, therefore, street-level bureaucrats *make* law and policy. Lipsky (2010:24) calls them "de facto policy makers," while Maynard-Moody and Portillo (2010:260) call them the "ultimate policymakers."

In China, basic-level courts are quintessential street-level bureaucracies, and their frontline judges are quintessential street-level bureaucrats. China's judiciary is undifferentiated from the rest of the state bureaucracy. Although judges enjoy a real measure of decision-making autonomy in their everyday work, the judiciary as a whole is subordinate and beholden to the needs and interests of the party-state (Fu 2014; Kinkel 2015; Peerenboom 2010). As civil servants without tenure, judges are duty-bound to support the party-state and its political priorities. At the same time, however, owing to their heavy caseloads and the highly discretionary nature of their work, judges develop creative methods of complying – or faking compliance – with shifting mandates and directives from above (Li, Kocken, and van Rooij 2016; Paneyakh 2014). According to Lipsky (2010:xiii), "the decisions of street-level bureaucrats, the routines they establish, and the devices they invent to cope with uncertainties and work pressures, effectively *become* the public policies they carry out" (emphasis in original). Judges' routine coping strategies, which so frequently diverge from the judicial ideal, "add up to street-level policy" (Lipsky 2010:86).

Judges in China's basic-level courts illustrate five defining hallmarks of street-level bureaucrats. First, owing to pervasive legal ambiguity, judges exercise enormous discretion at every stage of the civil litigation process. Chinese-language scholarship about China's civil justice system is replete with the words "discretionary" (裁量权), "subjective" (主观), and "arbitrary" (随意) for describing almost every type of judicial decision, and the words "flexible" (弹性 and 灵活) and "ambiguous" (笼统, 模糊, and 含糊) for describing decision-making rules. Throughout this book we have seen judges exercise discretion in the interpretation and implementation of ambiguous rules concerning: whether to issue a public notice to a defendant whose whereabouts are alleged to be unknown; whether to apply the simplified civil procedure (solo judge) or the ordinary civil procedure (collegial panel); whether to admit or exclude evidence; whether to affirm a litigant's claim of domestic violence on the basis of admitted evidence; whether to affirm a litigant's claim of a two-year physical separation; whether to affirm the breakdown of mutual affection; how to protect the best interests of the child in child custody determinations; and whether and how to broker informal compromises, settlements, and concessions between litigants. A judge in Anhui succinctly asserted that, compared to those who work on other kinds of civil cases, "Judges in domestic relations trials are distinguished by the relatively great deal of discretion they wield" (Zhou and Qiu 2018). Legal ambiguity allows judicial practice to decouple from laws that champion the freedom of divorce, gender equality, and the best interests of the child.

Second, the problem of "many cases, few judges" that characterizes China's court system extends to street-level bureaucracies everywhere. China's basic-level courts exemplify the universal challenges of public service agencies that face "extraordinary demand for resources relative to the supply" and are "under-staffed relative to the demands on them" (Lipsky 2010:132). "Street-level bureaucracies are labor-intensive in the extreme" (p. 5) because "demand for services is practically inexhaustible relative to supply" (p. 55). Toiling under the weight of heavy caseloads, street-level bureaucrats "cannot do the job according to the ideal conceptions of the practice" (Lipsky 2010:xvii). "Resources are chronically inadequate relative to the tasks workers are asked to perform" (p. 27n1) owing to "the scarcity of resources relative to the demands made upon them" (p. 83). "Street-level bureaucrats characteristically have very large case loads relative to their responsibilities. The actual numbers are less important than the fact that they typically cannot fulfill their mandated responsibilities with such case loads" (p. 29). The working conditions of China's basic-level courts, like those of other street-level bureaucracies, lead to worker burnout and attrition (p. xv).

Third, owing to their heavy caseloads, frontline public service workers such as Chinese judges are too busy to give each individual case the full consideration demanded by formal procedures. "The fact that street-level bureaucrats must exercise discretion in processing large amounts of work with inadequate resources means that they must develop shortcuts and simplifications to cope with the press of responsibilities" (Lipsky 2010:18). Their innovative "coping behaviors" and "coping mechanisms" allow them to complete their tasks, albeit often in ways that are contrary to organizational goals and service ideals (Lipsky 2010:xvii–xviii). China's basic-level courts have coped with their crushing workloads by developing various methods of optimizing scarce judicial resources: deputizing assistant judges and putting them to work on a greater share of cases; assigning a greater share of cases to solo judges, which entailed increasing simplified civil procedure utilization rates; expanding the pool of lay assessors and increasing their rates of participation on collegial panels; and, of course, clamping down on divorce by denying a greater share of first-attempt divorce petitions. Such routines, simplifications, and shortcuts "did not merely facilitate work; they determined outcomes divergent from the stated policy objective" (Lipsky 2010:84). The right of abused women to divorce is a clearly "stated policy objective" of the Chinese party-state that is fully supported by law but undermined by judges' routine practice of denying first-attempt divorce petitions.

Adjudicated denials in first-attempt divorce cases have significantly lightened judges' workloads while simultaneously supporting China's political priorities of marital preservation and stability maintenance. For these reasons, judges have denied divorce petitions across the board, regardless of whether they involved statutory wrongdoing. Although a fault-based claim of domestic violence can and should be lawful grounds for divorce, divorce petitions involving such a claim – which accounted for about 30% of all first-attempt divorce petitions – were no more likely to be granted than those which did not involve such a claim. When judges denied divorce petitions, they frequently and improperly misrepresented allegations of domestic violence as ordinary family conflict, mutual hitting, or aberrations from otherwise healthy marital behavior; cited abusers' contrition and unwillingness to divorce as evidence of mutual affection and reconciliation potential; and disaffirmed the admissibility and validity of supporting evidence. By doing so, judges routinely gaslighted domestic violence victims. Recasting as fundamentally healthy and hopeful – as a pretext for forcibly preserving – a toxically abusive marriage from which the victim seeks to exit is the very epitome of gaslighting.

Fourth, street-level bureaucrats triage and ration scarce resources by privileging help-seekers they deem to be more "deserving" and "worthy" of public services. They classify, sort, and differentiate applicants into categories of deservingness and worthiness shaped by cultural stereotypes (Lipsky 2010). Their "routines and simplifications are subject to workers' occupational and personal biases, including the prejudices that blatantly and subtly permeate society. The biases expressed in street-level work may be expected to be manifested in proportion to the freedom workers have in defining their work life and the slack in effective controls to suppress those biases" (Lipsky 2010:85). Chinese judges, like other street-level bureaucrats, make judgments about the credibility and truthfulness of applicants (Lipsky 2010:74), some of whom must bear "persistent assumptions of fraud and dishonesty" (p. 93). Empirical patterns presented throughout this book suggest that judges have regarded women (1) as more likely than men to file frivolous and impulsive divorce petitions, make bogus claims of the unknown whereabouts of the spouses they want to divorce, and exaggerate and fabricate claims of domestic violence, and therefore (2) as less deserving than men of divorce on the first attempt, the full due process afforded by the ordinary civil procedure, and child custody.

Fifth, street-level bureaucracies measure and evaluate the performance of their workers. Because the extent to which a worker's performance advances organizational goals generally eludes measurement, street-level bureaucracies set performance targets that are easier to measure. These "surrogate measures" take on a life of their own and "guide future performance" as street-level bureaucrats orient their behavior toward them (Lipsky 2010:52). In their efforts to maximize their professional rewards and minimize their professional sanctions, street-level bureaucrats carry out their work tasks according to how they are measured and evaluated. In the words of Lipsky (2010:51), "the behavior of workers comes to reflect the incentives and sanctions implicit in those measurements" and "behavior in organizations tends to drift toward compatibility with the ways the organization is evaluated." Although an organizational goal of courts everywhere is to deliver justice according to the law, judicial performance in China is evaluated primarily according to measures of case processing efficiency and litigants' acceptance of outcomes.

Endogenous institutional dynamics – including the conditions of work in street-level bureaucracies – help explain the limited impact of exogenous laws and legal norms. Let us now consider the theoretical and methodological implications of institutional decoupling in China's divorce courts.

THEORETICAL IMPLICATIONS

My empirical findings on marital decoupling in China shed theoretical light on institutional decoupling – the extent to which and reasons why legal systems that bear the symbolic hallmarks of global legal norms subvert them in practice. Decades of research on local compliance with global norms documents a ubiquitous gap between doctrinal law and on-the-ground practices, and the ubiquity of hollow and symbolic commitments to world society values. Do previous explanations for the extent and character of decoupling between global legal commitments and local legal practices in general help us make sense of decoupling in the specific context of Chinese divorce litigation? China's ratification of CEDAW, which scholars argue helps explain international variation in the gap between promises and practices (Englehart and Miller 2014; Htun and Weldon 2018; Wang and Schofer 2018), appears to have had little impact on the protection of Chinese domestic violence victims unilaterally seeking divorce in court. Of course, we have no way of knowing whether the plight of Chinese women seeking freedom from their abusive husbands would have been even worse in its absence. Furthermore, divorce litigation is only one piece of the larger puzzle of gender violence, and perhaps China's ratification of CEDAW has helped women in other institutional contexts.

Can we make sense of China's divorce twofer as a function of bureaucratic capacity (Cole 2015)? While increasing the supply of judges and other court personnel, by alleviating some of the pressures of crushing dockets that incentivize judges to deny first-attempt divorce petitions, might help women seeking divorce, the institutional roots of the divorce twofer also lie with the endogenous institutional logics of a political ideology of marital preservation and performance evaluation systems that incentivize adjudicated denials of divorce petitions. Can we attribute gender injustice in China's divorce courts to the absence of a strong and autonomous domestic feminist women's movement (Htun and Weldon 2018)? We can only speculate about the hypothetical ability of such a movement to diminish the impact of the patriarchal cultural beliefs and gender stereotypes shaping judges' decisions.

My Henan–Zhejiang comparison has illuminated contextual similarities and differences. The same gender injustices emerge in high relief from both provincial samples. Empirical patterns show remarkable consistency between the two provinces in the extent of and reasons for gender inequality in case outcomes. That the empirical patterns I presented are so consistent across two subnational contexts that differ in other ways suggests the power of the endogenous institutional logics at the heart of my argument.

With respect to regional differences, adjudicated divorce was far more restrictive in Zhejiang than in Henan. Zhejiang, as a coastal province adjacent to Shanghai in one of the most prosperous parts of China, is much more integrated with and proximate to world society than Henan is. Adherents of world society theory would have been hard-pressed to predict a judicial clampdown on divorce unfolding at precisely a place and time of intensifying global integration such as China in the mid-2000s. Nor would they have predicted the judicial clampdown on divorce to be earliest and most severe in an area of China closest to world society. Contrary to the expectations of world society theory, adjudicated divorce became increasingly difficult to obtain over time as court dockets across China swelled, and have been considerably more difficult to obtain in Zhejiang than in Henan in no small measure because court dockets have been so much heavier in Zhejiang. The contrast between Henan and Zhejiang in this regard also reflects a more general effect of urbanization: in both provinces, urban courts, which had heavier dockets than rural courts, were more inclined than rural courts to deny first-attempt divorce petitions.

At the same time, however, empirical findings partially support world society theory by revealing that gender injustices in both provinces were concentrated in rural areas further away from world society. In urban courts, female plaintiffs were at no disadvantage vis-à-vis male plaintiffs with respect to the probability of obtaining a divorce on the first try, and mothers enjoyed an advantage vis-à-vis fathers with respect to the probability of winning child custody when divorces were granted. Judges' biases toward female litigants appear to diminish with urbanization. Over time, the ongoing process of urbanization may help to exert gender-equalizing pressures on divorce litigation practices. During the time period covered by the court decisions I analyze in this book, however, predominantly urban areas accounted for only a small share of all divorce adjudications.

In the context of Chinese divorce litigation, the direction of institutional "drift" (Schofer and Hironaka 2005) has been away from at least as much as toward global norms. The "paradox of empty promises" is not courts' incremental enforcement of international legal commitments that hitherto were widely ignored, as Hafner-Burton and Tsutsui (2005) might expect. On the contrary, it is the extent to which courts are a primary obstacle to the realization of the promises enshrined in laws intended to protect women's freedom of divorce and to offer relief to victims of marital violence. The real paradox is that Chinese judges are *expected* to subvert and stretch beyond recognition domestic laws that are "constructed out of a common and universalistic world cultural frame" (Boyle and Meyer 1998:214) and are *rewarded* for doing so. We cannot understand Chinese courts' routine failure to offer relief from domestic violence as merely a matter of compliance failure. On the contrary, we should understand the judicial practices I have documented in this book as compliance success. Courts' routine failure to protect victims of domestic violence is a function of *purposeful institutional design*.

Judges' seemingly limitless discretion to assess marital quality, reconciliation potential, and evidence submitted by litigants is hardly a problem of implementation, much less an unintended consequence of institutional design flaws. It is an institutional *feature* as much as it is an institutional *bug*. The logic of the breakdownism standard is its flexibility for allowing judges to apply it in ways that support prevailing political priorities and pragmatic needs. China's enduring political priority of preventing frivolous divorce has a long legacy and has taken on renewed urgency since 2012. Judges' discretionary application of breakdownism supports the political goals of family preservation and social stability. Indeed, according to the deputy chair of the committee responsible for drafting the 1980 Marriage Law, this was precisely the legislative intent of breakdownism, which "at once maintains the principle of freedom of marriage [which includes the freedom of divorce] and also gives the courts considerable latitude" (Huang 2005:187). From a pragmatic standpoint, an overly rigid system risks breaking.

461

Discretionary flexibility helps judges complete their tasks and reap the rewards of hitting performance targets. As Lipsky (2010:19) puts it, "Lower-level participants develop coping mechanisms contrary to an agency's policy but actually basic to its survival."

METHODOLOGICAL IMPLICATIONS

According to Pope and Meyer (2016:289–90), "Decoupling exists because world models, which are suffused with meaning and cultural significance, interface with situated interests and practical concerns at the local level (Meyer and Rowan, 1977). Local actors may adopt the models for reasons of external legitimacy, but buffer the models from daily practices to maintain internal technical efficiency or solidarity." A key methodological task, then, is properly identifying and measuring the relevant local "situated interests" and "practical concerns." From the existing literature on the topic, we should expect that the extent to which China's commitments to women's rights, including the right to divorce, are decoupled from on-the-ground practices is a function, above all, of its links to world society, its bureaucratic capacity, and the strength and autonomy of its domestic feminist women's movement (Cole 2015; Englehart and Miller 2014; Htun and Weldon 2018; Wang and Schofer 2018). But, of course, we cannot assess the relative importance of multiple and potentially contradictory norms in a given institutional context before knowing what they are and how they work in theory and practice. As Drori and Krücken (2009:20) put it: "The research methodologies common to world society theory have not allowed for specific findings that explain different degrees of coupling or pointed to the cultural and historical specificity of the determining societal context."

Insofar as a key objective of macro-comparative cross-national research on states' promises and practices is to assess the relative importance of endogenous and exogenous influences, essential methodological ingredients include appropriate measures of endogenous influences well attuned to local contexts. Only after first inductively ascertaining the endogenous norms and practices – legal and otherwise – that pertain to a specific context would we know what to compare with exogenous world society norms and practices (Fourcade and Savelsberg 2006; Hagan, Levi, and Ferrales 2006; Halliday and Carruthers 2009). Might empirical findings in the world society literature consistently showing stronger exogenous effects be an artifact of dominant approaches to measuring endogenous influences? Any comparison of global and local effects will necessarily privilege the former if salient endogenous norms and practices obstructing the realization of exogenous institutional prescriptions are poorly measured or altogether omitted from the analysis. We will not find what we do not know to look for; we cannot assess what we do not know to include in the assessment. For example, in their cross-national research on divorce rates, Wang and Schofer (2018:20) find that global cultural norms valorizing "individual freedom, consent, and gender equality" trump local cultural and institutional barriers to divorce, which they measure as economic development, religious tradition, mass education enrollment (all of which theoretically drive cultural values conducive to divorce), and female labor force participation (which theoretically promotes women's financial wherewithal to divorce). China's perfect score of 3 out of 3 (over a period of almost 40 years) on a "divorce law equality" index (with higher scores meaning greater gender equality, constructed from components of Htun and Weldon's [2015] "family law index") belies the endogenous Chinese legal standard of breakdownism – altogether invisible in this scholarly literature – routinely used to deny first-attempt divorces to plaintiffs, and especially to female plaintiffs, particularly when they make claims of marital violence.

To be sure, China's rising divorce rates are consistent with Wang and Schofer's (2018:16) sanguine conclusion that "the legitimation of world cultural principles at the global level can propel local change." Global scripts, including "developmental idealism," may very well contribute to values of individualism, feminism, and equal rights in China and may thus influence *individual* behavior (Boyle, McMorris, and Mayra 2002; Thornton and Xie 2016; Yu and Xie 2015) in the context of marriage and divorce despite durable local *organizational* barriers to divorce rooted in endogenous institutional norms and practices that are orthogonal to world society models. Such local organizational barriers are the focus of this book. If we know what to look for and where to look for it, we will surely find similar decoupling processes in other contexts characterized by street-level bureaucrats who, for material, ideological, political, cultural, and cognitive reasons, faithfully enforce endogenous institutional norms hostile to the very elements of world society they simultaneously champion. Such decoupling processes are all too often obscured by the local embrace of world society norms captured in macro-comparative cross-national research because they are more conspicuous on the surface veneer of institutions.

A macro-comparative cross-national research design would have obscured our ability to discern these key local forces obstructing women's freedom of divorce in China. Macro-comparative cross-national generalizations come at the potential cost of missing the story in specific cases. Conversely, contextually specific explanations, even when they get the story right in a specific case, come at the potential cost of precluding generalizations. Even when they cannot be generalized, however, idiosyncratic stories can be of enormous theoretical utility insofar as they are exceptions that prove the rule or bring to the fore less common and therefore less conspicuous processes (Emigh 1997; Lieberman 2005; Pearce 2002). Macro-comparative cross-national research on the promises and practices of nation-states is self-avowedly and variously macro-sociological, macro-social, macro-cultural, macro-institutional, macro-structural, macro-historical, and macro-phenomenological (Bromley and Suárez 2013; Drori and Krücken 2009; Fourcade and Savelsberg 2006; Frank and Moss 2017; Hallett 2010; Meyer 2010; Pope and Meyer 2016; Schofer et al. 2012; Wotipka and Ramirez 2008). Scholars in this tradition have been forthright in acknowledging the methodological limitations of their approach. They are the first to admit that their images of the ground taken from the stratosphere are at best low resolution (e.g., Frank et al. 2009:279).

Country-level indicators of state responses to human rights and gender violence have gained currency and acquired legitimacy in policy and scholarly contexts. Ironically, such indicators are themselves institutionalized myths that are loosely coupled with what they ostensibly reflect. Human rights indicators not only shame autocrats by illuminating their human rights abuses, but also serve to buttress authoritarian regimes by obscuring their human rights violations (Zaloznaya and Hagan 2012). When social scientists use indicators to assess compliance with human rights treaties, they "transform a judgment-laden process into one that appeared technical, scientific, and therefore – in a context in which the treaty bodies' authority is often in doubt – more legitimate" (Rosga and Satterthwaite 2012:306). Standardized models for indicators and rankings have emerged and spread globally according to the same isomorphic pressures social scientists use such measures to study (Erkkilä and Piironen 2018; Merry 2016; Sauder and Espeland 2009).

Cases in point are the Cingranelli–Richards Human Rights Data Project's "physical integrity rights," "women's rights," and other related ordinal measures (Alexander and Welzel 2015; Cole 2012, 2015; Cole and Ramirez 2013; Englehart and Miller 2014; Wei and Swiss 2020). (For a review and assessment of an array of gender equality measures, see Liebowitz and Zwingel [2014] and Sundström et al. [2017].) Hafner-Burton and Tsutsui's (2005) ordinal measure of government repression of human rights and Hathaway's "fair trial index" (2002) use many of the same sources, most notably US Department of State human rights reports, which have "come to play an outsized role in academic research on human rights and state repression, as commonly used sources of cross-national data on state behavior" (Bagozzi and Berliner 2018:663; also see Gallagher and Chuang 2012; Innes de Neufville 1986). In the absence of measurement validity assessments (but with the occasional ceremonial reference to intercoder reliability to enhance their legitimacy), we are asked to take these indicators at face value as objectively accurate and free of political bias. Of similarly dubious validity and inscrutable construction is the "Caprioli index of physical security of women" measuring violence against women and available in the WomanStats database (Hudson, Bowen, and Nielsen 2011). We have only an incomplete picture of the "over 500 sources" used (Caprioli et al. 2009:5), the role of country experts, and the precise criteria for coding laws as, for example, "generally enforced" or "rarely enforced." In the same vein are the "index of sex equality in family law" (Htun and Weldon 2015, 2018:127–32; Wang and Schofer 2018) and the "index of government response to violence against women" (Htun and Weldon 2018:31–50). China's score of 12 out of 13 in "sex equality in family law" – with points for all three divorce components (Wang and Schofer 2018) – belies a key finding reported in this book: the unlikely and worsening prospects of getting divorced in court on the first attempt and women's disproportionate challenge in this regard. China's score of 2 out of 10 in "government action on violence against women" (Htun and Weldon n.d.) may accurately capture the limited on-the-ground impact of its "policy regime" but misses the broad scope and large scale of its official policy responses, including legal reforms reviewed in Chapter 2.

Similar concerns can be raised about some of the independent variables used to explain these outcomes measures. If "bureaucratic efficacy" does indeed account for variation in country-level human rights enforcement, are the International Country Risk Guide indicators used by Cole (2015), which include opaque ordinal "bureaucracy quality" and "corruption" measures constructed by research staff, sufficiently sensitive to local context? Is either tax collected as a proportion of

GDP (Englehart and Miller 2014) or government consumption as a percentage of GDP (Wang and Schofer 2018) a valid measure of state capacity in general and in the context of women's rights enforcement in particular?[1] Do such measures capture relevant endogenous institutional forces as effectively as the measures of exogenous influences against which their effects are typically compared? If we have reason to believe that the gap between the promises and practices of law stems from the concrete working conditions of street-level bureaucrats responsible for the disposition of justice, why would we assess the effects of measures of dubious relevance such as government tax revenue and consumption instead of relevant measures such as pressures from political ideology, caseloads, and performance targets? Instead of measuring what is conveniently available, should we not instead measure what we inductively ascertain from deep contextual knowledge to be salient and relevant?

As another case in point, does a code of 0 out of 2 for China in both the "strength" and "autonomy" of its feminist women's movement – constructed largely on the basis of "country and region-specific expert opinion" – sufficiently capture a relevant endogenous determinant of the effectiveness of women's divorce rights and legal protections against violence (Htun and Weldon 2018:52–58) that can be meaningfully compared with the exogenous influence of global legal norms as measured by CEDAW ratification (Htun and Weldon 2018:62–63)? Does a code for China's apparent establishment of a "low-level gender mainstreaming institution" in 1992 adequately capture the effect of endogenous "women's policy machinery" effectiveness on state responses to various dimensions of women's rights, including protection against violence through 2005 (Htun and Weldon [2018:59, 232], using codes from True and Mintrom [2001])? Scholars who use measures like these have not systematically confronted and grappled with such questions. Beyond raising measurement issues such as these, scholars have also critiqued dominant modelling strategies in this literature (Hug and Wegmann 2016).

In fairness, however, scholars who develop and use global indicators can hardly be faulted for their efforts to surmount the methodological

---

[1] Yasuda (2017:16–17) shows that state capacity measured as revenue as a proportion of GDP is a poor predictor of China's food safety record and introduces an alternative measure that takes country-level scale challenges into account. Lieberman (2002) and Hendrix (2010) assess the strengths and weaknesses of tax-related proxy measures of state capacity so widely used in macro-comparative cross-national research.

challenges inherent to macro-comparative cross-national research designs. "Lowest common denominator" strategies of using measures plausibly connected to the theorized mechanism of interest and available for the maximum number of cases are good-faith and unavoidable last resorts in analyses of pooled cross-sectional data from large samples of countries over long periods of time. Additional methodological strategies include the use of survey data of either general populations or sub-populations such as business managers about perceptions of, trust in, and experiences with institutions as proxies for institutional performance, including corruption. However, owing to one-size-fits-all instruments, perception bias, and desirability bias, the data they capture do not always reflect salient local institutional norms and practices (see Y. Wang [2013:108–9] for a review of such approaches). For example, scores and rankings of countries according to the World Justice Project's "rule of law index" (Urueña 2015) omit contextually specific endogenous institutional legacies such as mediation practices, which continue to dominate the Chinese justice system, including the courts (Huang 2016; Liu 2006).

A related methodological approach to cross-national comparisons of legal systems is to analyze vignette data (e.g., answers to questions about hypothetical disputes) collected by the Lex Mundi Project from lawyers around the world (Negro and Longhofer 2018). There is even a tradition of analyzing vignette data within the field of China studies to assess variation in court performance (Gallagher 2017; Gallagher and Yang 2017; Y. Wang 2013, 2014).[2]

A further limitation of macro-comparative cross-national research is its tendency to obscure subnational variation in institutional behavior by taking the country-year as the unit of analysis (Berkovitch and Gordon 2016). A research design limited to urban courts, which handle only a relatively small share of divorce litigation, would fail

---

[2] Yuhua Wang's (2013, 2014) indirect proxy measure of judicial corruption exemplifies the questionable validity of some prevailing measures of court performance. Using data from a 2003 nationally representative survey of the general population in 102 counties across China, he measures local courts' levels of corruption as the proportion of a small subsample of respondents in each locale who chose the category "courts are corrupt" as their answer to why they would not go to court in the hypothetical instance of a dispute. Leaving aside the issue of whether general perceptions of corruption are valid measures of actual corruption, a perhaps more critical issue is that, owing to complex skip patterns, respondents eligible to answer this question were limited to those who indicated a willingness to pursue the resolution of a hypothetical dispute in the first place and who then indicated an unwillingness to go to court. In other words, respondents who indicated they would not pursue any form of resolution or who indicated they would seek help in court – who together form a sizeable chunk of the sample – were removed from the pool of respondents asked about their perceptions of court corruption.

to reveal the important stories at the heart of this book. Failing to disaggregate urban and rural China, or focusing only on urban China, would thus limit our ability to identify key institutional forces animating divorce litigation.

In this book, rather than relying on indirect proxy measures of the gap between judicial promises and judicial practices, I scrutinized the actual behavior of over 250 courts in two provinces, directly observed the incidence of their use of competing legal standards in real-life rulings, and empirically assessed and explained the differential impact they have on female and male litigants. There is nothing abstract about these measures. They do not come from country experts, nor do they come from readings of US government reports about the behavior of Chinese courts. A court decision to deny a female plaintiff's first-attempt divorce petition means a real woman was unable to divorce (for at least some period of time). Had I measured China's "trial fairness" according to its formal laws and international treaty commitments summarized by the US State Department in its human rights reports (Hathaway 2002), I would have arrived at very different conclusions. Had I assessed Chinese court behavior according to vignettes presented to lawyers or to ordinary citizens (most of whom had never been to court; Negro and Longhofer 2018; Y. Wang 2014), or according to panels of regional and country "experts" (Cole 2012, 2015; Hafner-Burton and Tsutsui 2005; Htun and Weldon 2018), my conclusions would likewise have been different. Contrary to much of the literature on the diffusion and local penetration of global legal norms, my conclusions about judicial behavior and trial fairness come from empirical analyses of actual judicial behavior and actual trials.

Real decisions from real courts show both that, over time, adjudicated divorce became increasingly difficult in general and was disproportionately difficult for women in particular. My empirical findings show that the wide gender gap in the probability of getting an adjudicated divorce on the first attempt is explained in large measure by five correspondingly wide gender gaps in (1) the incidence of plaintiffs with domestic violence claims, (2) the incidence of plaintiffs whose spouses withheld consent, (3) judges' responses to plaintiffs' claims of domestic violence, (4) judges' responses to plaintiffs' claims of missing spouses, and (5) judges' responses to defendants' failure to appear in court for other reasons.

We must remain mindful of the substantive trade-offs of our methodological choices for other reasons, too. In-depth case studies such as this one are, by definition, poorly suited for generalizable research spanning wide swaths of time and place. They are also relatively narrow in the scope of the institutional issues they can address. In more concrete terms, the broader institutional issue of gender justice cannot be reduced to the specific issue of divorce practices in lower civil courts, the empirical focus of this book. Although this is a study of only one narrow slice of gender justice in one country, it provides a critical test for theories of local compliance with global norms. Is there a more likely place than the court system for the implementation of domestic laws such as China's that are so consistent with global legal norms? If a particular set of global legal norms embedded in domestic laws generally fails to penetrate the courts, perhaps we should harbor doubts about the prospects of world society penetration in other organizational contexts.

As the world's most populous country, China exerts a profound influence on the *worldwide* extent of world society penetration. All efforts to identify country-level determinants of compliance with global norms have treated small and large countries equally. No study of which I am aware paints a global portrait of the worldwide extent of local compliance with a given set of global norms. We know, for example, that rape-law reform is positively correlated with police reports of rape at the level of the country-year (Frank, Hardinge, and Wosick-Correa 2009). But we have no idea about the worldwide impact of rape-law reform. Likewise, studies of country-year correlates of the implementation of human rights (Cole 2015; Hafner-Burton and Tsutsui 2005) and women's rights (Htun and Weldon 2018) tell us little about their worldwide impact.

Two examples illustrate this point. First, insofar as rising levels of *income inequality* in most of the world coincides with rising levels of *income* in the poorest and most populous countries in the world, namely, China and India, treating all countries equally or weighting countries according to their populations lead to diametrically opposing conclusions about worldwide levels of income inequality. Either omitting China and India from the analysis or ignoring country-level populations shows an aggregate worldwide *increase* in income inequality, whereas including these two countries in a population-weighted analysis shows an aggregate worldwide *decrease* in income inequality (Firebaugh and Goesling 2004; Hung and Kucinskas 2011). Similarly, the choice to include or omit China from a pooled cross-national analysis of the feminization of legal professions would have dramatic consequences for our substantive conclusions about worldwide levels of lawyer feminization. Taking the unweighted country-year as the unit of analysis would vastly exaggerate lawyer feminization because doing so would treat small and large countries equally. Unusually low lawyer feminization levels in China and India suppressed the global impact of the rapid feminization of bars elsewhere in the world (Michelson 2013:1087, 1097). Although lawyer feminization has taken hold in a lot of countries around the world, results from a population-weighted analysis that includes China and India support the less-than-sanguine conclusion that "from a global perspective, the process of lawyer feminization has hardly begun" (Michelson 2013:1101). In short, the worldwide penetration of world society hinges to an important degree on the penetration of world society in China. World society theory will need to reckon with China.

WHITHER THE IMPACT OF CHINA'S 2015 ANTI-DOMESTIC VIOLENCE LAW?

The vast majority of court decisions in my collections predate China's 2015 Anti-Domestic Violence Law (Chapter 2). Nonetheless, we can look for early clues of its impact in the portion of decisions in my Zhejiang sample that were made after this new law took effect on March 1, 2016. Perhaps the grim picture I paint in this book began to change. Although all the decisions in my Henan sample predate the implementation of this law, 10,501 adjudicated divorce decisions in my full Zhejiang sample were made on or after March 1, 2016. In the solitary decision (one out of 10,501) in which this new body of law is cited, the plaintiff claimed to have been cut and injured in a knife attack by the defendant. In its written decision, the court cited this new body of law to justify denying the plaintiff's petition on the grounds that the plaintiff waited two years to file for divorce following the alleged attack and failed to submit evidence proving "frequent beatings and other violent behavior," and, above all, that the defendant both denied the plaintiff's claim of abuse and was unwilling to divorce (Decision #4687109, Haiyan County People's Court, Zhejiang Province, September 1, 2016).[3] A Chinese report cited by Amnesty International was similarly discouraging:

> 10 months after the enactment of the [Anti-Domestic Violence] law, of the 142 abuse-related divorce cases in the city of Jinan, only 14 cases

---

[3] Case ID (2016)浙0424民初2645号, archived at https://perma.cc/X876-G25A.

were allowed to get divorced [sic]. The reason these 14 cases were successful were invariably the same [sic]: the accused admitted to abusing the victim. In the rest of the cases, failure was also invariably due to the same reason: the accused denied allegations of domestic violence, and judges deemed the cases to have insufficient proof. (Lu 2018)

The enactment of this special body of law, so far at least, has apparently done more to signal a symbolic commitment to combatting domestic violence than to change judicial practices on the ground.

One way to assess the impact of this law is to assess the effectiveness of the system of personal safety protection orders it formalized (人身安全保护令; Chapter 2). Scholars have lamented the small number of applications for personal protection orders, low approval rates, and ineffective enforcement (J. Jiang 2019; Y. Jiang 2019). Many judges apply excessively high standards of proof to personal protection order applications even though the evidentiary standards for proving domestic violence are laxer for personal protection orders than for divorces (Du 2018:8). Many judges, rather than issuing protection orders, conduct mediation with the goal of persuading applicants to withdraw their requests (J. Jiang 2019). According to an SPC report, China's courts received 5,860 applications for personal protection orders and approved 3,718 of them between the time the Anti-Domestic Violence Law took effect in 2016 through the end of 2018 (Equality 2019). According to another government report, China's courts issued 5,749 personal protection orders through the end of 2019 (Equality 2020). These are paltry numbers considering the prevalence of domestic violence in such a large population.

Insofar as it represents a court's affirmation of domestic violence, judges should treat a personal protection order as proof of statutory wrongdoing in a divorce case. A decision to grant a divorce should thus be a no-brainer when a plaintiff submits a personal protection order as evidence of domestic violence. This is not so, however. Chapter 7 contains a case example in which a court, in its decision to deny a woman's divorce petition, disregarded a personal protection order it had issued to her only a week earlier. Chapter 3 also describes the Sisyphean plight of Ning Shunhua, whose divorce petitions were repeatedly denied after the same court had repeatedly granted her applications for protection orders. This is not an uncommon pattern. In another case, a court issued a personal protection order to a plaintiff on January 20, 2016, three days after she filed for divorce. On February 22, 2016, during the trial, the defendant stated to the court, "The plaintiff's claim of domestic violence is not factual. I never hit the plaintiff. The only time I ever hit her is when she made a date with another man and verbally provoked me." The court affirmed the following facts: "Beginning in August 2015, owing to the plaintiff's failure to return to and reside at home, the defendant's stalking the plaintiff, and other reasons, the two sides once again got into a fight, which led to physical conflict." The presiding judge, as judges so typically do, denied the plaintiff's divorce petition after representing her allegations of domestic violence as mutual fighting and holding that she had failed to provide evidence of the breakdown of mutual affection (Decision #4151585, Cixi Municipal People's Court, Zhejiang Province, February 22, 2016).[4]

To the extent that judges' tendency to ignore domestic violence in their haste to deny divorce petitions stems from their discretion and overwork, a reduction in either or both could shift their decision-making incentives to the benefit of vulnerable women. Likewise, to the extent that courts are sensitive and responsive to public outrage (Chapters 2 and 9), ongoing academic, journalistic, and public advocacy efforts to heighten public awareness within China of gender injustice in its divorce courts may also incentivize risk-averse judges to apply the law more faithfully and equitably in support of vulnerable women. Public sympathy for women who kill their abusive husbands can result in sentencing leniency (Chapter 9). Perhaps public sympathy for women seeking to divorce their abusive husbands in court can similarly result in a narrowing of the gap between legal promises and practices. Because the Anti-Domestic Violence Law was implemented only shortly before all courts were prohibited from publishing divorce decisions online in October 2016, we will need another source of data to assess its impact henceforth.

FINAL THOUGHTS

This book has chronicled the Sisyphean struggle of contested divorce in China, identified the institutional sources of this struggle, and assessed the extent of gender inequality with respect to outcomes of this struggle. It has documented the extent to which and provided reasons why women have borne the brunt of Chinese courts' clampdown on adjudicated divorce. Generally speaking, divorce is readily attainable outside the court system if both sides are willing and can agree on all terms.

---

[4] Case ID (2016)浙0282民初00647号, archived at https://perma.cc/H7SS-K55W.

Courts are the only place in China to which people can take contested, unilateral, ex parte divorces. China's divorce laws on the books provide strong protections to women seeking divorce. Chinese courts, however, routinely stretch these laws beyond recognition or altogether ignore them, and in so doing subvert China's own laws and international legal commitments. The evidence is clear: an apparent claim of domestic violence has no meaningful influence on whether a court grants an adjudicated divorce. In China's divorce courts, domestic laws and global legal norms concerning violence against women have been sidelined to the point of irrelevance. By privileging competing institutional imperatives, including judicial efficiency, the preservation of marriages, and social stability maintenance, courts serve the needs of political priorities more than the needs of gender justice. As political pressure to preserve marriages has grown, so too has courts' tendency to deny divorce petitions, even when – or especially when – they include claims of domestic violence. Just as proponents of the promarriage movement in the United States, in their efforts to reduce divorce, have ignored and obscured the pervasiveness of domestic violence (Catlett and Artis 2004), China's ideology of marital preservation undermines officially proclaimed commitments to combatting domestic violence. In prevailing political discourse, marital preservation serves the party-state's larger goal of social stability maintenance (Chapter 3; also see Wang 2020). By forcibly prolonging marriages, however, judges have enabled the persistence of domestic violence, which has sometimes escalated to suicide and homicide. Policies intended to promote social harmony and stability have therefore yielded unintended opposite effects.

Chinese judges deny first-attempt divorce requests for fear that plaintiffs, particularly female plaintiffs, embellish and lie; for fear that the approval process will slow the rate at which they clear cases; and for fear that angry husbands will retaliate, resulting in "extreme incidents" of social unrest. Undoubtedly, some plaintiffs do exaggerate and altogether fabricate their claims. The degree to which judges believe they do so, however, varies by plaintiff sex. Judges, biased by gender stereotypes, give greater credence to the claims of male plaintiffs and attach greater value to the rights of male defendants. When ruling on first-attempt divorce petitions, judges seem far more fearful of supporting a case without merit than denying a case with merit. On the whole, they would rather send a woman home with her abuser or force her into hiding than to grant a divorce to a woman who wants out of an unhappy marriage and may have thought spinning a poignant story about abuse would improve her chances of achieving her goal. Research on the veracity of women's domestic violence claims in the United States suggests that false negatives (true cases of domestic violence unrecognized as such) far outnumber false positives (fake cases of domestic violence falsely recognized as true). Whereas men's allegations of domestic violence are often false, women's are rarely exaggerated or fabricated (Haselschwerdt, Hardesty, and Hans 2011:1705–6, cited in Jeffries 2016:10; Jaffe et al. 2008:508). Even if some plaintiffs (however few) lie in court proceedings about abuse or the whereabouts of their spouses, is it better for judges to preserve the marriage than to dissolve it? Is the judicial error of dissolving the marriage of an unhappy woman who may have lied about or exaggerated abuse claims worse than the judicial error of exposing a battered woman to ongoing abuse by prolonging her marriage against her wishes? Would it not be better to err on the side of protecting women? Only exceedingly rarely have judges availed themselves of applicable evidentiary standards allowing them to give women who make allegations of domestic abuse the benefit of the doubt.

If, in one year alone, two-thirds of China's half a million plaintiffs in adjudicated divorce decisions are women, 40% of them experience domestic violence, and 70% of their petitions are denied, then over 90,000 female abuse victims seeking divorce remain exposed to their abusive husbands, typically for an additional year. The social and public health implications are palpable: China's institutionalized norm of denying a divorce request on the first attempt has spawned a sizable population of female marital violence refugees. In Henan and Zhejiang alone, thousands of women awaiting a second or third chance for an adjudicated divorce must choose from an array of similarly horrific options: further subjection to marital violence; separation from children, aging parents, and other kin while eking out an existence a safer distance from abusive husbands; and financial vulnerability and loss of child custody from concessions made to secure a divorce either in court or the Civil Affairs Administration.

In the grand scheme of domestic violence prevention in China, a 2015 criminal justice reform that led to greater leniency in the sentences of women who killed their abusive husbands (Chapter 9) is a clear case of "too little, too late." Women helped by criminal justice reforms are far outnumbered by women harmed by the divorce twofer. By the time domestic violence reaches the criminal courts, it has passed the point of no return. If China's leaders were serious about helping battered women, they would do their utmost to prevent domestic violence from escalating to the point of becoming matters for criminal courts. Vulnerable women seeking to divorce their abusive husbands would be better served by public authorities, including judges, who believe their allegations and provide effective intervention much further upstream. Until then, the Chinese women most in need of court protection are the least likely to get it.

REFERENCES

Ahl, Björn. 2020. "Why Do Judges Cite the Party? References to Party Ideology in Chinese Court Decisions." *China: An International Journal* 18(2):175–85.

Ahl, Björn and Daniel Sprick. 2018. "Towards Judicial Transparency in China: The New Public Access Database for Court Decisions." *China Information* 32(1):3–22.

Alexander, Amy C. and Christian Welzel. 2015. "Eroding Patriarchy: The Co-Evolution of Women's Rights and Emancipative Values." *International Review of Sociology* 25(1):144–65.

Alexy, Allison. 2020. *Intimate Disconnections: Divorce and the Romance of Independence in Contemporary Japan.* Chicago and London: The University of Chicago Press.

Alford, William P. and Yuanyuan Shen. 2004. "Have You Eaten? Have You Divorced? Debating the Meaning of Freedom in Marriage in China." In *Realms of Freedom in Modern China*, edited by W. Kirby, pp. 234–63. Stanford, CA: Stanford University Press.

All China Women's Federation Research Team. 2013. "全国农村留守儿童城乡流动儿童状况研究报告 (Research Report on China's Left-Behind Children and Migrant Children)." 中国妇运 (*Chinese Women's Movement*) (6):30–34.

Allison, Paul D. 1999. "Comparing Logit and Probit Coefficients Across Groups." *Sociological Methods & Research* 28(2):186–208.

Amato, Paul R. 2000. "The Consequences of Divorce for Adults and Children." *Journal of Marriage and Family* 62(4):1269–87.

Amato, Paul R. and Jacob E. Cheadle. 2008. "Parental Divorce, Marital Conflict and Children's Behavior Problems: A Comparison of Adopted and Biological Children." *Social Forces* 86(3):1139–61.

An, Chenxi (安晨曦). 2015. "民事诉讼立法预期与运行效果的背离及修正：以《民事诉讼法》新制度实施状况为范例的分析 (Gaps between Expectations and Outcomes of Civil Procedure Legislation and Their Remedies: An Analysis of the Implementation of the New Civil Procedure Law System)." 现代法学 (*Modern Law Science*) 37(6):173–84.

Anyang Municipal Intermediate People's Court Research Team (安阳市中级人民法院课题组). 2016. "人民陪审员事实审的庭审职权配置研究 (Research on the Functions and Allocation of People's Lay Assessors in Court Trials).” In 河南法治发展报告 (*Annual Report on Rule of Law Development in Henan*), edited by T. (丁同民) Ding and L. (张林海) Zhang, pp. 286–98. Beijing: 社会科学文献出版社 (Social Sciences Academic Press).

Artis, Julie E. 2004. “Judging the Best Interests of the Child: Judges’ Accounts of the Tender Years Doctrine.” *Law & Society Review* 38(4):769–806.

Attané, Isabelle, Lisa Eklund, M. Giovanna Merli, Michel Bozon, Tania Angeloff, Bo Yang, Shuzhuo Li, Thierry Pairault, Su Wang, Xueyan Yang, and Qunlin Zhang. 2019. “Understanding Bachelorhood in Poverty-Stricken and High Sex Ratio Settings: An Exploratory Study in Rural Shaanxi, China.” *The China Quarterly* 240:990–1017.

Bagozzi, Benjamin E. and Daniel Berliner. 2018. “The Politics of Scrutiny in Human Rights Monitoring: Evidence from Structural Topic Models of US State Department Human Rights Reports.” *Political Science Research and Methods* 6(4): 661–77.

Bai, Yu, Linxiu Zhang, Chengfang Liu, Yaojiang Shi, Di Mo, and Scott Rozelle. 2018. “Effect of Parental Migration on the Academic Performance of Left Behind Children in North Western China.” *The Journal of Development Studies* 54(7):1154–70.

Baidu. 2020. “人民法院民事裁判文书制作规范 (Specifications for Civil Decisions of the People’s Court).” Retrieved March 15, 2020 (https://perma.cc/M3H3-CJ4E).

Baker, Hugh D. R. 1979. *Chinese Family and Kinship*. London and Basingstoke: Macmillan.

Bartley, Tim. 2018. *Rules without Rights: Land, Labor, and Private Authority in the Global Economy*. Oxford and New York: Oxford University Press.

Bartley, Tim and Niklas Egels-Zandén. 2016. “Beyond Decoupling: Unions and the Leveraging of Corporate Social Responsibility in Indonesia.” *Socio-Economic Review* 14(2):231–55.

Basic Level Legal Artisan (基层法匠). 2016a. “中国各省份法院办案效率排行榜 (Chinese Provincial Rankings of Court Efficiency).” Retrieved January 11, 2020 (https://tinyurl.com/rqeluyn).

Basic Level Legal Artisan (基层法匠). 2016b. “各省、自治区、直辖市法院设置、人员配备等数据资料 (Data from Every Province, Autonomous Region, and Centrally-Administered City on Courts and Their Personnel).” Retrieved January 11, 2020 (https://tinyurl.com/uzacmzw).

Basic Level Legal Artisan (基层法匠). 2016c. “我国各省份民商事审判案源现状排行榜 (2008–2011) (China’s Provincial Rankings of Civil Cases and Their Sources).” Retrieved January 11, 2020 (https://tinyurl.com/uv6mcnz).

Baum, Richard. 1986. “Modernization and Legal Reform in Post-Mao China: The Rebirth of Socialist Legality.” *Studies in Comparative Communism* 19(2):69–103.

BBC. 2020. "Chinese Vlogger Dies After 'Set on Fire by Ex During Live Stream.'" *BBC.* Retrieved October 2, 2020 (www.bbc.com/news/world-asia-china-54380148).

Bemiller, Michelle. 2008. "When Battered Mothers Lose Custody: A Qualitative Study of Abuse at Home and in the Courts." *Journal of Child Custody* 5(3–4):228–55.

Berkovitch, Nitza and Neve Gordon. 2016. "Differentiated Decoupling and Human Rights." *Social Problems* 63(4):499–512.

Biland, Émilie and Hélène Steinmetz. 2017. "Are Judges Street-Level Bureaucrats? Evidence from French and Canadian Family Courts." *Law and Social Inquiry* 42(2):298–324.

Black, Donald J. 1989. *Sociological Justice.* New York: Oxford University Press.

Boli, John and Frank J. Lechner. 2001. "Globalization and World Culture." In *International Encyclopedia of the Social & Behavioral Sciences,* edited by N. J. Smelser and P. B. Baltes, pp. 6261–66. New York: Elsevier.

Boli, John and George M. Thomas. 1997. "World Culture in the World Polity: A Century of International Non-Governmental Organization." *American Sociological Review* 62(2):171.

Boyd, Christina L., Lee Epstein, and Andrew D. Martin. 2010. "Untangling the Causal Effects of Sex on Judging." *American Journal of Political Science* 54(2):389–411.

Boyle, Elizabeth Heger, Barbara J. McMorris, and Mayra Gómez. 2002. "Local Conformity to International Norms: The Case of Female Genital Cutting." *International Sociology* 17(1):5–33.

Boyle, Elizabeth Heger and John W. Meyer. 1998. "Modern Law as a Secularized and Global Model: Implications for the Sociology of Law." *Soziale Welt* 49(3):275–94.

Breitenbach, Esther and Fran Wasoff. 2007. *A Gender Audit of Statistics: Comparing the Position of Women and Men in Scotland.* Retrieved August 24, 2021 (https://era.ed.ac.uk/handle/1842/2797).

Brinig, MF and DW Allen. 2000. "'These Boots Are Made for Walking': Why Most Divorce Filers Are Women." *American Law and Economics Review* 2(1):126–69.

Bromley, Patricia and David F. Suárez. 2013. "Institutional Theories and Levels of Analysis: History, Diffusion, and Translation." In *World Culture Re-Contextualised: Meaning Constellations and Path-Dependencies in Comparative and International Education Research,* edited by J. Schriewer, pp. 139–59. London and New York: Routledge.

Bu, Xiaohong (卜晓虹), Xiaoting (黎晓婷) Li, and Xi (林曦) Lin. 2015. "'司法男权化'现象探析与解决之路：以基层法院离婚案庭审为视角 (An Analysis of and Solution to 'Judicial Patriarchalization': From the Perspective of Basic-Level Court Divorce Cases)." 法治论坛 *(Nomocracy Forum)* (4):3–18.

Buck, Pearl S. 1931. "Chinese Women: Their Predicament in the China of Today." *Pacific Affairs* 4(10):905–9.

Cai, Guoqin (蔡国芹) and Xianneng (蔡宪能) Cai. 1998. "民事审判方式改革中的程序非正当化倾向 (Tendencies Towards Procedural Unjustifiability in the Reform of Civil Trial Methods)." 嘉应大学学报 (*Journal of Jiaying University*) (5):30–34.

Cai, Lidong and Yingcheng Qi. 2019. "Judicial Governance of 'Fake Divorce' with Chinese Characteristics: Practical Rationality of the Chinese Courts in the Transitional Period." *The China Review* 19(2):99–123.

Cai, Xiaowei (蔡小伟) and Xiaohong (蒋小泓) Jiang. 2002. "维护公正: 神圣的职责 – – 湖州市中级人民法院自觉接受监督杜绝超审限案件纪事 (Protecting Justice: A Sacred Duty – Huzhou Municipal Intermediate People's Court Voluntarily Accepts Supervision to Correct Its Record of Cases Exceeding the Trial Time Limit)." 人民日报 (*People's Daily*), May 8, 12.

Cai, Yanmin (蔡彦敏). 2013. "中国民事司法案件管理机制透析 (An Analysis of China's Civil Judicial Case Management Mechanism)." 中国法学 (*China Legal Science*) (1):131–43.

Cancian, Maria and Daniel R. Meyer. 1998. "Who Gets Custody?" *Demography* 35(2):147–57.

Cancian, Maria, Daniel R. Meyer, Patricia R. Brown, and Steven T. Cook. 2014. "Who Gets Custody Now? Dramatic Changes in Children's Living Arrangements After Divorce." *Demography* 51(4):1381–96.

Cao, Yin. 2018. "Courts Put Domestic Disputes on Hold to Save Marriages." *China Daily*, August 13, 6.

Caprioli, Mary, Valerie M. Hudson, Rose Mcdermott, Bonnie Ballif-Spanvill, Chad F. Emmett, and S. Matthew Stearmer. 2009. "The WomanStats Project Database: Advancing an Empirical Research Agenda." *Journal of Peace Research* 46(6):839–51.

Catlett, Beth Skilken and Julie E. Artis. 2004. "Critiquing the Case for Marriage Promotion: How the Promarriage Movement Misrepresents Domestic Violence Research." *Violence Against Women* 10(11):1226–44.

Chai, Yongjun (柴用君) and Jingyuan (朱静渊) Zhu. 2005. "女子四次申请离婚遭法院驳回自杀抵抗家庭暴力 (Woman Denied Divorce by Court Four Times Commits Suicide to Defy Domestic Violence)." 兰州晨报 (Lanzhou Morning News), August 3. http://news.sohu.com/20050803/n226540723.shtml

Chang, Pi-Chuan, Huihsin Tseng, and Andrew Galen. 2018. "Chinese Segmenter v3.9.1."

Chang, Zhaojun (常照军). 2017. "夫妻琐事闹离婚法官倾心来调解 (Trivial Quarrel Causes Divorce Dispute, Judge Enthusiastically Mediates)." Retrieved August 16, 2018 (www.hncourt.gov.cn/public/detail.php?id=168994).

Chen, Chengjian (陈成建). 2002. "浙江义乌重视法院建设 (Zhejiang's Yiwu Attaches Importance to Court Construction)." 人民日报 (*People's Daily*), January 23, 11.

Chen, Elsie. 2020. "Fatal Domestic Attack Livestreamed in China." *The New York Times*, November 15, A16.

Chen, Fei (陈飞) and Dong (杨冬) Yang. 2016. "家暴案中受虐妇女'以暴制暴'行为的正当防卫适用 (The Application of Justifiable Self-Defense to Women Abused by Domestic Violence Who 'Combat Violence With Violence')." 云南大学学报法学版 (*Journal of Yunnan University Law Edition*) 29(5):20–30.

Chen, Feinian. 2005. "Residential Patterns of Parents and Their Married Children in Contemporary China: A Life Course Approach." *Population Research and Policy Review* 24(2):125–48.

Chen, Feinian, Guangya Liu, and Christine A. Mair. 2011. "Intergenerational Ties in Context: Grandparents Caring for Grandchildren in China." *Social Forces* 90(2):571–94.

Chen, Kun (陈琨). 2019. "扩大民事案件独任制适用范围的现实路径 －－基于B 省近3 年独任制适用情况的实践考察 (A Realistic Path to Expanding the Civil System of Solo Judging: A Study of the Practice of the Application of the System of Solo Judging in Province B Over the Past Three Years)." 法律适用 (*Journal of Law Application*) (15):105–15.

Chen, Lei (陈磊). 2013. "我国将改革人民陪审员制度 (China's Reform of the System of Lay Assessors)." 法治周末 (*Legal Weekly*), October 29. www.chinalawyeryn.com/xinwenzhongxin/20131031/17831.html

Chen, Min. 2014. "Anti-Domestic Violence Endeavors by Chinese Courts and the Bangkok Rules." In *Women in Prison: An International Symposium on the Bangkok Rules at the Centre for Comparative and Public Law at the Faculty of Law, University of Hong Kong, February 25–26*. Retrieved August 24, 2021 (https://wipsymposium.org/wip2/wp-content/uploads/2014/04/chen_en.pdf).

Chen, Min (陈敏). 2004. "受虐妇女综合症专家证据在司法实践中的运用 (Applying Expert Evidence on Battered Woman Syndrome in Judicial Practice)." 诉讼法论丛 (*Proceedings on Procedure Law*) (1):134–72.

Chen, Min (陈敏). 2009. "家庭暴力离婚案件不宜调解结案 (Mediation Is Inappropriate In Divorce Cases Involving Domestic Violence)." 法制日报 (*Legal Daily*), July 17. http://news.sohu.com/20090717/n265281817.shtml

Chen, Min (陈敏). 2013. "涉家庭暴力案件审理技能 (*Trial Skills in Cases Involving Domestic Violence*)." Beijing: 人民法院出版社 (People's Court Press).

Chen, Min (陈敏). 2018. "对谩骂和恐吓的分析、认定和应对 －－以反家庭暴力法为视角 (Analyzing, Affirming, and Responding to Abuse and Intimidation: From the Perspective of the Anti-Domestic Violence Law)." 人民司法 (*People's Judicature*) (7):4–9.

Chen, Ruihua (陈瑞华). 2016a. "法院改革中的九大争议问题 (Nine Controversial Issues in Court Reform)." 中国法律评论 (*China Law Review*) (3):211–20.

Chen, Ruihua (陈瑞华). 2016b. "法院改革的中国经验 (China's Court Reform Experience)." 政法论坛 (*Tribune of Political Science and Law*) 34(4):112–25.

Chen, Wei (陈苇) and Weiwei (段伟伟) Duan. 2012. "法院在防治家庭暴力中的作用实证研究 (Empirical Research on the Function of Courts in the Prevention of Domestic Violence)." 河北法学 (*Hebei Law Science*) (8):28–38.

Chen, Wei (陈苇) and Qinglin (张庆林) Zhang. 2015. "离婚诉讼中儿童抚养问题之司法实践及其改进建议 – – 以某县法院2011 – 2013年审结离婚案件为调查对象 (Judicial Practices of Child Custody in Divorce Litigation and Recommendations for Their Changes: A Survey of Divorce Cases from a County Court in 2011–2013)." 河北法学 (*Hebei Law Science*) (1):13–33.

Chen, Wei and Lei Shi. 2013. "Developments in China's Provisions for Postdivorce Relief in the 21st Century and Suggestions for Their Improvement." *Journal of Divorce & Remarriage* 54(5):363–80.

Chen, Wei, Lei Shi, and Wenjun He. 2014. "Empirical Research on Judicial Practice of the Post-Divorce Relief System – Targeted on Sampled Cases Handled in a Grass-Roots People's Court in Chongqing in 2010–2012 China." *International Survey of Family Law* 2014:51–70.

Chen, Wei, Lei Shi, and Xin Zhang. 2016. "The Divorce Damages System in China: Legislation and Practice." *International Journal of Law, Policy and the Family* 30(1):105–14.

Chen, Weidong (陈卫东). 2015. "公民参与司法: 理论、实践及改革 – – 以刑事司法为中心的考察 (Citizen Participation and the Judiciary: Theory, Practice, and Reform: An Investigation Based on Criminal Justice)." 法学研究 (*CASS Journal of Law*) (2):3–25.

Chen, Weidong (陈卫东). 2019. "诉讼爆炸与法院应对 (The 'Litigation Explosion' and the Court Response in China)." 暨南学报 (哲学社会科学版) (*Ji'nan Journal [Philosophy and Social Sciences]*) (3):13–22.

Chen, Weiqiang (陈炜强). 2013. "《婚姻法》第32 条第2 款新释: 基于社会与国家分离的视角 (A New Interpretation of Article 32, Item 2 of the Marriage Law from the Perspective of the Separation of State and Society." 西南科技大学学报 *Journal of Southwest University of Science and Technology* 30(1):8–11.

Chen, Xiaoyong (陈小勇). 2005a. "论离婚自由与反对轻率离婚 (On the Freedom of Divorce and Opposition to Frivolous Divorce)." 湖南科技学院学报 (*Journal of Hunan University of Science and Engineering*) (1):154–56.

Chen, Xiaoyong (陈小勇). 2005b. "论离婚自由的矛盾及解决办法 (Freedom of Divorce: Contradiction and Countermeasures)." 宿州学院学报 (*Journal of Suzhou College*) 20(4):22–24.

Chen, Xuefei (陈雪飞). 2007. "离婚案件审理中法官话语的性别偏向 (Gender Bias in Judges' Discourse during Divorce Trials)." 北大法律评论 (*Peking University Law Review*) 8(2):386–411.

Chen, Yali (陈雅丽) and Qianquan (徐前权) Xu. 2018. "编制内法官助理职能定位研究 (Research on the Functions of Judges' Clerks in the State Personnel System)." 长江大学学报 (社会科学版) (*Journal of Yangtze University [Social Sciences]*) 41(3):89–94.

Chen, Yongsheng (陈永生) and Bing (白冰) Bai. 2016. "法官、检察官员额制改革的限度 (The Limits of the Judge and Procurator Quota System Reform)." 比较法研究 (*Journal of Comparative Law*) (2):21–48.

Cheng, Chaoyang (程朝阳) and Xin (高鑫) Gao. 2019. "对'受虐妇女杀夫'类案件的法理分析 – – 以2014–2018年典型案例为样本 (A Jurisprudential Analysis of Abused Women Who Murder Their Husbands: A Sample of Typical Cases from 2014–2018)." 山东警察学院学报 (*Journal of Shandong Police College*) (167):11–20.

Cheng, Fengwei (程丰伟). 2020. "万万没想到：'离婚冷静期通知书'该冷静的是当事人还是法院? (I Never Expected This: Should 'Notices of Cooling-Off Periods' Apply to Litigants or Courts?)." Retrieved June 1, 2020 (https://new.qq.com/omn/20200523/20200523A0MV3W00.html).

Cheng, Le and Xin Wang. 2018. "Legislative Exploration of Domestic Violence in the People's Republic of China: A Sociosemiotic Perspective." *Semiotica* 2018(224):249–68.

Chinese Academy of Social Sciences Institute of Law Rule of Law Indicators Innovation Project Team. 2017. "司法大数据的建设、应用和展望 (Construction, Application, and Outlook of Judicial Big Data)." In 中国法院信息化发展报告 (*The Annual Report on the Informatization of Chinese Courts*), edited by L. (李林) Li and H. (田禾) Tian, pp. 88–100. Beijing: 社会科学文献出版社 Social Sciences Academic Press.

Chuncheng Evening News. 2018. "冲进法庭掀桌椅辱骂扬言杀法官 (Charging into Courtroom, Toppling Tables and Chairs, Cursing and Threatening to Murder the Judge)." 春城晚报 (*Chuncheng Evening News*), June 6, A09.

CLY (*China Law Yearbook* [中国法律年鉴]). Various years. Beijing: 中国法律年鉴社 (China Law Yearbook Press).

Cole, Wade M. 2005. "Sovereignty Relinquished? Explaining Commitment to the International Human Rights Covenants, 1966–1999." *American Sociological Review* 70(3):472–95.

Cole, Wade M. 2012. "Human Rights as Myth and Ceremony? Reevaluating the Effectiveness of Human Rights Treaties, 1981–2007." *American Journal of Sociology* 117(4):1131–71.

Cole, Wade M. 2013. "Strong Walk and Cheap Talk: The Effect of the International Covenant of Economic, Social, and Cultural Rights on Policies and Practices." *Social Forces* 92(1):165–94.

Cole, Wade M. 2015. "Mind the Gap: State Capacity and the Implementation of Human Rights Treaties." *International Organization* 69(02):405–41.

Cole, Wade M. and Francisco O. Ramirez. 2013. "Conditional Decoupling: Assessing the Impact of National Human Rights Institutions, 1981 to 2004." *American Sociological Review* 78(4):702–25.

Coltrane, Scott and Michele Adams. 2003. "The Social Construction of the Divorce 'Problem': Morality, Child Victims, and the Politics of Gender." *Family Relations* 52(4):363–72.

Cui, Lanqin (崔兰琴). 2015. "历史与比较视域下诉讼离婚理由及其伦理限制 (Divorce Litigation Holdings and Their Ethical Limitations in Historical and Comparative Perspective)." 河南财经政法大学学报 (*Journal of Henan University of Economics and Law*) (4):183–92.

Cui, Yongdong (崔永东). 2016. "法官责任制的定位与规则 (The Positioning of Judge Accountability and Its Rules)." 现代法学 (*Modern Law Science*) 38(3):28–36.

D'Attoma, Sara. 2019. "百年(不)好合! One Hundred Years of Marital (Un) Happiness! An Analysis of Divorce Proceedings Involving Domestic Violence and the Personal Protection Order System in China." *Journal of Comparative Law* 14(2):188–202.

Dahl, Gordon B. and Enrico Moretti. 2008. "The Demand for Sons." *Review of Economic Studies* 75(4):1085–120.

Davis, Deborah. 2010. "Who Gets the House? Renegotiating Property Rights in Post-Socialist Urban China." *Modern China* 36(5):463–92.

Davis, Deborah S. 2014. "Privatization of Marriage in Post-Socialist China." *Modern China* 40(6):551–77.

Dawson, Andrew and Liam Swiss. 2020. "Foreign Aid and the Rule of Law: Institutional Diffusion Versus Legal Reach." *The British Journal of Sociology* 71(4):761–84.

Deng, Li (邓丽). 2016. "2015年中国婚姻家庭法治 (China's Rule of Law in Marriage and Family in 2015)." In 中国法治发展报告 (*Annual Report on China's Rule of Law*), edited by L. (李林) Li and H. (田禾) Tian, 社会科学文献出版社 187–96. Beijing: Social Sciences Academic Press.

Deng, Li (邓丽). 2017. "身体与身份:家暴受害者在离婚诉讼中的法律困境 (Physical Rights and Marital Status: The Legal Dilemmas of Domestic Violence Victims in Divorce Litigation)." 妇女研究论丛 (*Journal of Chinese Women's Studies*) (6):106–15.

Dezalay, Yves and Bryant G. Garth. 2010. *Asian Legal Revivals: Lawyers in the Shadow of Empire*. Chicago and London: The University of Chicago Press.

Diamant, Neil J. 2000a. "Re-Examining the Impact of the 1950 Marriage Law: State Improvisation, Local Initiative and Rural Family Change." *The China Quarterly* 161:171–98.

Diamant, Neil J. 2000b. *Revolutionizing the Family: Politics, Love, and Divorce in Urban and Rural China, 1949–1968.* Berkeley, CA: University of California Press.

Diamant, Neil J. 2001. "Making Love 'Legible' in China: Politics and Society during the Enforcement of Civil Marriage Registration, 1950–66." *Politics & Society* 29(3):447–80.

DiMaggio, Paul J. and Walter W. Powell. 1983. "The Iron Cage Revisited: Institutional Isomorphism and Collective Rationality in Organizational Fields." *American Sociological Review* 48(2):147.

Ding, Pengchao (丁朋超). 2016. "我国民事合议制度内部关系的再改革 (The Re-Reform of the Internal Relations of China's Civil Collegial Panel System)." 时代法学 *(Presentday Law Science)* 14(6):82–93.

Dong, Wei (董巍) and Changsheng (纪长胜) Ji. 2016. "公告类离婚纠纷案件中的裁判问题 (Issues Concerning Judicial Decision-Making in Public Notice Divorce Disputes)." 天津法学 *(Tianjin Legal Science)* 128:88–93.

Drori, Gili S. and Georg Krücken. 2009. "World Society: A Theory and a Research Program in Context." In *World Society: The Writings of John W. Meyer*, edited by J. W. Meyer, G. Krücken, and G. S. Drori, pp. 3–35. Oxford and New York: Oxford University Press.

Du, Hu (杜虎). 2020. "'离婚冷静期'已成法律，保护弱势的机制得跟上 (The Cooling-Off Period Is Now Law, Mechanisms for Protecting the Vulnerable Must Catch Up)." Retrieved May 30, 2020 (www.sohu.com/a/398460236_665455).

Du, Wanhua (杜万华). 2008. "最高人民法院审判委员会委员、民事审判第一庭庭长杜万华在成都、汕头召开的民事审判专题座谈会上的讲话 (Speech at the Chengdu and Shantou Civil Adjudication Forum by Du Wanhua, Adjudication Committee Member and Chief of the Number One Civil Division of the Supreme People's Court)." Retrieved January 25, 2020 (www.cn-china.net/sfjs/news/sf/comprehensive/20081231/7821.html).

Du, Wanhua (杜万华). 2018. "论深化家事审判方式和工作机制改革 (On Deepening the Reforms of Trial Mode and Operating Mechanism for Family Justice)." 中国应用法学 *(China Review of Administration of Justice)* (2):1–9.

Duan, Chengrong (段成荣), Lidan (吕利丹) Lü, Jing (郭静) Guo, and Zongping (王宗萍) Wang. 2013. "我国农村留守儿童生存和发展基本状况－－基于第六次人口普查数据的分析 (Survival and Development of China's Left-Behind Children: An Analysis of Data from the Sixth Population Census)." 人口学刊 *(Population Journal)* 35(3):37–49.

Edelman, Lauren B. 2016. *Working Law: Courts, Corporations, and Symbolic Civil Rights.* Chicago and London: The University of Chicago Press.

Emigh, Rebecca Jean. 1997. "The Power of Negative Thinking: The Use of Negative Case Methodology in the Development of Sociological Theory." *Theory and Society* 15(3–4):631–54.

Englehart, Neil A. and Melissa K. Miller. 2014. "The CEDAW Effect: International Law's Impact on Women's Rights." *Journal of Human Rights* 13(1):22–47.

Engstrom, Nora Freeman. 2017. "The Diminished Trial." *Fordham Law Review* 86(5):2131–47.

Epstein, Deborah and Lisa A. Goodman. 2019. "Discounting Women: Doubting Domestic Violence Survivors." *University of Pennsylvania Law Review* 167(2):399–461.

Equality. 2019. *Three Year Monitoring Report on Implementation of the Anti-Domestic Violence Law of the People's Republic of China* 《中华人民共和国反家庭暴力法》实施三周年监测报告. Retrieved August 24, 2021 (www .equality-beijing.org/editor/attached/file/20190313/20190313181114_71 75.docx).

Equality. 2020. 《中华人民共和国反家庭暴力法》实施四周年监测报告 (*Four Year Monitoring Report on Implementation of the Anti-Domestic Violence Law of the People's Republic of China*). Retrieved August 24, 2021 (www .equality-beijing.org/editor/attached/file/20200704/20200704133754_71 00.pdf).

Erkkilä, Tero and Ossi Piironen. 2018. *Rankings and Global Knowledge Governance: Higher Education, Innovation and Competitiveness.* Palgrave Macmillan.

Fair, Katie. 2018. "Battered Spouse Syndrome: A Comparative Regional Look at Domestic Abuse and Self-Defense in Criminal Courts." *Lincoln Memorial University Law Review* 5(2):1–19.

Fallon, Kathleen M., Anna Liisa Aunio, and Jessica Kim. 2018. "Decoupling International Agreements from Domestic Policy: The State and Soft Repression." *Human Rights Quarterly* 40(4):932–96.

Fan, Mingzhi (范明志). 2010. "我国司法突发事件应急机制初探 (Exploration of China's Judicial Emergency Mechanisms)." 法学 (*Law Science*) (5):135–43.

Fan, Mingzhi (范明志) and Xiaodan (金晓丹) Jin. 2012. "关于人民法院 '案多人少'问题的调研分析 (Research Analysis Regarding the Problem of 'Many Cases and Few Judges' in People's Courts)." 中国审判新闻月刊 (*China Trial*) (71):98–101.

Fan, Xiancong (范贤聪). 2017. "我国农村离婚问题与对策探析 (An Analysis of China's Rural Divorce Problems and Countermeasures)." 法制 与社会 (*Legal System and Society*) (30):144–45.

Fan, Yu (范愉). 2008. "从诉讼调解到'消失中的审判' (From Judicial Mediation to 'The Vanishing Trial')." 法制与社会发展 (*Law and Social Development*) (5):60–69.

Fan, Yu (范愉). 2014. "人民陪审员制度与民众的司法参与 (The System of Lay Assessors and Public Judicial Participation)." 哈尔滨工业大学学报 (社会科学版) *Journal of HIT (Social Sciences Edition)* 16(1):50–55.

Fang, Hongwei (方宏伟). 2015. "法官流失及其治理研究 (Research on the Judge Attrition and Countermeasures)." 武汉理工大学学报 (社会科学版) (*Journal of Wuhan University of Technology [Social Sciences Edition]*) 28(3):470–78.

Fei, Xiao (小非). 2010. "'试离婚': 游走于法律边缘惹争议 ('Experimental Divorce': A Controversy on the Margins of the Law)." 法治与社会 (*Rule by Law and the Society*) (3):59–61.

Feng, Jiayun. 2020. "Court Denies Divorce to Woman After She Was Paralyzed from A Jump to Escape Domestic Violence." *SupChina.Com*. Retrieved July 29, 2020 (https://tinyurl.com/y6rzke7k).

Feng, Jiayun. 2021. "Four Divorce Petitions and Two Protective Orders Aren't Enough to Allow This Woman to Leave Her Abusive Husband." *SupChina. Com*. Retrieved August 3, 2021 (https://supchina.com/2021/04/15/four-divorce-petitions-and-two-protective-orders-arent-enough-to-allow-this-woman-to-leave-her-abusive-husband/).

Feng, Yuqing and Xin He. 2018. "From Law to Politics: Petitioners' Framing of Disputes in Chinese Courts." *The China Journal* 80:130–49.

Fincher, Leta Hong. 2014. *Leftover Women: The Resurgence of Gender Inequality in China*. London: Zed Books.

Finder, Susan. 1993. "The Supreme People's Court of the People's Republic of China ." *Journal of Chinese Law* 7:145–224.

Firebaugh, Glenn and Brian Goesling. 2004. "Accounting for the Recent Decline in Global Income Inequality." *American Journal of Sociology* 110(2):283–312.

Fourcade, Marion and Joachim J. Savelsberg. 2006. "Introduction: Global Processes, National Institutions, Local Bricolage: Shaping Law in an Era of Globalization." *Law & Social Inquiry* 31(3):513–19.

Frank, David John, Bayliss J. Camp, and Steven A. Boutcher. 2010. "Worldwide Trends in the Criminal Regulation of Sex, 1945 to 2005." *American Sociological Review* 75(6):867–93.

Frank, David John, Tara Hardinge, and Kassia Wosick-Correa. 2009. "The Global Dimensions of Rape-Law Reform: A Cross-National Study of Policy Outcomes." *American Sociological Review* 74(2):272–90.

Frank, David John, Ann Hironaka, and Evan Schofer. 2000. "The Nation-State and the Natural Environment over the Twentieth Century." *American Sociological Review* 65(1):96–116.

Frank, David John and Dana M. Moss. 2017. "Cross-National and Longitudinal Variations in the Criminal Regulation of Sex, 1965 to 2005." *Social Forces* 95(3):941–69.

Friedman, Sara L. 2006. *Intimate Politics: Marriage, the Market, and State Power in Southeastern China*. Cambridge, MA: Harvard University Asia Center, Harvard University Press.

Frohmann, Lisa. 1991. "Discrediting Victims' Allegations of Sexual Assault: Prosecutorial Accounts of Case Rejections." *Social Problems* 38(2):213–26.

Fu, Ailing and Jian Wang. 2019. "Till Death, Purchase of Another House, or Occurrence of Other Events Do Us Part: Interests-Oriented Fake Divorce Cases in China." *Journal of Divorce & Remarriage* 60(2):152–70.

Fu, Hualing. 2014. "Autonomy, Courts, and the Politico-Legal Order in Contemporary China." In *The Routledge Handbook of Chinese Criminology*, edited by L. Cao, I. Y. Sun, and B. Hebenton, pp. 76–88. Abingdon and New York: Routledge.

Fu, Yulin. 2018. "Court Management in Transformation China: A Perspective of Civil Justice." *Peking University Law Journal* 6(1):81–103.

Fu, Yulin (傅郁林). 2003. "繁简分流与程序保障 (Determining Ordinary or Simplified Procedure and Protecting Due Process)." 法学研究 (*CASS Journal of Law*) (1):50–63.

Galanter, Marc. 2004. "The Vanishing Trial: An Examination of Trials and Related Matters in Federal and State Courts." *Journal of Empirical Legal Studies* 1(3):459–570.

Gallagher, Anne T. and Janie Chuang. 2012. "The Use of Indicators to Measure Government Responses to Human Trafficking." In *Governance by Indicators: Global Power Through Classification and Rankings*, edited by K. Davis, A. Fisher, B. Kingsbury, and S. E. Merry, pp. 317–43. Oxford and New York: Oxford University Press.

Gallagher, Mary E. 2006. "Mobilizing the Law in China: 'Informed Disenchantment' and the Development of Legal Consciousness." *Law & Society Review* 40(4):783–816.

Gallagher, Mary E. 2011. "Users and Non-Users: Legal Experience and Its Effects on Legal Consciousness." In *Chinese Justice: Civil Dispute Resolution in Contemporary China*, edited by M. Y. K. Woo and M. E. Gallagher, pp. 204–33. Cambridge and New York: Cambridge University Press.

Gallagher, Mary E. 2017. *Authoritarian Legality in China: Law, Workers, and the State*. Cambridge and New York: Cambridge University Press.

Gallagher, Mary and Yujeong Yang. 2017. "Getting Schooled: Legal Mobilization as an Educative Process." *Law & Social Inquiry* 42(1):163–94.

General Office of the SPC. 2011. "《最高人民法院关于新形势下进一步加强人民法院基层基础建设的若干意见》的新闻发布稿 (Several Opinions of the Supreme People's Court on Strengthening the Construction of the Foundation of Basic-Level People's Courts Under the Current Situation)." Retrieved December 26, 2019 (www.court.gov.cn/shenpan-xiangqing-3179.html).

Geng, Xueqing (耿学清), and Yijun (王亦君) Wang. 2018. "全国现有农村留守儿童697万人 (There Are Currently 69.7 Million Left-Behind Children Nationwide)." 中国青年报 (*China Youth Daily*), October 31, 4.

Gieryn, Thomas. 2018. "Truth Is Also a Place." *Aeon*. Retrieved January 11, 2020 (https://aeon.co/essays/labs-courts-and-altars-are-also-traveling-truth-spots).

Glynn, Mary Ann and Ryan Raffaelli. 2013. "Logic Pluralism, Organizational Design, and Practice Adoption: The Structural Embeddedness of CSR Programs." In *Institutional Logics in Action, Part B*, edited by M. Lounsbury and E. Boxenbaum, pp. 175–97. Bingley, UK: Emerald.

Gong, Xikui. 1998. "Household Registration and the Caste-Like Quality of Peasant Life." In *Streetlife China*, edited by M. Dutton, pp.81–92. Cambridge and New York: Cambridge University Press.

Goodmark, Leigh. 2005. "Telling Stories, Saving Lives: The Battered Mothers' Testimony Project, Women's Narratives, and Court Reform." *Arizona State Law Journal* 37:709–57.

Gould, Jon B. and Scott Barclay. 2012. "Mind the Gap: The Place of Gap Studies in Sociolegal Scholarship." *Annual Review of Law and Social Science* 8(1):323–35.

de Graaf, Paul M. and Matthijs Kalmijn. 2003. "Alternative Routes in the Remarriage Market: Competing-Risk Analyses of Union Formation after Divorce." *Social Forces* 81(4):1459–98.

Gruijters, Rob J. and John Ermisch. 2019. "Patrilocal, Matrilocal, or Neolocal? Intergenerational Proximity of Married Couples in China." *Journal of Marriage and Family* 81(3):549–66.

Gu, Peidong (顾培东). 2014. "人民法庭地位与功能的重构 (Reconstruction of the Status and Function of the People's Tribunal)." 法学研究 (*CASS Journal of Law*) (1):24–42.

Guiyang Evening News (贵阳晚报). 2020. "女子不堪家暴跳楼致截瘫, 事发一年没能离成婚, 法院: 不再进行调解 (Case of the Abused Woman Who Jumped Out of a Building Causing Paraplegia, Unable to Divorce a Year Afterwards, Court Says: Will No Longer Mediate)." Retrieved July 30, 2020 (https://tinyurl.com/3wanp9k5).

Guo, Beibei (郭倍倍). 2016. "人民陪审员制度的核心问题与改革路径 (Core Problems and Reform Pathways of the System of Lay Assessors)." 法学 (*Law Science*) (8):92–99.

Guo, Caiyiling (郭彩懿凌). 2019. "受虐妇女反抗杀夫行为的司法认定探析 (Exploring Judicial Determinations of Abused Women Who Murder Their Husbands)." 中国新通信 (*China New Telecommunications*) (18):240–42.

Guo, Jianping (郭剑平). 2018. "我国离婚冷静期制度构建的法理学思考 (Reflections on the Jurisprudence of China's Divorce Cooling-Off Period)." 社会科学家 (*Social Scientist*) (7):26–34.

Guo, Qichao (郭启朝). 2009. "南阳众法庭竞赛零判决: 法官称标准定得有点高 (Courts in Nanyang Compete in a Zero Adjudication Contest: Judges Say Standards Are Too High)." 大河报 (*Dahe News*). Retrieved April 21, 2017 (www.dahe.cn/xwzx/sz/t20090219_1489499.htm).

Guo, Shilong (郭士龙). 2018. "浅议新民诉法解释对离婚案件审理的影响 (On the Influence of the New Civil Procedure Law Interpretations on Divorce Trials)." 法制与社会 (*Legal System and Society*) (1):112–13.

Hafner-Burton, Emilie M. and Kiyoteru Tsutsui. 2005. "Human Rights in a Globalizing World: The Paradox of Empty Promises." *American Journal of Sociology* 110(5):1373–1411.

Hafner-Burton, Emilie M., Kiyoteru Tsutsui, and John W. Meyer. 2008. "International Human Rights Law and the Politics of Legitimation." *International Sociology* 23(1):115–41.

Hagan, John, Ron Levi, and Gabrielle Ferrales. 2006. "Swaying the Hand of Justice: The Internal and External Dynamics of Regime Change at the International Criminal Tribunal for the Former Yugoslavia." *Law & Social Inquiry* 31(3):585–616.

Haley, Usha C. V. and George T. Haley. 2016. "Think Local, Act Global: A Call to Recognize Competing, Cultural Scripts." *Management and Organization Review* 12(01):205–16.

Hallett, Tim. 2010. "The Myth Incarnate: Recoupling Processes, Turmoil, and Inhabited Institutions in an Urban Elementary School." *American Sociological Review* 75(1):52–74.

Halliday, Terence C. and Bruce G. Carruthers. 2009. *Bankrupt: Global Lawmaking and Systemic Financial Crisis*. Stanford, CA: Stanford University Press.

Haltom, William and Michael McCann. 2004. *Distorting the Law: Politics, Media, and the Litigation Crisis*. Chicago and London: The University of Chicago Press.

Han, Su Lin. 2017. "China Has a New Domestic Violence Law. So Why Are Victims Still Often Unsafe?" Retrieved June 4, 2020 (www.chinafile .com/reporting-opinion/viewpoint/china-has-new-domestic-violence-law-so-why-are-victims-still-often).

Haselschwerdt, Megan L., Jennifer L. Hardesty, and Jason D. Hans. 2011. "Custody Evaluators' Beliefs about Domestic Violence Allegations during Divorce: Feminist and Family Violence Perspectives." *Journal of Interpersonal Violence* 26(8):1694–1719.

Hathaway, Oona A. 2002. "Do Human Rights Treaties Make a Difference?" *The Yale Law Journal* 111(8):1935–2042.

He, Jiahong. 2016. *Back from the Dead: Wrongful Convictions and Criminal Justice in China*. Honolulu: University of Hawai'i Press.

He, Jiahua (何家华) and Yansong (余岩松) Yu. 2015. "人民陪审员制度价值诉求与实践诉求分离和统合的实证研究： 以河南A县基层人民法院为例 (Empirical Research on the Separation and Integration of the Ideals and Practices of the People's Assessor System)." 法律社会学评论 (*Sociology of Law Review*) 243–55.

He, Qianyu (贺茜妤). 2019. "我国诉讼离婚冷静期制度研究 (Research on China's Divorce Litigation Cooling-Off Period)." 辽宁公安司法管理干部学院学报 (*Journal of Liaoning Administrators College of Police and Justice*) (5):91–96.

He, Weifang (贺卫方), Zhiming (张志铭) Zhang, Guoqin (沈国琴) Shen, Hang (高航) Gao, and Weiwei (张薇薇) Zhang. 2012. "《中华人民共和国法院组织法》修改报告 (Report on the Amendment of the Organic Law of Courts of the People's Republic of China)." Retrieved January 26, 2020 (http://heweifang.blog.caixin.com/archives/48154#more).

He, Xin. 2009. "Routinization of Divorce Law Practice in China: Institutional Constraints' Influence on Judicial Behaviour." *International Journal of Law, Policy and the Family* 23(1):83–109.

He, Xin. 2014. "Maintaining Stability by Law: Protest-Supported Housing Demolition Litigation and Social Change in China." *Law & Social Inquiry* 39(4):849–73.

He, Xin. 2016. "Double Whammy: Lay Assessors as Lackeys in Chinese Courts." *Law & Society Review* 50(3):733–65.

He, Xin. 2017. "'No Malicious Incidents': The Concern for Stability in China's Divorce Law Practice." *Social and Legal Studies* 26(4):467–89.

He, Xin. 2021. *Divorce in China: Institutional Constraints and Gendered Outcomes*. New York: New York University Press.

He, Xin and Fen Lin. 2017. "The Losing Media? An Empirical Study of Defamation Litigation in China." *The China Quarterly* 230:371–98.

He, Xin and Kwai Ng. 2013a. "In the Name of Harmony: The Erasure of Domestic Violence in China's Judicial Mediation." *International Journal of Law, Policy and the Family* 27(1):97–115.

He, Xin and Kwai Ng. 2013b. "Pragmatic Discourse and Gender Inequality in China." *Law & Society Review* 47(2):279–310.

He, Xin and Yang Su. 2013. "Do the 'Haves' Come Out Ahead in Shanghai Courts?" *Journal of Empirical Legal Studies* 10(1):120–45.

Heimer, Carol A. 1999. "Competing Institutions: Law, Medicine, and Family in Neonatal Intensive Care." *Law & Society Review* 33(1):17–66.

Henan High People's Court. 2018. "法院判决离婚案件标准精华版 (2018年最新) (Standards for Judging Divorce Cases, the Essential Version [the Newest from 2018])." Retrieved January 26, 2020 (www.hncourt.gov.cn/public/detail.php?id=174695).

Henan Provincial Academy of Social Sciences Research Team (河南省社会科学院课题组). 2017. "2016年河南法治建设状况与2017年展望 (Henan's Rule of Law Situation in 2016 and Outlook for 2017)." In 河南法治发展报告 (*Annual Report on Rule of Law Development in Henan*), edited by T. (丁同民) Ding and L. (张林海) Zhang, pp. 1–19. Beijing: 社会科学文献出版社 Social Sciences Academic Press.

Henan Provincial Bureau of Justice. 2014. 河南省基层法律服务工作者名录 (2014年度) (*Henan Provincial Roster of Legal Workers for 2014*). 河南省司法厅 (Henan Provincial Bureau of Justice).

Henan Provincial Bureau of Statistics. 2015. 河南统计年鉴 (*Henan Statistical Yearbook*). Beijing: China Statistics Press.

Henan Provincial Bureau of Statistics. 2019. 河南统计年鉴 (*Henan Statistical Yearbook*). Beijing: China Statistics Press.

Henan Provincial Bureau of Statistics. Various years. "Henan Statistical Datasheet." Retrieved (https://www.china-data-online.com/).

Henan Provincial High Court. 2016. "裁判文书上网的河南实践 (Henan's Practice of Posting Court Decisions Online)." In 河南法治发展报告 (*Annual Report on Rule of Law Development in Henan*), edited by T. (丁同民) Ding and L. (张林海) Zhang, pp. 167–72. Beijing: 社会科学文献出版社 Social Sciences Academic Press.

Hendley, Kathryn. 2009. "'Telephone Law' and the 'Rule of Law': The Russian Case." *Hague Journal on the Rule of Law* 1(2):241–62.

Hendley, Kathryn. 2017. *Everyday Law in Russia*. Ithaca and London: Cornell University Press.

Hendrix, Cullen S. 2010. "Measuring State Capacity: Theoretical and Empirical Implications for the Study of Civil Conflict." *Journal of Peace Research* 47(3):273–85.

Hengyang County Court. 2021. "衡阳县人民法院关于'宁顺花诉陈定华离婚纠纷案'的情况通报 (Notice on the Situation Concerning the Hengyang County People's Court's 'Ning Shunhua v. Chen Dinghua Divorce Case')." Retrieved August 3, 2021 (https://m.weibo.cn/status/4626303921946658?).

Higuchi, Koichi. 2020. "KH Coder: For Quantitative Content Analysis or Text Mining (v3.Beta.01e)." Retrieved July 6, 2020 (https://github.com/ko-ichi-h/khcoder).

Honig, Emily and Gail Hershatter. 1988. *Personal Voices: Chinese Women in the 1980s*. Stanford, CA: Stanford University Press.

Hou, Hongbin (侯虹斌). 2020. "'完美受害者'拉姆：杀死她的，不只是她前夫 (Lamu, the 'Perfect Victim': She Was Murdered Not Only by Her Ex-Husband)." Retrieved October 2, 2020 (https://perma.cc/452Z-36WC).

Hou, Jianbin (侯建斌). 2018. "构建家事审判改革协同机制 (Constructing a Domestic Relations Trial Reform Collaborative Mechanism)." 法制日报 (*Legal Daily*). Retrieved July 30, 2018 (www.legaldaily.com.cn/index_article/content/2018-05/19/content_7548459.htm?node=5955).

Hou, Meng (侯猛). 2017. "《人民法院组织法》大修应当缓行——基于法官制度的观察 (Major Revisions of the Organic Law of the Courts Should Be Slowed Down: Observations of the System of Judges)." 中国法律评论 (*China Law Review*) (6):46–54.

Hou, Shumei, and Ronald C. Keith. 2012. "A New Prospect for Transparent Court Judgment in China?" *China Information* 26(1):61–86.

Hou, Zhanglei (侯章磊). 2019. "社会工作介入农村留守儿童教育问题研究——以信阳市Y 小学农村留守儿童为例 (Research on Social Work Intervention Into Left-Behind Children's Education: The Case of Rural Left-Behind Children in Y Primary School in the City of Xinyang)." 社会与公益 (*Society and Public Welfare*) (2):66–71.

Hsia, Tao-tai and Constance Axinn Johnson. 1986. *Law Making in the People's Republic of China: Terms, Procedures, Hierarchy, and Interpretation.* Washington, DC: Library of Congress, Law Library.

Htun, Mala and S. Laurel Weldon. 2015. "Religious Power, the State, Women's Rights, and Family Law." *Politics & Gender* 11(3):451–77.

Htun, Mala and S. Laurel Weldon. 2018. *The Logics of Gender Justice: State Action on Women's Rights Around the World.* Cambridge and New York: Cambridge University Press.

Htun, Mala and S. Laurel Weldon. n.d. "Replication Files." Retrieved February 17, 2021 (https://malahtun.com/publications/).

Hu, Changming (胡昌明). 2015. "中国法官职业满意度考察: 以2660份问卷为样本的分析 (A Survey of Chinese Judges' Work Satisfaction: An Analysis of a Sample of 2,660 Questionnaires)." 中国法律评论 (*China Law Review*) (4):194–206.

Hu, Haipeng (胡海鹏). 2019. "离婚诉讼二次判离潜规则的批判与规制探究 – – 以离婚冷静期制度的构建为视角 (Critiquing and Regulating the Unwritten Rule of Granting Second-Attempt Divorce Petitions)." Retrieved December 31, 2019 (https://perma.cc/2RGE-DKBT).

Hu, Jingchao. 2015. "Ngender (v0.1.0)." Retrieved June 21, 2019 (https://github.com/observerss/ngender).

Hu, Mingyu (胡明玉). 2016. "离婚诉讼中的妇女儿童权益保障 – – 以海南省基层法院审结离婚案件为对象 (Guaranteeing the Rights and Interests of Women and Children in Divorce Litigation: Divorce Decisions in Hainan Province's Basic-Level Courts)." 中国统计 (*China Statistics*) (7):24–27.

Hu, Mingyu (胡明玉) and Xince (沈新策) Shen. 2016. "离婚诉讼中儿童权益法律保障情况实证调查研究 – – 以海南省三个基层法院审结离婚案件为调查对象 (Empirical Survey Research on the Situation of Legal Protections to the Rights and Interests of Children in Divorce Litigation: A Survey of Divorce Cases from Three Basic-Level Courts in Hainan Province)." 海南大学学报人文社会科学版 (*Humanities & Social Sciences Journal of Hainan University*) (3):122–31.

Hu, Ran, Jia Xue, Kai Lin, Ivan Y. Sun, Yuning Wu, and Xiying Wang. 2020. "The Patterns and Influencing Factors of Help-Seeking Decisions among Women Survivors of Intimate Partner Violence in China." *Journal of Family Violence* 36:669-681.

Huan, Xiaojun (郇小军). 2014. "离婚案件'首次判不离', 另一种法律规避 – – 兼论《婚姻法》第三十二条与现实的不兼容 (The 'First-Attempt Denial' of Divorce Cases as Another Type of Legal Evasion: The Incompatability of Article 32 of the Marriage Law and Current Practices)." Retrieved December 27, 2019 (http://jjzy.chinacourt.gov.cn/article/detail/2014/07/id/2614026.shtml).

Huang, Philip C. C. 2005. "Divorce Law Practices and the Origins, Myths, and Realities of Judicial 'Mediation' in China." *Modern China* 31(2):151–203.

Huang, Philip C. C. 2006. "Court Mediation in China, Past and Present." *Modern China* 32(3):275–314.

Huang, Philip C. C. 2016. "The Past and Present of the Chinese Civil and Criminal Justice Systems." *Modern China* 42(3):227–72.

Hudson, Valerie M., Donna Lee Bowen, and Perpetua Lynne Nielsen. 2011. "What Is the Relationship between Inequity in Family Law and Violence against Women? Approaching the Issue of Legal Enclaves." *Politics & Gender* 7(4):453–92.

Hug, Simon and Simone Wegmann. 2016. "Complying with Human Rights." *International Interactions* 42(4):590–615.

Hung, Ho-fung and Jaime Kucinskas. 2011. "Globalization and Global Inequality: Assessing the Impact of the Rise of China and India, 1980–2005." *American Journal of Sociology* 116(5):1478–1513.

Information Office of the State Council. 2015. "Gender Equality and Women's Development in China." Retrieved March 11, 2019 (www.scio.gov.cn/zfbps/ndhf/2015/Document/1449894/Image/201509221449894_336090.pdf).

Inglehart, Ronald F., Eduard Ponarin, and Ronald C. Inglehart. 2017. "Cultural Change, Slow and Fast: The Distinctive Trajectory of Norms Governing Gender Equality and Sexual Orientation." *Social Forces* 95(4):1313–40.

Inglehart, Ronald and Pippa Norris. 2003. *Rising Tide: Gender Equality and Cultural Change Around the World*. Cambridge and New York: Cambridge University Press.

Innes de Neufville, Judith. 1986. "Human Rights Reporting as a Policy Tool: An Examination of the State Department Country Reports." *Human Rights Quarterly* 8(4):681–99.

Jaffe, Peter G., Janet R. Johnston, Claire V. Crooks, and Nicholas Bala. 2008. "Custody Disputes Involving Allegations of Domestic Violence: Toward A Differentiated Approach to Parenting Plans." *Family Court Review* 46(3):500–522.

Jeffries, Samantha. 2016. "In the Best Interests of the Abuser: Coercive Control, Child Custody Proceedings and the 'Expert' Assessments That Guide Judicial Determinations." *Laws* 5(1):1–17.

Jia, Jianbing (贾建兵), Sanqi (陈三奇) Chen, Lirong (王利荣) Wang, Lin (赵琳) Zhao, and Bing (刘冰) Liu. 2014. "完善审判权运行机制着力化解涉诉信访――河南省三门峡市中院关于审判权运行与涉诉信访问题的调研报告 (Perfecting Adjudicatory Mechanisms for Reducing Petitions Generated by Litigation: Research Report on Henan Province's Sanmenxia Municipal Intermediate Court)." 人民法院报 *(People's Court Daily)*, May 1, 8.

Jiang, Feng (姜峰). 2015. "法院'案多人少'与国家治道变革: 转型时期中国的政治与司法忧思 (Courts' 'Many Cases, Few Judges' and National

Governance Change: Political and Judicial Concerns in China's Era of Transformation)." 政法论坛 (*Tribune of Political Science and Law*) 32(3):25–37.

Jiang, Jinliang (姜金良) and Zhenyuan (朱振媛) Zhu. 2014. "司法如何保护婚姻: 基于离婚案件二次起诉现象的分析 (How the Judiciary Protects Marriage: An Analysis Based on the Phenomenon of Second-Attempt Divorce Petitions)." 汕头大学学报 (人文社会科学版) *Shantou University Journal (Humanities & Social Sciences Bimonthly)* 30(2):81–88.

Jiang, Jue. 2019. "The Family as a Stronghold of State Stability: Two Contradictions in China's Anti-Domestic Violence Efforts." *International Journal of Law, Policy and the Family* 33(2):228–51.

Jiang, Quanbao, Marcus W. Feldman, and Shuzhuo Li. 2014. "Marriage Squeeze, Never-Married Proportion, and Mean Age at First Marriage in China." *Population Research and Policy Review* 33(2):189–204.

Jiang, Yongping (蒋永萍). 2016. "提高妇女地位国家机制的回顾与分析 (A Review and Analysis of Government Mechanisms for Raising the Status of Women)." In *2013–2015年: 中国性别平等与妇女发展报告* (*Annual Report on Gender Equality and Women's Development in China [2013–2015]*), edited by L. (谭琳) Tan, pp. 125–36. Beijing: 社会科学文献出版社 Social Sciences Academic Press.

Jiang, Yue (蒋月). 2009a. "改革开放三十年中国离婚法研究: 回顾与展望 (Looking Back and Ahead at China's Marriage Law After Thirty Years of Reform and Opening Up)." 法学家 (*The Jurist*) 1:63–84.

Jiang, Yue (蒋月). 2009b. "论我国现行法定离婚理由立法主义 (China's Current Statutory Grounds for Divorce)." 东方法学 (*Oriental Law*) 4:17–28.

Jiang, Yue (蒋月). 2019. "我国反家庭暴力法适用效果评析 – – 以2016 – 2018年人民法院民事判决书为样本 (An Analysis of the Application of China's Anti-Domestic Violence Law: A 2016–2018 Sample of People's Court Decisions)." 中华女子学院学报 (*Journal of China Women's University*) (3):13–22.

Jiangsu Province Nantong Municipal Intermediate People's Court Research Team (江苏省南通市中级人民法院课题组). 2013. "关于人民法院'事多人少'问题的调研报告 (Research Report on the Problem of 'Many Cases, Few Judges' in People's Courts)." 中国审判新闻月刊 (*China Trial*) (91):98–101.

Jin, Fucheng (靳付成) and Zheng (周正) Zhou. 2018. "兴也, 衰也?从数据看基层法律服务工作者的现状和未来 (Rising or Falling? Assessing the Current Situation and Future from Statistics on Basic-Level Legal Workers)." Retrieved August 16, 2018 (www.zhihedongfang.com/54468.html).

Jin, Ha. 2000. *Waiting*. Vintage.

Jin, Hao (靳昊). 2017. "'不要再让法袍染血' – – 从伤害法官事件看如何守护'守护者' (No More Bloodstains on the Robes of Justice: Incidents of

Harm To Judges as a Window on How to Guard the Guardians).” 光明日报 (*Guangming Daily*), March 1, 5.

Johnson, Kay Ann. 1983. *Women, the Family and Peasant Revolution in China*. Chicago and London: The University of Chicago Press.

Judicial Big Data Research Institute (司法大数据研究院). 2018. “司法大数据专题报告之离婚纠纷 (Judicial Big Data Special Topic Report: Divorce Disputes).” Retrieved June 13, 2019 (www.court.gov.cn/upload/file/2018/03/23/09/33/20180323093343_53196.pdf).

Kennedy, John James and Yaojiang Shi. 2019. *Lost and Found: The “Missing Girls” in Rural China*. New York: Oxford University Press.

Kinkel, Jonathan J. 2015. “High-End Demand: The Legal Profession as a Source of Judicial Selection Reform in Urban China.” *Law and Social Inquiry* 40(4):969–1000.

Kinkel, Jonathan J. and William J. Hurst. 2015. “The Judicial Cadre Evaluation System in China: From Quantification to Intra-State Legibility.” *The China Quarterly* 224:933–54.

Kuo, Lily. 2018. “Chinese Province Introduces ‘Divorce Test’ for Couples Planning to Split.” *The Guardian*. Retrieved January 24, 2020 (www.theguardian.com/world/2018/may/23/chinese-province-introduces-divorce-test-for-couples-planning-to-split).

Kuo, Lily. 2020. “Anger in China at Law Ordering ‘Cooling-Off’ Period Before Divorce.” *The Guardian*, May 29. Retrieved August 24, 2021 (www.theguardian.com/world/2020/may/29/anger-in-china-at-law-ordering-cooling-off-period-before-divorce).

Landis, J. Richard, and Gary G. Koch. 1977. “The Measurement of Observer Agreement for Categorical Data.” *Biometrics* 33(1):159–74.

Lang, Yanling (郎燕玲). 2016. “对离婚案件中留守儿童的法律思考 (Legal Thoughts On Left Behind Children In Divorce Cases).” 公民与法 (*Citizen and Law*) (12):29–41.

Law, Yik Wa, Melissa Chan, Huiping Zhang, Lianne Tai, Sandra Tsang, Patricia Chu, and Paul Yip. 2019. “Divorce in Hong Kong SAR, 1999–2011: A Review of 1,208 Family Court Cases.” *Journal of Divorce and Remarriage* 60(5):389–403.

Lazarus-Black, Mindie. 2007. *Everyday Harm: Domestic Violence, Court Rites, and Cultures of Reconciliation*. Urbana and Chicago: University of Illinois Press.

Ledeneva, Alena. 2008. “Telephone Justice in Russia.” *Post-Soviet Affairs* 24(4):324–50.

Lee, Ching Kwan and Yonghong Zhang. 2013. “The Power of Instability: Unraveling the Microfoundations of Bargained Authoritarianism in China.” *American Journal of Sociology* 118(6):1475–508.

Lei, Ya-Wen and Daniel Xiaodan Zhou. 2015. “Contesting Legality in Authoritarian Contexts: Food Safety, Rule of Law and China’s Networked Public Sphere.” *Law & Society Review* 49(3):557–93.

Li, Boyang (李波阳) and Min (贾敏) Jia. 2019. "对家暴受虐妇女杀夫案件量刑的实证分析 – – 以某省女子监狱24 起案例为样本 (An Empirical Analysis of Criminal Sentencing of Female Abuse Victims Who Murder Their Husbands: A Sample of 24 Cases of Female Inmates in Province X)." 犯罪研究 (Chinese Criminology Review) (5):61–71.

Li, Hongxiang (李洪祥). 2014. "离婚妇女婚姻家庭权益司法保障实证研究: 以吉林省中等发达地区某基层法院2010– 2012 年抽样调查的离婚案件为对象 (Empirical Research on the Judicial Protection of Women's Marriage and Family Rights in Divorce)." 当代法学 (Contemporary Law Review) (5):79–88.

Li, Hongxiang (李洪祥). 2015. "我国离婚率上升的特点及其法律对策 (Characteristics of and Legal Responses to China's Rising Divorce Rate)." 社会科学战线 (Social Science Front) (6):211–19.

Li, Hongxiang (李洪祥), Xiyuan (王希元) Wang, and Kaibo (郑凯波) Zheng. 2016. "离婚家庭儿童权益法律保障司法调查分析 – – 以吉林省经济发展程度不同地区离婚案件为例 (An Analysis of Protections of the Rights and Interests of Children in Divorce: Divorce Cases from Economically Diverse Parts of Jilin Province)." 中华女子学院学报 (Journal of China Women's University) (3):14–22.

Li, Huabin (李华斌). 2014. "三门峡法院: 建设新型合议庭规范审判权运行的探路者 (Sanmenxia Courts: Trailblazers of the New Collegial Panel)." 中国审判新闻月刊 (China Trial) (1):42–45.

Li, Jiahong (李桂红), and Feng (叶锋) Ye. 2015. "司法改革语境下司法辅助事务管理模式的构建 (The Formation of Models for the Administration of Trial Work Assistance in the Conext of Judicial Reform)." 上海政法学院学报(法治论丛) (Journal of Shanghai University of Political Science & Law [The Rule of Law Forum]) (4):102–12.

Li, Ke. 2015a. "Divorce, Help-Seeking, and Gender Inequality in Rural China." Ph.D. dissertation, Department of Sociology, Indiana University Bloomington.

Li, Ke. 2015b. "'What He Did Was Lawful': Divorce Litigation and Gender Inequality in China." Law & Policy 37(3):153–79.

Li, Ke. 2016. "Relational Embeddedness and Socially Motivated Case Screening in the Practice of Law in Rural China." Law & Society Review 50(4):920–52.

Li, Ke. 2020. "Land Dispossession and Women's Rights Contention in Rural China." China Law and Society Review 5(1):33–65.

Li, Ke. 2022. Marriage Unbound: Divorce Litigation, Power, and Inequality in Contemporary China. Stanford, CA: Stanford University Press.

Li, Ke and Sara L. Friedman. 2016. "Wedding Marriage to the Nation-State in Modern China: Legal Consequences for Divorce, Property, and Women's Rights." In Domestic Tensions, National Anxieties: Global Perspectives on Marriage, Crisis, and Nation, edited by K. Celello and H. Kholoussy, pp. 147–69. Oxford and New York: Oxford University Press.

Li, Ling. 2010. "Legality, Discretion and Informal Practices in China's Courts: A Socio-Legal Investigation of Private Transactions in the Course of Litigation." Ph.D. Dissertation, Faculty of Law, Leiden University.

Li, Qiongyu (李琼宇), Shufen (刘淑芬) Liu, and Lin (杨林) Yang. 2013. "家庭暴力在离婚诉讼案件中的认定与处断: 以贵阳市南明区人民法院2010 年度离婚案件为调查对象 (Affirming and Negating Domestic Violence in Divorce Litigation: An Investigation of Divorce Cases in the Nanming District People's Court of Guiyang City)." 哈尔滨学院学报 *Journal of Harbin University* 34(7):32–36.

Li, Shuming (李曙明). 2020. "热评: 检察院法院回应 '女子不堪家暴跳楼事件'逐渐清晰 (Commentary: Procuracy's Response to the 'Case of the Abused Woman Who Jumped Out of a Building' Gradually Clarifies)." *CCTV.Com.* Retrieved July 29, 2020 (https://tinyurl.com/y3ydnx44).

Li, Tiezhu (李铁柱). 2017. "四川发出首份离婚冷静期通知书 (Sichuan Issues Its First Notice of Cooling-Off Period)." 北京青年报 (*Beijing Youth Daily*), March 22, A10.

Li, Ting (李婷). 2018. "留守儿童心理状况研究 – – 基于河南省的实际 (Research on the Psychological Condition of Left-Behind Children: The Reality in Henan)." 行政事业资产与财务 (*Assets and Finances in Administration and Institution*) (14):39–40.

Li, Xiuping (李秀平). 2001. "《婚姻法》怎解离婚难题 (How to Resolve Difficult Issues in the New Marriage Law?)." 法律与生活 (*Law & Life*) 1:4–9.

Li, Xiuping (李秀平). 2003. "妻子, 被蹂躏与被掠夺 (Wives, Downtrodden and Preyed On)." 法律与生活 (*Law & Life*) (5):2–8.

Li, Xuejing (李雪菁). 2014. "基层一线法官的职业困境与对策 – – 以广西南宁市基层法院为例 (Frontline Judges' Plight and Countermeasures: The Case of a Basic-Level Court in Guangxi Province's City of Nanning)." 中外企业家 (*Chinese & Foreign Entrepreneurs*) (2):219–23.

Li, Yedan, Joris Kocken, and Benjamin van Rooij. 2016. "Understanding China's Court Mediation Surge: Insights from a Local Court." *Law & Social Inquiry* 43(1):58–81.

Li, Yongjun (李拥军) and Fangfang (周芳芳) Zhou. 2018. "我国判决说理激励机制适用问题之探讨 (On the Application of Incentive Mechanisms to Judgment Reasoning in China)." 法制与社会发展 (*Law and Social Development*) (3):57–69.

Liang, Xuguang (梁旭光). 1982. "反对轻率离婚 (Opposition to Frivolous Divorce)." 道德与文明 (*Morality and Civilization*) p.19.

Lieberman, Evan S. 2002. "Taxation Data as Indicators of State-Society Relations: Possibilities and Pitfalls in Cross-National Research." *Studies in Comparative International Development* 36(4):89–115.

Lieberman, Evan S. 2005. "Nested Analysis as a Mixed-Method Strategy for Comparative Research." *American Political Science Review* 99(03):435–52.

Liebman, Benjamin L. 2011a. "A Populist Threat to China's Courts?" In *Chinese Justice: Civil Dispute Resolution in Contemporary China*, edited by M. Y. K. Woo and M. E. Gallagher, pp.269–313. Cambridge and New York: Cambridge University Press.

Liebman, Benjamin L. 2011b. "A Return to Populist Legality? Historical Legacies and Legal Reform." In *Mao's Invisible Hand*, edited by S. Heilmann and E. J. Perry, pp. 269–313. Cambridge, MA and London: Harvard University Press.

Liebman, Benjamin L. 2013. "Malpractice Mobs: Medical Dispute Resolution in China." *Columbia Law Review* 113:181–264.

Liebman, Benjamin L. 2014. "Legal Reform: China's Law-Stability Paradox." *Daedalus* 143(2):96–109.

Liebman, Benjamin L. 2015. "Leniency in Chinese Criminal Law? Everyday Justice in Henan." *Berkeley Journal of International Law* 33(1):153–222.

Liebman, Benjamin L., Margaret Roberts, Rachel E. Stern, and Alice Z. Wang. 2020. "Mass Digitization of Chinese Court Decisions: How to Use Text as Data in the Field of Chinese Law." *Journal of Law and Courts* 8(2):177–201.

Liebowitz, Debra J. and Susanne Zwingel. 2014. "Gender Equality Oversimplified: Using CEDAW to Counter the Measurement Obsession." *International Studies Review* 16(3):362–89.

Lin, Hui (林辉). 2008. "论法官员额制度的推进 (On the Advancement of Judge Quota Systems)." 法制与经济 (*Legal and Economic*) (10):20–21.

Lin, Kai, Ivan Sun, Yuning Wu, and Jia Xue. 2021. "Chinese Police Officers' Attitudes toward Domestic Violence Interventions: Do Training and Knowledge of the Anti-Domestic Violence Law Matter?" *Policing & Society*. 31(7):878–94.

Lin, Xi (林曦), Xiaohong (卜晓虹) Bu, and Xiaoting (黎晓婷) Li. 2015. "司法担当论: 以离婚纠纷案件为视角 (Engaged Justice: From the Perspective of Divorce Cases)." 治理研究 (*Governance Studies*) (3):123–28.

Lipsky, Michael. 2010. *Street-Level Bureaucracy: Dilemmas of the Individual in Public Service*. 30th Anniv. New York: Russell Sage Foundation.

Liu, Baijun (刘百军) and Fei (石飞) Shi. 2016. "云南涉家暴刑案首次引入专家证人 (In Yunnan Criminal Domestic Violence Case First-Ever Admission of Expert Witness Testimony)." 法制日报 (*Legal Daily*), March 25, 3.

Liu, Hong and Ning Li. 1992. "Divorce in China." *Beijing Review* (September 7–13):28–30.

Liu, Jianqing (刘建清). 2017. "试论法官职业倦怠及其应对策略 (On Judge's Occupational Burnout and Its Countermeasures)." 新余学院学报 (*Journal of Xinyu University*) 22(4):63–67.

Liu, Junmei (刘君眉). 2016. "我市推行反家暴'告诫制度'底气更足 (Our City's Anti-Domestic Violence 'Warning System' Boosts Confidence)." 温州都市报 (*Wenzhou Metropolitan News*), March 1, 9.

Liu, Li (刘黎). 2013. "离婚案件中家庭暴力的认定与处理 (Affirming and Handling Domestic Violence in Divorce Cases)." 人民司法 (*People's Judicature*) (22):77–80.

Liu, Lianjun (刘练军). 2019. "'红'与'专': 法官职业认知的理念与规范叙事 ('Red' and 'Specialized': Perceptions and Rules about Judges)." 法治研究 (*Research on Rule of Law*) (5):95–110.

Liu, Lixia (刘立霞), and Rui (刘蕊) Liu. 2020. "家庭暴力下受虐妇女杀夫案的量刑研究 (Research on Criminal Sentencing in Cases of Abused Women Murdering Their Husbands)." 燕山大学学报 (哲学社会科学版) (*Journal of Yanshan University [Philosophy and Social Science]*) 21(2):43–50.

Liu, Meng and Cecilia Chan. 1999. "Enduring Violence and Staying in Marriage: Stories of Battered Women in Rural China." *Violence Against Women* 5(12):1469–92.

Liu, Min (刘敏). 2012. "二次离婚诉讼审判规则的实证研究 (Empirical Research on Patterns of Two-Trial Divorce Litigation)." 法商研究 (*Studies in Law and Business*) (6):80–84.

Liu, Sida. 2006. "Beyond Global Convergence: Conflicts of Legitimacy in a Chinese Lower Court." *Law and Social Inquiry* 31(1):75–106.

Liu, Sida. 2011. "Lawyers, State Officials and Significant Others: Symbiotic Exchange in the Chinese Legal Services Market." *The China Quarterly* 206:276–93.

Liu, Sida and Terence C. Halliday. 2016. *Criminal Defense in China: The Politics of Lawyers at Work.* Cambridge and New York: Cambridge University Press.

Liu, Sida, Lily Liang, and Ethan Michelson. 2014. "Migration and Social Structure: The Spatial Mobility of Chinese Lawyers." *Law & Policy* 36(2):165–94.

Liu, Wancheng (刘万成) and Yongjian (郑永建) Zheng. 2018. "家事审判中离婚冷静期的合理性证成与完善 (Justification and Improvement of the Reasonableness of the Domestic Relations Trial Reform's Cooling-Off Period)." 人民法院报 (*People's Court Daily*), July 11, 7.

Liu, Xiaobin (刘小斌). 2014. "民事简易程序适用效果不佳之程序外因素研究 (Research on Extra-Procedural Factors Behind Poor Outcomes in the Application of the Simplified Civil Procedure)." Retrieved October 6, 2020 (www.chinacourt.org/article/detail/2014/05/id/1291034.shtml).

Liu, Yahui (刘亚辉). 2016. "省十二届人大五次会议举行第二次大会 (Second Meeting of the Fifth Session of the 12th Henan Provincial People's Congress)." 河南日报 (*Henan Daily*), February 4, 1.

Liu, Ye, John Stillwell, Jianfa Shen, and Konstantinos Daras. 2014. "Interprovincial Migration, Regional Development and State Policy in China, 1985–2010." *Applied Spatial Analysis and Policy* 7(1):47–70.

Liu, Yu (刘瑜). 2011. "'被离婚'奇案,还是'再离婚'闹剧? – – '钢铁大王'杜双华家里那本难念的经 (A Case of 'Unwittingly Divorced' Or A Farce of 'Re-Divorced'? Steel Magnate Du Shuanghua's Family Skeleton in the Closet)." 民主与法制 (*Democracy and Legal System*) 16:38–41.

Long, J. Scott, and Jeremy Freese. 2014. *Regression Models for Categorical Dependent Variables Using Stata*. 3rd ed. College Station, TX: Stata Press.

Long, J. Scott, and Sarah A. Mustillo. 2021. "Using Predictions and Marginal Effects to Compare Groups in Regression Models for Binary Outcomes." *Sociological Methods & Research* 50(3):1284–320.

Lou, Bixian (娄必县). 2018. "法官职业危机的克服与豁免权构建 (Overcoming the Professional Crisis of Judges and Constructing the Judge's Immunity)." 武汉理工大学学报 (社会科学版) (*Wuhan University of Technology [Social Science Edition]*) 31(3):110–16.

Lu, Liya (卢利亚). 2017. "农村留守儿童的监护: 问题及对策 (Guardianship of Left-Behind Children in the Countryside: Problems and Countermeasures)." 当代教育理论与实践 (*Theory and Practice of Contemporary Education*) 9(5):1–6.

Lu, Pin. 2018. "Two Years On: Is China's Domestic Violence Law Working?" Retrieved June 21, 2019 (www.amnesty.org/en/latest/campaigns/2018/03/is-china-domestic-violence-law-working/).

Lü, Yuedu (吕岳督). 2015. "基层人民法院合议庭运行机制研究——以民商事审判为视角 (Research on the Operation of Basic-Level Collegial Panels: From the Perspective of Civil and Commercial Adjudication)." Retrieved January 26, 2020 (http://zzfy.hncourt.gov.cn/public/detail.php?id=22447).

Luo, Dongchuan (罗东川), and Bin (黄斌) Huang. 2011. "我国司法效率改革的实践探索: 立足于当前人民法院'案多人少'问题的思考 (Exploring China's Judicial Efficiency Reforms in Practice: Thoughts on the Current Problem of 'Many Cases, Few Judges' in People's Courts)." 法律适用 (*Journal of Law Application*) (3):8–13.

Luo, Ling (罗玲). 2016. "裁判离婚理由影响因素实证研究: 以 2010–2011 年河南省的部分离婚纠纷案件判决文书为样本 (An Empirical Study of the Factors Affecting the Legal Grounds for Divorce: A 2010–2011 Sample of Divorce Judgments from Henan Province)." 中华女子学院学报 (*Journal of China Women's University*) (1):14–23.

Ma, Chao (马超), Xiaohong (于晓虹) Yu, and Haibo (何海波) He. 2016. "大数据分析: 中国司法裁判文书上网公开报告 (Big Data Analysis: A Report of China Judgements Online)." 中国法律评论 (*China Law Review*) 4:195–246.

Ma, Mingyang (马名扬). 2018. "离婚冷静期通知书, 只想让你更懂得珍惜 (The Divorce Cooling-Off Notice Is Only to Help You Cherish What You Have)." 婚姻与家庭(社会纪实) (*Marriage & Family*) (2):16–18.

Ma, Yi'nan (马忆南). 2006. "婚姻法第32条实证研究 (Empirical Research on Article 32 of the Marriage Law)." 金陵法律评论 (*Jin Ling Law Review*) 1:20–27.

Ma, Yi'nan (马忆南) and Ling (罗玲) Luo. 2014. "裁判离婚理由立法研究 (Research on Court Holdings in Divorce Rulings)." 法学论坛 (*Legal Forum*) 29(4):34–44.

Maynard-Moody, Steven and Shannon Portillo. 2010. "Street-Level Bureaucracy Theory." In *The Oxford Handbook of American Bureaucracy*, edited by R. F. Durant, pp. 253–77. Oxford and New York: Oxford University Press.

McConville, Mike, Satnam Choongh, Pinky Choy Dick Wan, Eric Chui Wing Hong, Ian Dobinson, and Carol Jones. 2011. *Criminal Justice in China: An Empirical Inquiry*. Cheltenham, UK and Northampton, MA: Edward Elgar.

McHugh, Marry L. 2012. "Interrater Reliability: The Kappa Statistic." *Biochemia Medica* 22(3):276–82.

Meng, Chongyan (孟崇彦). 2012. "改革和完善我国法院调解制度的思考－－从比较法的角度 (Reflections on Reforming and Perfecting China's Judicial Mediation System: A Comparative Law Perspective)." 法制博览 (*Legality Vision*) (3):85–87.

Meng, Qingkui (孟庆魁). 1982. "要重视和加强民事审判工作 (Trial Work Must Be Given Attention and Strengthened)." 人民司法 (*People's Judicature*) (9):15–16.

Merry, Sally Engle. 1990. *Getting Justice and Getting Even: Legal Consciousness Among Working-Class Americans*. Chicago and London: The University of Chicago Press.

Merry, Sally Engle. 2006. *Human Rights and Gender Violence: Translating International Law into Local Justice*. Chicago and London: The University of Chicago Press.

Merry, Sally Engle. 2009. *Gender Violence: A Cultural Perspective*. Chichester, UK: Wiley-Blackwell.

Merry, Sally Engle. 2016. *The Seductions of Quantification: Measuring Human Rights, Gender Violence, and Sex Trafficking*. Chicago and London: The University of Chicago Press.

Meyer, John W. 2010. "World Society, Institutional Theories, and the Actor." *Annual Review of Sociology* 36(1):1–20.

Meyer, John W., John Boli, George M. Thomas, and Francisco O. Ramirez. 1997. "World Society and the Nation-State." *American Journal of Sociology* 103(1):144–81.

Meyer, John W. and Brian Rowan. 1977. "Institutionalized Organizations: Formal Structure as Myth and Ceremony." *American Journal of Sociology* 83(2):340–63.

Miao, Michelle. 2013. "The Politics of China's Death Penalty Reform in the Context of Global Abolitionism." *The British Journal of Criminology* 53(3):500–19.

Michelson, Ethan. 2006. "The Practice of Law as an Obstacle to Justice: Chinese Lawyers at Work." *Law & Society Review* 40(1):1–38.

Michelson, Ethan. 2007. "Lawyers, Political Embeddedness, and Institutional Continuity in China's Transition from Socialism." *American Journal of Sociology* 113(2):352–414.

Michelson, Ethan. 2008. "Dear Lawyer Bao: Everyday Problems, Legal Advice, and State Power in China." *Social Problems* 55(1):43–71.

Michelson, Ethan. 2010. "Family Planning Enforcement in Rural China: Enduring State-Society Conflict?" In *Growing Pains: Tensions and Opportunity in China's Transformation*, edited by J. C. Oi, S. Rozelle, and X. Zhou, pp. 189–226. Stanford, CA: Shorenstein Asia Pacific Research Center, distributed by Brookings Institution Press.

Michelson, Ethan. 2012. "Access to Lawyers: A Comparative Analysis of the Supply of Lawyers in China and the United States." *National Taiwan University Law Review* 7(1):223–55.

Michelson, Ethan 2013. "Women in the Legal Profession, 1970–2010: A Study of the Global Supply of Lawyers." *Indiana Journal of Global Legal Studies* 20(2):1071–137.

Michelson, Ethan. 2019a. "Decoupling: Marital Violence and the Struggle to Divorce in China." *American Journal of Sociology* 125(2):325–81.

Michelson, Ethan. 2019b. "Many Voices in China's Legal Profession: Plural Meanings of Weiquan." *China Law and Society Review* 4(2):71–101.

Michelson, Ethan. 2019c. "Supplemental Material." Retrieved February 14, 2020 (www.journals.uchicago.edu/doi/suppl/10.1086/705747).

Michelson, Ethan and Benjamin L. Read. 2011. "Public Attitudes toward Official Justice in Beijing and Rural China." In *Chinese Justice: Civil Dispute Resolution in Contemporary China*, edited by M. Y. K. Woo and M. E. Gallagher, pp. 169–203. Cambridge and New York: Cambridge University Press.

Miller, Arthur R. 2003. "The Pretrial Rush to Judgment: Are the Litigation Explosion, Liability Crisis, and Efficiency Cliches Eroding Our Day in Court and Jury Trial Commitments." *New York University Law Review* 78(3):982–1134.

Min, Tianyang (闵天阳). 2017. "关于当前离婚案件审判模式的思考 (Reflections on Contemporary Divorce Trial Modes)." 法制与经济 (*Legal and Economic*) (17):179–80.

Ministry of Civil Affairs of China. 2018. "2017 年社会服务发展统计公报 (2017 Social Services Development Statistical Report)." Retrieved June 13, 2019 (www.mca.gov.cn/article/sj/tjgb/201808/20180800010446.shtml).

Ministry of Civil Affairs of China. Various years. 中国民政统计年鉴 (*China Civil Affairs Statistical Yearbook*). Beijing: China Statistics Press.

Ministry of Justice. 2018. "律师、公证、基层法律服务最新数据出炉 (Newest Data on Lawyers, Notaries, and Basic-Level Legal Workers Are Fresh Out of the Oven)." Retrieved August 16, 2018 (www.moj.gov.cn/ government_public/content/2018-03/14/634_17049.html).

Minzner, Carl. 2009. "Judicial Disciplinary Systems for Incorrectly Decided Cases: The Imperial Chinese Heritage Lives On." *New Mexico Law Review* 39(1):63–87.

Minzner, Carl. 2011. "China's Turn Against Law." *American Journal of Comparative Law* 59(4):935–84.

Mize, Trenton. 2019. "Best Practices for Estimating, Interpreting, and Presenting Nonlinear Interaction Effects." *Sociological Science* 6:81–117.

Mnookin, Robert H. and Lewis Kornhauser. 1979. "Bargaining in the Shadow of the Law: The Case of Divorce." *The Yale Law Journal* 88(5):950.

Mo, Li. 2017. "Trends in the Divorce Rate and Its Regional Disparity in China." *Journal of Comparative Family Studies* 48(4):383–94.

Mortelmans, Dimitri. 2020. "Introduction." In *Divorce in Europe: New Insights in Trends, Causes and Consequences of Relation Break-ups*, edited by D. Mortelmans, pp. 1–14. Cham, Switzerland: SpringerOpen.

Moustafa, Tamir. 2014. "Law and Courts in Authoritarian Regimes." *Annual Review of Law and Social Science* 10(1):281–299.

Myers, Steven Lee and Olivia Mitchell Ryan. 2018. "Burying 'One Child' Limits, China Pushes Women to Have More Babies." *The New York Times*, August 12, A1.

Di Nallo, Alessandro. 2019. "Gender Gap in Repartnering: The Role of Parental Status and Custodial Arrangements." *Journal of Marriage and Family* 81(1):59–78.

National Bureau of Statistics of China. 2015. 中国人口和就业统计年鉴 (*China Population and Employment Statistical Yearbook*). Beijing: China Statistics Press.

Negro, Giacomo and Wesley Longhofer. 2018. "World Society, Legal Formalism, and Execution of Legal Procedures." *Social Forces* 97(2):649–73.

Ng, Kwai Hang and Xin He. 2014. "Internal Contradictions of Judicial Mediation in China." *Law and Social Inquiry* 39(2):285–312.

Ng, Kwai Hang and Xin He. 2017a. *Embedded Courts: Judicial Decision-Making in China*. Cambridge and New York: Cambridge University Press.

Ng, Kwai Hang and Xin He. 2017b. "The Institutional and Cultural Logics of Legal Commensuration: Blood Money and Negotiated Justice in China." *American Journal of Sociology* 122(4):1104–43.

Ni, Zijun (倪子钧). 2014. "农村地区离婚案件分析与思考 – – 以吉林省农安县为例 (Analysis of and Reflections on Divorce in Rural Areas: The Case of Nongan County, Jilin Province)." 法制与社会 (*Legal System and Society*) (21):213–14.

Ningbo Municipal Yinzhou District People's Court (宁波市鄞州区人民法院). 2014. "离婚纠纷案件审判白皮书 2009–2012年 (Divorce Dispute Case Trials White Paper 2009–2012)." Retrieved June 27, 2019 (www.nbyzfy.gov.cn/art/2014/7/11/art_3478_229265.html).

Pache, Anne-Claire and Filipe Santos. 2013. "Embedded in Hybrid Contexts: How Individuals in Organizations Respond to Competing Institutional Logics." In *Institutional Logics in Action, Part B*, edited by M. Lounsbury and E. Boxenbaum, pp.3–35. Bingley, UK: Emerald.

Palmer, Michael. 1995. "The Re-Emergence of Family Law in Post-Mao China: Marriage, Divorce and Reproduction." *The China Quarterly* 141:110–34.

Palmer, Michael. 2007. "Transforming Family Law in Post-Deng China: Marriage, Divorce and Reproduction." *The China Quarterly* 191:675–95.

Palmer, Michael. 2017. "Domestic Violence and Mediation in Contemporary China." In *Mediation in Contemporary China: Continuity and Change*, edited by H. Fu and M. Palmer, pp. 286–318. London: Wildy, Simmonds & Hill.

Pan, Qinglin (潘庆林). 2019. "民事案件繁简分流制度的完善 – – 基于对A 省基层法院的调研 (Improving the System of Designating Cases as Complex and Simplified: A Study of A Basic-Level Court in Province A)." 法学杂志 (*Law Science Magazine*) (9):124–30.

Pan, Yongzhang (潘涌燚). 2018. "陈敏: 专注于研究反家暴法律 (Chen Min: Immersed in Research on Anti-Domestic Violence Laws)." 温州新闻网 (*Wenzhou Online News*). Retrieved March 27, 2020 (http://news.66wz.com/system/2018/11/28/105131511.shtml).

Paneyakh, Ella. 2014. "Faking Performance Together: Systems of Performance Evaluation in Russian Enforcement Agencies and Production of Bias and Privilege." *Post-Soviet Affairs* 30(2–3):115–36.

Paradis, Cheryl. 2017. "Assessment of Intimate Partner Violence and the Battered Woman Syndrome." *Psychiatric Annals* 47(12):593–97.

Parish, William L., Tianfu Wang, Edward O. Laumann, Suiming Pan, and Ye Luo. 2004. "Intimate Partner Violence in China: National Prevalence, Risk Factors and Associated Health Problems." *International Family Planning Perspectives* 30(4):174–81.

Parish, William L. and Martin King Whyte. 1978. *Village and Family Life in Contemporary China*. Chicago and London: The University of Chicago Press.

Pearce, Lisa D. 2002. "Integrating Survey and Ethnographic Methods for Systematic Anomalous Case Analysis." *Sociological Methodology* 32(1):103–32.

Peerenboom, Randall, ed. 2010. *Judicial Independence in China: Lessons for Global Rule of Law Promotion*. Cambridge and New York: Cambridge University Press.

People's Court Media Office. 2019. "最高人民法院发布2019年第一季度审判执行工作数据 (Supreme People's Court Issues Trial and Enforcement Work Statistics for First Quarter of 2019)." Retrieved August 2, 2020 (www.court.gov.cn/zixun-xiangqing-157962.html).

Perrin, Ruth Leah. 2017. "Overcoming Biased Views of Gender and Victimhood in Custody Evaluations When Domestic Violence Is Alleged." *American University Journal of Gender, Social Policy & the Law* 25(2):155–77.

Pettit, Ellen J. and Bernard L. Bloom. 1984. "Whose Decision Was It? The Effects of Initiator Status on Adjustment to Marital Disruption." *Journal of Marriage and the Family* 46(3):587.

Pierotti, Rachael S. 2013. "Increasing Rejection of Intimate Partner Violence." *American Sociological Review* 78(2):240–65.

Pope, Shawn and John W. Meyer. 2016. "Local Variation in World Society: Six Characteristics of Global Diffusion." *European Journal of Cultural and Political Sociology* 3(2–3):280–305.

Qu, Xiangdong (屈向东), and Jiqiang (范继强) Fan. 2019. "论中国法官员额制的历史演进 (On the Historical Evolution of the Quota System of Chinese Judges)." 政法学刊 *(Journal of Political Science and Law)* (2):17–27.

Rathus, Zoe, Samantha Jeffries, Helena Menih, and Rachael Field. 2019. "'It's Like Standing on a Beach, Holding Your Children's Hands, and Having a Tsunami Just Coming Towards You': Intimate Partner Violence and 'Expert' Assessments in Australian Family Law." *Victims & Offenders* 14(4):408–40.

Raynard, Mia, Michael Lounsbury, and Royston Greenwood. 2013. "Legacies of Logics: Sources of Community Variation in CSR Implementation in China." In *Institutional Logics in Action, Part A*, edited by M. Lounsbury and E. Boxenbaum, pp. 243–76. Bingley, UK: Emerald.

Research Office of the Nanjing Municipal Intermediate Court. 1987. "谈判决不准离婚 (A Discussion of Adjudicated Denials of Divorce Petitions)." 人民司法 *(People's Judicature)* 10:16–18.

Ridgeway, Cecilia L. 2011. *Framed by Gender: How Gender Inequality Persists in the Modern World*. Oxford and New York: Oxford University Press.

Rivera, Echo A., Cris M. Sullivan, and April M. Zeoli. 2012. "Secondary Victimization of Abused Mothers by Family Court Mediators." *Feminist Criminology* 7(3):234–52.

Robel, Lauren K. 1990. "Caseload and Judging: Judicial Adaptations to Caseload." *Brigham Young University Law Review* (4):3–65.

Robinson, Jean. 1989. "Family Policies, Women, and the Collective Interest in Contemporary China." *Policy Studies Review* 8(3):648–62.

Rong, Weiyi (荣维毅). 2016. "反对针对妇女暴力领域法律政策回顾分析 (A Review and Analysis of Laws and Policies to Combat Violence against Women)." In *2013–2015年：中国性别平等与妇女发展报告 (Annual Report on Gender Equality and Women's Development in China [2013–2015])*, edited by L. (谭琳) Tan, pp. 203–14. Beijing: 社会科学文献出版社 Social Sciences Academic Press.

Rong, Weiyi (荣维毅). 2020. "消除一切形式对妇女的暴力 – – 对近五年中国治理对妇女暴力行动的评估 (Eliminating All Forms of Violence Against Women: An Assessment of China's Actions to Combat Violence Against Women in the Last Five Years)." 山东女子学院学报 *(Journal of Shandong Women's University)* (149):45–56.

Rongan County People's Court (融安县人民法院). 2019. "什么人?竟威胁办离婚案的法官'你们准备收尸'……(What Kind of Person Goes as Far as to Threaten Judge Who Decided Divorce to 'Prepare for Corpses'?)."

Retrieved December 24, 2019 (www.lzgd.com.cn/news/inliuzhou_view .ashx?id=68338).

Rosenfeld, Michael J. 2018. "Who Wants the Breakup? Gender and Breakup in Heterosexual Couples." In *Social Networks and the Life Course. Frontiers in Sociology and Social Research, Volume 2*, edited by D. F. Alwin, D. H. Felmlee, and D. A. Kreager, pp. 221–43. Springer.

Rosga, AnnJanette and Margaret L. Satterthwaite. 2012. "Measuring Human Rights: UN Indicators in Critical Perspective." In *Governance by Indicators: Global Power Through Classification and Rankings*, edited by K. Davis, A. Fisher, B. Kingsbury, and S. E. Merry, pp. 297–316. Oxford and New York: Oxford University Press.

Rothenberg, Bess. 2002. "The Success of the Battered Woman Syndrome: An Analysis of How Cultural Arguments Succeed." *Sociological Forum* 17(1):81–103.

Rothenberg, Bess. 2003. "'We Don't Have Time for Social Change': Cultural Compromise and the Battered Woman Syndrome." *Gender & Society* 17(5):771–87.

Runge, Robin. 2015. "Operating in a Narrow Space to Effect Change: Development of a Legal System Response to Domestic Violence in China." In *Comparative Perspectives on Gender Violence: Lessons from Efforts Worldwide*, edited by R. Goel and L. Goodmark, pp. 31–42. Oxford and New York: Oxford University Press.

Sandefur, Rebecca L. 2015. "Elements of Professional Expertise: Understanding Relational and Substantive Expertise through Lawyers' Impact." *American Sociological Review* 80(5):909–33.

Sauder, Michael and Wendy Nelson Espeland. 2009. "The Discipline of Rankings: Tight Coupling and Organizational Change." *American Sociological Review* 74(1):63–82.

Schofer, Evan and Ann Hironaka. 2005. "The Effects of World Society on Environmental Protection Outcomes." *Social Forces* 84(1):25–47.

Schofer, Evan, Ann Hironaka, David John Frank, and Wesley Longhofer. 2012. "Sociological Institutionalism and World Society." In *The Wiley-Blackwell Companion to Political Sociology*, edited by E. Amenta, K. Nash, and A. Scott, pp. 57–68. Chichester, West Sussex and Malden, MA: Wiley-Blackwell.

Shaffer, Martha. 1990. "R. v. Lavallee: A Review Essay." *Ottawa Law Review* 22(3):607–24.

Shandong Province Ji'nan Municipal Intermediate People's Court Research Team (山东省济南市中级人民法院课题组). 2018. "关于2015–2017年度山东省济南市法院离婚纠纷案件的调研报告 (Research Report on Divorce Disputes in Shandong Province's Ji'nan Municipal Courts, 2015–2017)." 山东法官培训学院学报 (*Shandong Judges Training Institute Journal*) 3:170–87.

Shangqiu Municipal Intermediate Court Research Team (商丘市中级人民法院课题组). 2017. "'让审理者裁判由裁判者负责'的实践探索：以商丘新型合

议庭改革为样本 (An Exploration of the Practice of 'Letting Judges Judge and Assigning Responsibility to Decision-Makers': The Case of Shangqiu Collegial Panel Reform)." In 河南法治发展报告 (*Annual Report on Rule of Law Development in Henan*), edited by T. (丁同民) Ding and L. (张林海) Zhang, pp. 49–67. Beijing: 社会科学文献出版社 Social Sciences Academic Press.

Shao, Chen (邵晨). 2015. "浅议法官独立 – – 以制度管理为视角 (On the Independence of Judges: From A System Management Perspective)." 襄阳职业技术学院学报 (*Journal of Xiangyang Polytechnic*) 14(1):36–40.

Sheehy, Elizabeth, Julie Stubbs, and Julia Tolmie. 2012. "Battered Women Charged With Homicide in Australia, Canada and New Zealand: How Do They Fare?" *Australian & New Zealand Journal of Criminology* 45(3):383–99.

Shi, Guang (时光). 2005. "18年离婚路, 她为何走不出家庭暴力的泥潭 (An 18-Year Divorce Road: Why She Couldn't Escape the Mire of Domestic Violence)." 现代妇女 (*Modern Woman*) (10):4–7.

Shi, Lei. 2020. "Reactive Law or Conservative Law? The Reform of Divorce Procedure in China." *International Journal of Law, Policy and the Family* 34(2):126–44.

Shih, Chih Yu. 1996. "China's Socialist Law Under Reform: The Class Nature Reconsidered." *American Journal of Comparative Law* 44(4):627.

Sichuan Online. 2017. "安岳法院发出首张'离婚冷静期'通知书 (Anyue Court Issues First Notice of 'Cooling-Off Period')." Retrieved June 2, 2020 (https://ziyang.scol.com.cn/ayx/201703/55854267.html).

Simon, Rita James and Linda Mahan. 1971. "Quantifying Burdens of Proof: A View from the Bench, the Jury, and the Classroom." *Law & Society Review* 5(3):319–30.

Smart, Carol. 1984. *The Ties That Bind: Law, Marriage, and the Reproduction of Patriarchal Relations*. London and Boston: Routledge & Kegan Paul.

Smil, Vaclav. 1993. *China's Environmental Crisis: An Inquiry Into the Limits of National Development*. Armonk, NY: M. E. Sharpe.

Sohu.com. 2003. "刘拴霞杀夫被判 '受虐妇女'杀夫不属正当防卫 (Court Rules Liu Shuanxia's Murder of Abusive Husband Is Not Justifiable Self-Defense)." Retrieved June 22, 2020 (http://news.sohu.com/17/02/news211910217.shtml).

Sohu.com. 2020. "遭家暴跳楼致截瘫女子已离婚, 孩子抚养权归原告, 等刑事判决结果 (Abused Woman Who Jumped Out of a Building Causing Paraplegia Is Now Divorced, Gets Child Custody, Now Awaiting Criminal Verdict)." Retrieved July 30, 2020 (www.sohu.com/a/410426453_120083964).

Sohu.com. 2021a. "第五次, 她离了! (Divorced on the Fifth Try!)." Retrieved August 3, 2021 (www.sohu.com/a/464151381_120046696).

Sohu.com. 2021b. "湖南女子5年5次起诉离婚被判返还彩礼8.5万!其表示不解 (Hunan Woman Who Filed for Divorce Five Times in Five Years Is Baffled by Court Order to Return Bride Price of ¥85,000)." Retrieved August 3, 2021 (www.sohu.com/a/481189925_161795).

Solomon, Peter H. 2010. "Authoritarian Legality and Informal Practices: Judges, Lawyers and the State in Russia and China." *Communist and Post-Communist Studies* 43(4):351–62.

Solomon, Peter H. 2012. "The Accountability of Judges in Post Communist States: From Bureaucratic to Professional Accountability." In *Judicial Independence in Transition*, edited by A. Seibert-Fohr, pp. 909–35. Berlin, Heidelberg: Springer.

Solomon, Peter H. 2015. "Post-Soviet Criminal Justice: The Persistence of Distorted Neo-Inquisitorialism" edited by G. Slade and M. Light. *Theoretical Criminology* 19(2):159–78.

Song, Peipei (宋镕培). 2016. "家暴刑案首次引入专家证人作证 (First-Ever Admission of Expert Witness Testimony in Criminal Domestic Violence Case)." 四川法制报 (*Sichuan Legal Daily*), April 7, A01.

Song, Yuansheng (宋远升). 2017. "精英化与专业化的迷失 – – 法官员额制的困境与出路 (The Loss of Professionalization and Specialization: The Predicament of the Judge Quota System and a Way Out)." 政法论坛 (*Tribune of Political Science and Law*) (2):101–17.

Song, Yueping, Jingwen Zhang, and Xian Zhang. 2020. "Cultural or Institutional? Contextual Effects on Domestic Violence against Women in Rural China." *Journal of Family Violence* 1–13.

SPC (Supreme People's Court). 2013. "最高人民法院详解最高法院裁判文书上网热点问题 (Supreme People's Court Explains in Detail Pressing Issues About China Judgements Online)." Retrieved December 30, 2020 (https://perma.cc/8UQG-Y9FD).

SPC (Supreme People's Court), ed. 2018. 人民法院司法统计历史典籍 1949–2016 (*People's Courts Compendium of Historical Judicial Statistics, 1949–2016*). Beijing: 中国民主法制出版 (China Legal Publishing House).

Sprick, Daniel. 2018. "Replacing Violence with Violence? A Functionalist Approach to Self-Defence in China." *Journal of Comparative Law* 13(2):283–307.

Stacey, Judith. 1983. *Patriarchy and Socialist Revolution in China*. Berkeley, CA: University of California Press.

Stanko, Elizabeth Anne. 1982. "Would You Believe This Woman? Prosecutorial Screening for 'Credible' Witnesses and a Problem of Justice." In *Judge, Lawyer, Victim, Thief: Women, Gender Roles, and Criminal Justice*, edited by N. H. Rafter and E. A. Stanko, pp. 63–82. Boston: Northeastern University Press.

Steensland, Brian. 2006. "Cultural Categories and the American Welfare State: The Case of Guaranteed Income Policy." *American Journal of Sociology* 111(5):1273–326.

Stern, Rachel E. 2013. *Environmental Litigation in China: A Study in Political Ambivalence*. Cambridge and New York: Cambridge University Press.

Stöckl, Heidi, Karen Devries, Alexandra Rotstein, Naeemah Abrahams, Jacquelyn Campbell, Charlotte Watts, and Claudia Garcia Moreno. 2013.

"The Global Prevalence of Intimate Partner Homicide: A Systematic Review." *The Lancet* 382(9895):859–65.

Su, Hucheng (苏湖城). 2011. "家庭暴力离婚诉讼如何取证 (How to Collect Evidence of Domestic Violence for Divorce Litigation)." 农家参谋 (*The Farmers Consultant*) 12:36.

Su, Li (苏力). 2010. "审判管理与社会管理－－法院如何有效回应'案多人少'? (Case Management and Social Management: How Can Courts Deal with 'Many Cases and Few Judges'?)." 中国法学 (*China Legal Science*) (6):176–89.

Su, Yunyun (苏云云). 2018. "家庭暴力对子女抚养权归属影响探究－－以美国相关制度为借鉴 (Research on the Influence of Domestic Violence on Child Custody Determinations: Drawing on the American System)." 北京化工大学学报 (社会科学版) (*Journal of Beijing University of Chemical Technology [Social Sciences Edition]*) (3):54–59.

Sun, Bo (孙波). 2010. "离婚案件缺席审判的思考 (Reflections on In Absentia Divorce Trials)." 大众商务 (*Popular Business*) 116:264.

Sun, Hang (孙航). 2019. "新收案件数持续增长 结案数同比大幅增加 整体运行态势稳中向好 (Numbers of New Cases Continues to Rise, Numbers of Closed Cases Significantly Increased Over Previous Year, and the Overall Situation Is Stable and Improving)." 人民法院报 (People's Court Daily), August 1, 1.

Sun, Yong (孙勇). 2006. "公告离婚的适用与完善 (The Application and Improvement of In Absentia Public Notice Divorce)." 理论月刊 (*Theory Monthly*) 1:121–23.

Sundström, Aksel, Pamela Paxton, Yi-Ting Wang, and Staffan I. Lindberg. 2017. "Women's Political Empowerment: A New Global Index, 1900–2012." *World Development* 94:321–35.

Suo, Xing (所行). 2020. "哈尔滨刺死法官者被批捕 (Man Who Stabbed Judge to Death Arrested)." 人民法院报 (*People's Court Daily*), November 18, 1.

Sweet, Paige L. 2019. "The Sociology of Gaslighting." *American Sociological Review* 84(5):851–75.

Swiss, Liam. 2009. "Decoupling Values from Action: An Event-History Analysis of the Election of Women to Parliament in the Developing World, 1945–90." *International Journal of Comparative Sociology* 50(1):69–95.

Tan, Dexiu (谭德修) and Yonghong (王永红) Wang. 2011. "公告离婚适用的困境与出路 －－ 兼评我国《婚姻法》第32 条第4 款之不足 (Dilemmas and Remedies in the Application of Public Notice Divorces: A Commentary on the Deficiencies of Article 32, Item 4 of the Marriage Law)." 湖南科技学院学报 (*Journal of Hunan University of Science and Engineering*) 32(8):115–18.

Tan, Lin (谭琳). 2016. "附录: 中国性别平等与妇女发展大事记 (Appendix: Major Events in Gender Equality and Women's Development in China)."

In *2013–2015年: 中国性别平等与妇女发展报告 (Annual Report on Gender Equality and Women's Development in China [2013–2015])*, edited by L. (谭琳) Tan, pp. 296–344. Beijing: 社会科学文献出版社 Social Sciences Academic Press.

Tan, Xu (覃旭). 2017. "农村离婚妇女探视权之保障 (Guaranteeing the Visitation Rights of Divorced Rural Women)." 法制博览 *(Legality Vision)* (18):270.

Tan, Zuocai (谭佐财), and Junbo (王俊博) Wang. 2016. "离婚诉讼中家庭暴力之证据认定: 以C 市基层法院103 份离婚案件判决书为分析样本 (The Affirmation of Evidence of Domestic Violence in Divorce Litigation: An Analysis of a Sample of 103 Divorce Cases from a District Court in C City) ." 法制与社会 *(Legal System and Society)* 10:184–85.

Tang, Jiaqing (唐嘉清). 1996. "浅析民事案件的预审 (An Analysis of Pretrial Civil Cases)." 人民司法 *(People's Judicature)* (9):19–21.

Tang, Liyi (汤立伊). 2017. "我国人民陪审员参审机制的反思与进路 (Reflections on and Ways to Advance China's People's Lay Assessor Mechanism)." 行政与法 *(Public Administration & Law)* (1):121–28.

Tang, Ren (唐牣). 2014. "民事简易程序适用改革的思考 (Thoughts on Reforming the Application of the Simplified Civil Procedure)." 山东审判 *(Shandong Justice)* (6):77–81.

Tang, Weijian (汤维建). 2016. "民事庭审程序优质化改革的理论与实践 (Optimized Reform of Civil Court Trial Procedures: Theories and Practice)." 贵州民族大学学报(哲学社会科学版) *(Journal of Guizhou Minzu University [Philosophy and Social Sciences])* (3):130–60.

Tang, Wenfang and William L. Parish. 2000. *Chinese Life Under Reform: The Changing Social Contract.* Cambridge and New York: Cambridge University Press.

Tang, Xuchao (唐旭超). 2017. "规范与重构: 基层法院民事审判庭设置的实证研究 (Standardization and Reconstruction: Empirical Research on Civil Divisions of Basic-Level People's Courts)." 法律适用 *(Journal of Law Application)* (5):96–102.

Tang, Yingmao (唐应茂). 2018. "领导意愿、机构能力和司法公开 (Leader's Will, Institutional Capacity, and Judicial Openness: Preliminary Research on Online Disclosure Rates of Court Decisions in Beijing, Shanghai, and Guangdong)." 中国法律评论 *(China Law Review)* 6:90–102.

Tang, Yingmao and John Zhuang Liu. 2019. "Mass Publicity of Chinese Court Decisions: Market-Driven or Authoritarian Transparency?" *The China Review* 19(2):15–40.

Tang, Zilong (汤梓龙). 2014. "法官员额制度研究 (Research on the Judge Quota System)." 法制与社会 *(Legal System and Society)* (9):44–45.

Tao, Jian (陶建), and Wei (卢茜) Lu. 2012. "农村离婚率上升的成因及法律思考 (Causes of and Legal Considerations for the Rise of Rural Divorce)." 法制与社会 *(Legal System and Society)* 19(7):65–66.

Tatlow, Didi Kirsten. 2015. "Battered Woman Is Spared Execution in China." *The New York Times*, April 25, A3.

Thomas, Natalie. 2016. "In China, Calls for End to Aggressive Child Custody Tactics." *Reuters*, December 28. Retrieved August 24, 2021 (www.reuters.com/article/us-china-custody-idUSKBN14I084).

Thornton, Arland and Yu Xie. 2016. "Developmental Idealism in China." *Chinese Journal of Sociology* 2(4):483–96.

Thornton, Patricia H., William Ocasio, and Michael Lounsbury. 2012. *The Institutional Logics Perspective: A New Approach to Culture, Structure, and Process*. Oxford and New York: Oxford University Press.

Tian, Xiangyu (田祥玉). 2016. "离婚应该慢慢来 (Take It Slowly With Divorce)." 婚姻与家庭 (社会纪实) (*Marriage & Family*) (8):25–27.

Tian, Yuan (田源) and Qun (王群) Wang. 2016. "基层人民法庭法官执业生态问题研究: 基于D 县法院6 处人民法庭的实证考察 (Research on Judges in Basic-Level People's Courts: An Empirical Investigation of Six Courts in County D)." 三峡大学学报(人文社会科学版) (*Journal of China Three Gorges University [Humanities & Social Sciences]*) 38(6):81–87.

Treiman, Donald J. 2012. "The 'Difference between Heaven and Earth': Urban–Rural Disparities in Well-Being in China." *Research in Social Stratification and Mobility* 30(1):33–47.

Trent, Katherine and Scott J. South. 2011. "Too Many Men? Sex Ratios and Women's Partnering Behavior in China." *Social Forces* 90(1):247–67.

Trevaskes, Susan. 2008. "The Death Penalty in China Today: Kill Fewer, Kill Cautiously." *Asian Survey* 48:393–413.

Trevaskes, Susan. 2010. "The Shifting Sands of Punishment in China in the Era of 'Harmonious Society'." *Law & Policy* 32(3):332–61.

Trevaskes, Susan. 2015. "Lenient Death Sentencing and the 'Cash for Clemency' Debate." *The China Journal* 73:38–58.

True, Jacqui and Michael Mintrom. 2001. "Transnational Networks and Policy Diffusion: The Case of Gender Mainstreaming." *International Studies Quarterly* 45(1):27–57.

Tsui, Ming. 2001. "Divorce, Women's Status, and the Communist State in China." *Asian Thought & Society* 26(77):103–25.

UNDP. 2014. "中国司法改革年度报告2013 (Annual Report on China's Judicial Reform 2013)." Retrieved August 8, 2018 (https://www.cn.undp.org/content/china/zh/home/library/democratic_governance/annual-report-on-china-s-judicial-reform-2013.html).

Urueña, René. 2015. "Indicators and the Law: A Case Study of the Rule of Law Index." In *The Quiet Power of Indicators: Measuring Governance, Corruption, and Rule of Law*, edited by S. E. Merry, K. E. Davis, and B. Kingsbury, pp. 75–102. Cambridge and New York: Cambridge University Press.

Van Rooij, Benjamin, and Carlos Wing-Hung Lo. 2009. "Fragile Convergence: Understanding Variation in the Enforcement of China's Industrial Pollution Law." *Law & Policy* 32(1):14–37.

Vaughan, Diane. 1986. *Uncoupling: Turning Points in Intimate Relationships.* Oxford and New York: Oxford University Press.

Walker, Lenore E. 2017. *The Battered Woman Syndrome. Fourth.* New York: Springer.

Wan, Xiaoying (万笑影), and Shangjun (林上军) Lin. 2020. "巡回审判, 开庭在基层 (Mobile Adjudication, Trials at the Grassroots)." 浙江日报 (*Zhejiang Daily*), June 24, 7.

Wang, Alex L. 2018. "Symbolic Legitimacy and Chinese Environmental Reform." *Environmental Law* 48(4):699–760.

Wang, Cheng-Tong Lir and Evan Schofer. 2018. "Coming Out of the Penumbras: World Culture and Cross-National Variation in Divorce Rates." *Social Forces* 97(2):675–704.

Wang, Chunxia (王春霞). 2016. "涉家暴刑事案件应引入专家证人 (Criminal Domestic Violence Cases Should Admit Expert Witness Testimony)." 中国妇女报 (*China Women's News*), March 11, A4.

Wang, Chunxia (王春霞) and Shuzhen (罗书臻) Luo. 2016. "家事审判改革为相关立法提供实践依据 – – 专访最高人民法院审判委员会专职委员杜万华 (Domestic Relations Trial Reform Provides Practical Basis for Related Legislation: An Interview with Du Wanhua, Full-Time Member of the Supreme People's Court's Adjudication Committee)." 人民法院报 (*People's Court Daily*), March 3, 1.

Wang, Cong (王聪). 2012. "审判组织: 合议制还是独任制? – – 以德国民事独任法官制的演变史为视角 (Adjudicatory Bodies: Collegial Panels or Solo Judges? From the Perspective of Historical Development of Germany's Civil Solo Judge System)." 福建法学 (*Fujian Jurisprudence*) (1):76–81.

Wang, Di. 2020. "Jia, as in Guojia: Building the Chinese Family into a Filial Nationalist Project." *China Law and Society Review* 5(1):1–32.

Wang, Jian. 2013. "To Divorce or Not to Divorce: A Critical Discourse Analysis of Court-Ordered Divorce Mediation in China." *International Journal of Law, Policy and the Family* 27(1):74–96.

Wang, Jun (王俊). 2021. "连城法院发出首张离婚冷静期通知书, 诉讼离婚能否适用冷静期? (Liancheng Court Issues First Notice of Cooling-Off Period, Can Cooling-Off Periods Be Used in Divorce Litigation?)." 新京报 (*The Beijing News*), January 8. Retrieved August 24, 2021 (www.bjnews.com.cn/detail/161009165615494.html).

Wang, Lusheng (王禄生). 2016. "法院人员分类管理体制与机制转型研究 (Research On the Transformation of Court Personnel Classification and Management Systems)." 比较法研究 (*Journal of Comparative Law*) (1):63–75.

Wang, Mengyao (王梦遥). 2018. "最高法: 离婚案最长可设3个月冷静期 (Supreme People's Court: The Longest Allowable Cooling-Off Period Is 3 Months)." 新京报 (*The Beijing News*), July 22, A01.

Wang, Qingting (王庆廷). 2015. "法官分类的行政化与司法化 – – 从助理审判员的'审判权'说起 (The Bureaucratization and Judicialization of the Judge Classification System: A Discussion of the Judicial Powers of Assistant Judges)." 华东政法大学学报 (*ECUPL Journal*) (4):72–81.

Wang, Shaoxia (王绍霞). 2013. "农村留守妇女离婚案评析 (A Comment on the Divorce Cases of Rural Left-Behind Women)." 民主与法制 (*Democracy and Legal System*) (3):174–76.

Wang, Shimei (王诗梅). 2014. "从民事诉讼角度谈我国自由心证制度的构建 (A Discussion from the Perspective of Civil Litigation of the Construction of China's System of Judging by Common Sense)." 鄂州大学学报 (*Journal of Ezhou University*) 21(3):20–22.

Wang, Xiangxian, Gang Fang, and Hongtao Li. 2013. *Research on Gender-Based Violence and Masculinities in China: Quantitative Findings*. United Nations Population Fund (UNFPA) China Office. Retrieved August 24, 2021 (https://china.unfpa.org/sites/default/files/pub-pdf/6.Research%20on%20Gender-based%20Violence%20and%20Masculinities%20in%20China%20_Quantitative%20Findings.pdf).

Wang, Xiaofen (王晓芬). 2017. "受虐妇女杀夫案件刑法问题研究 (A Study on the Criminal Law of Battered Women's Homicide)." M.A. Thesis, Zhengzhou University Law School.

Wang, Xiaoxiao (李潇潇). 2016. "我国民事一审撤诉的程序设计研究 (On System Design of First Instance Civil Withdrawal in China)." 中南大学学报(社会科学版) (*Journal of Central South University [Social Science]*) 22(2):51–60.

Wang, Xin (王新). 2015. "受虐妇女杀夫案的认定问题 (Conviction Issues in Cases of Abused Women Who Kill Their Husbands)." 法学杂志 (*Law Science Magazine*) (7):87–94.

Wang, Xiying, Dongping Qiao, and Liqiao Yang. 2013. *Hard Struggles in Times of Change: A Qualitative Study on Masculinities and Gender-Based Violence in Contemporary China*. United Nations Population Fund (UNFPA) China Office. Retrieved August 24, 2021 (https://china.unfpa.org/sites/default/files/pub-pdf/Hard%20Struggles%20in%20Times%20of%20Change%20-%20English.pdf).

Wang, Yaming (王亚明). 2017. "法官员额制的结构改革新探 (New Exploration of the Structural Reform of the Judge Quota System)." 法治研究 (*Research on Rule of Law*) (5):67–77.

Wang, Yanbin (王焰斌). 2015. "二七法院破解案多人少难题狠抓执法办案要务 (Dealing with the Urgent Task of Solving the 'Many Cases, Few Judges' Problem in the Erqi Court)." Retrieved July 8, 2018 (www.hncourt.gov.cn/public/detail.php?id=161482).

Wang, Yanhong (王艳红). 2013. "试论司法和谐政策对法官约束条件的影响 (Influence of Judicial Harmony Policies on Judges' Constraints)." 行政与法 *(Public Administration & Law)* (9):32–37.

Wang, Yueduan. 2019a. "Overcoming Embeddedness: How China's Judicial Accountability Reforms Make Its Judges More Autonomous." *Fordham International Law Journal* 43(4):737–66.

Wang, Yueduan. 2019b. "Reevaluating 'Countermeasure from Below': Evidences from Judicial Personnel Reforms in China." *Peking University Law Journal* 7(2):127–45.

Wang, Yuhua. 2013. "Court Funding and Judicial Corruption in China." *The China Journal* 69:43–63.

Wang, Yuhua. 2014. *Tying the Autocrat's Hands: The Rise of the Rule of Law in China.* Cambridge and New York: Cambridge University Press.

Wang, Yuyan (王玉燕). 2012. "浅议公告送达在离婚案件中的适用 (A Discussion of the Application of Public Notice Service in Divorce Cases)." 法制与社会 *(Legal System and Society)* 1:119–20.

Wang, Zhen. 2018. "Reassessing the Performance Evaluation System in the Xi Jinping Era: Changes and Implications." *East Asia* 35(1):59–77.

Wang, Zheng. 2014. "The Chinese Dream: Concept and Context." *Journal of Chinese Political Science* 19(1):1–13.

Wee, Sui-Lee. 2020. "Her Husband Abused Her. But Getting a Divorce Was an Ordeal." *The New York Times*, September 17, A1.

Wei, Qian, and Liam Swiss. 2020. "Filling Empty Promises? Foreign Aid and Human Rights Decoupling, 1981–2011." *The Sociological Quarterly* 1–20. www.tandfonline.com/doi/full/10.1080/00380253.2020.1828003

Weikart, Richard. 1994. "Marx, Engels, and the Abolition of the Family." *History of European Ideas* 18(5):657–72.

Welzel, Christian. 2013. *Freedom Rising: Human Empowerment and the Quest for Emancipation.* Cambridge and New York: Cambridge University Press.

Weng, Yijie (瓮怡洁). 2020. "论法官助理制度的功能定位与职权界分 (On the Function and Authority of the Judges' Clerks)." 政法论坛 *(Tribune of Political Science and Law)* 38(2):108–21.

Whyte, Martin King, ed. 2010. *One Country, Two Societies: Rural-Urban Inequality in Contemporary China.* Cambridge, MA and London: Harvard University Press.

Whyte, Martin King and William L. Parish. 1984. *Urban Life in Contemporary China.* Chicago and London: The University of Chicago Press.

Wimmer, Andreas. 2001. "Globalizations Avant La Lettre: A Comparative View of Isomorphization and Heteromorphization in an Inter-Connecting World." *Comparative Studies in Society and History* 43(3):435–66.

Wolf, Margery. 1985. *Revolution Postponed: Women in Contemporary China.* Stanford, CA: Stanford University Press.

Woo, Margaret. 2001. "Review of Neil J. Diamant's Revolutionizing the Family: Politics, Love, and Divorce in Urban and Rural China, 1949–1968." *American Journal of Sociology* 107(1):256–57.

Woo, Margaret Y. K. 2003. "Shaping Citizenship: Chinese Family Law and Women." *Yale Journal of Law and Feminism* 15:99–134.

Wotipka, Christine Min and Francisco O. Ramirez. 2008. "World Society and Human Rights: An Event History Analysis of the Convention on the Elimination of All Forms of Discrimination Against Women." In *The Global Diffusion of Markets and Democracy*, edited by B. A. Simmons, F. Dobbin, and G. Garrett, pp.303–43. Cambridge and New York: Cambridge University Press.

Wu, Guoping (吴国平). 2014. "论离婚案件中半流动家庭留守妇女权益的法律保护 (Legal Protections of the Rights and Interests of Left-Behind Women of Half-Floating Families in Divorce Cases)." 重庆工商大学学报(社会科学版) (*Journal of Chongqing Technology and Business University [Social Sciences Edition]*) 31(4):99–106.

Wu, Hongqi (吴洪淇). 2015. "法律人的职业化及其实现状况 – 以九省市实证调查数据为基础 (Legal Professionalization and the Extent of Its Realization: Empirical Survey Data from Nine Provinces and Cities)." 证据科学 (*Evidence Science*) 23(1):81–93.

Wudi. 2014. "Gender Guesser: Guess the Gender of Chinese Names (v0.10.0)." Retrieved June 21, 2019 (www.phpclasses.org/package/2701-PHP-Guess-the-gender-of-Chinese-names.html).

Xia, Jianghao. 2020. "The Best Interests of the Child Principle in Residence Disputes after Parental Divorce in China." *International Journal of Law, Policy and the Family* 34(2):105–25.

Xia, Yiwei, Tianji Cai, and Hua Zhong. 2019. "Effect of Judges' Gender on Rape Sentencing: A Data Mining Approach to Analyze Judgment Documents." *The China Journal* 19(2):125–49.

Xia, Yiwei, Yisu Zhou, Li Du, and Tianji Cai. 2019. "Mapping Trafficking of Women in China: Evidence from Court Sentences." *Journal of Contemporary China* 29(122):238–52.

Xiao, Jianfei (肖建飞), Yanwen (马艳雯) Ma, and Danting (妥丹婷) Tuo. 2014. "婚姻家庭纠纷审判中的裁判行为分析 (An Analysis of Judicial Decisions in Family Dispute Litigation)." 边疆经济与文化 (*The Border Economy and Culture*) 12:61–63.

Xiaoxiang Morning News (潇湘晨报). 2020. "女子不堪家暴跳楼致截瘫, 事发一年没能离成婚, 还曾遭到死亡威胁 (Women Jumps Out of Building Owing to Unbearable Domestic Violence, Becomes Paraplegic, Still Unable to Divorce A Year Later, Even Receives Death Threats)." Retrieved July 29, 2020 (https://tinyurl.com/y6qq4o8z).

Xiji County People's Court. 2013. "西吉县人民法院审理婚姻家庭案件裁量标准 (讨论稿) (Standards of the Xiji County People's Court for Ruling on

Marriage and Family Cases [Discussion Draft]).” Retrieved January 26, 2020 (http://xj.nxfy.gov.cn/xjfyxwzx/xjfyzdjs/201303/t20130306_1129168.html).

Xin, Chunying (信春鹰). 1999. 中国的法律制度及其改革 (*Chinese Legal System & Current Legal Reform*). Beijing: 法律出版社 (Law Press).

Xing, Hongmei (邢红枚). 2013. “论配偶暴力中受虐妇女杀夫案的量刑 (Criminal Sentencing of Abused Women Who Murder Their Husbands).” 中华女子学院学报 (*Journal of China Women's University*) (1):24–28.

Xinhua. 2011. “王胜俊详解困扰基层法院三大困难和三大问题 (Wang Shenjun Details Three Major Difficulties and Three Major Problems Plaguing Basic-Level Courts).” Retrieved December 26, 2019 (www.gov.cn/jrzg/2011-10/25/content_1978214.htm).

Xinhua. 2016. “习近平: 推动形成社会主义家庭文明新风尚 (Xi Jinping: Promote a New Ethos of Forming Civilized Socialist Families).” Retrieved August 9, 2018 (www.xinhuanet.com/politics/2016-12/12/c_1120103506.htm).

Xinhua. 2017. “婚姻登记下月起免费, 新人‘领证’还需准备点啥? (Marriage Registration Fees Waived Beginning Next Month, What Do Newlyweds Need to Bring to Get a License?).” Retrieved November 5, 2020 (www.xinhuanet.com//local/2017-03/25/c_1120693752.htm).

Xinhua. 2018. “China First Internet Court Handles Over 10,000 Cases.” *China Daily*. Retrieved September 7, 2020 (www.chinadaily.com.cn/a/201808/18/WS5b77c8f4a310add14f386801.html).

Xinhua. 2019. “Across China: Divorced Yet? Mediation Service Takes Aim at ‘Impulsive Divorce’.” Retrieved January 24, 2020 (www.xinhuanet.com/english/2019-05/18/c_138069644.htm).

Xiong, Xiangyu (熊翔宇). 2012. “诉讼离婚背后的法律问题及司法建议 (Legal Issues and Recommendations in Divorce Litigation).” 济源职业技术学院学报 (*Journal of Jiyuan Vocational and Technical College*) 11(4):69–72.

Xu, Anqi (徐安琪). 2000. “有无和好可能:夫妻感情是否破裂的判断标准 (Is There Reconciliation Potential? Assessment Standards in the Determination of the Breakdown of Mutual Affection).” 上海社会科学院学术季刊 (*Quarterly Journal of Shanghai Academy of Social Sciences*) (4):110–20.

Xu, Anqi (徐安琪). 2007. “离婚与女性地位及权益之探讨 (Exploring Divorce and the Status, Rights, and Interests of Women).” 浙江学刊 (*Zhejiang Academic Journal*) 1:198–206.

Xu, Chunbin (许春彬). 2012. “分居认定标准研究 – – 以 2009 – 2010 年河南省部分基层法院离婚纠纷案件判决书为样本 (Standards for Affirming Separation: An Empirical Study on Basic-Level Courts' Granting Divorce in Henan Province in 2009 and 2010).” 中华女子学院学报 (*Journal of China Women's University*) 1:38–44.

Xu, Kim Qinzi. 2019. “Changing Patterns and Determinants of First Marriage Over the History of the People's Republic of China.” *Population* 74(3):205–35.

Xu, Lijing (许莉静). 2012. "'形合实独'现象解析与对策选择 (Analysis and Countermeasures for the Phenomenon of 'Collegial in Form, Solo in Practice')." 商业文化 (*Business Culture*) (1):26–27.

Xu, Shuanggui (徐双桂). 2016. "离婚案件'首次判不离'现象普遍存在五方面原因 (Five Reasons for the Ubiquity of the Phenomenon of Denying First-Attempt Divorce Petitions)." Retrieved January 2, 2020 (http://ycyzfy.chinacourt.gov.cn/article/detail/2016/09/id/2137593.shtml).

Xu, Xin (徐昕), Yanhao (黄艳好) Huang, and Rongrong (卢荣荣) Lu. 2011. "2010年中国司法改革年度报告 (Annual Report on China's Judicial Reform in 2010)." 政法论坛 (*Tribune of Political Science and Law*) 29(3):133–53.

Xu, Xin (徐昕), Yanhao (黄艳好) Huang, and Rongrong (卢荣荣) Lu. 2015. "中国司法改革年度报告 (2014) (Annual Report on China's Judicial Reform 2014)." 政法论坛 (*Tribune of Political Science and Law*) 33(3):125–41.

Xu, Xin (徐昕), Yanhao (黄艳好) Huang, and Xiaotang (汪小棠) Wang. 2014. "中国司法改革年度报告 (2013) (Annual Report on China's Judicial Reform 2013)." 政法论坛 (*Tribune of Political Science and Law*) 32(2):83–102.

Xu, Xin (徐昕), Rongrong (卢荣荣) Lu, and Yanhao (黄艳好) Huang. 2012. "中国司法改革年度报告 (2011) (Annual Report on China's Judicial Reform 2011)." 政法论坛 (*Tribune of Political Science and Law*) 30(2):97–115.

Xu, Yixin (许一新) and Tao (江涛) Jiang. 2009. "法官助理制度的再思考 (Reconsiderations of System of Judges' Clerks)." 法治论丛 (上海政法学院学报) *Journal of Shanghai University of Political Science & Law* (5):100–105.

Xu, Yuezhen (徐月珍) and Tong (李彤) Li. 2011. "浅谈法官自由裁量权问题 (On the Problem of Judges' Discretion)." 哈尔滨职业技术学院学报 (*Journal of Harbin Vocational & Technical College*) (4):35–36.

Xue, Ninglan (薛宁兰). 2014. "离婚法的诉讼实践及其评析 (Analysis on Litigation Practice of Chinese Divorce Law)." 法学论坛 (*Legal Forum*) 29(4):15–23.

Xue, Shasha (薛莎莎). 2020. "河南柘城回应'女子遭家暴跳楼截瘫离婚案': 成立联合调查组 (Henan's Zhecheng Responds to 'Divorce Case of Paralyzed Abuse Victim Who Jumped Off Building': Joint Investigative Team Established)." *ThePaper.Cn.* Retrieved July 29, 2020 (www.thepaper.cn/newsDetail_forward_8420027).

Xue, Yongyi (薛永毅). 2019. "基层法院设立候补法官制度研究 – – 以法官养成及审判权二元配置为中心的分析 (Research on the Establishment of a System of Judges-in-Waiting: Analysis of a Dual Track Configuration of Adjudicatory Authority)." 渭南师范学院学报 (*Journal of Weinan Normal University*) 34(12):18–24.

xzqh.org. 2011. "2010年全国政区统计 (2010 Statistics on National Administrative Units)." Retrieved August 8, 2020 (www.xzqh.org/html/show/cn/4851.html).

Yan, Bo (严波). 2016. "平昌女子执意离婚三儿女跪求妈妈回家 (Pingchang Woman Insists on Divorce, Her Three Children Beg Her to Come Home)." 巴中晚报 (*Bazhong Evening News*), February 19, A4.

Yan, Ge (严戈) and Chunxiang (袁春湘) Yuan. 2015. "2014年全国法院案件质量评估分析报告 (2014 Report of An Analysis of Case Quality Assessment Systems Nationwide)." 人民司法 (*People's Judicature*) (9):82–84.

Yang, Dali L. 2017. "China's Troubled Quest for Order: Leadership, Organization and the Contradictions of the Stability Maintenance Regime." *Journal of Contemporary China* 26(103):35–53.

Yang, Jianwen (杨建文) and Dongsheng (陈东升) Chen. 2014. "人民法院网上公布裁判文书过程揭秘 (Uncovering the Secret History of People's Courts Posting Decisions Online)." 法制日报 (*Legal Daily*), January 8, 4.

Yang, Jinjing (杨金晶), Hui (覃慧) Tan, and Haibo (何海波) He. 2019. "裁判文书上网公开的中国实践: 进展、问题与完善 (China's Practice of the Public Disclosure of Court Decisions: Progress, Problems, and Perfection)." 中国法律评论 (*China Law Review*) (6):125–47.

Yang, Lixin (杨立新). 2011. "最高人民法院《关于适用〈婚姻法〉若干问题的解释（三）》的民法基础 (The Civil Law Foundation of the Supreme People's Court's Third Judicial Interpretation of Several Issues Concerning the Application of the Marriage Law)." 法律适用 (*Journal of Law Application*) (10):40–43.

Yang, Weiguo (杨卫国). 2014. "论民事简易程序系统之优化 (On the Optimization of the Civil Simplified Procedure System)." 法律科学(西北政法大学学报) (*Science of Law [Journal of Northwest University of Political Science and Law]*) (3):167–74.

Yang, Xinsen (杨鑫森). 2012. "我国民事诉讼简易程序的不足和完善 (Shortcoming with and the Perfection of China's Simplified Civil Procedure)." 改革与开放 (*Reform & Opening*) (12):16.

Yang, Xiuhua (杨秀华). 2014. "论民事诉讼中的法院调解之不足 (On the Shortcomings of Court Mediation in Civil Litigation)." Retrieved September 8, 2020 (www.chinacourt.org/article/detail/2014/12/id/1524111.shtml).

Yang, Yizhong (杨宜中). 2010. "法院管理越来越规范 (Court Administration Increasingly Standardized)." 人民法院报 (*People's Court Daily*), March 3, 1.

Yang, Yujing (杨玉静). 2016. "婚姻家庭领域法律政策回顾分析 (A Review and Analysis of Family Laws and Policies)." In *2013–2015年: 中国性别平等与妇女发展报告 (Annual Report on Gender Equality and Women's Development in China [2013–2015]*), edited by L. (谭琳) Tan, pp. 224–33. Beijing: 社会科学文献出版社 Social Sciences Academic Press.

Yao, Gaigai (姚改改). 2015. "'以暴制暴'案审判首现专家证人: 适用四部门'办理家暴刑事案件意见'的温州样本 (First Expert Testimony in 'Combatting Violence With Violence' Trial: Wenzhou Example of Application of 'Opinions Concerning the Handling of Criminal Domestic Violence Cases.'" 中国妇女报 (*China Women's News*), March 27, A4.

Yao, Silu (姚似璐). 2021. "《民法典》实施后浙江法院出具首份离婚冷静期通知书 (After the Civil Code Takes Effect Zhejiang Court Issues First Notice of Cooling-Off Period)." *ThePaper.Cn*, January 14. Retrieved August 24, 2021 (www.thepaper.cn/newsDetail_forward_10787826).

Yasuda, John K. 2017. *On Feeding the Masses: An Anatomy of Regulatory Failure in China*. Cambridge and New York: Cambridge University Press.

Ye, Feng (叶锋). 2015. "司法改革视野下审判辅助事务管理模式初探 (A Preliminary Exploration of Models for the Administration of Trial Work Assistance Under Judicial Reform)." 东方法学 (*Oriental Law*) (3):122–33.

Ye, Houqi (叶厚隽). 2007. "当前农村离婚现象和婚姻法适用中的问题考察 (An Investigation of Divorce and the Application of the Marriage Law in the Present-Day Countryside)." 天中学刊 (*Journal of Tianzhong*) 22(4):42–46.

Ye, Shengbin (叶圣彬). 2016. "司法改革背景下法官助理定位及相关问题研究 (Research on the Function of Judges' Clerks and Related Issues Against the Backdrop of Judicial Reform)." 法治社会 (*Law-Based Society*) (3):102–10.

Ye, Xiangyang (叶向阳). 2004. "对当前职业法官合议制实施情况的调查与思考 (A Survey and Reflections on the Current Situation of Implementing the System of Collegial Panels of Professional Judges)." 法律适用 (*Journal of Law Application*) (7):29–33.

Ye, Xiaohua (叶肖华). 2015. "零判决现象的反思与批判 (Rethinking the Phenomenon of 'Zero Judgment')." 政法论坛 (*Tribune of Political Science and Law*) 33(3):155–63.

Yi, Xingming (易兴明) and Daocai (童道才) Tong. 1998. "谈判决不准离婚的违法性 (A Discussion of the Illegality of Adjudicated Denials of Divorce Petitions)." 人民司法 (*People's Judicature*) 1998(10):38–39.

Yu, Deshui (禹得水), and Feng (高峰) Gao. 2015. "国家治理视野下的人民法庭(1949–2014) (People's Tribunals from a Governance Perspective)." 政法学刊 (*Journal of Political Science and Law*) 32(2):18–29.

Yu, Jia and Yu Xie. 2015. "Cohabitation in China: Trends and Determinants." *Population and Development Review* 41(4):607–28.

Yu, Jianhua (余建华) and Huanliang (孟焕良) Meng. 2016. "浙江全力打造'智慧法院'获点赞 (Zhejiang Praised for Its Full Commitment to Building a 'Smart Court')." 人民法院报 (*People's Court Daily*), February 6, 1.

Yu, Lang (余浪). 2009. "合议制独任化的问题与对策 (The Problem of the Solofication of the Collegial Panel and Countermeasures)." 法制与社会 (*Legal System and Society*) (12):156–57.

Yu, Long (于珑). 2013. "为生二胎离婚复婚不久又要离 (Divorced In Order to Have A Second Child, Remarried, Shortly Afterwards Tried to Divorce Again)." 都市晨报 (*City Morning News*), February 21, A13.

Yuan, Dingbo (袁定波). 2013. "全国法院5年156名法官因公牺牲 (Over the Past Five Years 156 Judges Sacrificed on the Job in Courts Nationwide)."

Retrieved August 14, 2020 (www.chinacourt.org/article/detail/2013/04/id/937260.shtml).

Yuan, Dingbo (袁定波) and Yuansen (丁元森) Ding. 2012. "2632家各级法院专设审管机构 (Case Management Offices Established in 2,632 Courts at Every Level)." 法制日报 (*Legal Daily*), December 27, 5.

Yun, Dan (贠丹). 2019. "对受虐妇女综合症专家证据的理论反思与路径建构 (Theory and Practical Steps Concerning Expert Evidence of Battered Woman Syndrome)." 妇女研究论丛 (*Journal of Chinese Women's Studies*) (156):75–85.

Zaloznaya, Marina and John Hagan. 2012. "Fighting Human Trafficking or Instituting Authoritarian Control? The Political Co-Optation of Human Rights Protection in Belarus." In *Governance by Indicators: Global Power Through Classification and Rankings*, edited by K. Davis, A. Fisher, B. Kingsbury, and S. E. Merry, pp. 344–64. Oxford and New York: Oxford University Press.

Zang, Emma. 2020. "When Family Property Becomes Individual Property: Intrahousehold Property Ownership and Women's Well-Being in China." *Journal of Marriage and Family* 82(4):1213–33.

Zeng, Congli (曾聪俐), Yuankai (姚元凯) Yao, Jie (胡杰) Hu, Gang (侯刚) Hou, and Jingjing (马晶晶) Ma. 2013. "我国农村'留守儿童'义务教育问题的调查与研究 – – 以甘肃省、贵州省、江西省以及山东省的抽样调查为依据 (Survey Research on Compulsory Education Among China's 'Left-Behind Children')." 法制与社会 (*Legal System and Society*) (6):234–35.

Zeng, Hui (曾辉) and Qiuyun (周秋云) Zhou. 2019. "婚姻案件中家庭暴力认定难的应对路径研究 – – 以证据规则的适用为视角 (Research on Resolving Difficulties Affirming Domestic Violence in Marriage Cases)." *Zhou, Qiuyun* (周秋云). Retrieved August 15, 2020 (www.pinlue.com/article/2019/04/1814/588718108749.html).

Zeng, Qiong (曾琼). 2008. "论离婚案件中的公告送达 (On Public Notice Service of Process in Divorce Cases)." 学海 (*Academia Bimestrie*) 2:161–65.

Zeng, Shaoyou (曾少友). 2013. "离婚案中农村妇女权益保护之窘境及对策之探讨 (Exploring Predicaments and Countermeasures in the Protection of the Rights of Rural Women in Divorce Cases)." 才智 (*Ability and Wisdom*) (14):242.

Zhan, Yufeng (詹玉锋). 2013. "'形合审离'合议制度运行现状及对策 (The Current Situation of 'Collegial in Form But Absent from Trials' in Judicial Panel System and Countermeasures)." Retrieved August 7, 2020 (www.chinacourt.org/article/detail/2013/04/id/938443.shtml).

Zhang, Cheng (章程). 2013. "女儿起诉离婚老爹出庭阻止法院判不准离婚 (When A Daughter Filed for Divorce in Court, Her Father Showed up to Prevent It, and the Court Denied Her Divorce Petition)." 广州日报 (*Guangzhou Daily*), August 2, AII1.

Zhang, Haifeng (张海峰), and Honggui (范红佳) Fan. 2011. "婚姻诉讼案件中判据离婚的衡量标准探析 (An Exploration of Standards for Divorce in Marriage Litigation Cases)." Retrieved December 24, 2019 (http://jzzy.hncourt.gov.cn/public/detail.php?id=4767).

Zhang, Honglin (张洪林). 2012. "反家庭暴力法的立法整合与趋势 (Legislative Integration and Trends of Anti-Domestic Violence Laws)." 法学 (Law Science) (2):43–52.

Zhang, Hongwei. 2014. "Domestic Violence and Its Official Reactions in China." In The Routledge Handbook of Chinese Criminology, edited by L. Cao, I. Y. Sun, and B. Hebenton, pp. 224–37. Abingdon and New York: Routledge.

Zhang, Jianyuan (张剑源). 2018. "家庭暴力为何难以被认定?以涉家暴离婚案件为中心的实证研究 (Why Is Family Violence Difficult to Affirm? An Empirical Study Focusing on Divorce Cases Related to Family Violence)." 山东大学学报(哲学社会科学版) (Journal of Shandong University [Philosophy and Social Sciences]) (4):103–11.

Zhang, Lianhan and Weimin Zuo. 2020. "Criminal Defense Rate and Underlying Wealth Effect: Data Analysis Based on Judgments of First Instance In Sichuan Province in 2015 and 2016." Wisconsin International Law Journal 37(2):441–68.

Zhang, Xianming (张先明). 2014. "设法解决法官流失问题 (Design Laws to Resolve the Problem of Judge Attrition)." 人民法院报 (People's Court Daily), March 13, 6.

Zhang, Qianfan. 2016a. "Judicial Reform in China: An Overview." In China's Socialist Rule of Law Reforms Under Xi Jinping, edited by J. Garrick and Y. C. Bennett, pp. 17–29. New York: Routledge.

Zhang, Qianfan (张千帆). 2016b. "如何设计司法? 法官、律师与案件数量比较研究 (How Should the Judiciary Be Designed? Comparative Research on the Caseloads of Judges and Lawyers)." 比较法研究 (Journal of Comparative Law) (1):52–62.

Zhang, Qing (张青). 2018. "基层法官流失的图景及逻辑: 以Y省部分基层法院为例 (A View and the Logic of Judge Attrition in Basic-Level Courts: Taking A Portion of Basic-Level Courts in Province Y as Examples)." 清华法学 (Tsinghua University Law Journal) 12(4):48–67.

Zhang, Rongli (张荣丽). 2017. "家暴致离婚案件子女抚养权归属审判研究 – – 从儿童保护法律视角对调研结果及典型案例的分析 (Research on the Assignment of Child Custody in Divorces Caused by Domestic Violence: Research Results And An Analysis of Typical Cases From the Perspective of Laws Protecting Children)." 妇女研究论丛 (Journal of Chinese Women's Studies) (1):46–53.

Zhang, Rui (张瑞). 2019. "法官助理的身份困境及其克服 (The Predicament of the Status of Judges' Clerks and Overcoming It)." 法治研究 (Research on Rule of Law) (5):111–21.

Zhang, Taisu. 2012. "The Pragmatic Court: Reinterpreting the Supreme People's Court of China." *Columbia Journal of Asian Law* 25:1–61.

Zhang, Taisu and Tom Ginsburg. 2019. "China's Turn toward Law." *Virginia Journal of International Law* 59:278–361.

Zhang, Wei (张伟). 2012. "家事纠纷解决机制的调查与研究 (Survey Research on Domestic Relations Dispute Resolution Mechanisms)." 河南财经政法大学学报 (*Journal of Henan University of Economics and Law*) (6):48–67.

Zhang, Wusheng (章武生). 2012. "我国民事简易程序的反思与发展进路 (Reflections on China's Simplified Civil Procedure and Its Future)." 现代法学 (*Modern Law Science*) 34(2):86–96.

Zhang, Xianming (张先明). 2015. "我国陪审制度的历史沿革与现状 (The History and Current Situation of China's Lay Assessor System)." 人民法院报 (*People's Court Daily*), April 21, 1.

Zhang, Xuejun (张学军). 2009. "婚姻法学研究三十年 (Thirty Years of Legal Research on Marriage Law)." 法学杂志 (*Law Science Magazine*) 2:26–29.

Zhang, Ying (张莹). 2011. "我国登记离婚法律制度的发展与完善 (Developing and Perfecting China's System for Registering Divorce)." 山东女子学院学报 (*Journal of Shandong Women's University*) (6):74–78.

Zhang, Yujia (张裕佳). 2017. "论立案登记制实施中的问题与完善: 以北京市法院为例 (On Problems in and the Perfection of the Implemention of the Case Filing and Registration System: Taking a Beijing Court as an Example)." 法制与社会 (*Legal System and Society*) (2):18–22.

Zhang, Yun (章蕴). 1957. "勤俭建国勤俭持家为建设社会主义而奋斗: 章蕴同志在中国妇女第三次全国代表大会上的报告 (Diligently Build the Nation and Diligently Grasp the Family for the Struggle of Socialist Construction: Zhang Yun's Report to the Third National Meeting of the All-China Women's Federation)." 人民日报 (*People's Daily*), September 9, 4.

Zhao, Chunlan (赵春兰), and Ming (揭明) Jie. 2008. "我国民事速裁程序适用过程 须明确的几个问题 (Some Issues In Need of Clarification in the Process of Applying China's Civil Expedited Procedures)." 政治与法律 (*Political Science and Law*) (1):153–57.

Zhao, Jianwen (赵建文). 2016. "中国人权报告: 性别平等与妇女发展状况 (China Human Rights Report: Gender Equality and Women's Development)." In 中国法治发展报告 (*Annual Report on China's Rule of Law*), edited by L. (李林) Li and H. (田禾) Tian, pp. 47–57. Beijing: 社会科学文献出版社 Social Sciences Academic Press.

Zhao, Li (赵莉), and Yu (丁钰) Ding. 2016. "离婚案件中涉及未成年子女抚养权归属存在的问题及对策 – 以南京市六家基层法院四年 (2011 – 2014 年) 离婚纠纷案件判决书为样本 (Issues and Countermeasures Concerning the Determination of Child Custody in Divorce Cases: A

Sample of Four Years [2011–2014] of Adjudicated Divorce Decisions from Six Basic-Level Courts I." 中华女子学院学报 *(Journal of China Women's University)* (1):24–34.

Zhao, Mingxing (赵明星). 2018. "论离婚诉讼的公告送达制度 (On the Public Notice Service of Process System in Divorce Litigation)." 思想政治与法律研究 *(Research on Ideology, Politics, and Law)* 9:187.

Zhao, Qiang (赵强). 2015. "不堪家暴砍死丈夫 她被判了5年 (Unable to Endure Domestic Violence, She Hacked Her Husband to Death, Sentenced to Five Years)." 河南商报 *(Henan Commercial Daily)*, May 22, A18.

Zhao, Ruohui and Hongwei Zhang. 2017. "Family Violence and the Legal and Social Responses in China." In *Global Responses to Domestic Violence*, edited by E. S. Buzawa and C. Buzawa, pp. 189–206. Cham: Springer.

Zhao, Shuhong (赵淑红). 2019. "苏南五市婚姻家庭纠纷的调研分析报告 (Report of An Analysis of Marriage and Family Disputes in Five Cities in Southern Jiangsu Province)." 法制博览 *(Legality Vision)* (25):154–55.

Zhao, Xiuju (赵秀举). 2017. "论民事和解协议的纠纷解决机制 (On the Dispute Resolution Mechanism of Civil Reconcilation Agreements)." 现代法学 *(Modern Law Science)* 39(1):132–44.

Zhao, Zejun (赵泽君) and Yanyu (赵雁雨) Zhao. 2011. "'民事普通程序简便审'不可取 (Simplifying the Ordinary Procedure Is Not the Way to Go)." 法制与经济 *(Legal and Economic)* (7):69–70.

Zhao, Zhengfu (赵政府). 2020. "嫌疑人携带剔骨刀捅刺法官." 生活报 *(Life Post)*, November 18, 6.

Zhejiang Provincial Bureau of Statistics. 2015. 浙江统计年鉴 *(Zhejiang Statistical Yearbook)*. Beijing: China Statistics Press.

Zhejiang Provincial High Court Research Team (浙江省高级人民法院联合课题组). 2019. "构建新型审判团队研究 (Research on Constructing A New Form of Trial Team)." 人民司法 *(People's Judicature)* (13):56–61.

Zheng, Chunyan, Jiahui Ai, and Sida Liu. 2017. "The Elastic Ceiling: Gender and Professional Career in Chinese Courts." *Law & Society Review* 51(1):168–99.

Zheng, Tiantian. 2015. "Intimate Partner Violence, Women, And Resistance in Postsocialist China." *Wagadu: A Journal of Transnational Women's and Gender Studies* 13:155–82.

Zheng, Yunbo (郑云波). 2018. "员额制框架下法院案多人少矛盾的解决－－以民事诉讼为主要视角 (Resolving the Contradictions of Many Cases and Few Judges Under the Quota System Framework: From the Perspective of Civil Procedure)." 天府新论 *(New Horizons from Tianfu)* (6):129–36.

Zhengzhou Municipal Intermediate Court Research Group. 2014. "基层法院'案多人少'问题研究: 以郑州地区为主要研究样本 (Research on the Problem of 'Many Cases, Few Judges' in Basic-Level Courts)." Retrieved June 8, 2018 (www.hncourt.gov.cn/public/detail.php?id=145295).

Zhou, Bin (周斌). 2014. "四大因素促法院办案保质保量 (Four Major Factors Promoting Court Case Quality)." 法制日报 (*Legal Daily*), March 13, 1.

Zhou, Bingyi (周冰一), and Yuanting (邱苑婷) Qiu. 2018. "家事法官眼中的离婚浮世绘 (Portraits of Divorce Through the Eyes of a Domestic Relations Judge)." 南方人物周刊 (*Southern People Weekly*) Retrieved August 24, 2021 (www.nfpeople.com/article/8705).

Zhou, Jiao (周姣). 2018. "关于离婚冷静期制度的思考 (Thoughts on a System for Divorce Cooling-Off Periods)." 法制与社会 (*Legal System and Society*) (1):35–36.

Zhou, Jing (周竟). 2013. "浙江温州出台家暴告诫制度: 轻微家暴也将被存档 (Zhejiang's Wenzhou Introduces Domestic Violence Warning System: Minor Domestic Violence Will Be Filed)." *Xinhua*. Retrieved April 26, 2020 (http://politics.people.com.cn/n/2013/1128/c70731-23688176.html).

Zhou, Viola. 2017. "More Divorces Combined with Fewer Marriages Seen as Threat to Family Life." *South China Morning Post, September* 6, p.5.

Zhou, Wanting (周婉婷). 2018. "离婚诉讼中二次起诉司法裁判研究 (Research on Second Trials in Divorce Litigation)." M.A. Thesis, Yunnan University School of Law.

Zhu, Suli. 2016. *Sending Law to the Countryside: Research on China's Basic-Level Judicial System*. Singapore: Springer.

Zhu, Yameng (朱雅萌). 2020. "我国法官员额制改革问题研究 (Research on the Issue of China's Judge Quota System Reform)." 法学研究 (*CASS Journal of Law*) (21):64–65,68.

Zhu, Xuan (朱轩). 2021. "衡阳妇联回应'女子5年4次起诉离婚被驳': 曾多次介入, 男方偏激 (Hengyang Women's Federation Responds to 'Woman Denied Divorce Four Times in Five Years': In Numerous Interventions, Her Husband Exhibited Extreme Behavior)." *ThePaper.Cn*. Retrieved August 3, 2021 (www.thepaper.cn/newsDetail_forward_12196008).

Zhu, Zhanwang (朱展望), and Songwen (邹松文) Zou. 2001. "民事简易程序适用过程中出现的问题及其对策 – – 以浙江省金华市两级法院为考察对象 (Problems and Countermeasures in the Application of the Simplified Civil Procedure: Taking Both Levels of Courts in Zhejiang's Jinhua Municipality as the Object of Investigation)." 法律适用 (国家法官学院学报) (*Journal of Applied Law [National Judges College Law Journal]*) (8):48–52.

Zou, Tiran (邹偶然). 2015. "女子不堪长期家暴杀夫获刑5年 (Woman Sentenced to Five Years After Murdering Her Abusive Husband)." 工人日报 (*Workers' Daily*), March 14, 6.

Zuo, Weimin (左卫民). 2018. "'诉讼爆炸'的中国应对:基于W区法院近三十年审判实践的实证分析 (The Chinese Response to a 'Litigation Explosion': An Empirical Analysis of Thirty Years of Adjudicatory Practice in District W Court)." 中国法学 (*China Legal Science*) (4):238–60.

Zuo, Weimin (左卫民). 2020. "通过诉前调解控制'诉讼爆炸' – – 区域经验的实证研究 (Controlling the 'Litigation Explosion' Through Pre-Trial Mediation: Empirical Research on a Region's Experience)." 清华法学 (*Tsinghua University Law Journal*) 14(4):89–106.

Zuo, Weimin and Jinghua Ma. 2013. "The Role of Criminal Defence Lawyers in China: An Empirical Study of D County, S Province." In *Comparative Perspectives on Criminal Justice in China*, edited by M. McConville and E. Pils, pp. 234–55. Cheltenham, UK and Northampton, MA: Edward Elgar.

INDEX

CAMBRIDGE STUDIES IN LAW AND SOCIETY

Law's Wars: The Fate of the Rule of Law in the US "War on Terror"
Richard L. Abel

Transforming Gender Citizenship: The Irresistible Rise of Gender Quotas in Europe
Edited by Eléonore Lépinard and Ruth Rubio-Marín

Muslim Women's Quest for Justice: Gender, Law and Activism in India
Mengia Hong Tschalaer

Children as 'Risk': Sexual Exploitation and Abuse by Children and Young People
Anne-Marie McAlinden

The Legal Process and the Promise of Justice: Studies Inspired by the Work of Malcolm Feeley
Jonathan Simon, Rosann Greenspan, Hadar Aviram

Gift Exchanges: The Transnational History of a Political Idea
Grégoire Mallard

Measuring Justice: Quantitative Accountability and the National Prosecuting Authority in South Africa
Johanna Mugler

Negotiating the Power of NGOs: Women's Legal Rights in South Africa
Reem Wael

Indigenous Water Rights in Law and Regulation: Lessons from Comparative Experience
Elizabeth Jane Macpherson

The Edge of Law: Legal Geographies of a War Crimes Court
Alex Jeffrey

Everyday Justice: Law, Ethnography, and Injustice
Sandra Brunnegger

The Uncounted: Politics of Data in Global Health
Sara L. M. Davis

Transnational Legal Ordering of Criminal Justice
Gregory Shaffer and Ely Aaronson

Five Republics and One Tradition
Pablo Ruiz-Tagle

The Law Multiple: Judgment and Knowledge in Practice
Irene van Oorschot

Health as a Human Right: The Politics and Judicialisation of Health in Brazil
Octávio Luiz Motta Ferraz